Targum Neofiti 1: Numbers

Targum Pseudo-Jonathan: Numbers

THE ARAMAIC BIBLE

• THE TARGUMS •

PROJECT DIRECTOR

Martin McNamara, M.S.C.

EDITORS

Kevin Cathcart • Michael Maher, M.S.C.
Martin McNamara, M.S.C.

EDITORIAL CONSULTANTS

Daniel J. Harrington, S.J. • Bernard Grossfeld

The Aramaic Bible

Volume 4

Targum Neofiti 1: Numbers

Translated, with Apparatus and Notes

BY

Martin McNamara, M.S.C.

Targum Pseudo-Jonathan: Numbers

Translated, with Notes

BY

Ernest G. Clarke

with the assistance of Shirley Magder

A Michael Glazier Book
THE LITURGICAL PRESS
Collegeville, Minnesota

About the Authors:

Martin McNamara, M.S.C., is Professor of Sacred Scripture at the Milltown Institute of Theology and Philosophy, Dublin. He has a licentiate in Theology from the Gregorian University, Rome, and a licentiate and doctorate in Sacred Scripture from the Biblical Institute, Rome. His doctoral dissertation was entitled *The New Testament and the Palestinian Targum to the Pentateuch* (1966; reprint 1978). His other publications on the Targums and Judaism include *Targum and Testament* (1972); *Palestinian Judaism and the New Testament* (1983); *Intertestamental Literature* (1983).

Ernest G. Clarke, M.A., B.D., Ph.D., is Professor Emeritus of Aramaic Language and Literature at the University of Toronto (Department of Near Eastern Studies). He received his early training at the University of Toronto and his doctorate from Leiden University, The Netherlands. He is the author of *The Selected Questions of Ishō bar Nūn* (1962), *The Wisdom of Solomon* (1973), and *Targum Pseudo-Jonathan of the Pentateuch: Text and Concordance* (1984).

Shirley Magder holds an M.A. degree from the Department of Near Eastern Studies, the University of Toronto.

First published in 1995 by The Liturgical Press, Collegeville, Minnesota 56321.

Library of Congress Cataloging-in-Publication Data

Bible. O.T. Numbers. English. McNamara. 1995.
Targum Neofiti 1, Numbers / translated, with apparatus and notes by Martin McNamara. Targum Pseudo-Jonathan, Numbers / translated, with notes by Ernest G. Clarke with the assistance of Shirley Magder.
p. cm. — (The Aramaic Bible ; v. 4)
"A Michael Glazier book."
Includes bibliographical references and index.
ISBN 0-8146-5483-5
1. Bible. O.T. Numbers. Aramaic. Targum Yerushalmi--Translations into English. 2. Bible. O.T. Numbers. Aramaic. Targum Yerushalmi—Criticism, Textual. 3. Bible. O.T. Numbers. Aramaic. Targum Pseudo-Jonathan—Translations into English. I. McNamara, Martin. II. Clarke, Ernest G. (Ernest George) III. Magder, Shirley. IV. Bible. O.T. Numbers. English. Clarke. 1995. V. Title. VI. Series: Bible. O.T. English. Aramaic Bible. 1987 ; v. 4.
BS709.2.B5 1987
[BS1263]
221.4'2 s—dc20
[222'.14042]
95-10270
CIP

Logo design by Florence Bern.
Typography by Graphic Sciences Corporation, Cedar Rapids, Iowa.
Printed and bound in the United States of America by Edwards Brothers, Inc., Ann Arbor, Michigan.

TABLE OF CONTENTS

EDITORS' FOREWORD

While any translation of the Scriptures may in Hebrew be called a Targum, the word is used especially for a translation of a book of the Hebrew Bible into Aramaic. Before the Christian era Aramaic had in good part replaced Hebrew in Palestine as the vernacular of the Jews. It continued as their vernacular for centuries later and remained in part as the language of the schools after Aramaic itself had been replaced as the vernacular.

Rabbinic Judaism has transmitted Targums of all books of the Hebrew canon, with the exception of Daniel and Ezra-Nehemiah, which are themselves partly in Aramaic. We also have a translation of the Samaritan Pentateuch into the dialect of Samaritan Aramaic. From the Qumran library we have sections of a Targum of Job and fragments of a Targum of Leviticus, chapter 16, facts which indicate that the Bible was being translated into Aramaic in pre-Christian times.

Translations of books of the Hebrew Bible into Aramaic for liturgical purposes must have begun before the Christian era, even though none of the Targums transmitted to us by rabbinic Judaism can be shown to be that old and though some of them are demonstrably compositions from later centuries.

In recent decades there has been increasing interest among scholars and a larger public in these Targums. A noticeable lacuna, however, has been the absence of a modern English translation of this body of writing. It is in marked contrast with most other bodies of Jewish literature, for which there are good modern English translations, for instance the Apocrypha and Pseudepigrapha of the Old Testament, Josephus, Philo, the Mishnah, the Babylonian Talmud and Midrashic literature, and more recently the Tosefta and Palestinian Talmud.

It is hoped that this present series will provide some remedy for this state of affairs.

The aim of the series is to translate all the traditionally-known Targums, that is those transmitted by rabbinic Judaism, into modern English idiom, while at the same time respecting the particular and peculiar nature of what these Aramaic translations were originally intended to be. A translator's task is never an easy one. It is rendered doubly difficult when the text to be rendered is itself a translation which is at times governed by an entire set of principles.

All the translations in this series have been specially commissioned. The translators have made use of what they reckon as the best printed editions of the Aramaic Targum in question or have themselves directly consulted the manuscripts.

The translation aims at giving a faithful rendering of the Aramaic. The introduction to each Targum contains the necessary background information on the particular work.

In general, each Targum translation is accompanied by an apparatus and notes. The former is concerned mainly with such items as the variant readings in the Aramaic texts, the relation of the English translation to the original, etc. The notes give what explanations the translator thinks necessary or useful for this series.

Not all the Targums here translated are of the same kind. Targums were translated at different times, and most probably for varying purposes, and have more than one interpretative approach to the Hebrew Bible. This diversity between the Targums themselves is reflected in the translation and in the manner in which the accompanying explanatory material is presented. However, a basic unity of presentation has been maintained. Targumic deviations from the Hebrew text, whether by interpretation or paraphrase, are indicated by italics.

A point that needs to be stressed with regard to this translation of the Targums is that by reason of the state of current targumic research, to a certain extent it must be regarded as a provisional one. Despite the progress made, especially in recent decades, much work still remains to be done in the field of targumic study. Not all the Targums are as yet available in critical editions. And with regard to those that have been critically edited from known manuscripts, in the case of the Targums of some books the variants between the manuscripts themselves are such as to give rise to the question whether they have all descended from a single common original.

Details regarding these points will be found in the various introductions and critical notes.

It is recognized that a series such as this will have a broad readership. The Targums constitute a valuable source of information for students of Jewish literature, particularly those concerned with the history of interpretation, and also for students of the New Testament, especially for those interested in its relationship to its Jewish origins. The Targums also concern members of the general public who have an interest in the Jewish interpretation of the Scriptures or in the Jewish background to the New Testament. For them the Targums should be both interesting and enlightening.

By their translations, introductions, and critical notes, the contributors to this series have rendered an immense service to the progress of targumic studies. It is hoped that the series, provisional though it may be, will bring significantly nearer the day when the definitive translation of the Targums can be made.

Kevin Cathcart   Martin McNamara, M.S.C.   Michael Maher, M.S.C.

PREFACE

This present volume is numbered Volume 4 in the whole series, even though two volumes (Volumes 1A and 1B) were required for the Targums of Genesis, other than that of Onqelos.

The original plan was to publish the entire corpus of Palestinian Targums (Neofiti, Neofiti glosses, Fragment Targums, Pseudo-Jonathan) in the first five volumes of this series—one volume for each of the books of the Pentateuch. It was also planned to have Neofiti, with its Apparatus and notes, on pages facing the corresponding text and notes of Pseudo-Jonathan. Detailed examination of the midrashim common to both would be in the Pseudo-Jonathan section, with reference to this in the notes to Neofiti. Such a presentation of texts and notes proved too cumbersome from the publishing point of view, principally because the space required for each of the two blocks would not correspond. It was finally decided to present each of the two (Neofiti and Pseudo-Jonathan) separately, and further, to devote a volume to each for Genesis (Volume 1A and 1B of this series). It has been found possible to combine both in one volume for Exodus, Leviticus, and Numbers.

The introduction to Neofiti treats briefly of Numbers in Jewish tradition and of the Book of Numbers and rabbinic midrash. It then goes on to examine in some detail the translation techniques in Targum Neofiti Numbers.

The text of Neofiti had already been translated by the present writer for the *editio princeps* under the editorship of Alejandro Díez Macho (1970). The editor has completely revised this translation for the present work.

In this translation, as in all volumes in this series, words in italics in the translation proper denote deviation in the Targum from the Hebrew Text.

This first part of the volume contains all the material of the Palestinian Targums of Numbers, with the exception of Pseudo-Jonathan. The Apparatus contains all the marginal variants in the manuscript of Codex Neofiti 1, apart from merely orthographical and grammatical ones. The significant variants of the other Palestinian Targum texts are also given. When it is perceived (as, for instance, Num 21:15) that other texts contain a recension worthy of reproduction in full, this is done. In such cases the reproduction of the simple variants would fail to do justice to the texts.

As in the case of Neofiti Genesis, Exodus, and Leviticus, notes to Neofiti Numbers concentrate on the features and peculiarities of Neofiti's text, with the minimum of reference required for an understanding of the midrash common to Neofiti and Pseudo-Jonathan. For fuller treatment the reader is referred to the notes on this latter.

This concentration on the peculiarities of Neofiti is a feature of all the books of the Pentateuch. From this it becomes clear that in good part, at least, Neofiti represents a unified approach to the understanding of the Torah.

Acknowledging once again our debt to Michael Glazier for the initiation of this series, we must also express gratitude to The Liturgical Press for having agreed so generously to continue it; to Mark Twomey, managing editor, for general supervision; and particularly to John Schneider, who took over the task of editing the volumes in this series and overseeing their publication. The quality of these volumes owes much to his exceptional editorial skills.

Ernest G. Clarke
Toronto, Canada

Martin McNamara, M.S.C.
Dublin, Ireland

ABBREVIATIONS

Ab. Zar.	Abodah Zarah
Ant.	Josephus, *Jewish Antiquities*
b.	Babylonian Talmud
B	First *Biblia Rabbinica.* Venice, Bomberg, 1517–18
BL	British Library
BM	British Museum (now British Library)
CTg (B, etc.)	Cairo Genizah (Pal.) Targum manuscript
Frg. Tg(s).	Fragment Targum(s)
Gen. R.	Genesis Rabbah
Giṭṭ.	Giṭṭin
Hall.	Hallah
HT	Hebrew Text
j.	Jerusalem (Palestinian) Targum
Kel.	Kelim
L	Fragment Targum Leipzig Manuscript
LAB	Ps.-Philo, *Liber Antiquitatum Biblicarum*
LXX	Septuagint
Meg.	Megillah
Mek.	Mekilta de R. Ishmael
Meturg.	Elias Levita's *Meturgeman*
MSmg	Marginal reading of Ps.-J. manuscript
MT	Masoretic Text

NEB	New English Bible
Nf	Neofiti
Nfi	Neofiti interlinear gloss
Nfmg	Neofiti marginal gloss
NJB	New Jerusalem Bible
N	Nürnberg Fragment Targum Manuscript
NRSV	New Revised Standard Version
Num. R.	Numbers Rabbah
Onq.	Onqelos
OT	Old Testament
P	Paris BN Fragment Targum Manuscript
Pal. Tg.	Palestinian Targum
Ps.-J.	Targum Pseudo-Jonathan
REB	Revised English Bible
RSV	Revised Standard Version
Sam. Tg.	Samaritan Targum
Shabb.	Shabbath
Shebi.	Shebiith
Sifre Deut.	Sifre to Deuteronomy
Sifre Num.	Sifre to Numbers
Sukk.	Sukkoth
Tanḥ.	Tanḥuma
Tg.	Targum
V	Vatican Library Fragment Targum Manuscript
VM	Philo, *De Vita Mosis*
Vulg.	Vulgate

Journals and Series

BASOR	Bulletin of the American Schools of Oriental Research
BibThB	Biblical Theology Bulletin
BiblZeit	Biblische Zeitschrift
CCL	Corpus Christianorum, Series Latina

EJ	Encyclopaedia Judaica
HUCA	Hebrew Union College Annual
ITQ	The Irish Theological Quarterly
JBL	Journal of Biblical Literature
JJS	Journal of Jewish Studies
JNSL	Journal of Northwest Semitic Languages
JPS	Jewish Publication Society
JQR	Jewish Quarterly Review
JSJ	Journal for the Study of Judaism
JSOT	Journal for the Study of the Old Testament
JSS	Journal of Semitic Studies
JTS	Journal of Theological Studies
MGWJ	Monatschrift für Geschichte und Wissenschaft des Judentums
NTS	New Testament Studies
PIBA	Proceedings of the Irish Biblical Association
PL	J. P. Migne, *Patrologia Latina*
RB	Revue Biblique
RevHistRel	Revue d'Histoire des Religions
RSR	Recherches de science religieuse
SBL	Society of Biblical Literature
TDNT	Theological Dictionary of the New Testament
VT	Vetus Testamentum
VTSuppl	Supplement to Vetus Testamentum
ZAW	Zeitschrift für die Alttestamentliche Wissenschaft

BRIEF INTRODUCTION
TO
THE PALESTINIAN TARGUMS OF NUMBERS

Martin McNamara, M.S.C.

I. THE BIBLICAL BOOK OF NUMBERS

It is generally recognized that the Book of Numbers is one of the least unified books of the Bible. It is a collection of censuses, laws, and traditions concerning the sojourn of the people of Israel in the wilderness and of the first conquests of the territories promised to it. In a sense it represents the end of a tradition, containing laws and material not found in other books. It has older traditions and the updating of earlier codes. Thus the inheritance rights of women were neglected in the other biblical codes. The right of daughters to inherit is set out in the test case of the daughters of Zelophehad in 27:1-11 (Zelophehad is mentioned in 26:33). In what looks to be a kind of codicil at the very end of the book (chap. 36), it is specified that daughters who so inherit must marry within their own tribe so that the total inheritance of the tribes of Israel may remain unaltered. Numbers thus looks like an articulating tradition in dialogue with the past and with itself.

It is usual to see the Book of Numbers as consisting of three great sections:

I. Further ordinances of God at Sinai (1:1–10:36).

II. Further sojourn in the wilderness (11:1–20:13; precise place of ending uncertain). A good part of this sojourn would appear to have been at a place called Kadesh (which some would identify with the present-day spring *en qdeš,* about forty-six miles south-southwest of Beersheba[1] as the crow flies).

III. Preparation for and beginning of the conquest (20:14–36:16).

Apart from the numbering, the censuses, and the laws, this biblical book contains the narrative of some notable events and incidents, carrying lessons for the original readership and audience and for later generations. Notable among these are the gifts of God to Israel in the wilderness (the cloud, the water miraculously provided, the well, the

[1]See M. Noth, *Numbers. A Commentary* (London: SCM Press, 1968) 106.

manna and quails, the bronze serpent); the Balaam narrative; the seduction by the Moabite and Midianite women; the division of the land across the Jordan and its frontiers. We cannot now determine what history already lay behind these individual pieces and how much the author of the Book of Numbers, as we have it, was recasting tradition to present a message for the Jews of his own day—generally assumed to be some time in the postexilic period. He was, in any case, articulating and reformulating traditions that would be further developed after his own day.

II. THE BOOK OF NUMBERS IN JEWISH TRADITION

1. *Jewish Non-Rabbinic Tradition*

We have a rather detailed retelling of the story of Numbers in three writers of the first century C.E., namely, Philo Judaeus (ca. 20 B.C.E to 54 C.E.), particularly in *The Life of Moses;* Josephus Flavius (ca. 37–100 C.E.), in his *Jewish Antiquities* (Book 4); and Pseudo-Philo, in his *Biblical Antiquities* (*Liber Antiquitatum Biblicarum,* abbreviated *LAB*). From these we can see how well developed the traditions had become and how they compare with the targumic and rabbinic evidence.

Num 11:27 speaks of Eldad and Medad prophesying in the camp, without giving us the content of their prophecy. An apocryphal writing under the name of *Eldad and Modad* (referred to in second-century C.E. sources) purported to contain these prophecies. The work, unfortunately, is known only from an early citation.[2]

The three sources already referred to also speak of the well of water, the cloud, and the manna. In targumic and rabbinic tradition these are connected respectively with Miriam, Aaron, and Moses. This same association is found already in *LAB* 20, 7.[3]

The manna had a rich tradition attached to it, one that has been studied in detail.[4]

The highly developed Jewish tradition with regard to Balaam begins with the Bible, in which there are at least two portraits of him, one hostile, the other less so (if not quite positive). According to Num 31:8; Josh 13:22, the Israelites killed Balaam, son of Beor, with the sword. He had given evil counsel to Balak (Num 31:16). See also Deut 23:5-6; Neh 13:2; Josh 24:9-10. In the narrative of Num 22–24, Balaam's conduct is not censured. The targumic and rabbinic tradition presents Balaam in a negative light, interpreting the main biblical narrative in the light of Num 31:8, 16.[5] This negative presentation is what we find in Philo, *Life of Moses,* 1, 48–54 (263–295), an indication of the antiquity of the targumic and rabbinic tradition. Curiously enough, it is not that followed by Josephus, *Ant.,* 4, 6, 1-6 (100–126) or Pseudo-Philo, both of whom present

[2]See E. G. Martin, "Eldad and Modad," in J. H. Charlesworth, ed., *The Old Testament Pseudepigrapha* 2 (London, 1985) 463–465.

[3]See the text below in the note to 12:12; also note to chap. 21.

[4]See B. J. Malina, *The Palestinian Manna Tradition. The Manna Tradition in the Palestinian Targums and Its Relationship to the New Testament* (Leiden, 1968).

[5]For a summary of the rabbinical evidence, see K. G. Kuhn, "*Balaam,*" in *TDNT* 1 (1964) 524f. See also McNamara, 1993.

Balaam as a noble character.[6] Kuhn notes that Josephus stresses all the favorable aspects (of Balaam) and either ignores or quickly passes over the rest. Josephus, in his opinion, must have had some interest in putting Balaam in the best possible light.[7]

What the motives of Josephus and Pseudo-Philo were in so presenting Balaam we cannot say. It is interesting that none of the three writers gives a detailed treatment of Balaam's oracle on the star to arise from Jacob (Num 24:17-24). This text may well have been the "ambiguous oracular pronouncement found in Holy Scripture that one of their country would at that time be given command over the world" (Josephus, *War,* 6, 312f.), which spurred on to action the insurgents to the revolt of 64–70 C.E. (See below, note 23 to Num 24:17.)

The manner in which the messianic-type elements of the Balaam oracles were understood in late pre-70 C.E. Judaism merits consideration.[8] This can be expected to have depended on the precise text being used by the interpreter and the expositor's own overall religious and world view. Philo used the Greek rendering, not the Hebrew original, and the Greek LXX rendering of Num 24 transforms the original to a greater or lesser degree. Speaking apparently of Jacob or Israel, the Hebrew Text of Num 24:7 says: "Waters shall flow from his buckets and his seed shall be in many waters, his kings shall be higher than Agag, and his kingdom shall be exalted." In the Greek LXX translation this becomes: "There shall come forth a man out of his seed, and he shall rule over many nations; and the kingdom of God shall be exalted and his kingdom shall be increased."

Philo uses this text (in *De praemiis et poenis,* 16 [95]), but not in a strictly militaristic sense: "For 'there shall come forth a man' (Num 24:7) says the oracle, and leading his host to war he will subdue great and populous nations, because God has sent to his aid the reinforcements which befit the godly, and that is dauntless courage of soul and powerful strength of body, either of which strikes fear into the enemy, and the two if united are quite irresistible." It has been noted that the messianic figure of this passage of Philo does not battle non-Jews but "some fanatics whose lust for war defies restraint or remonstrance" (*De praemiis et poenis,* 94).[9]

Philo's "messianism" cannot be taken as identical with a "nativist," Palestinian type. Qumran tradition appears to have had a special interest in the relevant "messianic" sections of the Balaam oracles. Num 24:17 is cited in the Damascus Rule (CD 7:9-21)[10] (ca. 100 B.C.E.?), which interprets the "star" as the Interpreter of the Law (Priestly Messiah?) and the "scepter" as Prince of the whole congregation.[11] Num 24:15-17 is

[6]In *LAB* 17, 4 Balaam, on receiving Balak's embassy, prays to God: "And now enlighten your servant if it be right to go forth with them." D. Harrington (*The Old Testament Pseudepigrapha* 2, 325) notes on this that Balaam's reply here puts him in a more favorable light than he receives in the OT.

[7]Kuhn, in *TDNT* 1 (1964) 524.

[8]For greater detail on this, see M. McNamara, "Early Exegesis in the Palestinian Targum (Neofiti 1) Numbers 24," *PIBA* 16 (1993) 57–79, esp. 57–67.

[9]See R. D. Hecht, "Philo and Messiah," p. 147, with reference to J. J. Collins, *Between Athens and Jerusalem. Jewish Identity in the Hellenistic Diaspora* (New York: Crossroad, 1983) 115. For the messianism of Josephus, see Lagrange, *Le messianisme,* 5–7; Story, "What Kind of Messiah . . .?" *Bibliotheca Sacra* 104 (1947) 485–487.

[10]For a study of this section see H. Kosmala, "Damascus Document 7:9-21," in *Essay in the Dead Sea Scrolls in Memory of E. L. Sukenik,* 1961, pp. 183–190.

[11]English translation in Vermes, *The Dead Sea Scrolls,* 3rd ed., 1987, p. 89.

also one of the texts in the Qumran Messianic Anthology or Testimonia (4Q175), dating to the early first century B.C.E.[12] Num 24:17-19 is cited as part of the liturgy in *The War Scroll* (1QM, 4QM), col. XI), ca. 10 B.C.E.–10 C.E.):[13] "Truly the battle is Thine and the power is from Thee! It is not ours. . . . This thou hast taught us from ancient times, saying, *A star shall come out of Jacob . . . The enemy shall be his possession and Israel shall accomplish mighty deeds.*"

While Josephus does not expand on the Balaam story, the opposite is true with regard to the Midianite women (cf. Num 31:16). This has been developed into a major moralizing section by Josephus (*Ant.,* 4, 6, 7-12, 131-155), with the message that sexual passions can lead to the rejection of the authority of tradition.[14] The theme of Balaam's advice to Balak to have Midianite women seduce Israel is also developed in Philo, *Life of Moses,* 1, 53–54 (294–298).

2. *Rabbinic Tradition*

Rabbinic traditions on episodes and narratives of the Book of Numbers (the manna, the well, Balaam, etc.) can be found scattered throughout rabbinic sources. We have two works in rabbinic literature with commentary on portions of Numbers, i.e., *Sifre Numbers* and *Numbers Rabbah.*

Sifre Numbers is an exegetical midrash (mainly halakic) on Numbers. It begins with 5:1, the first legal portion of Numbers. Longer narrative units (such as Num 13–14; 16–17; 20–24) are completely omitted but in the portions treated of the narrative parts are included, so that some haggadah is also provided. *Sifre Numbers* is not a homogeneous text and appears to combine material from two different Jewish exegetical schools. The most probable time for the formation of *Sifre Numbers* is a date after the middle of the third century.[15]

Numbers Rabbah consists of two very different parts. *Num. R.* I (with sections 1–14) and approximately three-quarters of the total work is a haggadic treatment of Num 1–7. *Num. R.* II (sections 15–23) is a homiletic midrash which discusses Num 8–36 much more briefly. The whole work was probably in the style of *Num. R.* II, and this may have originated in the ninth century or somewhat earlier. The lengthier *Num. R.* I seems to have been a later development. The connection of the two parts, to give us the present work, probably took place at the beginning of the thirteenth century.[16]

[12]English translation in Vermes, *The Dead Sea Scrolls,* p. 295.

[13]English translation in Vermes, *The Dead Sea Scrolls,* p. 116.

[14]See H. W. Attridge, *The Interpretation of Biblical History in the Antiquitates Judaicae of Flavius Josephus,* Harvard Dissertations in Religion (Missoula: Scholars Press, 1976) 128–132; W. C. van Unnik, "Josephus' Account of the Story of Israel Sin with Alien Women," in *Travels in the World of the OT* (Assen: Von Gorcum, 1974) 241–261.

[15]In the above I follow H. L. Strack and G. Stemberger, *Introduction to the Talmud and Midrash* (Edinburgh: T & T Clark, 1991) 290–293.

[16]See Strack-Stemberger, op. cit., 337–339.

III. TRANSLATION TECHNIQUES IN TARGUM NEOFITI NUMBERS

In the introduction and notes to Genesis in this series, some of the translation techniques of the Palestinian Targum as found in Codex Neofiti have been considered. In the introductions to Exodus and to Leviticus, special attention has been given to these translation techniques. In keeping with this, I here examine some of these same techniques as found in Nf Numbers.

1. *Hebrew šlmym, zbḥ šlmym, "peace offerings" becomes "sacrifices of holy things."* The Hebrew terms *šlmym* and *zbḥ šlmym* (RSV: "peace offering") are generally rendered in Nf as "sacrifices of holy things." See R. Hayward, Nf Lev, Introd. II, 1. Likewise in the occurrences in Numbers, for HT *šlmym* (6:14; 15:8; 29:39) and for HT *zbḥ šlmym* (6:17; chap. 7 passim; 10:10). See also below, note to Nf Num 6:14.

2. *Hebrew "fire offerings" ('iššeh) becomes "sacrifices" (qrbn).* As noted by R. Hayward (Introd. to Nf Lev II, 2), in Nf the Hebrew phrase "fire offerings (*'iššeh*) to the Lord" regularly becomes "sacrifice(s) to the name of the Lord." Thus also for the occurrences in Numbers (15:3, 10, 13, 14; 28:19).

3. *Hebrew Text terumah becomes "separated offering" ('pršw).* The word *terumah* of the HT ("contribution," "offering," etc.; RSV: "offering"; NRSV: "sacred donations") is in Nf invariably translated as *'pršw,* "separated offering," except in Exod 25:3 and 30:15, where *'pršh* (lit.: "separation") is used. Thus in Exod 25:2 (twice); 29:27, 28; 30:13, 14; 35:5 (twice), 21, 24; 36:3, 6; Lev 7:14, 32, 34; 10:14, 15; 22:12; Num 5:9; 6:20; 15:19, 20, 21; 18:8, 11, 19, 24, 26, 27, 28, 29; 31:29, 41, 52; Deut 12:6, 11, 17.

4. *Hebrew "to make, do" becomes "to sacrifice."* In certain contexts the Hebrew verb *'śh,* with the general meaning of "to make, to do," is used in the sense of "to offer" or "to sacrifice." See R. Hayward in Introd. Nf Lev II, 3. Thus also in the occurrences in this sense in Numbers (6:17, 21; 8:12; 15:3, 5, 6, 8, 14, 24; 28:4, 8, 31; 29:2, 39.

5. *Hebrew "burn, offer" (qṭr) becomes "set in order."* In Nf, this Hebrew word in the Hiphil (generally understood as "to burn incense") is invariably rendered by *sdr,* "to arrange, set in order." For Exodus and Leviticus, see Introd. Nf Exod III, 8, and R. Hayward in Introd. Nf Lev II, 4. The same holds true for the occurrences in Num 5:26; 17:5; 18:17.

6. *Hebrew "fill the hand" becomes "complete the offering of the hand."* The Targum expansion is probably intended to make the sense of the Hebrew clearer to a later generation. It is expanded in the same way in the occurrences in Nf Exod, Lev (see R. Hayward, Introd. Nf Lev II, 5), and in the sole occurrence in Numbers (3:3, rendered as "initiated").

7. *Treatment of Hebrew "sweet-smelling savor" used of sacrifice.* The HT often speaks of sacrificial offerings as being *ryḥ nyḥwḥ,* "a sweet-smelling savor." The Targum tends to soften this somewhat by reference in its translation to the offering being "received with good pleasure before the Lord" or "as an odor of good pleasure which is received before the Lord." For a discussion of this phrase see R. Hayward in Introd. Nf Lev II, 6, and the note on Nf Num 15:10 below. Nf Num follows its general translation technique in its paraphrase of the Hebrew terms (Num 15:3, 7, 10, 13, 14, 24; 18:17; 28:2, 6, 8, 13, 24, 27; 29:2, 6, 8, 13, 36).

8. *Addition of the phrase "without blemish," in reference to sacrificial animals.* When the HT speaks of sacrificial animals being "perfect" (*tm, tmym*), Nf invariably expands as "perfect without blemish." See note 18 to Nf Gen 6:9 (*The Aramaic Bible,* vol. 1A, p. 73). Thus also in Nf Num (HT *tmym:* 6:14; 19:2; 28:3, 9, 11, 19; 29:2, 8, 13, 19, 20, 23, 26, 29, 32, 36).

9. *Understanding of the verb "to offer up" ('lh).* As noted by R. Hayward, in the HT the root *'lh* is used in the Hiphil in the sense of "to offer up," and sometimes in Nf this is translated by *sdr,* "to set in order," just as the HT *qtr* is. It is tendered in this manner also in the two occurrences in Num 8:2, 3.

10. *Addition of "festival day" in description of feast.* Nf glosses the HT expression *mqr' qdš,* "holy convocation," with the words *ywm' ṭb',* "a festival." See R. Hayward, Introd. Nf Lev II, 10. The principle holds for the occurrences in Numbers (28:18, 25, 26; 29:1, 7, 12).

11. *The formulas "decree/statute of the Torah."* When the term *torah* of the HT refers to a specific regulation, not to the Mosaic dispensation as such, Nf may render as "decree of the law." Thus in Nf Num 5:29 ("decree of the law of jealousy"); 6:13, 21 ("decree of the law of the Nazirite"); 15:16 ("one decree of law"). The Hebrew equivalent *ḥqt twrh* is found in 19:14; 31:21, where Nf renders literally: "one decree of law." In Nf 9:14 and 35:29 the phrase occurs without the presence of *twrh* in the HT.

12. *Treatment of the Hebrew term mišpaṭ(im) ("judgment[s]).* As in the other books of the Pentateuch (see Introd. to Nf Exod III, 10; also R. Hayward, Introd. Nf Lev II, 12), Nf Num almost universally renders HT *mšpṭ(ym)* as *sdr(y) dynh.* Thus in Num 9:3, 14; 15:16, 24; 27:5, 21; 29:6, 33; cf. 36:13. For specific reasons it renders otherwise in Num 27:11; 35:12, 24, 29. In the translation here presented, *sdr(y) dynh* is generally rendered as "ordinance(s)." For a number of texts Sokoloff (1990, 368) translates as "legal decisions." For an understanding of the concepts involved, see also R. Hayward, Introd. Nf Lev II, 12.

13. *Addition of the adjective "precious/good" to "crimson."* Nf generally adds *ṭb,* "precious/good," to the term "crimson" in the many occurrences of the word in Exodus and in Lev 14:4, 6, 49, 52. See R. Hayward, Introd. Nf Lev II, 14. It does likewise for all the occurrences in Numbers (4:8; 19:6).

14. *The expression "remit and forgive."* This compound expression, *šry wšbq,* is found as a translation of HT *slḥ,* "pardon," in Nf Num 14:19, 20, and elsewhere in Nf. See Introd. to Nf Exod III, 21 (*The Aramaic Bible,* vol. 2, p. 5), and R. Hayward, Introd. Nf Lev II, 15, and note 9 to text. Elsewhere in Nf Num the Hebrew term is rendered by the simple *šbq* (Nf Num 15:25, 26, 28; 30:6, 9, 13). See note to Nf Gen 4:8 (*The Aramaic Bible,* vol. 1A, p. 66).

15. *Translation of Hebrew twldwt.* In Genesis this Hebrew term is generally rendered in Nf by the composite *yḥws twldwt.* See note 6 to Nf Gen 2:4 (*The Aramaic Bible,* vol. 1A, p. 56; see also pp. 25f.). In Numbers the Hebrew term occurs only in the combination *twldtm lmšpḥtm* (RSV: "their generations, by their families") in Num 1:20-42, where Nf renders as *yḥwsyhwn lzr'yythwn* and in 3:1, *twldt 'hrn,* where Nf retains the Hebrew form: *tldwwth d'hrn.*

16. *Translation of Hebrew śdh.* In Nf this term can be rendered in one of three ways; see note 9 to Nf Gen 2:5 (*The Aramaic Bible,* vol. 1A, p. 57). In Nf Num two of these

are used: *ḥql* in 16:14; 20:17; 21:22; 23:14; by *b-'py br'* in 19:16; 22:4, 23. In 21:20 it is rendered by *tḥwm,* "boundary."

17. *Translation of Hebrew zr'.* When referring to humans and human progeny, this Hebrew term is generally rendered in Nf as "sons." See note to Nf Gen 3:15 (*The Aramaic Bible,* vol. 1A, p. 61; see also p. 26). Thus also in Num 14:24; 18:19. In 5:28 it is rendered as "male son" and in 25:13 as *zr'yt,* ("descendants").

18. *Translation of Hebrew "elders" as "wise men."* In Nf the term *zkn,* "elder(s)," of the HT is translated "wise men." See Introd. Nf Exod, no. 12. Thus also in the occurrences in Num 11:16, 24, 25; 22:4.

19. *Translation of Hebrew "land flowing with milk and honey."* In Nf this Hebrew phrase is generally rendered as "a land producing good fruits, pure as milk and sweet as honey." Thus Exod 3:8, etc.; Lev 15:2; Deut 6:3. See notes to text. So also in the occurrences in Num 13:27; 14:8; 16:13, 14.

20. *Translation of Hebrew yštḥw.* For Nf's rendering of this term of the HT, see note 4 to Nf Gen 18:2 (*The Aramaic Bible,* vol. 1A, pp. 103f.). There are only two occurrences of the term in Numbers, the first (22:31) of Balaam, where a root cognate with the Hebrew is used; the second with reference to idols, where, as elsewhere in Nf (Exod 20:5; 23:24; 34:14), the verb "bow down to" (*šqd*) is used.

21. *Paraphrase of Hebrew ḥn.* When *ḥn* occurs alone in the HT, Nf generally paraphrases by adding *wḥsd;* see note 16 to Nf Gen 6:8 (*The Aramaic Bible,* vol. 1A, p. 73). Thus also in Nf Num 11:15; 32:5. In the third occurrence in Num (11:11), Nf has *ḥsd* only. With Nfmg we should probably correct to *ḥn wḥsd.*

22. *Addition of adjective "redeemed" with reference to the Exodus.* As elsewhere in Nf (see Introd., no. 23, to Nf Exod), when the HT mentions the Exodus from Egypt, Nf Num frequently inserts a reference to "redemption," e.g., "I brought you out redeemed. . . ." Thus in Nf Num 1:1; 9:1; 15:41 (twice); 24:8; 26:4; 33:1, 3, 38; see also 24:7, 19 (the Messiah a redeemer).

23. *Expansions through addition of "men of," "people of."* In keeping with its general practice, Nf Num tends to specify persons where the HT uses personal or tribe names, e.g., "the men of (the tribe of)," "the sons of." See Introd. Nf Exod III, 24. In Numbers, Nf generally prefixes "the people of" to HT *'dh,* "assembly"; thus 1:16, 53; 3:7; 4:34; 10:2, 3, etc. It does not, however, do likewise for the HT term *qhl,* "congregation." See also R. Hayward, Introd. Nf Lev II, 18.

24. *Paraphrase of Hebrew gr.* Unlike the case in Nf for other books of the Pentateuch (see Introd. to Nf Exod, no. 28) where there is ambiguity, there is no ambiguity in Nf Num with regard to the understanding of *gr* of the HT. In Nf it is universally rendered as *gywr,* "proselyte." Thus in 9:14; 15:15, 16, 26, 29, 30; 19:10; 35:15.

25. *Treatment of HT pqd.* In a study in 1958 E. A. Speiser remarked that "there is probably no other Hebrew verb that has caused translators so much trouble as *pqd.*" From a study of the cognate word *paqadum* in the Mari archives, he concluded that all the occurrences of PQD in the OT census passages must now be rendered simply "to record, to enroll." An earlier study of PQD by R. Holler opposed rendering PQD by "to count," and proposed instead that a basic meaning "to muster" developed in two directions, one "to make an inventory," hence "to number," and the other "to organize or "to assemble." In this sense, he believes, the qal passive participle *pequdim* is better trans-

lated by "inventory" than by "sum" or "number." Following on Speiser's conclusions, J. B. Van Hooser translated all the census passages of PQD as "to enroll, to record." In a specialized study on the theological meaning of PQD, J. Schabert concludes that PQD in its occurrences in the mustering protocol Num 1–4 and 26 is a *terminus technicus* of military and administrative language with the meaning of "to muster" for the verbal forms, and "the mustered" for the nominal forms.

B. Grossfeld has studied the manner in which the 356 occurrences of PQD in the biblical text have been translated in the ancient versions (LXX, Syr., Latin, Tgs.). His analysis yields a variety of twenty-six different meanings, which can further be broken down to four basic meanings, with eight sub-categories, as follows:

I. *Administrative-Legal:* (1) to appoint; (2) to deposit, commit, entrust, store; (3) to rule, to be in charge of; (4) to order.

II. *General:* (1) to remember, to inspect, review, examine, visit, look after; (2) to seek, to miss.

III. *Theological:* (1) to punish, avenge, accuse.

IV. *Military/Census:* (1) to count.

Turning now to the rendering of PQD in Nf Num, we may note that there are about 86 occurrences of the word in the book, as follows: 19 in chap. 1; 18 in chap. 2; 11 in chap. 3; 14 in chap. 4; 2 in chap. 14; 19 in chap. 26; 1 in chap. 27; 2 in chap. 31. In all these instances (with two exceptions), the HT term PQD is rendered by the Aramaic root *skm.* With this we may include the three instances of the Hothpael form of PQD in Num 1:47; 2:33; 26:62, "to be mustered, to be passed in review." This, too, is rendered in Nf by *skm ('stkm).* The two exceptions to the use of *skm* are Nf Num 14:18 (HT: *pqd,* "visiting the iniquity of the fathers on the children"), where Nf renders as "remembering," *mdkr,* and Num 27:16, where Nf renders by *mn',* "appoint." Furthermore, there is in the HT (Num 3:32, 36; 4:16, twice) the noun *pqdh (pequddah),* derived from PQD, requiring the meaning "office, charge." In Nf this term, too, is translated by *skm (skwm).*

The Aramaic *skm* does not have a wide range of meanings: *skm,* verb, "to count, to agree"; Ithpe., "to be counted"; *skwm,* noun, "number, total"; *skwmw,* "counting" (Nfmg, Frg. Tg. V, Num 16:29; Nfmg Num 4:16). See Sokoloff, 377–378. The choice of this single translation word by the Nf tradition in Numbers does not always make for smooth translation and occasionally fits badly in the context.

26. *Coins, weights and measures.* As is general in Nf, the HT term *sheqel* is rendered by *sl'* ("sela"). Thus Nf Num 3:47, 50; chap. 7 passim; 18:16; 31:52. Likewise, HT *'ph ('ephah)* is rendered as *mekiltah.*

IV. LIST OF PLACE NAMES IN TARGUMS NEOFITI AND PSEUDO-JONATHAN: NUMBERS

(Material on Ps.-J. from E. G. Clarke)

In the first volume of this series (*The Aramaic Bible* 1A, pp. 21–23), I gave a listing of toponyms in Greek and Latin in the Palestinian Targums of the Pentateuch, particularly in Codex Neofiti 1. Many of these were from the Book of Numbers. The Book of

Numbers is so rich in non-biblical place names that these merit listing and examination apart. That is what I do here, although many of them are also examined in the notes to the text.

Some of the biblical names of the Book of Numbers are found in other books of the Pentateuch as well. In these cases Nf's identification for the Book of Numbers is generally that found for the other books of the Pentateuch. The Book of Numbers has also a number of place names proper to itself, of which Nf often gives non-biblical equivalents. Together with this, Nf (as other Pal. Tg. texts) at Num 34:15 has an inserted section on the borders of the two and a half tribes, for which no border is indicated in the Hebrew Text. Five sources may be distinguished for the material used by the targumist in this section: Num 32:33-42 and Deut 3:1-17; Ezek 47, especially 47:15-17; material related to the Tannaitic border list; added glosses, some of a haggadic nature; a redactional stratum (see Alexander, 1974, 218–252). An early and Tannaitic list of border towns or locations is introduced in *Sifre Deut.* 51 (on Deut 11:24) as follows: "These are the boundaries of the Land of Israel as seized by those who came up from Babylonia: the Ashkelon junction. . . ." The list is also found in *t. Shebi.* 4:11, *j. Shebi.* 6, 36.[17] This Tannaitic list begins at Ashkelon, goes from southwest to north, northeast, southeast, and southwest (ending with Ashkelon). It has details only along the northern border.

Nf Num 34 gives a detailed indication of Israel's border, for the south, west, and north, following the lines indicated by the biblical text. Then, for 34:15 it gives its special list.

As in Num 34 (Nf) there is a detailed list of Israel's geographical borders, so in Ps.-J. Num 34:3-12 there is an extensive list of geographical names. These lists of names are related also to two other lists found in Josh 15:2-4 and Ezek 47:15-20. As one can see, Ps.-J. divides the list into places in the south (vv. 3-5), west (v. 6), north (vv. 7-9), east (vv. 10-12) relevant to the nine and a half tribes that crossed over to settle in the Promised Land. The territory of the three tribes Reuben, Gad, and Manasseh, who dwelt east of the Jordan, are described in Num 32:33-42 and Deut 3:1-17. As noted above, Nf has a geographical list in v. 15 similar in many ways to the general outline in 34:3-12 (Ps.-J.). Ps.-J. in v. 15 simply says, "Two and a half tribes received their inheritance on the other side of the Jordan, to the east."

1. **Antioch:** *'ntwky' ('Antokya).* Num 13:21; 34:8 (cf. Gen 10:18), rendering Hamath of HT. "From Taurus Umanos (Amanus) to the entrances of Antioch." HT: "From Mount Hor (*hor ha-har*) to the entrance of Hamath." The town in question is on Israel's northern border. Nf renders Hamath here, as in Num 13:21; see Gen 10:18: HT "Hamathites"; Nf "the Antiochenes." The identification of Hamath with Antioch is standard in early Jewish texts (see Alexander, 1974, 181, 207) but was not the sole identification. Josephus (*Ant.* 1,6,2 #138) and some rabbinic texts identified it with Amatha (modern Hama), also named Epiphaneia, and thus the Jews in general in Jerome's day,

[17]This text, with minor changes, has been found in the mosaic inscription in the synagogue at Rehob. For an English translation of this inscription, see J. Sussman, in his essay "The Inscription in the Synagogue at Rehob," in *Ancient Synagogues Revealed,* L. Levine, ed. (Jerusalem, 1982) 146–59. See also R. Hammer's note in his English translation of *Sifre Deut.* 51 (Hammer, 1986) 419.

although some of them identified it with Antioch: *Non nulli Antiochiam ita appellatam putant* (Jerome, *Hebr. quaest. in Gen.* 10:18; CCL 72,14). In Ps.-J. Antioch appears as the targumic identification of Hamat in Num 13:21, but in Num 34:8 Ps.-J. has Tiberias, which is an error for Antioch but may be Ps.-J.'s attempt to harmonize the text with Deut 3:17 (Ps.-J.).

2. **Apamea:** *'pmyh* (VN: *'pmyys;* Ps.-J.: *'pmy'h*). Num 34:10, 11. On the eastern border of Israel, translating HT: Shapham. "And you shall draw a line for the eastern boundary from Tirat Enwata (HT: Hazar-enan) to Apamea. And the boundary goes down from Tirat Enwata to Daphne" (HT: Riblah). There are two possibilities with regard to location. One is that the city originally intended was Apamea. There were a number of cities of this name in the Seleucid empire, two or three of which are mentioned in rabbinic literature. One of these was Apamea on the Orontes, more precisely referred to as "Syrian Apamea." There are solid arguments in favor of accepting this as the targumic identification of biblical Shapham. Josephus (*War* 2,28,5, #479) tells us that it had Jews among its population during the Jewish war, a fact borne out by *m. Hall.* 4:10-11, which classes it for first fruits as within the land of Israel. Jerome, moreover (*Comm. on Ezek.* 47:18; CCL 75,723; PL 25,478), says that the Jews of his day identified Shapham with Apamea. Some modern scholars believe that this is the city intended. However, the form *'pmyys* (Apameas) of the Frg. Tg. (VN) requires explanation. Other modern scholars, e.g., P. S. Alexander (1974, 212–213) and Le Déaut (1979, vol. 3, p. 323), as already J. Levy (p. 54) and M. Jastrow (p. 105), believe that the place intended is really Paneas in northern Galilee (i.e., Caesarea Philippi). The initial aleph would be prosthetic. The Greek letter *n* can be occasionally reproduced by a mem in Hebrew and Aramaic.

3. **Aulon (Aulos) of the Cilicians,** *'wwls dqylqy* (VN: *d-'wwl dqylq'y;* Ps.-J.: *l-'bls dqylq'y*). Num 34:8; HT: Zedad *ṣdd.* A town or place on the northern borders of Israel. "From Taurus Amanus . . . to the entrance of Antioch; and the boundary shall come out at the Aulon of the Cilicians." Like HT Zedad, this place name is found only in the Pal. Tg. Num 34:8. The second element clearly refers to Cilicia: "of the Cilicians," "Cilician." The first part, not found elsewhere in rabbinic texts, seems to be derived from the Greek *aulôn,* a term with varied related meanings. One is: "a narrow or hemmed-in place," "a cleft between mountains." That seems to be the meaning here. The "Cilician Aulôn" would thus mean the Pass of Beilon, or the Syrian Gates, between Antioch and Cilicia. This is probably the location intended in the Targum. The Greek term *aulôn* could also mean "a broad but enclosed plain," in which sense the "Cilician Plain" could refer to the coastal plain of Cilicia that opened beyond the Syrian Gates. Another meaning of *aulôn* is "a narrow stretch of water" or "straits." And, in fact, the stretch of water between Cyprus and Cilicia is referred to as the "Cilician Aulôn" (*kilikios aulôn*); see Ptolemy, *Geog.* 6,4,4; Pliny, *NH* 5,130.

The Aramaic form is Awlas (*'wwls*), or, as in Ps.-J. Ablas (*'bls;* representing the usual shift of ww>b). In either reading the final letter is *s,* not *n*—Awlas (Ablas) rather than Aulôn. This might represent Greek *aulas,* accusative plural form of *aulê* (Latin *aula*), "open court," etc., and Stephanus of Byzantium (145,19) mentions a place by the name of Aulai in Cilicia. It was a seaport near Tarsus, which does not suit the Targum context. An original reading *Aulôn* seems to be the most suitable. The final *s* (samech), in P. S. Alexander's opinion (Alexander, 1974, 208), may be an error for a similar-looking final mem. Other examples of such a misreading are known, e.g., *Hispania* as *'spmy'*; Paneas as *pmy's.*

In manuscripts of Josephus' *Antiquities* (13,15,4 #397) mention is made of a *Kilikên aulôn* in a list of places held by the Jews under Alexander Jannaeus. While this is thought to be a scribal error for an original *halykos aulôn* ("Valley of Salt"), the scribal error itself (if such it be) seems to indicate that the place name *Kilikên Aulôn* did exist.

See further Alexander, 1974, 207–209.

4. **Ayna:** *'yynh* ("The Spring)." Num 34:11; Ps.-J., VN: "The Springs"; 34:11 (16). Near Daphne (at Dan). Nf here has a simple rendering of the HT: "Ain." Ps.-J. and VN have the plural form. See Alexander, 1974, 217–218.

5. **Bar Sanigora.** Num 34:8 (Ps.-J.). According to Le Déaut, vol. 3, p. 322, n. 16, the word is a corruption of Zénodore. It is on the border between Syria and Palestine; see Alexander, 1971, 224–226.

6. **Bar Zoemah.** Num 34:8 (Ps.-J.). A city in the north between Syria and Palestine.

7. **Bathyra:** Nf: *btryh.* Num 34:15 (added paraphrase): ". . . the boundary went out for them to Qeren Zawwe (correct to: *qryy zkwt',* "villages of Zekhuta") to Bathyra, and (to) the whole Trachonitis of Beth-Zimra." Nf actually has: "(*qrn zwwy*) *dbtryh* (and all Trachonitis . . .)," which would ordinarily be translated: "(Qeren Z.) which is behind it (or: of Batreh) and all Trachonitis of Beth-Zimra." Nf's *qrn zwwy* is to be corrected (partly with Ps.-J.) to "Qirye Zekhuta," Beth-Zimra is to be connected with the person Zamaris, and *btryh* is to be understood as having been intended originally to designate Bathyra. Zamaris was the name of a Babylonian Jew appointed by Herod the Great as a leader of a colony of Babylonian Jews in Batanea, on the borders of Trachonitis. They were settled there to discourage the incursion of Trachonite Arabs into the settled land. See Josephus, *Ant.* 17,2,1-2, ##23-28; *Life* 2, 11 (#54). The chief town of the settlement was Bathyra (Josephus, *Ant.,* 17,2,2, #26): "he (Zamaris) built in it fortresses and a village, and named it Bathyra." It is the *bryrs/btyrh* of rabbinic texts. See I. Gafni, "Bathyra," in *EJ* 4(1972), col. 323; Alexander, 1974, 286.

8. **Beth ha-Jeshimon.** Num 21:20; 23:28. Rendering HT: Ha-Jeshimon. In Nf Num 33:49 the HT form is retained. Ps.-J. spells as Beth-Jeshimon only in 21:20 but Beth-Jeshimoth in 23:28 and 33:49.

9. **Beth Nimrin.** Num 32:3. HT: Nimrah. Ps.-J. has Beth Nimre.

10. **Beth Ramatha.** Num 32:36, rendering MT Beth-haran (occurring only here in the Pentateuch) as if it were *Beth ha-ram* (cf. Josh 13:27). No identification seems intended.

11. **Beth Sekel.** Num 34:9 (Ps.-J.).

12. **Beth Yeraḥ:** *byt yrh;* occurring in Pal. Tg. only in Num 34:15 (additional paraphrase). According to Nf, the border of the two and a half tribes went in part "to Chinnereth . . . to the fortress of Iyyon to the east of Beth Yeraḥ, and from east of the Sea of Beth Yeraḥ . . . to Yadyoqiṭa . . . ." The presence of the reference to Beth Yeraḥ in the present text may be due to an error. (See below under Iyyon.) Beth Yeraḥ itself, however, is identifiable. It was at the most southerly point of the Sea of Galilee (Lake of Tiberias). Beth Yeraḥ (near Yerah) was a twin town of Sennabris (texts in Jastrow, p. 595). In *Gen. R.* 98,17, to Gen 49:21, explaining Kinnereth of Deut 3:17, R. Eleazar (ca. 270 C.E.) says that it is Gennesaret; R. Samuel ben Nachman (ca. 260) that it is Beth Yeraḥ, while R. Judah ben Simon (ca. 320) says that it is Sennabris and Beth Yeraḥ. According to Josephus (*War* 3,9,7, #447), Sennaberis was about thirty stadia (three-quarters of a mile) from (the town of) Tiberias. See also Alexander, 1974, 228.

13. **Beth Zimra:** *byt zymr'.* Num 34:15 (added paraphrase). Beth Zimra is to be connected with the personal name Zamaris, the leader of the Babylonian Jews who settled on the borders of Batanea and Trachonitis, with Bathyra as chief town. See under "Bathyra."

14. **Butnin (Batanea):** *bwtnyyn* (*Botneyin*). Num 21:33; 34:15; also Deut 3:1, 3, 11; 4:10, 13f., 43, 47; 29:6; 32:14; 33:22; *Mwtnin* in Num 32:33; *Mtnyn* in Deut 1:4; HT: Bashan. The area known as Batanea in Roman times. The form Boteynin is proper to the Palestinian Targums. In other targumic texts Bashan is rendered as *Matnan.* Ps.-J. prefers the spelling "Matnan," representing the consonantal shift of b>m and sh>t.

15. **Caesarea (Philippi):** "Image of the Cock of Caesarea" (*ydywqyṭ'/ydywqyṭws* [correct to: *'yqwnyn*] *trngwl qsrywn*). Num 34:15 (added paraphrase); Nf reads: "Yadyoqitos (=Image of the) Cock of Caesarea, which is at the east of the (Cave) of Dan." "Upper Tarnegola of Caesarea" is also mentioned in the border lists of *Sifre Deut.* 51 on Deut 11:24 and *t. Shebi.* 4:11. The name Caesarea is also in Nf Gen 14:15 (HT: Dan). See also Alexander, 1974, 229.

16. **Cilicia, Aulon of.** Num 34:8. See under "Aulon of the Cilicians."

17. **Damascus, Springs of:** *'yynwwtyh.* Num 34:15 (added paraphrase): "the Mount of Snow, at the border of Lebanon, which is to the north of the Springs of Damascus." Mention of these springs may have been occasioned by *'nn* in the name Hazar-enon of the border list of Ezek 47:17.

18. **Daphne:** *dpny.* Num 34:11; HT: Riblah. On the northern border of Israel: "Their boundary went from Apamea (= Paneas, at Dan?) to Daphne." The identification of the biblical Riblah with Daphne is general in rabbinic tradition. There were a number of cities with the name Daphne (= "laurel"), one near Antioch, the other near Paneas/Dan. Rabbinic tradition identified Riblah (of the land of Hamath) of

Nebuchadnezzar's campaign (2 Kgs 25:20-21; Jer 52:26-27) with Daphne of Antioch. Jerome (*Comm. on Ezek.* 47:18; CCL 75,723; PL 25,478), apparently following Jewish tradition, identifies Riblah of Num 34:11 with Antioch, and the "spring" of Num 34:12 with Daphne of Antioch. It may be that it was this Jewish tradition which had the targumist identify Riblah of 34:11 with Daphne. The Daphne in question, however, by reason of the course of Israel's border being given, must be the Daphne near Dan/Paneas, not that of Antioch. This Daphne near Dan is mentioned by Josephus (*War* 4,1,1 #3). See Alexander, 1974, 214–217; Le Déaut, *Nombres,* p. 323, n. 25.

19. **Dirat Adarayya.** Num 34:4. This is Frg. Tg.'s (VN) rendering of the HT Hazar-addar, rendered Tirat Adarayya in Nf. See Ṭirat Adarayya below. Ps.-J. agrees with Nf here as well as in 34:9, 10.

20. **Divakinos.** Num 34:8 (Ps.-J.). Whether this word and Tarnegola are one or two places is questionable. Alexander (1971) considers the two words a corruption for "Image of the Cock." Divakinos is then a corruption of *dywq* or Greek *eikôn* ("image, idol"). The reference would be to such an image at Caesarea Philippi.

21. **Fortress of Nephahayya.** Num 21:30; HT: Nophah. Possibly no identification is intended, merely a transcription of the HT word, with the Aramaic plural ending, and the added description of "fortress." Ps.-J. presents a midrash on Dibon and the HT *nph,* "laid waste," rather than a place name; hence Ps.-J.'s "desolation."

22. **Gablah:** *gblh.* Num 24:18; also Gen 14:6; 32:4; 33:14; Deut 1:2, 44; 2:1, 5, 8, 12, 22. HT: (Mount) Seir. So also Frg. Tg., Ps.-J. and Sam. Tg. The home of Esau. The identification of Seir with Gabla (Gebal) is found in the *Genesis Apocryphon* (1QGenAp) 21,11,29 (first century B.C.E.): "The Hurrians who [were] in the mountains of Gebal [HT: "in Seir," Gen 14:6] until they reached El-Paran which is in the desert." It is the Gobolitis or Gebalene which according to Josephus (*Ant.* 2,1,2 #6) the sons of Esau occupied and was part of Idumaea; it was also connected with the Amalekites (*Ant.* 3,2,1 #40; 9,9,1 #188). In Nf Deut 32:2 "the mountains of Gablah" renders "Mount Paran" of the HT. A tradition apparently considered it located in Gablah; cf. Gen 14:6.

23. **Gennesar, Sea of:** *ym' dgnysr.* Num 34:11; also Deut 3:17; HT: Sea of Chinneret. The toponym Gennesar is found in 1 Macc 11:67, in the New Testament, and in Josephus.

24. **Graves of Those Who Were Desirous.** Num 33:16. A rendering of MT (RSV): Kibroth-hattavah. No identification seems intended.

25. **Hill of Hatmana.** Num 34:9 (Ps.-J.). Possibly modern 'Atman, north of Dera'a in Syria; see Alexander, 1971, 227.

26. **Huminas Ṭaurus.** Num 34:7. See below under Taurus Aminus.

27. **Idols of Peor.** Num 23:28; 25:5. See below under Peor, idols of.

28. **Italy:** *'yṭly'.* Num 24:24; also Gen 10:4; HT: Kittim. The Kittim mentioned in Dan 11:30 are generally understood as the Romans. In Num 24:24 the Vulg. renders as *Italia.* Ps.-J. expands on "Italy" to add "Rome" and "Constantinople."

29. **Iyyon, Fortress of:** (*krk' d-*) *'ywn.* Num 34:15 (added paraphrase). A border town in Nf's list for the two and a half tribes, east of the Jordan: "to Chinnereth . . . ; the boundary went out for them to the fortress of Iyyon to the east of Beth Yerah." This section of the paraphrase is not in the Frg. Tg. as found in VN.

The identification and localization of this fortress of Iyyon are connected with one's view on the nature of this section of Nf. The present text situates it to the east of Beth Yerah, that is, to the southern part of the Sea of Galilee. A. Díez Macho, with reference to I. Press (see below note 19 to Num 34:15), thinks it appears to be the present-day 'Ayyun ("Wells"), two and a half kilometers to the north of Al-Hamma and four kilometers to the east of the Sea of Galilee (Chinnereth). The reference to Beth Yerah in Nf, however (not in VN), may be an erroneous gloss, and Iyyon of the text seems to be connected with "depression of Iyyon" (*nqypt'* [corrected from *nqybt'*] *d'ywn*) of the border list of *Sifre Deut.* 21 (on Deut 11:24) and *t. Shebi.* 4:11; *j. Shebi.* 6,36c, where the border moves to ". . . Mesaf Sefarta, the depression of Iyyun, Upper Tarnegola of Caesarea (Philippi). . . ." Jastrow (p. 933), with reference to Hildesheimer, *Beiträge zur Geographie Palestinas* (Berlin, 1886, pp. 37ff.), identified this with Mardj 'Ayun in the north of Palestine. So also Alexander (1974, 229), Merdj 'Ayun being a plain lying about the town of Merdj 'Ayun, to which it gave its name, to the northeast of Baniyas. According to Alexander, "the fortress of Iyyon" (of Nf Num 34:15) is probably Tell Dibbin at the northern end of the plain, the biblical Iyyon (1 Kgs 15:20; 2 Chr 16:4).

30. **Kerak Tarnegolah:** lit. Fort Tarnegola, or Fortress of the Cock; Num 33:36; also Deut 2:8 (vocalized in CTg Br Dt 2:8 as Tornagala); HT: Ezion-geber. The border list of the two and a half tribes (and the rabbinic border lists) mention an Upper Tarnegola near Caesarea (Philippi). See under Caesarea, Yadyoqitas. This is hardly the place intended in Nf Num 33:36 and Deut 2:8. In these we probably have only an interpretative rendering of the HT Ezion-geber, *geber* in Hebrew = "cock" (in Aramaic *tornegola*).

31. **Keren Zekutha.** Num 34:9 (Ps.-J.). HT: Ziphron. Possibly modern Zakiye, southeast of Damascus; see Alexander, 1971, 227.

32. **Kinnereth.** Num 34:15. Here Nf leaves the HT name untranslated. VN identify as "the Sea of Gennesar," as do both Nf and VN in the other occurrence in Deut 3:17.

33. **Laḥayyath, Leḥawwath (Moab).** Num 21:15, 28 (*lḥwwt;* HT: Ar); 32:34 (*lḥyyt;* HT: Aroer). Also in Deut 2:9, 29 (HT: Ar); 2:36; 4:48 (HT: Aroer). Ps.-J. does not mention Lehayyath in Num 21:28.

34. **Liburnian ships.** Num 24:24. The Liburnians were dwellers of the Dalmatian coast and its offshore islands. See note 31 to 24:24. Ps.-J. has an entirely different text at 24:24 and does not mention Liburnian ships.

35. **Ma'alath.** Num 32:3 (Ps.-J.); HT: Elealeh.

36. **Madbashta.** Num 32:3 (Ps.-J.); HT: Dibon.

37. **Makhlalta.** Num 32:3 (Ps.-J.); HT: Ataroth. This place was assigned to Gad (Num 32:3, 34). In the Mesha Stone (lines 10-11): "The men of Gad dwelt in the land of Ataroth."

38. **Maresha:** *mryšh.* Num 22:39; HT (RSV): Kiriath-huzoth; Ps.-J: "Birosha." Nf may be an erroneous reading of "Birosha" but is much more probably a variant writing (mem for beth, as elsewhere; see above under "Aulon" and below under "Mikbar").

39. **Mera.** Num 32:3 (Ps.-J.); HT: Sebam.

40. **Mikbar:** *mkbr.* Num 32:1, 3; MT: Jazer. A district in Peraea. The MT Jazer is retained in Nf Num 21:32; 32:15. Ps.-J. renders the Hebrew name as Mikwar, spelled as Mikbar in 21:32. This is the usual consonantal shift of w>b.

41. **Motenim:** *mwtnyn.* Num 32:33; MT: Bashan. The MT Bashan is generally rendered as Butnin in Nf. See under "Butnin" above. Ps.-J. translates the HT "Bashan" as Matnan as usual. The Motenim in Nf seems to be a consonantal shift of b>m.

42. **Mount of Iron:** *twr przl'.* Num 34:4; MT: Zin (*Ṣin*). The HT reads: "and your boundary shall . . . cross to Zin, and the end shall be south of Kadesh-barnea." In Nf Zin is identified as "the Mount of Iron" and Kadesh-barnea as "Reqem de-Ge'a." Num 34:4 is the only place in the Pentateuch where Zin (Sin) occurs alone. In Num 13:21; 20:1; 27:14 (twice); 33:36; 34:3; Deut 32:51 we read of the Wilderness of Sin, identified as Kadesh in Num 33:36. In all these cases Nf reproduces the Hebrew form "wilderness of Zin," which it naturally identifies as "Reqem" in Num 33:36.

The "Mount of Iron" was a real geographical locality, mentioned in Josephus, *War* 4,8,2 #454, and *m. Sukk.* 3:1. See also 1 Henoch 67:4-5 and 1 Enoch 52. Josephus, describing the Transjordan, tells how a second range of mountains beginning at Julias "extends itself southwards as far as Somora, which borders on Petra in Arabia. In this ridge of mountains there is one called the Iron Mountain, that runs in length as far as Moab." See further Alexander, 1974, 189–191. Ps.-J. makes a distinction between the singular and the plural for the HT "Zin." In 33:36 and 34:3 Ps.-J. writes the plural for "Zin," and we have translated as the "desert of the palms," as does Le Déaut; see also Ezek 47:19.

43. **Mount of Snow:** *ṭwr tlgh.* Num 34:15 (in a free paraphrase); also Deut 3:8; 4:48, rendering HT "Mount Hermon." Also in VN, Num 34:15. In Nf Num 34:15 the Mount of Snow is given with the Lebanon as the northern border of Israel. Mount Hermon must be intended. Ps.-J. only makes reference to Mount of Snow in Deut 4:48; otherwise Ps.-J. uses Hermon.

44. **Naḥal Segula:** "the wadi of the cluster of Grapes." Num 13:23, rendering the HT: "Eschol," "cluster of grapes." Probably a simple translation, not indication of an actual place name, is intended. Ps.-J. as well as Onq. uses *'tkl'* rather than Nf *sgwlh;* see Le Déaut, vol. 3, p. 125, n. 11.

45. **Nephahayya, Fortress of.** Num 21:30; HT: Nophah. See under "Fortress" above.

46. **Nile of the Egyptians:** *nylws dmṣryy.* Num 34:5; HT: "the Brook (*nḥlh*) of Egypt." Also in Nf Gen 15:18: "the Nile of Egypt," rendering HT "River (*nhr*) of Egypt." Also Ps.-J.

47. **Passes of Abarayya:** *mgzt 'bryyh.* Num 21:11; 33:44; HT: *'yy h'brym;* RSV: Iye-abarim. Very probably no particular locality is intended in Nf, which merely attempts a translation of the first element and transcribes the second, with an Aramaic ending. See also "Tirat Adarayya" below. Ps.-J. in 21:11 reads "the plain of Megaztha," but in both 27:12 and 33:44 Ps.-J. agrees with Nf.

48. **Ocean:** *'wqyynws.* Num 34:6. In a targumic addition on the western boundary: "And the boundary of the Great Sea—Ocean; these are the Waters of the Beginning, its islands, its ports and its ships, with the primordial waters that are in it (*bgwwh;* or: 'in the midst'); this shall be for you the sea boundary." HT: "For the western boundary (*gbwl*), you shall have the Great Sea and (its) coasts; this shall be for you its western boundary (*gbwl*)." As western border, "the Great Sea" (Josh 1:4: "towards the going down of the sun"), like "the western sea" (Deut 11:24), might normally be taken as indicating the Mediterranean. The presence of "boundary/border" (*gbwl*) twice in Num 34:6 led to exegetical speculation among the rabbis; R. Judah ben Ilai (fourth century) maintained that the border intended must be the border of the Great Sea, which R. Judah took to be the Atlantic; see *b. Giṭṭ.* 8a. The targumic text may have been built up from a series of glosses, which, however, represent an exegetical tradition, one which probably represents a world view. Alexander (1974, 201) refers to Ps.-Aristotle, *De mundo* III (393a16), where the Mediterranean is called "the inner sea," as opposed to "the outer sea," or the Oceanus which surrounds the islands of the inhabited world. For this reason, in Nf we should probably read *bgwwh* (referring to the Mediterranean), with the meaning "in the midst" (= "the inner sea").

It is not clear how the expansions in Nf are linked to the geographical boundaries. A first level of translation and interpretation may have been that the western boundary was as far as the Great Sea, interpreted as the Atlantic, and included the Mediterranean, with its islands, ports, and ships. This led to the concept of Oceanus and the primordial waters—less quantifiable concepts which fit none too easily into earthly geographical boundaries.

See further Alexander, 1974, 200–203; below, note 8 to Num 34:6 and note 17 in Ps.-J.

49. **Pelusium:** *pylwswpyn* (probably an error for *pylwsyn*). Num 33:5; also as *pylwsyn,* Gen 47:11; Exod 12:37. HT: Rameses, the place of residence of the Israelites in Egypt.

50. **Peor, idols of:** *ṭ'wwth dp'r.* Num 23:28; HT here: "Top of Peor" (*r'š hp'wr*), a form occurring only here. HT Num 25:18 and 31:16 have Peor alone ("the affair of Peor") and in Num 25:3, 5 "Baal-Peor," in all of which instances Nf renders as "the idol of Peor." In Deut 3:29 and 4:46 HT "Beth-Peor" is rendered in Nf as "the idol of Peor." For Ps.-J. the distribution is somewhat different. In Num 23:28 and Deut 4:46 there is no mention of Peor. In Num 25:3, 18 and 31:16 Ps.-J. translates as HT. Only in Num 25:5 does Ps.-J. follow Nf.

51. **Qeren (?) Zawwe** (read: **Qryy zkwt'**): *qrn zwwy.* Num 34:15 (in an added paraphrase on the borders of the two and a half tribes): "From the Great River, the river Euphrates, the boundary went out for them to *qrn zwwy (Qeren Zawwe),* to Bathyra (*btryh*), the whole of Trachonitis of Beth-Zimra." VN have *qryn zwwt';* Ps.-J. *qrn zkwt'.* The original form of the name seems to have been *qryy zkwth,* "the villages of Zakhuta." The place in question seems to be connected with *skwth* (with initial samech), Sakutha, of the rabbinic border list in *Sifre Deut.* 51; *t. Shebi.* 4:11: "Sakutha, Nimrin. . . ." Alexander (1974, 227) proposes one of two possible identifications: Modern Zakiye, south-southwest of Damascus, or the Zakkaia of Ptolemy V,14,20.

52. **Qesem:** *qsm.* Num 34:4, 5; "(Shuq Masai at) Qesem." HT: (Hazar-addar to) Azmon (*'ṣmn*). The place is present-day el-Quseima, at the eastern end of the wadi el-Arish, and very probably the correct identification of the biblical Azmon. See Alexander, 1974, 199; Abel, *Géographie* I, 306.

53. **Raphion (Raphia):** *rpywn.* Num 34:15 (in added paraphrase on the border of the two and a half tribes), which in its final stage ". . . goes out to Raphion (*rpywn*), and to Shuq Mazai (*mzy*), and to the Cave of Ain Gedi until it reaches the border district of the Sea of Salt." VN have a similar text but read Raphia (*rpyh*) instead of Raphion: "it goes out to Raphia and to Shuq Mazai until it reaches the border of the Sea of Salt." In Nf Num 34:4 the southern border is described from the Ascent of Akrabbim, by the Mount of Iron, Reqem de-Ge'a, "and shall pass by the boundary of Shuq Masai (*msy*) at Qesem." (VN are similar, omitting the reference to Shuq Masai.) Qesem, as we have seen above, is at the southwest border, in the area of Gaza. If Shuq Mazai of 34:15 is the same as Shuq Masai of 34:4, Raphion would appear to have been in the same area. In this case Nf's reading (*rpywn*) is best corrected to VN's Raphiah (*rpyh*) and identified with Raphia, south of Gaza. Thus A. Díez Macho, 1974, 4 (*Números*), 322, with reference to Abel, *Géographie* 2, 172, and Avi-Yonah, 1951, 118 (= Avi Yonah 1977). However, the reference to Shuq Mazai in Nf and VN 34,15 may be an erroneous gloss, added because a glossator took an original Raphia to be the town in southern Palestine. Thus Alexander, 1974, 128. In this case, with a Transjordan location, Nf's reading "Raphion" can be kept, and the place possibly identified with the Raphion of 1 Macc 5:34 (= Josephus, *Ant.* 12,8,4 #342).

Another possibility, and a variant of the first, might be that the texts of Nf (and VN) are original, not glosses, but that what the compiler intended was to have the border list end as the larger border list began: at the southwest of Palestine. Thus, here two traditions would be combined: the rabbinic tradition beginning and ending the border list at the southwest with Ashkelon, and the list for the two and a half tribes, ending in some way at the Dead Sea.

54. **Reqem:** *rqm.* Num 13:26; 20:1, 14, 16, 22; 33:36, 37. Also in Gen 14:7; 16:14; 20:1; Deut 1:2, 19, 46; 2:14; 9:23. HT: Kadesh. Reqem is the constant identification of HT Kadesh in all Targums and in the Peshitta Pentateuch.

Reqem (*rqm*) was the Semitic name for Petra in Edom; see Josephus, *Ant.* 4,4,7 #82: Moses led his forces through the desert and came to a place in Arabia which the Arabs have deemed their metropolis, formerly called Arkê (read: Arkem), today named Petra. There Aaron ascended a lofty mountain range that encloses the spot . . . and died with the eyes of the multitude on him" (cf. HT Num 33:37-38; 20:22: "and they set out from Kadesh and encamped at Mount Hor . . ."). See likewise Josephus, *Ant.* 4,7,1 #161 (on the death of Rekem [LXX: Rokom], the Midianite king, Num 31:8): "the fifth (Midianite king) Rekem, the city which bears his name ranks highest in the land of the Arabs and to this day is called by the whole Arabian nation, after the name of its royal founder, Rekeme; it is the Petra of the Greeks." The Semitic form of the name has been confirmed by a Nabataean inscription, in which the city is designated as RQMW (the waw being a standard Nabataean ending). See Alexander, 1974, 192–199. Ps.-J. agrees with the references in Nf except that in Num 20:1 Ps.-J. does not contain Reqem.

55. **Reqem de Ge'a.** In Nf, Frg. Tgs. and Ps.-J. *rqm dgy'h* (or *gy''*), with an ayin; in Onq. and Pesh. *gy''* (with an aleph). Nf Num 32:8; 34:4; also in Deut 1:2, 19; 2:14; 9:23. This is the constant rendering of HT Kadesh-barnea in Nf, in all other Targums, and in Pesh. The name is also found in the rabbinic border lists of *Sifre Deut.* 51 and *t. Shebi.* 4:11, towards the end: ". . . Sakuta, Nimrin, the fort of Zariza, Reqem of Gaia (*rqm gy'h;* with aleph), the Garden of Ashkelon, and the great road leading to the wilderness."

The name Gi'a itself, without combination with Reqem, is found as the name of a place, city, or village one and a quarter miles east of Petra, at the upper end of Wadi Musa. It is called el-Gi in Arabic and is attested with the writings *gy'', gy', g'y'* (with aleph) in Nabataean inscriptions. The place indicated by these was probably a town. It may be that mentioned by Eusebius, *Onomasticon* 62,16: "*Gai:* a stage of the Israelites in the wilderness. There is to this very day a city called Gaia close to Petra." In connecting this with a stage in the wilderness, Eusebius was probably under the influence of LXX Num 33:44, 45, which renders HT 'Iyyim (with initial ayin) (of Moab) as Gai. The LXX translators, however, scarcely had a site near Petra in mind for this biblical place name, far removed from Petra. Gamma was a recognized transliteration of Hebrew ayin in certain words.

The targumic exegetical tradition clearly located the biblical Kadesh-barnea in the vicinity of Petra. Thus also Eusebius, *Onomasticon* 112,8: "*Kadesh-barnea:* the desert, stretching alongside the city of Petra in Arabia."

The linking of Ge'a to Reqem may have been intended to distinguish this particular area or place near Reqem from another, also well known, namely Reqem di-Hagra, also mentioned in rabbinic texts.

See further Alexander, 1974, 192–199.

56. **Sea of Gennesar.** Num 34:11. See above "Gennesar, Sea of."

57. **Shalmaites:** *šlmyyh.* Num 24:21; HT: Kenite (*kyny*); also in Gen 15:19 (*šlm'y*), HT: Kenizite (*kyny*). The same translation of HT Kenite is also in other Targums. The term is also found in rabbinic texts: *j. Shebi.* 6,36b (bottom); *Gen. R.* 44 (one view identifies the Kenizites as Shalmaites); *b. B. Bat.* 56a (identifying Kadmonites as Shalmaites); *j. Qidd.* 1, 61d (top; identifying the Kenites as Shalmaites). They are probably the *Salmani,* the Arabian people in or near Mesopotamia mentioned by Pliny, *Nat. Hist.* 6,26, #30; the *salmênoi* of Stephanus of Byzantium. In Ps.-J. this word appears in 24:22, not in 24:21.

58. **Shiran.** Num 32:3 (Ps.-J.); HT: Nebo.

59. **Shuq Masai** (at Qesem): *šwq msyy.* Num 34:4; see also 34:15. In 34:4 Shuq Masai is given as the extreme western end of Israel's southern border: "(the boundary . . . shall continue to) Tirat-Adarayya and shall pass by the boundary of Shuq Masai at Qesem . . . and . . . from Qesem to the Nile. . . ." HT: "to Hazar-addar and pass along to Azmon." In Nf HT Hazar-addar is identified as Tirat-adarayya, and Azmon as Qesem. The reference to Shuq Masai is extra. The Frg. Tgs. (VN) and Ps.-J. do not contain here the reference to Shuq Masai, and in the following verse HT Azmon is rendered in Nf simply by Qesem, without any reference to Shuq Masai. Here, apparently, Nf has incorporated a marginal gloss intended to identify Qesem. Shuq Masai here is the Sykamazon of Byzantine texts, a town and a district to the south of Gaza (between Gaza and Raphia), modern Khirbet Suq Mazen; see Abel, *Géographie,* II, 172. Shuq Masai is not elsewhere mentioned in rabbinic texts. The gloss would appear to date from Byzantine times, when Sykamazon seems to have been of some importance and to have had a bishop. See Alexander, 1974, 199; also above under "Qesem" and "Raphia." The word does not appear in Ps.-J.

60. **Shuq Mazai** (in the Transjordan)? A Shuq Mazai (with zayin) is also mentioned in Nf Num 34:15, but in connection with a Raphion (presumably in the Transjordan) and Ain Gedi at the Dead Sea, and towards the end of the boundary list of the two and a half tribes. One explanation is that both place names in Nf here are glosses erroneously inserted. Another is that the same places as in Nf Num 34:4 are intended to conclude the border list. The error in this case would be the connection with Raphion of the Transjordan. See above under "Raphion."

61. **Simath:** *symt* (with initial samech). Num 32:3. HT: Sebam, a word found only here in the Pentateuch. The Frg. Tgs. VN and Onq. reproduce the HT word. Frg. Tg. L_2 has *swbr';* Ps.-J. has Mera for the HT Sebam; see no. 39 above. The Aramaic term *symt* does not appear to be elsewhere attested.

62. **Springs of Damascus.** Num 34:15. See above "Damascus, Springs of."

63. **Tanis:** *ṭnys.* Num 13:22. HT: Zoan (MT: *ṣo'an*); also in Exod 1:11. HT: Pithom. In the Pentateuch Zoan occurs only here, and Pithom in Exod 1:11.

64. **Taurus Umanus (Taurus Amanus):** *ṭwwrws mns; wmns ṭwwrs.* MT: *Hor ha-har;* RSV: Mount Hor. Nf: ". . . from the Great Sea . . . to Huminas Taurus (*hwmyns ṭwwrws*); from Taurus Menos (*ṭwwrws mynws,* with yod deleted in manuscript) to the entrance of Antioch." The original reading of the Nf and Pal. Tg. tradition is uncertain, as texts differ. Ps.-J. has *ṭwwrys 'wmnys; ṭwwrws 'wmnys* (and in Num 33:37-38 *ṭwwrws 'wmnws*); P (34:8): *ṭwwrws mnws;* VN: *ṭwwrws mnws.*

Obviously the original reading from which these derive had a double rendering for HT *Hor ha-har,* the first element of which rendering was "Taurus." The second was a variant of "Amanus." It is agreed that the double name corresponds to the two distinct mountain ranges, the Taurus and the Amanus. In the Pal. Tg. these are given as the northern boundary of Israel. Josephus, too (*Ant.* 1,6,1-2 ##122, 130), makes the mountains of Taurus and Amanus the boundary between the sons of Japhet and the sons of Ham. Likewise, according to *t. Hall.* 2:11 (Zuckermandel, p. 99), on the question: "What is Israel and what is foreign territory?" the answer is: "Everything from the Taurus Amanus (*ṭwrws 'mnws*) downwards . . . is the land of Israel; from the Taurus Amanus and beyond is foreign territory." (See also *m. Hall.* 4:18; *m. Shebi.* 6:1, with simple Amanus.)

The Amanus range begins on the coast to the west of Antioch and runs in a north-northwesterly direction for about a hundred and fifty kilometers almost to Germanicia (modern Marash), where it is separated from the Taurus range by the gorge of Jihum. There are few passes through it, one being the Beilan Pass to the north of Antioch, which connects Syria and Cilicia, the Syrian Gates of antiquity (Ptolemy, *Geog.* 5,14,9). See Alexander, 1974, 204. The Amanus range was an important natural barrier, and, as noted, was given by Josephus as a frontier between Japhet and Ham.

P. S. Alexander (1974, 204) thinks that the original Pal. Tg. identification of the biblical Hor ha-Har of Num 34:7-8 may have been simply Mount Taurus at the Beilan Pass. Amanus would have been added later to specify the Taurus as Taurus of the Amanus range, and not the more famous and extensive Taurus range to the north. He notes that 1QGenap 30,16 places the "Mountain of the Bull" (*twr twr'*) on the northern border of the land of Israel, and the Taurus of Beilan is what is probably intended. Behind the Aramaic *twr'* ("Bull") of this text stood the Aramaic Targum form *twwrws.*

In this context it is worth noting that Jerome (*Comm. on Ezek.* 47:15-17; CCL 75,721; PL 25,477; written 411 C.E.) says that the Jews of his day maintained that *Hor ha-Har* of Num 34:8 was the Amanus or the Taurus (*uel Amanum montem significare uel Taurum*).

With regard to the other and southern Mount Hor (*hor ha-har*) where Aaron died (Num 20:22, 23, 25, 27; 21:4, 33-41; Deut 32:50), Nf retains the Hebrew in Aramaic form (*hr twr'*). Ps.-J.'s rendering is influenced by the Pal. Tg. identification in Num 34:7, 8.

65. **Taverns of Hiratha:** *pwndqy ḥyrth (ḥyrt').* Num 33:7, 8; also Exod 14:2, 9. HT: Pi-Hahiroth. Not found in Ps.-J. See notes 9 and 10 in chapter 33.

66. **Ṭirat Adarayya:** *ṭyrt 'dryyh.* Num 34:4. HT: Hazar-addar. The Frg. Tgs. (VN) 34:4 have: Dirat Adarayya (*dyrt 'dryyh*). In neither case is there a direct identification; both

simply translate the Hebrew *ḥṣr* and transliterate the second element, adding an Aramaic plural ending. *ṭyrh,* means "enclosure" (as in Nf Gen 25:16); *dyrt* means "a courtyard"; (see Sokoloff, 1990, 148), probably related to the Aramaic word *drh,* "courtyard, dwelling." See also under "Dirat Adarayya" above.

67. **Ṭirat Enwata:** *ṭyrt 'nwwth.* Num 34:9, 10. HT: Hazar-enan; VN, Nfmg: *dyrt 'nwwt'.* The targumist simply translated the Hebrew *ḥṣr* (as earlier in Hazar-addar) and read HT *'nn* as a plural. He must not have known any identification of the Hebrew place name. See Alexander, 1974, 219f. For the meaning of *ṭirah* and *dyrh,* see under Tirat Adarayya. Jerome may have known the targumic rendering of *hsr* as preserved in the Frg. Tg. tradition (*dyrh,* "courtyard"). Sometimes Jerome translates as "Villa Enon" (*Comm. on Ezekiel* 47:18; CCL 75, 721, 723), but occasionally also (as in *Comm. on Ezek.* 47:18, CCL 75,723) as *atrium Enan,* "the courtyard of Enan," (= targumic *dirat 'Enan,* of VN and Nfmg).

68. **Top of the Height:** Num 21:20; 23:14; also in Deut 3:27; 34:1. Probably not intended as an identifiable place name.

69. **Trachon(a):** *(kl) trkwn (byt zymr').* Num 34:15 (in an added paraphrase); also in Deut 3:4 (*ṭrkwnh;* with initial teth); 3:13, 14 (*trkwnh;* with initial tau). HT: Argob. It is Tracho (*ho Trachô*) of Josephus (*Ant.* 13,16,5 #427; etc.); Trachonitis of Luke 3:1.

70. **Valley of the Hebrews.** Num 21:11; cf. 27:12; see also **Fords of Abarayya:** Num 33:44.

71. **Yadyoqiṭa:** *ydwqyṭ', ydywqṭws.* Num 34:15, in an added paraphrase on the borders of the two and a half tribes: ". . . to the fortress of Iyyon to the east of Beth Yeraḥ; and from the east of the Sea of Beth Yeraḥ the boundary went out for them to Yadyoqiṭa, and from Yadyoqiṭas Tarnegol of Caesarea, which is on the east of the (Cave) of Dan, the boundary went out for them to the Mount of Snow." The text "the Sea of Beth Yeraḥ" (found in no other text of this paraphrase on Num 34:15) is probably an erroneous insertion in Nf. The point of departure for the boundary for "Yadyoqitos" would then have originally been Iyyon near Dan/Paneas. "Yadyoqiṭas," variously given in the texts (see Apparatus to verse, and note 20 to Num 34:15), is patently a corruption, and most probably of an Aramaic form of the Greek loan word *eikôn,* a likeness of any kind, whether a picture, a carving, or a free-standing statue. The form of this loan word in our sources is almost invariably corrupt, and presumably intentionally so, the image in question (of a rooster [*trngl*]) having been regarded as an abomination. This particular image was situated near Dan/Paneas/Caesarea (Philippi). Thus in all the texts (Nf, VN, Ps.-J., Nfmg).

"Tarnegola (the rooster) of Caesarea" (*trngla 'y'h dgysry*) is also given in the rabbinic border list *Sifre Deut.* 51; *t. Shebi.* 4:11: "the depression of Iyyun, upper Tarnegola of Caesarea, Beth Sukkot . . . ." See also Alexander, 1974, 229.

INDEX OF VERSES PRESERVED IN THE FRAGMENT-TARGUMS OF NUMBERS

The following list is taken from M. L. Klein, *The Fragment-Targums of the Pentateuch According to Their Extant Sources* (Rome: Biblical Institute Press, 1980), vol. I, pp. 246–247, and is reproduced by the kind permission of the publisher.

NUMBERS

Verse	P	V	N	L
1:21		V	N	
4:7	P	V	N	
4:9-10	P	V	N	
4:13		V	N	
4:20	P	V	N	
5:19		V	N	
5:22	P	V	N	
6:3		V	N	
6:5	P			
6:27	P			
7:3		V	N	
7:13	P	V	N	
7:14-17		V	N	
9:8		V	N	
10:35		V	N	L
10:36	P	V	N	L
11:5	P	V	N	L
11:8	P	V	N	L
11:12	P	V	N	L
11:15		V	N	L
11:20	P			
11:26	P	V	N	L
11:28	P			
11:32		V	N	L
12:1	P	V	N	L
12:7	P	V	N	L
12:11		V	N	L
12:12	P	V	N	L
12:13		V	N	L
12:16	P	V	N	L
13:20	P	V	N	
13:23	P	V	N	
13:30		V	N	
14:4	P	V	N	
14:9	P			
14:18		V	N	
14:20		V	N	
14:30		V	N	
14:44		V	N	
15:21		V	N	
15:31		V	N	
15:32	P	V	N	
15:34		V	N	
15:38		V	N	
16:1	P	V	N	L
16:13	P			
16:15	P	V	N	
16:22		V	N	
16:28	P	V	N	
16:29		V	N	
17:3	P	V	N	
17:10		V	N	
17:23	P	V	N	
17:27		V	N	
18:12		V	N	
19:6		V	N	
19:15		V	N	
20:2	P			
20:10	P			
20:11		V	N	
20:17		V	N	
20:21		V	N	
20:26		V	N	
20:29	P	V	N	
21:1		V	N	
21:6	P	V	N	
21:9	P	V	N	
21:14-15	P	V	N	
21:17-20	P	V	N	
21:22	P			
21:27		V	N	
21:28-30	P	V	N	
21:31		V	N	
21:32	P	V	N	
21:34	P	V	N	
22:5	P			
22:7	P	V	N	
22:21		V	N	
22:24	P	V	N	
22:30	P	V	N	
23:3		V	N	
23:7-10	P	V	N	
23:15		V	N	
23:19-24	P	V	N	

Verse	P	V	N	L
24:1	P	V	N	
24:3-10	P	V	N	
24:14-15	P	V	N	
24:16		V	N	
24:17-24	P	V	N	
24:25		V	N	
25:1-3		V	N	
25:4	P	V	N	
25:5-9		V	N	
25:12	P	V	N	
25:18		V	N	
26:11	P	V	N	
27:5		V	N	
27:16		V	N	
28:2	P	V	N	
28:7	P	V	N	
30:13-14		V	N	
30:17		V	N	
31:3		V	N	
31:22		V	N	
31:50	P	V	N	
32:1		V	N	
32:3		V	N	L
32:4		V	N	
32:7		V	N	
32:9		V	N	
32:14	P	V	N	
32:17	P	V	N	
32:24		V	N	
32:34-35		V	N	
33:3	P	V	N	
33:7		V	N	
33:9		V	N	
33:36	P			
33:52		V	N	
34:3-5		V	N	
34:6	P	V	N	
34:7		V	N	
34:8	P	V	N	
34:9-12		V	N	
34:13		V		
34:15		V	N	
35:2		V	N	
35:4		V	N	

CATALOGUE OF CAIRO GENIZAH FRAGMENTS OF PALESTINIAN TARGUMS OF NUMBERS

The following list is taken from M. L. Klein, *Genizah Manuscripts of Palestinian Targum to the Pentateuch* (Cincinnati: Hebrew Union College, 1986), vol. I, pp. xlvi–xlviii, and is reproduced by the kind permission of the publisher.

Num 19:1–20:13 . . . . MS AA
Num 28:16-31 . . . . MS F
Num 28:22-31 . . . . MS Y

Targum Neofiti 1: Numbers

Translation

CHAPTER 1

1. And[1] *the Memra*[2] of the Lord spoke with Moses in the wilderness of Sinai, in the tent of meeting, on the first[a] of the second month, in the second year,[b] at the time *the children of Israel*[3] had come forth[c] *redeemed* out of Egypt, saying: 2. "Take the *census*[d4] of the congregation of all the children,[e] of Israel according to their families,[f] according to their fathers' house, according to the number of their names, every male, head by head; 3. from twenty years and upwards, all in Israel who can go forth to the *army of war,*[g5] you and Aaron shall muster them according

Apparatus, Chapter 1

[a] Nfmg: "(on the first) day."
[b] Nfmg: "(on the) second (year)." In the text of Nf, "second" is in the masculine: cf. *šenin* (masc. plur. of *šenah*).
[c] Nfmg: "(in the second year) of the Exodus."
[d] Lit.: "take the sum total of the heads."
[e] Nfmg: "raise the head of all the people of the congregation of Israel."
[f] Nfmg: "according to their families" (written differently).
[g] I.e., every male useful for war.

Notes, Chapter 1

[1]Chapters 1–4 seem to have presented little of midrashic interest to the early Jewish expositors. Chap. 1 describes a census of Israel; chap. 2 gives the order of the tribes; chap. 3 is on the tribe of Levi; chap. 4 on Levite clans. The laws begin in chap. 5, and only here does the rabbinic midrashic commentary *Sifre on Num.* commence. Onqelos has very little expansive material in chaps. 1–4. Neither does Nf, apart from the occurrence of the usual translational techniques.

[2]"*the Memra*": In Nf Num *Memra* is used (1) as the subject of such verbs (not verb "to be") as "to be revealed" (*'tgly*), 22:9, 20; "say," 22:12, 23:4; "appoint" (*zmn*), 17:19; 23:3, 4, 16; "set" (*swy*), 23:5, 12, 16; "speak" (*mll*), 1:1; "come," 24:8; "multiply" (*sgy*), 23:8; (2) in the phrase "voice of the Memra," etc. ("according to the decree of the Memra," *'l pm gzrt mmr'*): 3:16, 39, 51; 4:37, 41, 45, 49; 9:18 (twice), 20 (twice); 9:23 (3 times); 10:13; 11:20; 13:3; 14:41; 20:24; 22:18; 24:13; 27:14; 33:2, 38; 34:5; 36:5; (3) "name of the Memra," 14:11; 18:9; 20:12; "my name," "my Memra," 6:27; (4) with preposition "in" (*b*), 10:29; 11:21; 11:17; 14:14; 14:21, 28; 6:27; (5) with the verb "to be," etc., 14:9; 23:21; 23:19; "after the Memra of the Lord," 14:24, 43; 32:12, 15; 21:5, 7; 13:11; "a memra" (command?) from before the Lord," 24:4, 16. See R. Hayward, 1981, 153f.

[3]"children of Israel," addition in Nf. HT: "they came out." See Introd. Nf Num III, 23.

[4]"the census"; lit.: "the head (= total) of the numbers"; "the sum total" (*ryš skwmyhwn*). The HT has "the head" (*r'š* = "total of"). Nf translates the HT ("take the *r'š* of . . .") in this context as: *r'š skwm(yhwn)* in Num 1:2, 49; 4:22; 26:2; and as *skwm(yhwn):* "the total," in 4:9. See also 4:2; 31:26, 49.

[5]"to the army of war" *(kl npqy) ḥyl qrb'*; HT: (*kl yṣ' ṣb'*). In the HT the verb *sb'* occurs rarely: with the meaning of rendering religious or liturgical service (in the tent of meeting: Exod 38:8; Num 4:23; 8:24) or in the sense of rendering military service, i.e., to fight, to war (Num 31:7; 31:42). The *noun ṣb'* (*ṣaba'*) is much more frequent, sometimes from the context to be understood as liturgical service in the tent of meeting (of the Levites; e.g., Num 4:3, 23, 30, 35, 39, 43; 8:24, 25; see also Dan 8:13), generally however in a military sense, "war," "host."

Since Exod 38:8 cannot be understood in a military sense, Nf renders in a religious sense by two different terms: "The just women who prayed at the door of the tent of meeting." Nfmg (with the Frg. Tg.) has: "the modest (*ṣny'*; or: 'retired') women who were modest (or: 'had retired')." In all the other cases Nf renders the verb *ṣb'* in the military sense: thus "the army (or: 'host') of war" (*ḥyl qrb'*) for the HT's *ṣb' ṣb'* (MT: *liṣbo' ṣaba'*) in Num 4:23; 8:24. It has a different rendering for the verb in Num 31:7, 42 (see notes to text).

Nf's rendering of the noun *ṣb'* differs somewhat according to context but is always with the root *ḥyl.* In the context "all who go out to *ṣb'* (war)," it is rendered by *ḥyl qrb',* "the army (or: 'host') of war" (e.g., Num 1:3; 4:3). In the context "according to (their) hosts" (*lṣb' tm*) and in parallel with *pqwd* ("as numbered. . ."), it is rendered by "hosts," "armies," "multitudes," *ḥyylwwn (-thwn)*, the plural of *ḥyl;* thus in 2:4, etc.

to their companies. 4. And there shall be with you a man from *each* tribe, a man who is the head of his father's house. 5. And these are the names of the men who shall stand with you: *from the tribe of the sons*[6] of Reuben, Elizur bar Shedeur; 6. *from the tribe of the sons*[6] of Simeon, Shelumiel bar Zuri Shaddai; 7. *from the tribe of the sons*[6] of Judah, Nahshon bar Amminadab; 8. *from the tribe of the sons*[6] of Issachar,[h] Nethanel bar Zuar; 9. *from the tribe of the sons*[6] of Zebulun, Eliab bar Helon; 10. from the sons of Joseph, *that is, (from) the tribe of the house*[7] of Ephraim,[i] Elishama bar Ammihud: *from the tribe*[j] *of the sons* of Manasseh, Gamaliel bar Bedahzur; 11. *from the tribe*[k] *of the sons* of Benjamin, Abdan bar Gideon; 12. *from the tribe*[m] *of the sons*[6] of Dan, Ahiezer bar Ammi Shaddai; 13. *from the tribe*[n] *of the sons*[6] of Asher, Pagiel bar Ochran; 14. *from the tribe of the sons*[6] of Gad, Elisaph bar Deuel;[o] 15. *from the tribe of the sons*[6] of Nephtali, Ahira bar Enam." 16. These were the appointed ones of *the people of* the congregation,[p] the princes of their fathers' tribes:[q] they are the heads of the thousands[r] of the children of Israel. 17. And Moses and Aaron took these men who had been set aside according to their names. 18. And they gathered all *the people of the* congregation[8] together on the first[s] of the second month, and they were enrolled according to their families,[9] according to their fathers' house, according to

Apparatus, Chapter 1

[h] Nfmg: "of Issachar: from the tribes of the sons of Joseph, who is from the tribe of the sons of Ephraim"; this marginal gloss passes from v. 8 to v. 10.

[i] Nfmg: "from the tribes of the sons of Joseph, who is from the tribe of the sons of Ephraim."

[j] Nfmg: "of Manasseh, Gamaliel."

[k] Nfmg: "from Benjamin."

[m] Nfmg: "from Dan, of the tribes of"; a gloss probably to be understood in this way: instead of the text: "from the tribe of the sons of Dan," the variant would be: "of Dan"; instead of the text: "of the tribe," the variant would be: "of the tribes of (Dan)." One can suspect, however, that "of the tribes of" is an error for: "of the sons of (Dan)."

[n] Nfmg: "from Asher."

[o] In Num 2:14: "Reuel."

[p] Nfmg: "these are the appointed ones of the congregation" (written differently).

[q] Nfmg: "(the princes of their fathers') tribe."

[r] Text: *'ynwn;* Nfmg: *hnwn* (variant writing).

[s] Nfi: "the (first) day."

Notes, Chapter 1

[6]"from the tribe of the sons of (Reuben, etc.)"; HT: "of Reuben (etc.)." An exegetical expansion in the style of Nf. See Introd. Nf Num III, 23.

[7]"of the house of (Ephraim)" instead of the usual phrase: "the sons of."

[8]"the people of the (congregation)," *'m knyšt';* HT: *'dh,* "congregation." For the addition "the people of," see above, Introd. III, 23. See also below, 16:11, 16: "the people of your congregation," *'m knyštk* RSV HT: "your assembly" (*'dtk*). Nf very frequently renders "assembly," *'dh* of the HT, by *'m knyšt',* especially in Numbers; thus: Nf Lev 4:15; 8:3, 4, 5; 10:6, 17; 16:5, 24; 14:6; Num 1:16, 18, 53; 3:7; 4:34; 10:2, 3; 14:1, 2, 10; 15:24, 35, 36; 17:6; 16:19, 19; 20:1, 2, 8 (twice), 11, 27, 29; 35:25 (twice). Other renderings in Nf are simple *knyšth; qhl knyšth* (Exod 12:6); *'dt knyšth* (Exod 16:2). Nf's expansion of HT: *'dh,* "congregation," seems to be the rule when the HT *'dh,* "congregation," refers to Israel in a positive sense and is not qualified by an adjective. Thus Nf Num 1:16, 18, 53.

[9]"their families," *lzr'yythwn;* HT: *mšpḥh.* Nf renders the frequently occurring Hebrew word *mšpḥh* by *zr'yth*, "family," "descendant," and *zr'yth dbnyn* (*bnwy,* etc.), "descendants of children," but more frequently by the former. The latter rendering is found in Nf Gen 10:32; Exod 6:14, 15, 19, 24; Num 3:21 (twice), 23, 27 (33 in Nfmg), 33, 35; 4:18, 24, 28, 33, 34, 36, 37, 38, 40, 41, 42, 45; 26:5, 5, 6, 6, 7; 12, 12, 13, 13, 15, 15, 16, 16, 17, 17, 18, 20.

the number of names, from twenty years and upwards, head by head. 19. As the Lord[t] had commanded Moses, he numbered[u][10] them in the wilderness of Sinai. 20. And the sons of Reuben, Israel's first-born, their descendants[w] according to their families, according to their fathers' house, according to the number of names, head by head, every male from twenty years and upwards, all who were able to go forth to war;[x] 21. the *total*[y][11] of the tribe *of the sons* of Reuben was forty-six thousand five hundred. 22. Of the sons of Simeon, their descendants according to their families, according to their fathers' house the total[z] according to the number of names, head by head, every male from twenty years and upwards, all who were able to go forth to war;[aa] 23. the *total*[bb][11] of the tribe of the sons of Simeon, fifty-nine thousand three hundred. 24. Of the sons of Gad, their descendants according to their families, according to their fathers' house, according to the number of names, from twenty years and upwards, all who could go forth to war:[cc] 25. the *total*[11] of the tribe *of the sons* of Gad, forty-five thousand six-hundred and fifty.[dd] 26. Of the sons of Judah, their descendants[ee] according to their families, according to their fathers' house, according to the number of names, from twenty years and upwards, all who could go forth to war: 27. the *total*[11] of the tribe of Judah, seventy-four thousand six hundred. 28. Of the sons of Issacher, their descendants according to their fathers' house, according to the number of names, from twenty years and upwards, all who could go forth to war: 29. the *total*[11] of the tribe *of the sons* of Issachar, fifty-four thousand four hundred.[ff] 30. Of the sons of Zebulun, their descendants, according to their families, according to their fathers' house, according to the numbers of names, from twenty years and upwards, all who could go forth to war: 31. the *total*[11] of the tribe *of the sons* of Zebulun, fifty-seven thousand four

Apparatus, Chapter 1

[t] Nfmg: "the Memra of the Lord."
[u] Nfmg: "he counted (them)."
[w] Nfmg: "their generations, their families" (cf. Onq.).
[x] Nfmg: "(in the) army" (cf. Onq., Ps.-J.).
[y] Lit.: "the totals," "the numbers."
[z] In the text: "its total" (*sekumeh*). The scribe, however, vacillates when writing the word, and it appears that one should read: "its sum totals," i.e., the sum totals of his house (*skwmwy*). Nfmg suppresses this word.
[aa] Nfmg: "(in the) army" (cf. note *x* to v. 20 above).
[bb] Lit.: "the totals," "numbers"; the same in v. 21 and following verses.
[cc] Nfmg: "(in the) army"; the same variant in the following verses, with similar construction (cf. note to v. 20 above).
[dd] Nfmg: "forty-five thousand six hundred."
[ee] Nfmg: "their generations, according to their families" (Onq. and Ps.-J.); a variant repeated in the following verses.
[ff] Nfmg: "forty-five thousand (and four hundred)."

Notes, Chapter 1

[10] "he numbered," *skm;* HT root, *pqd;* see next note.
[11] "the total," lit. "totals," *skwmy(hwn).* MT: *peqûd* (*-yhem,* etc.). RSV: "number." Nf renders the HT *pqd,* when used in the sense of "pass in review," "muster," by *skm,* "count," passive, "those counted, total." Thus in Num 1 (passim); 2 (passim), 3 (passim), 4 (passim), 14:29; 26 (passim); 31:14, 48. See also note to 31:49 and B. Grossfeld, 1984, and above, Introd. III, 25.

hundred. 32. Of the sons of Joseph, *that is the tribe of the house* of Ephraim, their descendants according to their families,[gg] according to their fathers' house (according to numbers of names),[hh] from twenty years and upwards, all who could go forth to war: 33. the *total*[11] of the tribe of[ii] Ephraim, forty thousand four hundred. 34. Of the sons of Manasseh, their descendants, according to their families, according to their fathers' house, according to number of names, from twenty years and upwards, all who could go forth to war: 35. the *total* of the tribe *of the sons* of Manasseh, thirty-two thousand two hundred. 36. Of the sons of Benjamin, their descendants, according to their families, according to their fathers' house, according to the number of names, from twenty years and upwards, all who could go forth to war: 37. the *total* of the tribe *of the sons* of Benjamin, thirty-five thousand four hundred. 38. Of the sons of Dan, their descendants, according to their families, according to the number of names, from twenty years and upwards, all who could go forth to war: 39. the *total*[11] of the tribe *of the sons* of Dan, sixty-two thousand seven hundred. 40. Of the sons of Asher, their descendants, according to their families, according to their fathers' house, according to the number of names, from twenty years and upwards, all who could go forth to war: 41. the *total* of the tribe *of the sons* of Asher, forty-one thousand five hundred. 42. *Of*[jj] the sons of Naphtali, their descendants, according to their families, according to their fathers' house, according to the number of names, from twenty years and upwards, all who could go forth to war: 43. the *total*[11] of the tribe *of the sons* of Naphtali, fifty-three thousand four hundred. 44. These are the *sum totals* of those whom Moses and Aaron numbered together with princes of Israel, twelve men each of whom was the *head*[kk] of his fathers' house. 45. And the *sum* totals of the children of Israel according to their fathers' house, from twenty years and upwards, all who could go forth to war,[mm] 46. the *sum* total was six hundred and three thousand five hundred and fifty. 47. But the Levites were not numbered[nn] among them according to their fathers' tribe. 48. And the Lord spoke[oo] with Moses, saying: 49. "Only the tribe of Levi you shall not number and the *census* of them[pp] you shall not take within the children of Israel; 50. and you shall appoint the Levites over the tabernacle of the testimony and of all its furnishings, and over all that belongs to it. They shall

Apparatus, Chapter 1

[gg] Nfmg: "of the tribe of the sons of Joseph, that is of the tribe of the sons of Ephraim, their generations according to their families."

[hh] These words are missing in the text but are added in the margin.

[ii] Nfmg: "(of the tribe) of the sons of (Ephraim)."

[jj] The corresponding Aramaic particle (*le*) is in the Hebrew *incipit* and in the text of Nf. It has, however, been erased from the Aramaic text to make it conform to the HT.

[kk] Nfmg: "a (head of his fathers' house)."

[mm] Nfmg: "(in the) army"; see note to v. 20.

[nn] Nfmg: "were (not) counted."

[oo] Nfmg: "the Memra of the Lord."

[pp] Lit.: "the head of their numbers"; Nfmg: "you shall not take their heads," i.e., you shall not make a census of them.

carry[qq] the tabernacle and all its furnishings, and they shall serve it and shall encamp around about the tabernacle. 51. And when the tabernacle[rr] sets out, the Levites shall take it down, and when the tabernacle is pitched[ss] the Levites shall set it up. And the *layman*[12] who draws near *to minister*[13] shall be put to death.[tt] 52. And the children of Israel shall encamp, every man by his own encampment, and every man by his standard, according to their hosts. 53. But the Levites shall encamp round about the tabernacle of the testimony, that there be no wrath upon *the people of* the congregation[uu] of the children of Israel; and the Levites shall take charge (of the tabernacle)[ww] of the testimony." 54. And the children of Israel did according[xx] to all that the Lord[yy] had commanded Moses, thus they did.

CHAPTER 2

1. And the Lord[a] spoke with Moses and with Aaron, saying: 2. "The sons of Israel shall encamp, every man according to his (own) standard, with the ensigns of his fathers' house; they shall encamp round about the tent of meeting,[b] facing it. 3. And those who encamp the first,[c] to the east, (shall be) the standard of the camp *of the tribe of the sons*[1] of[d] Judah, by their hosts. And the leader *of the tribe*[e][1] of

Apparatus, Chapter 1

[qq] Nfmg: "that it has. They shall bear (the tabernacle)."
[rr] Nfmg: "and in the going forth (lit.: 'setting out') of the tabernacle."
[ss] Nfmg: "and in the pitching."
[tt] Nfmg: "(and the layman) who shall draw near shall be put to death."
[uu] Nfmg: "(upon) the assembly (of the sons of)."
[ww] Nfmg: "the Levites (shall take) charge of the tabernacle of the testimony"; the word "tabernacle" is missing in the text.
[xx] Nfi: "all (that)."
[yy] Nfmg: "the Memra of the Lord."

Notes, Chapter 1

[12] "layman," *ḥlwnyy,* "non-priest." This is Nf's regular rendering of HT *zr,* "stranger, foreigner, outsider" (Num 1:51; 3:10, 38; 17:5; 18:4, 7; cf. also Exod 29:33; Lev 22:10, 12; 32:13; Deut 25:5).
[13] "to minister"; an addition in Nf.

Apparatus, Chapter 2

[a] Nfmg: "the Memra of the Lord."
[b] Nfmg: "he shall surround (reading: *yḥzwr*) the tent of meeting."
[c] *qdmyyn mn;* or: "in the vanguard"; cf. v. 9.
[d] Nfmg: "of the camp of the sons . . ."
[e] Nfi: "of the tribes of (Judah)."

Notes, Chapter 2

[1] The words in italics are additions to the HT.

the sons[f] of Judah[g] being Nahshon bar Amminadab, 4. his host in their numbers[h] being seventy-four thousand six hundred. 5. And those who encamp near to him (shall be) the tribe[i] *of the sons*[1] of Issachar. And the leader *of the tribe* of the sons[j] of Issachar (shall be) Nethanel bar Zuar, 6. his hosts, being numbered, fifty-four thousand four hundred. 7. And[k] the tribe[m] *of the sons* of Zebulun, <the leader *who had been appointed*[2] *over the camp*[n] *of* the tribe of Zebulun>[o] being Eliab bar Holon, 8. his hosts, being numbered, fifty-seven thousand four hundred. 9. The *whole*[1] number of the camp *of the tribe of the sons*[1] of Judah, according to their hosts, (is) one hundred and eighty-six thousand four hundred. These set out[p] first on the march. 10. The standard of the camp *of the tribe of the sons*[q1] of Reuben (shall be) to the south, (divided) according to their hosts, the leader *who had been appointed*[2] *over the tribe*[r] of the sons of Reuben: Elizur bar Shedeur. 11. And his hosts in their numbers: forty-five thousand five hundred. 12. And those who encamp near to him (shall be) the tribe[s] of the sons of Simeon, the leader *who had been appointed*[2] *over the camp*[t] *of the tribe* of the sons of Simeon being Shelumiel bar Zuri Shaddai, 13. his hosts, in their numbers being fifty-nine thousand three hundred. 14. And[u] the tribe *of the sons* of Gad: the leader *who had been appointed*[w2] *over the camp*[x] *of the tribe* of the sons of Gad being Eliasaph bar Reuel;[y] 15. and his hosts, in their numbers being forty-five thousand six hundred and fifty. 16. The *whole* number of the camp *of the tribe of the sons*[1] of Reuben: one hundred and fifty thousand four hundred and fifty[z] (divided) according to

Apparatus, Chapter 2

[f] Nfmg: "and as chief there had been appointed over the hosts of the tribe of the sons of . . ."

[g] Nfi: *hw-*, to be read probably as *hw'* = "he," or *hwh* = "he was," e.g., "was (?) (Nahshon)"; unless we read as "of Judah," a defective or abbreviated form of "Yehudah," "(Ye)hu(dah)."

[h] Lit.: "their totals," "their sum totals."

[i] Nfmg: "of (the tribe)."

[j] Nfmg: "and as chief there had been appointed over the hosts of the tribe of the sons of . . ."

[k] This "and" is not in the Hebrew text.

[m] Nfmg: "of the tribe (of the . . .)."

[n] Nfmg: "(over) the hosts (of the tribe . . .)."

[o] Missing in the text and added on the lower margin by the copyist of the colophon of the Neofiti MS. This added section has marginal notes (Nfmg) by the annotator of these folios.

[p] Nfmg: "they shall set out first."

[q] Nfmg: "the camp of the sons of . . ."

[r] Nfmg: "(over) the host of the tribe (of the sons . . .)."

[s] Nfmg: "of (the tribe . . .)."

[t] Nfmg: ("over) the hosts (of the tribe . . .)."

[u] Nfmg: "of the tribe (of the sons . . .)."

[w] Nfi: "(and the leader) who (had been) appointed."

[x] Nfmg: "(over) the hosts (of the tribe . . .)."

[y] Cf. Num 1:14: "bar Deuel."

[z] Nfmg: "one hundred and fifty-one thousand four hundred and fifty" (with HT).

Notes, Chapter 2

[2] "leader who had been appointed," *rbh dhwh mmny;* HT: *nśy'* (*naśî'*), "leader"; and thus in Nf Num 2:7, 10, 11, 14, 18, 22, 25, 27, 29; likewise Nf Num 1:16; 3:32; 7:2. In other texts Nf renders simply by "chief(s)" (*rb[rbyh]*), e.g., Num 3:24, 30, 35; 7:3, 18, (24), 30, 36, 42, 48, 54, 60, 66, 72, 78, 84; 13:2; 16:2.

their hosts. They set out[aa] second on the march. 17. Then the camp of the tent of meeting set out, the camps of the Levites, in the midst of the camp. In the same order as they had encamped, so did they set out; each according to his (proper) place,[bb] according to their standards. 18. The standard of the camp *of the tribe of the sons*[1] of Ephraim (shall be) *to the west* (divided) according to its hosts, the leader *who had been appointed*[2] *over the camp*[cc] *of the tribe* of the sons of Ephraim being Elishama bar Ammihud. 19. And their hosts, in their numbers: forty thousand five hundred. 20. And *those next to him*[dd] (shall be) the tribe of Manasseh,[ee] the leader *who had been appointed*[2] *over the camp of the tribe* of Manasseh being Gamaliel bar Pedah Zur.[ff] 21. And his hosts, in their numbers: thirty-five thousand four hundred.[gg] 22. And the tribe[hh] *of the sons* of Benjamin, the leader *who had been appointed*[2] *over the camp*[ii] *of the tribe* of Benjamin[jj] being Abidan bar Gideoni, 23. and his hosts in its number: thirty-five thousand four hundred. 24. The *whole* number of the camp *of the tribe of the sons*[1] of Ephraim: one hundred and eight thousand one hundred, (divided) according to their hosts. And[kk] they set out in the third place. 25. The standard of the camp *of the tribe of the sons*[1] of Dan (shall be) to the north, (divided) according to their hosts, the leader *who had been appointed*[2] *over the camp*[mm] *of the tribe* of the sons[nn] of Dan being Ahiezer bar Ammi Shaddai.[oo] 26. And their hosts in their numbers: sixty-two thousand seven hundred. 27. And those who encamp next to him[pp] (shall be) <the tribe>[qq] *of the sons* of Asher, the leader *who had been appointed*[2] *over the camp*[rr] *of the tribe* of the sons of Asher being Pagiel bar Ochran. 28. And their hosts, in their numbers: forty-one thousand five hundred. 29. And the tribe[ss] of Naphtali, the leader *who had been appointed*[2] *over the camp*[tt] *of the tribe* of the sons of Naphtali being Ahira bar Enan. 30. And their hosts, in their numbers: fifty-three thousand four hundred. 31. The entire numbers of the camp *of the tribe of the sons* of Dan:

Apparatus, Chapter 2

[aa] Nfmg: "and they set out," or: "raised the camp" (*wyṭlwn,* a different construction). It appears that this variant is to be placed here, even though the MS, by means of a "circellus," refers it to: "the tent of meeting set out" of the following verse. If this word refers to v. 17, the variant must be translated as "and they shall set out" (lit.: "raise the tent" or "camp").

[bb] Nfmg: "each according to his territory, according to their standards" (= Ps.-J.).

[cc] Nfmg: "(over) the hosts (of the tribe . . .)"; cf. same variant in v. 12.

[dd] Nfi: "to them."

[ee] Nfmg bis: "(the tribe) of the sons of (Manasseh)."

[ff] The name broken up into two component parts.

[gg] "thirty-five thousand four hundred," due to the influence of v. 23; in Nfmg: "(thirty-five thousand) two hundred," with HT.

[hh] Nfmg: "and of the tribe (of the sons . . .)."

[ii] Nfmg: "(over) the hosts (of the tribe . . .)."

[jj] Nfi: "of the sons of (Benjamin)."

[kk] Nfmg: "in the third place" (without "and").

[mm] Nfmg: "(over) the hosts of the sons (of Dan)."

[nn] Nfmg: "(over) the camp of the sons (of Dan)."

[oo] In two words; as one word in the HT.

[pp] Nfi: "and those who are near to him."

[qq] This text has erroneously: "the leader."

[rr] Nfmg: "(over) the hosts (of the tribe . . .)."

[ss] Nfi: "(and the tribe) of the sons (of Naphtali)."

[tt] Nfmg: "(over) the hosts (of the tribe . . .)."

one hundred and fifty-seven thousand *six hundred.*[uu] They were the last[ww] to set out, according to their standards." 32. These are the *numbers* of the children of Israel, according to their fathers' house. The *numbers* of the camps and of their hosts:[xx] six hundred and three thousand five hundred and fifty. 33. But the Levites were not numbered among the children of Israel, in accordance with what the Lord had commanded Moses. 34. And the children of Israel did all that the Lord[yy] commanded Moses; thus did they encamp by their standards[zz] and thus did they set out, each according to his families, according to his fathers' house.[a]

CHAPTER 3

1. These are the generations[a] of Aaron and of Moses, on the day that the Lord[b] spoke with Moses on Mount Sinai. 2. And these are the names of the sons of Aaron:[c] Nadab, the first-born, and Abihu, Eleazar, and Ithamar. 3. And these are the names of the sons of Aaron, the priests who were anointed, who were initiated[d] to *serve in the high priesthood.*[1] 4. And Nadab and Abihu died[e] when they offered foreign fire before the Lord in the wilderness of Sinai and they had no sons.[f] And Eleazar and Ithamar *served in the high priesthood*[g][1] during the lifetime of Aaron

Apparatus, Chapter 2

[uu] Nfmg: "of the camp of the sons of Dan one hundred and seventy-five thousand six (hundred)"; HT: "one hundred and fifty-seven thousand six hundred."
[ww] Nfmg: "the last" (different form of the same word); Nfi: "those of the rear-guard."
[xx] Nfmg: "the camps of the children of Israel, (divided) according to their hosts."
[yy] Nfmg: "the Memra of the Lord."
[zz] Nfmg: "in this manner used they encamp according to their standards."
[a] Nfmg: "(and thus) used they set out, each . . ."

Apparatus, Chapter 3

[a] *tldwwth;* or: "the descendants," or: "the genealogical history."
[b] Nfmg: "the Memra of the Lord."
[c] Thus in text, instead of Aaron.
[d] Lit.: "who completed the offering of their hands"; cf. Lev 8:33.
[e] The first "before the Lord" of the HT and Onq. is missing in the text, as in Vulg. and Sam. Tg.
[f] Nfmg: "(and) they had no male (sons)."
[g] Nfmg: as HT without the gloss, "in the high priesthood."

Notes, Chapter 3

[1] "to serve in high priesthood." HT: *lkhn,* RSV: "to minister in the priest's office." The HT Num speaks twice of the "high priesthood" (Num 35:25, 28). Elsewhere it speaks of "the priest" (in general: 3:3, 6; 5:8, 9, 10, 15, 18; 6:10, 20) or in the plural, "the sons of Aaron, the priests" (10:8); of "Aaron the priest" (3:6, 32; 4:16, 28, 33; 7:8; 17:2; 18:28; 26:64; 33:38); and "Eleazar (the son of Aaron) the priest" (17:2, 4; 19:3, 4, etc.). Nf introduces various references to the high priest. Aaron is called "the high priest" in 4:16, 28, 33. There is mention of Eleazar, the son of Aaron, the high priest, 17:1; 26:1; Phinehas, son of Eleazar, son of the high priest Aaron (25:11); an unnamed high priest (4:20). Nf Num 3:3, 4 speaks of the "high priesthood."

their father. 5. And the Lord[b] spoke with Moses, saying: 6. "Bring near the tribe of Levi and place it before Aaron the priest that they may serve him. 7. And they shall be at his service and at the service of all *the people of* the congregation, before the tent of meeting, performing the ministry of the tent. 8. And they shall have charge of all the furnishings of the tent and[h] attend to the worship of the children of Israel, performing the ministry of the tent. 9. And you shall give the Levites to Aaron and to his sons; they are given to him *as a gift* by the children of Israel. 10. And you shall equip[i] Aaron and his sons so that they may attend to their priesthood[j]; and a *layman*[2] who draws near *to serve*[3] shall be put to death."[k] 11. And the Lord[b] spoke with Moses, saying: 12. "And behold,[m] I have *separated*[4] the Levites from among the children of Israel instead of all the first-born that open *the first fruit of* the womb[n5] of the children of Israel; and the Levites shall be for *my Name.* 13. For all the first-born are for *my Name.*[o6] On the day that *I smote* all the first-born in the land of Egypt, I consecrated to my name all the first-born of Israel, from the sons[p] of man to the beasts. They shall belong to *my Name.* The Lord has said."[7] 14. And the Lord[q] spoke with Moses in the wilderness of Sinai, saying:

Apparatus, Chapter 3

[h] Nfi: "(and) all (the worship)."
[i] Nfmg: "you shall number."
[j] Nfmg: "their (priestly) services."
[k] Nfmg: "by the consuming fire before the Lord"; cf. Ps.-J.
[m] Nfi: "I am" (erroneous reading).
[n] Possibly we should read as follows: "the first-fruits of those that open the womb" (or: "the first-fruits of the doors of the womb"); Nfmg: "the first ones of those that open the womb" (or: "the first ones of the doors of the womb"). But perhaps "the first ones" (*qdmy*) is a variant of "for my Name" (first time) of the following verse, since "for my Name" has a circellus above it, whereas there is no corresponding variant in Nfmg; in this case *qdmy* should be rendered "before me." In this last hypothesis the reference "circellus" has erroneously been placed above "for my Name" (*l-šmy*) of v. 13 instead of being placed above *l-šmy* of v. 12.
[o] See Ps.-J.: "they shall be servants (they shall serve) before me"; cf. preceding note.
[p] Note that annotator 1 put in the graphic variant *m-b(ny)* and has erased it, an argument that the very frequent variants *m-x / mn-x* are not arbitrary; see Díez Macho, 1973, 47*f.
[q] Nfmg: "the Memra of the Lord."

Notes, Chapter 3

[2]"layman"; see note to Num 1:51.
[3]"to serve" (or: "to minister"); an addition in Nf.
[4]"separate" (the Levites); HT: "take"; also 3:41, 44; 8:6, 14.
[5]"(first-born) that open the first fruit (lit.: 'beginning') of the womb"; Aramaic: *(kl bwkryh) ptḥy šyrwy wwldh;* HT: *pṭr rḥm,* "first-born of the womb." The term *pṭr* alone occurs in the HT Exod 13:12, 13; 34:19, 20; *pṭr rḥm* ("first-born of the womb") in HT Exod 13:2, 12, 15; 34:19; Num 3:12; 18:15, and in Ezek 20:26. In some texts Nf renders as "everyone opening the womb" (*kl ptḥy wwldah*): Exod 13:2, 12 (second occurrence), 13, 15; 34:19 (second occurrence), 20. In the other cases Nf introduces the term *šyrwy,* "beginning" (="first-born"?): Exod 13:12 (first occurrence: "every beginning opening the womb," *kl šrwy ptḥe wwldh*); Exod 34:19 (first occurrence); Num 3:12; 18:15: *kl ptḥy šyrwy wwldh,* "everyone (everything) that opens, the beginning (first-born) of the womb." The significance of the introduction of *šyrwy* is not clear.
[6]"to my Name"; HT lit.: "to me" (="mine").
[7]"the Lord has said"; HT: "I am the Lord."

15. "Number the sons of Levi according to their fathers' house, according to their families; every male from a month upwards you shall number."[r] 16. And Moses numbered them[s] according to *the decree of the Memra* of the Lord,[8] as he had been commanded. 17. And these were the sons of Levi, according to their names: Gershon and Kohath and Merari. 18. And these are the names of the sons of (Gershon)[t] according to their families: Libni and Shimei. 19. And the sons of Kohath (according to their families):[u] Amram and Izhar and Hebron and Uzziel. 20. And the sons of Merari according to their families: Mahli and Mushi. These are the families[w] of Levi[x] according to their fathers' house. 21. To Gershon[y] (belongs) the family of *the sons*[z] of Libni and the family of *the sons* of Shinei. These are the families of *the sons* of the Gershonites. 22. Their *numbers,*[9] according to the number of all the males, from one month old[aa] and upwards, their *numbers* (were) seven thousand five hundred.[aa] 23. The family of *the sons* of the Gershonites encamped at the extremities[bb] of the tent, *to the west.*[cc] 24. And the leader of the fathers' house *of the tribe of the sons* of the Gershonites was Eliasaph bar Lael. 25. And the charge of the sons of Gershon[dd] in the tent of meeting was the tabernacle, and the curtain,[ee] and its covering,[ff] and the curtain[gg] for the door of the tent of meeting; 26. and the *poles*[hh][10] of the court, and the curtain for the door of the court which is near the tabernacle and near the altar, round about, and

Apparatus, Chapter 3

[r] Nfmg: "count."
[s] Nfmg: "and (Moses) counted them."
[t] "Levi" in the text, through the influence of v. 17.
[u] In Nfmg; missing in text.
[w] Nfmg: "those according to their families are the Levites."
[x] Nfi: "the families of the Levites."
[y] Nfi: "to the sons of Gershon."
[z] Nfmg: "(the family) of the tribe (of the sons)."
[aa] In Nfi orthographical and other variants.
[bb] HT: "behind."
[cc] Nfmg: "westwards" (another grammatical form; Hebrew?).
[dd] Nfmg: "of the Gershonites."
[ee] Or: "and its curtain"; or: "and the curtain"; or: "and its curtains"; HT: "and the tent"; Syr.: "and its curtains."
[ff] "and the covering(s)," with Sam., LXX, Vulg., Syr.; Nfmg: "its coverings," with HT.
[gg] Nfmg: "and the curtains at the entrance (of the tent)."
[hh] *w'ylwwt* (see note); unless there is question of a defective writing of "and the curtains"; Nfmg: *wwylwwt,* from Greek *bêlon;* HT: "and the door-curtains."

Notes, Chapter 3

[8] "according to the decree of (lit.: according to the mouth of the decree of) the Memra of the Lord"; HT lit.: "according to the mouth of Y." This HT phrase is rendered throughout in the same fashion by Nf: Num 3:16, 39, 51; 4:37, 41, 45, 49; 9:18, 20, 23; 13:3; 22:38; 23:12, 16; 27:21; 33:2; 36:5; likewise in Nf Num 4:27 with relation to Aaron.

[9] "their numbers" or "totals," *skwmyhwn;* see note to 1:21.

[10] "posts" or "doorposts" (of the court), *'ylwwt (drth);* also in 4:26; HT: *ql'y (hḥṣr).* Nf renders HT *ql'* in conjunction with *ḥṣr* in the same way in the other occurrence in Num 4:26; likewise in Exod 35:17. Elsewhere, however, in this same combination (Nf Exod 27:9; 35:17; 38:16, 18; 39:40), it renders by *w(y)lwn,* the Greek or Latin loan word (*bêlon, uelum*), "curtain," as it invariably does when not in conjunction with HT *ḥṣr* (Nf Exod 27:11, 12, 14, 15; 38:12, 14, 15). It is not easy to say what the original reading was in Nf Num 3:26; 4:26—"poles," "posts," or "curtain(s)"—as in Nfmg.

their cords:[ii] all the service pertaining to these. 27. And of *the sons of* Kohath[jj] were the family *of the sons*[kk] of the Amramites and the family *of the sons*[mm] of the Izharites, and the family[nn] *of the sons* of the Hebronites and the family *of the sons*[oo] of the Uzzielites. These are the families *of the sons* of the Kohathites. 28. According to the number of all the males from a month old[pp] and upwards (there were) eight[pp] thousand six hundred, entrusted with the charge of the sanctuary. 29. The family of the sons of Kohath encamped at the extremities of the tabernacle, to the south. 30. And the leader of the fathers' house of *the sons of the* Kohathites[qq] was Elizaphan bar Uzziel. 31. And in their charge were the ark, the table, the candlestick, and the altar,[rr] and the vessels of the sanctuary with which the ministry is performed, and the curtain,[ss] and all the service pertaining to it. 32. And the leader *who had been appointed*[11] over the princes of the *Levites* was Eleazar, son of Aaron the priest, (*to take*) *the number*[tt][9] of those who had charge of the service of the sanctuary. 33. Of Merari were the family *of the sons*[uu] of Mahli and the family *of the sons*[ww] of Musi. These are the families *of the sons* of Merari.[xx] 34. Their *numbers,*[9] according to the number of[yy] all the males from a month old and upwards, (were) six thousand two hundred.[yy] 35. And the leader of the fathers' house of the family[zz] *of the sons* of Merari was Zuriel bar Abihael. They encamped at the side[a] of the tabernacle, to the north. 36. And the total responsibility[b] of the sons of Merari was: the tables of the tabernacle, and its bars and its pillars and its clasps, and all its utensils and all its service; 37. and the pillars of the court round about and their clasps, their pegs and their cords.[c] 38. And those who first encamped before the tabernacle, before the tent of meeting, to the east, were Moses, Aaron[d] and his sons, charged with the service of the sanctuary, for the service of

Apparatus, Chapter 3

[ii] Nfmg: "its bars."
[jj] Nfmg: "and of Kohath."
[kk] Nfmg: "(the families) of the Amramites."
[mm] Nfmg: "(the clan) of the Izharites."
[nn] Nfmg: "(the clan) of the Hebronites."
[oo] Nfmg: "(the clan) of the Uzzielites."
[pp] In Nfmg orthographical variants, similar to those for v. 22 (note *aa* above).
[qq] Nfmg: "and the leader of the house of the family of the sons of the (Kohathites)."
[rr] "and the altar" (sing.) as in Syr.; Nfi: "and the altars," plural as in HT (altar of the burnt offerings, Exod 27:1-8, and of the sweet incenses, Exod 30:1-10).
[ss] Nfmg: "in all (its services)."
[tt] In HT *pqddt:* "the charge" (the one charged with . . .); cf. 3:36; see note to Nf Num 1:21. Nfmg: "(their responsibility) extended to . . ."
[uu] Nfmg: "(the family) of Mehli."
[ww] Nfmg: "(the family) of Mushi."
[xx] Nfmg: "these are the families of Merari."
[yy] In Nfmg orthographical and other variants as in vv. 22, 28. See above.
[zz] Nfmg: "and the leader of the house of the family (of the sons of . . .)."
[a] Lit.: "at the sides of" (*b-sṭrwy*); Nfmg: "at the skirts, lower parts of" (*špylwy*).
[b] *w-skwm mṭrt* . . . (see v. 32). Nfmg has *w-smkwt,* to be corrected to *skmwt* ("the counting of . . .") Frg, Tg. V Num 4:16; as Nfmg Num 16:29; see also Nfmg 3:32 (*smkwt,* corrected to *skmwt*).
[c] Nfmg: "and their bars."
[d] Nfi: "and Aaron," with HT.

Notes, Chapter 3

[11]"who had been appointed"; an addition in Nf.

the children of Israel. And any *layman*[12] who should draw near *to serve*[13] was[e] to be put to death. 39. And the *number*[9] of Levites whom Moses and Aaron numbered according to *the decree of the Memra* of the Lord,[8] by their families, all males from one month old and upwards, (was) twenty-two thousand. 40. And the Lord[f] said to Moses: "Number all the first-born males of the children of Israel, from one month old and upward, and take the number of their names. 41. And you shall *separate* the Levites for *my Name,*[14] *says*[g] the Lord,[15] instead of all the first-born of the children of Israel; and the cattle of the Levites instead of all the firstlings among the cattle of the children of Israel." 42. And Moses numbered all the first-born of the children of Israel according as the Lord[f] had commanded. 43. And all the first-born males, according to the *number*[9] of their names, from one month old and upwards, according to their numbers,[h] were twenty-four thousand two hundred and seventy-three. 44. And the Lord[f] spoke with Moses, saying: 45. "*Separate*[16] the Levites instead[i] of all the first-born of the children of Israel, and the cattle of the Levites instead of their cattle; and the Levites shall be for *my Name;* I, the Lord.[j] 46. And for the ransom of the two hundred and seventy-three first-born of the sons of Israel that remain[k] (in excess) of the (number of) the Levites, 47. you shall take five *selas*[17] for each head; *selas* of the sanctuary you shall take, *which is* twenty *ma'in*[18] to the *sela.*[17] 48. And you shall give the money to Aaron and to his sons as ransom for those that remain over in excess."[m] 49. And Moses took the ransom money from what exceeded the number of those ransomed by the Levites.[n] 50. He received[o] the money of the first-born of the children of Israel, one thousand three hundred and sixty-five *selas,*[17] in *selas* of the sanctuary. 51. And Moses gave the money of the ransomed to Aaron and to his sons according to *the decree of the Memra* of the Lord,[8] according as the Lord[p] had commanded Moses.

Apparatus, Chapter 3

[e] Nfmg: "who draws near should be put to death."
[f] Nfmg: "the Memra of the Lord."
[g] Nfmg: "the Levites for my Name, thus says . . ."
[h] Nfmg: "their number."
[i] Nfmg: "take the Levites instead of . . ."
[j] Nfmg: "thus says the Lord."
[k] Nfmg: "that are left over."
[m] Nfmg: "(for) those that are left over."
[n] Lit.: "from what exceeded the ransom of the Levites."
[o] Nfmg: "he took."
[p] Nfmg: "the Memra of the Lord."

Notes, Chapter 3

[12]"layman"; see note to 1:51 above.
[13]"to serve"; an addition in Nf.
[14]"for my Name"; HT: "for me."
[15]"says (the Lord)"; HT: "I am the Lord."
[16]"separate"; HT: "take."
[17]*Sela* is the constant rendering in Nf of the HT shekel. See Introd. Nf Gen (*The Aramaic Bible,* vol. 1A, pp. 32f.).
[18]*ma'in,* sing. *m''* (*me'a,* rendering *gerah* of the MT throughout (Nf Exod 30:13; Lev 27:25; Num 3:47; 18:16). A *me'a* was one-sixth of a denarius.

CHAPTER 4

1. And the Lord[a] spoke with Moses and with Aaron, saying: 2. "Take the census[b] of the sons of Kohath from among the sons of Levi, according to the families of their fathers' house, 3. from thirty years old up to fifty years old, all who are to enter *the army of war,*[c1] to perform the service in the tent of meeting. 4. This shall be the service of the sons of Kohath in the tent of meeting, *in the sanctuary:*[d2] 5. when the camp is to set out,[e] Aaron and his sons shall enter and remove[f] the veil of the curtain and shall cover the ark of the testimony with it. 6. And over it they shall put the covering of *sasgewan*[g3] skin and they shall spread above a cloth wholly[h] of blue and shall set its poles in place. 7. And over the table *of the bread* of Presence[i4] they shall spread a cloth of blue, and they shall put upon it the bowls and the dishes[j] and the libation jars[k] and the libation flagons; and the bread shall be *continually*[5] upon it. 8. And they shall spread over them a cloth of *precious*[6]

Apparatus, Chapter 4

[a] Nfmg: "the Memra of the Lord."
[b] Lit.: "receive the sum totals of . . ."
[c] *dy'wl lḥyl qrbh:* i.e., those useful for, or capable of, military service; Nfmg: the same meaning with a different grammatical form (*d'll*).
[d] Lit.: "in the house of the holy things"; HT, Onq., Ps.-J.: "the most holy things."
[e] Nfmg: "when (the camp) is to set out" (another form).
[f] Nfmg: "and they shall lower."
[g] *sasgewan* or *sasgona:* a word of uncertain meaning; it translates the Hebrew word *tahaš* ("dolphin").
[h] Nfmg: "(a cloth) of thread of blue."
[i] Nfi: "(bread) of arrangement." Cf. Exod 25:23-30 and see note.
[j] Nfmg: "the bowls and its dishes."
[k] Nfmg: "(the dishes) and the libation flagons." If this marginal gloss is placed in the right place, it suppresses "and the libation jars."

Notes, Chapter 4

[1]"army of war," *ḥyl grb';* see note to Nf 1:3 above.

[2]"in the sanctuary," or: "in his sanctuary," or: "in the house of the holy things" (*bbyt q(w)dšyh;* HT: *b'hl mw'd qdš hqdšym,* "in the tent of meeting: the most holy things," cf. RSV; lit.: "in the tent of meeting the holy of holies."

[3]*sasgewan* ("skin") 4:8, etc. The HT has (*'wr*) *tḥš* (MT: *taḥaš*), a word of uncertain meaning, variously rendered: RSV: "goatskin"; NRSV: "fine (leather)"; NEB: "porpoise-hide" (with marginal note: "*strictly* hide of sea-cow"); REB: "dugong-hide"; NJB: "fine leather." Nf renders HT *tḥš* throughout as *ssgwn(');* (thus Exod 25:5; 26:14; 35:7, 23; 36:19; 39:34; Num 4:6, 8, 10, 11, 12, 14, 25). Onqelos and Ps.-J. render with the same term as Nf. So also the Syriac translation. This targumic translation of *taḥăs* is noted in *b.* Talmud, *Shabb.* 28a: "that is the reason we translate (*taḥăs*) with *sasgona,* because it glistened with many colors; and in Tg. Cant 7:2 *sasgona* is mentioned as the name of an animal (of many colors), the skin of which was used for covering the tabernacle. M. Klein (for CTg D Exod 39:34, *s'sgwn*) renders: "multicolored" (Klein, 1986, 2, 300); B. Grossfeld (in Onq., *The Aramaic Bible,* vols. 7, 8) translates as "scarlet."

[4]"of the bread," an addition in Nf; HT: "table of the Presence", *šlḥn hpnym;* RSV: "table of the bread of the presence." The bread of the presence was arranged in two rows (Lev 24:6), hence the name "bread of the arrangement" (1 Chr 9:32; 23:29, etc.).

[5]"bread . . . continually," *lḥm btdyrh.* The HT has *lḥm tmyd,* "the bread of continuity" (RSV: "the continual bread"). Nf renders the *tmyd* adverbially. Elsewhere the HT speaks of *'lh tmydh* (Num 28:3, 6, 10, 18, 23, 24, 31; 29:6, 11, 16, 19, 22, 25, 28, 31, 34, 38), "a continual offering," where Nf renders literally: "a continual burnt offering" (RSV).

[6]"precious"; an addition in Nf.

crimson material, which they shall cover with a covering of *sasgewan*[m][3] skin, and they shall set its poles in place. 9. And they shall take a cloth of blue and shall cover the candlestick of the illumination and its lamps and its snuffers[n] and its tray,[o] and all the utensils for the *service*[p] with which it is used.[q] 10. And they shall put it and all its utensils within a covering[r] of *sasgewan*[3] skin and shall place it upon the carrying frame. 11. And over the golden altar[s] they shall spread[t] a cloth of blue, and they shall cover it with a covering of *sasgewan*[3] skin, and they shall *cover*[u][7] its poles. 12. And they shall take all the vessels of the service,[w] which they use within[x] the sanctuary, and they shall place them (within a cloth of blue[y] and shall cover them with a covering of *sasgewan* skin and thev shall put it)[z] upon the carrying frame; 13. and they shall (clear away the) grease[aa] (from) the altar[bb] and spread over it[cc] a purple cloth; 14. and they shall put upon it all its utensils with which service is made: the trays and the forks[dd] and the shovels and the sprinkling basins,[ee] all the utensils of the altar; and they shall spread upon it a covering of *sasgewan* skin, and they shall put its poles in place. 15. And when Aaron and his sons have finished covering the holy things[ff] and all the utensils of the holy things, as the camp sets out,[gg] after that the sons of Kohath shall enter to be laden[hh] *with the tabernacle,*[8] but they shall not touch the sanctuary,[9] lest they die.[ii] These are the burdens[jj] of the sons of Kohath in the tent[kk] of meeting. 16. And the duty[mm] of Eleazar, the son of Aaron, the *high* priest, shall be the oil for the illumination and

Apparatus, Chapter 4

[m] Nfmg: "with a covering of *sasgewan* skins."
[n] *mlqṭṭh;* Nfmg: "its snuffers" (another form, *mlqṭyh,* that found in plur. in N, and in sing. in V).
[o] Or: "its receptacles for cut wicks" (snuff dishes); or: "ashtrays"; cf. v. 14.
[p] "for the service" (*šimmušah*); thus with various texts of Onq. and Ps.-J., against "(vessels) for oil" (*šamnah*) of the HT and LXX.
[q] Lit.: "that they serve it by them"; Nfmg: "by it."
[r] Nfmg: "its utensils in a covering"; cf. Onq., Ps.-J.
[s] the altar of fragrant incenses; cf. Exod 30:1-6.
[t] Nfi: "they shall clothe."
[u] Nfmg: "they shall place," with HT; the text: "and they shall cover" is probably incorrect (dittography).
[w] This expression of v. 12 ("these vessels of the service") could be the reason why it is introduced in v. 9; see note *p* above.
[x] Nfmg: "(that they use) in the sanctuary."
[y] Nfmg: "above a thread of blue."
[z] Omitted in text through homoeoteleuton; added in margin.
[aa] Lit.: "and they shall satisfy," rendering HT *w-dššnw* (piel) ("and they shall clear away the fat ashes"); same word used by Nf to render Hebrew (qal) in Deut 31:20; Nfmg, and VN: "and they shall remove ashes from (the altar)."
[bb] The altar of burnt offerings.
[cc] Nfmg: "over them"; this variant, however, is probably to be referred to the last "upon it" of the next verse.
[dd] "and the forks," with "and," not in HT.
[ee] Nfmg: "(and) its sprinkling basins."
[ff] Nfmg: "the sanctuary."
[gg] Nfmg: "(and all) the utensils of the sanctuary as the camp sets out."
[hh] Nfi: "(to be laden) but (they shall) not . . ."; "with the tabernacle," dittography; Nfmg: "to bear but (they) shall not . . ."
[ii] Nfmg: "since they would die."
[jj] in plur.; HT sing.
[kk] Nfmg: "(of Kohath); the tent . . ."
[mm] See 3:32-36.

Notes, Chapter 4

[7]HT: "put (in)."
[8]"with the tabernacle"; an addition in Nf.
[9]Lit.: "house (place) of holiness."

the aromatic incense and the continual cereal offering[nn] and the anointing oil—the oversight duty[mm] for the whole tabernacle and all that which is in it, in the sanctuary[oo] and in its utensils." 17. And the Lord[pp] spoke with Moses and with Aaron, saying: 18. "You shall not *blot out*[qq][10] the tribe of the families *of the sons*[11] of the Kohathites[rr] from among the Levites. 19. Do this[ss] to them so that they may live and not die when they draw near the most holy sanctuary: Aaron and his sons shall go in and *settle*[tt][12] each of them to his task and to his burden. 20. But they shall not enter[uu] to look when *the high priest*[ww][13] is covering[14] *all the utensils* of the sanctuary, *lest* they die." 21. And the Lord[xx] spoke with Moses, saying: 22. "Take also the *census*[yy][15] of the sons of Gershon, according to their fathers' house, according to their families. 23. From thirty years old and upwards to fifty years old you shall number them, all that may enter the *army of war,*[16] to render service in the tent of meeting. 24. This shall be the service of the families *of the sons*[17] of Gershon, for serving and for bearing burdens:[zz] 25. they shall carry[a] the curtains of the tabernacle and the tent of meeting, its covering and the covering of *sasgewana*[3] (which covers it and the curtain)[b,c] of the door of the tent of meeting, 26. and *the posts*[d][18] of the enclosure and curtain[e] of the door of the court which is

Apparatus, Chapter 4

[nn] Nfmg: "the perpetual cereal offering (*minḥah*) and the oil," or: "the oblation (*minḥah*) of ther perpetual offering and the oil."
[oo] Nfmg: "(and all that) is in the sanctuary."
[pp] Nfmg: "the Memra of the Lord."
[qq] Nfmg: "you shall (not) be blotted out."
[rr] Nfmg: "of Kohath."
[ss] Nfmg: "(this) remedy (or: 'ordinance') you shall do (give) (to them): that they turn away their eyes from the sanctuary"; cf. Ps.-J.
[tt] Nfmg: "and they shall set (them)." The text is probably to be corrected in accordance with Nfmg.
[uu] Nfmg: "the Levites (shall not enter) when the priests cover the holy utensils"; PVN: "and the Levites shall not enter to see (= to look) when the priests are concealing the utensils of the sanctuary, lest they die."
[ww] Nfmg: "(when) the priests are concealing the utensils of the sanctuary, lest they die" = PVN.
[xx] Nfmg: "the Memra of the Lord."
[yy] Lit.: "take also the number of heads of . . ."
[zz] Nfmg: "of the Gershonites for the serving and for carrying."
[a] Nfmg: "they shall bear."
[b] Nfmg: "(and) the curtain of" (another word).
[c] Omitted in text through homoeoteleuton; added in Nfmg.
[d] Cf. 3:26; we should probably read: "(and) the curtains," with Nfmg and HT.
[e] Nfmg: "(and) the curtains of" (another word).

Notes, Chapter 4

[10]"blot out"; HT: "cut off."
[11]"the high priest"; an addition in Nf; see note to 3:3 above. HT: "when he is covering."
[12]"settle," *šryn;* HT: *śmw,* "put."
[13]"high priest"; see note to 3:3 above.
[14]"is covering" is Nf's paraphrase of the problematic single term *kbl'* (as if from root *bl',* lit.: "to swallow," "devour") of the HT; now generally understood to mean: "even for a moment." The Frg. Tg. renders similar to Nf (see Apparatus); so also Ps.-J. and in substance Onq.
[15]"census"; HT lit.: "the head."
[16]"army of war"; see note to 1:3 above.
[17]An addition in Nf.
[18]"the posts," or "poles." See note to 3:26 above and Apparatus.

near the tabernacle and near the altar round about, and their cords[f] and all the utensils for their service; and all that must be done with regard to these things they shall do. 27. All the service of the sons of the Gershonites, with regard to all their burdens[g] and all their services, shall be at *the command*[19] of Aaron and of his sons; you shall assign[h] to them all their burdens in the ministry.[i] 28. This shall be the service of the family of the sons of the Gershonites in the tent of meeting, and their ministry shall be under (the command)[j] of Ithamar, the son of Aaron, the *high* priest. 29. And for the sons of Merari, you shall number them according to their families, according to their fathers' house. 30. From thirty years old and upward to fifty years old you shall number them, all that may enter the *army of war,*[16] to do the work of the tent of meeting. 31. And this is the ministry of their burdens,[k] in accord with their entire service in the tent of meeting: the tables of the tabernacle and its bars[m] and its pillars and its clasps; 32. and the pillars of the court round about and their clasps and their pegs and their cords,[n] with all[o] their utensils and with all[o] their service. And you shall assign by their name all the objects they are charged to carry.[p] 33. This shall be the service of the families of the sons of Merari; in all their service in the tent of meeting they shall be under the command of Ithamar, the son of Aaron the *high*[20] priest." 34. And Moses and Aaron and the leaders *of the people* of the congregation[21] took[q] the numbers of the sons of the Kohathites according to their families, according to their fathers' house, 35. from thirty (years) old and upward to fifty (years)[r] old, all that may enter the *army of war,*[16] to serve in the tent of meeting. 36. And their *numbers,*[22] according to their families, was two thousand seven hundred and fifty. 37. These were the *numbers*[22] of the families *of the sons* of the Kohathites, all that should serve in the tent of meeting, which Moses and Aaron numbered, according to *the decree of the Memra*[23] of the Lord through Moses. 38. And the *numbers* of the sons of Gershon,

Apparatus, Chapter 4

[f] Nfmg: "(and) their bars."
[g] Nfmg: "their burdens" (a different word).
[h] Nfmg: "(and) you shall determine (for them)."
[i] Nfmg: "in (the) ministries all their burdens."
[j] Missing in text.
[k] Nfmg: "(the ministry) of their burdens" (another word).
[m] Nfmg: "their bars" (without "and").
[n] Nfmg: "and their bars."
[o] Lit.: "for all," "and for all," a literal translation of the HT. However, the *lamed* of the HT, reproduced in Nf (rendered "for" in translation), seems to be emphatic, for which reason it is not to be rendered by "for."
[p] Nfmg: the same as note *k* to v. 31 above.
[q] Nfmg: "and they counted," or: "and they assigned."
[r] Missing in text; supplied from parallel passages.

Notes, Chapter 4

[19] "at the command"; lit.: "at the degree of the mouth of Aaron"; HT lit.: "according to the mouth of." See note to 3:16 above.
[20] "high"; an addition in Nf. See note to 3:3 above.
[21] "the people of the congregation"; HT: *'dh,* RSV: "congregation". For the addition "the people of," see above Introd. III, 23 and note to 1:16 above.
[22] "their numbers," *skwmyhwn;* HT: *pqdyhm.* See note to 1:21.
[23] "decree of the Memra of"; see HT: "according to the mouth of." See note to 3:16.

according to their families, according to their fathers' house, 39. from thirty years old and upward to fifty years old, all who should enter the *army of war,* to[s] serve <in> the tent of meeting: 40. the *numbers* according to their families, according to their fathers' house, were two thousand six hundred and thirty. 41. These were the numbers of the families of the sons of Gershon, all who should serve in the tent of meeting, which Moses and Aaron numbered[t] in accordance with *the decree of the Memra*[23] of the Lord. 42. And the *numbers* of the families of the sons of Merari according to their families, according to their fathers' house, 43. from thirty years old and upward to fifty years old, all who should enter the army of war, to[u] serve in the tent of meeting—44. their *numbers* according to their families were three thousand *five hundred.*[w24] 45. These were the *numbers* of the families of the sons of Merari which Moses and Aaron numbered in accordance with *the decree of the Memra* of the Lord through Moses. 46. All those who were numbered of the Levites, whom Moses and Aaron and the leaders of Israel numbered, according to their families, according to their fathers' house, 47. from thirty years old and upward to fifty years old, all who should enter[x] to render the work of service and the service of bearing burdens in the tent of meeting, 48. their *numbers* were eight thousand five hundred and eighty. 49. In accord with *the decree of the Memra* of the Lord, through Moses they assigned each to his own task and to his burden. And the task of each was that which the Lord[y] had commanded *through* Moses.[25]

CHAPTER 5

1. And God[a] spoke with Moses, saying: 2. "Command the children of Israel that they put out of the camp everyone who is leprous and everyone who has a flux and

Apparatus, Chapter 4

[s] Nfmg: "(of war), the ministry to serve the tent."
[t] Nfmg: "they counted," or: "they assigned."
[u] Nfmg: "(of war) the ministry to serve."
[w] Nfmg: "(three thousand) two hundred," with HT, Onq., Ps.-J., LXX.
[x] Nfmg: "(all) who should enter to render the work of service and the work of service in the tent of . . ."
[y] Nfmg: "the Memra of the Lord."

Notes, Chapter 4

[24]"three thousand five hundred"; HT: three thousand two hundred. See Apparatus.
[25]"through Moses"; lit.: "by the hands of M."; HT, Onq., Ps.-J.: "which the Lord had commanded Moses."

Apparatus, Chapter 5

[a] Nfmg: "the Memra of the Lord."

everyone who is unclean *through the defilement of a human* corpse.[b][1] 3. Male or female, you shall put them out; you shall put them outside the camp, lest they render unclean their camps within which I dwell."[c] 4. And the children of Israel did so, and they put them outside the camp; as the Lord[a] had spoken with Moses, thus did the children of Israel do. 5. And the Lord spoke with Moses, saying: 6. "Speak with the children of Israel: 'Should a man or a woman commit any of the sins of man,[d] by deceiving in *the name*[2] of the Lord,[e] that person shall be guilty. 7. And he shall confess the sin he has committed and repay his guilt in the full,[f] and he shall add a fifth[g] for it, and he shall give it to him against whom he has sinned.[h] 8. And if the man has no redeemer[i] to whom restitution can be made for the sin, the restitution to be made to the Lord[j] shall belong to the priest in addition to the ram of expiation, with which[k] expiation shall be made for him. 9. And every *separated offering*[3] of any of the holy things of the children of Israel, which they shall offer to the priest, shall be his,[m] 10. and the holy things of a man shall be his;[n] and what a man gives to the priest shall be his.'" 11. And the Lord[o] spoke with Moses, saying: 12. "Speak with the children of Israel and say to them: 'If any man's wife turns aside and acts unfaithfully against him, 13. and if a man has carnal relations with her and the affair remains hidden from the eyes of her husband and she re-

Apparatus, Chapter 5

[b] Lit.: "the uncleanness of the corpse of a son of man."
[c] Nfmg: "(lest they) render impure your camps, for the glory of my Shekinah dwells among you."
[d] Lit.: "any of the debts of a son of man." Translation of an objective genitive ("any sin against men") by a subjective genitive. Nfmg: "(should a man or a woman commit any of the sins of) the sons of man." The "circellus" (over "sins of") marking the place of this variant is, however, probably badly placed.
[e] Nfmg: "the name of the Memra of the Lord."
[f] Nfmg: "(he shall repay) the capital (lit.: 'in the head') and he shall add fifths (read:? 'a fifth') of its price (lit.: 'in its principal')"; cf. Ps.-J.
[g] Nfmg: "a fifth of its price."
[h] Nfmg: "to the one to whom the sin offering belongs."
[i] Nfmg: "a man redeemer," i.e., "(if) a man (has no) redeemer" (?); cf. Onq.; or: "if he has (no) man (as) redeemer"?
[j] Nfmg: "to be made (repaid) to the name of the Lord."
[k] Lit.: "that atonement shall be made for him to it"; Nfmg: "by it," as in HT, Onq., Ps.-J.
[m] Nfmg: "they shall be for him."
[n] Nfmg: "it shall be for him; (what) a man . . ."
[o] Nfmg: "the Memra of the Lord."

Notes, Chapter 5

[1]"through the defilement of a human corpse." RSV: "through contact with the dead." (HT: "with a nefesh.") Onq: lit.: "defilement of a nefesh of a son of man." Same rendering of HT in Nf Lev 22:4.

[2]"by deceiving in the name of the Lord. . ." HT: *lm'l m'l bYHWH* (RSV: "by breaking faith with the Lord"); also in Lev 5:15; 5:21; 26:90; Num 5:12, 27; Deut 32:51. Nf renders by the same throughout and adds "in the name of" also in Lev 5:21 (parallel to Num 5:6) where there is mention of the Lord in the HT.

[3]"separated offering," *'pršw;* the invariable rendering of MT *terumah* (RSV: "offering") in Nf throughout, except in Exod 25:3 and 30:15, where *'pršh* (lit.: "separation") is used. Thus in Exod 25:2, 2; 29:27, 28; 30:13, 14; 35:5, 21, 24; 36:3, 6; Lev 7:14, 32, 34; 10:14, 15; 22:12; Num 5:9; 6:20; 15:19, 20, 21; 18:8, 11, 19, 24, 26, 27, 28, 29; 31:29, 41, 52; Deut 12:6, 11, 17. See above Introd. III, 3.

mains undetected although she has defiled herself, and there is no witness against her and she has not been seized (in the act); 14. and if the spirit of jealousy comes upon him, and he is jealous of his wife who has defiled herself; or if the spirit of jealousy comes upon him and he is jealous of his wife although she has not defiled herself, 15. then, the man shall bring his wife to the priest and he shall bring for her the offering required for her, a tenth of a *mekilta*[4] of barley flour. He shall not pour upon it (oil, nor place)[p] frankincense upon it, because it is the cereal offering of jealousy, a cereal offering of remembrance,[q] bringing sin to remembrance. 16. And the priest shall bring her near and shall set her before the Lord; 17. and the priest shall take *pure* water in[r] an earthen vessel, and the priest shall take some of the dust which is at the sides of the tabernacle[s] and he shall put it into the water; 18. and the priest shall set the woman before the Lord and shall disarrange the hair of the woman's head, and in the palm *of her hand*[5] he shall place the cereal offering of remembrance, which is the cereal offering of jealousy. And in the hands of the priest[t] shall be bitter waters that bring curses. 19. Then the priest shall make her swear, and he shall say to the woman: If no man has lain with you and if you have not turned aside, becoming unclean, *outside the authority*[6] of your husband, you shall be free[u] from these bitter waters which bring curses.[w] 20. But if you have turned aside, *outside*[x] *the authority*[6] of your husband, and have become unclean, and if a man other[y] than your husband has lain[z] with you—21. then, the priest shall make the woman swear the oath of the curse and the priest shall say to the

Apparatus, Chapter 5

[p] Missing in text and in Nfmg.
[q] Nfmg: "of memorial, recalling."
[r] Nfmg: "holy (water) within."
[s] Nfmg: "and from the dust which is under a plank which is in the foundations of the tabernacle."
[t] Nfmg: "the cereal offering of remembrance—and (? with the sign of the accusative) it is the cereal offering of jealousy—; and in the hands of the priest shall be the investigating waters to investigate." We should probably correct the central part to read: "which is the cereal offering of jealousy."
[u] *tydky (mymy');* or "justified," "purified."
[w] Nfmg: "(and if) you have (not) turned aside, becoming unclean, while under the authority of your husband, you shall be free (or: 'justified') from these investigating waters which investigate"; cf. VN: "be acquitted (or: 'purified') by these investigating waters which investigate (lit.: 'waters . . . to investigate')."
[x] Nfmg: "(being) under (the authority of your husband)"; or: "instead of"; cf. v. 29.
[y] Nfmg: "under," or: "instead of"; see preceding note.
[z] Lit.: "and a man gave sexual intercourse"; Nfmg 1° (to "gave"): "placed," "appointed," "put" (the use of the bed); Nfmg 2° (to "use"): "(and a man gave the use of) his couch outside the authority of your husband."

Notes, Chapter 5

[4]"mekilta," which means: "a measure of capacity." HT: "ephah." This is Nf's invariable rendering of the HT "ephah" (Exod 16:36; Lev 5:11; 6:13; 19:36, Num 5:15; 28:5; Deut 25:14, 15).
[5]"palm of her hand"; HT: "in her palm."
[6]"outside the authority"; HT: "(while you were) under (your husband's) authority."

woman: May the Lord give you over to (be) a curse and an oath[aa] among your people, when the Lord makes your thigh melt away and your belly[bb] swell; 22. may this water which bring curses[cc] enter into your belly to make your belly[dd] swell and your thigh melt away. And the woman shall say: Amen, Amen, Amen that I have not been defiled; Amen that I shall not be defiled.[ee] 23. And the priest shall write these curses in a book and shall wash (them) off into the bitter waters;[ff] 24. and he shall make the woman drink the bitter waters that bring curses;[gg] and the waters that bring curses shall enter into her to bring *her* bitterness. 25. And the priest shall take the cereal offering of jealousy out of the woman's hand,[hh] and shall wave the cereal offering before the Lord, and shall bring it upon the altar. 26. And the priest shall take a fistful of the cereal offering, its memorial portion, and *shall arrange*[7] it on top of the altar, and after this he shall make the woman drink the water. 27. And when he has made her drink the water, if she has defiled herself and has been unfaithful to her husband, the water that brings curses shall enter into her to cause *her* bitterness, and her stomach shall be swollen[ii] and her thigh shall melt away, and the woman shall become a curse among the people. 28. And if the woman has not defiled herself and is guiltless, *she shall conceive and bear a male son.*[jj][8] 29. This is *the decree of* the law[9] of jealousy[kk] when the wife[mm] turns aside *outside*[nn] *(the authority of)* her husband and defiles herself, 30. or when the spirit of jealousy comes upon a man and he gets jealous of his wife, and sets the woman

Apparatus, Chapter 5

[aa] Nfmg: "and an oath" (*mwmy,* a different word) = Onq.
[bb] Nfmg: "(among) your people when the Memra of the Lord makes your thigh melt away and your stomach swell."
[cc] Nfmg: "these investigating (waters)."
[dd] Nfmg: "your stomach."
[ee] P: "and the woman shall say: Amen, Amen. Amen if I have been defiled; Amen if I shall be defiled in the future"; VN: "and the woman shall say: Amen that I have not been defiled; Amen if I shall be defiled in the future."
[ff] Nfmg: "in the investigating waters."
[gg] Nfmg: "the investigating waters to investigate shall enter into her (text: 'him')."
[hh] Nfmg: "the hands of (the woman)."
[ii] Nfmg: "the investigating waters to investigate and (her stomach) shall be melted away."
[jj] Nfmg: "and she is guiltless (or: 'justified'), she shall conceive a son."
[kk] Nfmg: "(this) is the instruction of jealousy."
[mm] Nfi: "that a wife turns aside."
[nn] Nfmg: "instead of her husband."

Notes, Chapter 5

[7]"shall arrange it," "set it in order"; HT: "shall burn it" (*hqṭr,* root *qṭr*). Nf invariably renders "burn" (*hqṭr* of HT) as "shall arrange." Thus in all occurrences in Nf Num (5:26; 17:5; 18:17). See Nf Lev, Introd. II, 4 and above Num, Introd. III, 5.

[8]"she shall conceive and bear a male son;" HT lit.: "she shall be free and she shall be sown (= impregnated) (with) seed (or: 'produce seed')." Nf specifies that the offspring would be male; so also Ps.-J. The birth of male children is also mentioned in the comments on this verse in *Sifre Num.* Par. 19 (end).

[9]"decree of the law." HT: "the law" (*tôrah*). When *tôrah* is used in this restricted sense in the HT, Nf renders by "decree of the law." Thus in Nf Num 5:29; 6:13, 21. The corresponding Hebrew expression is found in HT Num 19:2, 14; 31:21 (RSV: "statute of the law"), where Nf also translates by "decree of the law." See above, Introd. III, 11.

before the Lord. And the priest shall exercise on her all *these statutes* of the law.[oo][10] 31. Thus shall the man be free from her sin,[pp] and that woman shall receive (the punishment of) her sin.'"

CHAPTER 6

1. And the Lord[a] spoke with Moses, saying: 2. "Speak with the children of Israel and say to them: 'If a man or woman[b] expressly vows the vow of naziriteship to consecrate himself before the Lord, 3. he shall drink neither *new* wine *nor old,*[c][1] he shall drink neither vinegar of *new* wine nor of *old wine,*[d][1] nor shall he drink any grape juice,[e] nor eat fresh or dried grapes. 4. In all the days of the *vow* of his naziriteship he shall eat nothing that is made from the grapevine, not even *raisins or pips.*[f][2] 5. All the days of the vow of his naziriteship a razor[g] shall not *come up* to his head; until the days that he has consecrated himself *before* the Lord have been completed he shall be a holy person;[h] the hair of his head shall grow[i] in long locks. 6. All the days of his consecration to *the name of* the Lord,[3] he shall not go near a

Apparatus, Chapter 5

[oo] Nfmg: "(all) this praiseworthy law"; lit.: "(all) the praise of this law."

[pp] Nfmg: "(from) sins"; lit.: "debts."

Notes, Chapter 5

[10]"these statutes of the law"; HT: "all this law" (*tôrah*). For a slightly different rendering, see note to 5:29 above.

Apparatus, Chapter 6

[a] Nfmg: "the Memra of the Lord."
[b] Lit.: "the woman"; Nfmg: "a woman."
[c] VN: "he shall abstain (lit.: 'be restrained') from wine, new and old; he shall not drink vinegar of new wine or vinegar of old wine, nor shall he drink any grape wash"; Nfmg: "(from wine new and old) he shall abstain; wine (correct to: vinegar) of new wine" = VN.
[d] Nfmg: "nor vinegar (a different word) of wine" = VN.
[e] Nfmg: "grape wash" = VN.
[f] Lit.: "from raisins to pips"; Nfmg: "(from) the kernels to the skins (he shall) not (eat)."
[g] Nfmg: "a razor (*glp=glb*) shall not pass over . . ."
[h] Nfmg: "(he shall be) a sacred object."
[i] Nfi: "and it grows."

Notes, Chapter 6

[1]"new wine nor old" (*ḥmr ḥdt w'tyq*). HT: *yyn wškr* (RSV: "wine and strong drink"). Nf renders this Hebrew phrase in the same manner in the other occurrences (Lev 10:9; Deut 29:5); otherwise, in isolation *yyn* is rendered simply by *yyn,* and *škr* in isolation simply by *ḥmr.*

[2]"raisins or pips," *mn kmyšn 'd pgn;* rendering two Hebrew terms, *mḥrṣnym w'd-zg,* found only here in the Hebrew Bible.

[3]"to the name of the Lord"; HT: "to the Lord."

body[j] of a dead person. 7. He shall not make himself unclean for his father or for his mother,[k] for his brother or for his sister at their death,[m] because *the crown*[n][4] of his God is upon his head. 8. All the days of his naziriteship he *shall* be holy *before*[o] the Lord. 9. And should a dead man who is near him have died suddenly[p] *without his knowing it,*[5] he renders the hair of his consecrated head unclean,[q] and he shall shave his head on the day of his purification; on the seventh day he shall shave it. 10. On the eighth day he shall bring two turtledoves or two young pigeons to the priest at the entrance of the tent of meeting; 11. and the priest shall *offer* one as a sin offering and the other as a burnt offering, and he shall make atonement for him, for what he has sinned by reason of[r] the dead body;[s] and he shall consecrate his head on that day. 12. And he shall consecrate himself *before* the Lord for the days of his naziriteship, and he shall bring a year-old lamb as a guilt offering; but the former days shall be void because *the crown* of his naziriteship[7] has been defiled.[t] 13. And this is *the decree of* the law[8] of the nazirite:[u] On the day that he finishes

Apparatus, Chapter 6

[j] Nfmg: "(of his consecration) before the Lord, (he shall not go near) the defilement of a dead body."
[k] Nfmg: "and (or) for his brother"; "and" (or) is not in the HT.
[m] Nfmg: "at their death" (another form).
[n] *klyl;* Nfmg: "the crown" (= the long hair of the nazir) (a different word: *nzyr* = Heb. *nzr*).
[o] Nfmg: "he shall be a sacred object before . . ."
[p] Nfmg: "(and should) there die near him a dead person whom one has an obligation to bury" (lit.: "a dead man of the precept," or: "a dead man of charity"); cf. *j. Meg.* 3b: "suddenly (and he is) forced (to defilement)."
[q] Nfmg: "it (or: 'he') shall be rendered unclean."
[r] Nfmg: "through (lit.: 'from') which he has become guilty by reason of . . ."
[s] Nfmg: "through (lit.: 'from') which he has sinned by reason of a man (lit.: 'a son of man') who died and whom he buried."
[t] Nfmg: "(because) he has defiled the head of his naziriteship."
[u] Nfmg: "(this) shall be the instruction of the naziriteship: on the day."

Notes, Chapter 6

[4]"the crown (*klyl*) of his God"; HT: "the *nzr* (RSV: 'separation to') of his God." The same word *klyl',* "crown," also occurs in a variant in Onq. In HT *nzr,* in the sense of "consecration," occurs in Lev 21:12; Num 6:4, 5, 7, 8, 9, 12, 13, 18, 19, 21. In all instances in Num 6, except in 6:7 and 6:19, Nf renders as "naziriteship"; in 6:19 as "crown of his naziriteship." In the HT the word is used in what is regarded the sense of "diadem" in Exod 29:6; 39:30; Lev 8:9. Nf renders as "crown" in Exod 29:6; 39:30, and Lev 6:19, "crown of the sanctuary," "of house of holiness" (in all texts HT: "crown of holiness" = holy crown), Lev 8:9 (in all three HT "crown of holiness"). In Num 6:19 Nf renders as "crown of naziriteship," paraphrasing HT "cut off, *'t-nzrw*"; ((RSV: "cut off the hair of his consecration").

[5]"Suddenly (*btkyp*) without his knowing," HT. *bpt' pt'm,* the two words in combination occurring only here in the Hebrew Pentateuch (cf. Isa 29:5; 30:13). The RSV renders as: "very suddenly." *bpt'* occurs in HT Pent. only in Num 6:9 and 35:22. In Num 35:22 Nf renders again as *btkwp* (= *btkyp*). In the HT Pent. *pt'm* occurs only in Num 6:9; 12:4. In 12:4 Nf renders by *btkwp.* In Deut 4:42 Nf prefaces *btkwp* (as Frg. Tg. V) to "without his knowing it" of the HT.

[6]"the crown of his naziriteship"; HT: "his *nzr,*" in the sense of "his consecration"; see note to 6:7.

[7]"offer up"; HT lit.: "shall make."

[8]"decree of the Law"; HT: "the law;" see note 5:29 above, and Introd. III, 11.

the days of his naziriteship, he shall be brought to the entrance of the tent of meeting, 14. and he shall offer as his offering *before* the Lord one male year-old lamb, perfect, *without blemish,* [9] as a burnt offering, and one female year-old lamb, perfect, *without blemish,* [9] as a sin offering, and one ram, perfect, *without blemish,* [9] as a *sacrifice of holy things,* [10] 15. and a basket of cakes of unleavened bread of fine flour soaked in oil and unleavened rolls anointed with oil, and their cereal offerings and their drink offerings. 16. And the priest shall offer them before the Lord, and he shall offer his sin offering and his burnt offering. 17. And he shall offer the ram as a *sacrifice of holy things* [10] before the Lord together with the basket of unleavened bread, and the priest shall *offer* his cereal offering and his drink offering,[w] 18. and the nazirite shall shave his consecrated head at the door of the tent of meeting, and (he shall take the hair from his consecrated head)[x] and put it in the fire which is under the sacrifice of *the holy things.* [10] 19. And the priest shall take the boiled[y] shoulder from the ram and one unleavened cake from the basket and one roll which is unleavened, and shall put it on the palm[z] *of the* nazirite's *hands* after he has shaved *the crown*[aa] of his naziriteship,[11] 20. and the priest shall raise them as a wave offering[bb] before the Lord; they are a holy thing for the priest, together with the (breast)[cc] of the wave offering and the thigh of the *separated offering;* and after this the nazirite may drink wine. 21. This is *the decree*[dd] *of* the law[12] of the nazirite. He who vows an offering to the Lord beyond his naziriteship, apart from what he can afford,[ee] he shall do so in accordance with his vow beyond the requirements of his naziriteship.'" 22. And the Lord[ff] spoke with Moses, saying: 23. "Speak with Aaron and with his sons, saying: 'Thus shall you bless[gg] the chil-

Apparatus, Chapter 6

[w] Nfmg: "his drink offerings."
[x] Missing in text; added in margin.
[y] Nfmg: "(the shoulder) which is boiled."
[z] Nfmg: "the palm."
[aa] *klyl;* Nfmg: "the crown" (another word, *nzyr,* that in Nfmg to v. 7, note *n* above).
[bb] *'npw;* MT: *tenuphah.*
[cc] Text: *m';* "belly." Read *ny'h,* "breast," with Nfmg, Aruch and Nf Exod 29:27.
[dd] Nfmg: "the instruction of . . ."
[ee] Lit.: "apart from what his hand may find." Nfmg: "he may find between his hands."
[ff] Nfmg: "the Memra of the Lord."
[gg] Nfmg: "in this order shall you bless."

Notes, Chapter 6

[9] "perfect, without blemish"; HT: "perfect" (*tmym*), in keeping with Nf's translation technique. See above Introd. III, 8. Thus in Nf Num 6:14, 19:2; 28:3, 9, 11, 19, 31; 29:2, 8, 13, 17, 20, 23, 26, 29, 32, 36.
[10] "sacrifice of holy things"; HT: "(as) *šlmym.*" This is Nf's usual rendering of HT *zbḥ(y) šlmym* (in Num 6:17, 18; 7:17, 23, 29, 35, 41, 47, 53, 59, 65, 71, 77, 83, 88; 10:10; 15:3, 5, 8; 25:2) and of *šlmym* alone in Num 6:14; 15:8; 29:39. So also for other books. See above Introd. III, 1 and Introd. to Exodus II, and Leviticus II, 1.
[11] "crown of his naziriteship." See note to 6:7.
[12] "decree of the law." See note to 5:29, 6:13 above, and Introd. III, 11.

dren of Israel:—*Moses went forth from my Name and said* to them:[hh][13] 24. [ii] THE LORD BLESS YOU AND KEEP YOU; 25. THE LORD MAKE HIS FACE SHINE UPON YOU AND BE GRACIOUS TO YOU; 26. THE LORD LIFT UP HIS COUNTENANCE UPON YOU, AND GIVE YOU PEACE.'[14] 27. So shall they put my Name,[jj][15] *my Memra,* upon the children of Israel, and I, *in my Memra,* shall bless them."

Apparatus, Chapter 6

[hh] Or: "Moses went forth from his Name and said to them"; Nfmg: "and say (to them)." Note that the LXX translates v. 27, which speaks of "my Name" at v. 20. We should possibly read *min šemayya,* "from heaven."

[ii] Verses 24-25 are in Hebrew, without Aramaic translation. See note to verse.

[jj] P: "and they shall put my holy Name upon the children of Israel, and I in my Memra will bless them. However, it is not possible for the priests to serve before me in the high priesthood until such time as they are thirty years old. And you, my people, children of Israel, must not criticize (lit.: 'think in your hearts after') the priests, saying: So and so committed acts of violence and so and so committed robbery, so as not to receive from them the order of blessings with which they bless you. And I, in my Memra, am peeping and looking from the lattices, from between the fingers of the priests, and I in my Memra will bless you"; Nfmg: "(my) holy (Name upon the children)"; cf. P.

Notes, Chapter 6

[13]"Moses went forth from my name (*mn šmy*) and said. . ." This is an addition to the HT, which has: "Thus shall you bless the children of Israel, saying to them: The Lord bless you. . ." Nf's insertion is unexpected and difficult to understand. A. Díez Macho (*Neophyti 1,* 1974, 4, 53) suggests reading *šmy',* "(from) heaven," instead of *šmy,* "(from) my name," an emendation with which B. Barry Levy, 1987, 2, 67f. disagrees. Nf, he notes, has understood *'mr* (of *'mr lhm* of the HT v. 23) as a 3rd masc. sing. perfect verb ("he said to them") rather than as an imperative ("say to them," and the paraphrase "and Moses went forth. . .") in order to stress the interpretation that the words are those of Moses. The two words *mn šmy* ("from my name") are assumed to be an intrusion and should perhaps be associated with v. 27 ("put my Name. . ."). A difficulty against this interpretation is that the HT in v. 23 actually has the fuller spelling *'mwr* (with a waw), which would less easily be taken as a perfect.

[14]In Nf left in Hebrew without any Aramaic translation. The blessing of the priests is included, together with the story of Reuben (Gen 35:22) and the second story of the (golden) calf (Exod 32:21-35), in early lists of texts to be read out but not translated. Thus Mishnah, *Meg.* 4:10; Babylonian (*b. Meg.* 25b) and Palestinian (*j. Meg.* 75c) Talmuds. However, the original prohibition seems to have concerned the actual reading of the text of Num 6:24, 26 by the priests, not the translation in the Synogogue. See further M. Klein, "Not to be translated in public—*l' lmtrgm bsybwr,*" *JJS* 39 (1988) 80–91, esp. 80f., 90f. (with bibliography p. 81 note); P. Alexander, "The Rabbinic List of Forbidden Targumim," *JJS* 27 (1976) 178–191. Some MSS of Onq. translate the priestly blessings, while others (including the important MS Vat. Ebr 448) give them in Hebrew only. The two texts of Ps.-J. contain both the Hebrew and Aramaic translation. The Frg. Tg. does not have the verse.

[15]"my Name, my Memra"; a double rendering of the HT: "my Name." Onq. and Ps.-J. have: "the blessing of my Name," probably in an effort to avoid direct contact of God's name with mankind; see the note of B. Grossfeld to Onq. Num 6:27 (*The Aramaic Bible,* vol. 8, p. 89). The Frg. Tg. (P) and Nfmg have: "my holy Name."

CHAPTER 7

1. And on the day that Moses had finished setting up the tabernacle, he anointed it and consecrated it and all its utensils (and the altar and all its utensils).[a] And when he had anointed them *with the anointing oil*[1] and had consecrated them, 2. the princes[b] (of Israel, the heads of their fathers' house)[c] made an offering, (these were the princes)[c] of the tribes, those, namely, who *had been appointed over*[d2] the census.[3] 3. And they brought their offerings before the Lord: six *yoked*[4] wagons[e] and twelve bulls; one wagon for two princes[f] and a bull for *each* one; and they brought them near before the tabernacle. 4. And the Lord[g] spoke with Moses, saying: 5. "Accept them[h] from them and let them serve for the service of the tent of meeting and give them to the Levites, to each man according to the measure of his service." 6. And Moses took the wagons and the bulls and gave them to the Levites. 7. And *Moses* gave two wagons and four bulls to the sons of Gershon, according to the measure of their service. 8. And *Moses*[5] gave four wagons and eight bulls to the sons of Merari, according to the measure of their service, under the direction of Ithamar the son of Aaron the priest.[i6] 9. And to the sons of Kohath *Moses* gave *neither wagons nor bulls,*[7] because theirs was the service of the sanctuary: they had to carry the *ark* on *their*[8] shoulders. 10. And the princes also offered the offering for the dedication[j] of the altar on the day they anointed it. And the princes brought near their offering before the altar. 11. And the Lord[k] said to Moses: "A prince *from each tribe*[9] shall *each* day offer their offering for the dedication of the

Apparatus, Chapter 7

[a] Missing in text and margin; omitted by homoeoteleuton.
[b] Nfi: "magnates" (or: "princes") (another word).
[c] Missing in text; omitted through homoeoteleuton; added in margin.
[d] Nfmg: "these were the princes of Israel, those (namely) who (were) established and appointed over the census."
[e] Nfmg: "loaded with tapestries when they are covered."
[f] Nfmg: "from two princes" (or: "magnates").
[g] Nfmg: "the Memra of the Lord."
[h] Nfmg: "take (them) from (them)."
[i] Nfmg: "the high (priest)."
[j] Nfmg: "the anointing of the altar."
[k] Nfmg: "the Memra of the Lord."

Notes, Chapter 7

[1]"with the anointing oil"; an addition to the HT.
[2]"who had been appointed (over)," *mmnyn* HT: "who stood over," *h-'mdym.* Nf employs the same term to expand the simple *'l,* "over," in Num 10:22.
[3]"census"; lit.: "the numbers."
[4]"yoked"; rendering *ṣb,* "covered," of HT, found only here in the Pentateuch; Onq. and Ps.-J. "covered"; likewise the Vulg.
[5]"Moses"; HT: "he."
[6]"the priest"; Nf often adds "high" to priest (see note to 3:3), but not here; Nfmg, however, does.
[7]"neither wagons nor bulls"; an addition to the HT, providing an object to the verb.
[8]"ark . . . their"; not in HT.
[9]"from each tribe"; an explanatory addition to HT.

anointing[m] of the altar."[10] 12. And the one[n] who offered his offering[o] on the first day was Nahshon bar Amminadab, of the tribe of *the sons*[11] of Judah. 13. And[12] his offering *which he offered*[13] was one silver bowl, whose weight was one hundred and thirty *selas, in selas of the sanctuary,*[p14] one silver sprinkling basin, *whose weight* was seventy *selas,* in *selas* of the sanctuary; he *offered these* two *utensils—the bowl and the sprinkling basin*[15]—full of fine flour soaked[q] in oil, as a cereal offering; 14. one dish,[16] ten *selas of silver its weight* made, *but it was* of gold,[r] which *he offered* full of the *chief* incenses, *precious perfumes,*[s] *blended and pure, for the incense;*[t] 15. one young bull,[17] *three years old;* one ram, *two (years) old;* and one year-old lamb, *the three of which he offered* as a burnt offering;[u18] 16. one male

Apparatus, Chapter 7

[m] This lit.; possibly to be understood as: "for the dedication, the anointing, of . . ."
[n] Nfmg: "(and) he (who)."
[o] Nfmg: "the offerings."
[p] Nfi: "(in) holy (selas)."
[q] Nfmg: "mixed" = VN.
[r] VN: "one dish, (in) weight ten selas, which was of gold, which he offered, full of choice precious perfumes, blended and pure, for the incense of the aromas (or: 'incense offering')"; Nfmg: "(one dish) of ten selas in weight which was of gold" = VN.
[s] Nfmg: "(full of the chief) aromas" = VN.
[t] Nfmg: "for the incense of the aromas" = VN.
[u] VN Nfmg: "(one lamb) a year old (lit.: 'of its year')"; the three of them (VN omit 'the three of them') the chief of the tribe offered up as a burnt offering"; cf. also vv. 21, 27, 33, 39, 45, 51, 57, 63, 69, 75, 81.

Notes, Chapter 7

[10]"for the dedication of the anointing of (*lḥnwkt rbwth*) the altar"; HT: "for the anointing of (*lḥnkt*) the altar." Nf uses the double word *ḥnwkt rbwth* (lit.: "the dedication of the anointing") to translate the simple HT *ḥnkh.* (Nf Num 7:11, 84, 88); Onq. retains the HT terms (*ḥnwkah*) in all three cases. Ps.-J. has the double term as in Nf; Nf (and Ps.-J.) introduces the phrase for each of the days of the dedication (vv. 18, 24, 30, 36, 42, 48, 54, 60, 66, 72, 78.

[11]"of the sons"; an expansion in the style of Nf; see above Introd. III, 23.

[12]According to the Mishnah, *Meg.* 3:6, in the (synagogue) liturgy at Hanukkah (the Feast of Dedication) the passage "The Princes" (Num 7:1-49) was read. The additions in vv. 13-17 add little of substance but are in rather stark contrast with the more literal rendering in Nf Num chaps. 1–6, and Nf Numbers in general outside of the evident cases of midrash. It may be that these expansions in Nf (and VN) Num 7:13-17 are due to liturgical usage. See further B. Barry Levy, 1987, 2, 71. For the relationship of the Frg. Tg. to the liturgy, see M. Klein, 1980, 1, 19–23 (p. 20 for Hanukkah). See also B. Barry Levy, 1987, 2, 71 (on 7:17).

[13]"which he offered"; an explanatory addition to HT: "his offering," as in vv. 14, 16, 17.

[14]"(130 selas) in selas of the sanctuary." Added here in Nf, but found in HT in v. 13b.

[15]"he offered these in utensils . . . basin." This explanatory expansion to the HT is repeated for each of the eleven days: vv. 19, 25, 31, 37, 43, 49, 55, 61, 67, 73, 79.

[16]There are many expansions in Nf's paraphrase of this verse (v. 14). The HT has: "one golden dish of ten shekels, full of incense." The HT text, and Nf's paraphrase, is repeated for each of twelve days (vv. 20, 26, 32, 38, 44, 50, 56, 62, 68, 73, 80).

[17]The HT specifies the age only for the lamb, and leaves unclear whether the one-year-old male lamb or all three animals are for the burnt offering. The question is discussed in *Sifre Num,* par. 50 and 56 (on Num 7:15, 87), stressing that all three animals are suitable for the whole burnt offering. Nf does likewise and also (unlike *Sifre,* Onq., or Ps.-J.) assigns ages to the other two animals. VN paraphrase as Nf.

[18]The substance of v. 15, and Nf's paraphrase, is repeated for each of the other eleven days (vv. 21, 27, 33, 39, 45, 51, 57, 63, 69, 75, 81).

goat,[19] *which he offered* as a sin offering,[w] *for the remission of sins and for sins unwittingly committed,*[20] *to expiate by the blood of the male goat for his (own) sins and for the sins of the tribe unwittingly committed;* 17. and for the *sacrifice of holy things*[x][21] he offered two bulls, five rams, five kid goats, five male lambs, a year old. This was his offering *which the prince of the tribe of the sons of Judah,* Nahshon bar Amminadab, *donated*[y] and *offered from his own riches.* 18. On the second day *of the dedication of the anointing of the altar,* Nethanel bar Zuar, the prince *of the tribe of the sons* of Issachar, made an offering. 19. He offered as his offering[z] one silver bowl, whose weight was one hundred and thirty *selas in selas of the sanctuary,*[aa] one silver sprinkling basin *weighing seventy selas in selas of the sanctuary;*[aa] *he offered those two utensils—the bowl*[bb] *and the sprinkling basin*[cc]—full of fine flour soaked in oil, as a cereal offering; 20. one dish, ten *selas of silver its weight* made[dd] *but it was*[ee] of gold, *which he offered* full of the chief incenses, *precious perfumes,*[ff] blended and pure, for the incense;[gg] 21. one young bull, *three years old;*[hh] one ram, *two*[ii] (years) *old;* and one year-old lamb, *the three of which he offered* as a burnt offering;[jj] 22. one male goat, *which he offered* as a sin offering,[kk] *for the remission of sins and for sins unwittingly committed, to make atonement by the blood of the male lamb for his (own) sins and the sins of the tribe unwittingly committed;*

Apparatus, Chapter 7

[w] Nfmg: "(which) the chief of the tribe (offered) as a sin offering" = VN.

[x] VN: "and for the sacrifice of holy things he offered two bulls, five (text: 'two') rams, five kid goats, five (male) lambs a year old. This was his offering which the prince of the tribe of the sons of Judah, Nahshon bar Amminadab, arranged and offered from his riches."

[y] The reason for adding this word ("he donated," *tndb*) in Nf is to explain the name Amminadab through paronomasia; Nfmg: "(which) he arranged" = VN.

[z] Nfmg: "and he offered."

[aa] Nfi 1° and Nfi 2°: "(in) holy (selas)."

[bb] Nfmg: "(in selas of the sanctuary) two full—a bowl." (*pyylyh,* indeterminate; in text determined, *pyyltyta;* a Greek loan word).

[cc] Nfi: "and one sprinkling basin."

[dd] Nfmg: "(one dish) of ten (selas) of gold, full of incense."

[ee] Nfmg: "(one dish) ten selas (in weight) which was of gold."

[ff] Nfmg: "(full of) the chief aromas."

[gg] Nfmg: "for the incense of the aromas."

[hh] Nfmg: "(one young bull), one ram, one year-old lamb for a burnt offering."

[ii] Nfmg: "two" (a different form).

[jj] Nfmg: "(which three) the chief of the tribe offered as a burnt offering."

[kk] Nfmg: "(which) the chief of the tribe offered as a sin offering."

Notes, Chapter 7

[19]In v. 16 Nf has elaborate expansion. The HT simply has: "one male goat for a sin offering." Nf's expansion seems to have borrowed elements from Lev 16:17. This formula is repeated for the remaining days of the celebration: v. 22 (day 2), 28 (day 3), 34 (day 4), 40 (day 5), 46 (day 6), 52 (day 7), 58 (day 8), 64 (day 9), 70 (day 10), 76 (day 11), 82 (day 12).

[20]"remission of sins . . . committed." The HT in v. 17 has: "and for the sacrifice of peace offerings (*zbḥy šlmym*) two oxen, five rams, five male goats and five male rams a year old. This was the offering of (Nahshon . . .)." The invariable part of this formula is repeated in HT and in Nf's paraphrase for the other days of the celebration (vv. 23, 29, 35, 41, 47, 53, 59, 65, 71, 77, 83).

[21]"sacrifice of holy things." See note to 6:14; also above Introd. III, 1.

23. and for the sacrifice of *holy things he offered* two bulls, five rams, five kid goats, five male lambs, a year old. This was his offering *which the prince of the tribe of the sons of Issachar,* Nethanel bar Zuar, *donated*[mm] *and offered from his own riches.* 24. On the third day *of the dedication of the anointing of the altar,* Eliab bar Helon (the prince of)[nn] *the tribe* of the sons of Zebulun, *made an offering.* 25. The offering[oo] *which he offered*[pp] (was) one silver bowl, whose weight was one hundred and thirty *selas in selas of the sanctuary;*[qq] one silver sprinkling basin *weighing* seventy *selas* of the sanctuary;[qq] *these* two utensils—*the bowl and the sprinkling basin*[rr]—he offered[ss] full <of fine flour>[tt] soaked[uu] in oil, as a cereal offering; 26. one dish, ten *silver selas its weight*[ww] made, but it was of gold,[xx] *which he offered* full of *the chief (incenses),*[yy] *precious perfumes,*[zz] *blended and pure for the incense;*[a] 27. one young bull, *three years old;* one ram, *two (years) old;* and one year-old lamb, *the three of which he offered* as a burnt offering;[b] 28. one male goat, *which he offered* as a sin offering, for the *remission of sins and for sins unwittingly committed, to expiate by the blood of the male goat for his (own) sins and for the sins of the tribe unwittingly committed;*[c] 29. and for the sacrifice *of holy things he offered* two bulls, five rams, five kid goats, five male lambs, a year old. This was his offering *which the prince of the tribe of the sons of Zebulun,* Eliab bar Helon, *donated and offered from his own riches.*[d] 30. On the fourth day of the *dedication of the anointing of the altar,* Elizur bar Shedeur, the prince *of the tribe* of the sons of Reuben, *made an offering.* 31. His offering *which he offered* (was) one silver bowl, whose weight was a hundred and thirty *selas, in selas of the sanctuary,* one silver sprinkling basin *weighing* seventy *selas* in *selas* of the sanctuary; *these two utensils—the bowl and the sprinkling basin—he offered* full of fine flour soaked in oil, as a cereal offering; 32. one dish, ten *silver selas its weight* made, *but it was of gold, which he offered* full of *the chief incenses, precious perfumes, blended and pure, for the incense;* 33. one young bull, *three years old;* one ram, *two (years) old;* and one year-old lamb, *the three of which he offered* as a burnt offering; 34. one male goat, *which he offered* as a sin offering, *for the remission of sins and for sins unwittingly committed, to expiate by the blood of the male goat for his (own) sins and for the sins of the tribe unwittingly committed;* 35. and for the sacrifice of *holy things he offered* two bulls, five rams, five kid goats, five male lambs, a year old. This was his offering *which* Elizur bar Shedeur, *the prince of the tribe of the sons of Reuben,*

Apparatus, Chapter 7

[mm] Nfmg: "(which) he arranged."
[nn] Missing in text.
[oo] Lit.: "his offering."
[pp] Nfmg: "he offered his offering."
[qq] Nfi: "(in) holy (selas)."
[rr] Nfmg: "and a sprinkling basin."
[ss] Nfmg: "(the two objects he offered) full."
[tt] Omitted in text and margin.
[uu] Nfmg: "mixed."
[ww] Nfmg: "(one dish) of ten (selas) of gold full of incense."
[xx] Nfmg: "(a dish) of ten selas (in weight) which was of gold."
[yy] This appears to be missing from the text; cf. parallel passages.
[zz] Nfmg: "(full of) the chief aromas."
[a] Nfmg: "for the incense of the aromas."
[b] The same variants of v. 21.
[c] The same variants of v. 22.
[d] For the variants of this verse and of vv. 30-83 in Nf see the translation of the earlier parallel verses.

donated and offered from his own riches. 36. And on the fifth day *of the dedication of the anointing of the altar,* Shelumiel bar Zuri Shaddai, the prince *of the tribe* of the sons of Simeon, *made an offering.* 37. And his offering *which he offered* was one silver bowl, whose weight was a hundred and thirty *selas, in selas of the sanctuary;* one silver sprinkling basin, *whose weight was* seventy *selas,* in *selas* of the sanctuary; *he offered those* two *utensils—the bowl and the sprinkling basin*—full of fine flour soaked in oil, as a cereal offering; 38. one dish, ten *silver selas its weight* made, *but it was* of gold, *which he offered* full of *the chief* incense, *precious perfumes, blended and pure, for the incense;* 39. one young bull, *three years old;* one ram, *two (years) old;* and one year-old lamb, *the three of which he offered* as a burnt offering; 40. one male goat, *which he offered* as a sin offering, *for the remission of sins and for sins unwittingly committed, to expiate by the blood of the male goat for his (own) sins and for the sins of the tribe unwittingly committed;* 41. and for the sacrifice of *holy things he offered* two bulls, five rams, five kid goats, five male lambs, a year old. This was his offering *which* Shelumiel bar Zuri Shaddai, *the prince of the tribe of the sons of Simeon, donated and offered from his own riches.* 42. On the sixth day *of the dedication of the anointing of the altar,* Eliasaph bar Deuel, the prince *of the tribe* of the sons of Gad, *made an offering.* 43. And his offering *which he offered* was one silver bowl, whose weight was a hundred and thirty *selas, in selas of the sanctuary;* one silver sprinkling basin, *whose weight* was seventy *selas* of the sanctuary; *he offered these* two *utensils—the bowl and the sprinkling basin*—full of fine flour soaked in oil, as a cereal offering; 44. one dish, ten *silver selas its weight* made, *but it was of gold, which he offered* full of *the chief* incenses, *precious perfumes, blended and pure, for the incense;* 45. one young bull, *three years old;* one ram, *two (years) old;* and one year-old lamb, *the three of which he offered* as a burnt offering; 46. one male goat, *which he offered* as a sin offering, *for the remission of sins and for sins unwittingly committed, to expiate by the blood of the male goat for his (own) sins and for the sins of the tribe unwittingly committed;* 47. and for the sacrifice of *holy things he offered* two bulls, five rams, five kid goats, five male lambs, a year old. This was his offering *which* Eliasaph bar Deuel, *the prince of the tribe of the sons of Gad, donated and offered from his own riches.* 48. On the seventh day of *the dedication of the anointing of the altar,* Elishama bar Ammihud, the prince *of the tribe* of the sons of Ephraim, *made an offering.* 49. And his offering *which he offered* was one silver bowl, whose weight was a hundred and thirty *selas, in selas of the sanctuary;* one silver sprinkling basin, *whose weight* was seventy *selas* of the sanctuary; *he offered these* two *utensils—the bowl and the sprinkling basin*—full of fine flour soaked in oil, as a cereal offering; 50. one dish, ten *silver selas its weight* made, *but it was of gold, which he offered* full of *the chief* incenses, *precious perfumes, blended and pure, for the incense;* 51. one young bull, *three years old;* one ram, *two (years) old;* and one year-old lamb, *the three of which he offered* as a burnt offering; 52. one male goat, *which he offered* as a sin offering, *for the remission of sins and for sins unwittingly committed, to expiate by the blood of the male goat for his (own) sins and for the sins of the tribe unwittingly committed;* 53. and for the sacrifice of *holy things he offered* two bulls, five rams, five kid goats, five male lambs, a year old. This was his offering *which* Elishama bar Ammihud, *the prince of the tribe of the sons of Ephraim, donated and offered from his own riches.* 54. On the eighth day of the *dedication of the anointing of the altar,* Gamaliel bar Pedah Zur, the prince *of the tribe* of the sons of Manasseh, *made an offering.* 55. And his offering *which he offered* was one silver bowl, whose weight was a hundred and thirty *selas, in selas of the sanctuary;* one silver sprinkling basin, *whose weight* was seventy *selas* of the sanctuary; *he offered these* two *utensils—the bowl and the sprinkling basin*—full of fine flour soaked in oil, as a cereal offering; 56. one dish, ten *silver selas its weight* made, *but it was of gold, which he offered* full of *the chief* incenses, *precious perfumes, blended and pure, for the incense;* 57. one young bull, *three years old;* one ram, *two (years) old;* and one year-old lamb, *the three of which he offered* as a burnt offering; 58. one male goat, *which he offered* as a sin offering, *for the remission of sins and for sins unwittingly committed, to expiate by the blood of the male goat for his (own) sins and for the sins of the tribe unwittingly committed;* 59. and for the sacrifice of *holy things he offered* two bulls, five rams, five kid goats, five male lambs, a year old. This was his offering *which* Gamaliel bar Pedah Zur, *the prince of the tribe of the sons of Manasseh, donated and offered from his own riches.* 60. On the ninth day *of the dedication of the anointing of the altar,* Abidan bar Gideoni, the prince *of the tribe* of the sons of Benjamin, *made an offering.* 61. And his offering *which he offered* was one silver bowl, whose weight was a hundred and thirty *selas, in selas of the sanctuary;* one silver sprinkling basin, *whose weight* was seventy *selas* of the sanctuary; *he offered these* two *utensils—the bowl and the sprinkling basin*—full of fine flour soaked in oil, as a cereal offering; 62. one dish, ten *silver selas its weight* made, *but it was of gold, which he offered* full of *the chief* incenses, *precious perfumes, blended and pure, for the incense;* 63. one young bull, *three years old;* one ram, *two (years) old;* and one year-old lamb, *the three of which he offered* as a burnt offering; 64. one male goat, *which he offered* as a sin offering, *for the remission of sins and for sins unwittingly committed, to expiate by the blood of the male goat for his (own) sins and for the sins of the tribe unwittingly committed;* 65. and for the sacrifice of *holy things he offered* <two> bulls, <five rams, five kid goats,> five male <lambs>, a year old. This was the offering *which* Abidan bar Gideoni, *the prince of the tribe of the sons of Benjamin, donated and offered from his own riches.* 66. On the tenth day *of the dedication of the anointing of the altar,* Ahiezer bar Ammi Shaddai, the prince *of the tribe* of the sons of Dan, *made an offering.* 67. And his offering *which he offered* was one silver bowl, whose weight was a hundred and thirty *selas, in selas of the sanctuary;* one silver sprinkling basin, *whose weight* was seventy *selas* of the sanctuary; *he offered these* two *utensils—the bowl and the sprinkling basin*—full of fine flour soaked in oil, as a cereal offering; 68. one dish, ten *silver selas its weight* made, *but it was of gold, which he offered* full of *the chief* incenses, *precious perfumes, blended and pure, for the incense;* 69. one young bull, *three years old;* one ram, *two (years) old;* and one year-old lamb, *the three of which he offered* as a burnt offering; 70. one male goat, *which he offered* as a sin offering, *for the remission of sins and for sins unwittingly committed, to expiate by the blood of the male goat for his (own) sins and for the sins of the tribe unwittingly committed;* 71. and for the sacrifice of *holy things he offered* two bulls, five rams, five kid goats, five male lambs, a year old. This was his offering *which* Ahiezer bar Ammi Shaddai, *prince of the tribe of the sons of Dan, donated and offered from his own riches.* 72. On the eleventh day of *the dedication of the anointing of the altar,* Pagiel bar Ochran, the prince *of the tribe* of the sons of Asher, *made an offering.* 73. And his offering *which he offered* was one silver bowl, whose weight was a hundred and thirty *selas, in selas of the sanctuary;* one silver sprinkling basin, *whose weight* was seventy *selas* of the sanctuary; *he offered these* two *utensils—the bowl and the sprinkling basin—* full of fine flour soaked in oil, as a cereal offering; 74. one dish, ten *silver selas its weight* made, *but it was of gold, which he offered* full of *the chief* incenses, *precious perfumes, blended and pure, for the incense;* 75. one young bull, *three years old;* one ram, *two (years) old;* and one year-old lamb, *the three of which he offered* as a burnt offering; 76. one male goat, *which he offered* as a sin offering, *for the remission of sins and for sins unwittingly committed, to expiate by the blood of the male goat for his (own) sins and for the sins of the tribe unwittingly committed;* 77. and for the sacrifice of *holy things he offered* two bulls, five rams, five kid goats, five male lambs, a year old. This was his offering *which* Pagiel bar Ochran, *the prince of the tribe of the sons of Asher, donated and offered from his own riches.* 78. On the twelfth day *of the dedication of the altar, of its anointing,* Ahira bar Enan, the prince of the *tribe of the* sons of Naphtali, *made an offering.* 79. And his offering *which he offered* was one silver bowl, whose weight was a hundred and thirty *selas, in selas of the sanctuary;* one silver sprinkling basin *whose weight* was seventy *selas* of the sanctuary; *he offered these* two *utensils—the bowl and the sprinkling basin*—full of fine flour soaked in oil, as a cereal offering; 80. one dish, ten *silver selas its weight* made, *but it was of gold, which he offered* full of *the chief* incenses, *precious perfumes, blended and pure, for the incense;* 81. one young bull, *three years old;* one ram, *two (years) old;* and one year-old lamb, *the three of which he offered* as a burnt offering; 82. one male goat, *which he offered* as a sin offering, *for the remission of sins and for sins unwittingly committed, to expiate by the blood of the male goat for his (own) sins and for the sins of the tribe unwittingly committed;* 83. and for the sacrifice of *holy things he offered* two bulls, five rams, five kid goats, five male lambs, a year old. This was his offering *which* Ahira bar Enan, *the prince of the tribe of the sons of Naphtali, donated and offered from his own riches.* 84. This was the dedication *of the anointing*[22] of the altar, on the day in which it was anointed, offered by the princes of *the children* of Israel: twelve silver bowls, twelve silver sprinkling basins, twelve dishes <of gold>.[e] 85. *The weight of* each silver bowl[f] was a hundred and thirty *selas,* and of each sprinkling basin seventy; all the silver of the utensils, two thousand four hundred *selas,* in *selas* of the sanctuary; 86. the twelve

Apparatus, Chapter 7

[e] In text: "of silver."

[f] Nfmg: "one bowl."

Notes, Chapter 7

[22] "the dedication of the anointing" (*ḥnwkt rbwth . . .*). See note to 7:11.

golden dishes, full of incense,[g] each dish (weighed) ten *selas,* in *selas* of the sanctuary; all the gold of the dishes was one hundred and twenty (*selas*).[h] 87. All the bulls for the burnt offering, twelve bulls; rams, twelve; year-old lambs, twelve; with their cereal offerings; and twelve male goats for the sin offering; 88. and all bulls for the sacrifice of *holy things* were twenty-four bulls; rams, sixty; male goats, sixty; year-old lambs, sixty. This was the dedication *of the anointing* of the altar, after it had been anointed. 89. And when Moses used to enter the tent[i] of meeting to speak with him, he heard the voice of the *Dibbera*[j23] speaking[k] with him from above the mercy seat which was upon the ark of the testimony, from between the two cherubim. *From there the Dibbera* used to speak with him.[m24]

CHAPTER 8

1. And the Lord[a] spoke with Moses, saying: 2. "Speak with Aaron and say to him: 'When you *arrange*[1] the lamps, the seven lamps shall give light in front of the lampstand.'" 3. And Aaron did so; he *arranged*[1] the lamps in front of the lampstand, as the Lord[a] had commanded Moses. 4. And this was the workmanship of the lampstand, a hammered work of gold; from its vase to its lilies, it was hammered work. According to the appearance which the Lord had shown[b] Moses, thus did *Bezalel*[c2] make the lampstand. 5. And the Lord spoke with Moses, saying:

Apparatus, Chapter 7

[g] Nfmg: "full of incenses, of precious aromas, of twelve . . ."
[h] Nfmg: "selas"; in text of Nf, with HT, "selas" is absent.
[i] Nfmg: "and at Moses' entry into the tent of . . ."
[j] *dbyrh.* See note.
[k] Nfi: "it (or: 'he') spoke."
[m] Nfmg: "with Moses."

Notes, Chapter 7

[23]"the voice of the Dibbera"; HT: "the voice." The "Dibbera" was God conceived of as communicating his will to his people. See also M. McNamara in *The Aramaic Bible,* vol. 1A, p. 38, and note to Nf Exod 19:3 (*The Aramaic Bible,* vol. 2, p. 79).
[24]"from between the two cherubim. From these the Dibbera . . . "; HT: "from between the two cherubim, and it spoke to him."

Apparatus, Chapter 8

[a] Nfmg: "the Memra of the Lord."
[b] Nfmg: "(that) the Memra of the Lord had shown."
[c] Nfi: without the name Bezalel.

Notes, Chapter 8

[1]"arrange"; HT (RSV): "set up."
[2]"did Bezalel"; HT: "did he," i.e., Moses. The precise agent is given in Nf, according to Exod 31:2-11. It was Bezalel rather than Moses who was responsible for the art work.

6. "Separate the Levites from among the children of Israel and cleanse them. 7. And thus shall you do to them[d] to cleanse them: sprinkle the water of expiation upon them and they shall pass the razor over all their body and wash their clothes and they shall be clean. 8. And they shall take a young bull and a cereal oblation of fine flour soaked in oil; and you shall take a second young bull for a sin offering. 9. And you shall bring the Levites near before the tent of meeting, and you shall bring together the entire congregation of the children of Israel.[e] 10. And when you bring the Levites near before the Lord, the children of Israel shall lay their hands upon the Levites, 11. and Aaron shall offer the Levites as a wave offering before the Lord from the children of Israel, and theirs shall be to do the service of the Lord. 12. And the Levites shall lay their hands upon the heads[f] of the bulls; and you shall *offer*[g][3] one as a sin offering and the other as a burnt offering *before*[4] the Lord, to make atonement for the Levites. 13. And you shall set the Levites before Aaron and before his sons, and you shall offer them as a wave offering *before* the Lord. 14. And when you have separated the Levites from among the children of Israel, the Levites shall belong to *my Name.*[5] 15. And after that the Levites shall go in to serve the tent of meeting; and you shall have cleansed them and offered them as a wave offering, 16. because they are given to me as *a gift* from among the children of Israel: instead of *those who open* every womb, the first-born of all of the children of Israel, I have *set* them *aside*[6] for *my Name.*[5] 17. Because all the first-born of the children of Israel, both in the sons of man[h] and in beast, belong[i] to *my Name.*[5] The day that I *slew* all the first-born in the land of Egypt, <I consecrated>[j] them to *my Name,*[5] 18. and I took the Levites instead of all the first-born[k] of the children of Israel; 19. and I gave the Levites[m] as *a gift* to Aaron and to his sons, from among the children of Israel, to do the service of the children of Israel in the tent of meeting and to make atonement for the children of Israel, so that there may be no wrath among the children of Israel when the children of Israel draw near[n] the sanctuary." 20. And Moses and Aaron and all the congregation[o] of the children of Israel did so to the Levites; the children of Israel did all that the

Apparatus, Chapter 8

[d] Nfmg: "and according to this rite."
[e] Nfmg: "(the entire) assembly of the people of the congregation."
[f] Nfmg: "(upon) the head of the . . ."
[g] Nfmg: "and he shall offer."
[h] I.e., "men"; Nfi: "both of men."
[i] Nfmg: "(because) I have set apart for my Name."
[j] Omitted through forgetfulness and added in the margin in square letters proper to the text; Nfmg: "I have set (them) apart."
[k] Nfi: "(of every) first-born."
[m] Nfmg: "(and I gave) to the Levites given to Aaron."
[n] Nfmg: "(so that there be no) devastating death when the children of Israel draw near."
[o] Nfmg: "(and all) the people of the . . ."

Notes, Chapter 8

[3]"shall offer . . . before the Lord"; HT "shall make to the Lord."
[4]"before the Lord"; HT: "to the Lord."
[5]"to my Name"; HT: "to me."
[6]"set aside" or "separate"; HT: "take." See note to 3:12 above.

Lord[p] had commanded Moses concerning the Levites. 21. And the Levites purified themselves and washed their clothes, and <Aaron[q] offered[r] them as a wave offering before the Lord, and Aaron made[s] atonement for them>[t] to cleanse them.[u] 22. And after this the Levites went in to perform their service in the tent of meeting before Aaron and before his sons. According as the Lord[w] had commanded Moses concerning the Levites, thus they did to them. 23. And the Lord[w] spoke with Moses, saying: 24. "This is what *you shall do* to the Levites:[7] From *twenty* years[x][8] old and upwards he[9] shall enter into the *army*[y] *of war,*[10] to serve *in* the tent of meeting.[11] 25. And from the age of fifty years, he shall return from the *army of war*[10] and shall serve no more;[z] 26. he shall, however, minister to his brethren in the tent of meeting, to keep the charge, but he shall do no service. According[aa] to *this order* shall you do to the Levites, in their charge."

Apparatus, Chapter 8

[p] Nfmg: "the Memra of the Lord."
[q] This word is missing in text and margin.
[r] Nfmg: "and he offered as a wave offering" (another writing); or: "he shall offer as a wave offering."
[s] Nfmg: "and he shall make atonement."
[t] "Aaron . . . for them" missing in text; added in margin, except for first word.
[u] Nfi: "to cleanse (them)" (another form).
[w] Nfmg: "the Memra of the Lord."
[x] Nfmg: "this is the service that there is for the Levites; from twenty."
[y] Nfmg: "into the service to perform the ministry in the tent . . ."
[z] Nfmg: "(from the work) of the service and shall serve no more"; thus with HT, from which Nf text disagrees.
[aa] Nfmg: "to discharge (or: 'watch'), but perform liturgical services he shall not do; according to this . . ."

Notes, Chapter 8

[7]Verse 24 in the HT (RSV) reads: "This is what pertains to the Levites: from twenty-five years old and upward . . ."

[8]"from twenty (years)"; unique (error?). HT and versions: "from twenty-five." Unlike the Levites, no age limit is fixed for the priestly service; see *Sifre Num* 63, on Num 8:26; *t. Hull.* 1:16; Luke 1:18 and texts in Strack-Billerbeck, 2, 89. In some cases, however (*Sifra Lev* 21, 17 [95b 2ff.] = *b. Hull* 24b) twenty years is given as the lower limit for priestly service; cf. also Num 1:3, 22, 24; 1:26, 28, 30, 32, 34, 36, 38, 40, 42.

[9]"he," i.e., they.

[10]"the army of war," *l-ḥyl qrbh;* HT: *lṣb' ṣb';* RSV: "to perform the work" (in the service of the tent of meeting). In the present context the HT terms are generally taken to refer to liturgical service. As elsewhere, Nf understands in a military sense; see note to 1:3 above.

[11]"to serve in the tent of meeting," HT: "in the service of (*b'bdt*) the tent of meeting." The same expression occurs in Num 4:23, and Nf renders as here.

CHAPTER 9

1. And the Lord[a] spoke with Moses in the wilderness of Sinai in the second year, at the time *the children of Israel*[1] came forth[b] *redeemed*[2] out of Egypt, in the first month, saying: 2. "The children of Israel[c] shall keep the Passover[d] at its appointed time. 3. You shall keep it on the fourteenth day of this month[e] at twilight,[f] at its appointed time, you shall keep it according to all its statutes and according to all its *ordinances.*"[3] 4. And Moses spoke with the children of Israel to keep the Passover. 5. And they kept the Passover on the first *month,*[4] on the fourteenth day of the month, at twilight,[f] in the wilderness of Sinai. <According to> all that the Lord[a] had commanded Moses, thus the children of Israel did. 6. And there were certain men who were unclean[g] through the *defilement*[5] of the corpse of a man,[h] and they could not keep the Passover on that day; <and they drew near before Moses and before Aaron on that day>.[i] 7. And those men said to him:[j] "We are unclean through the *defilement* of the corpse of a man;[h] why should we be impeded from offering the Lord's offering at its appointed time amongst the children of Israel?"

Apparatus, Chapter 9

[a] Nfmg: "the Memra of the Lord."
[b] Nfmg: "(second year,) at the coming forth (of the children of Israel)."
[c] Nfi: "Israel (shall keep).
[d] Nfmg: "the sacrifice (?) of the Passover"; cf. Ps.-J.
[e] Nfi: "in (this) month"; Nfmg: "in the month of Nisan, between . . ."
[f] Lit.: "between the two suns."
[g] Nfmg 1°: "and there were some men there who were unclean"; Nfmg 2°: "and there were some men who had been laden with the coffin of Joseph, and who had been laden with Nadab and Abihu, the sons of Aaron, and it was not possible for them to keep the Passover."
[h] Lit.: "a son of man."
[i] Missing in text and margin.
[j] Nfmg: "(they said) to Moses."

Notes, Chapter 9

[1]"the children of Israel came forth"; HT: "at their coming forth."
[2]"redeemed," added in keeping with the tendency of Nf; see above Introd. III, 22.
[3]"ordinances," *sydry dynwy;* HT: *mšpṭ(yw).* For Nf's rendering, see above Introd. III, 12.
[4]"month"; an addition in Nf.
[5]"defilement of the corpse of a man"; lit.: "d. of the nefesh of a son of man." HT: "defiled by the nefesh of a man" (*'dm). Nephesh,* a term rich in meaning, is used in the HT in the sense of "deceased person" (with or without the qualification *mt,* "dead"—with *mt* in Num 6:6; Lev 21:11; without *mt* but with *'dm* in Num 9:6, 7; 19:11, 13 (*nefeš 'dm*), and simply *npš* in Lev 19:28; 21:1; 22:9; Num 5:2; 6:11; 9:10. In all cases Nf retains the Hebrew term, apparently with the meaning "a dead person." In Lev 22:4; Num 5:2; 9:10, Nf adds *(npš) dbrnš;* and in Lev 19:28; 21:1, it adds "of a dead person."

8. And he said[k] to them: *This is one of the four legal cases*[6] *which came up before Moses; in two of them*[m] *Moses was quick and in two of them Moses was slow.*[n] *In (the case of) the unclean persons who were not able to keep the Passover at its appointed time and in the case of*[o] *the daughters of Zelophehad, Moses was quick because their cases were civil cases.*[7] *In (the case of) the wood-gatherer who willfully profaned the sabbath, and in the case of the blasphemer who pronounced the sacred Name with blasphemies,*[p] *Moses was slow because their cases were capital cases,*[q8] *to teach the judges*[r] *to arise after Moses that they be quick in civil cases*[7] *and slow in capital cases,*[s] *lest they precipitately put to death someone who should be executed by law,*[9] *and lest they be ashamed*[t] *to say: 'We have not heard,' since Moses our master*

Apparatus, Chapter 9

[k] Nfmg: "Moses (said): Arise now and I will have you hear what is established before the Lord to do to you; this is one . . ."; VN: "This is one of the four legal cases that came in before Moses; in two of them Moses was quick, and in two of them Moses was slow. In (the case of) the unclean persons who were not able to keep the Passover at their appointed times and in the case of the daughters of Zelophehad, Moses was quick because their cases were civil cases (lit.: 'cases, judgments, of wealth'). And (in the case of) the blasphemer who blasphemed the holy Name and in (the case of) the wood-gatherer who willfully profaned the sabbath, Moses was slow because such cases were cases of capital sentence. And in both one and the other Moses said: I have not heard, to teach the judges who were to arise after Moses to be quick in civil cases and slow in cases of capital sentence, so that they should not be ashamed to say: I have not heard. Truly our master Moses said: I have not heard. And he said to them: Arise and hear what the Memra of the Lord will command you."

[m] Nfmg: "which came in before Moses, our master; in two of them . . ."; cf. VN.

[n] Nfmg: "slow" (another form, that in VN).

[o] Nfmg: "(in its appointed time) and on account of (the daughters of Zelophehad)"; = VN.

[p] Nfmg: "(concerning wealth;) in the case of the blasphemer who blasphemed the name of the Lord with blasphemies and in the case of the wood-gatherer who profaned the sabbath willfully, Moses was (slow)."

[q] Lit.: "judgments of lives."

[r] Nfmg: "(judgments of capital sentence) and in these he said: I have not heard, to teach the judges that were to arise after Moses to be quick in civil cases (lit.: 'cases, judgments, of wealth') and slow . . ."; = VN.

[s] I.e., civil cases.

[t] Nfmg: "(that they should not) be ashamed to say: We have not heard; truly our master Moses said . . ."; = VN (with "I have not heard").

Notes, Chapter 9

[6]The inserted midrash is found again, with slight variations, in Nf Lev 24:12; Num 15:34 and 27:5, at each occurrence of the four key texts. In the present context the midrash has been inserted inelegantly into the translation ("and he said to them. This is . . . "), the paraphrastic translation being given fully after the midrash. The HT has: "And Moses said to them: Arise and I will make (you) hear what the Lord will command concerning you." For a study of this midrash and a bibliography on it, see A. Jaubert, "Les séances du sanhédrin et les récits de la passion," *RevHistRel* 166 (1964) 143–169; 167 (1965) 1–33, esp. 167 (1965) 26–30). See also B. Barry Levy, 1987, 2, 44–47 (on Lev 24:12).

[7]"civil cases"; lit.: "cases (judgments) of wealth;" Sokoloff (p. 147): "fiscal cases."

[8]"capital cases"; lit.: "judgments (cases) of lives."

[9]Lit.: "who is worthy (destined) to be put to death in judgment."

said: 'I have not heard'": and Moses said to them: "Arise *now* and I will make *you* hear what *is established before* the Lord *to do to you.*" 9. And the Lord[u] spoke with Moses, saying: 10. "Speak with the children of Israel saying: 'If any one of you or of your (future) generations is unclean through the *defilement*[5] of the corpse of a *man*[w] or is afar off on a journey, he shall keep the Passover before the Lord. 11. They shall keep it on the second month on the fourteenth day at twilight.[x] They shall eat it with unleavened bread and with bitter herbs. 12. They shall leave none[y] of it over until the morning,[10] and they shall not break a bone in it.[z] According to all the statutes of the Passover they shall do. 13. But the man who is pure and is not *afar* off on a journey and refrains[aa] from keeping the Passover, that person shall be blotted out from the midst of his people; because he did not offer the offering of the Lord at its appointed time, that man shall receive (the chastisement of) his sins. 14. And if an orphan[bb] resides[cc] with you and will keep the Passover before the Lord, he shall keep it according to the statutes of the Passover and according to its *ordinances;*[11] there shall be one decree *of law*[dd] for you, both for the sojourner and for the native[ee] of the land.'" 15. And on the day that *Moses* set up the tabernacle, the cloud covered the tabernacle of the testimony; and in the evening it was over the tabernacle as the appearance of fire until the morning. 16. Thus it will be continually; the cloud will cover[ff] it and by night the appearance of *inextinguishable*[12] fire.[gg] 17. And *at the time* the cloud was taken up[hh] from above the tabernacle, immediately afterwards the children of Israel set out; and in the place that <the cloud>[ii] came to rest,[jj] there the children of Israel encamped. 18. According to *the decree of the Memra*[13] of the Lord the children of Israel shall set out, and according to *the decree of the Memra*[13] of the Lord the children of Is-

Apparatus, Chapter 9

[u] Nfmg: "the Memra of the Lord."
[w] Lit.: "a son of man."
[x] Lit.: "between the two suns."
[y] Nfmg: "and they (shall) not (leave)."
[z] Nfmg: "and you shall not neglect (to fulfill) with it the precept; according to all the statutes of the Passover . . ."
[aa] Nfmg: "and ceases from keeping"; = Ps.-J.
[bb] *gyzr* or *gyzl;* the text is probably corrupt and is to be emended to "an orphan" or "a sojourner" (*gywr*).
[cc] Nfmg: "sojourns"; "resides as a sojourner."
[dd] Nfmg: "there shall be one instruction."
[ee] Nfmg: "for the sojourners and for the natives (of . . .)."
[ff] Nfmg: "(the cloud) of the glory will cover (it)."
[gg] Lit.: "fire devouring fire"; cf. Tg. Gen 38:25. Nfmg: "and during the night as the appearance of fire."
[hh] Nfmg 1°: "and according as it was taken up" (lit.: "and according to the elevation of . . .").
[ii] Thus Nfmg; in text: "the tabernacle."
[jj] Nfi: "(and where) the fire shall (come to rest)."

Notes, Chapter 9

[10]HT: "They shall leave none of it until morning, and a bone in it they shall not break. According to all the statutes of the Passover, they shall keep (lit.: 'do') it." Cf. Exod 12:40: HT: ". . . and a bone you shall not break in it"; rendered literally in Nf; cf. John 19:36 and Le Déaut, 1963, esp. 202ff. In Nf Num 9:12, the final word "they shall do" is written twice, and the final word of HT (*'tw* = "it") left untranslated. Note the paraphrase of Nfmg.

[11]"ordinances"; *sdry dynwy;* HT: *mšpṭw;* see above to 9:3, and Introd. III, 12.

[12]"inextinguishable fire"; lit.: "fire eating fire"; "a fire which consumes fire"; also in Pal. Tg. Gen 38:26 (on fire of Gehenna); Nf Exod 24:17, Deut 9:3. See also *b. Yoma* 21b.

[13]"decree of the Memra of the Lord"; HT: "the mouth of the Lord."

rael shall encamp; all the days that the cloud *rests*[14] over the tabernacle they shall[15] remain encamped. 19. And when the cloud stands still[kk] <many days over the tabernacle, the children of Israel shall[15] keep the charge of the Lord and shall> not[mm] set out. 20. And there will be *times*[16] that the cloud will be[nn] a short number of days over the tabernacle; according to *the decree of the Memra*[13] <of the Lord>[17] they shall[15] encamp, and according to *the decree of the Memra*[13] of the Lord they shall[15] set out. 21. And *there are times* when the cloud remains[oo] from evening until morning, and when the cloud will[15] be taken up in the morning they will[15] set out; or that it remains for the day and the night, and when the cloud will be taken up, they will set out. 22. And whether it be two days or a month or *many*[18] days[pp] that the cloud tarries over the tabernacle, dwelling over it, the children of Israel shall[15] remain encamped and shall[15] not set out; and when *the cloud*[qq][19] is taken up, they shall[15] set out. 23. According to *the decree of the Memra*[13] of the Lord they shall[15] encamp, and according to the *decree of the Memra* of the Lord they shall[15] set out. They kept the charge of the Lord according to *the decree of the Memra*[13] of the Lord (given) through Moses.

Apparatus, Chapter 9

[kk] Nfmg: "and when it is taken up."
[mm] Missing in text; added in margin.
[nn] Nfmg: "and times that (the cloud) will be."
[oo] Nfmg: "and times that (the cloud will be)."
[pp] Nfmg: "many days in the tarrying (of the cloud)."
[qq] Nfmg: "and when (the cloud) is taken up (lit.: 'at its being taken up'), they shall set out."

Notes, Chapter 9

[14]"rests"; *d-šry;* HT has imperfect, *yškn.*

[15]"will cover," etc. In the HT in vv. 16-23 most of the verbs are in the imperfect, which modern versions generally render by the past tense: "the cloud covered"; "the people of Israel set out," etc. (Note, however, NRSV: "they would set out"; "they would encamp.") So also Tg. Onq. (generally using participles, which B. Grossfeld renders as consuetudinal: "would set out," etc.). Ps.-J. and Vulg. render likewise, as past tense. Nf, however, retains the imperfect form, which I have rendered as future, although in biblical Aramaic (as in literary Aramaic) the imperfect can be rendered as past imperfect. The LXX, however, renders these imperfects in vv. 18-23 as future.

[16]"there will be (are) times that"; HT: "it will be that."

[17]"of the Lord" is probably to be added to the first occurrence of "of the Memra"; HT: "the mouth of the Lord."

[18]"many"; an expansive addition.

[19]"when the cloud"; HT: "when it . . ."

CHAPTER 10

1. And the Lord[a] spoke with Moses, saying: 2. "Make yourselves two silver trumpets; (of) hammered work you shall make them, and they shall serve you for summoning *the people*[1] *of* the congregation and for breaking camp. 3. When they blow them, all *the people*[1] *of* the congregation shall come together beside you at the entrance of the tent of meeting. 4. But if they blow only one,[b] the princes shall come together beside you, the princes[c] of the thousands of Israel.[d] 5. If they blow an alarm, the camps which encamp[e] on the east shall set out.[f] 6. If they blow an alarm a second *time,* the camps that encamp[e] on the south shall set out; they shall blow an alarm as they set out. 7. But when the assembly is brought together, you shall blow (the trumpet) but you shall not sound an alarm. 8. And the sons of Aaron, the priests, shall blow the trumpets. And (these things) shall be an eternal statute for you throughout your generations. 9. And when you enter battle array in your country against your enemies,[g] *against the foe*[2] that oppresses[h] you, you shall blow your trumpets, and you shall be remembered before the Lord your God, and you shall be *redeemed*[i][3] from your enemies. 10. And on the day of your gladness, at *the times*[4] of your festivals, at the beginnings of your months, you shall blow the trumpet over your burnt offerings and over the sacrifices of *your holy things,*[5] and they shall serve you as a *good* memorial before your God. I, the Lord, your God."[j] 11. And in the second year, <in the second month,>[6] on the twentieth of the month, <the cloud>[k] was taken up from above the tent of meeting, 12. and the children of Israel set out on their journeyings from the desert of Sinai, and the cloud settled down in the desert of Paran. 13. And they set out at first[m] according

Apparatus, Chapter 10

[a] Nfmg: "the Memra of the Lord."
[b] Nfmg: "(one) of them."
[c] Nfi: "all (the princes)."
[d] Nfi: "(of the thousands) of the sons of (Israel)."
[e] Nfi: "which have encamped."
[f] Nfmg: "and they set out."
[g] Nfmg: "(against) the foe that oppresses you, you shall sound the alarm on the trumpets and you shall be remembered."
[h] Nfi: "that oppresses you" (written differently).
[i] Nfmg: "and you shall be delivered from the hand of (your) enemies."
[j] Nfmg: "thus says the Lord."
[k] Missing in text; is in Nfmg ("a cloud").
[m] Nfmg: "(and they set out) from the beginning according to (the decree)."

Notes, Chapter 10

[1]"the people of the congregation; HT: "the congregation"; see above Introd. III, 23.
[2]"against your armies, against the foe that oppresses you." A double translation of the HT. A single translation in Nfmg and Ps.-J. ("against the oppression that oppresses you)." A similar double translation in Nf Exod 23:22; see also Nf Num 10:35.
[3]"redeemed." See Introd. III, 22.
[4]"at the times of . . ."; HT: "at your festivals."
[5]"(sacrifices) of holy things," HT: "of peace (offerings, *šlmym*)"; see above Introd. III, 1.
[6]"in the second month"; absent from Nf; probably to be restored with HT, Onq., Ps.-J.

to *the decree of the Memra*[n7] <given> through[o] Moses. 14. The standard of the camp of the sons of Judah set out first[p] by their hosts; and *the chief who had been appointed*[8] over the hosts *of the tribe of the sons of Judah*[9] was Nahshon bar Amminadab. 15. And over the hosts of the tribe of the sons of Issachar was Nethanel bar Zuar. 16. And over[q] the hosts of the tribe of the sons of Zebulun was Eliab bar Helon. 17. And after the tabernacle had been taken apart,[r] the sons of Gershon and the sons of Merari set out carrying[s] the tabernacle. 18. And the standard of the camp *of the sons* of Reuben, in their hosts, set out;[t] and *the chief who had been appointed*[8] over the hosts *of the tribe of the sons of Reuben*[9] was Elizur bar Shedeur. 19. And over the hosts[u] of the tribe of the sons of Simeon was Shelumiel bar Zur Shaddai. 20. And over the hosts[u] of the tribe of the sons of Gad was Eliasaph bar Deuel. 21. And *the sons*[10] of the Kohathites carrying the tabernacle set out, and before their arrival the tabernacle was set up. 22. And the standard of the camp *of the tribe*[11] of the sons of Ephraim set out[w] in their hosts, and *the chief who had been appointed*[8] over the hosts *of the tribe of the sons of Ephraim*[9] was Elisama bar Ammihud. 23. And over the hosts[u] of the tribe of the sons of Manasseh was Gamaliel bar Pedah Zur. 24. And over the hosts[x] of the tribe of the sons of Benjamin was Abidan bar Gideoni. 25. And the standard of the camp of the sons of Dan, according to their hosts, set out,[y] as rear-guard of all the camps; and *the chief who had been appointed*[8] *over* its hosts[z] was Ahiezer bar Ammi *Nadab.*[aa] 26. And over the hosts[u] of the tribe of the sons of Asher was Pagiel bar

Apparatus, Chapter 10

[n] *mmr, memar.* The text can be read as *mymr(')* (the Memra) or *mymr(h)* ("his Memra"). Since the word ends a line, it is more probable that it is the latter, with letters for the divine name YYY ("the Lord") missing; thus: "the Memra of the Lord."

[o] Lit.: "by the hand of Moses"; Nfmg: "by the hands of Moses."

[p] Nfmg: "(set out) from the beginning according to their hosts."

[q] Nfmg: "and the chief who had been appointed over (the hosts of . . .)."

[r] Nfmg: "and when the tabernacle had been taken down they (i.e., Gershon and the sons of Merari) set out."

[s] Nfmg: "bearing."

[t] Nfmg: "and the standard of the tribe of (Reuben) shall set out."

[u] Nfmg: "and the chief who had been appointed over the hosts of . . ."

[w] Nfmg: "and the standard of the camp of the sons of (Ephraim) shall set out."

[x] This word is written in Hebrew in the text, a mistake noted by a small stroke placed above it.

[y] Nfmg: "and the standard of the camp (of the sons of Dan) shall set out."

[z] Nfmg: "(who had been appointed over) the hosts of the tribe of the sons of Dan."

[aa] Most probably an error for Ammi Shaddai of biblical text; cf. 1:12; 2:25: 7:66, 71.

Notes, Chapter 10

[7]"to the decree of the Memra"; HT: "according to the mouth of the Lord." See also Apparatus, note *n*.

[8]"the chief who had been appointed over . . . Judah"; HT: "and over his host (was)." Similarly in vv. 18, 22; cf. also v. 25.

[9]An expansion in Nf.

[10]"the sons of"; an expansion. See Introd. III, 23.

[11]"of the tribe"; an expansive addition. See Introd. III, 23.

Ochran. 27. And over the hosts[u] of the tribe of the sons of Naphtali was Ahira bar Enan. 28. Those were the journeys of the children of Israel according to their hosts; *in accordance with this order*[12] they used to set out.[bb] 29. And Moses said to Hobab bar Reuel, the Midianite, the father-in-law of Moses: "We are setting out for the place, of which the Lord[cc] said: 'I will give it to you.' Come with us and we will do you good, for the Lord[dd] *in his Memra* said[13] that *he would bring* good *and consolation* upon Israel." 30. But he said: "I will not <go>;[ee] rather shall I go to my land and to my kindred." 31. And he said *to him:* "Do not forsake us, I pray,[ff] because since you know[14] *the marvels that the Lord*[gg] *has worked with us in every place* we have encamped or while *traveling* in the wilderness, you shall be *testimony*[15] for us. 32. And if you come with us, whatever good with which the Lord[hh] will favor us we shall bestow on you." 33. And they journeyed from the mount *of the sanctuary* of the Lord,[ii][16] a journey <of three days, and the ark of the covenant of the Lord went before them>,[jj] a three days' journey, *to prepare*[kk] for them a place of

Apparatus, Chapter 10

[bb] Nfmg: "according to their hosts they set out."

[cc] Nfmg: "(of which) the Memra of the Lord (said): I shall give it to you. Come with us and we will do you good, since the Memra of the Lord has spoken (i.e., decreed to bring) good things on Israel."

[dd] Nfmg: "since it has been decreed from eternity (lit.: 'from the days of the world,' or: 'of eternity') to bring good things on Israel."

[ee] Missing in text and margin.

[ff] Nfmg: "I beseech."

[gg] Nfmg: "for this you know our encampments in the wilderness . . . and you shall be for us the indicator of the crossroads (or: 'of sources')"; Ps.-J.: "as the pupil of our eye" (*Sifre*).

[hh] Nfmg: "the Memra of the Lord."

[ii] Nfmg: "from the Mount of the Lord."

[jj] Missing in text and margin; omitted through homoeoteleuton.

[kk] Nfmg: "to show (them)."

Notes, Chapter 10

[12]"in accordance with their order"; an addition to HT, which simply has: "and they used to set out," as in Nfmg.

[13]HT: "for the Lord had promised (lit.: 'has spoken') good to (or: 'upon') Israel."

[14]MT (RSV): "for you know we are to encamp in the wilderness, and you will serve as eyes for us." For Nf's "the marvels the Lord works for us," see *Sifre Num* 80, on Num 10:31 ("signs and wonders in the wilderness)." For Hobab's (= Jetro) knowledge of these marvels, see Exod 18:1-11.

[15]"testimony," i.e., the fact that Hobab bar Reuel (identified in Jewish tradition as Jetro) came with Israel to the promised land as a proselyte will be evidence that the door is open to proselytes; see *Sifre Num* 80 (on Num 10:31).

[16]HT: "from the mount of the Lord," *hr yyy* of HT. A similar translation of "the mountain of God" (*hr 'lhym*) in Nf Exod 4:27; a different rendering in Nf Exod 3:1; 18:5; 24:13.

encampment.[17] 34. And the cloud *of the Glory of the Shekinah* of the Lord[mm][18] *was a shield* during the day when they set out[nn] from the camp. 35. And whenever the ark set out, Moses *used to pray,*[19] saying: "Arise, *I pray you,* O Lord, and let your enemies be scattered,[oo] and let those who hate you flee from before you." 36. And when it came to rest, *Moses used to pray,* saying: "Return, *now,* O Lord *from the might of your anger and come back to us in your good mercies, and make the Glory of your Shekinah dwell in the midst of* the thousands and myriads; *let the myriads be multiplied and bless the thousands of the children* of Israel."[pp][20]

Apparatus, Chapter 10

[mm] Nfmg: "(and the cloud) of the glory of the Lord (was) over them."

[nn] Nfmg: "when they set out" (a different form).

[oo] Nfmg: "(and) when the ark used to set out, Moses used to raise his hands in prayer and say: Arise, now, O Memra (of the Lord) (text: *memreh,* 'his Memra,' but correct with VN) in the might of your power and let (+ with VN: the enemies of your people) be scattered"; = VN, which continues as Nf does.

[pp] VN, Nfmg: "and when the ark used to come to rest, Moses used to lift his hands in prayer and say: Return (VN: come back), now, O Memra of the Lord, from the might of your anger (VN + and return to us in your mercies) and bless the myriads and multiply the thousands of the children of Israel."

Notes, Chapter 10

[17]"to prepare for them a place of encampment" (*lmtqnh lhwn 'tr byt mšrwy*); also in Nf Frg. Tg. Gen 46:28. HT *ltwr lhm mnwḥh*; RSV: "to seek out a resting place for them." Nf Exod 33:14; Lev 25:29. Ps.-J. translates as Nf; Onqelos has "to prepare a site for a resting place" (*'tr byt mšryh*). For a possible relationship with the Fourth Gospel, see M. McNamara, "'To Prepare a Place for You.' A Targumic Expression and John 14:2f.," *Milltown Studies* 2 (Dublin, 1979) 100–108; *Palestinian Judaism and the New Testament* (Wilmington, Del.: 1983) 239–241.

[18]HT: "and the cloud of the Lord was over them . . ." For a study of the "cloud" vocabulary of the OT and the midrashic development of its symbolism to the end of the Aramaic period, and the significance of these for NT passages, see J. Luzarraga, 1973. Here, as in Nf Exod 40:38 "the cloud of the Lord" is paraphrased as "the cloud of the glory of the Shekinah of the Lord." The "cloud" is an image used rather frequently (about 50 times) in the Pentateuch as a symbol of the divine presence. In Nf most of these are rendered without paraphrase. Where the need is felt to clarify or to soften the HT expression, however, Nf expands somewhat, generally by the insertion of "the Shekinah of the Lord" or "the glory of the Shekinah of the Lord." The HT Exod 16:10 says: "the glory of the Lord appeared in the cloud." Here Nf simply adds "of the Shekinah" to "glory." Exod 34:5 (HT: "the Lord descended in the cloud") becomes: "the glory of the Shekinah of the Lord was revealed in the cloud." Similarly, in Nf Num 10:34; 11:25; 12:5, "The cloud abode upon it" (i.e., the tent of meeting) of Exod 40:35 becomes: "the glory of the Shekinah of the Lord dwelt upon it." "I will appear in the cloud" of Lev 16:2 becomes in Nf: "In my cloud, the glory of my Shekinah, my Memra is revealed." In Num 12:5 HT, "your cloud stands over them" becomes in Nf: "the cloud of the glory of your Shekinah was upon them." For the "glory of the Shekinah of the Lord" in Nf, see Introduction to Nf Genesis, *The Aramaic Bible,* vol. 1A, pp. 36f. and J. Luzarraga, 1973.

[19]"used to pray saying"; Nf introduces the reference to prayer; HT: "used to say."

[20]This is a meticulously balanced paraphrase of the very difficult HT text: "And when it rested he said: Return, O Lord; Israel's myriads (of) thousands." There is a discussion of Num 10:35-36 in *Sifre Num* 104 (on Num 10:35-36) and *Sifre Deut* 11 (on Deut 1:11), where other related biblical texts, especially with reference to myriads and thousands, are invoked; e.g., Deut 1:11: "May the Lord make you a thousand times as many as you are and bless you"; and Ps 68:17(18): "with mighty chariotry." Num 10:36 is variously rendered in the Targums: Onq.: "Return, O Lord, and reside in your Glory among Israel's myriads of thousands"; Ps.-J.: "Return, now (or: I pray), O Memra of the Lord, in your good mercies and lead your people Israel and make the glory of your Shekinah dwell between them and love the myriads of Jacob, shield (of) the thousands of Israel." The Frg. Tgs. (PVN) and Nfmg (for which see the Apparatus) are close to Nf's paraphrase. Nf gives a double paraphrase of "return": "return from your anger" (following Exod 32:12 and Nf rendering), and "return in your mercy." As in rabbinic tradition, the myriads and thousands are understood as referring to Israel, to the divine presence and blessing (cf. Deut 1:11).

CHAPTER 11

1. And the people murmured, meditating evil *in the hearing* of the Lord; and it *was heard before*[a1] the Lord and his anger grew strong, and the fire *from before*[2] the Lord burned among them and consumed the extremities of the camp. 2. And the people cried out *before* Moses; and Moses prayed *before* the Lord and the fire was swallowed up.[b] 3. And *Moses*[3] called the name of that place The Place of Burning[c4] because the fire *from before*[2] the Lord burned among them there. 4. And the conglomeration[5] (of foreigners)[d] that was among them had a strong craving, and the children of Israel also wept again, saying: "*Oh!* Who will give us meat to eat![e] 5. We remember the fish we used to eat in Egypt free of charge, the cucumbers, the melons, the leeks,[f] the onions, and the garlic. 6. And now our soul[g] is *empty;*[h6] *we have* nothing except this manna>,[i] *from which* our eyes[j] *depend.*"[k8] 7. And the manna[7] was like a coriander seed,[m] and the sight of it[n] was like the appearance of bdellium.[o] 8. And the people *began* to gather it[p] and to grind it, (in

Apparatus, Chapter 11

[a] Nfmg: "(was heard) before the Lord and was manifest before (the Lord)."
[b] Nfmg: "was swallowed up" (lit.: 'sank, went down'; cf. Onq.).
[c] Nfmg: "(of the plague) *Taborah* (burning) because there was burned."
[d] Nfmg: "and the motley multitude that was among them."
[e] Nfmg: "Oh, that we had someone who would give us (meat) to eat."
[f] Nfmg: "the cucumbers, the melons (Greek word: *molopepôn,* a species of melon: *cucurbis citrullus*) and the leeks"; = PVN.
[g] Nf uses the same words as the HT (*nefeš*), for which reason I translate as "soul" (with LXX, Vulg.), although the Hebrew in this instance is best rendered as "throat," "strength."
[h] Nfmg: "it is dry; (we have) not."
[i] Missing in text; added in Nfmg.
[j] See Ps.-J.: "this manna which we look on as the poor man who looks to a mouthful from the hands."
[k] Nfmg: "except the manna which your eyes see."
[m] Nfmg 1°: "(and the manna) was (like the seed) of white coriander"; Nfmg 2°: "(and the manna) was like white coriander seed."
[n] Nfmg: "and its appearance was like the appearance of bdellium."
[o] See Ps.-J., MS BL Add. 27031, fol. 152b, with extensive paraphrase.
[p] *šrwn;* corr. to (?): *sṭyn;* = "roamed about" (as if from Hebrew *sṭh*); VN: "and the people used to roam about (*syyṭyn*) and collect (it) and grind it in a mill (or: 'in mills,' *dḥwt',* V; *rḥwtt',* NL Nfmg; *mdwkt',* Nf), or pounded it under foot in mortars, and they used to boil it in stew-pots (also in P) and make it into cakes (*'wgyn;* Nf *ḥwrrn*) and its taste was like the taste of pancakes with honey" (ending = Tg. Exod 16:31, Nf); Nfmg: "the people used to roam about (*sṭyn*) and collect it"; = VN.

Notes, Chapter 11

[1]"heard before the Lord" (*šm' qdm*); HT: "the Lord heard."
[2]"fire from before the Lord"; HT: "fire of the Lord."
[3]"Moses called"; MT: "he called."
[4]"the place of burning"; *bet yeqidta;* MT: Taberah.
[5]"conglomeration" or "mixed multitude"; text: *'rbwbh,* correct to *'rbrwbh,* with Nfmg, and Nfmg VB Exod 12:38.
[6]"is empty"; HT: "is dry." Cf. Nfmg.
[7]On the manna tradition see B. J. Malina, 1968.
[8]"this manna from which our eyes depend"; HT *(blty). 'l hmn 'ynynw;* "(save that) our eyes are toward the manna."

mills),[q] (and they ground it in mortars and boiled[r] it in pots),[s] and they made cakes[t] out of it; and its taste was like the taste of *pancakes*[u] *with honey.*[9] 9. And when the dew came down on (the camp)[w] at night, the manna used to come down upon it. 10. And Moses heard the voice of the people, (which was) crying, according to their families, each one at the door of his tent; and the anger of the Lord grew very strong; and Moses was displeased.[x] 11. And Moses said *before* the Lord: "Why, *I pray,* have you made your servant dispirited?[y] And why, *I pray,* have I not found grace in your sight[z] that you should set upon me the burden of this entire people? 12. Have I, perchance, conceived[aa] this entire people or have I given them birth[bb] that you should say to me: 'Carry them in your bosom as the *nurse*[10] carries the suckling,[cc] to the hand that I swore to their fathers?'[dd] 13. From where do I get meat to give to all this people? For they cry out *before* (me),[ee] saying: 'Give us meat that we may eat.' 14. I alone[ff] am not able to bear the *discomfort*[11] *of* this entire people, for *they are* stronger than I am. 15. And if it is thus you act with me, kill me, *now,*[gg] (with) death, if I have found grace *and favor*[12] in your sight,[hh] that I may not see the misery *of your people.*"[13] 16. And the Lord[ii] spoke with Moses: "Gather

Apparatus, Chapter 11

[q] Missing in text but is in Nfi and VN.
[r] Nfmg: "and they cooked (it) in it."
[s] Missing in text; added in Nfmg.
[t] Nfmg: "pancakes"; = VN.
[u] Nfmg: "(and its taste was) like pancakes soaked in (lit.: 'of the juice, humidity, of') oil."
[w] In the text: "on the tabernacle."
[x] Nfmg: "displeased" (another word).
[y] Nfmg: "have you dispirited" (or: "have you given this displeasure"—the same verb written differently).
[z] Nfmg: "(have I not found) grace and benevolence (*ḥesed:* 'faithful love') before you."
[aa] Nfmg: "have I made" (variant due to confusion of *'brt* with *'bdt*).
[bb] Nfmg: "or have I given (them) birth" (another form, that of VN).
[cc] Nfmg: "bear them in your bosom as the nurse (Greek loan word *paidagôgos*) bears the suckling to (the land)"; = PVN.
[dd] Nfmg: "to his fathers"; = VN.
[ee] Nfmg: "near him"; Nfi: "before me," with MT; in the text of Nf: "before him"; confusion of *waw/yod?* 3rd per. for 1st?; or: "before him" (i.e., before God)?
[ff] In the text: "he alone."
[gg] Or: "I pray"; Nfmg: "I beseech (you)."
[hh] Nfmg: "before you."
[ii] Nfmg: "the Memra of the Lord."

Notes, Chapter 11

[9] "pancakes with honey"; HT (RSV): "cakes baked with oil." See also B. Grossfeld's note 8 on Onq. on this verse (*The Aramaic Bible,* vol. 8, pp. 100f.).

[10] "nurse," *pydgwgh* (masc.); a Greek loan word, *paidagôgos,* rendering *'mn ('omen)* of the HT; the word is also used to translate *'mn* of Prov 8:30 in *Gen. R.* par. 7 (on Gen 1:1). By reason of etymology, the Aramaic (and rabbinic Hebrew) word would seem best translated by "instructor, guardian, (youth's) governor." Thus Sokoloff, 1990, 430 ("instructor"). However, in the present context it seems to denote "nurse." The HT term designating Rebekah's foster-mother or nurse (HT: *mnqh;* Nf: *mynqth*) Deborah (Gen 24:59; 35:8) is translated as *pedagog* in Nfmg Gen 24:59, and "nurse" (*mrbyth*) in Nfmg Gen 35:8. See also M. McNamara, in PIBA 15 (1992), 22.

[11] "discomfort (of all this people)"; HT: "carry this entire people."

[12] "grace and favor"; HT: "grace"; cf. above Introd., III, 21; note to Nf Gen 6:16 (*The Aramaic Bible,* vol. 1A, p. 30); also Nf Gen 18:3; 30:27; Exod 33:13, etc. Nf Num 11:11 is an exception in not adding "and favor."

[13] "misery of your people"; see also Nfmg in Apparatus. HT: "my own wretchedness," a text rendered literally in Onq. and Ps.-J. With the tradition of Nf and VNL compare *Sifre Num* 91 (on Num 11:15): "it is better for me that you kill me first that I may not see the retribution that is ready to come upon them." A scribal emendation (*tiqqun*) maintained that the original reading was "thine own wretchedness"; another rabbinic tradition held that the original reading was: "their wretchedness." On this see C. McCarthy, *The Tiqqune Sopherim,* 1981, esp. pp. 123–126.

for me seventy men from the *wise men*[jj][14] of Israel, whom you know[kk] to be the *wise ones*[14] of the people, and their commanders; and bring them to the tent of meeting and let them stand in readiness there with you. 17. And *I will be revealed in my Memra*[15] and I will speak with you there; and I will *increase*[mm][16] some of the *holy* spirit[nn][17] that is with you and will set it upon them; and they shall bear[oo] the burden of the people with you and you shall not bear (it) alone.[pp] 18. And you shall say to the people: 'Sanctify[qq] yourselves for tomorrow and you shall eat meat, for you have cried in the hearing of the Lord saying: *Oh,*[rr] who can give us meat, because it was good for us in Egypt! And the Lord will give you meat and you shall eat. 19. You shall not eat one day, nor two days, for five days nor twenty days, 20. but for a month of days, until such time as it comes out from your nostrils and it becomes an abomination for you, for the reason that you have rebelled *against*[18] *(what was) according to the decree of the Memra of* the Lord, the *Glory* of *whose Shekinah* dwells among you[ss] and because you cried before me saying: Why, then, have we come out[tt] *of the land* of Egypt?'" 21. And Moses said: "The people among whom *I dwell* (number) sixty myriads[uu] of foot*men,*[ww] and you *in your Memra* have said: 'I shall give you meat and they shall eat for a month.'[xx] 22. If (flocks)[yy] and

Apparatus, Chapter 11

[jj] Nfmg 1°: "(from) the wise men and they shall teach"; Nfmg 2°: "(from) the wise men" (a different construction).

[kk] Nfmg: "(when) you know" (a different word) "that they are."

[mm] Nfmg: "I shall cause (some of the holy spirit) to pass."

[nn] Cf. Ps.-J.: "spirit of prophecy."

[oo] Nfmg: "and they shall carry."

[pp] Nfmg: "(and) you shall (not) carry it alone."

[qq] Nfmg: "and to the people you shall say: Sanctify yourselves."

[rr] Nfi: "and if (or: 'and would that')"; Nfmg: "we had someone who would give us to eat."

[ss] Nfmg: "for the reason that you have despised the glory of the Shekinah of the Lord which is among you."

[tt] Nfmg: "(why, then,) did he bring us out of Egypt?"

[uu] This rendering takes *'štyn ('ăstin)* of the text as "sixty" (plur. of *'št'* = *št'*) (as Frg. Tg. [PVNL] and Nf Num 12:16; see also lexica). Other possible renderings: "six hundred thousand footmen, males"; or: "the men (or: 'heroes') of the people . . ."; or: "six hundred thousand men of the infantry" (cf. Ps.-J.).

[ww] Nfi: "sixty hundred thousand"; Nfmg: "as sixty (*'štyn*) myriads of footmen."

[xx] Lit.: "a month of days."

[yy] Text has erroneously: "peoples." Nfmg: "if flocks and herds (were sacrificed . . . ; the continuation of the variant is here missing), if all the fish of the Great Sea (= the Mediterranean) were gathered together for them, would all (this) suffice for them?"

Notes, Chapter 11

[14]"wise men"; HT: "elders" (of Israel), in keeping with Nf's translation technique (Num 11:16, 24, 25, 30; 16:25. See above Introd. III, 18). The same translation is followed for the "elders of Midian" in Nf Num 22:4; in Num 22:7, however, Nf renders as "princes."

[15]"I will be revealed in my Memra"; HT: "I will descend."

[16]"I will increase" or: "I will anoint," *'rby;* HT: "I will withdraw," *w-'ṣlty.* Onq. and Ps.-J. render in the same manner as Nf.

[17]"some of the holy spirit"; HT: "some of the spirit."

[18]"rebelled against . . . dwells among you"; see Nfmg (Apparatus). HT: "you have rejected the Lord who is among you."

herds were slaughtered for them, would there be sufficient for them? If all the fish of the sea[zz] were gathered for them, would there be sufficient for them?" 23. And the Lord[a] said to Moses: "*Is there deficiency*[b] *before* the Lord? Now shall *you* see whether my word comes true for you or not." 24. And Moses went out and spoke *all* the words of the Lord with the people, and he brought together seventy men from among *the wise men*[c] of the people[d] and set them round about the tent.[e] 25. And *the Glory of the Shekinah of* the Lord *was revealed* in the cloud[19] and spoke with him. And *it increased*[f20] some of the *holy* spirit[g] that was upon him and set it upon the seventy *wise men.*[14] And it happened that when the *holy* spirit[h] rested on them[21] that they prophesied; and they did not *cease.* 26. And two men remained in the camp; the name of one was Eldad and the name of the second was Medad, and the *holy* spirit rested upon them.[i] *Eldad* prophesied *and said:* "Behold,

Apparatus, Chapter 11

[zz] Nfmg: "if (all the fish of) the Great (Sea) were gathered together for them, would all (this) be sufficient for them?"
[a] Nfmg: "the Memra of the Lord."
[b] Nfmg: "is it possible that there be deficiency before the Lord?"
[c] Nfi: "the sages of (the people)."
[d] Nfmg: "the wise men of Israel and he set (them)."
[e] Nfmg: "(round about) the camp."
[f] Nfmg: "and he caused to pass."
[g] Nfmg: "(the spirit) of the sanctuary"; cf. Ps.-J. according to MS Add. 27031: "the spirit of prophecy."
[h] Ps.-J.: "spirit of prophecy."
[i] P: "and two men remained in the camp, the name of one was Eldad and the name of the second Medad, and the holy spirit (*rwḥ qwdš'*) rested upon them. Eldad prophesied and said: Quail come up from the sea and become a stumbling block for the children of Israel. And Medad prophesied and said: Moses, the scribe of Israel, is to be gathered from the midst of the world and Joshua bar Nun who is his (MS: 'the') attendant receives (the gift of) prophecy after him. And the two of them prophesied together and said: In the very end of the days God and Magog and their (lit.: 'his') hosts go up to Jerusalem and by the hands of King Messiah they fall, and for seven years of days the children of Israel enkindle fire from their weapons, and they will not go out to the woods nor will they cut trees. And these were from the seventy (*šwb'ty* = *šwb'yty*) wise men who were mentioned by name

Notes, Chapter 11

[19]HT has: "and the Lord came down in the cloud."
[20]HT: "withdrew"; see v. 17.
[21]The HT says that the spirit rested on Eldad and Medad and that they prophesied in the camp, giving no details on the contents of their prophecies. The lacuna was filled by tradition with regard to the prophecies and persons of Eldad and Medad. These traditions are found in rabbinic writings, e.g., *b. Sanh.* 17a; *Num. R.* 15:19; cf. also *b. Sanh.* 96b-97a; 98a; *Sifre Num* 96 on Num 11:26. The apocryphal work *The Book of Eldad and Modad* was used in the early Church, but the only known citation from it is (in Greek) in Hermas, *Vision* 2, 3.4 (3rd cent. C.E.?): "The Lord (*kyrios*) is near (*engys*) to those who turn to him, as is written in the (Book of) Eldad and Modad, who prophesied in the desert to the people." See further E. G. Martin in *The Old Testament Pseudepigrapha,* vol. 2, pp. 463–465; J. Charlesworth, *The Pseudepigrapha and Modern Research,* 1976, pp. 94f. This is very close to a text in Ps.-J., Num 11:26: "The Lord (*qyrys,* a Greek loan word) is near (*'tymws,* the Greek loan word *etymos*) to them in the hour of distress." There is nothing of the midrash in Onq. Ps.-J. has a more developed form of the midrash than Nf and Frg. Tg. or Nfmg. For the prophecy on the quails, see Num 11:31-33. The prophecy on Joshua as successor to Moses (see Num 27:18-23) is cited in *Sifre Num* 95, end, *in loc.*: "Of Eldad and Medad it says that they prophesied. . . . And what did they say?: 'Moses dies and Joshua brings Israel into the land.'" The text with the prophecy on the advent and defeat of Gog and Magog in Jerusalem depends on Ezek 39, esp. 39:9-10. Sections of this paraphrase containing prophecies appear to be metrical, like biblical prophecy. It may be poetry. For a study of this aspect of the text, see B. Barry Levy, 1987, 2, 79–84; 1986, 1, 64–69, esp. 66.

quail come up from the sea and shall become[j] *a stumbling-block for Israel.*" *And Medad prophesied and said: "Behold, Moses the prophet is taken up from the midst of the camp, and Joshua bar Nun exercises his leadership in his stead." And both of them prophesied together, saying: "At the very end of the days Gog and Magog ascend on Jerusalem, and they fall at the hand of King Messiah, and for seven years the children of Israel shall kindle fires from their weapons; and they will not have to go out (to) the forest.*" And these were from *the seventy wise men who were set apart.* And the seventy wise men did not leave *the camp while Eldad and Medad* were prophesying in the camp.[22] 27. And a young man hurried[k] and told Moses, saying: "Behold, Eldad and Medad are prophesying in the camp." 28. And Joshua bar Nun, Moses' minister[m] from his youth,[n] answered and said: "My master Moses, withhold[o][23] *the holy spirit*[p] from them." 29. And Moses said to him: "Are you jeal-

Apparatus, Chapter 11

(or: set aside, designated). And the seventy (*šwb'ty*) wise men did not go out from within the camp as long as Eldad and Medad were prophesying in the camp"; VN: "And two men remained in the camp. The name of one of them was Eldad and the name of the second Medad, and the holy spirit rested upon them. Eldad prophesied and said: Behold the prophet Moses, the scribe of Israel, is being gathered from the midst of the world, and Joshua bar Nun, his disciple (MS: 'his disciples') serves the camp after him. Medad prophesied and said: Behold quails come up from the sea and become a stumbling block to the children of Israel. And both of them prophesied together and said: At the very end of the days Gog and Magog and their (MS: 'his') hosts go up to Jerusalem and by the hands of King Messiah they fall, and for seven years of days the children of Israel enkindle fire from their weapons. They will not go out to the woods nor will they cut down a tree. And these were from among the seventy (*swb'ty*) wise men. And the seventy wise men did not go out from the tent while Eldad and Medad were prophesying in the camp."

[j] Nfmg: "and shall become a stumbling block for the children of Israel. And Medad prophesied and said: Moses, Israel's scribe, shall be gathered from the world, and Joshua, the son of Nun, who is the attendant, shall receive his prophecy after him. And behold, they were from the seventy (*šwb'ty* = *šwb'yty*) elders who had been set aside by name (lit.: 'by their names'), and the seventy (*šwb'yt*) elders did not come out of the camp while Edlad and Medad prophesied in the camp"; (for the first part cf. P).

[k] Nfmg: "ran."

[m] Nfi: "the minister" (another word, that of P).

[n] Nfmg: "from his youth" (another word, that of P).

[o] Nfmg 1°: "separate"; = P; Nfmg 2°: "beseech before the Lord concerning them and interrupt their prophecy."

[p] Cf. Ps.-J.: "the spirit of prophecy."

Notes, Chapter 11

[22]"And these . . . were prophesying in the camp"; HT: "And they (Eldad and Medad) were among those enrolled (*bktbym*), and they did not go out to the tent and they prophesied in the camp"; (RSV: "but they had not gone out so they prophesied in the camp"). A question arising from the biblical evidence and debated in the schools was whether Eldad and Medad were members of the original group of seventy-two (six for each tribe), later reduced to seventy (cf. Num 11:16, 24, 25). Nf says Eldad and Medad were "designated," "set apart" (*mtpršyn;* Nfmg: *'tpršw bšmhwn*) members of the seventy sages (elders), but goes on to state (somewhat ambiguously) that the seventy remained in the camp while Eldad and Medad prophesied—as if there was question of two groups. Nf (and Frg. Tg.) seems to be a well-constructed and original unit. Ps.-J. has the same essential midrash as Nf, with some additions. See notes to Ps.-J.

[23]"withhold the holy spirit . . ."; HT: "forbid (restrain) (them)."

ous for me? *Oh,* who will make all the people[q] of the Lord prophets, the Lord[r] putting his holy spirit[s] upon them?" 30. And Moses retired to the camp, he and the wise men of Israel. 31. And a wind arose from *before* the Lord and carried quail from the sea <and spread[t] them over the camp for a distance of a day's *journey* in one direction>[u] and for the distance of a day's *journey* in the other direction, round about[w] the camp, to a *height* of two cubits[x] above the face of the earth. 32. And the people arose all that day and all that night and all the next day and gathered the quails.[y] He who collected least collected ten *kors;* and they spread them out for themselves in layers[z] round about the camp. 33. The meat was still between their teeth, before it was *consumed,* when the anger of the Lord grew strong against the people and (the Lord)[aa] smote very many of them.[bb] 34. And he called the name of that place *The Graves of the Desires*[cc][24] because there they buried the people who had the craving. 35. From "*The Graves of the Craving*"[dd] the people journey to[ee] Hazeroth, and they remained in Hazeroth.[ff]

Apparatus, Chapter 11

[q] Nfmg: "(all) the congregation."
[r] Nfmg: "that the Memra of the Lord gave."
[s] Cf. Ps.-J.: "his spirit of prophecy."
[t] Nfmg: "and cast (them)"; cf. Onq.
[u] Missing in text; supplied in Nfmg.
[w] Nfmg: "(over the camp for the distance of the journey of) one day to one side, and for the distance of one day's journey to the other side round about."
[x] Nfmg: "(the camp) and to the height of two (cubits: erased) they flew above (the . . .)."
[y] Nfmg (reading *msṭr* and rearranging somewhat): "striking (the quails) with the palm of the hand."
[z] Nfmg: "in layers" (another word).
[aa] Added, taking it from Nfmg.
[bb] Nfmg and Nfi: "the Lord (smote) the people with great death" (or: "plague," *mth,* reconstructing a gloss from isolated words of Nfmg and Nfi; see Ps.-J.).
[cc] Nfmg: "*tḥmdnh*" ("[the Graves of the] Appetites").
[dd] Nfmg: "*tḥmdnyyh*" ("of the appetites." This variant is mistakingly assigned to *mtḥmnyn* of the preceding verse).
[ee] Nfmg: "(the people journeyed) from Hazeroth."
[ff] Nfmg: "and they encamped (at Hazeroth)."

Notes, Chapter 11

[24]*qbry š'lth;* MT: Kibroth-hattavah (= "graves of desires"), a name which occurs again in 11:35, where Nf renders as *qbry tḥmwdh,* "the Graves of (the) Craving." The same name also occurs in Num 33:16-17 and Deut 9:22. In Num 33:16 Nf renders as *qbry š'ly š'lth* ("the Graves of the ones who were desirous)" and in Num 33:17 as *qbry twḥmdth.* In Deut 9:22 Nf renders as *qbry š'lth.* It appears that both translations of the Hebrew were quite acceptable.

CHAPTER 12

1. And Miriam and Aaron spoke[a] against Moses concerning[1] the Cushite woman that he had married; *and behold,*[b] the Cushite[c] woman[d] *was Zipporah, the wife of Moses; except that as the Cushite woman is different in her body*[e] *from every other creature, so was Zipporah, the wife of Moses, handsome in form and beautiful in appearance*[f] *and different in good works*[g] *from all the women of that generation.*[h] 2. And they said: "Has the Lord spoken only with Moses?[i] Has he not also spoken

Apparatus, Chapter 12

[a] *mllt;* VN: "spoke" (a different word, *'yst'w*).

[b] Taking *whlw* to be the same as *w-'rw* of Dan 7:6, 7, 13, or *w-'lw* of Dan 2:31; PVN: *h'l'* ("But, now," M. Klein).

[c] Nfmg: "and behold (*whlw*) she was not a (Cushite) woman." Nfi: "not (a Cushite woman)," cf. PVN.

[d] Nfmg: "(except) that this Cushite distinguishes his flesh from" = VN; P: "the Cushite is different in appearance from every other."

[e] Lit.: "in her form"; Nfmg: "in her forms" (features); P: "handsome in appearance and beautiful in form."

[f] Lit.: "in her appearance."

[g] Nfmg: "and distinguished in good work (or: 'in her good work')"; cf. VN.

[h] P adds at the end of v. 1: "and thus did David prophesy and say: Shiggaion of David which he sang to the Lord concerning Cush, a Benjamite (in Hebrew; Ps 7:1). And would you say that Saul, king of Israel, was a Cushite man? Rather, just as this Cushite's flesh is different from all human beings (lit.: 'sons of man'), thus was Saul, king of Israel, beautiful in form and handsome in appearance and different in his good works from every human being (lit.: 'all sons of man') of that generation. And thus did Jeremiah prophesy and say: And Ebed-Melech the Cushite heard (in Hebrew; Jer 38:7). And would you say that Baruch, the son of Neriah, the pious man, was a Cushite man? Rather, just as this Cushite's flesh was different from all other human beings (lit.: 'sons of man'), thus was Baruch, the son of Neriah, a man handsome in form and beautiful in appearance and different in his good works from every human being (lit: 'all sons of man') which there was in that generation. And thus did Amos prophesy and say: Are you not to me like the Cushites, O sons of Israel (in Hebrew; Amos 9:7). And would you say that the descendants of Abraham and the descendants of Isaac and Jacob were evil in deeds? Rather, just as this Cushite is set apart and divided from every other creature, so also did the merciful One distinguish and sanctify the children of Israel as a heave offering (*terumah, trwmt'*) from the threshing floor and a loaf from the dough (cf. Num 15:20); and he called them (lit.: 'him') sons of his people, his portion and his inheritance" (cf. Deut 32:9). See note and *Sifre Num,* par. 99.

[i] Nfmg: "behold, the Memra of the Lord has spoken not only with Moses."

Notes, Chapter 12

[1]"concerning *('l 'sq)* . . . that generation." HT: "because of the Cushite woman whom he had married, for he had married a Cushite woman." The reference in the HT is probably to Moses' wife Zipporah, a Midianite (Exod 2:21). The repeated mention of Moses' marriage to a Cushite led to speculation as to the meaning of "Cushite," at least in its second occurrence. Thus *Sifre Num* 99 (on Num 12:1): as the Cushite is different in the color of the skin, so are all individual members of the chosen people (Zipporah, David, Saul, Baruch) different in beauty and good works. Nf's paraphrase is in this tradition. Moses' wife is identified in the paraphrase as Zipporah, outstanding in beauty and good works. The paraphrase of the Frg. Tgs. (PVNL) is almost identical with that of Nf apart from an addition to P which clearly relates to *Sifre Num* 99. See further on this B. Barry Levy, 1987, 2, 85f.; Onq and Ps.-J. differ from this paraphrase but are also in rabbinic tradition. See B. Grossfeld, on Onq. Num 12:1 (*The Aramaic Bible,* vol. 8, p. 103) and note of E. Clarke to Ps.-J., below, p. 222, n. 2.

with us?" And (this) *was heard before*[j2] the Lord. 3. Now the man Moses was very meek, more so than any of the sons of man upon the face of the earth. 4. And the Lord[k] said suddenly to Moses and to Aaron <and to Miriam: "Go outside, the three of you, to the tent of meeting">;[m] and the three of them went out. 5. And *the Glory of the Shekinah* of the Lord *was revealed* in the pillar of cloud,[3] and stood at the door of the tent and called Aaron and Miriam; and the two of them went out. 6. And he said: "Hear my words,[n] I pray. Should there be a prophet *among you,* I, the Lord, will be *revealed* to him in visions, and in dreams[o] I will speak with him. 7. My servant Moses[4] is not like *any of the (other) prophets;*[p] in *my whole world*[q] *which I have created,* he is faithful.[r] 8. *Speech to speech*[s5] (I spoke) with him in visions and not in appearances,[t] and a resemblance *from before* the Lord he used to contemplate. Why, then, do you not fear to speak against my servant, against Moses?" 9. And the anger of the Lord was enkindled against them and he departed.[u] 10. And the cloud turned aside[w] from above the tabernacle, and behold, Miriam was leprous <like the snow.[x] And Aaron saw Miriam and behold, she was leprous>.[y] 11. And Aaron said to Moses: "I beseech you, my master; do not, I

Apparatus, Chapter 12

[j] Nfmg: "it has spoken also with us. And it was manifest and known before (the Lord)"; Nfi: "(with us) it conversed."
[k] Nfmg: "the Memra of the Lord."
[m] Missing in text and margin.
[n] Nfmg: "hear my words (another form), I pray: if . . ."
[o] Nfmg: "(should there be) a prophet of yours, (I) the Lord, will make myself known to him in a vision; in a dream I will speak . . ."
[p] Nfi: "(he is not) like any (other) prophet."
[q] *bkl 'wlmy; or:* "among all my young men whom . . ."
[r] P: "there is none like the person (lit.: 'son of man'), my servant Moses, in the entire royal court (Latin loan word *comitatus,* possibly through Greek *komitaton*) of Israel. Of all (or: 'for all') the scribal clerks (*lblr';* Latin loan word *librarius*) of my royal court he is most trustworthy"; VN: "there is no one like my servant Moses in all the royal court (*komitaton*), head of the officials (?; *kyldyn* = Chaldeans?; error for *librarii,* scribal clerks?), my royal court, he is faithful." Possibly in both P and VN the text between "royal court" and "is most trusted" represents glossing. The original may have been as Nfmg: "my servant Moses, in my whole court, he is most trusted."
[s] Or: "speech against (*lqbl*) speech." Nfmg has variant *kl wqbl,* as in Nf Deut 34:10.
[t] Nfmg: "in vision and not in secret and the appearance (of the Lord) . . ."
[u] Nfmg: "against them and he withdrew (lit.: 'was taken up')."
[w] Nfmg: "passed."
[x] Nfmg: "(and, behold, Miriam) was punished with leprosy, (she became) white like snow."
[y] Missing in text; supplied in margin.

Notes, Chapter 12

[2]"was heard before . . ."; HT: "the Lord heard."
[3]The HT has: "and the Lord came down in the pillar of cloud"; see note to 10:34.
[4]The HT (RSV) has: "not so with my servant Moses. He is entrusted with (or: 'the working in') all my house." In Nf "house" of the HT is interpreted as the entire world. Onq. understands as: "by all my people"; Ps.-J.: "all Israel my people." Frg. Tg. (PVNL), Nfmg as: "in all my royal court" (see Apparatus).
[5]"speech to speech" (*mmll qbl mmll*) or "speech corresponding to (opposite) speech"; HT: "mouth to mouth," *ph 'l ph.* The same phrase occurs in Nf Exod 33:11 (HT: "face to face," *pnym 'l pnym*); Deut 5:4 (HT: *pnym bpnym*) and Deut 34:10 (*mmll kl wqbl mmll;* HT: "*pnym 'l pnym*). There is an almost identical paraphrase in Onq. and Ps.-J. ("speech with speech"), all intended to soften somewhat the anthropomorphism of the HT.

pray, set upon us the offense[z] which through error we have committed and which we have sinned.[aa] 12. Let not *Miriam,*[bb] I pray, be *unclean in the camp* like the dead;[cc][6] *for behold, she is like the child who has passed nine months*[7] *in* the womb[dd] of its mother *in water and in fire, without a mishap, and when the appointed time for it* to come forth *into the world* arrived, half of its flesh is eaten.[ee] *Thus,*[ff] *when we were enslaved in Egypt, and again driven about in the desert, our sister saw (us) in our bondage; and when the time has come to possess the land, why*[gg] *must she be withheld from us? Pray*[hh] *for the dead flesh*[ii] *that is on her that it may live. Why*

Apparatus, Chapter 12

[z] Lit.: "debt."

[aa] Nfmg: "we have sinned" (or: "we have incurred guilt") (another verb).

[bb] PVN: "Let not Miriam our sister, I pray, be(come) leprous, causing defilement (missing in P) in the tent like a dead person. For just like this infant (or: 'offspring, embryo') that was in its mother's womb nine months in water and in fire, and was not harmed; and when the appointed time came for it to come forth from its mother's womb, half of its flesh is eaten up. Thus has Miriam our sister been driven about with us in the wilderness and she has been with us in our tribulation, and now that the appointed time has come to enter (P: to take possession of) the land of Israel, why is she withheld from us? Pray, now, over her dead flesh that it may live and that we may not cause (*nybd*) her merit to be lost" (unless *nybd* is formed under the influence of the Hebrew Nifal, thus: "that her merit may not be lost"). Thus VN ending. P ends: "Pray, now, for this dead flesh that it may live for she is our sister and our close blood (lit.: 'flesh') relation. Why, I pray, should her merit be lost (*nwbd;* or: 'why, I pray, should we cause her merit to be lost')"; Nfmg: "let not Miriam our sister, I pray, become like the pregnant woman who has turned leprous in her pregnancy and when the time comes for her to give birth, the child dies in her womb. Has not Miriam suffered with us? And now the time has come to see the consolation. Let her not be removed far (from us) now."

[cc] Nfi: "(in the tent) of the dead."

[dd] Nfmg: "leprosy in the tent like a dead person, for (she is) like this child who was in the womb"; cf. PVN, with: "thus like this child."

[ee] Nfmg: "(to come forth) from the womb of its mother, is eaten"; = PVN.

[ff] Nfmg: "thus was Miriam our sister driven about in the wilderness and was with us in the end (*'qb';* with PVN read: *'qn',* "distress") when . . ."; cf. PVN.

[gg] Nfmg: "(and when) the appointed time (lit.: 'times') to enter the land of Israel (has come), why . . . ?"; = VN.

[hh] Nfmg: "(pray) now" (or: "pray then"); = PVN.

[ii] Nfmg: "this (dead flesh) and it shall live that we may not make her merit (or: 'her righteousness') perish" (*nwdb;* or: "that her merit/righteousness may not be lost").

Notes, Chapter 12

[6]The HT has: "Let her not be as one dead, of whom the flesh is half consumed when he comes out of his mother's womb." The Frg. Tg. Nfmg and Ps.-J. have essentially the same paraphrase as Nf. In this paraphrase the image of the fetus, safe in the womb for nine months and dying just before childbirth, is spelled out. This is then understood of Israel and Miriam; the period of conception and gestation are understood as the enslavement in Egypt and the desert wandering, childbirth as possession of the land. Miriam had suffered with her people in the former; why should she die just before her birth to possession of the land? Onq.: "Let now not this one be kept away from us, for she is our sister; pray not for this dead flesh that is in her that she may be cured."

[7]"nine months in the water and in fire (or: 'in the fire')." For Jewish traditions in Miriam, see R. Le Déaut "Miryam, soeur de Moïse, et Marie, mère du Messie," *Biblica* 45 (1964) 198–219 (202f. for Num 12); L. Díez Merino, "Maria, hermana de Moises en la tradición targumica," *Scripta de Maria* 7 (1984) 33–61.

should (we lose) her merit?"[8] 13. And Moses *prayed*[9] *before* the Lord *and* said: "I beseech, *by the mercies before you, O Lord gracious and merciful* God, heal her."[jj] 14. And the Lord[kk] said to Moses: "*Had* indeed her father *rebuked*[10] her severely, it *would be just*[11] that she be humbled *before him* for seven days. Let her be shut up outside the camp for seven days,[mm] and after this she will be *healed*."[nn] 15. And Miriam was shut up[oo] outside the camp for seven days; and the people did not journey until such time as Miriam was *healed*.[12] 16. *Although*[pp][13] *Miriam the prophet-*

Apparatus, Chapter 12

[jj] Nfmg: "saying: O God, you who heal every evil (corr: 'all flesh')"; the *r* of *byśrh* is to be found in *'śry* (corr.: *'śy*), "cure her"; text as corrected; = VNL.

[kk] Nfmg: "the Memra of the Lord."

[mm] Nfmg: "if (her father) had become seriously angry with her, it would be just that she should be banished from before him seven days; let her be locked up (or: 'banished') for seven days."

[nn] Nfmg: "(and after) this she shall be readmitted"; with HT.

[oo] Or: "banished."

[pp] PVNL: "although the prophetess (P + Miriam) was sentenced to become leprous, there is in it (lit.: 'in us'; P: 'with [it]') plentiful teaching in the commandments and for the observers of the precepts; (P + for the sake of) a small precept which a man does, he receives because of it a plentiful reward, and as the prophetess Miriam stood by the bank of the river for a small hour to see what would be the end of (= what would finally happen to) Moses, the children of Israel became sixty myriads, which amount to eight legions (Latin loan word, *legio*); and the clouds of Glory and the well did not move nor set out from their place until such time as Miriam the prophetess was healed from leprosy. And after Miriam had been healed from leprosy, after that the people set out from Haseroth and settled in the wilderness of Paran"; Nfmg: "and because Miriam waited for Moses by the river one hour, the Shekinah of the Lord of the world waited for her and all Israel and the tabernacle for seven days."

Notes, Chapter 12

[8]"Why should (we lose) her merit?"; correcting Nf with Nfmg, Frg. Tg. and Ps.-J. See Apparatus. The various benefits conferred on Israel through the merits of Miriam are noted in Tg. Nf: "Because she stood at the bank of the river to see the fate of Moses, Israel became sixty myriads" (Nf Num 12:16); while she was leprous the clouds of glory and the well did not move (Nf Num 12:16); for her merits the well used to come up for them in the desert journeyings (Nf Num 21:1; see notes to text), and ceased to do so at her death. This targumic tradition is already clearly expressed in Pseudo-Philo, *LAB* 20, 7 (trans. D. Harrington, *The Old Testament Pseudepigrapha,* 2, 329): "And these are the three things that God gave to his people on account of (? = *bzkwt;* or: 'for the merit of') three persons; that is, the well of water of Marah for Miriam and the pillar of cloud for Aaron and the manna for Moses. And when these come to their end, these three things were taken away from them." See further R. Le Déaut, art. cit., *Biblica* 45 (1964), esp. 202–213. For *bzkwt,* "merits, on account of,"; see notes to Nf Gen 12:3, 13 (*The Aramaic Bible,* vol. 1A, pp. 86–87).

[9]"Moses prayed . . ."; HT: "And Moses cried to the Lord, Hear her, O God, I beseech you." The formulaic expression is in keeping with Nf's interest in prayer; see Introd. to Neofiti, *The Aramaic Bible,* vol. 1A, pp. 40f., and M. Maher, 1990, 226–246. For "gracious and merciful God," cf. Exod 34:6.

[10]"rebuked" or "chastised"; HT: "if her father had but spit in her face."

[11]"it would be just, etc."; HT: "should she not be shamed for seven days?"

[12]"healed"; HT: "she may be brought in again."

[13]The HT for v. 16 has: "And after that the people set out from Hazeroth and encamped in the wilderness of Paran." Before the translation of v. 16 is given, Nf takes occasion of the mention in v. 15 of the seven day delay due to the Miriam's detainment to present a midrash on the merits of Miriam. First there is a reflection on the lessons to be drawn from Miriam's leprosy. A general principle (of rabbinic theology) is stated on the great reward given for the observance of even a small precept of the Law. (See also Nf and Pal. Tg. Gen 15:1.) The principle is illustrated from Miriam's life. Her standing by the Nile to see what would become of Moses (Exod 2:4) merited Israel becoming sixty myriads, i.e., 600,000—a round number for the total of 603,550 given in Num 1:45-46, or eighty legions of 7500 men each, somewhat higher than the generally reckoned number in a legion (3000 to 6000 men). The second effect of Miriam's merit was that the clouds and well did not move, persumably a cloud which led Moses, and a cloud to lead the people. The well giving the Israelites water in the desert was especially associated with Miriam in early Jewish tradition and is known as Miriam's well. See note to v. 12.

ess was sentenced to become leprous, there is much teaching (in this) for the sages and for those who keep the law, that for a small precept which a man does, he receives for it[qq] a great reward. *Because*[rr] *Miriam stood on the bank of the river to know what would ultimately become of Moses, Israel became sixty myriads—which is a total of eighty legions. And the clouds of the glory and the well did not move nor journey from their places until such time as the prophetess Miriam was healed of her leprosy. <And after the prophetess Miriam was healed of her leprosy,>*[ss] after this the people moved from Hazeroth and camped in the wilderness of Paran.

CHAPTER 13

1. And the Lord[a] spoke with Moses, saying: 2. "Send men that they may spy out the land of Canaan, which I gave to the children of Israel; you shall send one man according to each of their fathers'[b] tribes; all the princes[c] that are among them you shall send." 3. And he sent[1] them from the wilderness[2] according to *the decree of the Memra*[3] of the Lord; all of them were leading men of the children of Israel. 4. And these were their names: From the tribe *of the sons*[4] of Reuben, Shammua bar Zaccar; 5. from the tribe *of the sons*[4] of Simeon, Shaphat[d] bar Hori; 6. from the tribe *of the sons*[4] of Judah, Caleb bar Jephunneh; 7. from the tribe *of the sons*[4] of Issachar, Igal bar Joseph; 8. from the tribe *of the sons*[4] of Ephraim, Hoshea bar Nun; 9. from the tribe *of the sons*[4] of Benjamin, Palti bar Raphu; 10. from the tribe *of the sons*[4] of Zebulun, Gaddiel bar Sodi; 11. from the tribe *of the sons*[4] of Joseph, that is Manasseh,[e] Gaddi bar Susi; 12. from the tribe *of the sons*[4] of Dan, Ammiel bar Gemalli; 13. from the tribe *of the sons*[4] of Asher, Setur bar Michael; 14. from the tribe *of the sons*[4] of Naphtali, Nahbi bar Vophsi; 15. from the tribe *of the sons*[4] of Gad,[f] Geuel bar Machi. 16. These were the names of the men whom

Apparatus, Chapter 12

[qq] Nfi: "for them."
[rr] Nfi: "plentiful (reward) and because."
[ss] Missing in text, but is in Nfmg.

Apparatus, Chapter 13

[a] Nfmg: "the Memra of the Lord."
[b] Nfmg: "his fathers."
[c] Nfmg: "the princes" (another word from the same root).
[d] In text: "Shaphar."
[e] Nfmg: "which is of the tribe of the sons of Manasseh."
[f] In text: "oath."

Notes, Chapter 13

[1]"he sent"; HT: "Moses sent."
[2]"from the wilderness"; HT: "from the w. of Paran."
[3]"decree of Memra of the Lord"; "mouth of the Lord."
[4]"of the sons of (Reuben), etc." An expansion in the usual style of Nf; cf. Introd. III, 23. HT: "Reuben," etc.

Moses sent to spy out the land *of Canaan.* And Moses called Hoshea bar Nun Joshua. 17. And Moses sent them to spy out the land of Canaan; and *Moses*[5] said to them: "Go up this[g] (way) to the south, and (then) you shall go up into the mountain; 18. and you shall see what kind that land is, and whether the people who dwell in it are strong or weak, whether they are few or many;[h] 19. and whether the land in which they dwell is good or bad; and whether the cities in which they dwell are *village settlements*[6] or are fortified;[i] 20. and what the land is like; whether its fruits are fat or lean;[j] whether or not there are trees in it. Be of good courage and take some of the fruits of the land." And those days were the days of the first fruits of the grapes. 21. And they went up and spied out the land from the wilderness of Zin to Rehob, at the entrance[k] of *Antioch.*[m7] 22. And they went up by[n] the south, and Caleb arrived[o8] as far as Hebron; and Ahiman, Shesshai, and Talmai, the sons of Anak the Giant,[p] were there. And Hebron was built seven years[q] before *Tanis*[9] of Egypt. 23. And they arrived at[r] *Nahal Segula*[s10] and gathered[t] from there a branch and (also) one cluster of grapes;[u] and they carried it in a basket[w] between two (of them),[x] and likewise some pomegranates and figs. 24. And that place was called Nahal Segula because of the cluster of grapes which the children of Israel gathered[y] from there. 25. And after they had spied out[z] the land, they returned at the end of forty days. 26. And they went their way and came in[aa] to Moses and

Apparatus, Chapter 13

[g] In text: "outside" (*br'* for *b-d'*).
[h] Nfmg: "(or) weak, whether they are small (in number) or many."
[i] Nfmg: "in which (they dwell), whether they are villages or fortresses."
[j] Nfmg 1°: ": "(whether) its fruits are lean"; Nfmg 2°: "(fat or) hard" (= "without sap"); = PVNL.
[k] Nfmg: "as you enter (Antioch)" (= in the direction of Antioch).
[m] MT: "*Le-bo'-Ḥamat,*" or: "the entrance of Hamath."
[n] Nfi: "to the south."
[o] Nfmg: "and they came."
[p] Nfmg: "the sons of Ephron the giant (or: 'the hero')."
[q] Nfmg: "(and Hebron) was built (seven years) before Tanis of Egypt was built."
[r] Nfmg: "and they came"; = PVNL.
[s] I.e., the Valley of the Cluster of Grapes (HT: *Nahal 'Eshkol,* with same meaning).
[t] Nfmg: "and they cut"; = PVNL.
[u] Nfmg: "and a cluster of grapes on it"; = PVNL.
[w] Nfmg: "and they bore it on a pole" (Greek loan word *asilla*).
[x] Nfmg: "between two men"; = PVNL.
[y] Nfmg: "they cut."
[z] Nfmg: "(from) spying out."
[aa] Nfmg: "and they came" (another verb).

Notes, Chapter 13

[5]"And Moses said"; HT: "and he said."
[6]"village settlements or are fortified"; HT (RSV), "camps or strongholds."
[7]"Antioch"; HT: Hamath. Nf is here as in the other occurrence of the word in Num 34:8; see also Nf Gen 10:18. See M. McNamara, 1972, 191.
[8]"And Caleb arrived"; HT: "and he arrived." Despite the general context, the fact that the singular form of the verb (*yb',* "he arrived") is used in the HT, coupled with Josh 14:13-14, which gives Hebron as an inheritance to Caleb, Nf interprets as if only one person reached Hebron, this person being identified as Caleb. Onq., too, renders as singular, but without identification; Ps.-J. as plural.
[9]"Tanis"; HT: Zoan (*ṣ'n*), the sole occurrence of the word in the Pentateuch. In Exod 1:11 Nf renders HT Pithom as Tanis.
[10]*Nahal Segula:* ("the wadi of the cluster of grapes"); HT: Eschol (= "cluster of grapes").

Aaron and to the congregation of the children of Israel,[bb] at the wilderness of Paran, at *Reqem;*[11] and they gave word to them and to all *the people* of the community, and they showed them the fruits of the land.[cc] 27. And they related to him saying: "We have entered[dd] the land to which you have sent us, and truly it is *a land producing good fruits,*[12] *pure as* milk *and sweet as* honey; and behold, some of *its* fruits. 28. Yet the people who dwell in the land are indomitable,[ee] the towns are strong and very large;[ff] and we also saw sons of Anak *the Giant*[gg] there. 29. The Amalekites dwell[hh] in the south country; the Hittites, the Jebusites, and the Amorites dwell in the mountain, and the Canaanites dwell by the sea and by *the passes*[13] of the Jordan."[ii] 30. And Caleb silenced the people *before* Moses and said: "Let us truly go up and take possession of it,[jj] for we shall indeed be able to do it." 31. But the people who *went*[kk] with him said: "We are not able to go up against the people; for they are stronger than we." 32. And they brought *before* the children of Israel an evil report[14] of the land which they had spied out, saying: "The land through which we have gone to spy it out is a land which devours its inhabitants; and all the people we saw in it are *masters*[mm] *of evil eyes,*[nn][15] *giants* of stature.[16] 33. And we say the *giants*[17] there, the sons of Anak, (descendants) of *the giants,*[17] and in our own sight we were as locusts, and so were we in their sight."

Apparatus, Chapter 13

[bb] Nfmg: "the assembly of the congregation of Israel."

[cc] Nfmg: "(Reqem) de-Gia and they informed them (lit.: 'brought back word'; 'word' is missing in Nfmg, but is in Nfi) and all the people of the congregation, and they showed them the fruits of the land."

[dd] Nfmg: "we have come."

[ee] Nfmg: "this people which inhabits (the land) is strong."

[ff] Nfmg: "and its fortified cities (very) large."

[gg] Nfmg: "(the sons) of Ephron, the giant."

[hh] Nfmg: "were dwelling in the (south) country."

[ii] Nfmg: "(from the sea) to the border (or: 'territory') of the Jordan."

[jj] Nfmg: "and we shall take possession of them."

[kk] Nfmg: "(who) had gone up."

[mm] Nfmg: "that we have seen there possess (evil) eyes (lit.: 'are masters of eyes')" (a different grammatical construction).

[nn] Nfmg: "are men of evil ways"; but possibly a gloss to "giants"; see Ps.-J.

Notes, Chapter 13

[11]"Reqem," as also in Onq. and Ps.-J. HT: Kadesh. Nf invariably identifies HT Kadesh as Reqem (Nf Num 20:1, 14, 16, 27; 27:14; 32:8; 33:36, 37; 34:14), which is identified with Petra by Josephus. See note to Ps.-J. Gen 14:7; McNamara, 1972, 199f.; G. I. Davies, "Additional Note on Reqem," *VT* 22 (1972) 152–163; also above, Introd. IV, 54.

[12]"a land producing good fruits . . ."; HT: "a land which flows with milk and honey"; Nf's regular translation of the HT phrase; see Exod 3:8, 17; 13:5; 33:3; Lev 20:24; Num 13:27; (14:8); 16:13, 14; Deut 6:3. See above, Introd. III, 19.

[13]"the passes of the Jordan"; HT: "along (*'l yd*) the Jordan."

[14]"evil report," *ṭybh; ṭyb(')* II, cf. Jastrow, 1950, 529. Thus in Nf Gen 37:2; Num 13:32; 14:36, 37, rendering HT *dbh (dibbah).* Sokoloff, 1990, 219, understands these texts in the sense of Jastrow *ṭyb(')* I, "nature, character." The present context seems to favor the sense of "(evil) report." See also note to Nf Gen 37:2 (*The Aramaic Bible,* vol. 1A, p. 17).

[15]"masters of evil eyes"; i.e., sorceress, magicians; an addition not found in other Tg. texts of this verse and apparently intended as a rendering of HT "men of stature," of which Nf apparently gives a double rendering.

[16]"giants of stature"; HT: "men of stature." Nf paraphrases according to the targumic and rabbinic principle that HT *'yš* (plur. *'nšym*) means more than an ordinary man. See notes to Nf Gen 12:20; 32:7 (*The Aramaic Bible,* vol. 1A, pp. 88, 157).

[17]"giants," HT: "the Nephilim."

CHAPTER 14

1. Then *the people*[1] of the congregation[a] raised[b] their voice, and the people wept that night. 2. And all the children of Israel murmured[c] against Moses and against Aaron, and all *the people*[1] of the congregation said to them: "Would that we had died[d] in the land of Egypt! Or in this wilderness, would that we had died! 3. Why, then, is the Lord[e] bringing us into this land to die by the sword? Our wives and our little ones will become booty. Would it not be better for us that we go back[f] to Egypt?" 4. And each one said[g] to his fellow:[h] "Let us set a *king*[2] *over us* and go back to Egypt." 5. And Moses and Aaron *prostrated themselves*[i3] on their faces before the congregation[j4] of the children of Israel. 6. And Joshua bar Nun and Caleb bar Jephunneh, who were from among the explorers of the land,[k] rent their garments 7. and said to all the congregation[m] of the children of Israel: "The land through which we have passed to spy it out is a very good land[n] indeed. 8. If the Lord delights in us, he will bring us[o] to this land and will give it to us, a land which *produces good fruits,*[5] *pure as* milk *and sweet*[p] *as* honey. 9. Only do not rebel against *the Glory*[6] *of the Shekinah* of the Lord;[q] and you shall not fear the people of

Apparatus, Chapter 14

[a] Nfmg: "and all the people of the congregation raised."
[b] Lit.: "gave."
[c] Nfmg: "and contended."
[d] Nfmg: "(and) the children of Israel (said): Would that we had died. . . !" The "circellus" is probably wrongly placed over *lhwn,* "to them."
[e] Nfmg: "The Memra of the Lord brings (us) in."
[f] Nfmg: "to go back."
[g] Nfmg: "and they said."
[h] Nfmg: "to others" (lit.: "to his brothers").
[i] Nfmg: "and they bowed down" (lit.: "and he bowed down"); lit. in text: "and he prostrated himself."
[j] Nfmg: "(before) the assembly of the people."
[k] The original text "of the explorers of the land" has been corrected by adding in the margin in square characters, proper to the text: "(of the explorers) who had spied out the land"; for this correction the particle *d('ar'a)* has been erased. With this correction made, the variant in Nfmg: "(from among the explorers) of the land" is understandable.
[m] Nfmg: "(to all) the people of the assembly."
[n] *lhdh lhdh.* In Nfmg we have *hdh,* a defective variant of *(l)hdh* ("very"), as in Nf Gen 17:2, 6. See also CTg B Gen 7:19. *ḥdh lḥdh.*
[o] Nfmg: "(if) the Memra of the Lord is well pleased in us, he will bring us into . . ."
[p] Nfmg: "and tasty."
[q] Nfmg: "against the Name of the Lord."

Notes, Chapter 14

[1]"the people of the congregation"; HT: "all the congregation."
[2]"a king" (*mlk*); HT: *r'š;* RSV: "a captain"; a term generally rendered in Nf by the cognate *ryš.* Frg. Tg. as Nf (*mlk*); Onq. *ryš';* Ps.-J. composite *mlyk lryš:* "a king as head."
[3]"prostrated (*'sth*); HT: "fell upon their faces."
[4]"before the congregation," *knyšth;* HT: "before all the assembly of the congregation." *(kl qhl 'dt),* omitting the translation of "all." The composite Hebrew expression occurs again in Exod 12:6, where Nf renders literally as *kl qhl knyšt'.*
[5]"produces good fruits . . ."; see above Introd. III, 19, and note to 13:27.
[6]"against the glory . . ."; HT: "against the Lord."

the land, for[r] *as it is easy*[7] *for us to eat bread, so do they appear easy to us to blot them out.*[s] Their (protecting) shadow has passed from them, and *the Memra* of the Lord is with us; do not fear them."[t] 10. But all the congregation *of the people* said to stone them with stones. And the Glory *of the Shekinah* of the Lord[8] *was revealed* in the tent of meeting to all the children of Israel. 11. And the Lord said to Moses: "How long[u] will this people be angry before me? And how long will they not believe in the *Name of my Memra*[9] in spite of all the signs *of my miraculous wonders*[10] which I have worked among them? 12. I will *slay*[11] them with the pestilence and blot them out,[12] and *it is possible before me*[13] to constitute you a people[w] greater and mightier than they." 13. But Moses said *before* the Lord: "Then the Egyptians[x] will hear that you in your might have brought up this people from among them; 14. and they will tell[y] the inhabitants of this land. They have heard[z] that you are he, *the Glory of whose Shekinah*[14] is in the midst[aa] of this people; that, *appearance*[15] to *appearance,* you have been revealed[bb] *in your Memra,* O Lord, and (that) the cloud of the *Glory of your Shekinah*[16] was upon them[cc] and (that) in the

Apparatus, Chapter 14

[r] Nfmg: "(because) they (shall be) our food (reading: *mzwnn*), as if their shadow had passed (= vanished?)" (= the shadow which stopped them from dissolving like manna at sunrise; Exod 16:21).

[s] P: "they are little to blot them out"; otherwise P = Nf.

[t] Nfmg: "the Memra of the Lord (shall be) at our aid; do not fear"; cf. Ps.-J.

[u] Nfmg: "How long?" (another form).

[w] Nfmg: "and I will constitute you, Moses, a people . . ."

[x] Nfmg: "behold, the Egyptians hear it . . ."

[y] Lit.: "and they say to."

[z] "(and) the inhabitants of the country (will say): We have heard . . ."

[aa] Nfmg: "between"; there is no reference "circellus" for this variant.

[bb] Nfmg: "for (in) vision have you been revealed."

[cc] Nfmg: "standing over."

Notes, Chapter 14

[7]"it is easy (*qlyl*) . . . eat bread . . ."; HT: "for they are bread to us." Nf's paraphrase avoids any reference to cannibalism and seems influenced by the description of the manna in Num 21:5; RSV: "we loathe this worthless (*qlql*) food" ("bread"), which Nf renders as "the bread the nourishment of which is little" (*qlyl*).

[8]HT: "the glory of the Lord appeared" ("was seen").

[9]"Believe in the name of my Memra"; HT: "believe in me."

[10]"signs of my miraculous wonders," *nyšy pryšty,* as in Nf Exod 15:18. HT Num 14:11, *'twt.* Nf is probably influenced by the HT expression *'tt whmwptym,* Deut 34:11 and elsewhere. See also Nf Num 14:22 and note to Nf Deut 34:11.

[11]"slay"; HT: "strike."

[12]"blot out"; HT: verb *yrš,* in this context "disown," "disinherit"; the same Hebrew word also means "inherit." When the root *yrš* means "disinherit," Nf generally translates with the root *šyṣy,* "blot out," "destroy." Thus in Exod 15:9; 34:24; Num 14:12; 21:32; 32:21, 39; 33:52, 53, 55; Deut 7:17; 9:3, 4. The Hebrew word is rendered differently in Nf Deut 9:5, 25; 18:12, by the Aramaic *ṭrd,* "drive out."

[13]"It is possible before me . . ."; HT: "I will make you." Nf renders the HT phrase in the same way in Exod 32:10 and Deut 9:14. See also note to Nf Gen 18:14 for use of "Is it possible?" in relation to God.

[14]"the glory of whose Shekinah was"; HT: "your cloud stands over them." See note to Num 10:34.

[15]"appearance to appearance (*ḥzyw bḥzyw*) you have been revealed in your Memra"; HT: "you are seen eye to eye" (an expression occurring only here in the Pentateuch).

[16]"not possible before the Lord"; HT: "the Lord was not able."

pillar of cloud you[dd] walked[ee] before them during the day and in the pillar of fire by night. 15. Now, if you kill[ff] this people as one man, the nations who have heard your fame[gg] will say: 16. 'Because it was not possible *before* the Lord to bring this people into the land which he swore to them, he has slain them in the wilderness.' 17. And now, *O Lord,* let your might grow strong,[17] I pray, according as you have spoken,[hh] saying: 18. 'The Lord is long-suffering,[ii][18] *far removed with regard to anger*[jj] *and near with regard to mercy* and generous *in performing* steadfast love;[kk] *forgiving and remitting* sins[mm][19] *and pardoning* rebelliousnesses *and effacing*[nn] sins; but he will by no means acquit (the guilty).[oo] *On the day of the great judgment*[20] he will recall[pp] the sins[mm] of the wicked fathers upon the *rebellious* sons, upon the third and upon the fourth *generation.'*[qq] 19. Forgive, I pray,[rr] *and remit*[21] the sins (of)[ss] this people according[tt] to the greatness of your steadfast love, and according

Apparatus, Chapter 14

[dd] Nfi: "(. . . you) behold you walk."
[ee] Nfmg: "you lead."
[ff] In text *wtqṭl,* imperf., with *ṭ* interlineated; Nfmg: *mqtl* (passive) Ithp. participle; correct to *mqṭl,* active participle (with same meaning as text).
[gg] Nfmg: "(your) great (fame)."
[hh] Nfmg: "(as) he spoke."
[ii] Lit.: "long of (= prolonging) spirit" (*'ryk rwḥ*), i.e., slow to get angry. VN: "the Lord is long-suffering" (lit.: "long of mercies," *'ryk rḥmyn;* read as Nf: *'ryk rwḥ*), far removed with regard to anger and near with regard to mercy and generous in performing steadfast love and truth, but the Lord certainly will not acquit (or: 'justify') the guilty in the day of the Great Judgment, recalling the sins of the wicked fathers upon the rebellious sons."
[jj] "far removed from anger," *w-rḥyq rgz;* see note.
[kk] Nfmg: "(steadfast love) and truth and justifying . . ."; "steadfast love and truth" corresponds to the Hebrew *ḥsd w-'mt,* i.e., goodness and unbreakable solidarity.
[mm] Lit.: "the debts."
[nn] Lit.: "atoning for"; i.e., condones, pardons, expiates.
[oo] Missing in text, as in Exod 34:7 (parallel passage); Nfmg: "the Lord (does not acquit) sinners; (in the day)."
[pp] Nfmg: "he shall visit."
[qq] Nfmg: "(generation) to those who hate me."
[rr] Nfmg: "and remit, the sins of . . ."
[ss] In the text erroneously "and."
[tt] Nfmg: "for the greatness . . ."

Notes, Chapter 14

[17]HT: "And now, I pray thee, let the power of the Lord (*'dny*) be great . . ."
[18]"long suffering . . . anger . . . mercy," *YYY 'ryk rwḥ, wrḥyq rgz wqryb rḥmyn.* The HT v. 18 has: "The Lord is slow to anger (*'rk 'pym*), abounding in steadfast love, forgiving iniquity and transgression, but will by no means clear the guilty." See Exod 34:6-7. Nf, as in Exod 34:6-7, gives a triple paraphrase of HT *'rk 'pym,* one being *rḥyq rgz,* "remote, far removed, from anger." Tg. Joel 2:13 renders the same HT text as *mrḥyq rgz, "removing anger";* see note by K. Cathcart in *The Aramaic Bible,* vol. 14, p. 69. So also *j. Taan.* II, 65b; cf. Jastrow, p. 1448.
[19]"forgiving and remitting," *šry wšbq:* HT: *nś' 'wn (wpš').* See also note to Nf Gen 4:7, *The Aramaic Bible,* vol. 1A, p. 66, and above, Introd. III, 14. See also M. McNamara, 1972, 129f.; note 8 to Nf Gen 4:8 (*The Aramaic Bible,* vol. 1A, p. 66).
[20]"On the day of great judgment . . . generation"; HT: "visiting the iniquity of fathers upon children, upon the third and upon the fourth generation." Parallel passages occur in HT Exod 20:5; Deut 5:9; and Exod 34:6-7 and are in general translated by Nf in like manner. The reference to the day of Great Judgment in this context is found only here and Nf Exod 34:7.
[21]"forgive and remit," *šry wšbwq;* HT: *slḥ* (*l'wn*). This is Nf's usual rendering of this HT term (in Qal and Niphal): Exod 34:9; Num 14:19, 20; 15:25 (in all three texts of Num Nfmg has "forgive and remit"); Lev 14:20, 31; 5:10, 13, 16, 18; 19:22; Deut 29:19 (not so in Num 15:26, 28; 30:6, 9, 13; Lev 4:35; 5:26, where the single passive *yštbq* ("remitted") is used.

as you have borne this people from Egypt until now." 20. And the Lord[uu] said: "*Behold,* I forgive *and remit* as *you have spoken.*[ww22] 21. But, (as) I live *and endure in my Memra for ever,*[23] and the glory of *the Shekinah of* the Lord[24] fills the whole earth:[xx] 22. none of the men who saw my glory and the signs *of my wonders*[25] which I worked in Egypt and in the wilderness, and have put me to the test these ten times and have not listened to my voice,[yy] 23. shall see the land which I swore to their fathers; and no one[zz] who provoked before me[a] shall see it. 24. But my servant Caleb, because a *holy* spirit[26] was with him and he followed[b] *my Memra* faithfully, him shall I bring into the land into which he went, and his children[c] shall possess it.[d] 25. Now, the Amalekites and the Canaanites dwell in the Plain; turn tomorrow and journey[e] to[f] the wilderness by the way of the Reed Sea."[g] 26. And the Lord[h] spoke with Moses and with Aaron, saying: 27. "For how long (shall it be) for this evil congregation[i] who murmur *before me* against me?[j27] <The murmurings of the children of Israel which they murmur against me> *have been heard before* me.[k28] 28. Say to them: '(As) I live *and endure in my Memra,*' says the Lord, 'as they have spoken in my hearing, so shall I do to them! 29. Your dead bodies shall fall in this wilderness, and of all of you of whom a census has been taken,[m] and of all who have been numbered of you from twenty years old and upwards, who have murmured *before* me, 30. not one shall come into the land in which, with my

Apparatus, Chapter 14

[uu] VN: "and the Memra of the Lord said: Behold, I forgive and remit according to your word"; Nfmg: "the Memra of the Lord said"; cf. VN.

[ww] Nfmg: "(and remit) according to your word"; = VN.

[xx] Nfmg: "(. . . I,) thus says the Lord, and (the earth) is full of the glory . . ."

[yy] Nfmg: "the voice of my Memra."

[zz] Nfmg: "(and none) of those who provoked me."

[a] I.e., "blasphemes before me," or: "provoked me to anger."

[b] Lit.: "fulfilled." Nfmg: "because a spirit of wisdom dwelt upon him and he fulfilled . . ."

[c] Nfmg: "and the descendants of his sons."

[d] Nfmg: "(shall possess) them."

[e] Nfmg: "and journey" (another form of the same word).

[f] Nfi: "in the wilderness."

[g] Or: "the Red Sea."

[h] Nfmg: "the Memra of the Lord."

[i] Nfmg: "(how long shall) the people of (thus evil) congregation . . ."

[j] Nfmg: "(which murmurs) against me. The murmurings of the children of Israel who murmur against me are manifest before me."

[k] Missing in text; supplied in margin.

[m] Nfmg 1°: "according to all (. . . of whom a census has been taken)"; Nfmg 2°: "and according to all."

Notes, Chapter 14

[22]"as you have spoken"; MT: "according to your word."

[23]"as I live and endure in my Memra for ever"; HT: "I live" (*ḥy 'ny*). Nf renders in the same way in the other occurrences of the HT phrase (see Gen 3:22; 27:27; Num 14:28; Deut 32:40, *ḥy 'nky,* and Sokoloff, 1990, 490).

[24]"glory of the Shekinah of the Lord"; HT: "the glory of the Lord."

[25]"signs of my wonders"; HT: "my signs." See note to 14:11.

[26]"a holy spirit"; HT: "a different the spirit."

[27]"before me against me"; HT: "against me."

[28]"have been heard before me"; HT: "I have heard."

hand[n] uplifted, *I swore* to make you dwell, except Caleb bar Jephunneh and Joshua bar Nun. 31. And your little ones whom you have said would be booty, those shall I cause to enter, and they shall see the land[o] which you have rejected. 32. But as for you, your dead bodies shall fall in this wilderness. 33. And your children shall go astray[p] in the wilderness for forty years, and they shall receive (the chastisement of) your abomination until your dead bodies[q] are exterminated in the wilderness. 34. According to the number of days that you were spying our (the land), forty days, for each day one year, you shall receive[r] (the chastisement of) your sins for forty years, and you shall know the (consequences of) murmuring against me.' 35. I, the Lord, have spoken; surely, this will I do to all this[s] evil congregation[t] which has murmured *before* me.[u] In this wilderness they shall be exterminated and there shall they die." 36. And the men whom Moses sent to spy out the land, and who came back and stirred up[w] the whole congregation against him, spreading a *great evil* report[x][29] concerning the land, 37. (these) men who spread an evil report concerning the land died by a sudden death before the Lord. 38. And Joshua bar Nun and Caleb bar Jephunneh (remained alive)[y] from among these men who went to spy out the land. 39. And Moses spoke these words with all the children of Israel, and the people mourned greatly. 40. And they rose early in the morning and went up to the top of the mountain, saying: "Behold, we are here; we will go up[z] to the place which the Lord has promised, because we have sinned." 41. And Moses said: "Why, I pray, are you transgressing *the decree of the Memra*[30] of the Lord, for that will not succeed? 42. Do not go up, for *the glory of the Shekinah of* the Lord[31] does not dwell upon you, lest[aa] you be struck down before[bb] your enemies. 43. For

Apparatus, Chapter 14

[n] Lit.: "in which I lifted my hand in an oath"; Nfmg: "I raise up my hands"; = VN.

[o] Nfmg: "(you have said) they would be (booty), I shall cause to enter and they shall know the land."

[p] Nfmg: "(your children) shall nourish themselves for the merits of their fathers on manna for forty years and there shall remain (or: 'they shall bear'?) all your sins (lit.: 'debts') (until)."

[q] Nfmg: "(until) the last (lit.: 'the end') of your corpses (are exterminated in the wilderness)."

[r] Nfmg: "(one) year, you shall bear (your sins)."

[s] Nfmg: "this" (lit.: "these"). The demonstrative is in the plur., in agreement with *'mmh.*

[t] Nfmg: "(all) the people of (this evil) generation."

[u] Nfmg +: "against me."

[w] Nfmg: "and they murmured."

[x] Nfmg: "those (men) who spread an evil report of the land."

[y] Added above the text by the annotator in red ink, which is the ink of Nfmg and Nfi from v. 27. Nfmg 1°: "those were (from among)"; Nfmg 2°: "these."

[z] Nfi: "we will go up" (a different writing); Nfmg: "we go up."

[aa] Lit.: "that you be not struck down (lit.: 'broken')"; Nfi: "and (that you may) . . ."

[bb] Nfmg: "(lest) you be delivered into the hand (of your enemies)."

Notes, Chapter 14

[29]"a great evil report," *ṭbh rbh byš.* HT: *dbh (dibbah);* see note to Nf Num 13:32. Perhaps the addition of *rbh* here (not occurring in v. 37) is an error.

[30]"decree of the Memra"; HT: "mouth."

[31]"the glory of the Shekinah does not dwell"; HT: "for the Lord is not among you."

the Amalekites and the Canaanites are there before you,[cc] and you shall fall by the sword because you have turned back from *the Memra* of the Lord and the Lord[dd] will not be with you." 44. And they went up *secretly*[ee][32] to the top of the mountain, but the Ark of the covenant and Moses did not move from[ff] the camp. 45. And the Amalekites and the Canaanites who dwelt[gg] in that mountain came down and smote them and crushed[hh] them to *destruction*.[ii][33]

CHAPTER 15

1. And the Lord[a] spoke with Moses, saying: 2. "Speak with the children of Israel and say to them: 'When you come into the land, your dwelling-place,[b] which I give to you, 3. and you *offer* from the herd or from the flock as *an offering before*[1] the Lord a burnt offering or a sacrifice for an express vow, or as a freewill offering, or *on the occasion of*[2] your appointed feasts,[c] *making offering* as a pleasing odor *before* the Lord, 4. then the one who offers shall offer (as) his offering before the

Apparatus, Chapter 14

[cc] Nfmg: "(before me) that you may not serve before them."
[dd] Nfmg: "the Memra of the Lord (shall not be) at your aid."
[ee] Nfmg: "and they hastened"; = VN.
[ff] Nfmg: "(from) within."
[gg] Nfi: "who dwelt" (a different grammatical construction); Nfmg: "the Amalekites and the Canaanites, who dwelt."
[hh] Nfmg 1°: "and they slew (them)"; Nfmg 2°: "and they blotted them out."
[ii] MT and Onq.: "as far as Hormah."

Notes, Chapter 14

[32]"went up secretly"; HT (RSV): "they presumed" (*w-y'plw,* only here in the Pentateuch) to go up."
[33]"crushed them to destruction"; HT (RSV): "pursued them even to Hormah—*wyktwm 'd hḥrmh.* The definite article before *ḥrmh* makes Nf take it as a common name rather than a place name. See the translation of the root *ḥrm* in Num 21:3, where the toponym is written *ḥrmt.*

Apparatus, Chapter 15

[a] Nfmg: "the Memra of the Lord."
[b] Nfmg: "of your encampments."
[c] Nfmg: "burnt offerings or sacrifices for an express vow (lit.: 'distinct expression of a vow') or as a freewill offering or at the time of the rites (lit.: 'orders') of your solemnities."

Notes, Chapter 15

[1]"you offer . . . an offering before . . ."; HT: "and you make an offering by fire to the Lord." See above Introd. III, 2.
[2]"on the occasion of" (or: "at the time of"); HT: "at."

Lord an oblation of one tenth of a *mekilta*[2] of fine flour,[3] soaked in a fourth of a *hin*[4] of oil;[d] 5. and wine for the drink offering,[e] a fourth of a *hin, you shall offer*[5] with the burnt offerings or for *the sacrifice of holy things,*[f6] for each lamb.[g] 6. Or if there is question of a ram,[h] *you shall offer* as an oblation two tenths of fine flour soaked in one third of a *hin* of oil; 7. and for a drink offering[i] you shall offer a third of a *hin* of oil, as a pleasing odor *before* the Lord. 8. And *if you offer*[7] a young bull as a burnt offering, or as a sacrifice[j] for an express vow,[k] or as *a sacrifice of*[m] *holy things*[8] to *the name of* the Lord,[9] 9. with[n] the young bull there shall be offered an oblation of three tenths of fine flour soaked in half a *hin* of oil; 10. and as a drink offering you shall offer[o] half a *hin* of wine, as *an offering*[10] *acceptable* as a pleasing odor[11] *before* the Lord.[p] 11. After *this manner* shall *you make the offering* with each bull or with each male goat or lamb: lambs *or kids* or goats.[q] 12. According to the number which you prepare, you shall *offer* with each one after

Apparatus, Chapter 15

[d] Nfmg: "a tenth (of a *mekilta* of fine flour) soaked in oil, of oil of pressed olives a quarter of a *hin.*"
[e] Nfmg: "for libations."
[f] Nfmg: "for the sacrifices of holy things."
[g] That is, "for each lamb"; Nfmg: "(for) one . . ." (written differently); Nfi: "(for) one (lamb)" (masc.; in other texts fem.).
[h] Nfmg: "or for a ram."
[i] Nfmg: "for libations."
[j] Nfi: "(or in) the libation (corr.: 'sacrifice')."
[k] Nfmg: "as burnt offerings or libations (corr.: 'sacrifices') for an express vow (lit.: 'distinct expression of a vow')."
[m] Nfi: "of the holy things."
[n] Nfmg: "besides (the young bull)."
[o] Nfmg: "for a libation you shall offer."
[p] Nfmg: "(an agreeable odor) for the name of the Lord."
[q] Nfmg: "for one (= each) bull or for one (= each) ram or for a lamb of the lambs (= of the flocks of sheep) or of kids of the goats (= of the flocks of goats)."

Notes, Chapter 15

[3]"one tenth of a mekilta of fine flour" (*'śrwn mklth dlt; [slt = swlt, sûlet*]; *mekilta* is a measure (of capacity). It is generally used in Nf as a translation of the HT "ephah." Here the HT has: *slt 'śrwn,* "fine flour a tenth."
[4]"a hin,"; as in the HT.
[5]"you shall offer" HT: "you shall make" or "do." See above, Introd., III, 4.
[6]"holy things"; an addition in Nf; HT: "the sacrifice."
[7]"you offer"; HT: "you make." See above, Introd., III, 4.
[8]"a sacrifice of holy things." This is Nf's usual translation of HT: *šlmym* ("peace offerings"); see above, Introd., III, 1.
[9]"to the name of the Lord"; HT: "to the Lord."
[10]"an offering," *qrbn;* HT: *'ššh;* MT: *'iššeh.* Generally understood as related to *'š ('eš),* "fire," and rendered "an offering (made) by fire." However, Nf invariably renders by *qrbn,* "offering," without mention of fire, and so also Onq., Ps.-J., and other Pal. Tg. texts. The LXX, too, occasionally (e.g., Exod 30:20) renders as "holocaust," otherwise as *karpôma* (Exod 29:25, 41; Lev 1:9, 13) or *thysia,* "sacrifice" (Lev 2:2, 3, 11). The Vulg. renders as *oblatio* in Exod 29:18, 25, 41; 30:20; Lev 21:17; as *holocausta* in Lev 1:9, 13. See also above, Introd. III, 2.
[11]"an offering acceptable as a pleasing odor"; *qrbn mtqbl lryḥ dr'wḥ;* HT: *ryḥ nyḥt;* RSV: "a pleasing odor." The HT phrase is translated as here in Nf Lev 1:9, 13, 17; 2:2, 9 (cf. 2:12); 3:5; 23:13, 18; (cf. 26:31); Num 15:10, 13, 14; 18:17; (cf. 28:2, 13, 24); 29:6; 29:13, 36. It is rendered by "as an odor of good favor (*lryḥ dr'w'*) in Nf Exod 29:18, 25; Lev 4:31; 6:8, 14; 8:21, 28; 17:6; Num 15:24; 28:8, 27; 29:2, 8; as "(an offering) as an odor of good pleasure," *(qrbn) lryḥ dr'wh,* in Nf Lev 3:16; Num 15:7. See also above, Introd. III, 7.

this manner. 13. All the citizens shall do these things in like manner[r] when they offer *an offering acceptable* as a pleasing odor *before* the Lord.[s] 14. And if a sojourner dwells[t] with you, or *anyone* who is among you, throughout your generations, wishes *to offer* an *offering acceptable* as a pleasing odor *before* the Lord,[u] as you do, so shall he do.[w] 15. The assembly—you and the sojourner who sojourns among you—will have only[x] <one> decree *of* law,[y] a perpetual statute throughout your generations; as you are, so shall the sojourner[z] be before the Lord. 16. There shall be *one decree of* law[aa][12] and one ordinance of judgment[13] for you and for the sojourner who sojourns among you.'" 17. And the Lord[bb] spoke with Moses, saying: 18. "Speak with the children of Israel and say to them: 'When you come into the land to which I bring you, 19. when you eat[cc] of the food[dd] of the land, you shall put aside *a separated offering* for *the name of* the Lord.[14] 20. As the first fruits of your kneading troughs[ee] you shall set aside a cake as *a separated offering;*[ff][15] as *a separated offering*[ff] *of grain* from the threshing floor, *and wine*[gg] *from the wine press,*[16] thus shall you set it aside. 21. Of the first fruits of your kneading troughs[ee] you shall set aside[hh] *a separated offering*[ff] to *the Name of* the Lord[17] throughout your generations. 22. But if by inadvertence you err[ii] and do not perform all these precepts[jj] which (the Lord)[kk] has spoken[mm] with Moses,

Apparatus, Chapter 15

[r] Nfmg: "and all the citizens (= natives of the land) shall offer according to this order."

[s] Nfmg: "(agreeable odor) to the name of the Lord."

[t] Nfmg: "dwells as a sojourner."

[u] Nfmg: "to the name of the Lord ('as' is missing) you do."

[w] The subject of "thus shall he (or: 'it') do" is probably "the assembly" of the following verse; Nfmg: "thus shall it be done."

[x] This word, which is in Nfmg with MT, Ps.-J, and Onq is missing.

[y] Nfmg: "one sole teaching (or: 'interpretation')."

[z] Nfmg: "thus the sojourners."

[aa] Nfi: "(one) law"; Nfmg: "(one sole) teaching (or: 'interpretation')."

[bb] Nfmg: "the Memra of the Lord."

[cc] Nfmg: "at the time you eat."

[dd] Nfmg: "(of the) food."

[ee] Or: "dough"; Nfmg: "(of) your dough (or: 'kneading troughs')": the same word with the confusion of *ayn/aleph;* Nfi employs the same word also with the confusion of *b/ww.*

[ff] Lit.: "as separation" (of something for an offering).

[gg] "wine," correcting the text ("palm tree," "date palm") with Nfi; it could also be rendered: "and as *terumah*" (i.e., as an offering for the priest), correcting the original with *wtmrh.*

[hh] Nfmg: "you shall give"; = VN.

[ii] Nfmg: "you forget" or "you overlook."

[jj] Nfmg: "commandments."

[kk] Missing in text.

[mm] Nfmg: "(which) the Memra of the Lord commanded."

Notes, Chapter 15

[12] "one decree of law"; HT: "one law" (*tôrah*). See above note to 5:29 and Introd. III, 11.

[13] "ordinance of judgment," *sdr dyn;* or: "legal decision"; HT: *mšpṭ,* RSV: "ordinance." See above note to 9:3 and Introd. III, 12.

[14] "the name of the Lord"; HT: "the Lord."

[15] "separated offering," *'pršw.* See note to 5:9 above.

[16] "you shall offer . . . wine press"; HT: "as an offering (*terumah*) from the threshing floor, thus shall you present (*trymw*) it."

[17] "to the Name of the Lord"; HT: "to the Lord."

23. all that the Lord[nn] has commanded you through[oo] Moses from the day that the Lord gave command and onward throughout your generations, 24. if, without the congregations[pp] seeing it, it was done inadvertently, all *the people of* the congregation *shall offer*[18] one bull as a burnt offering, as an agreeable odor to *the Name of* the Lord,[qq19] together with its oblation and its drink offerings according to the ordinance, and one male goat for a sin offering. 25. And the priest shall make atonement for all the congregation[rr] of the children of Israel, and they shall be forgiven,[ss] because it was inadvertence, and they have brought their offering before the Lord, and their guilt offering before the Lord for their inadvertence. 26. And all the congregation[tt] of the children of Israel shall be forgiven,[uu] and the sojourner who sojourns among them,[ww] because it was the entire people that sinned by inadvertence.[xx] 27. If one person sins,[yy] he shall offer a female goat a year old as a sin offering.[zz] 28. And the priest shall make atonement[a] before the Lord for the person who sinned by inadvertence,[a] to make atonement for him,[b] and he shall be forgiven. 29. For the citizens of Israel and for the sojourner who dwells among you, for the person who sins by inadvertence[c] you shall have *one decree of* law.[d20] 30. But a person[e] who does anything *with head uncovered,*[f21] whether he be from among the citizens or of the sojourners, is a blasphemer *before* the Lord, and that person shall be blotted out from the midst of the people. 31. Because he despised the word[g] of the Lord and has desecrated his precept,[h] that person[i] shall be blotted

Apparatus, Chapter 15

[nn] Nfmg: "the Memra of the Lord."
[oo] Lit.: "by the hands of."
[pp] Nfmg: "(if) without seeing it (lit.: 'outside the eyes of . . .') the people of the congregation."
[qq] Nfmg: "(an agreeable odor) before the Lord."
[rr] Nfmg: "(for all) the people of the congregation."
[ss] Nfmg: "and it shall be pardoned and forgiven (them)."
[tt] Nfmg: "(all) the people (of the congregation)."
[uu] Nfmg: "and it shall be pardoned and forgiven."
[ww] Nfmg: "among you."
[xx] Nfmg: "(because all the people) of the congregation was in error."
[yy] In the text (after "sins") and glosses, "through inadvertence" is missing, which is in MT, Ps.-J., Onq., and Tg. Sam.
[zz] Or: "for the sin offering" (*l-ḥṭ'th*); Nfmg: *lḥṭt,* "for a sin offering."
[a] Nfmg: "who sinned by inadvertence before the Lord; and he shall make atonement for him and they shall be pardoned and forgiven."
[b] Nfi: "to make atonement" (a different form).
[c] Lit.: "what he did in error."
[d] Nfmg: "one same teaching."
[e] Nfmg: "but the person."
[f] Nfmg: "(what he does) with a high hand (= in a provocative manner, arrogantly), whether they be from among the citizens or from among the sojourners, (blasphemes) the Memra of the Lord."
[g] Nfmg: "the words of . . ."
[h] Nfmg: "his commandments."
[i] Lit.: "the soul"; VN: "his soul."

Notes, Chapter 15

[18]"shall offer"; HT: "shall make." See above Introd. III, 4.
[19]"to the name of the Lord"; HT: "to the Lord."
[20]"one decree of law"; HT: "one law." See note to 5:29 and Introd. III, 11.
[21]"with head uncovered," (*bryš gly*), i.e., "openly, publicly"; HT: *byd rmh,* "with a high hand." Nf translates the HT occurrences of *byd rmh* (Exod 14:8; Num 15:30; 33:3) by *bryš gly.* The Aramaic expression also occurs in a free paraphrase in Nf Gen 40:18 (in relation to the Exodus) and in Nfmg Lev 26:13 (again in relation to the Exodus). For a possible bearing of the phrase on NT interpretation, see McNamara, 1966, 176–177.

out; *he shall receive* (the chastisement of) his sin.'" 32. When the children of Israel were in the wilderness, they found a man gathering sticks on the sabbath day. 33. And those who found him gathering sticks brought him to Moses and to Aaron and to all the congregation[j] *of the children* of Israel. 34. *This is one of the four legal cases*[22] *which came up*[k] *before Moses our master. In two of them Moses was quick*[m] *and in two of them Moses was slow.*[n] *And in each of those Moses said: "I have not heard." In the case of the unclean persons who could not keep the Passover at its (appointed) time and in the case of the two daughters of Zelophehad, Moses was quick, because the cases were civil cases. But in the case of the wood-gatherer who profaned the sabbath willfully, and in the case of the blasphemer who pronounced the holy Name blasphemously, Moses was slow, because these cases were cases of capital sentence, to teach the judges who were to arise after Moses that they should be quick in civil cases and slow in cases of capital sentence, so that they would not put to death precipitately someone who should by law be executed; so that they would not be ashamed to say: "We have not heard," since Moses our master has also said: "I have not heard."* And they put him in prison *until such time* as it would be explained[23] to them *before the Lord* what should be done to him. 35. And the Lord[o] said to Moses: "That man shall surely die.[p] All *the people of* the congregation shall stone him with stones outside the camp." 36. And all the people of the congregation brought him outside the camp and stoned him with stones; and he died as the

Apparatus, Chapter 15

[j] Nfi: "(all) the people (of the congregation)"; Nfmg: "(all) the people of the congregation" (a different grammatical construction).

[k] Nfmg: "which came in before (Moses)"; VN: "this is one of the four cases, etc., written above; in (the case of the) blasphemer, and in (the case of) the unclean person (through contact with) the dead. And they put him aside in custody until such time as it was made clear to them from before the Lord what was to be done to him in these cases."

[m] Nfmg: "circumspect."

[n] Cf. text and Nfmg of Lev 24:12 for the same paraphrase; also found in Num 9:8 and 27:5. Nfmg: "(. . . was) quick. In the case of the wood-gatherer, who profaned the sabbath arrogantly, and in the case of the one who blasphemed the holy Name with blasphemies, Moses was slow because their cases were cases of capital punishment; and in the case of the unclean who could not keep the Passover at the (appointed) time, and in the case of the daughter of Zelophehad Moses was quick because their cases were civil cases (lit.: 'cases of wealth'). And in each one of these he said: I have not heard; to teach the judges who were to arise after Moses to be slow in cases of capital punishment and quick in civil cases (lit.: 'cases of money'), so that they would not be ashamed to say: We have not heard; Moses, our master, also said: I have not heard. And they locked him up. . . ."

[o] Nfmg: "the Memra of the Lord."

[p] Nfmg: "he shall surely be put to death."

Notes, Chapter 15

[22]This midrash occurs again in Nf Lev 24:12 and in Nf Num 9:8. See to Num 9:8, and the note of B. Barry Levy, 1987, 2, 44–47 (to Lev 24:12). Here, unlike Nf Num 9:8, the paraphrase proper of the HT comes at the end and is not broken in two by the inserted midrash.

[23]The HT has (RSV): "and they put him in custody, because it had not been made plain (MT: *ky lô poraš*) what should be done to him." The translator may have understood God to be the subject of *prš*.

Lord[q] had commanded Moses. 37. And the Lord spoke to Moses, saying: 38. "Speak with the children of Israel and say to them <to make tassels[r] on the borders[s] of their cloaks throughout their generations, and to set[t] upon> tassels[u] of the *borders of the cloak* a cord[w24] of blue. 39. And they shall be for you turbans,[x] and you shall see them[y] and shall recall all the precepts[z] of the Lord and shall do them; and you shall not (go astray)[aa] after *the thoughts of your heart* and after the *vision of* your eyes,[25] after which you (are wont to) go astray. 40. Thus you shall recall all my commandments and be holy[bb] *before the Lord*[26] your God. 41. <I am the Lord, your God>[cc] who *redeemed*[27] you and led you forth from the land of Egypt to be for you[dd] a *Redeemer*[27] God: I,[ee] the Lord, your God."

Apparatus, Chapter 15

[q] Nfmg: "the Memra of the Lord."
[r] *ṣyṣyn;* MT: *ṣiṣit,* "fringes," "tassels"; Onq.: *kraspedon* (a Greek loan word).
[s] Nfmg: "on the borders of their cloaks, a twisted thread of blue."
[t] Nfmg: "they shall put"; = VN.
[u] Omitted in text through homoeoteleuton; added in the margin by the annotator [A] in red maroon ink, different from the ink which he uses in these pages. Above two words of the text added by [A], [LL] puts "circelli" (one over each word), which indicate the Nfmg. Therefore [A], who is the first copyist of Nf, completes the text of [LL], who is the third copyist, while [LL] in his turn annotates the text supplied by [A].
[w] *šy' (tklth).* See note. VN: "and they shall make for themselves tassels on the borders of their cloaks throughout their generations, and they shall put upon the tassels of their cloaks a twisted thread of blue."
[x] Nfmg: "and they shall be for you tassels."
[y] Lit.: "(and you shall see) it"; cf. MT.
[z] Nfmg: "the commandments of . . ."
[aa] Reading *tsṭwn* with Ps.-J.
[bb] Nfmg: "(and be) a people of holy ones for your God."
[cc] Missing through homoeoteleuton.
[dd] Nfmg: "(that) my Memra (be for you a Redeemer God)."
[ee] Nfmg 1°: "(I) am (the Lord)"; Nfmg 2°: "thus says the Lord."

Notes, Chapter 15

[24]"the tassels of the borders of the cloak, a cord"; HT (RSV): "the tassels of each corner a cord." The Aramaic word rendered cord (*šy'*) translates *ptyl* of the HT, a word occurring elsewhere in the HT and generally rendered by Nf (Exod 28:28, 37; 39:3, 31) and in the Frg. Tg. by *šzr,* "twisted thread, cord." The Aramaic *šy'* generally means "plaster," "sealing clay," and thus in Nf Num 19:15, where it renders *ptyl* of the HT. Here we should probably render "carded (or "twined") stuff." See also Sokoloff, 1990, 548.

[25]"the thoughts of your heart . . . vision of your eyes." HT: "your own heart, your own eyes."

[26]"before your God"; HT: "to your God."

[27]"redeemed, redeemer"; additions, in the manner of Nf, referring to the Exodus. See above, Introd. III, 22.

CHAPTER 16

1. And Korah the son Izhar, son of Kohath, son of Levi, (and Dathan)[a] and Abiram the sons of Eliab,[1] and On the son of Peleth,[1] sons of Reuben,[b] were at strife,[c2] 2. and rose up before Moses[d] together with two hundred[e] and fifty men of

Apparatus, Chapter 16

[a] In text *rttn,* with correction signs over both *t*'s; correct to *ddtn.*

[b] Nfmg: "(Peleth) of the tribe of the sons of (Reuben)."

[c] MT: "took"; Nfmg 1°: "and Korah (. . . and Dathan . . .) took evil counsel and quarreled"; Nfmg 2°: "and (Korah . . .) took counsel (*'yṣh*) and divided . . ." = VN; P same except with *'yṭ'* for *'yṣh.* P prefaces the following to the rendering of v. 1a: "Three harsh prophets prophesied in their anger and denied (or: 'belied') their (own) prophecies in despair (? *pryn';* a word of uncertain meaning; = *pwnryyh* of parallel passage of *j. Sanh.* 10:1 [28a] = [?] Greek *poneria*): Moses and Elijah and Micaiah. Moses prophesied in his anger and said: If these men die according to the death (*mwtn',* lit.: 'evil death, plague') that the sons of man die, and by the decree that is decreed against the sons of man, (then) the Memra of the Lord has not spoken with me, and I am not from among the Lord's prophets nor was the Law of the Lord brought down through me. A heavenly voice (*bath qol*) came forth and said: Moses son of Amram, just as the tribe of Levi made petition before you, and you had no compassion of them and did not show pity to them, so eventually you are to make petition before me; and as you exalted yourself over them, so will I exalt myself over you. You have said to them: It is much for you, sons of the tribe of Levi; so will it be said (to you): It is much for you. Do not speak further. Elijah prophesied and said: Answer me, O Lord, answer me, and let all this people know that you are their God, first God and last God, and that all the gods that they worship in your presence (lit.: 'before you') are false gods. And if you do not answer me and show the miracles (or: 'signs') of your might in this hour, (then) it will be you who have hardened their necks and turned them backwards, and made their hearts to stray backwards. A heavenly voice went forth and said: Elijah, Elijah, why have you permitted the creditor to collect his debt? That prayer has (already) been heard before me. Micaiah bar Imla prophesied in his anger and said: If Ahab return safely, I am not from among the Lord's prophets, and the Memra of the Lord has not spoken with me. A heavenly voice went forth and said: Micaiah bar Imla, I have fulfilled your decree, but I have (also) received Ahab's repentance; I have fulfilled your decree that Ahab should not return safely, and I have received Ahab's repentance so as not to bring about the evil in his days, and I have fulfilled the decree (or: 'word,' *mymr*) of my mouth: Just as the dogs have eaten the blood of Naboth, thus shall the dogs eat the blood of Ahab in the portion of Jezreel. End." (For biblical references in order, see Num 16:29; Num 16:7; Deut 3:6; 1 Kgs 18:37; 1 Kgs 22:28; 1 Kgs 22:19; 22:38; 2 Kgs 9:36.)

[d] Nfmg: "and they rose up impudently against Moses."

[e] Nfi: "one hundred (and fifty)."

Notes, Chapter 16

[1]"Eliab . . . Peleth"; cf. Num 26:5, 8, 9. Eliab was the son of Pallu, Reuben's son. In Nf text Dathan is erroneously written as "Tathan."

[2]"were (was) at strife," *plyg,* or: "were divided," "at variance"; so Nf Num 26:9 (twice), with the same verb rendering HT *b-hṣtm* (root *nṣh,* Hiphil, "to struggle)." The HT, with *lqḥ,* "took," without an object, creates difficulties (cf. RSV, "took men"; NJB, "were proud," interpreting through Arabic *yaqah*). Ancient versions render variously: LXX, "spoke"; Syr. (with Tgs.): "was divided" (strove); Vulg.: "behold" (*?ecce autem*). The problem was debated by the rabbis, and various solutions were offered. See note by B. Grossfeld on Onq. (*The Aramaic Bible,* vol. 8, p. 113), one being that the verb *lqḥ* signifies "strife." Thus *Num. R.* 18, 3, and *Tanh.* (B), Qorah V, p. 86. "Hence it is written: Korah took *(wayyiqqaḥ); wayyiqqaḥ* can only signify an expression of discord" (*peliga'*). Onq. renders as "separated himself" (*'tplg*). The Frg. Tgs. and Nfmg have a double rendering: "took and was (were) in strife" (*plg*).

the children of Israel, the *princes*[3] of the congregation,[f4] the chosen ones of *the assembly,*[g5] distinguished men of renown. 3. And they were gathered together[h] against Moses and against Aaron and said[i] to them: "It is too much from you,[j] because all the congregation,[k] all of it, is holy[m] and *the Shekinah*[n] *of* the Lord[6] *dwells* among them. Why, then, do you lord it over the assembly of the Lord's *congregation?*"[o7] 4. And Moses heard it and *prostrated himself*[8] upon[p] his face. 5. And he spoke with Korah and with all his congregation,[q] saying: "In the morning the Lord will make known who is his and[r] (who are) his holy ones, and will cause (them) to come near to him; and him in whom he *is well pleased* he will cause to draw near to him. 6. Do this: Take censers for yourselves, Korah, and all his congregation;[s9] 7. and put[t] fire in them, and tomorrow put[u] incense[w] upon them before the Lord; and the man in whom the Lord is *well pleased* shall be the holy one.[x] You have gone too far, sons of Levi!"[y] 8. And Moses said to (Korah):[z] "Hear, then, sons of Levi: 9. Is *it* too small a thing for you that the God of Israel had separated you from the congregation[aa] of Israel, to bring you near to himself, to do service in the Lord's tent of *meeting*[10] and to stand before the congregation[bb] to serve

Apparatus, Chapter 16

[f] Nfmg: "(princes) of the people of the congregation."
[g] Nfmg: "(the chosen ones) of the tent."
[h] Nfmg: "and they gathered."
[i] Lit.: "and they say to them."
[j] Nfmg: "you have gone too far."
[k] Nfmg: "(all) the people of the congregation are holy."
[m] Lit.: "all of them are holy"; Nfmg: "are righteous."
[n] Nfmg: "the glory (of the Shekinah of . . .)."
[o] Nfmg: "(the assembly) of the people of the congregation . . ."
[p] Nfmg: "and he fell down in prayer upon."
[q] Nfmg: "(and with) all the people of the congregation."
[r] Nfmg: "all that is his and (who are his holy ones)."
[s] Nfi: "(and all) the people of the congregation"; Nfmg: "(and all) his company."
[t] Nfmg: "and put" (written differently).
[u] Nfmg: "and they shall put"; or: "and there shall be put."
[w] Nfmg: "incenses."
[x] Nfmg: "(in whom) the Memra of the Lord (is well pleased), is the holy one."
[y] Nfmg 1°: "it is enough for you"; Nfmg 2°: "the office is enough for you, O sons of Levi."
[z] In text: "you," without the error being corrected or noted.
[aa] Nfmg: "of the assembly of the congregation."
[bb] Nfmg: "of the tent of meeting and to stand before the people of the congregation."

Notes, Chapter 16

[3]"princes," *rbrbny(n),* or "great men" (Sokoloff, 1990, 515); HT: *nśy'y(m).* In some instances Nf renders *nśy'* ("prince") of the HT in this manner: Gen 17:20; 25:16; Exod 34:31; 35:27; Num 1:16, 44; 3:32; 4:34, 46; 7:2 (twice), 3, 10; 10:4; 13:2; 16:2; 17:17, 21; 36:1. More frequently, however, and in almost all other cases, Nf renders by *rb,* "chief." In Lev 4:22 it renders by "the anointed priest."

[4]"congregation," *knyšth*; HT: *'dh.*

[5]"assembly," *qhlh;* translating HT *mw'd.*

[6]"Shekinah of the Lord," HT: "the Lord." See Introduction to Neofiti, *The Aramaic Bible,* vol. 1A, pp. 36–37.

[7]"assembly of the Lord's congregation." *'l qhl knyšth dYYY;* HT: *'l qhl YYY.*

[8]"prostrated himself"; HT: "fell."

[9]"his congregation" (of Korah), *knyštyh,* in keeping with Nf's general rendering of the HT *'dh.* Elsewhere in reference to Korah, Nf employs a different word ("counsel") to render this Hebrew word (Num 26:9; 27:3).

[10]"the Lord's tent of meeting"; HT: "the Lord's tent."

them? 10. And he has brought you near him, and all your brothers the sons of Levi with you; and you wish *to assume* the *high* priesthood[11] also![cc] 11. *On oath,* you and all *the people*[dd] of your congregation[ee][12] which you have summoned *before* the Lord:[ff] of *what account* is Aaron that you have murmured against him?" 12. And Moses sent to call Dathan and Abiram, the sons of Eliab; and they said: "We do not come up. 13. Is it a small thing that you have brought us up[gg] from a land that *produces good fruits, pure as* milk *and sweet*[hh] *as* honey,[13] to kill us in the wilderness, that you also lord[ii] it over us? 14. Moreover, you have not brought us into[jj] a land *producing good fruits, pure as* milk *and sweet*[kk] *as* honey;[13] nor have you given us possession of fields and vineyards. Will you blind the eyes of these men? We do not go up."[mm] 15. And it *grieved* Moses[14] very much and he said *before* the Lord: "Do not *receive* their offering favorably.[nn] I have not put a load[oo] on a donkey of any of them, nor have I done evil[pp] to one of them." 16. And Moses said to Korah: "Be present,[qq] you and all *the people of* your congregation,[rr] before the Lord, you (and they)[ss] and Aaron, tomorrow. 17. And take each one of you a censer;[tt] and you shall put incense[uu] on them, and each one shall present his censer before the Lord, two hundred and fifty censers; you also and Aaron, each with his censer." 18. And

Apparatus, Chapter 16

[cc] Nfmg: "likewise."
[dd] Or: "the men."
[ee] Nfi: "(and all) your congregation" (i.e., company).
[ff] Nfmg: "in truth (= *incipit* of Hebrew text). I swear (lit.: 'of an oath'): you, Korah, and all the people of your congregation, those who have rebelled against the glory of the Shekinah of the Lord . . ."
[gg] Nfmg: "(that) you have brought (us) up."
[hh] Nfmg: "and tasty."
[ii] Nfmg: "that you should also lord it (or: 'desire to lord it') . . ."
[jj] Nfmg: "I have been brought in" (?; *'t'lyt*).
[kk] Nfmg: "and tasty."
[mm] Nfmg: "even if you burned (out) the eyes of these men, we do not go up." By "these men," "us" is meant.
[nn] Nfmg: "do (not) look on their gift (*dôron,* Greek loan word); nor have I taken a gift (of any of them)"; = PVN.
[oo] Nfmg: "I have taken"; = VN.
[pp] Nfmg: "I have (not) done evil (written differently, as in VN) to anyone . . ."; cf. 1 Sam 12:1-4.
[qq] Nfi: "they shall be present"; Nfmg: "in readiness before . . ."
[rr] Nfi: "(and all) your congregation."
[ss] Nfi and Nfmg: "and they"; missing in text.
[tt] Lit.: "his censer."
[uu] Nfi: "incense" (the Hebrew word); Nfmg: "incenses."

Notes, Chapter 16

[11]"wish to assume the high priesthood"; MT (RSV): "seek the priesthood." See the note to 3:3 above.

[12]"the people of your congregation," *'m knyštk;* HT (RSV): "your assembly," *'dtk.* Nf very frequently renders company *'dh* and the HT by *'m knyšt',* especially in Numbers; thus Nf Lev 4:15; 8:3, 4, 5; 10:6, 17; 16:5, 24; 14:6; Num 1:16, 18, 53; 3:7; 4:34; 10:2, 3; 14:1, 2, 10; 15:24, 35, 36; 16:19, 19; 17:6; 20:1, 2, 8 (twice), 11, 27, 29; 35:25 (twice). Other renderings in Nf are simple *knyšth, qhl knyšth* (Exod 12:6); *'dt knyšth* (Exod 16:2). See also above, Introd. III, 23.

[13]"a land that produces . . . honey." Nf's invariable rendering of HT: "a land flowing with milk and honey." See above Introd. III, 19, and note to 13:27.

[14]"it grieved Moses" (*b'yš l-m*). HT: *wyḥr;* RSV: "Moses was angry." Nf has the same rendering of HT in other occurrences of root *ḥrh l-*: Gen 4:5, 6; cf. Gen 34:7 and 45:5 with double rendering (not, however, in Gen 31:36; but see Gen 31:35).

every man took his censer, and they put fire upon them[ww] and set incense upon them,[xx] and they stood at the entrance of the tent of meeting with Moses and Aaron. 19. And Korah assembled against them all *the people of* the congregation at the entrance of the tent of meeting; and the Glory of *the Shekinah of* the Lord was revealed upon all *the people of* the congregation. 20. And the Lord[yy] spoke with Moses and Aaron, saying: 21. "Separate yourselves from the midst of *the people of* this congregation,[zz][15] for in a little while I am going to blot them out." 22. And they *prostrated themselves*[a][16] on their faces and said: "O God, *you who rule*[17] *the breath*[b] of all flesh,[c] behold one man sins and will *there be anger* on the congregation?"[d][18] 23. And the Lord[e] spoke with Moses, saying: 24. "Speak with *all*[19] the congregation,[f] saying: 'Withdraw from round about the tent of Korah, Dathan and Abiram.'" 25. And Moses rose and went to Dathan and Abiram; and after him the *wise men*[20] of Israel went. 26. And he spoke to the congregation,[g] saying: "Turn aside, I pray, from the tent of those sinful men[h] and do not draw near to anything that belongs to them, lest you perish[i] with all their sins." 27. And they withdrew from round about the tent of Korah, Dathan and Abiram. And Dathan and Abiram arose[j] and stood at the entrance of their tents with their wives[k] and their sons and their little ones. 28. And Moses said: "In this[m] shall you know that I have been sent *from before* the Lord[n] to do all these works,[o] and that it has not been of my own *designing.*[p] 29. If these die the death that all[q] the *sons of* man die,

Apparatus, Chapter 16

[ww] Nfi: "in them."
[xx] Nfmg: "incenses."
[yy] Nfmg: "the Memra of the Lord."
[zz] Nfmg: "separate yourselves from among the assembly of (this) congregation."
[a] Nfmg: "and they bowed down"; = VN.
[b] Lit.: "the spirits," "the souls"; cf. MT.
[c] Nfmg: "God, O God, [words erased] (by whom) the soul of all flesh is given"; cf. Ps.-J.
[d] Nfmg: "the people of the congregation"; VN: "one man sins and there is anger on all the people."
[e] Nfmg: "the Memra of the Lord."
[f] Nfmg: "the people of the congregation."
[g] Nfmg: "with the people of the congregation."
[h] Nfmg: "(from) the tents of (these) men."
[i] Nfmg: "(lest you) be blotted out."
[j] Nfmg 1°: "they came out"; Nfmg 2°: "they came out with blasphemous words and stood . . ."; cf. Ps.-J.
[k] Nfmg: "(their tents) their wives."
[m] Nfmg: "in this" (another form).
[n] Nfmg: "(that) the Memra of the Lord has sent me."
[o] Lit.: "work," as a collective noun; Nfmg: "works" (another form).
[p] Nfmg: "(that) I have not invented them of myself" (lit.: 'out of my heart')"; = PVN.
[q] Nfmg: "of the death of which all die"; VN: "of the death of which the sons of man die."

Notes, Chapter 16

[15]"people of the congregation"; see note to 16:11.
[16]"they prostrated themselves"; HT: "they fell"; as in 16:4.
[17]"you who rule. . . ," etc.; HT: "O God, the God of the spirits of all flesh."
[18]"on the congregation"; HT: "on all the congregation."
[19]"all"; an addition in Nf.
[20]"wise men"; Nf's invariable rendering of HT's "elders." See note to 11:16 and Introd. III, 18, above.

and *if the decree that has been decreed* upon all *creatures*[21] has been decreed upon them,[r] (then) I have not been sent *from the Lord.*[s] 30. But if the Lord[t] creates a *new* creation[u22] and the earth opens its mouth and swallows them and everything that belongs to them and they go down to Sheol,[w] you shall know that these men *have caused anger before* the Lord." 31. And it happened that when he had finished[x] speaking all these words, the earth that was beneath them[y] was opened. 32. And the earth opened its mouth and swallowed them and their houses and all <the *creatures* that were with Korah[z] and all *that*>[aa] *belonged to them.*[bb23] 33. And they, and all that they possessed, went down alive to Sheol,[cc] and the earth covered over them and they were blotted out from the midst of the assembly. 34. And all the Israelites[dd] who were round about them fled at their cry, because they said: "Lest the earth swallow (us)[ee] up." 35. And fire came forth from before the Lord and devoured[ff] the two hundred[gg] and fifty men who had *arranged* incense.[hh]

Apparatus, Chapter 16

[r] Nfmg: "and the sentence of all the sons of man has been pronounced upon them"; = VN.
[s] Nfmg: "(that) the Memra of the Lord has not sent me."
[t] Nfmg: "the Memra of the Lord, and (the earth) opens . . ."
[u] Nfmg: "if from the days of the world (= from the creation of the world, or: from eternity) death was created in the world, behold, for this world it is a good thing; if not let it be created now; and let (the earth) open . . ."; cf. Ps.-J. Num 22:28.
[w] Nfmg: "alive in Sheol."
[x] Nfmg: "when they had finished."
[y] Nfmg: "which was beneath them" (a different grammatical construction).
[z] Nfmg: "(and all) the sons of man who were in the counsel of Korah."
[aa] Omitted in text through homoeoteleuton; added in margin.
[bb] Nfmg: "(and all) their wealth."
[cc] Nfmg: "(all) that they had. They (went down) alive into Sheol."
[dd] Lit.: "Israel."
[ee] Thus with MT, Onq., Ps.-J.; in text: "them."
[ff] Nfmg: "and swallowed up."
[gg] Nfi: "two hundred" (another form).
[hh] Nfmg: "who offered incense and perfumes."

Notes, Chapter 16

[21] *bryyth,* "creatures" or "creations."

[22] "creation," *bryyh,* "creation" or "creature." See also Gen 2:1; 7:4; Num 12:1; 16:32; 21:6; "new," an addition in Nf.

[23] "all that belonged to them"; HT (RSV): "all their goods," *rkws,* a term rendered in Nf in all other occurrences by *mmwn* (as here in Nfmg: "wealth"), apart from Gen 15:14, where it is rendered *nksyn,* "possessions."

CHAPTER 17

1. And the Lord[a] spoke with Moses, saying: 2. "Say to Eleazar,[b] the son of Aaron, the *high*[1] priest, that he take up the censers from the flames[c] and that he scatter the fire far away,[d] for they have been made holy. 3. And the censers of these sinners *who have sinned*[2] at (the cost of) their lives[e] they shall make into hammered plates[f] as a covering for the altar, for since they offered them before the Lord, they have been made holy; and they shall be a sign for the children of Israel." 4. And Eleazar the priest[g] took the bronze censers which those who were burned had offered; and they hammered them out as a covering for the altar, 5. to be a *good*[3] reminder to the children of Israel, so that no *layman,*[4] who is not of the *sons* of Aaron,[h] should draw near to *arrange*[5] incense[i] before the Lord, lest he become like Korah and his congregation[j6]—according to what the Lord[k] spoke to him through Moses. 6. And on the next day all *the people of* the congregation[7] of the children of Israel murmured against Moses and Aaron, saying: "You have killed the people *of the congregation*[8] of the Lord." 7. And when *the people of the* congregation[8] gathered together against[m] Moses and Aaron, they turned towards[9] the tent of meeting; and behold, the cloud covered it, and the Glory of *the Shekinah of* the Lord was

Apparatus, Chapter 17

[a] The first fifteen verses of this chapter belong to chap. 16 (16:36-60) in the Greek.
[b] Nfmg: "the Memra of the Lord."
[c] Lit.: "burnings"; "blazes" or "fireplaces."
[d] *Aruk:* "scatter [imperative] far away"; Nfmg: "(and) throw (the fire) far away."
[e] Nfmg 1°: "(of those who have sinned) against life"; Nfmg 2°: "(of those who have sinned) it is a blaze of fire against life."
[f] I.e., fine; Nfmg: "they shall make them into hammered plates" (a different construction; cf. MT).
[g] Nfmg: "the high (priest)."
[h] Nfmg: "the descendants (of Aaron)."
[i] Nfmg: "incenses."
[j] Nfmg: "and like the people of his congregation."
[k] Nfmg: "the Memra of the Lord."
[m] Nfmg: "when the assembly gathered together against."

Notes, Chapter 17

[1]"high priest"; HT: "priest." See note to 3:3.
[2]"who have sinned"; an addition in Nf.
[3]"a good reminder"; *dkrn ṭb.* The addition *ṭb,* "good" (also in Nf Exod 17:14; Lev 23:24; Num 10:10; 29:31 and Frg. Tg. Exod 12:14. It is in keeping with the phrase *dkyr lṭb,* "remembered for good," common in early Palestinian ossuary inscriptions; see M. Sokoloff, 1990, 149f.; J. Naveh, *On Stone and Mosaic* (Jerusalem, 1978) 7 (in Hebrew); J. A. Fitzmyer and D. J. Harrington, *A Manual of Palestinian Aramaic Texts* (Rome, 1978); J. B. Frey, *Corpus Inscriptionum Judaicarum,* vol. 2 (Rome, 1952).
[4]See note to 3:38 above.
[5]"arrange (incense)"; HT: "burn incense." See above, note to 5:6, and Introd. III, 5.
[6]"(Korah and) his congregation," *knyštyh;* see note to 16:6 above.
[7]"people of the congregation": see note to 1:16; 16:11, 16, and Introd. III, 23.
[8]"the people of the congregation"; Nf has achieved a uniform text by adding "of the congregation" in v. 6 and prefacing "the people of the" in v. 7.
[9]"turned towards" or "directed themselves towards"; *w-kwwn,* rendering the HT root *pnh.* Nf renders this same Hebrew verb with the same Aramaic verb also in Gen 18:22; Exod 7:23; 16:10; 32:15; Num 21:33; Deut 1:40.

revealed.[10] 8. And Moses and Aaron went in to the front of the tent of meeting. 9. And the Lord[k] spoke with Moses, saying: 10. "Separate yourselves from the midst *of the people* of this congregation,[n] for in a little while I am going to destroy them." And they *prostrated themselves*[11] upon[o] their faces. 11. And he said to Aaron: "Take the censer and put upon it fire from off the altar and set incense, and carry it quickly into the midst *of the people*[12] of the congregation and make atonement[p] for them, for wrath has gone forth from before the Lord;[q] the destruction[r] has begun to *destroy*[s] *the people.*"[13] 12. So Aaron took (it) as Moses had spoken[t] and ran into the midst of the assembly, and, behold, the destruction had begun *to destroy* the people; and he put on[u] the incense and made atonement[w] for the people. 13. And he stood[x] among the dead, *begging mercy for* the living;[14] and the plague ceased. 14. And the dead[y] *who died* from the plague were fourteen thousand seven hundred, besides the dead[z] who had died for (having adhered) to *the counsel* of Korah.[15] 15. And Aaron returned to Moses at the entrance of the tent of meeting: and the plague had ceased.[aa] 16. And the Lord[bb] spoke with Moses, saying: 17. "Speak with the children of Israel and receive[cc] from them, from all the princes according to their fathers' house: twelve rods. You shall write each man's name upon his rod, 18. and you shall write the name of Aaron upon the rod of Levi, for there shall be one rod for the head of each father's house.[dd]

Apparatus, Chapter 17

[n] Nfmg: "separate yourself from (lit.: 'from between') the people of (this) congregation"; = VN.
[o] Nfmg: "and they fell down in prayer upon"; = VN and Ps.-J.
[p] Nfmg: "incenses and go immediately to the people of the congregation and make atonement . . ."
[q] Nfi: "and behold (the destruction has begun)."
[r] Nfmg: "the destroyer (has begun)."
[s] Nfmg: "the destroyer [another form] (has begun) to destroy."
[t] Nfi: "(as) he had commanded."
[u] Nfmg: "and he placed" (lit.: "and he shall place"); cf. next note.
[w] Nfmg: "and he shall make expiation"; or: "and expiation was made"; or corr.: "and he made expiation."
[x] Nfmg: "Moses (stood).
[y] Nfmg: "those who died."
[z] Nfmg: "(besides) those who died."
[aa] The correct rendering of the Hebrew would be: "for the plague had been checked."
[bb] Nfmg: "the Memra of the Lord."
[cc] Nfmg: "and take from them a rod for each . . ."
[dd] *'l;* correcting error in text (*rl*).

Notes, Chapter 17

[10]"the glory of the Shekinah . . . was revealed"; HT: "the glory of the Lord was seen (or: 'appeared')." See Introduction to *The Aramaic Bible,* vol. 1A, pp. 36f.

[11]17:10: "prostrated themselves"; HT: "fell," as elsewhere in Nf.

[12]"the people of"; an addition; cf. note to 16:11, 16 and Introd. III, 23.

[13]"destruction has began to destroy the people"; HT: "the plague has begun"; Nf's addition ("to destroy the people") may be due to the HT in v. 12 ("the plague has begun among the people"). Nf renders the same in both cases.

[14]The HT has: "and he stood between the dead and the living."

[15]"the counsel of Korah"; HT: "the affair (*dbr*) of Korah." In Num 31:15 Nf renders the HT *dbr bl'm* ("the affair of Balaam") in like manner ("the counsel of Balaam"). See also *Num. R.* 20, 23 (on Num 25:1-2): "They followed Balaam's counsel."

19. And deposit them[ee] in the tent of meeting before the testimony, where *my Memra* meets[ff16] with you. 20. And the rod of the man in whom I am *well pleased*[17] shall turn green;[gg] and I will make to cease from me the murmuring[hh] of the children of Israel, who have murmured against you." 21. And Moses spoke with the children of Israel; and all their princes gave him a rod for each prince[ii] according to their father's house, twelve rods; and the rod of Aaron was among[jj] their rods. 22. And Moses deposited the rods before the Lord in the tent of the testimony. 23. And on the following day Moses went into the tent of the testimony: and behold, the rod of Aaron for the house of Levi had sprouted and put forth flowers and brought forth blossoms, and had matured[kk] and *produced* almonds,[mm18] the *produce of a night.* 24. And Moses brought out all the rods from before the Lord to all the children of Israel; and they saw (them) and each one took his own rod. 25. And the Lord[nn] said to Moses: "Put back[oo] the rod of Aaron before the testimony[pp] as a keeping,[qq19] as a sign from the rebellious sons, that their murmurings end[rr] from me, lest they die." 26. And Moses did (so); as the Lord[nn] had commanded him, thus he did. 27. And the children of Israel said[ss] thus:[tt] "Behold, we have come to an end; we have been blotted out, all of us perish;[20] *some of*

Apparatus, Chapter 17

[ee] Nfmg: "and you shall deposit (them)."
[ff] Nfmg: "meets" (written differently).
[gg] Nfmg: "It shall flower."
[hh] Nfmg: "the murmurings of . . ."
[ii] Nfmg: "a rod for each tribal prince."
[jj] Nfmg: "between (their rods)."
[kk] Nfmg: "and it had matured" (a different word, *ḥsl;* that of VN).
[mm] I.e., "and had produced mature almonds"; Nfmg: "and the same night it had bloomed blossoms and sprouted flowers and matured (i.e., produced mature) almonds"; VN as Nf except ending: "and matured (*ḥsl*) almonds, a son of almonds (*br lwzy'* [= Levita, *Meturg.*]: corr. with Nf to *br lyly'*: "overnight."
[nn] Nfmg: "the Memra of the Lord."
[oo] Nfmg: "put back" (another form).
[pp] Or: "the ark of the covenant."
[qq] I.e., to be kept.
[rr] Nfmg 1°: (the sons of the) testimony and let it (i.e., their murmuring) cease . . ."; ("testimony" should be corrected to "presumption" or "rebelliousness"); Nfmg 2°: "and let (their murmuring) cease."
[ss] Nfmg: "to Moses," with MT, Onq., and Ps.-J.; it is missing, however, in VN.
[tt] Lit.: "saying."

Notes, Chapter 17

[16]"my Memra meets"; HT: "I will meet."
[17]"am well pleased"; HT (RSV): "whom I shall choose."
[18]"produced almonds, the produce of a night"; HT (RSV): "it bore ripe almonds." The miraculous nature of the produce is also found in the paraphrases of Frg. Tg. (VNL, P; Nfmg and Ps.-J.) and also in various midrashim, e.g., *Num. R.* 18, 23 (on Num 17:23).
[19]"as a keeping," *l-mṭrh,* rendering HT *l-mšmrt.* Nf in general renders this word of the HT (which has a variety of senses—"guard," "watch," "keeping," "preserving," "injunction") with this same Aramaic word (cf. Nf Exod 12:6; 16:25, 32, 33, 34; Deut 11:1. See also Gen 26:5).
[20]The HT has: "and the people of Israel said to Moses: Behold we perish, we are undone, we are all undone," *gw'nw, 'bdnw, (klnw) 'bdnw,* which verbs Nf first translates as *spynn, 'štyṣynn, kln 'bdnn,* and then goes on to illustrate the threefold mention of destruction by examples of punishment from their recent experiences: plague (Num 14:12; 15:32-38); opening of the ground (Num 16:32-33); fire (16:35).

us have died of the plague, some of us the earth has devoured, and against others fire[uu] has come forth; 28. everyone who draws near to make an offering to the tent[ww] of the Lord shall die. Behold, we have come to an end of! *Behold, we are* blotted out!"[21]

CHAPTER 18

1. And the Lord[a] said to Aaron: "You and your sons and *the men of* your house[1] with you shall accept (the responsibility of) the[b] sins committed in connection with <the holy *things;* and you and your sons with you shall accept the responsibility of>[c] your priesthood.[d] 2. And bring your brethren near you[2] also, the tribe of Levi, the tribe of your father, and they shall join you and serve you,[e] while you and your sons with you are before the tent of the testimony. 3. And they shall attend to your service and to the service of all the tent, but they shall not come near to the vessels of the sanctuary nor to the altar,[3] and (thus) neither they nor you shall die.[f]

Apparatus, Chapter 17

[uu] Nfmg: "(. . . has devoured,) we all perish, we have been blotted out; there are some of us who have died in the plague; and there are some of us whom the fire has consumed, and there are some of us whom the earth, opening its mouth, has swallowed up"; VN as Nf save ending: "we have been made an end of; and we have all perished. There are some of us who have died in the plague, and there are some of us, whom the earth, opening its mouth, has swallowed up."

[ww] Nfmg: "(everyone) who draws near to make an offering in the tent . . ."

Notes, Chapter 17

[21]"behold we have come to an end, behold we are blotted out"; HT: *h'm tmnw lgw',* "Are we destroyed to expiry?"; RSV: "Are we all to perish?" Nf understands as two independent verbs and renders in the light of the occurrence of the verbs in v. 27.

Apparatus, Chapter 18

[a] Nfmg: "the Memra of the Lord."

[b] Nfmg: "(you . . .) and your father's house with you shall bear (the responsibility of . . .)."

[c] Omitted in text and margin through homoeoteleuton.

[d] Nfmg: "of your service."

[e] Nfmg: "(and they shall serve) with you."

[f] Nfmg: "neither they nor you" (expressed differently).

Notes, Chapter 18

[1]"the men of your house"; HT: "your father's house." Elsewhere Nf retains the HT expression.

[2]Lit.: "(near) to you" (*lwwtk*); HT: "(near) with you" (*'tk*).

[3]"to the vessels of the sanctuary nor to the altar"; lit.: "to the vessels of the sanctuary and next to (*'l gby*) the altar they shall not draw near" (*qrbwn*).

4. And they shall join you and shall attend to the service of the tent of meeting for all *the service of* the worship; and no *layman*[g4] shall come near you. 5. And you shall attend to the service of the sanctuary and to the service of the altar, that there be no wrath[h] upon the children of Israel. 6. And as for me, behold I have *separated*[5] your Levite brethren from the midst of[i] the children of Israel; *they are* a gift for you; they are given to the *Name of* the Lord,[6] to the service of the tent of meeting. 7. And you and your sons with you shall attend to your priesthood[j] in all that concerns the altar and (what is) within the veil; you shall perform the service. As a gift[k] I give (you) your priesthood[m] and a *layman*[4] who draws near *to serve*[n7] shall be put to death."[o] 8. And the Lord[p] spoke with Aaron and said: "Behold, I have given you charge of my separated[q] offerings;[8] all the consecrated things of the children of Israel I give you as *an anointing*[r9] and to your sons as a perpetual statute. 9. This shall be for you from the most holy place, from (the sacrifices by) fire; all their offerings, all their oblations, all their sin offerings and all their guilt offerings which they return to *the name of my Memra*[s10] are holy; they shall belong to you[11] and to your sons. 10. You shall eat[t] in the most holy place; every male may eat of them; they shall be holy *to you.*[11] 11. And this shall be yours: the *separated offering*[8] of (their)[u] gifts, all the wave offering of the children of[w] Israel; I have given (them)[x] to you, and to your sons and to your daughters with you, as a perpetual statute; every one who is clean among *the men*[y] *of* your house[z] may eat of it. 12. All *the best of* the oil and all *the best of* the grain and of the wine, the first fruits

Apparatus, Chapter 18

[g] Nfmg: "(for all) the service of the tent; and (no) layman . . ."
[h] Nfi: "again"; Nfmg: "any more."
[i] Nfmg: "Levites from amongst the sons of . . ."
[j] Nfmg: "your services."
[k] I.e., as a privileged service.
[m] Nfmg: "your services."
[n] Nfi: "to serve" (another verb).
[o] Nfmg +: "by a burning fire from before the Lord."
[p] Nfmg: "the Memra of the Lord."
[q] *'pršwty;* see note.
[r] I.e., as anointing rights; cf. Lev 7:35.
[s] Nfmg: "to my Name as most holy things."
[t] Nfmg: "as most holy things you shall eat them."
[u] Correcting the text which reads: "your gifts."
[w] Nfmg: "(and it shall be) for you; the separated offering of their gifts, in every separated offering of the sons of . . ."
[x] "them" is missing in the text; it is in Nfmg.
[y] In the sense of "persons," man or woman; the same in v. 13.
[z] Nfmg: "(every one who is clean) in your house may eat (of it)."

Notes, Chapter 18

[4]"layman" (*ḥylwny*), i.e., non-priest or non-Levite; HT: *zr,* "stranger," "outsider," etc.
[5]"separated"; HT: "taken."
[6]"the name of"; an addition in Nf.
[7]"draw near to serve"; HT: "draw near."
[8]"separated offering"; see note to 5:9, and Introd. III, 3.
[9]"anointing," *l-rbw;* rendering HT: *l-mšḥh* (MT: *l-mošḥah*) as if *l-mišḥah.* The Hebrew word *mošḥah* of this verse (as *mišḥah* of Lev 7:35) is generally understood to mean "portion."
[10]"the name of my Memra"; HT: "to me."
[11]"to you" (*lkwn*), plur.; HT: "to thee" (sing.).

of their land[aa][12] which they *set aside* for *the name*[bb] *of* the Lord,[13] I give you. 13. The first fruits of everything that is in their[cc] land, which they bring to *the name of* the Lord, shall be yours;[dd] every one who is clean among *the men of your house*[ee][14] may eat of it. 14. Every *separated*[ff] *thing* that is in Israel shall be yours.[gg] 15. All the first-born[hh] of every flesh, whether of man or of beast, which they offer to *the name of* the Lord, shall be yours; only that you must surely redeem[ii] the first-born of the sons of man; and you shall redeem the first-born of unclean beasts. 16. And with regard to their redemption,[jj] at a month old you shall redeem them at the value of five *selas* of silver, according to the *selas* of the sanctuary; twenty *main* make[kk] a *sela.*[15] 17. But you shall not redeem the first-born of the cows,[mm] or the first-born of sheep, or the first-born[nn] of goats; they are a holy thing.[oo] You shall throw their blood[pp] upon the altar and *arrange*[16] their fat pieces as an *offering acceptable*[17] as a pleasing odor to *the name of* the Lord.[18] 18. And their flesh[qq] shall be yours,[rr] as the beast[ss] of the wave offering and the right thigh is yours. 19. Every *separated offering*[tt][19] of the holy things which the children of Israel set

Apparatus, Chapter 18

[aa] Uncertain rendering of *šrwy brthwn;* MT: *re'šîtam* ("their first fruits"), unique use in the Pentateuch of Hebrew word with suffix. See note.

[bb] Nfmg: "(all the best) of the wheat and all the best of the wine and oil, their first fruit which they give to the name of . . ."; VN: "all the best of the wheat and all the best of wine and the oil—their first fruits," (*šyrwyyhwn*).

[cc] Nfi: ""(that is in) your land."

[dd] Nfmg: "for you."

[ee] Nfmg: "(everyone who is clean) in your house."

[ff] Nfmg: "(every) separated thing of Israel"; cf. Lev 27:28.

[gg] Nfmg: "for you."

[hh] Nfmg: "the first who open the womb."

[ii] Nfmg: "they shall be for you, only that you must redeem."

[jj] Nfmg: "and regarding its redemption."

[kk] Lit.: "twenty *main,* that is a sela"; Nfi: "are (a sela)."

[mm] Lit.: "of the bulls."

[nn] Nfi: "the first-born of a cow (or) the first-born of a sheep (or) the first-born . . ." In text "first-born" is the plural form; in Nfi the singular.

[oo] Nfmg: "of the goats you shall not redeem; they are a holy (= consecrated) thing. And (their blood . . .)."

[pp] Nfi: "their blood" (another form).

[qq] Nfmg: "and of their flesh."

[rr] Nfmg: "shall be for you."

[ss] Nfmg: "as the breast" (written differently); Nfi: "as the stomach" (corr.: "as the breast").

[tt] *'pršwt (qdšyh).* See note.

Notes, Chapter 18

[12]"first fruits of their land," *šyrwy brthwn.* The meaning of *brthwn* (rendered "their land") is quite uncertain and an addition to the HT. Nfmg, VN, and Ps.-J. simply read *š(y)rwhwn,* "their first fruits." On *šyrwy,* see above note to 3:12.

[13]"set aside for the name of the Lord"; HT: "give to the Lord."

[14]"the men of your house"; HT: "your house." The addition is in the usual translation manner of Nf.

[15]"twenty main make a sela"; lit.: "twenty main are a sela"; HT: "(the shekel of the sanctuary) which is twenty gerahs." The term *gerah* (one twentieth of a shekel) is rendered as *m''* (plur. *m'yn* in Nf Exod 30:13; Lev 27:25; Num 3:47; 18:16). Shekel is invariably rendered as *sela';* see note to Num 3:47; Nf Gen 23:15 and *The Aramaic Bible,* vol. 1A, pp. 32f.

[16]"arrange"; HT: "burn." See above, Introd. III, 5, and note to 5:26.

[17]"offering acceptable . . ."; see note to Nf Num 15:10; HT: "a pleasing odor."

[18]"to the name of the Lord"; HT: "to the Lord."

[19]"separated offering"; MT: *terumah.* See note to Nf Num 5:9 and Introd. III, 3.

aside for *the name of* the Lord I give you, and to your sons and to your daughters with you, as a perpetual statute; it is a perpetual covenant of salt before the Lord, for you and for your *sons after* you."[uu][20] 20. And the Lord[ww] said to Aaron: "You will have no inheritance in their land nor will you have any portion among them. *My Memra* is your portion and your inheritance among the children of Israel.[xx] 21. And to the sons of Levi, behold, I have given all the tithes[yy] of Israel[zz] as an inheritance, in return for the service which they serve, the service of the tent of meeting. 22. And the children of Israel shall not again[a] come near the tent of meeting *to make offerings,*[21] burdening themselves with sins thereby, *lest* they die. 23. But the Levites, they shall do the service of the tent of meeting, and they shall receive (the responsibility of) their sins;[b] it is a perpetual statute for *their*[22] generations; and in the midst of the children of Israel[c] they shall not possess inheritance,[d] 24. for I have given as inheritance to the Levites the tithes[e] of Israel which they set aside as a *separated offering*[f] for *the name of* the Lord. For this reason I have said to them: 'Among the children of Israel they shall not possess inheritance.'" 25. And the Lord[g] spoke with Moses, saying: 26. "And you shall speak with the Levites[h] and shall say to them: 'When you receive the tithe from the children of Israel which I give you from them for your inheritance, you shall set aside from it the separated offering[i] of the Lord: a tithe of the tithe. 27. And your *separated offering*[19] shall be reckoned for you as *the separated offering*[19] *of* grain from the threshing floor and as wine from the wine press. 28. So shall you also set aside the *separated offering*[19] of the Lord from all your tithes which you shall receive from the children of Israel, and from them you shall give the *separated offering*[19] of the Lord to Aaron the priest.[j] 29. Out of all the gifts given to you, you shall set aside all the *separated*

Apparatus, Chapter 18

[uu] Nfmg: "for the descendants of your sons after . . ."
[ww] Nfmg: "the Memra of the Lord."
[xx] Nfmg: "behold, I am your portion and your inheritance among the sons of Israel."
[yy] Nfmg: "the tithe," correcting the reading of Nfmg: "the produce."
[zz] Nfi: "in Israel."
[a] Nfmg: "any more."
[b] Nfmg: "they shall bear (the responsibility of) their sin."
[c] Nfmg: "and among Israel."
[d] Nfmg: "they shall (not) be put in possession."
[e] Nfmg: "the tenth of . . ."
[f] I.e., as an offering.
[g] Nfmg: "the Memra of the Lord."
[h] Nfmg: "and (you shall speak) to the Levites."
[i] Nfi: "(you shall set aside) the separated offering . . ."
[j] Nfmg: "the high (priest)."

Notes, Chapter 18

[20]"your sons after you"; HT: "your seed with you." Nf almost invariably paraphrases *zr'* ("seed") of the HT, when human progeny is intended, as "sons"; (see *The Aramaic Bible,* vol. 1A, p. 26). Exceptions are Gen 22:18; Exod 33:1; Lev 20:4; Num 25:13; Deut 30:6; 31:19, 21, and 34:21 (the ending of Deut in the present Codex Neofiti possibly represents a different translation from the body of the work). With Nf's paraphrase here compare Deut 4:40; 12:25, etc., where the HT has (in another context): "your sons after you."
[21]"to make offerings"; an addition to HT.
[22]"their"; HT: "your."

offering[19] of the Lord: of all its fat,[k23] *the choice part* of it.'[m24] 30. And you shall say[n] to them; 'When you have set aside *the choice part*[25] of it, it shall be reckoned for the Levites as *the separated offering of grain*[26] from the threshing floor and *of wine* from the wine press. 31. And you may eat it in every place, you and *the men*[o] *of* your houses; for it is your wages in return for your work in the tent of meeting. 32. And when you have made the separation of *the choice part*[25] of it, you shall not receive[p] (the responsibility of) sins[q] because of it; and you shall not profane[r] the holy things of the children of Israel, lest you die.'"

CHAPTER 19

1. And the Lord[a] spoke with Moses and with Aaron, saying 2. "This is the *decree*[b] of the law[1] which the Lord[a] commanded, saying: 'Speak with the children of Israel, and they shall take *and bring* to you a red cow, perfect,[2] in which there is

Apparatus, Chapter 18

[k] I.e., its best part.
[m] Nfmg: "(of all its fat) the best, what has been consecrated of it." The *circellus* is probably badly placed, and we should probably translate Nfmg: "(of all), the best (lit. 'its best'), what has been consecrated of it."
[n] Ps.-J. adds: "to the priests."
[o] "men," in the sense of persons: men and women.
[p] I.e., "you shall not incur"; Nfmg: "you shall (not) bear."
[q] Nfmg: "the sin."
[r] Nfmg: same as text but erroneously writing *tspwn* for *tpswn*.

Notes, Chapter 18

[23]"its fat," *trbh;* HT: *hlbw.* Onq. renders as "its best part" (*šwpryh*); Ps.-J. has dual rendering *špr ṭwbyh* ("very best").
[24]"the choice part (of it)"; *ṭwbk (mnh);* HT: *mqdšw* (*mmnw*); "the hallowed past." See Nfmg in Apparatus.
[25]"the choice part" (*ṭwbh*); HT: *ḥlbw* ("fat," "best"). See note to 18:29.
[26]"separated offering of grain . . ."; HT: "has as produce of the threshing floor and as produce of the wine press."

Apparatus, Chapter 19

[a] Nfmg: "the Memra of the Lord"; = CTg AA.
[b] Nfmg: "the instruction (of the Law)"; cf. Ps.-J.: "the decree of the instruction of the law."

Notes, Chapter 19

[1]"decree of the law"; HT: "the statute of the law"; (*ḥqt h-twrh*), as in the other occurrence in Num 31:21. In Nf the same Aramaic phrase translates *torah* of the HT when individual laws (not the Torah itself) are intended; see Nf Lev 6:2, 7, 18; 7:1, 11, 37, 46; 12:2, etc.; Num 5:29; 6:13, 21. See above note to 5:29 and Introd. III, 11.
[2]"(red cow,) perfect," *šlmh;* HT: *tmymh.* When the HT *tm(ym)* ("perfect") refers to sacrificial animals, Nf almost invariably adds "without blemish." (See note to Nf Gen 6:9; *The Aramaic Bible,* vol. 1A, p. 73, and above, Introd. III, 8.) Not so here. It was argued in rabbinic discussion that physical defects did not make the red heifer (cow) unacceptable for the sacrifice. See *Sifre Num.,* par. 123, 6.

no blemish, upon which *the servitude of* a yoke[3] has not come. 3. And you shall give her to Eleazar the priest[c] and he shall take her outside the camp and sacrifice her before him.[d] 4. And Eleazar the priest[e] shall take some of her blood with his finger and sprinkle some of her blood seven times opposite the front of the tent of meeting. 5. And he shall burn[f] the cow before him;[g] her skin, and her flesh and her blood with her excrements[h] shall be burned. 6. And the priest shall take cedar wood and hyssop and *precious*[4] crimson material,[i] and he shall *throw*[j] and cast[5] them into the midst of the burning[k] of the cow. 7. And the priest shall wash[m] his clothes and bathe his body in water, and afterwards he shall come into[n] the camp; and the priest shall be unclean *and removed*[o] *from the holy things*[6] until evening.[p] 8. And he who burns[q] her shall wash his clothes in water and shall bathe his body in water, and shall be unclean[r] until evening. 9. And a man who is clean shall gather up the ashes of the cow[s] and deposit them outside the camp in a clean place; and the congregation[t] of the children of Israel shall have them for the ritual use of the waters of aspersion.[u] She is a sin offering. 10. And he who[w] has gathered the ashes of the cow shall wash his clothes and shall be unclean until evening. And (this) shall be[x] a perpetual statute for the children of Israel and for the sojourners who sojourn among *you.*[7] 11. Everyone who touches[y] a dead person,[z] everyone

Apparatus, Chapter 19

[c] Nfmg: "the high (priest)"; = CTg AA.
[d] Nfmg: "and another priest shall sacrifice it in the sight of Eleazar"; CTg AA: "and another priest shall sacrifice it before him while he watches."
[e] CTg AA: "the high priest."
[f] I.e., "she shall be burned"; cf. Ps.-J.: "and another priest shall burn."
[g] Nfmg: "in the sight of Eleazar."
[h] Nfmg: "(with) her excrements" (another form of the word, that in CTg AA).
[i] CTg AA: "a strip (lit.: 'tongue') of precious crimson material."
[j] A superfluous verb (not in CTg AA), to be eliminated from the text.
[k] Nfmg: "into the ashes of the burning (of the cow)"; = VN.
[m] Nfmg: "he shall wash" (the same verb, written differently: *ww/b*).
[n] Nfmg: "to the camp."
[o] Nfmg: "(unclean) so that he cannot eat (the holy things)."
[p] Nfmg: "(until) the morning."
[q] Nfmg: "(and he) who burned (her)."
[r] Nfmg: "and he shall be rendered unclean"; = CTg AA.
[s] Nfmg: "the ashes of the burning of the cow."
[t] Nfmg: "the people of the congregation"; = CTg AA.
[u] Nfmg: "of the aspersion. [A different writing.] It is a sin offering."
[w] CTg AA: "and everyone who (gathers)."
[x] In text masc. form; in Nfmg and CTg AA fem. form.
[y] Since the verb *qrb* signifies not only "to draw near" but also "to touch" (Heb. *ng'*).
[z] Nfmg: "(who touches) an unclean (corpse)"; CTg AA: "anyone who touches a dead person, the unclean corpse of a son of man, shall be rendered unclean seven days."

Notes, Chapter 19

[3] "servitude of a yoke"; HT: "a yoke."
[4] "precious"; an addition in Nf.
[5] "throw and cast"; a double rendering of HT: *hšlyk*, "throw."
[6] "removed from the holy things"; an addition in Nf.
[7] "among you"; HT: "among them."

who touches an unclean corpse of a son of man, shall be unclean[aa] for seven days. 12. And *he shall be aspersed*[bb] on the third day and on the seventh day, and he shall be clean; but if he is not *aspersed*[cc][8] with them on the third day and on the seventh day, he shall not be clean. 13. Anyone who touches a dead person, an unclean corpse, of a son of man who has died, and who is not *aspersed,*[dd][8] defiles the tent of the Lord, and that person shall *be blotted out* from Israel. Because he did not sprinkle[ee] the waters of aspersion on himself, he is[ff] unclean. His uncleanness is still upon him. 14. This is *the decree*[gg] *of* the law:[9] When a man dies in the tent, everyone who comes into[hh] the tent and everyone who *is*[ii] in the tent shall be unclean for seven days. 15. And every open *earthen*[10] vessel that does not have a *clay stopper*[jj][11] infixed on it is unclean. 16. And anyone who in the open field touches one killed[kk] by the sword, or a dead person, or a man's bone, or a grave, shall be unclean seven days. 17. And for the unclean person they shall take some of the

Apparatus, Chapter 19

[aa] Nfmg: "he shall be rendered unclean for seven . . ."; = CTg AA.
[bb] Aramaic: *ytdy;* Nfmg: "he shall asperse" (*ydy*); CTg AA: "he shall be cleansed" (*ydky*).
[cc] *ytdy;* CTg AA: "he shall be cleansed" (*ydky*).
[dd] *ytdy;* CTg AA: cleanse himself" (*ydky*); Nfmg: "asperses (*ydy*)."
[ee] Nfmg: "has (not) sprinkled" (a different form of the same verb; that in CTg AA).
[ff] Nfmg: "shall be"; = CTg AA.
[gg] Nfmg: "(this is) the instruction of the law."
[hh] Nfmg: "who might enter"; = CTg AA.
[ii] Or: "all that is in the tent"; Nfmg: "(all) that is [a different construction] in the tent shall be rendered unclean seven (days)"; cf. CTg AA.
[jj] In text *gwph dšy'*, taking *gwph* identical with *mgwph, mgwpt'* forms in Ps.-J., Onq. (from *gwp 1,* "to close, lock up"; cf. also *m. Kel.* 9:1; 10:1, etc. One might also render: "and every open container that does not have a stopper infixed round about," reading *gwph* as = *gyph,* "the (clay) border"; Nfmg: "whose mouth (is not) sealed (*mš't;* corr. to: *mš''* ptc. of *š'y, š''*) above with clay"; VN: "and every open earthen vessel, that does not have a stopper (? *pwryt';* Greek loan word, *phoreion*?) sealed (*mš''*) on it is unclean." *mš''* renders *ṣmyd* of the HT, a hapax in this sense: pass. ptc. of *ṣmd,* "cover, covering, covered," and thus *mš''* taken as ptc. of *š'y:* "paste over," "smooth over," "plaster"; also possibly; = *m-šy',* i.e., plaster, cement, sealing clay. Elias Levita, *Meturg.,* knew variant readings: "stoppers of clay (*pwrytt' dš'h*) upon it and in several books I found *gwph*"; CTg AA: "and every open container which does not have (*some words omitted*) round about on it is unclean."
[kk] Nfmg: "(who touches) one killed" (a different construction); = CTg AA.

Notes, Chapter 19

[8]"(he shall be) aspersed"; *ytdy,* HT: "he shall purify himself" (*ytht'*). Nf translates the HT term in like manner in 19:13, 20, but with verb *dky,* "purify," in the other occurrences (Nf Num 8:21; 31:19, 20, 23).

[9]"decree of the law"; HT: "law." See above to 19:1.

[10]"earthen"; an addition in Nf.

[11]"clay stopper"; *gwph dšy'* (Sokoloff, 1990, 124, renders as "a plaster plug"); HT: *ṣmyd* (only here in this sense in HT); RSV: "cover." Onq. renders as *mgwpt šy'* (B. Grossfeld, "the clay-seal"). For a discussion of the various translations of the Hebrew *ṣamid,* and on rabbinic views on the text, see B. Grossfeld's note in *The Aramaic Bible,* vol. 8, p. 123. See also note *jj* in the Apparatus.

ashes of the burning[mm] of *the cow,*[12] and they put on them *pure*[13] spring waters[nn][14] within an *earthen*[13] vessel.[oo] 18. And a ritually unclean man shall take hyssop and dip it in water and asperse it upon the tent and upon all its utensils and upon all the persons that are there, and upon *any one* who has[pp] touched[qq] a bone or one killed or a dead person or a grave.[rr] 19. And the ritually clean person shall make aspersion upon the unclean person on the third day and on the seventh day; and on the seventh day he shall be cleansed[ss] and he shall wash his clothes and bathe in water, and at evening he shall be cleansed. 20. But a man who is unclean and who is *not aspersed,*[tt] that person shall *be blotted out* from the midst of the assembly, because he has defiled the sanctuary[uu] of the Lord; he has not sprinkled[ww] upon himself the water of aspersion; he is unclean. 21. It shall be a perpetual statute for them. And he who sprinkles the waters of aspersion shall wash his clothes; and he who touches the waters of aspersion shall be unclean[xx] until evening. 22. And everything the unclean person touches[yy] shall be unclean; and the person who touches him shall be unclean[zz] until evening.'"

Apparatus, Chapter 19

[mm] Nfmg: "to cleanse the unclean (person) (they shall take) dust from the burning . . ."; CTg AA: "they shall take some dust of the burning of the sin offering."
[nn] Nfmg: "(from) a vessel."
[oo] Nfmg: "spring water within a vessel (of clay)"; CTg AA: "living water from an earthen vessel."
[pp] Nfmg: "who have been there, everyone who has touched . . ."
[qq] Nfi: "who touches."
[rr] Lit.: "the grave"; Nfmg: "a grave"; = CTg AA. Though CTg AA uses absolute and determinate cases with clear distinction, occasionally Nf uses determinate cases in an absolute sense.
[ss] Nfmg: "and he shall cleanse (him)"; = CTg AA.
[tt] *ytdy;* CTg AA: "and does not cleanse himself" (*ydky*).
[uu] Lit.: "the house of the sanctuary (or: 'of holiness')"; Nfi: "the sanctuary" (one word); = CTg AA.
[ww] Nfi: "sprinkled" (a different verbal form); = CTg AA.
[xx] Nfmg: "everyone who touches the waters of aspersion shall be unclean . . ."; cf. CTg AA.
[yy] Nfi: "he who touches."
[zz] Nfmg: "shall be rendered unclean until . . ."; = CTg AA.

Notes, Chapter 19

[12]"burning of the cow"; HT: "of the burning of (= burnt) sin offering."
[13]"pure"; "earthen"; additions in Nf.
[14]"spring water"; HT: "living (= spring) water."

CHAPTER 20

1. And the children of Israel, all *the people of* the congregation,[1] came into[a] the wilderness of Zin in the first month,[b] and the people encamped at *Reqem;*[c] and Miriam died there, and was buried there. 2. And there was no water[d] for *the people of* the congregation,[1] and they gathered together[e] against Moses and against Aaron. 3. And the people, *the people of the congregation,*[f2] contended and said thus:[g] "Oh that we had *died,*[3] *as* our brothers[h] *died*[3] before the Lord! 4. Why, now,[i] have you brought[j] the assembly *of the congregation*[k4] of the Lord into this wilderness to have both us and our cattle die there? 5. And why, *now,*[i] have you brought us up[m] out of Egypt to bring us into[n] this evil place? It is not a good place as a place for seed—*without plants,*[5] without fig trees, without[o] vines, and without pomegranates. Nor is there *even* water[p] *for us* to drink!" 6. And Moses and Aaron came[q] from before the assembly to the door of the tent of meeting and prostrated themselves upon[r] their faces; and the Glory *of the Shekinah of* the Lord was revealed[6] to them.

Apparatus, Chapter 20

[a] Nfmg: "came (to)"; = CTg AA.
[b] Cf. Ps.-J.: "the tenth day of the month of Nisan."
[c] I.e., Petra; MT: Kadesh.
[d] CTg AA: "no water there"; P: "there was no water there for the people of the congregation because Miriam the prophetess had died and the well had been hidden away, and there were gathered together (or: 'and they had gathered together') against Moses and Aaron."
[e] Nfmg: "and they were gathered together"; as in CTg AA and P.
[f] Nfmg: "the people of the congregation" (*'m knyšth*) is probably an erroneous reading, originating in v. 1; with MT, CTg AA, Onq., and Ps.-J. it should read: "(and the people contended) with Moses" (*'m mšh*).
[g] Lit.: "and they said saying."
[h] Nfmg: "Would that we had died of the plague that our brothers died (of)"; = CTg AA.
[i] or: "then."
[j] Nfmg: "have you brought the assembly into . . ."; CTg AA: "have you brought the people of the congregation . . . into."
[k] Nfi: "of the people (of the congregation)"; cf. CTg AA.
[m] Verb *slq;* CTg AA: "brought us in (verb *'ly;* Hebrew *'lh,* 'brought [us] up') from the land of Egypt."
[n] *lmy'l;* in Nfmg and CTg AA form *lm'lh.*
[o] Nfmg: "(it is not a place) which is good to be sown, or to plant in it, without fig trees and without . . ."; CTg AA: "it is not a place for sowing seeds; it has neither figs nor vines."
[p] Nfi: "(and neither is there water) so that (we might drink."
[q] Nfmg: "and (Moses and Aaron) went in . . ."
[r] Nfmg: "and they fell down in prayer upon . . ."; CTg AA: "and they fell down upon their faces."

Notes, Chapter 20

[1]"the people of the congregation"; Nf's regular paraphrase of HT "congregation" (*'dh*). See above, note to 16:11 and Introd. III, 23.

[2]"and the people, the people of the congregation *('mh 'm knyšth,* with *y* superscript) contended." HT: "and the people contended with Moses" *(h'm 'm mšh).* Perhaps *kn(y)šth* is an error for *mšh,* and we should understand as the HT. See Apparatus.

[3]"died"; root *mwt;* HT: "expire" (*gw'*).

[4]"of the congregation"; an addition in Nf.

[5]"without plants"; not in HT; probably a double translation of HT *zr',* "seed."

[6]HT has: "the glory of the Lord appeared."

7. And the Lord[s] spoke with Moses, saying: 8. "Take the rod and bring *the people of* the congregation[7] together, you and your brother Aaron; and speak with the rock *before them,* before their eyes, that it give its water; and you shall bring water out of the rock for them, and you shall give drink to *the people of* the congregation and to their cattle." 9. And Moses took the rod from before the Lord, as he had commanded him.[t] 10. And Moses and Aaron gathered the congregation together before the rock[u] and said to them: "Hear then,[w] *O people, who teach its teachers*[x] *who need to learn;*[y7] shall we bring water forth for you from this rock?" 11. And Moses raised[z] his *rod,*[aa] and with his rod he struck the rock the second time[bb] twice, and abundant water came forth *from it,* and *the people of* the congregation[cc7] and their cattle drank. 12. And the Lord[dd] spoke with Moses and with Aaron: "Because you have not believed in me, in *the Name*[ee] *of my Memra,*[8] to sanctify *my Name*[9] in the eyes of the children of Israel,[ff] *of an oath,*[10] for this reason you shall not bring[gg] this assembly into the *place*[hh] which I have given them." 13. These are the Waters of the Quarrel[ii] which the children of Israel disputed[jj] *before* the Lord,[kk] and he sanctified *his Name*[mm11] by them. 14. And Moses sent messengers from *Reqem*[12]

Apparatus, Chapter 20

[s] Nfmg: "the Memra of the Lord."
[t] Nfmg: "had been commanded."
[u] CTg AA: "and Moses and Aaron gathered the people of the congregation together opposite the rock."
[w] P: "Hear, then, O people who teach their masters, who refused to learn; I have been commanded to bring forth water from this rock."
[x] Nfi: "your masters"; CTg AA: "who teaches its masters and is not faithful."
[y] "teaches," "its masters," "to learn": a paraphrase originating in the understanding of *hmrym* ("O rebels") of the MT as "masters"; Nfmg: "O rebellious sons."
[z] Nfmg: "and (Moses) lifted up"; = VN.
[aa] Nfi: "his hand"; CTg AA: "his hands."
[bb] We should probably eliminate this word *tnyn* from the text, as Nfi does; absent also in CTg AA.
[cc] Nfmg: "abundant water and the people of the congregation drank" (written differently).
[dd] Nfmg: "the Memra of the Lord"; = CTg AA.
[ee] Nfmg: "(believed) in the name of . . ."
[ff] Nfmg: "(my) glorious (Name) in the midst of my people, the children of Israel"; CTg AA: "because you have not believed in me to sanctify me in the midst of my people the children of Israel."
[gg] Nfmg: "(of an oath) you shall not bring in"; CTg AA: "of an oath you shall not bring in this people to the land I have given to them."
[hh] Nfmg: "to the land"; = CTg AA.
[ii] MT: "of Meribah." Cf. Exod 17:17. In Gen 14:7 Kadesh is called *'En Mišpat:* "fountain of judgment."
[jj] Nfmg: "these are the Waters of Wrangling (over) which the children of (Israel) wrangled."
[kk] CTg AA: "quarreled with the Lord, and his anger grew strong against them."
[mm] Nfmg: "with which my glorious Name was sanctified."

Notes, Chapter 20

[7]"O people who teach its masters, who need to learn"; HT: "O rebels"—*mrym (morîm)*, from *mrh;* "to rebel." The paraphrase, which is also in P and CTg AA (see Apparatus), takes HT *mrh* (*moreh*) as deriving from *yrh* (moreh = "teacher") rather than from *mrh,* "rebel."
[8]"in the name of my Memra"—an expansive paraphrase of "in me."
[9]"to sanctify my name"; HT: "to sanctify me."
[10]"of an oath"; an addition in Nf.
[11]"sanctified his name"; HT: "he showed (himself) holy."
[12]"Reqem" (= Petra); HT: "Kadesh." See note to 13:26, and M. McNamara, 1972, 199–200.

to the king of (the Edomites):[nn] "Thus says *your* brother Israel: '*You, you know*[oo][13] all the troubles that have come upon us; 15. for our fathers went down to Egypt and we dwelt in Egypt many days, and the Egyptians treated us and our fathers badly.[pp] 16. And we *prayed before*[14] the Lord and he heard the voice *of our prayer;*[15] and he sent <an angel>[qq] of *mercy* and *delivered*[rr][16] us from Egypt and behold, we are in *Rekem,*[12] a city *which is on the*[ss] borders of your territory. 17. Now, let us pass through your land. We will not pass through[tt] fields or vineyards, nor will we drink water *from cisterns.*[17] We shall walk along the King's Highway, and we shall not turn aside to the right or to the left until we have passed through your territory.'" 18. <And *the king*[uu] of the Edomites[18] said *to them:* "*You* shall not pass the borders, lest I have to come out to meet *you* with the sword>."[ww] 19. And the children of Israel said to him: "We will go up by *the King's Highway,*[xx][19] and if we drink of your waters, *we* and *our* cattle, we will give you *money for the purchase of them;*[yy][20] indeed, nothing *evil*[zz][21] (is intended); *we* will pass through on foot." 20. And he said: "You shall not pass through."[a] And the Edomites went out to meet them with a strong gathering[b] and an *uplifted* arm. 21. And the Edomites refused to allow[c] Israel to pass through their territory: and

Apparatus, Chapter 20

[nn] Erased by censor, as text and Nfmg in Gen 15:12, owing to identification of Edom with Rome; cf. Exod 12:42, where text skips the word "and King Messiah from Rome," apparently for fear of censorship; cf. Num 24:19. Nfmg omits "Rome," but P indicates its presence in the text.

[oo] Nfmg: "you know" (another verb).

[pp] In Nfmg the same verb with interchange of *'alef/'ayn.*

[qq] Missing in text.

[rr] Nfmg: "and brought (us) out."

[ss] Nfmg: "of the borders of."

[tt] Nfmg 1°: "we shall (not) oppress the bethrothed ones (cf. 22:15), nor shall we seduce virgins, nor shall we seek men's wives; we shall go by the king's public road (Greek loan word *strata*); we shall not turn aside . . ."; = VN, which continues as in Nf. Nfmg 2°: "we shall not seduce virgins nor oppress men's wives; we shall go by the way of the king of the world" (cf. Ps.-J.: "of the king who is in heaven").

[uu] In text *mlkyhwn (d'dm-),* for normal *mlkhwn;* Nfmg: "the Edomite (lit.: 'the Edomites') (said to him): You do not pass through my territory lest (I go out to meet you) with a people of drawn sword."

[ww] Missing in text; added in margin.

[xx] Nfi: "we will go by the king's public road" (Greek or Latin loan word *strata*).

[yy] Nfi: "purchase of it"; Nfmg: "we will give you the money of its value."

[zz] Paraphrase influenced by underlying HT; Nfmg: "an evil word (or: 'thing')" (a different Aramaic term).

[a] Nfmg: "you do not (shall not) pass" (plur.; in text sing.).

[b] Lit.: "people"; Nfmg: "with a strong people and a strong hand."

[c] Nfmg: "and the Edomite refused to permit . . ."

Notes, Chapter 20

[13]"you know" (plur.). In HT, sing.

[14]"we prayed before"; HT: "we called out to."

[15]"the voice of our prayer"; HT: "our voice."

[16]"angel of mercy and delivered"; HT: "an angel and brought us out."

[17]"from cisterns"; an addition in Nf.

[18]"the king of the Edomites"; HT: "Edom."

[19]"King's Highway," influenced by v. 17; HT: "highway" (*mslh*).

[20]"money for the purchase of them"; HT: "their price."

[21]Lit.: "no bad thing"; HT: "nothing (more)."

Israel turned aside from them, *because they had been commanded by their Father who is in heaven*[d] *not to set battle* array[e] *against them.*[22] 22. And they departed from *Reqem,*[12] and the children of Israel, the whole congregation,[f] reached Hor the Mountain. 23. And the Lord[g] said to Moses and to Aaron at Hor the Mountain, near the territory of the Edomites, saying,[h] 24. "Aaron shall be gathered to his people; for he shall not enter the land that I have given to the children of Israel, because you have rebelled against *the decree of my Memra by reason of the* Waters[23] of the Quarreling.[i] 25. Take Aaron and Eleazar his son, and bring them up to Hor the Mountain; 26. and strip[j] Aaron of his garments; and you shall put them on Eleazar his son;[k] and Aaron shall be gathered (to his people) and shall die there." 27. And Moses did as the Lord[m] has commanded, and they went up to Hor the Mountain in the sight[n] of the whole *people of* the congregation.[1] 28. And <Moses>[o] stripped Aaron of his garments and put them on Eleazar his son; and Aaron died there on the top of the mountain, and Moses and Eleazar came down from the mountain. 29. And all *the people of* the congregation saw that Aaron had died,[p] and the whole house[q] of Israel wept for Aaron thirty days.

Apparatus, Chapter 20

[d] Same paraphrase in VN; cf. Ps.-J.: "before the Memra of the heavens."
[e] Nfmg: "that they should not set (battle) array"; Nfi: "wage war on them."
[f] Nfmg: "(all) the people of the congregation at Hor."
[g] Nfmg: "the Memra of the Lord."
[h] Nfmg: "(near) the land of the Edomites, saying."
[i] Nfmg: "against the command (*or:* word, *mymr*) of his mouth at the Waters of the Quarreling."
[j] Nfmg: "(and) you shall strip"; = VN.
[k] Nfmg: "his sons."
[m] Nfmg: "the Memra of the Lord."
[n] Lit.: "to the eyes of"; Nfmg: "seeing (him)."
[o] Missing in text; in Nfmg ("and Moses stripped") as in HT, Ps.-J., Onq.
[p] Nfmg: "(of the congregation saw) Moses coming down from the top of the mountain, his clothes rent and ashes upon his head, and he was weeping and said: Woe is me because of you, Aaron my brother, column of the prayer of the children of Israel, who made expiation for them once every year. At that very hour the children of Israel believed that Aaron had died"; = VN (which is almost identical with P). VNP continue: "and all the people of the congregation of the children of Israel wept for Aaron for thirty days."
[q] Nfi: "(all) of the house (of)."

Notes, Chapter 20

[22] According to the additional paraphrase found in Nf, V, N, and Ps.-J., Israel avoided war with Edom at the divine command; see also Deut 2:5, 19. According to Nf and VN, the command was from their Father in heaven; according to Ps.-J. "from (before) the Memra of the heavens." On "Father in heaven" in Nf, see Introduction to Neofiti Genesis, *The Aramaic Bible,* vol. 1A, pp. 35f.

[23] "against the decree of the Memra concerning (*'l 'sq*) the waters . . . "; HT: "(against) my mouth (= command) at the Waters. . . "

CHAPTER 21

1. And the Canaanite, the king of Arad, who was dwelling in the south, heard[1] *that Aaron, the pious man for whose merits*[2] *the clouds of the glory used to lead Israel forth, had been removed;*[a][3] *and that Miriam the prophetess, for whose merits the well used to come up for them had been removed;* that Israel had reached the route *through which the spies*[b] *had come up.*[4] And they waged war on Israel and took captives[c] from among them. 2. And Israel vowed a vow to the Lord[d] and said:[e] If you will indeed deliver this people into our hands, I will *blot out* their cities."[f] 3. And the Lord heard the voice *of* Israel's *prayer*[5] and delivered the Canaanites

Apparatus, Chapter 21

[a] I.e., died; lit. "had been taken up."

[b] HT: *Ha-Atarim,* a place name; same translation ("spies") also in Ps.-J., Nfmg, VN, Onq., Sam. Tg., Vulg.

[c] Nfmg: "(that) Aaron had died and that the column of the cloud had been taken up and that Miriam the prophetess (had died) and that the well had been hidden. He answered and said to the people: Come, you who make war, and let us go up; let us set battle array against those of the house of Israel, for they have reached the way by which spies come in, and let us set battle array against those of the house of Israel and let us take many captives from them"; VN: "And the Canaanite, the king of Arad who was dwelling in the south, heard that Aaron the pious man had died, for whose merit (or: 'sake') the clouds of glory had protected Israel, and (that) the pillar of cloud had been taken up (or: 'departed'), and that Miriam the prophetess had died, for whose merits (or: 'sake') the well had accompanied them, and that the well had been hidden. He answered and said: O fighting men, come out and let us wage war against Israel, for they have found (?; *msynn*) the way by which the spies enter. And they set battle array against Israel and took many captives from them."

[d] Nfi: "before the Lord."

[e] Lit.: "and they say" = "and they said." Nfmg 1°: "and (Israel) said"; Nfmg 2°: "saying"; the *circellus,* however (erroneously, it would seem), refers the variant *'m[ ]* to the verb *tmswr,* which, according to such a variant, would be *'mswr* ("if indeed I shall deliver"; lit.: "if delivering I shall deliver").

[f] Nfmg: "I will blot out both them and their cities."

Notes, Chapter 21

[1]"(heard) that Aaron. . .had been removed"; the midrash is artificially inserted into the translation and breaks the syntax; the end of the translation ("that Israel. . .") takes up naturally after the insertion. The inserted midrash is on the connection of the clouds of glory with Aaron and of the well with Miriam. The tradition linking the well with Miriam and the cloud with Aaron (and the manna with Moses), and the cessation of each with the death of the person in question, is very old, already clearly stated in *LAB* 20, 8 (1st cent. C.E.?). On Nf Num 21, see McNamara, 1991.

[2]"for whose merits"; *d-bzkwt. . . ;* the Aramaic term can be understood as "for whose sake" or "for whose merit." Sometimes the Aramaic is to be rendered simply as "because of." However, when there is reference to the patriarchs or the mothers of Israel, it is probably to be rendered as "for whose merits." See note to Nf Gen 12:3, 13 (*The Aramaic Bible,* vol. 1A, pp. 86–87).

[3]"had been removed"; *'stlq(t);* lit.: "had been taken up." Here it means: "had departed"; "had died."

[4]"through which the spies had come up"; HT: "(the way of) Atharim." (*drk h-'trym*), a place name of unknown meaning. All the Targums (Onq., Ps.-J., Nf, VN, Nfmg) understand the Hebrew as derived from *twr,* "to seek out, spy out, explore"; likewise the Syr. and Vulg. (*per exploratorum viam*).

[5]"voice of Israel in prayer." The explicit mention of divine response is in keeping with Nf's style of translation. See note to 12:13 above.

into their hands, and they *blotted out*[g] them and their cities;[h] and they called the name of the place[i] Hormah. 4. And they journeyed from Hor[j] the Mountain by the way of the Red Sea to go around the land of the Edomites: and the soul of the people was *distressed* on the way. 5. And the people spoke against[k] *the Memra of the Lord*[m6] and *murmured against* Moses: "Why, now, have you brought us up from Egypt to kill us[n] in the wilderness? For *we have* neither bread *to eat* nor water *to drink,* and our soul is distressed[o7] by this bread, *the nourishment of which* is little." 6. *The Bath Qol*[p8] *came forth from the earth and its voice was heard on high:*[q] *"Come, see, all you creatures; and come, give ear,*[r] *all you sons of the flesh: the serpent was cursed from the beginning and I said to it: 'Dust shall be your food.' I*

Apparatus, Chapter 21

[g] Nfmg: "the Canaanites and they blotted (them) out."
[h] Nfmg: "their cities and he called."
[i] Nfmg: "that (place)"; Hormah = Destruction.
[j] With Nfmg; text: "from the mountain" (*mn ṭwr'*).
[k] Lit.: "after."
[m] Nfmg: "and the people spoke against the name of the Memra of the Lord and against Moses: Why . . ."
[n] Nfi: "to kill (another form) them."
[o] Nfmg: "(for we have no) food and there is no water and our soul is afflicted by (this) bread."
[p] *brt ql',* = Heb. *bat qol* (lit.: "daughter of a voice"), the technical term for the heavenly voice; Nfmg: "and the Lord sent a heavenly voice" (*brt ql'*).
[q] Nfmg: "in the heights."
[r] PVN: "Come see (VN: see), all you sons of men and give ear and hear all you sons of the flesh"; Nfmg: "sons of men, and give ear and hear all."

Notes, Chapter 21

[6]"against the Memra of the Lord . . . Moses"; HT: "against God and against Moses."
[7]"(our soul) is distressed"; HT: "loathes" (*qṣh*). Nf here, as in the other occurrences (Gen 27:46; Exod 1:12; Lev 20:22; Num 21:5; 22:3) translates HT *qwṣ* ("loathe") through the verb *'wq,* "to be distressed."
[8]The *bath Qol,* or "heavenly voice." For the tradition on the serpent, a study of this midrash, and its bearing on the NT, see Hans Maneschg, 1981. A thorough examination of the manna tradition has been made by Bruce J. Malina, 1968, pp. 42–93, for "The Manna Tradition in the Palestinian Targums"; pp. 67–70 for Pal. Tg. Num 21:5-6. As regards v. 6, he notes (p. 68) that the (manna) haggada there seems to be proper to the Pal. Tg. tradition. Its date would have to be that of the origin of these Targums, since there is no datable rabbinic tradition, to our knowledge that might serve as a parallel. For a detailed literary and textual study of the midrash in Nf Num 21:6, see B. Barry Levy, 1987, 2, 107–111. He considers the opening four lines as rhymed, parallel stichs. The point of the midrash is that the snake of Gen 3 will dominate the ungrateful people. God cursed the serpent of Gen 3 but blessed his people through the gift of the Exodus, the manna, the well, and the quails. But while the serpent did not complain about dust being given it as its food, the people complain about the manna. Hence, the serpent will rule over the people.

The midrash makes clear reference to other biblical texts: Gen 3:14 (HT: "and dust shall you eat"), which it gives as paraphrased in Nf (and the Pal. Tg. except in Ps.-J., which is influenced by Onq.); Num 11:26; Exod 16; 17:1ff. There is a clear connection between the paraphrase of Gen 3:14 ("dust shall be your food") here and Nf Gen 3:14, whether by direct dependence of one on the other or dependence of both on a common translation is less certain. The rendering of Gen 3:14 apart, significant linguistic differences have been noted between the bulk of this midrash and Nf's usual style. This may indicate that the midrash originated outside of the Neofiti tradition; see B. Barry Levy, 1987, 2, 111. The gifts of food through manna, water, and quails are also linked together in Exod 16–17; Ps 78:20ff., and Ps 105:40-41. "Its voice was heard on high" seems to echo Jer 31:15. While the midrash is on the serpent (of Gen 3:14) ruling over Israel, it is linked with the central idea of Num 21:6, and it serves as an introduction to the narrative of the fiery serpents, even though these are not said to be "descendants" of, or related to, the serpent of the Genesis narrative.

brought my people up from the land[s] *of Egypt*[t] *and I had manna come down*[u] *from heaven, and I made a well come up for them from the abyss, and I carried quail from the sea for them; and my people has turned*[w] *to murmur before me concerning the manna, that its nourishment is little. The serpent which does not murmur concerning its food will come*[x] *and rule over the people which has murmured*[y] *concerning their food." Wherefore* the Lord[z] let loose[aa] burning serpents among the people: and they bit the people, and many people[bb] of Israel died. 7. And the people came to Moses and said: "We have sinned, for we have *murmured*[9] against[cc] you. Pray *before* the Lord that he make the serpents[dd] pass from us."[ee] And Moses prayed for the people.[ff] 8. And the Lord[gg] said to Moses: "Make *a bronze serpent*[10] and set it on *an elevated place;*[11] <and it shall come to pass that every one who is bitten by the serpent and looks on it, shall live."[hh] 9. And Moses made a bronze serpent and put it on *an elevated place*>;[ii] and if the serpent bit anyone, he used to look on the bronze serpent and live.[jj] 10. And the children of Israel (set out)[kk] and encamped in Oboth. 11. And they set out from Oboth and encamped in the Passes of

Apparatus, Chapter 21

[s] Nfmg: "(your food) and it did not murmur against its food; I brought my people redeemed out of Egypt"; = PVN (P: ". . . out of the land of Egypt").

[t] Nfi: "(my people), from Egypt"; = VN.

[u] Nfi: "I had (manna) come down" (without "and"); = P.

[w] Nfmg: "(the manna); I carried quail from the sea for them; I made a well come up for them from the abyss; my people has turned . . ."; = PVN.

[x] Nfmg: "(concerning the manna) saying: Our soul is afflicted by the bread, the nourishment of which is light. Wherefore there will come . . ."; = PVN.

[y] Nfmg: "and he will bite the people that murmured . . ."; = P; cf. VN.

[z] Nfmg: "(its food) and the Memra of the Lord let loose . . ."; = PVN.

[aa] In text "created," *bry;* corr. to *gry.*

[bb] Nfmg: "and they bit the people and great multitudes (Greek loan word *ochlos*) died from them . . ."; = PVN.

[cc] Lit.: "behind"; Nfmg: "against the name of the (Memra of . . .)."

[dd] Nfmg: "the serpents" (the same word in fem. plur.).

[ee] Nfmg: "and against the name of your Memra. Pray, therefore, and let him make (the serpents) pass from us."

[ff] Lit.: "for the hands of the people"; Nfmg: "for (or: 'concerning') (the people)."

[gg] Nfmg: "the Memra of the Lord."

[hh] Nfmg: "on high and it shall come to pass that anyone who is bitten by the serpent shall look upon the bronze serpent and live (lit.: 'and be alive')."

[ii] Missing in text; supplied in Nfmg by [A]; the *circellus* over one word of the annotator [A], however, was added later by the annotator [LL] in red ink; v. 9a in PVN.

[jj] Nfmg: "a bronze serpent and set it ['on high' is missing], and it came to pass that anyone who was bitten by the serpents used to look on the bronze serpent and live (lit.: 'be alive')"; P: "and it was that when the serpent bit him he raised his eyes in prayer to his Father who is in heaven"; VN: "and Moses made a bronze serpent and set it on a high place, and anyone who was bitten by the (or: 'a') serpent would raise his face in prayer to his Father who is in heaven and would look at the bronze serpent and live."

[kk] Missing in text and in margin.

Notes, Chapter 21

[9] "murmured"; HT: "spoken."

[10] "a bronze serpent"; HT: "a seraph."

[11] "on an elevated place"; HT: *'l ns;* RSV: "on a pole"; Nf renders *ns* in Exod 17:14 as *ns* ("sign, miracle") and in Num 26:10 as *nsywn,* "a trial"; "a test."

Abarayya,[mm] [12] in the wilderness which is opposite the Moabites towards the sunrise. 12. They set out from there and encamped in the wadi of Zered.[nn] 13. They set out from there and encamped beyond the Arnon, which is in the wilderness, which goes forth from the boundaries of the Amorites; for the Arnon is the boundary of the Moabites, between the Moabites and the Amorites. 14. For this reason[13] *written*[oo] *and explained in the Book of the Law of the Lord—which is compared to the Book of the Wars—are the wonders*[pp] *which the Lord*[qq] *wrought with Israel when they stood by the Red Sea, and the mighty deeds he worked with them when they crossed* the wadis[rr] of the Arnon.[14] 15. *When Israel was crossing the wadis of the*

Apparatus, Chapter 21

[mm] *Megizat 'Ibrayya;* MT: 'Iyye ha-'Abarim; cf. Num 27:12; 33:44; and Deut 32:49.

[nn] Nfmg: "(in the torrent) *šrwwyyh*" (meaning uncertain; possibly = *šyr'* [= *šyrywnh*]; cf. Jastrow, 1569, 1631; ? = "of the coat of mail"). The meaning of *syr'* in Pal. Tg. Exod 28:32; 39:23 is quite uncertain: "coat of mail" (Jastrow, 1569; Klein, 1980, 2, 137, rendering VN Exod 28:32); "woven garment" (Sokoloff, 376).

[oo] Nfi: "it is said"; PVN: "for this reason it is said (P: 'said, written and explained') in the book of the Law of the Lord, which is compared to the book of the Wars, the signs and mighty deeds which the Lord (P: "Memra of the Lord") performed for his people the children of Israel when they were standing by the Reed Sea; he acted (P: 'he shall act') likewise with them when they were crossing (P: 'when they cross') the wadis of the Arnon."

[pp] Nfmg: "and the mighty deeds"; = PVN.

[qq] Nfmg: "the Memra of the Lord"; = PVN.

[rr] Nfmg: "(by the Reed Sea,) thus (the Memra of) the Lord shall do to them when they pass over the wadis of the . . ."; = PVN. Note the translation of HT's *b-swfh:* "by the Sea of Suph" in Nf, Onq., and Vulg. Vulg. renders as Nfmg: *Sicut fecit in Mari Rubro, sic faciet in torrentibus Arnon.*

Notes, Chapter 21

[12]"Passes of the Hebrews"; MT: *'Iyye ha-'Abarim;* cf. Num 27:12; 33:44; Deut 32:49.

[13]The HT (RSV) has: "wherefore it is written in the Book of the Wars of the Lord: 'Waheb in Shaphah, and the valleys of the Arnon, (13) and the slope of the valleys that extends to the seat of Ar, and leans to the borders of Moab.'"

[14]Apart from the introductory words, these verses in the Hebrew text are particularly difficult. Nonetheless, from the central unity in the targumic renderings (Onq.; Pal. Tgs., Ps.-J.) it appears that a targumic exegesis of the verses came into being very early. Verse 14 is rendered in the RSV: "Wherefore it is written in the Book of the Wars of the Lord: "Waheb in Shaphah (*'t whb bswph*) and the valleys of the Arnon" (*w't hnḥlym 'rnwn*). For a study of Nf text, see B. Barry Levy, 1987, 2, 112–115.

In 21:14 we are moving more deeply into a feature of the Pal. Tg. treatment of Num 21, which is that the paraphrase is a free development of a deep understanding of the text and instead of being translated, the underlying HT is woven into free-flowing midrash. "Written and explained," *ktyb wmprš,* or "explicitly written" (Sokoloff, 1990, 51, taking the last word as coming from *prš* 4, "to specify"). In Nf the paraphrase occurs generally to introduce a Scripture citation: Nf Exod 28:17; Lev 22:27; Deut 27:8 (a related formula is: *dkn ktbh mprš w'mr,* "for Scripture specifically says", Frg. Tg. Gen 35:9).

"The Book" of the HT is identified in Nf (and Pal. Tg.) as "the Book of the Law of the Lord." The HT *spr mlḥmt yyy* is generally taken by scholars today as one phrase: the Book of the Wars of the Lord. The targumic traditions seem to have taken "book" as in the absolute case, and the "wars of the Lord" as the book's content; cf. Onq.: "the Book concerning the Wars"; for the Pal. Tgs. (Nf, Frg. Tg.) these wars are the wonders of "Suph" and "Arnon," Suph being understood as "the Sea of Suph," i.e., of Reeds, and Arnon as the River Arnon. Thus also Onq. and Vulg. The Pal. Tg. tradition (Nf, P, V) and also Onq., omit *'t whb* of the HT.

Arnon, [15] *the Amorites hid themselves within the caves of the wadis of the Arnon, saying: "When the children*[ss] *of Israel*[tt] *are crossing, we will go out against them and kill them." But the master of all worlds, the Lord, who knows what is in the hearts, and before whom what is in the kidneys is manifest, made a signal; he signaled to the mountains, and their summits*[uu] *were joined one to the other and crushed the heads*

Apparatus, Chapter 21

[ss] Nfi: "(when) Israel (is crossing)."

[tt] Nfmg: "(of the Arnon,) the Amorites hid themselves in the caves saying one to the other: When Israel (is crossing)"; cf. similar text of P, which adds: "which are in the wadis of the Arnon" after "caves"; VN: "when the children of Israel were crossing the wadis of the Arnona the Moabites (P: 'the Amorites') hid in the caves which are in the wadis, saying: When the children of Israel are crossing we will go out against them and kill them. The master of all the world, the Lord, who knows what is in the hearts and before whom what is in the kidneys is manifest motioned to the mountains and they knocked their heads one against the other and they crushed the heads of their warriors and the valleys ran red with the blood of their dead. And Israel was marching above on the tops of the mountains and was unaware of the miracles and mighty deeds which the Lord had worked with them in the wadis of the Arnon. And Lehayyath, the city that was not a partner in their counsel, was spared (lit.: 'was spared for them'), and behold it is near the borders of the Edomites"; P: "when the Israelites were crossing the wadis of the Arnon, the Amorites were hidden in the caves that are in the wadis of the Arnon, saying one to the other: When the Israelites are crossing over the wadi of the Arnon we will go out against them and blot them out, and kill kings and rulers. But the master of all the world, the Lord, who knows what is in the hearts and before whom what is in the kidneys is manifest, signaled to the mountain tops and they knocked their heads one against the other and cracked the heads of their warriors and the wadis flowed with their blood and the Israelites were not aware of the miracles and mighty deeds which were performed with them in the wadis of the Arnon. And afterwards the mountains were separated and returned to their places, and the Israelites came to know of the miracles and mighty deeds which were done for them in the wadi of the Arnon. And Lehayyath, the city which was not in their counsel, was spared and behold it is near the borders of the Moabites."

[uu] Nfmg: "before them and we shall blot them out and we shall slay kings and rulers. In that same hour the Lord signaled to the mountains and the summits were joined"; cf. P.

Notes, Chapter 21

[15]In v. 15 we move more deeply still into the characteristic texture of Nf (Pal. Tg.) Num 21, with the underlying HT scarcely recognizable in the paraphrase. At first sight, the Targum in v. 15 would seem to have little connection with the Hebrew text. The contact with the Hebrew is probably to be found towards the end: "and the torrents overflowed with their blood." Behind this probably lies HT *w'šd nḥlym,* rendered in the RSV as "and the slope of the valleys." The HT word *'šd* is understood through the Aramaic root *'šd,* "pour out" (cf. Nfmg Deut 24:6; *'šdwt,* shedding [innocent blood]) and rendered *stp:* "the wadis were awash with their blood" (Sokoloff, 545). Onq. understood the HT in the same manner: "and the flowing (*špwk*) of the streams," but not in the sense of shedding blood, as Nf (and the Pal. Tg.) does.

Ar of the HT (*nṭh lšbt 'r;* RSV: "that extends to the seat of Ar"), is taken to be Ar Moab, a natural understanding in this context. Ar Moab of Deut 2:9, 29, and Aroer of Deut 2:36; 4:48 are rendered in Nf (and the Pal. Tg.) as Lehayyath (*lḥyt, lḥyyt*) Moab, as is Ar of Num 21:15, 28. It is also so rendered in Onq. Num 21:28 and as Leḥayyath in Onq. Num 21:15. Leḥayyath seems to be a place name. Its root meaning is uncertain. M. Jastrow (s.v., pp. 702–703) gives as meaning "palisades, in general fortresses," instancing Tg. Esth. 9:27. Likewise J. Levy, 1881, 408. The word is not registered in M. Sokoloff (op. cit.). The HT *wnš'n lgbwl mw'b,* RSV: "and extends to the borders of Moab" is rendered "and behold it is near the boundaries of the Moabites." In keeping with this basic paraphrase of the verse, Nf (and the other Pal. Tg. texts) insert a midrash on miracles believed to have been worked for the Israelites when crossing the Arnon, a tradition found in other Jewish (and also in Christian) texts. See also Num 21:24, 26, 28, 36; Deut 2.

of their heroes; and the torrents overflowed[ww] *with their blood; but they did not know the wonders and mighty deeds that the Lord had wrought with them in the wadis (of the Arnon); and after that they were explained (to them), and they went to their places. Lahavath,*[xx] *the city*[yy] *that was not in their counsel, was spared;*[zz] *and behold* it is near the boundaries of *the* Moab*ites.* 16. And from there[16] *the well*[17] *was given to them.* This is the well of which the Lord[a] said to Moses: "Gather the people together and I will give them water." 17. Then[b] Israel sang this song *of praise:*[c][18] "Spring up, O well";[d] they sang to it; *and it sprang up.*[19] 18. It is the well which the princes[20] *of the world, Abraham, Isaac, and Jacob,* dug *from the beginning;*[e] *the intelligent ones of the people perfected it, the seventy*[f] *sages who were*

Apparatus, Chapter 21

[ww] Nfi: "and emptied themselves"; Nfmg: "and the torrents flowed with their blood and Lehayyath the city . . ."

[xx] The word means "fortresses"; HT: Ar, capital of Moab.

[yy] Nfmg: "(the torrents) with the blood of their slain. And the Israelites walked upon the tops of the mountains above, and they did not know the wonders in the wadis of the Arnon. And Lehayyath, the city." For "Lehayyath the city," cp. Ar of HT, which in 22:36 is *'Ir Moab,* "the city of Moab."

[zz] Nfi: "was spared for them"; = VN.

[a] Nfmg: "(and from there) the well came up, that is the well (of) which the Memra of the Lord said . . ."

[b] Nfmg: "behold (then)"; = VN; cf. P.

[c] Nfmg: "the praises of this song"; = PVN.

[d] Nfmg: "(spring up,) O well! spring up, O well!"; = P.

[e] VN: "the well which the princes of the world dug from the beginning; Abraham, Isaac, and Jacob perfected it; the intelligent ones of the world, the Sanhedrin, the seventy sages, who were distinguished, found it with their staffs, Moses and Aaron the scribes of Israel. And from the wilderness it was given to them as a gift"; P: "the well which the princes of the people dug from the beginning; Abraham, Isaac, and Jacob perfected it, the seventy wise men, the Sanhedrin of Israel, the scribes with their staffs, they are the scribes of Israel, Moses, and Aaron. From the wilderness it was given to them as a gift."

[f] Nfmg: "the Sanhedrin of Israel, the seventy (. . . perfected it)"; Nfi: "the intelligent ones of the world, the seventy . . ."

Notes, Chapter 21

[16] This is a midrash on the well that was believed to have followed the Israelites during the desert wanderings. It is inserted into the present context and developed especially through the interpretation of place names as common names, beginning with the place name Beer (meaning "well") in v. 16. While the greater part of vv. 16-17 is translated, very little of the original of vv. 18, 19, 20a remains unchanged. In this v. 19 in particular represents a further stage in the transformation of the original Hebrew in the interests of midrash, already in evidence in earlier verses. The Pal. Tg. paraphrase is for the greater part found also in Onq., in Pseudo-Philo, *LAB* (10:7; 11:15; 20:8), and the Tosefta, all evidence of its early date of composition.

[17] Verse 16 in the HT reads: "And from there to Beer"; Beer in Hebrew meaning "well." Onq. (and Ps.-J.) understand as Nf and the Pal. Tg.: "At that time the well was given to them." See G. Vermes, 1963, 159–169, reproduced in G. Vermes, 1975, 127–138.

[18] "song of praise," Nf's usual translation of *šyr(h)* of the HT; also in Nf Exod 15:1; Deut 31:19, 22, 32, 34. (*šbḥ šyrth,* "praise of (this) song"). There is a different rendering, however, in Nf Deut 21:30.

[19] "and it sprung up"; an addition in Nf.

[20] The HT (RSV) has: "The well which the princes, which the nobles of the people delved, with the scepter (*bmḥqq;* MT *bimḥoqeq*) and with their staves. And from the wilderness they went on to Mattanah." In the Pal. Tg. midrash the princes of the HT are understood as the patriarchs, and the nobles as the sages. HT *meḥoqeq* is taken as deriving from *ḥq,* "statute," and rendered as "scribe"; so also in the other two occurrences of the word, Gen 49:10 and Deut 33:21. Onq. is similar, Num 21:18: "the leaders of the people dug, the scribes with their staffs." There is a similar interpretation in the Damascus Document (CD V 1, 7): "the Mehoqeq is the interpreter of the Torah"; see G. Vermes, 1975, 45–55.

distinguished; the scribes of Israel, Moses, and Aaron[g] *measured it* with their rods; and from the wilderness[21] *it was given to them* (as) a gift.[h] 19. *And after the well had been given to them as a gift,*[i] *it went on to become for them swelling torrents; and after it had become swelling torrents, it went on to go up with them to the tops of the mountains and to go down with them to the deep*[j] *valleys;* 20. *and after it had gone up with them to the tops of the high mountains*[k][22] and had gone down with them to the deep valleys, it was hidden[m] from them in the valley which is at the *boundaries* of *the* Moab*ites,* the top *of the height*[n] *which* looks out[o] opposite *Beth*

Apparatus, Chapter 21

[g] Nfi: "Moses and Aaron the scribes of Israel"; Nfmg: "the two scribes."

[h] Ps.-J.: "it was given to them as a gift"; Nfmg: "as the gift." The Aramaic translator renders the place names *Midbar* and *Mattanah* of the MT respectively as "wilderness" and "present" or "gift." VN: "and after the well had been given to them as a gift, it went on to become for them overflowing, swelling torrents. It went on to go up to the top of the mountains and went down with them to the deep valleys"; P: "and after it had been given to them as a gift, it went on to become for them overflowing torrents, and after it had gone on to become for them overflowing torrents, it went on to go up with them to the top of the mountains and went down with them to the deep valleys."

[i] Once again *Mattanah* is rendered by a common noun, and *Nahaliel* as "swelling torrents," and *Bamot* as "tops of the mountains."

[j] Nfmg: "(for them) overflowing torrents, it turned to go down (corr. to: 'go up') with them to the tops of the mountains and to go down with them to the deep ravines (or: 'torrents')"

[k] Nfmg: "after it had turned to go up with them to the tops of the mountains and to go down with them to the deep ravines (or: 'torrents'), the well was hidden from them <. . .> that (is) in the frontiers of the Moabites, on the top of the height which looks towards Beth-Jeshimon"; P: "and after it had come to have gone up with them to the top of the mountains and had gone down with them to the deep valleys, there was hidden from them the well [Nfmg: in the valley] that is on the border of the Moabites, Resh Ramatha [= the Top of the Height] that looks out opposite Beth-Jeshimon"; VN: "the well was hidden from them <in the glen?> which is on the border of the Moabites, Resh Ramatha which looks out opposite Abeth-Jeshimon." MT has: "and from Bamoth to the valley of the Plain of Moab, to the top of Pisgah, which dominates Jeshimon."

[m] Nfi: "it was cut off"; Nfi, however, should probably be corrected in conformity with the text.

[n] Nfi: "on the top of the height that is at the borders of the Moabites and behold, it looks . . ."

[o] Nfi: ""looks"; from the root *ṣuf;* in the text from the root *sfy.*

Notes, Chapter 21

[21]"And from the wilderness it was given to them (as) a gift. . ." The HT has a series of place names: "And from the wilderness (to) Mattanah. And from Mattanah to Nahaliel and from Nahaliel to Bamoth." The paraphrase of the place names of Num 21:18b-19 in the light of the well midrash is found already in *LAB* (10:7) "for forty years he brought forth a well of water to follow them"; *LAB* 11, 15. "And it followed them in the wilderness forty years and went up to the mountain with them and went down into the plains." So also Onq. Num 21:19: "Now since it was given to them, it went down with them to the valleys, and from the valleys it went up with them to the high country." The paraphrase of Num 21:19 is also found in *ṭ. Sukk.* 3, 11: "traveling with them up the mountains and going down with them to the valleys," going on to cite Num 21:18 in Hebrew. On 21:19-20 see also B. Barry Levy, 1987, 2, 117f.

[22]The HT (RSV) has: "And from Bamoth to the valley lying in the region of Moab by the top of Pisqah which looks down upon the desert" (*ha-yešimon*). The paraphrase in Nf (and Pal. Tg.), continues the description of the well of v. 19 and again treats the biblical narrative rather freely, in the overall interest of the midrash, which is to give a rather full account of the well and insert it here by reason of the occurrence of the name Beer in 21:17. In one tradition the well ("Miriam's well") ceased to come up at the death of Miriam, which occurred at Kadesh (i.e., Reqem; i.e., Petra) (Num 20:1), while here its disappearance is said to have been at the boundaries of the Moabites.

Jeshimon. 21. And Israel sent messengers to Sihon, the king of the Amorites, saying: 22. "I would *now* pass through your land;[p] we will not turn aside into fields or vineyards,[q] nor will we drink water[r] *of the cisterns.*[23] We will walk on the King's Highway[s] until such time as we have passed through your territory." 23. But Sihon did not permit Israel to pass through his territory; and Sihon gathered together all his people and went out against Israel into the wilderness, and he came[t] to Jahza[u] and they waged war with Israel. 24. And Israel *blotted* him *out*[w] at the edge of the sword and took possession of his land from the Arnon to the Jabbok, to the *borders*[x][24] of the children of Ammon;[y] for the border[z] of the sons of the Ammonites was strong. 25. And Israel took all these cities, and Israel dwelt in all the cities of the Amorites, in Heshbon and in all its *villages.*[25] 26. For Heshbon was the city of Sihon, the king of the Amorites, and he had waged war[aa] with the first king[bb] of the Moabites[26] and had taken the land from him[cc] as far as the Arnon. 27. For this reason the *composers of parables*[dd][27] say: "Go into Heshbon, let it be built, and let the city of Sihon be perfected.[ee] 28. For *a people*[ff] *of heroes*[28] *burning like* the fire[gg]

Apparatus, Chapter 21

[p] P: "I would now pass through your land; we shall not commit acts of violence (or: 'rape'); we shall not seduce virgins, nor shall we seek out married women. Along the Royal Road (Greek loan word *strata*) we shall go until such time as we shall have passed through your territory."
[q] Nfmg: "neither into field nor into vineyard."
[r] Nfmg: "(nor will we drink) from (cisterns)." This differs from HT.
[s] Nfmg: "by the royal road (lit.: 'road of the king') we shall go"; = P.
[t] Nfmg: "and they came."
[u] MT: Jahaz; cf. Josh 13:18, etc.
[w] Nfmg: "and Israel slew him."
[x] Or: "to the territory."
[y] Nfmg: "(Jabbok; to the) sons of the Ammonites."
[z] In the text, *tḥwmyhwn; tḥwm,* "border," "territory."
[aa] Nfmg: "(had set battle) array."
[bb] *mlkyhwn dm'b-.*
[cc] Nfmg, Nfi: "from his hand."
[dd] Lit.: "those who make proverbs (or: 'comparisons')."
[ee] Lit.: "shall be constructed and perfected." The Aramaic translator has not grasped the temporal value of the archaic Hebrew verbal tenses: the *yiqtol (yaqtalu)* as an indicative narrative mode of the past or present.
[ff] Nfmg: "(For) an impudent king has come forth like fire from Heshbon, and warring legions have come forth like flames of Gehenna from the city of Sihon, (destroying) Lahayyath of the Moabites . . ."; PVN: "For a people of warriors burning like fire have gone forth from Heshbon; fighting men like flames of fire from the city of Sihon, king of the Amorites (P: 'of the Moabites'; VN: 'went forth from the city of Sihon. They killed the kings of the Amorites'). They blotted out Lahayyath, the city of the Moabites. They killed their priests who were worshiping and sacrificing (VN: 'who were sacrificing') before the idols of the Arnon."
[gg] Nfmg: "like fire."

Notes, Chapter 21

[23]"of the cisterns," *gwbyn,* as in 20:17; HT: "from a well."
[24]"boundaries," *tḥwmyhwn* (instead of *tḥwmhwn*), plur.; HT sing. This is one of the many instances in Nf in which the *yod* is probably intended to indicate a vocalic shewa. An *aleph* is used for the same purpose in Nf Gen 26:1.
[25]"villages"; HT, lit: "daughters."
[26]"king of the Moabites," *mlkyhwn d-,* normally "kings (of the Moabites," *mlkyhwn dmw'byy*). As in 21:24 (see note), the *yod* merely denotes a vocalic shewa.
[27]*mtlyyh,* also in VN; HT: *mšlym* (RSV: "ballad singers)."
[28]"a people of heroes. . .like fire; fighting men. . . like flame"; "fire" and "flame" of the HT are taken as symbols for warriors.

have gone forth from Heshbon; *fighting men*[hh] *have gone forth like* the flame from the city of Sihon; *they have blotted out Lehawwath*[ii][29] of the Moab*ites* (and *slain the priests*)[jj][30] *who sacrificed before the bamoth*[kk] of the Arnon. 29. Woe[mm] to you, Moabites! The people *who have sacrificed before*[nn] *the idol*[oo] Chemosh have come to an end, have been *blotted out;* he has handed over their sons *chained in neck-irons*[pp][31] and their daughters in captivity to the king[qq][32] of the Amorites, Sihon. 30. And *the kingdom has ceased*[33] for Heshbon *and the dominion*[rr] *for* Dibon,[ss] and *its highways are devastated*[34] as far as the *Fortress of Nephahayya,*[tt][35] *which is near* Medeba." 31. And Israel dwelt in the land of the Amorites. 32. And Moses sent to spy out Jazer and they conquered[uu] its *villages*[ww] and *blotted out* the

Apparatus, Chapter 21

[hh] Nfi: "the war."
[ii] Nfmg: "Lahayyath of the Moabites."
[jj] Erased by the censor because the word *kwmr* means "priest" in the pejorative sense (of idols, etc.).
[kk] Nfmg: "the idols"; = PVN.
[mm] Nfmg: "Woe!"; written differently, as in VN; PVN: "Woe to you Moabites! the worshipers of the idol Kemosh have come to an end and are lost; you have handed over your sons bound in prisoners' chains (Latin loan word *collarium*) and your daughters into captivity to Sihon, king (*mlkyhwn*) of the Amorites."
[nn] Nfi: "(before) Kemosh."
[oo] Nfmg: "you have come to an end, you are lost, (you) who worship idols"; = PVN.
[pp] Nfmg: "you have handed over your sons bound in a collar"; = PVN.
[qq] *mlkyhwn.*
[rr] Nfi: "and the dominion" (another form of the same word).
[ss] Nfmg: "and (the kingdom has ceased) from the house of Heshbon and the dominion from the house of Dibon."
[tt] = of the smiths; Nfmg: "the cit(ies) as far as the market place of Nefahayya (= of the smiths)."
[uu] Nfmg: "(to spy out) Makwar and they conquered"; = PVN.
[ww] Nfi: "the villages"; = VN.

Notes, Chapter 21

[29]"blotted out Lehawwath"; HT: "it devoured Ar of Moab." As in 21:15, in PVN and Nfmg, we should probably read "Lehayyath." See note to 21:15.
[30]"slain the priests. . .bamoth," HT: "the lords of the heights of the Arnon," the "heights," *bamoth,* being understood as the cultic high places, and the "lords" as their priests.
[31]"chained in neck-irons," *qwlry';* a Greek or Latin loan word (*kollarion, collare*); HT: "he has made his sons fugitives." There is a similar understanding in Onq.
[32]"king of. . . ," *mlkyhwn d'mwryy.* Here again the *yod* is intended to indicate a vocal shewa; see 21:24.
[33]"the kingdom has ceased," etc. In the HT v. 30 (*wnyrm 'bd ḥšbwn 'd dybwn wnššym 'd npḥ 'šr 'd-mydb'*) has a number of obscurities and has been variously understood and rendered. Nf takes *nyrm* (? "we have shot at them") as deriving from *nyr,* in Aramaic, "a yoke," but apparently as a symbol of royalty. It joins *ḥšbwn* ("Heshbon") with this and gives its translation a poetic symmetry. Onq. understands here as Nf; "royalty has ceased at Heshbon." Nf inserts *wšlṭwn,* "dominion," for poetic balance (*mlkw* and *šlṭwn, mlk wšlyṭ* often occurring as a pair in Nf). See B. Barry Levy, 1987, 2, 119f. In general Onq. for this verse is in the same interpretative tradition but keeps closer to the underlying HT.
[34]Nf understands *w-nššym* (RSV, margin: "we have laid waste"), as derived from *šmm,* "to lay waste," and expands by inserting as subject "its highways." Onq. understands in a similar manner: "and desolation was laid."
[35]"The Fortress of Nephahayya"; MT: "Nophah." The name occurs only here in the HT and Targums. Possibly Nf is a mere transformation of the HT name and is not intended as an actual identification. Onq. has: "Nophah."

Amorites who *were dwelling* there.[xx] 33. And they turned and went up[36] towards[yy] *Butnin;*[zz 37] and Og, the king of *Butnin,* came out against them,[a] he and all his people, to wage war[b] at Edrei. 34. *And it came to pass that when Moses saw Og, the king of Butnin, he feared and trembled before him, and said:*[c] *"Is not this Og*[d] *who jeered at*[e] *Abraham*[f] *and Sarah, saying to them:*[g] *'Abraham and Sarah are like beautiful trees standing beside springs*[h] *of water, but producing no fruit.'" Because of this the Lord has preserved him alive until he saw their children and their children's children; and he came and fell into their hands.* And *after this* the Lord said to Moses: "Do not fear *before* him, for I have delivered him and all his people[i] into your hand; and you shall do to him as you have done to Sihon, the king of the Amorites who dwelt in Heshbon. 35. And they *blotted out*[j] him and his sons and all his people until there was not a survivor[k] left to him,[m] and they took possession of his land.

Apparatus, Chapter 21

[xx] Nfmg: "(who were) there"; = PVN.

[yy] Lit.: "and they directed themselves and went up."

[zz] Nfmg: "Botnayyim"; another form of the Aramaic name for Bashan of HT.

[a] Nfmg: "(the king) of Butneyin to meet us"; cf. Ps.-J.

[b] Nfmg: "to arrange battle array (= to wage war) in Edrei."

[c] Nfmg: "When Moses saw the wicked Og, he feared and trembled before him. He said"; VN: "And it was that when Moses saw Og [portion of text may have been omitted here; cf. V Deut 3:2 and 3:27] and he said: Are not you the wicked Og who used to taunt Abraham and Sarah and say: Abraham and Sarah are like beautiful trees that stand beside springs of water but bear no fruits. For which reason the Lord, the Holy One, may his name be blessed, kept him alive for many years until such time as he had seen their children and their children's children, and it came about that he fell into their hands. And the Lord said to Moses: Do not fear him, because I have delivered him into your hand, with all his people and the land; and you shall do to him as you have done to Sihon, the king of (*mlkyhwn*) the Amorites who dwelt in Heshbon"; P: "And when Moses saw Og, the wicked king, he shook and trembled before him and said: Is not this the wicked Og who used to taunt (marg. gl.: 'jeer at'; = Nf) Abraham and Sarah, saying: Abraham and Sarah, you are like beautiful trees planted and standing beside springs of water, but who do not produce fruits. For this reason the Holy One, blessed be he, may his name be praised, kept him alive and waited for him many years until such time as he had seen their children and their children's children, numerous as the dust of the earth, and he fell into their hands. And the Memra of the Lord said to Moses: Do not fear him, because I have delivered him into your hand with all his people and all his land. And you shall do to him as you have done to Sihon, king of (*mlkyhwn*) the Amorites who dwelt in Heshbon."

[d] Nfmg +: "the wicked" as P.

[e] Nfi: "this is Og who jeered."

[f] Nfmg: "our fathers, Abraham . . ."

[g] Nfi: "saying: Abraham."

[h] Nfmg: "(saying to them:) You appear planted beside the sources."

[i] Nfi +: "and his land."

[j] Nfmg: "and they slew."

[k] Nfmg: "(until there was not) a survivor left" (different forms).

[m] Nfi: "(not left) to him."

Notes, Chapter 21

[36]"turned (and went up)"; or: "they directed themselves to." HT: *pnh,* rendered here, as elsewhere in Nf (e.g., Num 14:25; 17:7), by *kwyn,* "turned, directed (themselves) towards."

[37]*Butnim* (written *btnyn* and *bwtnyn*); HT: Bashan; in Nf Num 32:33 *mwtnyn.* This is the regular rendering of Bashan in Nf (apart from Num 32:33, which has *mwtnyn*)—*bwtnyn:* Num 21:33; Deut 1:4; 3:3, 4, 10, 11, 13, 14; 11:43; 29:6; *bwtnyyn:* Num 34:15; Deut 3:1; 4:47; 33:2; *bny btnyy* in Deut 32:14. It is rendered *Batnin* in the Sam. Tg.; as *Matnan* in Onq. and as *Matnin* in the Syr. See note on Onq. Num 21:31 in B. Grossfeld, *The Aramaic Bible,* vol. 8 (1988), 129, with reference to D. Raphael, *Beth Miqra* 96 (1983) 73 (in Hebrew). See also McNamara, 1972, 192.

CHAPTER 22

1. And the children of Israel set out and encamped in the plain of Moab, at[a] the ford of the <Jordan>[b] of[c] Jericho. 2. And Balak, the son of Zippor, saw all that Israel had done to the Amorites. 3. And the Moabites feared greatly before the people because they were *strong,*[1] and the Moabites were distressed before the children[d] of Israel. 4. And the Moabites said[e] to the *wise men*[2] of the Midianites: "Now *this*[3] assembly[f] *will blot out*[g4] all *the cities*[5] round[h] about[i] as the ox *with its tongue licks up the grass of the face*[j] of the field." And Balak, the son of Zippor, *was* king[k] of *the* Moab*ites* at that time.[m] 5. And he sent messengers to Balaam, the son of Beor, *the interpreter*[n] *of dreams,*[6] who was by *the bank of* the River[o] (in)[7] the land of the sons of his people,[p] to call him, saying: "Behold, a *numerous*[8] people has come out of Egypt and behold, it has covered the face of the land and behold, they are dwelling opposite me. 6. And now,[q] come, I pray,[r] curse this people (for me), because they are stronger than we; perhaps I will be able to *blot* them *out,* and I will drive[s] them from the land; for I know that (what)[t] you bless will be blessed

Apparatus, Chapter 22

[a] Nfmg: "from the ford of the Jordan."
[b] In text by mistake: *lyrḥ'* ("to Jericho").
[c] Or: "opposite Jericho."
[d] Nfmg: "(because) they were many and the Moabites were distressed for their lives before the people of the sons of . . ."
[e] Lit.: "and they say."
[f] Nfmg: "and the Moabites said to the wise men (MT, Onq., Ps.J.: 'to the elders') of the Midianites: Now (or: 'Thus') will this assembly lick."
[g] Nfmg: "they shall be blotted out."
[h] Nfmg: "(the cities) around."
[i] Nfmg: "(around) us."
[j] Nfmg: "which is upon the face of."
[k] Nfmg: "the king."
[m] hour = time; MT, Onq., Ps.-J.: "at that time."
[n] Reading *ptwrh* of text, with Nfmg, as *ptwr;* P: *ptyr.*
[o] The Euphrates, as explicitly said in Ps.-J.
[p] Translating HT place name *'mw* (RSV: Amaw) as a common name. Sam. Tg., Vulg., and P have "Ammon."
[q] Nfmg: "and now" (another form)."
[r] *k'n* (lit.: "now") is the ordinary translation of HT *-n',* cohortative.
[s] Lit.: "(perhaps) we can set battle array against them and I will drive (them) out."
[t] Nfi: "what" (absent from text).

Notes, Chapter 22

[1]"strong"; HT: "many" (*rb*).
[2]"wise men"; HT: "elders." As general in Nf's translation; see above Introd. III, 18.
[3]"this"; an addition in Nf.
[4]"blot out"; HT (RSV): "lick up." Nf gives a literal translation to the second occurrence of the verb in this verse.
[5]"the cities"; "with its tongue"; additions in Nf.
[6]"the interpreter of dreams"; HT: "to Pethor." The place name is retained in the LXX, Onq., and Syr. The Pal. Tg. (Nf, P) interprets through the Aramaic root *ptr* (Hebrew *pšr*), "to interpret dreams." So also *LAB* 18, 2: (*interpretem somniorum*); Vulg. (*ariolum,* "a soothsayer"); Josephus, *Ant.* 4, 6, 2, 9, #104; Philo, *VM* 48, 8, 264. Both place name and interpretation combined in Ps.-J., and *Num. R.* 20, 7. For a detailed study of Num 22–24 in the Targums and in Jewish tradition, see G. Vermes, "The Story of Balaam—The Scriptural Origin of Haggadah," in *Scripture and Tradition in Judaism. Haggadic Studies,* Studia Post-Biblica 4 (Leiden: Brill, 1961; rev. ed. 1973), pp. 127–177; in part earlier "Deux traditions sur Balaam—Nombres xxii.2-21 et ses interprétations midrashiques," *Cahiers Sioniens* 9 (1955) 289–302.
[7]"by the bank of the river"; HT: "by the river."
[8]"numerous"; an expansion in Nf.

and what you curse[u] is cursed."[w] 7. And the *princes* of the Moabites and the *princes*[9] of the Midianites[x] went with the *wages*[y] *of* divination *sealed*[z] in their hands;[10] and they came to Balaam and spoke the words of[aa] Balak with him. 8. And he said to them: "Lodge here *this day and* tonight[11] and I will bring back word[bb] to you according as it is spoken with me *from before*[12] the Lord." And the princes of the Moabites dwelt with[cc] Balaam. 9. And *the Memra of the Lord was revealed*[13] to Balaam and said: "Who are those men[dd] *who are* with you?" 10. And Balaam said *before the Lord:*[14] "Balak, the son of Zippor, the king of the Moabites, has sent to me (saying): 11. 'Behold, a *numerous* people[15] has come out[ee] of Egypt and has covered the face of the land; *and* now, come I pray,[ff] curse them for me; perhaps I shall be able to wage war against them and[gg] I shall drive them out.'" 12. And *the Memra of the Lord*[16] said to Balaam: "You shall not go with them and you shall not curse the people, for they are blessed." 13. And Balaam rose in the

Apparatus, Chapter 22

[u] Nfmg: "(and) the one you curse."
[w] Nfi: "they shall be (cursed)."
[x] Nfmg: "the wise men of the Moabites and the wise men of the Midianites"; = VN (with "Moab"). VN: "and the wise men of the Moabites and the wise men of the Midianites went and letters (*w'grn*) sealed (*ḥtymyn;* corr. to: *ḥtymn*) in their hands and they came to Balaam and spoke with him the word of Balak." Possibly we should correct *w'grn* ("letters") to *w'gryn* ("wages"). P: "and letters (correcting *w'gdn,* of uncertain meaning: "sealed packets" [?]; "staff of divination" [?] to *w'grn*) "sealed in their hands."
[y] "wages," emending *gryn* of text to *'gryn;* perhaps text should be read (as in *Aruk*) as *gdyn (dqsmyn)*: "the sealed staffs of divination (in their hands)" (thus J. Levy). There is great variety with regard to reading of word in question: *'grn* ("letters") in VN Nfmg; *gdyn* in *Aruk* and Ps.-J., (London MS, BL Add. 27031; *mygdyn* Ps.-J., ed. Venice, 1591; *mgdyn,* Musafia; *gydwnyn* and *'ygwryn* in *Met.* MS Angelica.
[z] Nfmg: "and wages (? *'grn;* or: "letters," reading as *'iggaran;* or: "staffs," correcting to *'gdn*) sealed in their hands."
[aa] Nfmg: "the words of" (a different term).
[bb] Nfmg: "this night and I shall answer."
[cc] Nfmg: "(according as) the Memra of the Lord speaks to me and the princes of Moab stayed with."
[dd] Nfmg: "(and he said) to him: Who are (these) men?"
[ee] Nfmg: "Behold, the people has come out."
[ff] Lit.: "now"; cf. v. 6 and note.
[gg] Nfmg: "(perhaps) we can set battle array against them and . . ."

Notes, Chapter 22

[9]"the princes" (*rbrbny*); HT: "the elders." In v. 4 (as in general; see above, Introd. III, 18) Nf translates the HT as "wise men"; and so also VN and Nfmg in v. 7.

[10]"the wages of divination sealed (*ḥtymyn*) . . . in their hands"; HT: "divinations (*qsmym*) in their hands"; "wages" correcting *gryn* of Nf text to *'gryn.* There is a great variety of readings with regard to the original Aramaic word. Another well-attested reading is *'grn* (*ḥtymn*) = *'iggaran,* "letters (of divination, sealed"). In favor of the reading *'gryn,* "wages," we have Vulg. (*divinationis pretium*) and the strong tradition of the presence of gifts, gain, wrongdoing in the interpretation of this verse; cf. Philo, *VM* 48, #266; Jude 11; 2 Pet 2:15. For the bearing of this Tg. tradition on NT exegesis, see Vermes, 1973, 130, 135, 172; A. Díez Macho, 1964, 160; R. Le Déaut, 1969, 20; D. Muñoz León, 1972, 60–65; M. McNamara, 1966, 168; 1971, 516.

[11]"this day and tonight"; HT: "tonight."

[12]"spoken from before. . ."; HT: "as the Lord will speak."

[13]"the Memra. . .revealed"; HT: "And God came to Balaam."

[14]"before the Lord"; HT: "to God."

[15]"a numerous people"; HT: "the people."

[16]"Memra of the Lord"; HT: "God."

morning and said to the princes of Balak: "Go to your land, *for there is not good pleasure before*[17] the Lord to permit me come with you."[hh] 14. And the princes of the Moabites rose and came to Balak and said: "Balaam refused to come with us." 15. And again[ii] Balak sent *messengers,*[18] more numerous and honorable than they.[jj] 16. And they came to Balaam and said to him: "Thus says Balak, the son of Zippor: 'Let nothing withhold you, now,[kk] from coming to me; 17. for I will surely honor you greatly, and whatever you say to me I will do; and come, now, curse this people for me.'" 18. And Balaam answered and said to the servants of Balak: "Though Balak were to give me full of his house of silver and gold, it is not *possible*[mm] to go beyond the word[nn] *of the decree of the Memra*[19] of the Lord, my God, to do a thing small or great. 19. And, now, go up; remain[oo] here, I pray, you also, this night, that I may know what further is spoken[pp] with me *from before* the Lord."[qq] 20. And *the Memra of the Lord*[rr] was *revealed*[20] to Balaam at night[ss] and said to him: "If the men[tt] have come to call you, rise, go with them; but only what I speak[uu] with you, that shall you do." 21. And Balaam rose in the morning and *prepared* his donkey and went with the princes of the Moabites.[ww] 22. And *the Lord's*[21] anger was enkindled because he went; and the angel of the Lord placed himself in the way to impede him; and he was riding[xx] on his donkey and his two young men with him. 23. And the donkey saw the angel of the Lord standing in the road with a sword unsheathed in his hand; and the donkey turned aside and went into the open field;[yy] and Balaam struck the donkey to direct it[zz] into the road. 24. And the angel of the Lord stood[a] between the *hedges* of the vineyards, (with) a

Apparatus, Chapter 22

[hh] Nfmg: "(for) the Memra of the Lord has refused to allow me come with you."
[ii] Nfi: "once more" (the same idea with a different word: *twb*).
[jj] Nfmg: "to send more numerous and more powerful messengers than they."
[kk] Nfmg: "I beseech."
[mm] Nfi adds "for me."
[nn] Lit.: "the mouth."
[oo] Nfmg 1°: "and now remain"; Nfmg 2°: "remain" (written differently).
[pp] Nfi: "(that I may know what more) he has to speak."
[qq] Nfmg: "the Memra of the Lord."
[rr] Nfi: "the Lord"; note that "the Lord" is usually in the text, "Memra of the Lord" in the glosses.
[ss] Nfmg: "in the visions of the night."
[tt] Nfmg: "if these men have come to call you . . ."
[uu] Nfmg: "that I have spoken."
[ww] VN: "of Moab."
[xx] Nfmg same, with different construction (use of auxiliary verb *hwwh*).
[yy] Nfmg: "(and went) in the field and he struck."
[zz] Nfmg: "the donkey to turn her aside . . ."
[a] Nfi: "the angel (stood)" (without *lyh;* = VN).

Notes, Chapter 22

[17]"there is not good pleasure before. . ."; HT: "the Lord has refused. . ."
[18]"messengers"; HT: "princes."
[19]"decree of the Memra"; HT: "the mouth (= command) of the Lord."
[20]"the Memra was revealed"; HT: "And God came to Balaam," as in v. 9.
[21]"the Lord's"; HT: "God's." Throughout, the Pal. Tg. renders "Elohim" of the HT as "the Lord." See note to Nf Gen. 1:1 (*The Aramaic Bible,* vol. 1A, p. 52; also note 2 to Ps.-J. Gen 1:1 (*The Aramaic Bible,* vol. 1B, p. 16).

hedge on this side and a hedge on the other.[b] 25. And the donkey saw the angel of the Lord and pressed against the wall and pressed Balaam's foot against the wall;[c] and he struck her again. 26. Then the angel of the Lord passed on and stood in a narrow place[d] *in which* there was no way to turn aside,[e] either to the right or to the left. 27. And the donkey saw the angel of the Lord and lay down under[f] Balaam, and he hit the donkey with his staff. 28. And the Lord[g] opened the mouth of the donkey and she said[g bis] to Balaam: "What have I done to you that you have struck me these three times?"[h] 29. And Balaam said to the donkey: "Because you have been false to me. If I had a sword in my hand, I would kill you now." 30. And the donkey said to Balaam:[i 22] "*Where*[j] *are you going, wicked Balaam? You lack understanding! What! If you are not able*[k] *to curse me who am an unclean beast, and die in this world and who do not enter the world to come, how much less are you able*[m] *to curse the sons of Abraham, of Isaac and Jacob, on whose account the world was cre-*

Apparatus, Chapter 22

[b] I.e., "between two hedges"; Nfmg: "in the middle of (or: 'between') the vineyards, a hedge at one side and a hedge on the other side . . ."; = PVN.

[c] Nfi: "and she saw"; the *incipit* of the HT.

[d] Nfi: "(and stood) in a (narrow) place" (without *lyh*).

[e] Nfmg: "there was no way (to the right . . .)"; the variant, however, probably refers to the preceding words.

[f] Nfi: "and lay down under . . ." (without *lh*).

[g] Nfmg: "the Memra of the Lord."

[g bis] Text: "he said."

[h] Nf lacks the paraphrase with which Ps.-J. begins, but does know of the tradition of the existence of the well from the beginning; cf. Nf Num 21:18.

[i] PVN: "and the donkey said to Balaam: Woe to you wicked Balaam, lacking in understanding; no wisdom or knowledge (VN: 'and no wisdom') is to be found in you (lit.: 'by you'). Now, what if I am (VN: "Behold I am") an unclean animal (which) dies in this world and does not come to the world to come and you are unable to curse me through the wisdom of your understanding, how much more so the children of Abraham, Isaac, and Jacob for whose merit (or: 'sake') the world was created from the beginning—how shall you go and be able to curse them? And as to your having deceived these people, saying to them: This is not my donkey, she has been borrowed by me—indeed, I am your donkey on which you rode from your youth to this day. Have I indeed been accustomed to do so to you? And he said: No."

[j] Nfmg: "Am I not the donkey that you rode . . ."; = PVN. Nfmg does not know Nf's paraphrase.

[k] Nfi: "(to come, you are) unable."

[m] Nfi: "(how) are you going (to curse)"; = PVN.

Notes, Chapter 22

[22]"contrived"; Nf has *mtkwwn,* root *kwn,* rendering HT *skn* (*h-hskn hskntу*), a word found only here in the Pentateuch and generally rendered "accustomed." The HT for the passage has: "Am I not your donkey on which you have ridden all your life long to this day? Was I ever accustomed to do so to you?" The midrash is intended to introduce the donkey's words, translated rather literally into Aramaic at the end. It makes the point that if Balaam has no power to curse her, an impure creature without a future in the new age, how much less has he power over Israel? Then, with apparent reference to Balaam's accusation that the donkey was false to, deceived, him (v. 29), it is implied that Balaam said the donkey was not his own but borrowed, a statement made so as to be denied by the donkey's words in v. 30. The midrash of Nf is found substantially the same in the Frg. Tg. (P, V, N) with some differences, e.g., only Nf has: "and for whose merits it is remembered before them," and the presence in Nf of some terms in Hebrew (*mn r'š,* "from the beginning," PVN, *mn šyrwy'h; 'l 'ḥt kmh wkmh;* PVN: *'l ḥd* "how much more." See B. Barry Levy, 1987, 2, 126.

ated from the beginning, and for whose merits it is remembered[n][23] *before them? And with regard to your having taken undue advantage*[o] *of these men (saying): This is not my donkey; she is borrowed:*—am I not the donkey upon which you have ridden from your *youth* until[p] this day? Have I in truth ever contrived[q] to do so to you?" And he said:[r] "No." 31. And the Lord opened the eyes[s] of Balaam and he saw the angel of the Lord *standing,* set,[24] in the road and his sword unsheathed in his hand; and he prostrated himself upon his face. 32. And the angel of the Lord said to him: "Why[t] have you struck your donkey these three times? Behold, I have come out to oppose you[u] because the way has turned aside against me; 33. and the donkey saw me and turned aside before me these three times. If she had not turned aside before me, I would have now killed you[w] and let her live." 34. And Balaam said to the angel of the Lord: "I have sinned, for I did not know that you *stood* placed before me in the way: and now if it is evil in your sight, I will return *to my place.*"[x][25] 35. And the angel of the Lord said to Balaam: "Go with the men; but only the word which will I speak[y] with you, that shall you speak." And Balaam went with the princes of Balak. 36. When Balak heard that Balaam had come, he went out to meet him *to the land*[26] of the Moabites which *is near* the border of the Arnon,[z] at

Apparatus, Chapter 22

[n] Or: "it is governed" (*mdbr;* in text *mdkr*).
[o] Lit.: "you have oppressed (or: 'deceived'; *tlmt*) the faces of these men"; Nfi: "(with regard to what) you have said to (these) men."
[p] Nfmg: "(until) the time of (this day)."
[q] In text *mtkwwnt* (ptc., "to have intended; to have done deliberately"); Díez Macho, 1974: "been accustomed"; cf. HT. Ps.-J. *mthnyyty,* "I have taken pleasure." PVN as Nf.
[r] Nfmg: "thus; and he said: No"; = P; cf. VN.
[s] Nfmg: "and the Memra of the Lord opened the eyes, etc."
[t] Nfmg: "for what reason?"
[u] Nfmg: "to oppose (myself to you)."
[w] Nfmg: "now (I would have killed) you also"; a gloss erroneously attached to the following verse; cf. Ps.-J.
[x] Nfmg: "now if it is displeasing (lit.: 'evil') before you (= if it displeases you), I will return to my place."
[y] Nfmg: "(what) I have spoken."
[z] Nfmg: "(near) the territory of the Arnon."

Notes, Chapter 22

[23]"and for whose merits it is remembered (*mdkr*) before them," i.e., possibly before the patriarchs. The sentence is absent from other Pal. Tg. texts (Ps.-J., PVN, Nfmg) and may be an insertion by Nf. If "remembered" (*mdkr*) is original, the reference may be principally to the Binding of Isaac, recalled in this context (with Abraham and Jacob) in *LAB* 15, 5: ". . .his offering was acceptable before me, and an account of his blood I chose them." But perhaps, as suggested by Díez Macho (*Neophyti* 1, IV, 215), we should amend to *mdbr,* "is guided," is "governed." "Creation" (*'tbr'*) and (divine) "guiding" (providence) are found together elsewhere in Nf and the Pal. Tg., e.g., Nf Gen 4:8; also Num 23:9. We should possibly correct "before them" of this v. (22:3) to "before him."

[24]"standing set," *qym mt'td;* HT: *nṣb* ("stationed"); Nf renders the HT *nṣb* by the root *qwm* alone in Gen 18:2; 28:13; 37:7; 45:1; Exod 5:20; 15:8; 18:14; 33:8; by a word from the root *'td* alone in Exod 7:15; 33:21; 34:2; Num 22:23; 23:6; 23:17, and in the other occurrences by the double *qwm 'td (qyym m'td, qyym mt'td,* etc.): Gen 24:13, 43; Exod 17:9; Num 16:27; 22:31, 34; Deut 29:9.

[25]"to my place"; an addition in Nf.

[26]"to the land of the Moabites"; HT: "to the city of Moab."

the extremities[aa] of the territory. 37. And Balak said to Balaam: "Have I not indeed sent to you to call you? Why, *then,*[bb] have you not come to me? Am I, in truth, not able to honor you?"[cc] 38. And Balaam said to Balak: "Behold, I have come to you. Am I now really[dd] able to speak anything at all? The word[ee] which *the Lord*[ff][27] puts in my mouth, that will I speak." 39. And Balaam went with Balak and they entered the *royal* city, *that is Maresha.*[gg][28] 40. And Balak sacrificed oxen and sheep and sent (them) to Balaam and to his princes who were with him.[hh] 41. And then in the morning Balak took[ii] Balaam and brought him up to the altars of Baal;[jj] and from there he saw a section of the people.[kk]

CHAPTER 23

1. And Balam said to Balak: "Build for me here seven[a] altars and prepare for me[b] here seven bulls and seven rams." 2. And Balak did as Balaam had spoken;[c]

Apparatus, Chapter 22

[aa] Nfmg: "(to meet them,) to the city of Moab which is opposite the Arnon which is on the borders of . . . ," translating *'Ir Moab* (= 'Ar Moab).

[bb] Lit: "now."

[cc] Nfmg: "in truth is it not possible for me to honor you."

[dd] Nfmg: "can we (= I) really."

[ee] Nfmg: ". . . speak anything at all? The word . . ." This and the preceding note probably form only one gloss.

[ff] Nfmg: "the Memra of the Lord."

[gg] We should probably correct to Birosha, as in Ps.-J.; Nfmg: "and they came to the city which is in 'Two Markets' (*tryn šwqh*), that is, Beth Dibon." "Two Markets" is a translation of (*Qiryat*) *Ḥusot* (*ḥus,* "square," "market").

[hh] Nfmg: "and to the princes who were with him" (a different grammatical construction).

[ii] Nfmg: "took" (a different word).

[jj] Translating *Bamoth-Baal;* Nfmg: "(to) the idols (of) Peor, and he saw (lit.: 'its idol[s], Peor, and he saw')"; see G. Vermes, 1961, 142, for different renderings in Jewish tradition.

[kk] "a section," *mn qṣt;* cf. Nf Gen 47:2 with variant *syypy.* Nfmg: "a part (*syypy*) of the people"; see also Num 23:13.

Notes, Chapter 22

[27]"the Lord"; HT: "God." See note to 22:22 above.

[28]"the royal city, that is Maresha"; HT (RSV): "Kiriath-huzoth." Ps.-J. has "(the big city that is the city of Sihon, that is) Birosha" (on Birosha; see Ps.-J. Num 32:37). For *aryšh* (Moresa or Moresha) in Nf we should possibly read *bryšh* (as in Ps.-J.), unless the M(em) is but a variant reading of this (cf. Mutnin and Butnin; and note to Nf Num 21:33.

Apparatus, Chapter 23

[a] In text "bulls" is added to "seven," but deleted by the scribe himself.

[b] Nfmg: "and prepare (for me)" (another form of the word).

[c] Nfmg: "spoke."

and Balak and Balaam[1] offered a bull and a ram upon *each* altar. 3. And Balaam said to Balak: "Stand[d] beside your burnt offering and I will go; perhaps *the Memra of* the Lord[2] will come out to meet me; and whatever the Lord shows me, I will relate to you." And *Balaam* went with a *single-minded,*[e] *easy*[f] *heart to curse Israel.*[3] 4. And *the Memra of the Lord*[g4] met Balaam; and he said to him: "I have arranged the seven altars and offered a bull and a ram on *each* altar." 5. And *the Memra of* the Lord[2] put a word in Balaam's mouth and said: "Return to Balak and thus shall you speak."[h] 6. And he returned to him and behold, he was stationed[i5] beside his burnt offering, he and all the princes of the Moabites. 7. And he took up his *prophecy*[6] *in a* parabolic discourse:[j] "From Aram[k] Balak has taken me, the king[m] of the Moabites from the mountains of the East: 'Come,[n] curse Jacob[o] for me, and come, *diminish*[p] *for me those of*[q] *the house of* Israel.' 8. How can I curse[r] when the *Memra of the Lord*[s4] (blesses)?[t] How can I *diminish*[7] *them*[u] when *the Memra of* the

Apparatus, Chapter 23

[d] Nfmg, Nfi: "stand" (written differently).

[e] Or: "solitary." It is one way in which *šepi* (a place that is "solitary," solitude, bare, i.e., of trees) of the MT is translated. Onq.: "and he went solitary" (*yḥydy*); Nfmg, VN: "with an easy (*špy*) heart"; Nf has most likely a conflated reading.

[f] That is, "tranquil"; cf. Nfmg Gen 22:6, 8; in Nf text Gen 22:6, 8: "perfect heart," as in a variant of the Sam. Tg. Cf. Ps.-J.: "(and he went away) creeping like a serpent" (an allusion to Gen 3:15—*šfy-šwf?*); see Vermes, 1961, 144.

[g] Ps.-J. and Onq.: "the Memra (Onq.: a Memra) from before the Lord met Balaam."

[h] Nfmg: "and in this manner shall you speak."

[i] Nfmg: "(and behold,) he was ready" (*hw' m'td*).

[j] PVN, like HT, adds: "and said."

[k] P: "from Aram Naharaim."

[m] Nf and PVN have writings *mlkyhwn*.

[n] PVN +: "now" (or: "I pray").

[o] Nfi: "those of the house (of Jacob)"; = PVN.

[p] That is: "defeat."

[q] PVN: "the tribes of."

[r] Nfi: "(to curse) them"; PN: "how can I curse those of the house of Jacob?"

[s] Nfmg: "the Lord"; see note *rr* to Num 22:20.

[t] Thus PVN ("blesses them") and Ps.-J.; in the text "multiply," but with two small strokes by the scribe, which indicate that the word is wrong.

[u] PVN: "diminish those of the house of Israel."

Notes, Chapter 23

[1]Both the king and Balaam sacrifice as in HT, Onq., Ps.-J. According to the LXX, only one sacrifices, as in Philo, Josephus, Ps.-Philo, *LAB* 18, 10. See Vermes, 1961 (1973), 143.

[2]"Memra of the Lord"; HT: "the Lord."

[3]"And Balaam . . .Israel." HT: "And he went to a bare hill" (*špy*). The term *špy* occurs only here in the Pentateuch. Nf's reading may be conflate. See Apparatus. For the expression "an easy (*špy*) heart," cf. VNL, Nfmg, Gen 22:8 (P, Nf: "a perfect heart)." "To curse Israel" is an interpretative expansion.

[4]"The Memra of the Lord"; HT in 23:4: "God"; in 23:5: "the Lord."

[5]"stationed," *'t'td;* Nf's rendering HT: *nṣṣb* (MT: *niṣṣab*); see note to 22:31.

[6]"his prophecy. . .discourse," *bmtl nbwth;* HT: "He took up his (parabolic) discourse and said." Nf omits the translation of "and said."

[7]"diminish (*z'r;* or: 'curse') for me those of the house of Israel"; HT: "curse (*z'm*) Israel"; "curse, denounce," Nf, like the HT, chooses a synonym for *lwṭ*, "curse," used in the first part of the verse.

Lord[2] multiplies them?[8] 9. For I see *this people being led and coming*[w] *for the merits of the just fathers who are comparable to the* mountains,[9] *Abraham, Isaac, and Jacob;* and *for the merits of the just mothers who are comparable*[x] *to the* hills, *Sarah, Rebekah, and Leah.* Behold *this* people[10] dwell by themselves and they are not *mixed in with* the *customs*[y] *of the* nations.[z] 10. Who *can* count[11] *the young men* of *the house of* Jacob, *of whom it has been said that they would be blessed*[aa] like the dust *of the earth? Or who can number* one of the four *arrangements*[bb] *of the camp of the children* of Israel,[cc] *concerning whom it has been said: 'They shall be numerous*[dd] *like the stars of the heavens'"? And Balaam said in his prophetic parabolic discourse: "Were Israel to kill him by the sword, Balaam himself proclaims that he has no portion in the world to come; but if*[ee] *Balaam* were to die[ff][12] an upright *death,*[gg] *would*

Apparatus, Chapter 23

[w] PVN all lack "and coming."
[x] PVN: "for the merit of the (VN add: 'four') mothers who are comparable."
[y] Greek loan word *nomos;* also in PVN.
[z] PVN: "Who can count the young men of the house of Jacob, concerning whom it has been said that they will be numerous like the stars of heaven? Balaam the wicked said in his prophetic parabolic discourse: If Israel were to kill him by the sword, Balaam announces that he has no portion in the world to come. However, if Balaam were to die an upright death (PVN: *mwtnyn qšyṭyn;* Nf: *mwtnyn qšyṭyn*), would that his final end be like the least among them."
[aa] Nfmg: "blessed" (another form).
[bb] Greek loan word *taxis;* also in Nfmg.
[cc] Nfi: "(the camp) of Israel."
[dd] Nfmg: "that they should be multitudes."
[ee] Nfi: "that if (he were to die)."
[ff] Nfi: "(if) he (were to die)."
[gg] Lit.: "upright deaths" (*mwtyn qšyṭyn*); PVN (see note *z* above) *mwtnyn qšyṭyn,* lit.: "upright pestilences." All texts are probably corrupt, and "the death of the upright" is intended. Nfi: "the death (of the upright)."

Notes, Chapter 23

[8]The HT (RSV) has: "How can I curse whom God has not cursed? How can I denounce whom the Lord has not denounced?" Note Nf's use of "increase" and "diminish," as in v. 7. B. Barry Levy, 1987, 128, says it is not clear that Nf, v. 8, should be read as questions. The verse may also be seen as containing two statements.

[9]The HT has: "for from the top of the mountains (*ṣrym*) I see him, from the hills (*gb'wt*) I behold him." Nf's paraphrase understands "the top of the mountains" (*ṣrym,* masc.) of the patriarchs and the hills (*gb'wt,* fem.) of the Mothers of Israel. This interpretation of the mountains (*hrym; ṣrym*) and hills is very common in rabbinic literature (e.g., *Num. R.* XX, 19; *Tanh. B.,* IV. 143; *b. Rosh Hash.* 11a; *j. Sanh.* 10:1; cf. PVN, Nfmg Gen 49:26. The role of the merits of the patriarchs in the Balaam cycle is found already in Nf Num 22:30, with possible mention of God's leading (*mdbr*) his people; see note to Nf Num 23:30.

[10]"Behold this people. . .customs of the nation"; HT: "lo, a people dwelling alone, and not reckoning itself among the nations."

[11]The underlying HT (RSV) on which Nf's paraphrase is based reads: "who can count the dust of Jacob, or number (*mspr;* MT: *mispar*) the fourth part (*rb'*) of Israel?" The mention of "dust" leads to the reference to "young men" and to the recalling of God's promise to the patriarchs (Gen 22:17; 15:5; 26:4; Exod 32:13). The "fourth part" (*rb'*) is interpreted of the four Israelite camps traveling together in the wilderness (Num 2), with a reference to Gen 15:5, etc.

[12]In the HT Balaam expresses a desire to share in Israel's destiny: "Let me die the death of the righteous, and let my end be like his!" In the paraphrase Balaam's wish is put in the third person, and apparently a distinction is made: Should Balaam die by the sword (i.e., as a malefactor; according to Num 31:8; Josh 13:22, the Israelites slew Balaam, son of Beor, with the sword) his end will be like that which his donkey professed his own end was (Nf, Num 22:30), with no part in the future age. Should, however, his wish come true, in his dying an upright death (*qšyṭyn,* rendering HT *yšrym;* cf. Nf Deut 32:4; "death of the upright"), the prayer of somebody (not necessarily Balaam) is that his fate may be as that of the least in Israel: cf. Matt 11:12; Luke 7:28. Thus with regard to the paraphrase in Nf; there are slight differences in Ps.-J. text.

that his end, would that *his* latter end,[hh] were as (that of) *the least among* them." 11. And Balak said to Balaam: "What have you done to me? I brought you to curse my enemies and behold, you bless *them!*" 12. And he answered and said: "Must I not take heed to speak what his *Memra*[13] puts[ii] in my mouth?" 13. And Balak said to him: "Come, now,[jj] with me to another place from where you will see them; you will see only a section *of the people* and you will not see them all; and you shall curse them[kk] for me from there." 14. And he took him to the Field of Watchtowers,[mm] to the top of *the height;*[nn][14] and he built seven altars and offered a bull and a ram on *each* altar. 15. And he said to Balak: "Stand here beside your burnt offering and I will meet you here."[oo] 16. And *the Memra of* the Lord[pp][15] met Balaam and put a word in his mouth, and said: "Return to Balak and thus shall you speak." 17. And he came to him and behold, he was stationed[qq][5] beside his burnt offering and the princes of the Moab*ites*[rr] with him. And Balak said to him: "What *has been spoken*[ss] *from before* the Lord?" 18. And he took up his *prophecy* in parabolic discourse and said: "Rise, Balak, and hear: give ear, *now, to my words,* O son of Zippor; 19. The *Memra*[tt] *of the Lord* is not like the *memra*[uu] of the sons of man;[16] *nor are the works of the Lord*[ww] *like the work of the sons of man;*[xx] *the sons of man say and do not act; they decree and fulfill not; and they go back and deny*

Apparatus, Chapter 23

[hh] Nfmg: "(of the upright) would that his latter end . . ."

[ii] Nfi: "has put."

[jj] In Nf *k'n* = *kdwn* ("now") in Ps.J. = *-n'* in HT.

[kk] Nfi: "and curse (them)."

[mm] MT: Sedeh Sophim; Nfi: "of the sentinels."

[nn] MT: Pisgah.

[oo] VN: "and I in my Memra will honor you." Note use of Memra with human as subject, unless the Targumist took God as speaker to Balak.

[pp] Nfi: "and the Lord met."

[qq] Nfmg: "(and behold he was) placed"; Nfi: "placed" (another form).

[rr] Nfi: "(of) Moab."

[ss] Note use of passive instead of active.

[tt] PVN: "the Memra of the living God"; Nf has: "Memra of YYY."

[uu] Lit.: "like the *memar* (memra) of." Note use of *memar* (memra) with human as subject, and see note *oo* above.

[ww] PVN: "of God"; Nf has: "of YYY."

[xx] Nfi: "of the son of man" (= "of a man"). Note that in sing. ("son of") *nš* is used and almost always *'nš(')* in the plur. ("sons of man"). (However, note that P here has *nš'* in plur.; *bny nš'*.)

Notes, Chapter 23

[13]"his Memra"; HT: "the Lord."

[14]"top of the height"; HT: "top of Pisgah," as in the other occurrences in (Nf) Num 21:20; Deut 3:27; 34:1.

[15]"Memra of the Lord"; HT: "the Lord."

[16]HT (RSV): "God is not man that he should lie, or a son of man that he should repent. Has he said, and will he not do it? Or has he spoken, and will he not fulfill it?" The Nf paraphrase is found almost identically in PVN; for difference see Apparatus. The paraphrase, as usual, avoids the metaphor of the HT, thus in part avoiding the problem of its theological language, including the mention of a lie (even negatively) in relation to God. *Memar* (of God, of the sons of man) is probably to be understood in its fundamental sense of "speech," "statement" (cf. Nf Deut 30:14; 32:1; also Nf Deut 17:6) rather than in its specific theological targumic sense or with the meaning "person." The paraphrase of Onq. is similar to that of the Pal. Tg. It reads: "The *memra* of God is not like the words of (*mly*) the sons of man. The sons of man speak and lie. And it is also not like the deeds of the sons of flesh, who decree that things are to become but change their minds. He says and it is done and every *memar* of his is established." See note by B. Grossfeld to Onq. (*The Aramaic Bible* vol. 8, pp. 133f.); and also B. Barry Levy, 1987, 2, 133–135.

their words. God, however, says and does; he decrees and fulfills, *and his prophetic words are established forever.*[yy] 20. Behold *I have been brought*[zz][17] to bless; I shall bless *Israel* and *a blessing*[a] I shall not withhold[b] *from them.* 21. *I* see no *servants* of falsehood[c][18] among *those of the house of* Jacob, and no *servants of foreign worship* among *those of the house of* Israel; *the Memra of* the Lord their God is with them, and the acclaim[d] *of the splendor of the glory of their* king[e][19] *is a shield above* them. 22. God is he who brought them out[20] *of the land*[f] of Egypt; to him[21] belong *the power, the praise, and the majesty.*[g] 23. For *I see* none[h] *who observe omens*[22] among

Apparatus, Chapter 23

[yy] PVN: "and his decrees stand forever."

[zz] It translates HT as passive (*luqqaḥti*) with Vulg. (*adductus sum*) and Pesh., and not as active (*laqaḥti*) as in MT, Onq., and Ps.J.

[a] Nfmg and Nfi: "and blessings"; = PVN.

[b] Nfi: "I shall (not) go back" (= "I shall [not] repent"; or "I shall (not) take back" (correcting *tyyb* to *ytyb* + *'tyb*).

[c] Or: "doers (workers, *'bdy*) of lies . . . of foreign worship"; PVN: "I see no servers of (*plḥy*) lies among those of the house of Jacob, nor servers of (*plḥy*) foreign worship among the tribes of the children of Israel. The Memra of the Lord (P adds: their God) is with them and the acclaim (lit.: trumpet sound) of the splendor of (*zyw;* VN: the acclaim from, *mn,* corr. to *zyw,* with P and Nf) the glory of their king is a shield above them."

[d] Lit.: "trumpet sound."

[e] *mlkyhwn:* which might also mean "of their kings"; cf. Ps.-J.: "the trumpet sound of King Messiah."

[f] PVN: "who redeemed and brought them out redeemed from Egypt."

[g] Or: "exaltation"; "to him belong . . . and majesty" translates HT: "is for them as the horns (lit.: 'the eminences') of the buffalo"; *r'm* is read as *rwm* ("exaltation").

[h] PVN: "For I see none who observe omens (VN: 'who perform an omen') among those of the house of Jacob, and likewise none who practice divination among the tribes of the children of Israel. At that time it will be said to Jacob: What good things and consolations the Lord (P: 'the Memra of the Lord') is about to bring (VN: 'to relate,' 'tell'; *corr.:* to P) upon you (P: 'upon them') of the house of Jacob. Thus (P: 'Indeed') he said in his prophetic parabolic discourse: Blessed are you, just ones! What a good reward is prepared for you beside your Father who is in heaven for (or: 'in') the world to come."

Notes, Chapter 23

[17] "I have been brought," or: "I have been taken," *'dbryt,* rendering (like the Vulg.) HT *lqhty* (MT: *laqaḥtî*) as passive (*luqaḥtî*). Other elements, noted in italics, are expansive.

[18] "I see no servants of falsehood . . . of foreign worship"; HT: "he has not beheld misfortune (*'wn*) . . . nor divination." Like other ancient translations (with the exception of the LXX), Nf renders *'wn* ("mischief, evil"), a hapax in the Pentateuch, as a *nomen agentis.* Likewise with regard to "divination."

[19] "the acclaim . . . king"; HT: "the acclamation (shout) of a king." Ps.-J.'s paraphrase is explicitly messianic, and apparently those of Nf and the Pal. Tg. are implicitly so.

[20] PVN, as Nf often elsewhere, adds "redeemed" in this Exodus context. See above Introd. III, 22.

[21] The HT *ktw 'pt r'm lw:* "there is to him (= he has), like the eminence (= horns?) of a wild ox" requires interpretation and explanation. Does it refer to God or Israel? In the Targums it is seen as referring to God, *tw'ph* taken of his glory and *r'm* ("wild ox") understood as *rwm,* "eminence." This understanding of the passage is expressed in language redolent of liturgical formulae (similar to text of 1 Chr 29:11), one often found in Exodus contexts; see McNamara, 1966, 214–217.

[22] The HT can be rendered: "For there is no magic in Jacob and no divination in Israel. Now it shall be said of (or: 'to') Jacob and of (or: 'to') Israel: What has God done (or: 'how great is the work of God')." In its usual manner Nf makes concrete the abstract "magic" and "divination," and specifies twice what the "work" of God to be announced to Israel is, namely, the "good things" the (messianic) consolation (cf. Pal. Tg. Gen 49:1); the reward in store for Israel in the world to come. On the "good things" and the messianic consolation, see note to Nf Gen 49:1 (*The Aramaic Bible,* vol. 1A, p. 216, with bibliographical references); also M. McNamara, 1972, 137–141; Matt 7:11; Rom 3:8; 10:15 (= Isa 52:7); Heb 9:11; 10:1.

those of the house of Jacob, and none who *practice divination* among *those of the house of* Israel. At *this* time[i] *the good things and the consolations that are destined to come*[j] *upon you* and (upon) *those*[k] *of the house of* Israel will be announced to *the house of* Jacob." *Balaam said in his prophetic parabolic discourse: "Blessed are you, just ones! What a good reward is prepared for you before the Lord*[m] *for the world to come!* 24. Behold, the people[23] (of Israel);[n] like the lion they *lie down* and like the lioness they rise up;[o] *for as the lion* does not rest *or sleep* until it has eaten what has been torn and has drunk blood,[p] *so (with) this people;*[q] *they do not rest nor are they at ease*[r] until they slay[s] <their>[t] *enemies and have poured out the blood*[u] of *their slain like water.*" 25. And Balak said to Balaam: "You neither curse them at all nor bless them at all." 26. And Balaam answered and said to Balak: "Have I not spoken with you saying: 'All that the Lord says,[w] that shall I do?'" 27. And Balak said to Balaam: "Come, now, and I will lead you to another place; perhaps there may be *good pleasure before the Lord*[24] that you curse them for me from there." 28. And Balak took Balaam to the top of *the Idols* of Peor,[25] which looks out towards *Beth-ha-Jeshimon.*[x][26] 29. And Balaam said to Balak: "Build for me here seven altars and prepare for me here seven bulls and seven rams." 30. And Balak did as Balaam had said, and offered a bull and a ram on *each* altar.

Apparatus, Chapter 23

[i] Nfi: "at that (time)."
[j] Nfmg: "(are) to come" (another construction).
[k] Nfi: "(upon you,) house of (Israel)."
[m] See rendering of PVN, note *h* above.
[n] PVN: "Behold this people; like the lion they lie down (or: encamp) and like the lioness they bounce up (or: 'grow strong'; *mtgbryn;* Nf: *mtnṭlyn*). Just as the lion neither rests nor is at ease (*šdyk*) until it has eaten and torn flesh and drunk blood, thus (P: 'indeed') this people neither rests nor is at ease (*šdykyn*) until the time that they have killed their enemies and have poured out like water the blood of the slain of those who hate them."
[o] Nfi: "(and like the lioness) which rises up."
[p] Nfi: "the blood."
[q] Nfi: "these peoples."
[r] Nf: *škdyn;* correct to *šdkyn* with PVN.
[s] Nfi: "(until) the time in which they have slain"; cf. PVN.
[t] In text: "your."
[u] Nfi: "(the) blood" (*dm;* in text, and in PVN: *'dm*).
[w] Nfi, Nfmg: "(all that the Lord) has spoken."
[x] MT: "Yeshimon."

Notes, Chapter 23

[23]The HT speaks of a people, which is apparently compared to a lioness and lion. "It does not lie down till it devours the prey and drinks the blood of the slain." It is not clear in the HT whether it is the people or the animal that so acts. The paraphrase attributes the actions literally to the lion and figuratively to the people, and transforms "eating prey" and "drinking blood" into slaying and pouring out their blood.

[24]"good pleasure before the Lord"; HT: "be right in the eyes of God."

[25]"the idols (*ṭ'wwth*) of Peor"; HT: "to top of Peor" (*r'š hp'wr*), a name or phrase occurring only here. In Num 25:18; 31:16 we have Peor alone ("the affair of Peor") and in Num 25:3, 5, Baal-Peor, which is rendered in Nf in all instances in the same way: "the idol of Peor"; likewise *byt p'wr* as "the Idols of Peor" in Deut 3:29; 4:46.

[26]"Beth ha-Jeshimon"; HT: "Ha-Jeshimon"; so also in Nf Num 21:20. Onq. renders likewise in both cases (cf. Beth-Jeshimoth of the HT, Num 33:49, which is retained in Nf).

CHAPTER 24

1. And Balaam saw[1] that it was good *before* the Lord to bless Israel, and he did not go towards diviners as *he used to go on every occasion,*[2] *to consult through ghosts,*[a3] but *he went*[4] and set his face towards the desert *and recalled for them*[5] *the affair of the calf.*[b] 2. And Balaam lifted up his eyes and saw Israel encamped in its *formations.*[6] And a *holy* spirit[c7] *from before the Lord* came upon him. 3. And he took up his *prophecy*[8] in parabolic discourse[d] and said: "Says Balaam, the son of

Apparatus, Chapter 24

[a] *Lit.:* "to consult (*lmš'lyh*) by his phallus" (*dᵉkireh*); cf. J. Levy, 1, 176. It means to make necromantic consultation; *š'l* originally used for "to consult," like (*drš*, both God and diviners, and then for "to seek"); Nfi: "(to seek) the blessings" (*or:* "[consult] pure things"); Nfmg: "(all and) every other time to seek the blessings"; PVN: "at all and every other time to allow himself to be inquired of (*lmšt'lh;* or: 'to answer, issue an oracle') by his phallus."

[b] I.e., the golden calf; PVN add: "he sought to curse Israel."

[c] "holy spirit" is the "spirit of prophecy," as in Ps.-J. here and in other passages; Onq. also translates here as "spirit of prophecy."

[d] Sam. Tg.: "he lifted up his power," translating *mšl* by *šlt.*

Notes, Chapter 24

[1]The paraphrase of this verse (24:1) is identical in Nf or PVN, except that PVN at the end add: "he sought to curse Israel"; and P lacks *bdkyrh,* the Aramaic word here rendered "ghosts." On Nf Num 24, see McNamara, 1993.

[2]"as he used to go on every occasion"; same paraphrase in PVN; HT: "as at the other times," *kp'm bp'm.*

[3]"towards diviners to consult through ghosts"; lit.: "(on every occasion) to consult through his phallus towards diviners"; *lmš'lyh bdkyrh lqdmwt qsmyh;* this paraphrases the HT (*kp'm bp'm*) *lqr't nḥšym* "(as at other times) towards omens (or: 'spells')"; RSV: "to look for omens." What exact lexical form Nf *l-mš'lyh* is, is uncertain (see Golomb, 1985, 151; it is not noted in Sokoloff, 1990). PVN have *mšt'l',* Itpe., "to inquire (of diviners)," Sokoloff, 1990, 533. Other variants are *lš'l;* see Apparatus. The term *dkyr* is not registered by Jastrow or Sokoloff. J. Levy, 1866, 1, 176, understands Frg. Tg. 24:1 to mean "*membrum virile,*" and probably to be corrected to *dkwr',* "to consult through his *membrum virile*"; probably to make necromantic consultation, to seek apparitions of the dead in this manner. There is quite a variety of readings with regard to form of the term: Nf, VN *dkyrh;* Elias Levita, *Meturg.,* ed. Isny, (*lmš'l*) *bdkwrw.*

[4]"he went"; addition in Nf.

[5]"he recalled for (or: 'to,' *lhwn*) them the affair of the calf," i.e., the golden calf, Exod 32: he either reminded God of this against Israel (thus Vermes, 1961, 155), as explicitly in Ps.-J., or he reminded Israel itself, in order to break down their defenses (thus B. Barry Levy, 1987, 2, 138f.). The reference to the golden calf is in all Pal. Tg. texts (Nf, PVN) and in Ps.-J. It is also in some MSS of Onq. (MSS G, V, a, D), but not in the main text translated in the Aramaic Bible. See B. Grossfeld, *The Aramaic Bible,* vol. 8, p. 134.

[6]"in its formations"; *lṭksyhwn,* root *ṭks,* from the Greek *taxis.* HT: "according to its tribes." The Aramaic word *ṭks* (rarely *ṭqs*), elsewhere in Nf (Num 2:10, 17, 18, 25, 31, 34; 10:14, 22) renders *dgl* of the HT. Despite its Greek origins, Sokoloff, 1990, 224, renders the Aramaic term *ṭks* as "banner" (rather than "formation, batallion").

[7]"a holy spirit from before the Lord"; HT: "the spirit of God." See Introduction to Nf Genesis, *The Aramaic Bible,* vol. 1A, pp. 38f.

[8]The HT presents a very difficult text: "And he took up his discourse (*mšlw*) and said: The oracle (*n'm;* MT: *ne'um*) of Balaam, the son of Beor" (*bnw b'r*). In its usual fashion Nf renders *mšlw* as (*nṭl*) *bmtl nbwth* (cf. Nf Num 23:7, 18; 24:3, 15, 20, 21, 23); which I render: "(he took up) his prophecy in a parabolic discourse." Sokoloff, 1990, 377, renders: "in his prophetic theme."

Peor;[e] says[f9] the man *who is more honorable than his father:*[g10] *what has been hidden*[11] *from all the prophets*[h] *has been revealed to him.* 4. The utterance of one who has heard a *Memra*[i] *from before the Lord Most High,*[12] of the one who saw a vision of Shaddai. *And when he used to see,*[j] *he used to prostrate himself upon his face and the mysteries of prophecy* were revealed to him. *And he prophesied concerning himself,* that he would fall *by the sword; and his prophecy was eventually*[k] *to be fulfilled.* 5. How *beautiful*[m] are the tents of *the house of* Jacob,[n13] *for the merit of*

Apparatus, Chapter 24

[e] MT and other Tgs. here and v. 15: "Beor."
[f] *'mr* (=? *'ymr*); HT: *n'm.* See note.
[g] PVN: "than his brothers."
[h] This paraphrase interprets *šetum* of the MT as *setum* = "hidden" and *šetum* = "open"; cf. G. Vermes, 1973, 156f.
[i] In text: *mymr,* which can also be rendered "order," "command"; PVN have *mmll,* "speech"; Nfi: "the Memra." PVN: "the utterance of a man who heard speech from before the Lord and who saw (P: *ḥm';* VN: *ḥz'*) from before Shaddai a vision (?; VN: *ḥzy;* P: *ḥmy*), and when he fell down upon his face (P; VN: "and when he desired he would prostrate himself—*nš[tt] ḥ,* correcting text—upon his face") and the secrets of the prophecy would be revealed to him. And he prophesied concerning himself that he would fall by the sword, and ultimately the prophecy was to be fulfilled."
[j] Nfi: "to seek"; Ps.-J. adds: "that it be revealed to him."
[k] Lit.: "and the end of his prophecy was that it be fulfilled"; Nfmg: "(and the end of his prophecy was that it would be) valid (or: 'enduring')."
[m] Nfmg: "how good are your schools, (you) of the house of Jacob; and your synagogue (you) of the house of Israel"; PVN: "How good are tents in which Jacob your father prays, and tents which you made for the Lord's name (P; VN: 'for my name') and your tents round about, you of the house of Israel."
[n] Nfi: "those of the sons of Jacob."

Notes, Chapter 24

[9]Nf and most ancient versions understood *n'm* ("oracle") as a verb: "he said"; (LXX, Vulg., Onq., Syr.).

[10]"The man. . .who is more honorable than his father"; thus also Ps.-J.; PVN have: "than his brother"; HT: "the man," *h-gbr;* the Hebrew word *gbr* is, apparently, taken as an honorable title. See Vermes, 1961 (1973), 58–60, 63; also note to Nf Gen 12:20; 32:7.

[11]"what has been hidden. . .revealed to him." HT: *stm h'yn,* "*štm* of the eye." The Hebrew word *štm,* occurring only in 24:3, 15, could in later Hebrew be understood as "to open, unseal, bore" (*štm*), or as "to close, to stop up" (*stm,* with *samech* or *sin*). The Pal. Tg. makes use of both meanings in its paraphrase: "hidden, revealed." See B. Grossfeld, note to Onq. Num 24:3 (*The Aramaic Bible,* vol. 8, p. 136). What was hidden from the prophets but revealed to Balaam would be the redemption to come (Tg. Num 24:17-20), the reward in store for Israel in the world to come (Tg. Num 23:23), divine revenge on the wicked (Tg. Num 24:23). The paraphrase of this section of Nf Num is to be compared with Pal. Tg. Gen 49:1. For a comparison of Tg. Num 24:4 with Matt 13:17 and Luke 10:24, see McNamara, 1972, 139–141.

[12]The HT reads: "The oracle of him who hears the words of God, who sees the vision of Shaddai, falling down but having his eyes uncovered" (see RSV). The single word "falling down" (*npl*) is paraphrased at length, and the phrase "his eyes uncovered" is taken to refer to the mysteries of prophecy revealed to him. The contents of his prophecies are then added. Balaam made reference to the possibility of his death by the sword already in Tg. Num 23:10.

[13]The HT (RSV) has: "How fair are your tents (*'hlk*), O Jacob, your encampments, O Israel." The term *'hl* ("tent") is used in different contexts in the Hebrew Bible: tents in which the Israelites lived, the tent of meeting, tents mentioned in connection with Jacob, called "a man of tents" (Gen 25:27). Furthermore, in rabbinic tradition *'hl* was interpreted as "academy" or "school house." The Hebrew *'hl* is translated by *mškn* in the Pal. Tgs. in general, a normal rendering, since *mškn* in Aramaic means "tent." Onq. here renders *'hl* as "land," and *mškn* as "dwelling place." (See note by B. Grossfeld in *The Aramaic Bible,* vol. 8, p. 136f.) Syr. renders *'hl* as "tent" (*mškn*) and *mškn* as "dwelling place" (*mšrwyh*). The various Pal. Tg. texts (Nfmg, PVN) in this particular instance (see Apparatus) paraphrase in keeping with the various meanings and associations of the two key terms. Nf is unique in giving a triple paraphrase, each based on the two key words. The first and third begin with "How" (*mh*), the second with "what" (*kmh*). See further B. Barry Levy, 1987, 2, 140–142.

the tents in which Israel your[o] *father resided! What good things and what consolations is his Memra to bring upon you who are*[p] *of the house of Jacob, for the merit of the school houses*[q] *in which Israel your father*[o] *served!* How *beautiful is the tent of meeting which encamps among you who are*[p] *of the house of Jacob; and* <*your*> tents are *round about it, (you) of the house of* Israel.[r] 6. Like *overflowing* torrents,[14] *so*[s] *shall Israel overflow on your enemies.*[t] Like gardens *planted* beside *sources of water, so shall*[u] *their cities be producing sages and sons of the Law.* Like *the heavens* <which God has spread out>[w] *as the house of his Shekinah,*[x] *so shall Israel live and endure for ever beautiful and praised,* and like the water cedars, *praised and exalted among his creatures.*[y] 7. *Their king*[z] *shall rise up from among them and their*

Apparatus, Chapter 24

[o] Nfi: "their father."

[p] Nfi: "(you,) house (of Jacob)."

[q] Nfi: "(of) the schools"; in the Targums *mdrš* occasionally occurs instead of *byt mdrš.*

[r] In the text *dy* has been wrongly crossed out, so that the literal translation is: "and the tents (lit.: 'their tents'), which are round about it, of the house of Israel." More probably, however, *dy* should be retained and "their tents" should be corrected to "your tents," and the translation given as in text; cf. Ps.-J.

[s] "so," "thus," *kdn;* PVN have variant *k(y)n.*

[t] PVN: "on their enemies."

[u] Nfi, Nfmg: "thus shall the synagogues of Israel bring forth wise men and masters of the Law. Like the heavens which the Lord has spread out and perfected as a house for his Shekinah, thus shall . . ."; PVN: "their cities bring forth scribes and teachers of the Law."

[w] The text of Nf is corrupt; reconstructed according to Nfi, Nfmg (note *u* above) and PVN: "and like the heavens which the Memra of the Lord has spread out."

[x] The Pal. Tgs., the Sam. Tg., and other versions (not Onq.) read *'ahalim* ("aloes") as *'ohalim* ("tents"); the Pal. Tgs. speak of the heavens because they are the tent of God; cf. Ps 19:4 and Vermes, 1961, 158.

[y] "his creatures": *bbrywth;* Nfmg: "(thus shall Israel be) high and exalted above all the nations, beautiful and praised as the water cedars, and exalted among creatures" (correcting *bybdwyyt'* to *bybrywt'*); PVN end paraphrase of verse: "(of water cedars and exalted, PVN) among creatures," *bbrywt',* P; "through his pain/suffering," *bkkywtyh,* VN (to be corrected to P?). The *Aruk* has: "of water (cedars) and exalted like the cedar"—*kbryt',* corrected to *k-brt',* with Jastrow 1, 195a and Levy 1, 118b. The original reading from which all descend may have been as the *Aruk.*

[z] In Nf, PVN: *mlkyhwn, lit.:* "their kings."

Notes, Chapter 24

[14]The HT has a description of "the tents of Jacob" of v. 5: "like wadis (*nḥlym*) that stretch afar, like gardens beside a river, like aloes (*'hlym;* MT: *'ahalîm*) that the Lord has planted (*nt'*), like cedar trees beside the waters." Nf explains the first three similes of Israel but leaves the fourth unexplained. The word *nḥl,* "wadi" (overflowing or dry), is understood as in spate, overpowering; the river (water) is understood as the Law, or the study (of the Law). The HT *'hlym,* (= *'ahalim,* "aloes") is read as *'oholîm,* "tents," a symbol of the heavens (cf. Ps 19:4-5), and *nṭ',* "planted," apparently seen as connected with *nṭh,* "to stretch out," and paraphrased as "his tent, his dwelling place"; cf. Pss 19:1-6; 104:2; Isa 40:22. The cedar is symbolic of dignity, and this is implicit in "praised and exalted (among his creatures)." A paraphrase of the ending "like cedar trees beside the waters" would give a text very similar to that of v. 6b ("like gardens beside a river"), and for this reason the present ending may have been purposely chosen; cf. B. Barry Levy, 1987, 2, 143. However, there is a problem with regard to the original form of the final word: Nf, MS has *k-brywth;* ed. A. Díez Macho, *b-brywth;* VN, *b-krywtyh;* Nfmg, *bybdwyyt'* (which Díez Macho corrects to *bybrywt'*); an *Aruk* citation has *k-bryt'.* Sokoloff, 1990, 112b, tentatively renders Nf as: "(exalted) in strength" (*bryw;* root *bry* 2, "to be strong"). Others understand as if = *brywth* = *bryyth* (Heb. pl. *brywt* "(among his) creatures"; "mankind." Jastrow, 195a, 198a), notes the *Aruk* reading and corrects Frg. Tg. Num 24:6 to an original *brt'* (so also Levy, 1, 118b), plur. of *brt,* "cypress, pine tree." Thus, the original of all would have been "praised and exalted like the cypress"; see also Klein, 1980, 2, 76. The emendation, however, seems doubtful.

redeemer[aa][15] *shall be from them(selves).*[bb] He shall gather their exiles for them from the provinces of their enemies, and his children[cc] *shall rule over* many *nations.*[dd] He shall be stronger than *Saul,* who <had pity> on Agag, the king *of*[ee] *the Amalekites,* and the kingdom *of the King Messiah* shall be exalted.[ff][16] 8. To the God who brought them *redeemed* out of Egypt[gg] belong *the power,*[hh] *praise*[ii] *and exaltation.*[jj][17] *The children of Israel* shall eat up *the possessions* of the nations, their enemies, and their *warriors*[kk] *they shall slay, and their cities they shall take and divide.* 9. *They* repose and rest[mm] like the lion and like the lionessess,[nn] *and there is no nation or kingdom*[18] which stands up *against* <them>. *He who* blesses *them*

Apparatus, Chapter 24

[aa] The paraphrase is also in PVN.

[bb] PVN: "of them(selves) and in them(selves)."

[cc] Lit.: "his children"; PVN: "their children"; MT: *zar'ô,* "his seed."

[dd] PVN: "he shall rule nation" (without "many").

[ee] Nf, PVN: *mlkyhwn.*

[ff] PVN: "shall become great." The paraphrase of v. 7 is otherwise practically identical in Nf and PVN. In Agag the Sam. Tg. sees King Gog of the last days: "and his king shall raise up Gog and his (i.e., the Messiah's) kingdom shall be exalted."

[gg] PVN: "God who redeemed and brought out redeemed from the land of Egypt."

[hh] Nfi: "his power."

[ii] Nfi: "and his praise."

[jj] In text and Nfi: "his exaltation"; "exaltation" (and possibly also "power") paraphrase *re'em* ("buffalo") of MT; cf. 23:22.

[kk] PVN, Nfi: "and their cities they shall divide and their warriors they shall blot out"; for "warriors," MT has *'aṣmotehem,* "their bones"; PVN: "the children of Israel shall eat the (P adds: "remnants of the") booty of their cities and their mighty ones shall be slain (P; VN: 'they shall slay'), and what remains of them they shall divide up."

[mm] Nfmg: "(and rest) in the midst of war like the lion and like the lioness. There is not"; PVN: "Behold this people lies down (or: 'dwells') like the lion and like the lioness it grows strong. Whoever blesses them (VN: P: 'blesses Israel') will be blessed like Moses the prophet, the scribe of Israel, and whoever curses them will be cursed like Balaam the son of Beor."

[nn] Cf. 23:24; probably "like the lioness," correcting the text to *k'rywt'.*

Notes, Chapter 24

[15]The HT paraphrased may be rendered (RSV): "water shall flow from his buckets (*mdlyw*) and his seed (*zr'hw*) shall be in many waters." Nf (and the Pal. Tg. texts) understand the text messianically, and so probably also Onq., which renders: "The king who will be anointed from among his sons shall become great and rule over many nations." Nf's paraphrase is gotten by understanding "water" as "the king" (below identified as King Messiah); cf. Isa 45:8: "let righteousness flow" (same verb) and Amos 5:24 (righteousness like a stream); Jer 23:5; 33:15 (the Messiah a righteous branch). Israel is "the bucket" (*mdlyw*), unless the Targums have read or interpreted the HT through *mdlywtyw,* "(from) his branches"; see Vermes, 1961 (1973), 159f. The first stichos of the HT is interpreted twice in Nf, the second time with the introduction of a reference to the messianic ingathering of the exiles. In regular targumic fashion "his seed" (*zr'-zar'ô*) is interpreted as "his children," with, however, inclusion of an understanding of the HT root as *zaroa',* "arm," "power" (rule). The Vulg. and Syr. apart, ancient versions understood the present HT *mym* ("waters") as "nations" (LXX; Onq.; Ps.-J.; Pal. Tg.; Philo, *Life of Moses,* 52, 290). The original reading may have been *'mym,* "nations."

[16]The HT has: "his king shall be higher than Agag, and his kingdom shall be exalted." Nf, in keeping with its overall paraphrase of the context, interprets messianically but retains a historical reference to Agag and Saul (1 Sam 15:9).

[17]"power, praise, exaltation"; see note to 23:22.

[18]"there is no nation or kingdom. . ."; HT: "who will rouse him up?" The HT text and Nf paraphrase are similar to those in Gen 49:9; see note to Nf Gen 49:9 (*The Aramaic Bible,* vol. 1A, p. 219).

shall be blessed, *and he who* curses *them* shall be cursed."[oo] 10. And the anger of Balak was enkindled against Balaam, and he clapped on the palm of his hands; and Balak said to Balaam: "I brought you to curse my enemies and behold, you have blessed *them* these three times.[pp] 11. And now, *go* to your place; I said that I would surely honor you and behold, the Lord has held back the honors from you." 12. And Balaam said to Balak: "Did I not also speak to your messenger[qq] whom you sent to me, saying: 13. 'If Balak should give me full of this house of silver and gold, I would not be able to go beyond *the decree of the Memra of* the Lord[rr][19] to do either good or evil of my own *knowledge.*[ss] What the Lord will speak,[tt] that will I speak.' 14. And now behold,[20] I am going to my people; come[uu] I will give you counsel:[ww] *cause them to sin, otherwise you will not be able to rule them;*[xx] *these, however,* this people *are to rule* over your people at the end of the last days."[yy] 15. And he took up his *prophecy* in a parabolic discourse and said:[21] "Says[zz] Balaam, the son[a] of Beor,[b] says the man *who is more honored than his father;*[c] *what was hidden from all the prophets*[d] *has been revealed to him.* 16. The utterance of him who[e] heard a *Memra*[f] *from before the* Lord and got knowledge *from before* the Most High,[g] and saw visions of Shaddai.[22] *And when he made petition he prostrated himself*[h] *upon his face, and the mysteries of prophecy were* revealed *to him. And he*

Apparatus, Chapter 24

[oo] Nfmg: "(stand up) against them. He who curses them shall be cursed like Balaam, the son of Peor (*sic*); and he who blessed them shall be blessed (like) the prophet Moses, the scribe of Israel"; cf. PVN and Gen 12:3.
[pp] PVN: "I brought you (VN; P: 'your people,' corr. to VN) to curse those who hate me, and you have only blessed (them)."
[qq] Nfi: "to your messenger" (another form).
[rr] Cf. 22:18.
[ss] The text, and Nfi, should probably be corrected with Onq., Ps.-J: "of my own will" (*m-r'wty*); see, nevertheless, 16:28.
[tt] Nfi: "what (the Lord) has spoken."
[uu] PVN: "come, now."
[ww] Nfi, PVN add: "that you shall do to (PVN: 'in') this people."
[xx] PVN: "you will not rule this people."
[yy] Lit.: "(at) the end of the heel of the days."
[zz] *'mr;* or: "oracle/utterance of" (*'ymr*); cf. v. 4 above.
[a] Nfi: "sons of . . ."
[b] V and in v. 3: "Peor."
[c] PVN: "than his brothers"; see note *g* to v.3.
[d] Nfi: "(from every) prophet."
[e] PVN: "of the man who"; cf. to v. 3.
[f] PVN: "speech" (*mmll*); cf. note *i* to v. 4.
[g] Nfmg: "(of) the Most High and the vision"; PVN: "from before the Most High; who saw a vision from Shaddai and when he desired he would prostrate himself upon his face"; cf. note *i* to v. 4 above.
[h] Nfi: "(and when) he prostrated himself"; cf. PVN, Ps.-J. and v. 4 above.

Notes, Chapter 24

[19]"decree of Memra of the Lord"; HT: "the mouth (= command) of the Lord."
[20]The HT has: "And now, behold, I am going to my people; behold, I will let you know what this people will do to your people in the satter days." The Pal. Tg. translates the beginning of the verse literally and gives the substance of the ending. In between the two it inserts Balaam's advice to Balak to cause Israel to sin. Such advice is mentioned in Num 31:16 and is the substance of a developed midrash found in Pseudo-Philo, *LAB* 18, 13; Philo, *Life of Moses* 53, 294–298; Josephus, *Ant.*, 4, 6, 6, 126–130. The texts are given in Vermes, 1961 (1973), 162–164. The tradition has influenced Onq. and Vulg., and is found in all Pal. Tg. texts of Num 24:14.
[21]See notes to 24:3.
[22]The HT here is identical with 24:4. See to 24:4; and see comments of B. Barry Levy, 1987, 2, 146f., for differences of spelling and word usage in Nf's translation.

prophesied concerning himself that he would fall *by the sword; and his prophecy was eventually to be fulfilled.* 17. I see him,[23] but he is not here now; I observe him, but he is not nigh. *A king is to arise* from *those of the house of* Jacob, *and a redeemer and ruler* from *those of the house of* Israel; and he *shall kill the mighty ones of the* Moab*ites* and *blot out* all the sons of Sheth, and *he shall cast out the owners[i] of property.*[24] 18. And Edom shall be[j] an inheritance, and *the mountain of Gablah*[k][25] shall be an inheritance for its enemies. And Israel *shall prosper in abundant riches.*[m] 19. *A king is to arise*[26] from *those of the house of* Jacob, *and he will blot out the one who has sinned*[n] *from the sinful city,*[o] *that is* <. . . . .>"[p] 20. And he

Apparatus, Chapter 24

[i] "masters" = *mry;* possibly in this name, by reading *rmy,* there is a veiled allusion to "Rome"; cf. PVN: ". . . of the Moabites and he shall eject (lit.: 'empty, drain'; VN add: 'and blot out') all the children of the east."

[j] Nfmg: "is," or: "shall be."

[k] Nfi: *mwl* = "limit"?; perhaps it should be corrected to *gbwl,* "Gabla"; or possibly to *mzl,* "lot," "possession," and a displaced variant from the following verse: *yrtw* ("inheritance").

[m] PVN: "and Israel shall grow strong (or: 'overpower [them]') with great might."

[n] PVN: "everyone who has remained."

[o] *krkh:* "fortress," frequently "capital."

[p] PVN: "the sinful city, that is Rome." Nf ends the verse without identification of the city, putting the *sof pasuq* (:) after "that is." The copyist then leaves almost an entire line blank, possibly indicating that his original had the name of the city, which he omitted through fear of censorship, or because the identification was already censored, and erased, in his original. After the next verse, part of the line remains blank, without there being any reason to suppose that text is missing. For Ps.-J.'s rendering, see text and corresponding note.

Notes, Chapter 24

[23]This verse gets a clear messianic interpretation: "star" of the HT is rendered as "king," and "scepter" as "redeemer and ruler." The "scepter" is also interpreted messianically in the LXX and Syr., and both "star" and "scepter" are understood messianically in Onq. and the Pal. Tg. The messianic prophecy of this star was believed to have been fulfilled in Bar Cosba (Kosiba) by R. Aqiba (*j. Taan* 68d; see also Rev 22:16). The messianic interpretation is probably older still, for instance by the Zealots of 64–70 C.E. and earlier. Josephus (*War* 6, 5, 4, 312f.) tells us that among the causes of the final rebellion against Rome stood "an ambiguous oracular pronouncement, which had been found in Holy Scripture, that one from their country would at that time be given command over the world. This they applied to a member of their own people and many wise men erred in their interpretation" (see also Tacitus, *Hist.* 5, 13; Suetonius, *Vesp.* 4, 5). The biblical text on which the interpretation referred to by Josephus was based is a matter of debate. Some scholars favor Dan 7:13ff. as the text. Others, with greater probability, opt for the present text of Numbers (vv. 24ff.). The star to arise out of Israel would first subjugate the surrounding nations, and finally apparently (24:24) destroy all world powers; see M. Hengel, 1989, 237–240, and McNamara, 1993.

[24]"he shall cast out the owners of property"; (*mry nksyyh;* the same expression occurs in Nfmg Gen 4:20). An addition in Nf; PVN have a different addition. See Apparatus.

[25]"the mountain of Gablah"; HT: "Seir." Nf's regular rendering of Seir, the home of Esau. See McNamara, 1972, 194.

[26]The HT of v. 19 may be rendered "One will come down (or: 'shall dominate'; *w-yrd*) from Jacob and the fugitive from a city (or: 'the city') shall perish." Nf (as PVN), in keeping with its approach, interprets the text messianically. The Hebrew *wyrd* is understood of dominion and royal power. All the Targums identify the city as an important one or a capital: Onq. as "the city of the nations"; Ps.-J. as Constantinople; PVN as "the guilty city, that is Rome." So, too, undoubtedly Nf's original. Nf ends the verse without identification of the city, putting the *sof pasuq* (:) after "that is." The copyist then leaves almost an entire line blank, possibly indicating that his original contained the name of the city, which he omitted through fear of censorship or because the identification had already been censored and erased in his original. After the next verse, in the MS of Nf, part of the line remains blank, without there being any reason to suppose that text is missing. For Ps.-J.'s rendering see text and corresponding note.

saw[q] the Amalek*ites* and took up his *prophecy in a* parabolic discourse and said: "The first[27] of the nations *who waged (war)*[r] *with*[s] *Israel were the* Amalek*ites,*[t] and *in the last days, in the days of Gog and Magog,*[u] *they are to wage war against them;* but their end shall be destruction, *and their destruction shall be for ever.*"[w] 21. And he saw[x] *the Shalmaites*[y][28] and took up his *prophecy* in a parabolic discourse and said: "*How* strong is your encampment; and in the *cleft of* the rock[z] you have set *your dwelling.* 22. But if *the Shalmaite* is to *be despoiled,* it is still the Assyrian who will take you captive."[aa] 23. And he took up his *prophecy* in a parabolic discourse and said: "Who would live[bb][29] *in those days when*[cc] *the Lord sets his mighty anger to take vengeance of the wicked, to give the reward*[dd] *of the just ones, and when he*

Apparatus, Chapter 24

[q] The subject "Balaam" is understood.

[r] This word, missing in text, is in PVN.

[s] PVN: "against."

[t] PVN: "those of the house of Amalek."

[u] PVN: "in the end (lit.: 'in the heel'), in the end of the days."

[w] Nfmg: "(and said): The first of the kings and the nations who waged war on the house of Israel were those of the house of Amalek. Joshua bar Nun of those of the house of Ephraim smashed them. The second who made war on them was Saul bar Kish, and he destroyed them (or: 'when they made war on them a second time, Saul bar Kish destroyed them'); but their end will be destruction for ever."

[x] *ḥm';* Nfmg: "and he saw" (another verb; *ḥz'*).

[y] Translating "Kenites" of MT, as in Gen 15:19.

[z] *b-nyqr';* thus also P, Ps.-J.; VN: "like a cattle fold" (*k-bqrt;* to be corrected to P?).

[aa] *'rwm 'n yhwwy šlmyh lbyzh 'd k'n 'šwryy mšby ytk.* A. Díez Macho, 1974, 4, 240, renders: "The Salmites, however, will not be despoiled until the Assyrians take you captive"; Le Déaut, 1974, 448: "Because if the Shalmite must be despoiled (this will not be) until the Assyrians lead you into captivity." P: "Because if (*'yn*) the Shalmaite is to be despoiled, it is (?; *'d k'n*) (that) the Assyrian arises and takes him captive" (*šby*); VN: "Because if the Shalmaite is to be destroyed, it is (?; *'d k'n*) that the Assyrian is to arise and break (*šbyr,* Hebrew) you" (correct to: *šby;* "take you captive"?).

[bb] Nfi: "Woe"; P: "Woe to you sinners (lit.: 'debtors') who have incurred guilt. When God comes to exact vengeance from them, from the wicked, and to give a good reward to the just, and when he lets loose the kingdom(s) of the nations one against the other"; VN: "Who would be alive when the Memra of the Lord sets <words omitted?> to give a good reward to the just and to exact vengeance from the wicked."

[cc] Nfmg: "when the Lord establishes his throne to exact vengeance and sets."

[dd] Nfi: "rewards."

Notes, Chapter 24

[27]"the first . . . who waged war with Israel"; Nf makes specific the more generic HT: "Amalek was the first of the nations." See also Onq. Nf also specifies HT: "in the end," as in the days of Gog and Magog (cf. Ezek 38–39, etc.).

[28]"Shalmaites"; the identification of HT "Kenite" here and Gen 15:19. The same identification is found in Onq. and rabbinic texts. See note by B. Grossfeld to Onq. Gen 15:19 (*The Aramaic Bible,* vol. 6, p. 71); also above, Introd. IV, 57.

[29]"who would live. . ."; rendering the HT *'wy my yḥyh msmw* (MT: *miśśumô;* from the root *śwm?*) The word *mśmw* is taken by some scholars as the infinitive *śwm,* with *acc. rei* = "set, ordain"; thus RSV: "Alas, who shall live when God does this." Many modern versions emend the MT variously. Onq. interprets as: "Woe to sinners who shall be alive when God does these things." Nf, like other Pal. Tg. texts, seems to understand by reading a dual sense in *m-śmw:* (1) "to set," and (2) as if from, or related to, the Hebrew word *šmm, šmmh,* "to be desolated, to appall; devastation": "when God sets (*yšwwy*) his mighty anger to take vengeance. . . ." (The theme of God's punishment of the wicked and rewarding of the good occurs elsewhere in Nf, e.g., Gen 3:19, 24; 4:8; 49:1.) The civil strife among nations may be a further expression of this desolation (*šmm, šmmh*). Belief in the coming eschatological strife, (e.g., Gog and Magog (Nf Num 24:20) may stand behind it. The LXX renders v. 23a as: "and seeing Og . . . he said."

lets kingdoms loose one against the other? 24. Numerous multitudes[ee][30] *shall come forth*[ff] <*in Liburnian ships*[gg][31] of *insolent*> *language from the region of Italy*[hh] that is <. . .>.[ii] And many *legions of* <*the Romans*>[jj] *shall join with them,* and they shall enslave the Assyrians and afflict (the region) *beyond the River; and their end shall* be destruction *and their destruction shall be for ever.*"[kk] 25. And Balaam went and returned to his place, and Balak also returned to his place and *set up his daughters*[mm] as *prostitutes.*[nn][32]

Apparatus, Chapter 24

[ee] Greek loan word *ochlos*.

[ff] MT *wṣym;* text translated as if *yṣym* (Sam. Pent.); thus also LXX, Pesh., Vulg., Onq., and Pal. Tgs.

[gg] Greek or Latin loan word *liburnika, liburnia:* light barks. In Nf this and words following erased by censor. VN: "and numerous multitudes in Liburnian ships (*lbrny'*) will come from the province of Italy and many legions from the south (*mdrwm';* or: 'from those of the Romans,' or: 'of Rome') and they will subdue the Assyrians and afflict all the children of (the land) Beyond the River (*Abar Nahara*). However, the end of both one and the other is destruction, and the destruction will be forever": P: "and numerous multitudes, with mixed multitudes (*'rbrbny';* cf. VN Exod 12:38) will come forth from the province of Italy, that is Rome, and numerous legions from Rome will join (or: 'be joined') with them, and the Assyrians will be subdued and they will afflict all the children of (the land) Beyond the River (*Abar Nahara*). However, the end of both one and the other is destruction, and their destruction is for ever."

[hh] Word erased, but can still be read.

[ii] As in Pal. Tg. citation in the *Aruk* ("Italy, that is Rome"), we should read "Rome" as the continuation; cf. v. 19 and PVN; the scribe, however, passes to the following word without giving the name of Rome or leaving any space.

[jj] Word erased and substituted by points as far as the margin.

[kk] Nfmg: "numerous (armies shall come forth) from (Liburnia, from the region of Italy) [*these last words, or words similar to them, have been erased by the censor*] and shall subdue the Assyrians and shall end with the inhabitants of the bank of the Euphrates; but the end of both one and the other is destruction; (with) eternal (destruction) they shall perish."

[mm] Nfmg: "his daughters" (written differently); or: "the daughters," i.e., "the young maidens"; cf. Num 25:1 and Ps.-J.

[nn] Lit.: "for to increase (and) multiply," *prh wrbh,* i.e., for propagation (an allusion to HT Gen 1:28).

Notes, Chapter 24

[30]The HT of v. 24 may be rendered: "But ships (shall come) from Kittim (*wṣym myd ktym*) and shall afflict Asshur and Eber; and he shall also come to destruction." The advent of ships of Kittim (*ṣyym ktym*) is mentioned again in Dan 11:30, in which text the Kittim are generally understood to be the Romans. In the later Qumran writings, too, Kittim means the Romans. The Vulg. renders Num 24:24 as: "*Venient trieribus de Italia*" ("They shall come in triremes from Italy"). For "of insolent language" (*'zy lšwn*—actually two Hebrew words), see Dan 8:11 (*'z pnym,* "bold countenance)," and Deut 28:50.

[31]"Liburnian ships," *b-lbrnyyh* (HT: *ṣym,* "ships"; also in Nf Deut 28:68, HT, *'nywt,* "ships"). A Latin (*[nauis] liburna*) or Greek (*libyrnê, libernion,* etc.) loan word. See D. Sperber, *Nautica Talmudica,* Ramat Gan/Leiden, 1986, 137–138. In rabbinic sources "Liburnian" often glosses the Hebrew term for "noble (gallant) ship" (e.g., Isa 33:21). The term is found in Greek (under the form *libernos*) in the first century C.E.; see F. T. Gignac, 1955, 1, 222. "The *liburnian* was a fast two banked galley adapted from a craft developed among the Liburnians, piratical-minded dwellers of the Dalmatian coast and its offshore islands" (Sperber, citing L. Casson, 1971, 141–142). According to the *b. B. Mez.* 80b the capacity of a large *Liburnian* was some 900 *kors* (over 2500 cubic meters), which has been reckoned as some ten tons. On the *liburnian,* see also S. Panciera, *Epigraphica* 18 (1956), 130–156, and his entry "Liburna," in *Dizionario epigrafico di antichità romane,* s.v. (1958).

[32]"and set up his daughters as prostitutes"; an addition in Nf; in keeping with the advice given by Balaam according to Pal. Tg. Num 24:14; see note to 24:14. Here the addition serves to introduce the narrative of Israel's seduction by the Midianite women in Num 25. See *LAB* 18, 14: "On saying this, Balaam turned away and returned to his place. And afterwards the people were seduced after the daughters of Moab. For Balac did everything that Balaam had showed him." For a detailed study of the Balaam legend and its development, see Vermes, 1961 (1973), esp. 169–177.

CHAPTER 25

1. And Israel[a] dwelt in Shittim, and the people began to fornicate with the daughters of the Moabites.[b] 2. And they invited the people to the sacrifices of their *idols,* and the people ate and bowed down to their *idols.*[1] 3. And Israel yoked itself to *the idol*[c] *of* Peor,[2] and the anger of the Lord was enkindled against Israel. 4. And the Lord[d] said to Moses: "Bring[e] all the chiefs of the people and *set them up*[3] *in a Sanhedrin before* the Lord *and* let *them become judges.*[f] *Everyone who is guilty of death*[g] *they shall crucify*[h] *on a cross*[4] and bury his corpse at sun*set.*[5] *In this manner the might* of the Lord's anger will turn back from Israel." 5. And Moses said to the judges[i] of Israel: "Let every one kill[j] the men *of his people* who yoked themselves *to the worshipers of the idol* of Peor."[6] 6. And behold, a man of the children of Israel came and brought the Midianite woman to his brothers, in the sight of[k] Moses and in the sight of[k] the whole congregation of the children of Israel, while they were weeping at the door of the tent of meeting. 7. And Phinehas bar Eleazar, the son of Aaron the priest,[m] saw (it), and he rose from the midst of the congregation[n] and took a spear in his hand.[o] 8. And he went after the Israelite man within the

Apparatus, Chapter 25

[a] Nfmg: "the children of Israel."
[b] With Nfi; Nf lit.: "of the Moabite."
[c] VN: "and Israel clung to the worshipers of the idol of Peor."
[d] PVN: "the Memra of the Lord."
[e] PVN: "take."
[f] PVN: ". . . a Sanhedrin and let them crucify (or possibly: 'impale') anyone who is guilty, who is (condemned) to be killed and with sunset let them take down his corpse (P: 'their corpses') and bury them . . ."
[g] Nfi: "to be killed."
[h] Nfi: "you shall crucify"; cf. Ps.-J.: "you shall crucify them . . ."
[i] VN: "and Moses said to the commanders of Israel: Let everyone kill the men of his (own) house, those who clung to the worshipers of the idol of Peor."
[j] Nfi: "put to death."
[k] VN: "before."
[m] VN: "the high priest."
[n] "the assembly."
[o] See also the paraphrase of Ps.-J.

Notes, Chapter 25

[1]"their idols"; HT: "their gods."
[2]"idol of Peor"; HT: "Baal-peor."
[3]"set them up. . . Crucify on a cross"; HT: "Hang (*hwq'*) them in the sun to (= before) the Lord." The term translated "hang" (from root *yq'*) is a rare word (in the Qal in Gen 32:26, "be dislocated"). In Num 25:4 and 2 Sam 21:6 it is used in the Hiphil of a solemn form of execution, without its precise meaning being clear ("expose with legs and arms broken"?). See also 1 Chr 10:10. In Nf's paraphrase, the Sanhedrin is presumed to have the power of passing the death sentence.
[4]"crucify on a cross," root *ṣlb,* or "impale on a pole;" see Nf Gen 40:19; 41:13; Deut 21:22.
[5]"at (lit.: "with) sunset"; *'m mṭm' šmš';* HT: *ngd hšmš,* "against the sun," RSV: "in the sun," i.e., in broad daylight. B. Barry Levy, 1987, 2, 154 believes that Nf means here "only in daylight," before nightfall, based on Deut 21:23.
[6]"to the worshipers of the idol of Peor"; HT: "to the Baal of Peor."

assembly[p] and pierced both of them, the Israelite man and the woman, through the bowels.[q] And the plague was stopped from the children of Israel. 9. And the dead *who died* from the plague were twenty-four thousand. 10. And the Lord[r] spoke with Moses, saying: 11. "Phinehas bar Eleazar, son of the *high* priest Aaron, has turned back my wrath from the children of Israel in that he was jealous with my jealousy among them, and I have not *blotted out* the children of Israel in my jealousy. 12. *On oath,* say:[s] 'Behold, I give to him my covenant of peace. 13. And it shall be for him and for his descendants after him a covenant of priesthood for ever, in return for his having been jealous for *the Name of* his God, and for having made atonement for the children of Israel.'" 14. And the name of the *slain* Israelite man, who was *slain* with the Midianite woman, was Zimri ben Salu, the chief of a father's house *of the sons*[7] of the Simeonites. 15. And the name of the *slain* Midianite woman was Cozbi, the daughter of Zur, who was head of peoples of a father's house in Midian. 16. And the Lord[t] spoke with Moses, saying: 17. "Surround the Midianites and *slay* them; 18. for they have distressed you by their deceits which have deceived you in the affair of *the idol of* Peor and in the affair of Cozbi, the daughter of the chief of Midian, their sister[u] who *was slain* on the day of the plague because of the affair of *the idol of* Peor." 19. And after the plague,

Apparatus, Chapter 25

[p] We should possibly read: "within the room" (*kwl'*) with *Aruk;* same word in Ps.-J. Num 24:25. Nfmg: *lwwt hwṣ',* correcting to *ḥwṣ'* (*ḥuṣa'*) (with Ps.-J., London MS, BL Add. 27031), "to the street" ("outside"), or retaining text (*huṣa'*), "to the hedge"; VN: an Israelite man into the tent of prostitution (*qwbt'*) and he pierced both of them, the Israelite man and the woman in indignation (?;*b-qpd',* a word of uncertain meaning; = *qwbt'?;* or: *qwl'?*) (Hebrew).

[q] Nfmg: "through the bowels" (sing; in text plur.); cf. *byt twrph,* "pudenda."

[r] Nfmg: "the Memra of the Lord."

[s] PVN: "of an oath, go Moses (P adds: 'in my name') and say to Phinehas (VN continues): Behold, I give him."

[t] Nfmg: "the Memra of the Lord."

[u] I.e., the sister of the Midianites.

Notes, Chapter 25

[7]"house of the sons of"; following the translation pattern set in Nf Num 1; HT: "(chief of) a father's house belonging to the Simeonites." See also note to 1:10 above.

CHAPTER 26

1. The Lord[a] said to Moses and to Eleazar, the son of Aaron, the *high* priest,[1] saying: 2. "Take the *total*[2] of the numbers of all the congregation from twenty years old and upward, by their fathers' house, all who are able to go forth to war in Israel." 3. And Moses and Aaron the priest spoke (with) them[b] in the plains of Moab, near the Jordan of Jericho,[c] saying: 4. "From twenty years old and upward," as the Lord[a] had commanded Moses. And (these were) the children of Israel who came forth *redeemed*[3] from the land of Egypt:[d] 5. Reuben, the first-born of Israel; the sons of Reuben: Hanoch of the family[e] *of the sons*[4] of Hanochites; for Pallu, the family *of the sons*[4] of the Palluites; 6. for Hezron, the family *of the sons*[4] *of* the Hezronites; for Carmi, the family *of the sons* of the Carmites; 7. these are the families *of the sons*[4] of Reuben.[f] And their *numbers*[5] were forty-three thousand seven hundred and thirty. 8. And the sons of Pallu: Eliab. 9. And the sons of Eliab: Nemuel, Dathan, and Abiram, that is, Dathan and Abiram the appointed ones of the congregation who were at strife[g6] *before the Lord*[7] against Moses and Aaron in the counsel of Korah,[8] when they made a schism[g] *before* the Lord, 10. and the earth opened its mouth and swallowed them up together with Korah *the time the people* of the congregation died, when the fire consumed the two hundred and fifty men; and they became a sign. 11. And the children of Korah, *for the reason*[9] *that*

Apparatus, Chapter 26

[a] Nfmg: "the Memra of the Lord."
[b] In text and in Onq.: "(spoke) them," reading *'tm* of HT as *'otam.*
[c] I.e., opposite or near Jericho.
[d] Nfmg: "from the land of the Amorites"; probably a mistake for: ". . . of the Egyptians."
[e] We should probably translate: "for Hanoch, the family of . . . ," as in vv. 23, 26, 30, 31, 32; cf. Nfi: "the family," not: "of the family."
[f] Nfi: "(of the sons of) the Reubenites."
[g] Lit.: "who divided."

Notes, Chapter 26

[1]"high priest"; HT: "priest"; See note to Nf Num 3:3.
[2]"total (of the numbers)"; HT lit.: "the head of all the congregation," *r'š kl-'dt.*
[3]"redeemed"; an expansive addition in the usual style of Nf; see above Introd. III, 22.
[4]"family of the sons"; HT: "family," *mšpḥh.* See note to 1:2 and Introd. III, 23.
[5]"(and of) their numbers"; *skwmyhwn;* HT: "root *pqd;* Nf renders the HT *pqd* in this context by *skm;* see note to Nf Num 1:19 and Introd. III, 25.
[6]"(who) were at strife"; *plgw;* HT: *hṣw* (root *nṣh,* Hiphil); a rare term, in Hiphil only here and in Ps 60:2. The same Aramaic word is used of Korah in Nf Num 16:1, rendering a different Hebrew term; see note to 16:1.
[7]"before the Lord"; an addition in Nf.
[8]"in the counsel of Korah," *b-'ṣth dqrḥ,* rendering HT *b-'dt (qrḥ)* as in 27:3. The Hebrew term is rendered differently ("in the congregation of K.") in Nf in the other occurrences. See note to 16:6.
[9]"for the reason that. . ."; HT simply has: "and the sons of Korah did not die." Nf supplies the reason why, possibly influenced by 27:3.

they were not in the counsel of[h] *their father,* did not die.[i] 12. And the sons of Simeon according to their families: for Nemuel, the family of the Nemuelites;[j] for Jamin, the family *of the sons of the* Jaminites; for Jachin, the family *of the sons*[4] *of the* Jachinites; 13. for Zerah, the family *of the sons*[4] *of the* Zerahites; for Shaul, the family *of the sons*[4] *of* the Shaulites. 14. These are the families of Simeonites:[k] twenty-two thousand two hundred.[m] 15. The sons of Gad according to their families: for Zephon, the family *of the sons* of the Zephonites; for Haggi, the family of the[n] Haggites; for Shumi, the family *of the sons*[4] of the Shumites; 16. for Ozni, the family of the sons of the Oznites; for Eri, the family of the sons of the Erites; 17. for Arod, the family of the sons of the Arodites; for Areli, the family of the sons of the Arelites. 18. These are the families of the sons of Gad according to the numbers: forty thousand five hundred. 19. The sons of Judah: Er and Onan; and Er and Onan died in the land of Canaan. 20. The sons of Judah according to their families were: for Shelah, the family of the sons of the Shelanites; for Perez, the family *of the sons*[4] of the Perezites; for Zerah, the family of the sons of the Zerahites. 21. And the sons of Perez were: for Hezron, the family *of the sons*[4] of the Hezronites; for Hamul, the family *of the sons*[4] of the Hamulites. 22. These are the families *of the sons*[4] of Judah, according to their *number:*[5] seventy-six thousand five hundred. 23. The sons of Issachar according to their families: (for)[o] Tola, the family *of the sons*[4] of the Tolaites; for Puvah, the family of the sons of the Punites; 24. for Jashub, the family *of the sons*[4] of the Jashubites; for Shimron, the family *of the sons*[4] of the Shimronites. 25. These are the families *of the sons*[4] of Issachar[p] according to their numbers: sixty-four thousand three hundred. 26. The sons of Zebulun according to their families: for Sered, the family *of the sons*[4] of the Seredites; for Elon, the family *of the sons* of the <Elonites>;[q] for Jahleel, the family *of the sons*[4] of the Jahleelites. 27. These are the families *of the sons*[4] of Zebulunites according to their *numbers:*[5] sixty thousand and five hundred. 28. The sons of Joseph according to their families: Manasseh and Ephraim. 29. The sons of Manasseh: for Machir, the family *of the sons*[4] of the Machirites; and Machir begot Gilead; for Gilead, the family *of the sons*[4] of the Gileadites. 30. These are the sons of Gilead: (for)[r] Iezer, the family *of the sons*[4] of the Iezerites; for Helek, the family *of the sons*[4] of the Helekites; 31. (for)[r] Astiel, the family *of the sons*[4] of the Astielites; and (for)[r] Shechem, the family *of the sons*[4] of the Shechemites; 32. and (for)[r] Shemidah, the family *of the sons* of the Shemidaites; and (for)[r] Hepher, the

Apparatus, Chapter 26

[h] Nfi: "of Korah their father."

[i] Nfmg: "(of their father) and they followed the teaching of Moses, their master, they did not die of the plague, nor were they punished by the burning nor did they sink down when the earth swallowed up" (lit.: "at the earth's swallowing"); cf. Ps.-J.

[j] Nfi: "of the sons of (the Nemuelites)."

[k] Nfi: "of the sons of (the Simeonites)."

[m] Nfi: "and two hundred" (another form).

[n] "sons of the (Haggites)" is probably missing.

[o] Missing as in the case of Hanoch (v. 5 and vv. 23, 26, 30, 31, 32).

[p] Nfmg: "the families of Issachar."

[q] In the text by mistake: "of the Jahleelites."

[r] Missing: in vv. 5, 23, 26, 30, 31, 32.

family *of the sons*[4] of the Hepherites. 33. And Zelophehad, the son of Hepher, had no sons, but only daughters; and the names of the daughters of Zelophehad were Nahlah, Noah, Haglah, Milcah, and Tirzah. 34. These were the families *of the sons*[4] *of* Manasseh; their numbers were fifty-two thousand seven hundred. 35. These are the sons of Ephraim according to their families: for Shuthelah, the family *of the sons*[4] of the Shuthelahites; for Bechar, the family *of the sons*[4] of the Becherites; for Tahan, the family *of the sons*[4] of the Tahanites. 36. And these are the sons of Shuthelah: by Eran, the family *of the sons*[4] of the Eranites. 37. These are the families *of the sons*[4] of Ephraim according to their *numbers:*[5] thirty-two thousand five hundred. These are the sons of Joseph according to their families. 38. The sons of Benjamin according to their families: for Bela, the family *of the sons*[4] of the Belaites; for Ashvel, the family *of the sons*[4] of the Ashvelites; for Ahiram, the family *of the sons* of the Ahiramites; 39. for Shephupham, the family *of the sons*[4] of the Shephuphamites; for Hupham, the family *of the sons* of the Huphamites. 40. And the sons of Bela were Ard and Naaman; (for Ard),[s] the family *of the sons*[4] of the Ardites; for Naaman, the family *of the sons*[4] of the Naamanites.[t] 41. These are the sons of Benjamin according to their families, according to their *numbers:*[5] forty-five thousand six hundred. 42. These are the sons of Dan according to the families: for Shuham, the family *of the sons* of the Shuhamites. These are the families *of the sons* of Dan according to their families. 43. All the families *of the sons*[4] of the Shuhamites[u] according to their *numbers:* sixty-four thousand. 44. The sons of Asher according to their families: for Imnah, the family *of the sons*[4] of Imnah; for Ishvi, the family *of the sons*[4] of the Ishvites; for Beriah, the family *of the sons*[4] of the Beritites. 45. For the sons of Beriah: for Heber, the family *of the sons* of the Heber; for Malchiel, the family *of the sons*[4] of the Malchielites. 46. And the name of the daughter[w] of Asher was Serah. 47. These are the families of the sons of Asher according to their *numbers:*[5] fifty-three thousand four hundred. 48. The sons of Naphtali according to their families: for Jahzeel, the family *of the sons*[4] of the Jahzeelites; for Guni, the family *of the sons*[4] of the Gunites; 49. for Jezer, the family *of the sons*[4] of the Jezerites; for Shillem, the family *of the sons*[4] of the Shillemites. 50. These are the families *of the sons*[4] of Naphtali according to their families, and[x] their numbers: forty-five thousand four hundred. 51. These are the *numbers*[y5] of the children of Israel: six hundred, one thousand seven hundred and thirty. 52. And the Lord spoke with Moses, saying: 53. "To these *tribes* the land will be divided as an inheritance according to the

Apparatus, Chapter 26

[s] Missing in Nf, with HT, Onq., Ps.-J; is found in Sam. Tg., where the first part of the verse is missing.

[t] Nfi: "(of the sons of) Naaman."

[u] Nfmg: "(all) the families of Shuham."

[w] Nfi: "the son." See what is narrated of her in Ps.-J.

[x] Nfi: "according to their totals."

[y] I.e., "this is the total" (lit.: "these are the totals," i.e., the sum totals).

number of their names. 54. To *the tribe of* many *people you*[10] shall give a larger inheritance, and to *the tribe of* fewer *people you* shall give a smaller inheritance; each according to its numbers shall be given its inheritance. 55. But the land shall be divided by lots; according to the names of their fathers' tribes they shall inherit. 56. According[z] to lots shall their inheritance be divided between the *tribe* of many *people* and between the *tribe*[aa] of fewer *people*." 57. And these are the *number* of the Levites[bb] according to their families: for Gershon, the family *of the sons*[4] of the Gershonites; for Kohath,[cc] the family *of the sons*[4] of the Kohathites; for Merari, the family *of the sons*[4] of the Merarites. 58. These are the families *of the sons*[4] of Levites:[dd] the family *of the sons* of the Libnites, the family *of the sons*[4] of the Hebronites, the family *of the sons*[4] of the Mahlites, the family *of the sons*[4] of the Mushites, the family *of the sons*[4] of the Korahites. And Kohath begot Amram. 59. The name of Amram's wife was Jachebed, the daughter of Levi, whom (his wife) bore[ee] to Levi in Egypt; and to Amram she bore Aaron and Moses and Miriam their sister. 60. And to Aaron were born Nadab, Abihu, Eleazar, and Ithamar. 61. And Nadab and Abihu died when they offered foreign[ff] fire before the Lord. 62. And their *numbers*[5] were twenty-three thousand: every male from a month old and upward. But they were not numbered among the children of Israel, because no inheritance was given to them among the children of Israel. 63. These are the *sum* totals of (the census) Moses and Eleazar the priest, who numbered the children of Israel in the plains of Moab, which is near the Jordan of Jericho. 64. And among those there was not a man from the *numbers* made by Moses and Aaron the priest, who had numbered the children of Israel in the wilderness of Sinai. 65. For the Lord had said to them: "You shall surely die in the wilderness." And not a man of them was left except Caleb bar Jephunneh and Joshua bar Nun.

Apparatus, Chapter 26

[z] Nfi: "(according to) the word of."
[aa] Nfi: "the tribes."
[bb] Nfi: "of Lèvi"; or: "of the Levite."
[cc] In the text, by mistake: "for the Kohathite."
[dd] Nfi: "of Levi"; or: "of the Levite."
[ee] I.e., "who was born"; a literal translation of the HT.
[ff] Cf. Lev 10:1ff. and Tg.

Notes, Chapter 26

[10]"to the tribe of many. . .fewer people"; the HT has simply the ambiguous *lrb . . . lm'ṭ*, "to the large . . . the few"; cf. RSV: "to a large tribe, to a small tribe."

CHAPTER 27

1. Then there drew near the daughters of Zelophehad bar Hepher, bar Eliad, bar Machir, bar Manasseh, from the families of Manasseh, the son of Joseph; and these are the names of his daughters: Mahlah, Noah, Hoglah, Milcah, and Tirzah. 2. And they stood[a] before Moses, and before Eleazar the priest, and before the princes, and *before* all *the people*[1] of the congregation, at the door of the tent of meeting, saying: 3. "Our father died in the wilderness, and he was not among *the people of*[1] the congregation that rebelled *before* the Lord in the *counsel* of Korah,[2] but died for his own sins; and he had no *male*[3] sons.[b] 4. Why, *now*, should the name of our father cease from the midst of his family because he had no *male* son? Give us inheritance among our father's[c] brothers." 5. *This is one of the four cases*[d4] *that came up before Moses. In two of them Moses was quick and in two of them Moses was slow. And in each of these Moses said:*[e] *"I have not heard." In (the case of) the unclean persons who could not keep the Passover at its (appointed) time and in (the case of) the two daughters of Zelophehad he was quick, because their cases were civil cases.*[f] *And in (the case of) the wood-gatherer who profaned the sabbath willfully and in (the case of) the blasphemer who pronounced the holy Name blasphemously, Moses was slow, because their cases were cases of capital sentence—to teach the judges that would arise after him*[g] *that they (should) be quick in civil cases and slow in cases of capital sentence, so that they would not put to death hastily one worthy in judgment to be put to death, and so that they would not be ashamed to say: "We have not heard (a similar case)," since Moses their master said: "I have not heard."* And Moses brought the *procedure* to be followed in their case before the Lord. 6. And the Lord[h] said to Moses: 7. "The daughters of Zelophehad have spoken *rightly;*[i5] you shall surely give them inheritance and possession among their father's brothers,

Apparatus, Chapter 27

[a] Lit.: "and they stand"; an atemporal participle; the context determines the time ("they stood").
[b] Nfi: "(he had) no (sons)."
[c] Nfmg: "(of) our fathers."
[d] Cf. 15:34 and Lev 24:12.
[e] Nfmg: "and in each of these Moses said."
[f] Lit.: "cases of wealth"; Nfmg: "case."
[g] Nfi: "after Moses."
[h] Nfmg: "the Memra of the Lord."
[i] Nfmg: "thus the daughters."

Notes, Chapter 27

[1]"people of"; an expansion in the style of Nf; see Introd. III, 23.
[2]"the counsel (*b'ṣth d*) of Korah"; HT: "in the company of (*b'dt*) Korah;" see note to 26:9.
[3]"male" could be intended as emphasis in the present context, dealing with sons. However, Nf often renders "son" (*bn*) of the HT as "male son."
[4]This is the fourth insertion of this midrash in Nf; it is found also at the other three key texts: Lev 24:12; Num 9:8; 15:24. Here, as in 15:24, the verse is translated at the end of the midrash.
[5]"rightly," *kdyn;* HT: *kn,* which ordinarily is to be rendered "thus," but here and in some other cases as "right." Thus in Pentateuch in the present text (*dbr kn;* likewise Num 36:5; Gen 42:11, 19, 31, 33f. Nf renders in Genesis as "trustworthy," and in Num 36:5 as (*lmymr*) *y'wt,* "(to speak) right." Onq. and Ps.-J. in Num 27:7 also render by *y'wt.*

and *you* shall pass on the inheritance of their father. 8. And you shall speak with the children of Israel, saying: 'If a man dies and has no *male* son, he shall cause his inheritance to pass to his daughter. 9. And if he had no daughter, you shall give the inheritance to his brothers. 10. And if he has no brothers, you shall give his inheritance to his father's brothers. 11. And if his father has no brothers, you shall give his inheritance to the *blood* relation[6] who is nearest to him of his family, and he shall inherit it.'" 12. And the Lord said to Moses: "Go up into this mountain of Ibrayya[j 7] and see[k] the land that I have given to[m] the children of Israel. 13. And when you have seen it, you also shall be gathered to your people, as Aaron your brother was gathered, 14. (because)[n] you have rebelled against *the decree of my Memra*[8] in the wilderness of Zin at *the Waters* of the Contention[9] *of the people*[1] of the congregation[o]—to sanctify *my Name*[10] before them *in the affair*[p] of the waters"—that is, the Waters of the Contention of *Reqem*[q 11] of the wilderness of Zin. 15. And the Lord spoke with Moses, saying: 16. "Let the Lord God *who rules* the spirits[12] of all flesh appoint a *trustworthy*[13] man over *the people of*[1] the congregation, 17. who shall go out before them and who shall enter before them, and who shall lead them out *to the array of battle,*[14] and who shall bring them in *from the array of battle in peace;* that the congregation of the Lord may not be like a flock which has no shepherd." 18. And the Lord said to Moses: "Take Joshua bar Nun, *upon whom a holy* spirit[r] *from before the Lord rests,*[15] and you shall lay your hand

Apparatus, Chapter 27

[j] = "of the Hebrews." In the MT there is question of the mountains of Abarim to the east of the Dead Sea.

[k] In text: "and you shall see" = "and see"; Nfmg: "and see" (imper.).

[m] Nfi: "of the sons."

[n] Lit.: "as"; a literal translation of *ka'ašer* of the MT.

[o] Translation of "the waters of Meriba" of MT; cf. 20:13. Another possible translation: "the Waters of the Judges."

[p] The word *'sq* ("affair") probably also suggests the sense of "dispute"; cf. 20:13.

[q] The Targums translate the place names Kadesh and Kadesh-barnea as Reqem and Reqem dy Gi'a.

[r] HT: "spirit"; in such cases Nf normally paraphrases as "holy spirit," Ps.-J. as "spirit of prophecy."

Notes, Chapter 27

[6]"blood relation"; lit.: "flesh relation"; HT (RSV): "kinsman."

[7]"mountain of Ibrayya"; MT: *har ha-'abarim,*

[8]"decree of my Memra"; HT: "my mouth" (= command).

[9]"(waters) of the contention"; HT: "(at) Meribah."

[10]"my Name"; HT: "me."

[11]"Reqem"; HT: Kadesh; see note to Num 13:26.

[12]"who rules the spirits. . ."; HT: "the God of the spirits of all flesh."

[13]"a trustworthy man"; HT: "a man," *'yš,* this Hebrew term being generally taken in the Pal. Tg. as meaning more than an ordinary person; see note to Nf Gen 12:20; 32:7 (*The Aramaic Bible,* vol. 1A, pp. 88, 157).

[14]"lead them. . . to the array, from the array. . ."; HT: "lead them out and bring them in."

[15]"upon whom a holy spirit . . .rests"; HT: "in whom is the spirit."

upon him. 19. And you shall cause him to stand before Eleazar the priest, and *before the princes,*[16] and before all *the people of*[1] the congregation, and you shall give him command[s] before them. 20. And you shall put the garment[t] of your dignity[17] upon him so that all the congregation[u] may hearken[w] to him. 21. And he shall stand before Eleazar the priest, and he shall inquire for him by the ordinance of the Urim[x] before the Lord. According to *the decree of*[18] his mouth they shall go out, and according to *the decree of*[18] his mouth they shall come in, he, the children[y] of Israel[z] with him, and all *the people of*[1] the congregation." 22. And Moses did as the Lord[aa] had commanded him; and he took Joshua and made him stand before Eleazar the priest and before all *the people of*[1] the congregation. 23. And he laid his hands upon him and gave him command:[bb] what the Lord[cc] had commanded through Moses.

Apparatus, Chapter 27

[s] Nfi: "and give (him) command."

[t] Or: "instrument"; translation takes *mn* as *m'n* ("instrument," "dress," as in Syriac). Possibly *yat* (sign of accusative) of text should be suppressed, *mn* read as "from," "of" ("part of"), and the passage translated as: "and you shall put (part) of your dignity" (or change text to *yt zyw rbwtk:* "the splendor of your glory"). Onq.: "(part) of your splendor"; Ps.-J.: "(part) of the splendor of your glory."

[u] Nfi: "of the sons of Israel."

[w] The word corresponding to "hearken, listen" of Nf in Onq. and Ps.-J., here and in other places, is "to receive" (*qbl*).

[x] Cf. Exod 28:30; Lev 8:8; Deut 33:8.

[y] Nfi: "(he) and all (the children)."

[z] Nfmg: "(he,) the people (of the children of Israel)."

[aa] Nfmg: "the Memra of the Lord."

[bb] We should probably read, with Nfi: "according as . . ."

[cc] Nfi: "according as the Memra of the Lord had commanded."

Notes, Chapter 27

[16]"before the princes"; an addition in Nf; cf. v. 2.

[17]"put the garment of your dignity," *yt mn rbwtk;* HT: "with some of your authority," *mhwdk.* A. Díez Macho suggests that we suppress *yt* or read *mn* as *m'n,* with the meaning "instrument," "clothes" (cf. Syriac). In favor of the reading *mn* = *m'n* one might instance Nf Num 19:15 (HT: *kly* and Lev 11:34). The word *m'n, mn* can also have the meaning "garments," "clothing," but only in the plur.; cf. Sokoloff, 1990, 288b. If we understand *mn* as garment, the transfer of authority (with the mantle) from Moses to Joshua would be as from Aaron to Eleazar, and from Elijah to Elisha; see B. Barry Levy, 1987, 2, 156f. B. Barry Levy thinks that *yt mn* is possibly a double translation of Heb. *m-* (*mn*). Others, as R. Le Déaut, 1979, 3 (*Nombres*), 124f., favor suppressing *yt,* rendering: "you shall put on him some (a part) of your dignity."

[18]"the decree of his mouth"; HT: "his mouth."

CHAPTER 28

1. And the Lord[a] spoke with Moses, saying: 2. "Command the children of Israel and say to them:[1] 'My offering, my bread,[2] *the bread of the arrangement*[b] *of my table, what you offer before me*[c]*—behold, it is the fire which consumes it; and it shall be received from you*[d] *before* me as an agreeable odor.[3] *My people, children of Israel, take heed* to offer it[e] at its due time.' 3. And you shall say to them: 'This is *the ordi-*

Apparatus, Chapter 28

[a] Nfmg: "the Memra of the Lord."
[b] I.e., the bread of the Presence (Exod 25:30), called "bread of the arrangement" in the Targum (Exod 25:30; Lev 24:6, etc.) because it was arranged in two rows (Lev 24:6); cf. note to Exod 25:30. The transmission of v. 2 seems imperfect; cf. Ps.-J.; PVN: "my offering, the bread of arrangement."
[c] PVN: "before me on top of the altar."
[d] P: "from them" (corr. to PVN).
[e] PVN: "before me."

Notes, Chapter 28

[1]According to *m. Meg.* 3:6, Num 28:11-15 was read on the New Moon (the beginning of the month), and *m. Meg* 4:2 notes that on this day the Law section is read by four (each of which reads three verses), and that no reading from the prophets followed. Since Num 28:11-15 is too small for twelve verses, the reading was extended to 28:1-15. See B. Barry Levy, 1987, 2, 157–159; McNamara, 1972, 42–44.

This liturgical use may explain the presence in Nf (and the Pal. Tg.) of the phrase "My people, children of Israel" (v. 2). This phrase occurs in Nf about fifty times (Exod 12:45; 20:2, 3, 7, 8, 12, 13, 14; 22:17, 21, 27; 23:2, 3, 19; 34:17, 26; Lev 19:11, 26; 22:28. It is found also (in parallel to Exod 22:3-14) in Deut 5:6, 7, 11, 12, 16, 17, 18; 14:3, 11, 20, 21, 22; 15:1; 16:9, 16; 18:13, 14; 22:10; 24:6, 9; 25:5, 17, 19; 28:3, 4, 5, 6; 33:29. While it is not always found in a liturgical context nor introducing extensive midrashim (see Díez Macho, *Neophyti 1,* I, 63*), it is often found in such contexts and suits texts designed for catechesis. See the list of texts (not including Nf Num 28:2) with comment in M. M. Kasher, 1983, 2, 154–169 (p. 161, summary for Neofiti 1). Díez Macho believes that the transmission of v. 2 has been defective and refers us to Ps.-J. (*Neophyti 1,* IV, 263); likewise Le Déaut, 1987, 3 (*Nombres*), 266, n. 1, who says that Nf v. 2 is to be corrected according to Ps.-J., whose text distinguishes the showbread from the whole burnt offering (with reference to Geiger, *Urschrift,* 477). Ps.-J. differs from Nf on the following points: (1) it omits "my bread," and (2) after "of my table" it inserts: "the priests shall eat"; and (3) continues: "and what you offer on my altar, it is not permitted to anyone to eat of it. Is it not the fire which will (= must) devour it?" etc. However, no such emendation in Nf seems necessary; see notes below for details and B. Barry Levy, 1987, 2, 157–159.

[2]HT has: "my offering, my food (*lḥmy*) for "my offerings by fire (*l'šy*), my pleasing odor. . ." The term *lḥmy,* "my bread" or "my food" in God's mouth presented a problem: God does not need or eat food. *Num R.* XXI, 16-19 treats of it at length, with reference to Ps 50:12 and other texts. Nf seems to address this problem by saying that *lḥmy,* "my food" or "my bread" of the HT, is "the bread of the arrangement," *lḥm sdwr.* This is in keeping with Nf's rendering of HT's *lḥm pnym* as *sdwr lḥm 'py'(h)* in Exod 25:30; 35:13; 39:36 (always in conjunction with the "table" (*ptwr'*). The terminology is already prepared for in HT 1 Chr 28:16, 2 Chr 2:4; 29:18, where the showbread is called "the arrangement," *m'rkh,* and 1 Chr 9:32; 23:29; 2 Chr 13:11; Neh 11:33 with the phrase "the bread of arrangement," *lḥm m'rkh.* This bread was eaten by the priests each sabbath (Lev 24:5-9); only the incense was burned. Thus also Ps.-J. in Num 28:2. Nf seems to say that the fire (i.e., not God directly) consumed it, paraphrasing HT *l'šy,* "for my (offering of) fire." In this Nf differs from its usual rendering of the HT term *'ššh* as *qrbn,* "offering" (see above, note to 15:10 and Introd. III, 2). Nf (and PVN) in this verse, while not good exegesis, may be original, and Ps.-J. 3 a corrected version.

[3]"it shall be received. . .agreeable odor." This reflects the HT: "my pleasing odor", *ryḥ nyḥḥy,* in keeping with Nf's usual paraphrase of HT *ryḥ nyḥwḥ* (Exod 29:18, 25; Lev 1:9, 13, 17; 2:2, 9, 12; 3:5, 16, 31, etc., generally with *'šh;* Lev 1:9, 13, 17; 2:9; 3:5; (8:21, holocaust); 23:13, 18; Num 15:10, 13, 14 (15:24, holocaust); 18:17, [28:23], 28:6, 8; (28:13 holocaust); 28:24 (*lḥm*) 29:6; 29:13, 36. See Introd. III, 7.

nance of the offering[4] which you shall offer *before* the Lord: each day two lambs, a year old, perfect, *without blemish,*[5] as a perpetual[f] burnt offering. 4. One of the lambs *you shall offer* in the morning, and the second lamb *you shall offer* between the two suns. 5. And for the *minhah* (offering),[g] a tenth of a *mekilta*[h6] of fine flour soaked in a fourth of a hin of pressed oil. 6. It is a perpetual burnt offering *like that which was offered*[i] on Mount Sinai as an agreeable odor, *an offering acceptable*[7] *before* the Lord.[j] 7. And with each of the lambs *you shall offer* the corresponding libations *of wine:*[8] a quarter of a hin; the libation of *choice wine* to *the name of* the Lord shall be poured out in the vessels of the sanctuary. 8. And the second lamb *you shall offer* (between)[k] the two suns; like the *minhah* of the lamb of the morning and like its libations, thus *shall you offer it;* it is *an offering acceptable*[9] as an agreeable odor *before* the Lord.[m] 9. On the sabbath day *you shall offer*[10] two lambs, a year old, perfect, *without blemish,* and two tenths of fine flour soaked in oil, as a *minhah,* these and their *corresponding* libations. 10. *You shall offer*[10] the burnt offering of the sabbath *on the sabbath day;*[11] *it shall be offered beside* the burnt offering of the perpetual sacrifice[n] and its libations. 11. And at the beginnings of your months you shall offer a burnt offering *before* the Lord: two young bulls,[12] one ram, <seven>[o] lambs a year old, perfect, *without blemish;* 12. and *you shall offer*[13]

Apparatus, Chapter 28

[f] Cf. Exod 29:38ff.
[g] Cf. Exod 29:40ff.
[h] Nfmg: "a tenth of an *ephah*"; Onq., Ps.-J.: "a tenth of three *se'in;* Sam. Tg.: "a tenth of a *se'ah.*"
[i] Nfmg: "which you had been offered."
[j] Nfmg: "(an offering) acceptable for the name of the Lord."
[k] Missing in text; supplied, but incorrectly, in Nfi.
[m] Nfmg: "(. . . you shall offer it) as an agreeable odor: an offering acceptable to the name of the Lord."
[n] Nfi: . . . "the (perpetual) burnt offering" (*tamid*).
[o] Missing in text and margin, but is in HT and versions.

Notes, Chapter 28

[4]"ordinance of the offering," HT: "(this is) the offering."
[5]("perfect) without blemish"; Nf's usual expansion of HT "perfect" in such condition. See note to Nf Gen 6:9 and Introd. III, 8.
[6]"mekilta"; HT: ephah (*'yph*). This is Nf's constant rendering of this HT word (Exod 16:16; Lev 5:11; 6:13; 19:36; Num 5:15; 28:5; Deut 25:14, 15.
[7]"an offering acceptable. . . ."; The HT has: "it is a perpetual burnt offering which was made (*h'śyh; ha-ʿaśûyah;* RSV: 'ordained') at Mount Sinai, for an odor of good favor (RSV: 'pleasing odor'), an offering by fire (*'šh*) to the Lord."
[8]"you shall offer. . . of wine"; an addition in Nf; cf. Lev 23:13.
[9]"an offering acceptable. . ."; HT: "an offering by fire (MT: *'iššeh*), a pleasing odor to the Lord."
[10]"(you) shall offer"; an addition in Nf.
[11]"on the sabbath day"; HT: "on its sabbath."
[12]"two young bulls"; Nf's text has *twryn bny šthwn twryn tryn,* "bulls a year old two bulls," rendering HT *prym bny bqr šnym.* Nf, in keeping with its rendering of the HT wording elsewhere (e.g., Num 7:15, 21, etc.; 29:13, 17), should read: *twryn bny twryn tryn.* The word *šthwn* was introduced through its occurrence at the end of the verse.
[13]"according to this ordinance my people. . ." An addition in Nf, possibly occasioned by the liturgical use of the passage; see note to 28:1.

three tenths of fine flour as a *minhah* soaked in oil, for each bull; and two[p] tenths of fine flour as a *minhah,* soaked in oil, with each ram; 13. and *you shall offer* a tenth of a *mekilta* of fine flour as a *minhah,* soaked in oil, with each lamb; it is a burnt offering of agreeable odor, *an offering acceptable*[q] *before* the Lord.[r] 14. And as regards their libations—*that which you shall offer with them*[s]—of wine[t] you shall offer[u] half a hin with the bull, and *you shall offer* a third of a hin with the ram, and *you shall offer* a quarter of a *hin* with the lamb. This is the burnt offering *you shall offer at every beginning* of a month, as it is renewed.[w] *According to this ordinance,*[13] *my people, you shall make offerings at every* beginning of the months of the year. 15. And *you shall offer before* the Lord a male goat[x] for the sin offering;[y] *it shall be offered* beside the burnt offering of the perpetual sacrifice and its libations. 16. And in the first month, on the fourteenth day of the month, is *the sacrifice*[z] *of* the Passover[14] *before* the Lord. 17. And on the fifteenth day of this month is the feast. Seven days *you* shall eat unleavened bread. 18. On the first day (there shall be) *a feast day*[15] and a holy convocation; you shall do no servile work. 19. And you shall offer *offerings* as holocausts *before*[aa] the Lord: (two)[bb] young bulls, one ram, and seven lambs, a year old; they shall be[cc] for you perfect, *without blemish.*[5] 20. And as their *minhah you shall offer* three tenths of fine flour, soaked in oil <with the bull, and two tenths for the ram>.[dd] 21. *You* shall offer a tenth of a *mekilta* with each lamb. *According to this ordinance you shall offer* the seven[ee] lambs;[16] 22. and one male goat for a sin offering to make atonement[ff] for you. 23. *You shall offer* these besides the burnt offering of the morning,[gg] which is the

Apparatus, Chapter 28

[p] Nfmg: "(. . . in oil) you shall offer with each bull, and two . . ."
[q] Nfi: "(an offering) which is eaten."
[r] Nfi: "(an offering) acceptable to the name of the Lord."
[s] I.e., with the aforementioned animals.
[t] Nfmg: "of the burnt offering."
[u] Nfmg suppresses this verb (first occurrence).
[w] Nfi adds: "in its time"; Nfmg: "(. . . month) to the place (lit.: 'house'; = to the Temple?) of its renewal at its (due) time and according to this . . ." We should, however, probably correct and read Nfmg thus: "at its renewal, at its (due) time and according to this . . ."
[x] Nfmg: "one (male goat)."
[y] Nfmg: "for a sin offering."
[z] Nfmg: "(is) a sacrifice" (another form).
[aa] Nfmg: "(as) an offering, (as) a burnt offering before . . ."; CTg F: ". . . offerings as a holocaust before the Lord."
[bb] Missing in text; is in Nfi.
[cc] Nfi: "it shall be."
[dd] Omitted in the text through homoeoteleuton; supplied in Nfmg; CTg F: "with each ox . . . with each ram."
[ee] Nfmg: ". . . you shall offer for the number (or: 'the count') of the seven"; = CTg F.
[ff] Nfi: "to make atonement" (another form).
[gg] Nfmg: "(the burnt offering) which is near (= accompanies) the perpetual (= daily) burnt offering"; = CTg F; cf. CTg Y.

Notes, Chapter 28

[14]"sacrifice of the Passover"; *nkst psḥ';* HT: "Passover"; *psḥ;* the same expansion of *psḥ* in Nf Exod 12:11; Lev 23:5 "sacrifice of *psh* (*zbḥ psḥ*) in HT Exod 12:12; 34:25.

[15]"a feast day"; HT: "a holy convocation," *mqr' qdš.* The same double rendering "a feast day (*ywm ṭb*) and a holy convocation" occurs in Nf: Num 28:18, 25, 26; 29:1, 7, 12. Likewise in Nf Exod 12:16; Lev 23:2 (cf. 23:3), 4, 7, 21, 24, 27, 36. It is rendered simply by "holy convocation" in Nf Lev 23:8, 35.

[16]"according to this order you shall offer with the seven lambs." The HT for the verse simply has: "a tenth shall you offer (lit.: 'do') for each of the seven lambs"; cf. vv. 14, 29; 29:4, 14, etc.

continual burnt offering. 24. According to this *ordinance,* each day of the seven days you shall offer food, *an offering acceptable*[hh][17] *in good pleasure*[ii] *before* the Lord; *it shall be offered* beside the continual burnt offering and its libations. 25. And on the seventh day (there shall be) *a feast day,*[15] and you shall have a holy convocation; you shall do no servile work. 26. And on the day of the first fruits, when you offer a *minhah* of the new fruits *before* the Lord, *at the time of*[18] *your feast of* Weeks,[jj] (there shall be) *a feast day*[15] and you shall have a holy convocation. You shall do no servile work. 27. And you shall offer a burnt offering as an agreeable odor *before*[kk] the Lord: two young bulls and one ram, seven lambs a year old; 28. and *you shall offer* their *minhah* of fine flour soaked[mm] in oil; you shall offer three tenths with each bull, two[nn] tenths with the (one) ram. 29. *You shall offer* a tenth of a *mekilta* for each lamb;[oo] *according to this ordinance you shall offer*[pp] the seven lambs;[19] 30. (and) one[qq] male goat to make atonement for you 31. Besides the continual burnt offering and its *minhah,* you *shall offer* them—they shall be[rr] perfect, *without blemish* for you—and their libations."

CHAPTER 29

1. "And in the seventh month, on the first[a] of the month, you shall have *a feast day*[1] and a holy convocation; you shall do no servile work. It shall be for you a day

Apparatus, Chapter 28

[hh] Nfmg: "which is acceptable."
[ii] Nfi: "as an agreeable odor"; = CTg F and CTg Y.
[jj] Cf. Exod 23:15f.; 34:22; Lev 23:15-21.
[kk] CTg Y: "to the name of."
[mm] Nfmg: "mixed."
[nn] Nfmg: "(with) one (bull) and two . . ."
[oo] Nfmg: "(with) the lambs."
[pp] Nfmg: "you shall offer for the number (or: 'count') of the seven lambs"; CTg F: "you shall offer before me, O my people, to (or: 'for') the number (or: 'count') of the seven lambs."
[qq] Nfmg: "and (one) male goat."
[rr] Nfi: "it shall be."

Notes, Chapter 28

[17]"an offering acceptable. . ."; HT: "an offering by fire (*'iššeh*), a pleasing odor."
[18]"at the time of. . ."; HT has: "at your feast of weeks." See Exod 23:15-16; 34:22; Lev 23:15-21.
[19]For this verse (29) the HT simply has: "a tenth for each of the seven lambs."

Apparatus, Chapter 29

[a] Nfmg: "day."

Notes, Chapter 29

[1]"a feast day and a holy convocation"; HT: "a holy convocation"; see note to 28:25.

for the blowing[b] *of the shofar* and *alarm.*[c2] 2. And you *shall offer*[3] a burnt offering, a pleasing odor *before* the Lord: one young bull, one ram, seven lambs a year old, perfect, *without blemish.*[4] 3. And as their *minhah* of fine flour soaked in oil, three tenths *you shall offer with* the bull;[d] *you shall offer* two tenths *with the*[e] ram. 4. And *you shall offer*[5] one tenth of a *mekilta*[f] with each lamb.[g] *According to this ordinance*[6] *you shall offer* the seven[h] lambs. 5. And offer a male goat for a sin offering,[i] to make atonement for you. 6.—besides the burnt offering for the new moons with its *minhah* and its libations, according to the ordinance for them—as an agreeable offering; it is *<an offering>*[j] *acceptable*[7] *before* the Lord. 7. The tenth day of this seventh month shall be a *feast day;*[1] and you shall have a holy convocation, and *on it* you shall impose fast on yourselves.[k] You shall do no work.[m] 8. And you shall offer a burnt offering *before* the Lord as an agreeable odor: one young bull, one ram, seven lambs a year old; they shall be to you perfect, *without blemish.*[4] 9. And as their *minhah* of fine flour soaked in oil, *you shall offer* three tenths with the bull, two[n] tenths with the (one) ram. 10. *You shall offer a* tenth of a *mekilta* with each lamb. *According to this ordinance*[6] *you shall offer* with the seven[o] lambs. 11. *And offer* one male goat for a sin offering,[p] besides the sin offering of atonement and the burnt offering of the perpetual sacrifice with its *minhah* and

Apparatus, Chapter 29

[b] Nfmg: "it shall be for you (a day for) the sounding of the *shofar,* with connected (*tqy'h*) and disconnected (*ybbw*) notes." The *circellus* is probably badly placed and we should read: "it shall be for you a day for sounding with disconnected notes." Ps.-J. adds: "to confound Satan who comes to accuse you."

[c] Cf. Num 10:5, 9; 31:6.

[d] Nfmg: "one (bull) and two . . ."

[e] Nfmg: "one (ram)."

[f] Nfmg: "(and) you shall offer one (tenth)."

[g] Nfmg: "(with) one lamb" (corr. from "lambs").

[h] Nfmg: "you shall offer for the number (or: 'count') of the seven . . ."

[i] Nfmg: "(and a male goat) to make atonement (for you)," or better: "(and a male goat for a sin offering) to make atonement . . . ," i.e., in Nfmg "offer" of Nf text is suppressed with HT and versions.

[j] Missing in text; is in Nfmg and 27:6. Nfmg 1°: "an offering acceptable as an agreeable odor for the name of the Lord"; Nfmg 2°: (a variant of Nfmg 1°): "(an offering acceptable) to the name (of the Lord)."

[k] See Ps.-J. for details.

[m] Nfmg: "servile."

[n] Nfmg: "and two."

[o] Nfmg: "and you shall offer for the number (or: 'count') of the seven . . ."

[p] Nfmg: "(and one male goat) for the sin offering," i.e., in Nfmg "offer" of the text is suppressed; cf. v. 5 and note *i* above.

Notes, Chapter 29

[2]"the blowing of the trumpet and the alarm," *tqy'h dšwpr wybbw.* HT: *trw'h,* "blowing of the trumpet." The text of Nf refers to two kinds of blowing of the shofar, connected (*tqy'h*) and disconnected (*ybbw*). Nf probably has a double translation, as in Lev 23:24. The HT word is translated by *ybbw* alone in Nf Lev 25:9; Num 10:5, 6; 31:6.

[3]"You shall offer"; HT lit.: "you shall make"; in the other verse the explicit mention of offering is an addition in Nf (thus in vv. 4, 9, 11, 14, 15, 17, 19, 20, 21, 24, 25, 26, 27, 29, 30.

[4]"perfect without blemish"; HT: "perfect"; see above, Introd. III 8; notes to Num 28:3 and to Nf Gen 6:9.

[5]The HT for the verse has: "and one tenth each for the seven lambs."

[6]"according to their ordinance. . ."; a recurring addition in Nf; cf. Num 28:14, 21, 29; 29:4, 14, 15, 39. A similar phrase also occurs in the HT; see 9:3.

[7]"an offering acceptable . . ."; HT: "an offering by fire (*'iššeh*) to the Lord"; see above Introd. III, 2 and notes to 28:2 and 15:10.

their libations. 12. On the fifteenth day of the seventh month you shall have a *feast day*[1] and a holy convocation. You shall do no servile work, and you shall keep a feast *before* the Lord seven days. 13. And you shall offer a burnt offering, *an offering acceptable*[7] as an agreeable odor *before* the Lord: three young bulls, two rams, fourteen lambs a year old; they shall be perfect, *without blemish.*[4] 14. And as their *minhah* of fine flour soaked[q] in oil, *you shall offer* three tenths with each bull. *According to this ordinance*[6] *you shall* offer the three bulls.[r] You shall offer two tenths with each ram. According to this ordinance you shall offer the two[s] rams. 15. And *you shall offer* one tenth of a *mekilta* with each lamb. *According to this ordinance*[6] *you shall offer* with the fourteen.[t] 16. And *you shall offer* one male goat as a sin offering,[u] besides the burnt offering of the perpetual sacrifice, its *minhah* and its libations. 17. On the second day *of the feast of Booths,*[8] *you shall offer* <twelve young bulls and two rams>,[w] fourteen lambs a year old, perfect, *without blemish,*[4] 18. and their *minhah* and *the wine*[9] *of* their libations, *which you shall offer with them:* with the bulls, with[x] the rams, with[y] the lambs, according to their number, according to the ordinance. 19. And *offer* one male goat for the sin offering,[z] besides the burnt offering of the perpetual sacrifices, and its *minhah* and their libations. 20. On the third day *of the feast of Booths you shall offer* eleven bulls, two[aa] rams, fourteen lambs a year old, perfect, *without blemish,*[4] 21. and their *minhah* and their libations[bb]—*which you shall offer with them*—with the bulls, with the rams, with[y] the lambs, according to their number, according to the ordinance; 22. and one male goat for a sin offering, besides the burnt offering of the perpetual sacrifice, and its *minhah* and its libation.[cc] 23. On the fourth day *of the feast of Booths you shall offer* eleven bulls, two rams, fourteen lambs a year old, perfect, *without blemish,* 24. and their *minhah* and their libations[bb]—*which you shall offer with them*—with the bulls, with[x] the rams, with[y] the lambs, according to their number, according to the ordinance. 25. And *offer* a male goat for a sin offering,

Apparatus, Chapter 29

[q] Nfmg: "mixed."

[r] Nfmg: "(with each bull) for the number (or: 'count') of the three bulls."

[s] Nfmg: "(with each ram:) for the number (or: 'count') of the two (rams)."

[t] Nfmg: "(according to this ordinance) you shall offer for the number (or: 'count') of the fourteen lambs."

[u] Nfmg: "for the sin offering."

[w] Missing in the text; supplied in Nfmg by the person who added the glosses; "twelve and rams" is found in another Nfmg.

[x] Nfmg: "and with (the rams)."

[y] Nfmg: "and with (the lambs)."

[z] Nfi: "(and one male goat) for the sin offering"; without "offer"; cf. vv. 5, 11; Nfmg: "for a sin offering."

[aa] Nfmg: "and (two) rams."

[bb] Nfmg: "and wine of libation."

[cc] Nfmg: "and their libations."

[dd] Nfmg: "twelve."

[ee] "the rams" is twice in the margin to the supplied text.

[ff] Missing in the text; supplied in the margin.

[gg] Nfmg: "twelve (bulls) and (two) rams."

[hh] Nfmg: "and the water."

Notes, Chapter 29

[8] "on the feast of Booths"; an addition in Nf, as in vv. 20, 23, 26, 29. The section 29:12-38 concerns the feast of Booths.

[9] "the wine"; an addition in Nf; not added in Nf in vv. 21, 24, 27, 30, 33, 37 but is in Nfmg.

besides the burnt offering of the perpetual sacrifice, and its *minhah* and libation.[cc] 26. And on the fifth day *of the feast of Booths you shall offer* nine[dd] bulls, two rams, fourteen lambs a year old, perfect, *without blemish,* 27. (and their *minhah* and their libations[bb]—*which you shall offer with them*—with the bulls, with[x] (the rams),[ee] with[y] the lambs, according to their number, according to the ordinance);[ff] 28. and a male goat for the sin offering, besides the burnt offering of the perpetual sacrifice, and its *minhah* and its libation. 29. And on the sixth day *of the feast of Booths you shall offer* eight[gg] bulls, two rams, fourteen lambs a year old, perfect, *without blemish,* 30. and their *minhah* and their libations[bb]—*which you shall offer with them*—with the bulls, with the rams and with the lambs, according to their number, according to the ordinance; 31. and one male goat for the sin offering, besides the burnt offering of the perpetual sacrifice, *and a flask of water,*[10] *which is offered*[11] *on the sixth day upon the altar as a good memorial of the fructification of the rain,*[hh] (its *minhah*)[ii] and its libation, *and the libation of the water.*[jj][12] 32. And on the seventh day *of the feast of Booths you shall offer* seven bulls, two rams, fourteen lambs a year old, perfect, *without blemish,*[4] 33. and their *minhah* and their libations[bb]—*which you shall offer with them*[13]—with the bulls, with[x] the rams, with[y] the lambs, according to their number, according to the ordinance, 34. and one male goat for the sin offering, besides the burnt offering of the perpetual sacrifice, and its *minhah* and its libation.[kk] 35. And on the eighth day *you shall be gathered*

Apparatus, Chapter 29

[cc] Nfmg: "and their libations."
[dd] Nfmg: "twelve."
[ee] "the rams" is twice in the margin to the supplied text.
[ff] Missing in the text; supplied in the margin.
[gg] Nfmg: "twelve (bulls) and (two) rams."
[hh] Nfmg: "and the water."
[ii] This word and the preceding one ("the rain") added in the margin; one is missing in the text.
[jj] Nfmg: "(for the sin offering,) apart from the holocaust of the sin offering, and their *minhahs,* and their libations."
[kk] Nfmg: "one . . . goat for the sin offering, beside the burnt offering of the perpetual sacrifice, and its *minhah* and their libations."

Notes, Chapter 29

[10]"flask of water. . .rain." This is an addition in Nf, in keeping with the water libation observed at this feast. The HT (RSV) for v. 31 has: "also one male goat for a sin offering; besides the continual burnt offering, its cereal offering, and its drink offerings." The rite concerning the bringing of the water from the pool of Siloam to the altar each of the seven days of the feast of Booths is described in *m. Sukk.* 4:9 (and *t. Sukk.* 3:3-14). The water was poured into one of the two silver vessels by the altar; the other vessel was for wine. The libation of wine and water on the feast of Booths is also mentioned in Ps.-J. Gen 35:14. Note the addition of "wine" to "libations" of HT in Nf Num 29:18 and in Nfmg Num 29:21, etc. See note to 29:18. For the possible bearing of these traditions on John 7:37-39, see P. Grelot, 1963, 43–51; McNamara, 1972, 146; and extra bibliographical reference in Forestell, 1979, no. 196 (p. 43 and also 97).

[11]"which is offered," *dhwwt mtqrbh*"; or possibly: "which used to be offered up"; see also Nf (and Pal. Tg.) Lev 22:27, which Golomb, 1985, 205 renders as: "which are being offered."

[12]"its libations and the libation of the water." An expansion in Nf in keeping with the liturgical setting of the text. The HT has: ("its cereal offerings) and its drink offerings"; thus also Nfmg. See Apparatus.

[13]"which you shall offer with them"; an addition in Nf.

together, [14] *from your booths within your houses in joy,* [mm] *gathered together so that* [nn] *you may give alms.* You shall do no servile work. 36. And you shall offer as a burnt offering,[oo] *as an offering acceptable* as an agreeable odor before the Lord, one bull, one ram, seven lambs a year old, perfect, *without blemish,* 37. and their *minhahs* and their libations[pp]—*which you shall offer with them*[qq][13]—with *the* bulls and with the rams, and with the lambs, according to their number, according to the ordinance; 38. and one male goat for the sin offering, besides the burnt offering of the perpetual sacrifice, and[rr] its *minhah* and[rr] its libation. 39. <These>[ss] you *shall offer before* the Lord in your feasts,[tt][15] *according to this ordinance,*[6] besides your vows and (your)[uu] voluntary offerings, for your burnt offerings and for your *minhahs* and (your)[ww] libations, and for <your>[xx] *sacrifices of holy things.*"[16]

Apparatus, Chapter 29

[mm] Nfmg: "the eighth (day) you shall gather together with joy, going out from your tents into the interior of your houses; it shall be a joyful gathering."

[nn] Or: "that you may give alms"; Nfi: "alms" (sing.); lit.: "the precept," i.e., what has been commanded, almsgiving.

[oo] Nfmg: "(as) an acceptable (burnt offering)."

[pp] Nfmg: "and the wine of their libations."

[qq] Nfi: "for them"; or: "to them" (i.e., to the things which you shall offer).

[rr] Note the faithfulness of Nf in translating "and" with the HT; Nfmg: "its *minhah,*" without "and."

[ss] Missing in the text; supplied in the margin in the square characters proper to the text.

[tt] Nfmg: "these things you shall offer before the Lord at the time of the festivals of your feast days."

[uu] In text and in Nfi: "their."

[ww] In text: "their."

[xx] Thus Nfmg; in text "their."

Notes, Chapter 29

[14]The HT of v. 35 reads: "on the eighth day you shall have an *'sṛt* (MT: *'aśeret*). You shall do no servile work." This Hebrew term, in its Aramaic form *asartha,* became a technical name for Shavuot, the feast of Weeks (Booths). Thus already in Josephus, *Ant.,* 3, 10, 6 (par. 252). Thus also in Nf Deut 16:10, where the HT "feast of Weeks" of the HT is paraphrased as "the feast of Weeks, that is Asarta"; likewise in Nf Exod 34:22, with the same HT and Nf paraphrase. In contexts such as the present, the fundamental sense of the HT term *'śrt* or *'śrh* is generally taken to be "assembly," "gathering" ("festival of ingathering"). Thus explicitly in *Sifre Num.* 151 (on Num 22:35), *'yn 'śyrh 'l' knysh,* "*'śyrh* always means gathering/assembly" (ed. Horowitz, par. 151, p. 196), which text, however, is considered by K. G. Kuhn, 1964, 607, as a gloss interpolated into the text of *Sifre Num.* In Nf the HT term *'srt* is understood and rendered as "gathering" (*knyšth*) and further, as a joyful gathering (assembly). Thus in Nf Deut 16:8 the phrase "an *'srt* to the Lord your God" (referring to the seventh day of Passover), becomes in Nf: "a joyful assembly" (*knyštt ḥdwh*); likewise in Nf Lev 23:36, where HT *'srt* is rendered "a joyful assembly" (*knyšt ḥdwwh*). In the present text Nf seems to have a double rendering of the HT "You shall have an *'śrt*": (1) "You shall be assembled from your booths within your houses in joy"; (2) "assembled that you may have meritorious deeds" (?*knyšyn dmṣwwn tyhwwy lkwn;* or: "You shall have assemblies of commandment," i.e., for almsgiving. B. Barry Levy, 1987, 2, 162, notes that the use of *lkm* ("for yourselves") in the MT may have prompted the comment that on the eighth day the people should gather in their houses rather than in their *sukkot.*

[15]The HT lit. has: "These shall do to the Lord at your appointed feasts, beside . . ."

[16]"Your sacrifices of holy things"; HT: "your peace sacrifices," *šlmykm,* the usual Nf translation. See above Introd. III, 1.

CHAPTER 30

1. And Moses said[a] to the children of Israel all[b] that the Lord[c] had commanded Moses. 2. And Moses spoke with the heads of the tribes of the children of Israel, saying: "This is what the Lord[c] had commanded. 3. If a man vows a vow *to the name of* the Lord, or swears[d] an oath *to fulfill an obligation*[e] *to the Name of the Lord,*[1] he shall not fail to fulfill his word; he shall do all that proceeds out of his mouth[f] 4. And if a woman[g] vows a vow *before* the Lord and *obliges herself with an obligation*[h] in the house of her father, in her youth, 5. and her father hears of the vow and of *the obligation*[e] with which she *has obliged* herself and says nothing to her, every vow of hers shall stand and every *obligation* with which she *obliged* herself shall stand.[i] 6. But if her father dispenses her on the day that he hears[j] (of it), no vow of hers and no *obligation*[e] of hers by which *she obliged* herself shall stand; and from *before* the Lord she will be forgiven,[k] for her father dispensed her. 7. And if she *is given as wife* to a man[m] while there is upon her her vow or a *distinct expression* of her lips[n] by which *she has obliged* herself, 8. and her husband hearing of it, says nothing to her on the day that he hears of it, her vows shall stand, and the obligations[o] with which she *has obliged* herself <shall stand>.[p] 9. <But if her husband dispenses her on the day that her husband hears of it, he shall annul the vow that is upon her and the *distinct expression* of her lips by which *she obliged* herself>;[p] and she shall be forgiven *from before* the Lord.[q] 10. And a vow of a widow and of a divorced woman, all that by which she *has obliged* herself, shall stand against her. 11. And if she vowed in her husband's house, or *obliged* herself by any *obligation* under oath, 12. and her husband heard of it and said nothing to her and did not dispense her, every vow of hers and every *obligation*[e] of hers by which she *obliged herself, shall stand.*[i] 13. But if her husband annuls them on the day that he hears of it, then any *distinct expression*[r] of her lips with regard to a

Apparatus, Chapter 30

[a] Nfmg: "and (Moses spoke)."
[b] Nfmg: "according to all (that . .)."
[c] Nfmg: "the Memra of the Lord."
[d] Nfmg: "(or) if he has sworn."
[e] *qyym:* "oath," "promise," "vow."
[f] Nfmg: "(an oath) upon himself, he shall not break (or: 'profane') his words: all that has come forth from his mouth . . ."
[g] Lit.: "the woman"; Nfmg: "a woman."
[h] Nfmg: "and she has taken an oath."
[i] Nfmg: "they shall stand" (i.e., be valid).
[j] Nfi: "that they hear."
[k] Nfmg: "they shall not stand (= be valid) and (before) the Memra of the Lord it shall be forgiven and remitted"; cf. v. 9.
[m] Nfmg: "(and if) she is surely for a man."
[n] Nfi: "(of) her lips" (written differently).
[o] Lit.: "the obligation"; "the oath"; cf. HT.
[p] Omitted in the text; supplied by the annotator.
[q] Nfmg: "and (before) the Memra of the Lord it shall be forgiven and remitted (her)."
[r] Nfmg: "(the expression) which comes out . . ."

Notes, Chapter 30

[1]"(to fulfill an obligation) to the name of the Lord," HT: "(to bind) himself," *'l npšw.* Nf's text probably an error due to the beginning of the verse. The proper reading may be *'l npšh,* "(or) himself"; cf. Nfmg.

vow[s] and with regard to an *obligation* on herself shall not stand;[i] her husband has annulled them[t] and before the Lord she will be forgiven.[u] 14. Any vow and any oath which implies an *obligation* to afflict oneself, her husband may establish and her husband may annul.[w] 15. But if her husband says nothing to her day *after* day, then he establishes[x] them because he has said nothing to her on the day that he heard of them. 16. But if *her husband*[2] annuls them after he has heard of them, then he shall receive[y] her sin."[z] 17. These are the statutes that the Lord[aa] commanded Moses as between a man and his wife, and between a father and his daughter (while) in her youth[bb] in her father's house.

CHAPTER 31

1. And the Lord[a] spoke with Moses, saying: 2. "Carry out the vengeance of the children of Israel on the Midianites; and after this you shall be gathered[b] to your people." 3. And Moses spoke with[c] the people, saying: "Arm men from among you for the army *of war,* and let them go against Midian to set[d] the Lord's vengeance on Midian. 4. You shall send a thousand from each tribe, a thousand from each of the tribes of Israel, to the army *of war.*" 5. And there were enlisted[e] in the army from the thousands of Israel a thousand from every tribe, twelve thousand (men) armed for war.[f] 6. And Moses sent them, a thousand from each tribe, to the army *of war;* these and (Phinehas, the son of)[g] Eleazar the priest,[h] to the array of battle, with the

Apparatus, Chapter 30

[s] Nfmg: "(. . . expression) of a vow (lit.: 'to make a vow')."
[t] The copyist read: "the lady (*b'lh*) has annulled" (with fem. verb) instead of "her husband (*b'l-h*) has annulled"; VN: "her husband has broken (or: 'profaned') them."
[u] Nfmg: "(her husband) has broken (or: 'profaned') them and (before) the Memra of the Lord it shall be forgiven and remitted (her)."
[w] Nfmg: "(her husband) may break (them)"; VN: "a husband may break (or: 'profane') them."
[x] Nfmg: "(any) obligation (or: 'vow') that may be on her; he establishes them (because . . .)."
[y] that is: it shall be his responsibility.
[z] Nfmg: "his sins."
[aa] Nfmg: "the Memra of the Lord."
[bb] Nfmg: "in the days of her youth" (*ṭlywth;* same word as in VN; cf. also Ps.-J.; text: *rbywth*).

Notes, Chapter 30

[2] "her husband," in imitation of v. 13; the HT has: "he."

Apparatus, Chapter 31

[a] Nfmg: "the Memra of the Lord."
[b] Nfi: "he is gathered," or: "he will be gathered."
[c] Nfi: "to the."
[d] Nfmg: "(against) the Midianites to set."
[e] *'tḥylw;* cf. Nfmg v. 7 (notes *i, j*) below.
[f] Nfmg: "(for) the army of war."
[g] Added interlinearly.
[h] Nfmg: "the high (priest) for the army of war."

vessels of the sanctuary and the trumpets of the alarm in his hand. 7. And *they warred*[i] against Midian as the Lord had commanded[j] Moses, and slew every male. 8. And they slew the kings of the Midianites together with (the rest of) their slain: Evi, Reqem, Zur, Hur, and Reba, the five kings of the Midianites; and they slew Balaam, the son of Beor, with the sword.[k] 9. And the children of Israel took captive the women of the Midianites and their little ones; and they took as booty their animals[m] and all their cattle[n] and all their wealth. 10. And all the cities in their dwelling places[o] and all their *prefectures,*[p1] they burned with fire. 11. And they took all the booty and all the spoil, (both in men[q] and in beasts). 12. (And they brought the captives)[r] and the booty to Moses and to Eleazar the priest and to the congregation of the children of Israel, at the camp in[s] the plains of Moab near the Jordan of Jericho. 13. And Moses and Eleazar the priest and all the princes of the congregation[t] went out to meet them[u] outside the camp. 14. And Moses grew angry with the numbers[w2] of the army, the captains of the thousands and the captains of the hundreds who had come from the army of war.[x] 15. And Moses said to them: "Behold, you have let every female live.[y] 16. Behold, these were a *stumbling block*[z3] for the children of Israel, by the *counsel*[aa4] of Balaam, playing falsely in the name of the Lord[bb] in the affair of *the idol of* Peor, bringing the plague on *the people of*[5] the congregation of Israel. 17. And now, kill every male among the little ones, and kill every woman who has known a man in male intercourse.[cc] 18. And all the little ones among the women who have not known male intercourse,[dd] keep

Apparatus, Chapter 31

[i] Nfmg: *w-'tyyḥlw* (read: *w-tḥyylw*), "and there were enlisted"; or "and they moved into war."

[j] Nfmg: *w-'tyyḥlw* (read: *w-'tḥyylw*), "and there were enlisted (or: and they moved into war) against the Midianites as the Memra of the Lord had commanded."

[k] Nfmg: "at the edge of the sword."

[m] Nfmg: "all (their)."

[n] Nfmg: "their herds."

[o] Nfmg: "their cities and their encampments."

[p] Nfmg: "their fortresses."

[q] Lit.: "in the sons of man."

[r] Missing in the text; supplied in the margin.

[s] Nfmg: "to the plains."

[t] Nfmg: "of the people (of the congregation)."

[u] Nfmg: "to meet him."

[w] The other Targums' translations: "with the leaders."

[x] Nfmg: "(and the captains) of the hundreds who came from before" (*mn qdm;* corr. to [?]: "from the war," *mn qrb'*).

[y] Nfmg: "(every) daughter."

[z] Nfmg: "these are they who were a stumbling block"; cf. Ps.-J.

[aa] Nfmg: "in the question (of . . .)."

[bb] Nfmg: "in the name of the Memra of the Lord."

[cc] Nfmg: "(and) kill (every woman who has known) man in carnal intercourse."

[dd] Nfmg: "(known) carnal intercourse, keep alive."

Notes, Chapter 31

[1]"prefectures"; Greek loan word *eparchia.*

[2]"numbers," *skwmy-*; see Apparatus note to 1:3 and above, Introd. III, 25.

[3]"stumbling block"; an addition in keeping with the end of chap. 24.

[4]"counsel"; for HT: "affair." The HT has: "Behold, these became (= were the cause) for the children of Israel in the affair of Balaam (to act treacherously. . ." (correcting or thus understanding HT *lmsr-m'l*). Nf renders "affair of Balaam" as "the counsel of B." Note Nf's rendering of "the congregation of Balaam" in 26:9 and 27:3 as "the counsel of B."

[5]"the people of"; an expansion common in Nf. See Introd. III, 23.

alive for yourselves. 19. And you, dwell outside the camp seven days; every one who has killed any person, every one who has drawn near to any slain, purify yourselves on the third day, you and your captives. 20. And you shall purify every garment and every article of skin, and every work of goats' hair and every article of wood." 21. And Eleazar the priest said *to the people* who had waged war, who had come in *from* the army *of war*: "This is the *decree* of the law[6] which the Lord has commanded Moses: 22. Only the gold and silver, and[ee] the bronze and[ee] the iron and[ee] *the tin*[ff7] and the lead—23. all[gg] that can go into the fire—you shall pass through the fire and it shall be clean; but it shall (also) be purified in the waters of aspersion;[hh] and anything that cannot go into the fire you shall pass through the water. 24. And you shall wash your clothes on the seventh day and you shall be clean; and after this you shall enter within[ii] the camp." 25. And the Lord[jj] said to Moses, saying: 26. "Take (the count)[kk] of the spoil of the booty in both men and beasts, you and Eleazar the priest and the heads of the fathers' (houses)[mm] of the congregation.[nn] 27. And divide the spoil between the warriors who went out to the army *of war* and between *the people of*[5] the congregation. 28. And *you* shall set aside the *separated offering*[8] to *the name of* the Lord from the people who make war[oo] who went forth to the service[pp] *of war*, one soul out of five hundred, of the men,[qq] of the oxen, and of the donkeys and of the flock. 29. You shall take (it) from their half, and you shall give (it) to Eleazar the priest as the *separated offering*[8] of the Lord. 30. And from the people of Israel's half take one detached[rr] from (every) fifty, of people, and of the oxen, and of the donkeys, and of the flocks and of all the cattle; and you shall give them to the Levites who have the charge of

Apparatus, Chapter 31

[ee] With "and," which is not in the HT.
[ff] Lit.: "and the tin and the *ksyṭr*" (Greek loan word *kassiteros*, "tin"); "tin" is thus written twice, the second time with the Greek loan word; Nfi has variant writing *qs(yṭr')*; = VN.
[gg] Nfmg: "(every) thing" (*ptgm*).
[hh] Nfmg: "it shall be purified (by the) sprinkling (waters)."
[ii] Nfi: "(enter) to the (camp)."
[jj] Nfmg: "the Memra of the Lord."
[kk] Missing in the text; taken from Nfmg.
[mm] Nfi: "(of) your (fathers' family)."
[nn] Nfmg: "of the people of the congregation."
[oo] Lit.: "from the people who make war."
[pp] Nfmg: "(from the people) of the battle lines who went forth to the army (or: 'host') of . . ."
[qq] Lit.: "of the sons of man"; Nfi: "of the people."
[rr] Nfmg: "taken."

Notes, Chapter 31

[6]"decree of the law"; HT: "the statute of the law." See above Introd. III, 11.

[7]Lit.: "the iron and the tin and the tin," *b'ṣh wyt ksyṭr'*. A double rendering of HT *hbdyl*, in Aramaic and in Greek. See Apparatus. The LXX has also *kassiteros*, but in last place, "lead and tin."

[8]"separated offering," *'pršw*, here translating HT *mks* ("tribute"), as in the other occurrences of the word (Num 31:37, 38, 39, 40). Elsewhere in Nf (e.g., Num 6:20; 15:19, 20, 21; 18:8, 11, 24, 27; 31:29, 41, 52; Exod 25:3, etc.; Lev 7:14, etc.) this Aramaic word renders HT *trwmh*, the root of which (*rwm*) is used with *mks* in Num 31:28 ("to raise a tribute"). Note also the conjoining of both in 31:41. *mks trwmt yyy*, "the tribute of the heave offering" or "the tribute which was the *terumah* (= offering) of YYY," where Nf translates *mks* as *tlš* (=*tlyš*), "fraction, portion," a term Nf uses to translate HT *'ḥwz* ("drawn out") in Num 31:30, 47.

the tent of the Lord." 31. And Moses and Eleazar the priest[ss] did as the Lord[tt] had commanded Moses. 32. And the spoil, the remainder[uu] of the booty that *the people* who made war[ww] had captured, was six hundred and seventy-five thousand[xx] sheep, 33. and seventy-two thousand oxen, 34. and sixty-one thousand donkeys; 35. and persons,[yy] of women who had not known male intercourse, the total number of persons was thirty-two thousand. 36. And the half, the portion of *the people* who had gone out to the army *of war*, was in number three hundred and thirty-seven thousand five hundred sheep;[zz] 37. and the *separated offering*[8] to *the Name of* the Lord of sheep was six hundred <and seventy-five>.[a] 38. And (the oxen)[b] were thirty-six thousand; and their *separated offering*[8] for *the Name of* the Lord[c] was seventy-two *oxen:* 39. and thirty thousand five hundred donkeys; and the *separated offering*[8] of these for *the Name of* the Lord[d] was sixty-one *donkeys;* 40 and sixteen thousand persons;[yy] and the *separated offering*[8] of these for *the Name of* the Lord was thirty-two persons. 41. And Moses gave the fraction,[9] the *separated offering*[8] of the Lord,[e] to Eleazar the priest, as the Lord[f] had commanded Moses. 42. And from the people of Israel's half, which Moses had divided from (that of) the men who had been enlisted in the army,[g] 43. (this) half belonging to *the people of*[5] the congregation, was three hundred and thirty-seven thousand five hundred (sheep),[h] 44. and thirty-six thousand oxen, 45. and thirty thousand five hundred[i] donkeys, 46. and sixteen thousand persons.[j] 47. From the children of Israel's half Moses took what was detached, one from (every) fifty[k] of the persons[m] and of the beasts and gave them to the Levites who kept the charge of the tent of the Lord, as the

Apparatus, Chapter 31

[ss] Nfmg: "the priest" (with Hebrew word).
[tt] Nfmg: "the Memra of the Lord."
[uu] Nfmg: "the remnant" (a different word).
[ww] Nfmg: "(the people) of the army (of war)."
[xx] The text says: 670,000 (+) 50,000, instead of 670,000 (+) 5,000; unless we assume that by *ḥmšyn* is intended 5, not 50; cf. Dalman, 1905, 125.
[yy] Lit.: "and the soul of a son of man"; Nfmg: ". . . of the sons of man."
[zz] Nfmg: "sheep: 300,000 + 30,000 + 70,000 (corr.: 7,000) + 500."
[a] "and seventy-five" is missing in the text; the entire verse is added in square characters in the margin.
[b] Missing in the text; added in square characters in the margin.
[c] Nfmg: "and the Lord's separated offering seventy-two."
[d] Nfmg: "and the Lord's separated offering sixty-one."
[e] Lit.: "the detached (portion) of the separated (offering) of the Lord"; Nfmg: "the separation of the separated portion."
[f] Nfmg: "the Memra of the Lord."
[g] Nfmg: "(of the men) of the army of war."
[h] The text has erroneously: "of the people."
[i] Nfmg: "(thirty thousand) and six (hundred)"; the reading, however, is suspect and appears to belong to the following verse.
[j] Cf. v. 35; Nfmg: "of the sons of man (1)6,(000)."
[k] Lit.: "the detached (portion) of one from fifty."
[m] Lit.: "of the sons of man."

Notes, Chapter 31

[9]"the fraction"; see note to 31:28.

Lord[n] had commanded Moses. 48. And the total[o10] of those *who had been* appointed over *the census of* the army,[p] the captains of thousands and the captains of hundreds, drew near to Moses, 49. and they said to Moses: "Your servants have taken[q] the census *of the people* who make war who are under our command,[r] and not one of *them* has been counted.[s11] 50. And we have offered the offering of the Lord,[12] each one (of us) *when we went into*[t] *the houses of the Midianites, into the bedchambers of their kings; and (we saw)*[u13] *their daughters, pretty and beautiful,*

Apparatus, Chapter 31

[n] Nfmg: "the Memra of the Lord."

[o] I.e., "the sum total"; lit.: "the totals," "the sum totals." This is how Nf renders the Hebrew *hapequdim* ("the officers"). See note.

[p] Nfmg: "(the numbers) of the thousands" (lit.: "which are [for] the thousands") of the army of war."

[q] = "have made (the census)."

[r] Lit.: "under our hand"; Nfi: "in our hands."

[s] HT, Onq., Ps.-J.: "and not one is missing"; Nfmg: "(your servants) have taken the census of the heads (lit.: 'the head of the censuses') of the people of the army of war which is in our hands. None of us had been enrolled."

[t] "when we went in": corr. *mdhwwynn* ("as soon as [we went in]") of text to *kd hwwynn,* with Nfmg, PVN; Nfmg: "(of the Lord) when we went into the houses of the Midianite kings and into their sleeping quarters, and we saw the daughters of the Midianite kings pretty and tender; and we removed from them the gold crowns (PVN add: 'from their heads') and the rings (PVN add: 'from their ears') and the signet rings from their fingers; and the torques from their arms, and the (gold) hooks from their breasts; far be it from us, O Moses our master; one of us did not look at one of them and none of us was joined with (PVN: 'to') one of them, so that we may not be partner(s) with her in Gehenna in the world to come. Let this stand up for us on the day . . ."; = VN; P has the same except for omission of "and into their sleeping quarters" and "(pretty) and tender." PVN continue: "(the day) of the great judgment to atone for our souls before the Lord."

[u] The text has erroneously: "and we desired."

Notes, Chapter 31

[10]"and the census (totals) of. . . ," *skwmy. . . ,* rendering HT *pqwdym* (root *pqd*), generally rendered in this context as "officers." See note to 31:1 above, and Introd. III, 25.

[11]"has been counted" (thus Sokoloff, 1990, 378) or "agreed upon," the Aramaic *'stkm* (root *skm*), rendering HT *npqd,* the Niphal of *pqd.* The Hebrew term *pqd* has various meanings: (1) attend to; (2) visit; (3) register, muster; (4) appoint, and occasionally in the Niphal "be missed"; "lacking." Thus here, Num 31:49, and 1 Sam 20:18, 19; 25:7; 1 Kgs 20:39; 2 Kgs 10:18, 19; Jer 23:4; and with *mn* ("from"), Judg 21:3; 1 Sam 25:21; 2 Sam 2:30. The other Targums and ancient translations of Num 31:49 recognize the different meaning. Not, however, Nf in Num 31:49, which renders as it does elsewhere by *skm,* "to be counted." See also above note to Nf Num 1:21, Introd. III, 25, and B. Grossfeld, 1984, 83–102.

[12]The HT (cf. RSV) for v. 50 reads: "And we have brought the Lord's offering, (what) each man found, articles of gold, armlets and bracelets, signet rings, earrings, and beads, to make atonement for ourselves before the Lord." The opening and concluding words of Nf translate the corresponding sections of the HT, while the central section weaves a midrash around the key HT terms. The midrash contains, in a sense, the antithesis of Balaam's suggestion to Balak in Num 24:25 and seems influenced by the principle of Deut 21:10-14 on the self-discipline required on occasions such as this. The list of jewelry is reminiscent of Nf Gen 49:22 and Exod 35:22. The concluding section of the midrash, on fidelity in this world in order to avoid punishment in Gehenna, is to be compared with Nf Gen 39:10 and Gen 38:25. See further B. Barry Levy, 1987, 2, 164–167.

[13]"we saw," with Díez Macho, 1974, 295 correcting *ḥmdyn* ("we desired"; "lusted after)" of text to *ḥmyyn.* B. Barry Levy, 1987, 2, 166, sees no reason to emend in this way, even though "we saw" is attested in Ps.-J. and the Frg. Tg.

delicate and tender: and we unfastened the garlands,[14] *the crowns of gold, from their heads;* rings *from their ears,* necklaces *from their necks,* chainlets *from their arms,* chains *from their hands,* signet rings *from their fingers,* clasps *from their breasts. Nevertheless, not one of us was joined with one of them in this world, so as not to be*[w] *with her in Gehenna in the world to come. On the day of great judgment this will stand up in our favor,* to make atonement for us before the Lord." 51. And Moses and Eleazar the priest took the gold from them, every wrought article.[x] 52. And the gold of the *separated offering*[8] which they set aside to *the Name of* the Lord was sixteen hundred and fifty[y] *selas,* from the captains of thousands and from the captains of hundreds. 53. But the men of war had taken booty, every man for himself.[z] 54. And Moses and Eleazar the priest took the gold from the captains of thousands and the captains of hundreds, and brought[aa] it to the tent of meeting, as a *good* memorial for the children of Israel before the Lord.

CHAPTER 32

1. And the sons of Reuben and sons of Gad had numerous cattle,[a] very numerous indeed; and they saw the land of *Mikbar*[b 1] and the land of Gilead, and behold,

Apparatus, Chapter 31

[w] Nfi: "(so that) he may (not) be . . ."
[x] Nfmg: "(all) the wrought articles" (lit.: "the articles of work").
[y] Nfmg: "seventeen (thousand seven hundred and fifty)."
[z] Nfmg: "the people (= the troops) of the host of war took booty one (for) the other."
[aa] Nfmg: "and they took them within the tent of. . ."

Notes, Chapter 31

[14]"we unfastened the garlands, the crowns of gold." The text has: *whwwynn šryn qryh klylyyh ddhbh.* The term *qryh* (ordinarily meaning "a city") presents a problem, and A. Díez Macho, 1974, 4, 295, suggests reading (or understanding as) *qrnh* = (a loan word) *corona,* even though he refers us to P, which has *qwryy'* (also in VN). B. Barry Levy, 1987, 2, 167, noting that the *n* in *šryn(qryh)* is medial, suggests reading as one word *šrynqryh,* possibly denoting some feminine ornament, e.g., a "choke." Sokoloff, 1990, 506, takes *qryh (qryyh)* of Nf and Nfmg Num 31:50 in the sense of *qryyh* 3, "head ornament" ("golden head ornaments") = Mishnaic Hebrew *'yr šlzhb* (lit.: "golden city") of *m. Shab.* 6:1 (with reference to S. Lieberman, 1955, 8, 767). In a note on "golden city" (*'yr šlzhb*) of *m. Shab.* 6:1 (also in *m. Eduy* 2:7; *m. Kel.* 11:8). H. Danby, 1933, 104, 1 n. 13, calls it "a tiara shaped like Jerusalem." See *m. Shab.* 6:1 for a list of female ornaments not to be worn abroad on the sabbath.

Apparatus, Chapter 32

[a] Nfmg: "they had herds."
[b] MT: Jazer (*Ya'zer*); cf. Num 21:32.

Notes, Chapter 32

[1]"land of Mikbar"; MT: "land of Jazer." Thus also in Nf Num 32:3. The MT "Jazer" is retained in Nf Num 21:32; 32:35. *Mikbar* (also written *mikwar*) is a district in Peraea; not Machaerus. See Jastrow, p. 781b.

the place was *good for pasture.*[c2] 2. And the sons of Gad and the sons of Reuben came and said to Moses and to Eleazar the priest, and to the princes of *the people of*[3] the congregation, saying: 3. "(Ataroth and Dibon),[d] *Mikbar* and *Beth Nimrin*[4] and Heshbon and Elealeh and *Simath*[5] and Nebo and Beon, the land which the Lord subdued before the congregation[e] of Israel, is *pasture* land;[f] and your servants have *many* cattle."[g] 5. And they said: "If we have found[h] grace *and favor*[6] in your sight,[i] let this land be given to your servants for a possession. Do not make us cross the Jordan." 6. And Moses said to the sons of Gad and to the sons of Reuben: "Do your brothers go to battle while you remain[j] here? 7. Why, now will you discourage the heart[k] of the children of Israel from going over to the land that the Lord[m] has given to them? 8. Thus your fathers did when I sent them from *Reqem di-Ge'a*[7] to see the land; 9. they went up[n] to the Valley of the Cluster of Grapes,[o] and saw the land, and discouraged the heart[p] of the children of Israel from going into the land which the Lord[m] had given them. 10. And the anger of the Lord grew strong on that day, and he swore *an oath,* saying: 11. 'The men who came up from Egypt, from twenty years old and upward, shall not see the land that I swore (to give) to Abraham, to Isaac, and to Jacob, because <they have not walked perfectly after me>;[q] 12. except Caleb bar Jephunneh the Kenizzite and Joshua bar Nun, be-

Apparatus, Chapter 32

[c] Nfmg: "the land of Mikwar and the land of Gilead(ah) and behold, the place was a place of herds"; VN: "Maklalta and Dubashta, and Mikwar and Beth-Nimrin and Heshbon and Elealah and Sebam and Nebo and Beon"; L has two distinct versions of the verse as follows: "*Ataroth:* Maklalta and Madbashta, and facing between Nineveh and Qetolayya (= the slain ones), and Beth-Ataroth, Merod and Sebam and the burial place of Moses, and Beon. A(nother) T(argum) O(nqelos) (*t"* = *targum Onqelos 'aher):* Maklalta and Madbashta, Shophakh and Be(th)-Nimrin and Beth-Hushbenayya and Baal-Dibon and Subera, and the (bur-)ial place of Moses, and Beon." A scribal note following on this says: "And p(erhaps) one v(ersion) is Targum Yerushalmi." The text is not known as any variant to Onqelos. See Klein, 1980, 2, 165, note 87.

[d] Missing in text; added in Nfi.

[e] Nfmg: "the Memra of the Lord before the assembly of the congregation."

[f] Nfmg: "is a land of herds"; = VN.

[g] Nfmg: "(have) many herds."

[h] Nfmg: "we have found" (another word).

[i] Nfmg: "before you."

[j] Nfmg: "shall you remain (here)?"

[k] Lit.: "break the heart . . ."; Nfmg: "the hearts of the . . ."

[m] Nfmg: "the Memra of the Lord" (in v. 9 in Nfi).

[n] Lit.: "and they went up."

[o] MT: Nahal Eskol; cf. 13:23.

[p] Lit.: "broke the heart"; Nfmg: "the hearts of the . . ."

[q] Missing in text; in Onq. and Ps.-J.: "they did not walk perfectly after the fear of me."

Notes, Chapter 32

[2]"place good for pasture"; HT: "place for cattle."

[3]"people of"; an expansion common in Nf. See Introd. III, 23.

[4]"Beth Nimrin"; HT: Nimrah; only here in MT, Pentateuch. In HT Num 32:36 the name Beth Nimrah occurs, a form retained in Nf.

[5]"Simath"; MT: "Sebam," a name found in Pentateuch only here and in Num 32:38, where Nf has *sbmh.*

[6]"grace and favor"; *ḥn wḥsd.* HT *ḥn.* This is Nf's usual expansion of the HT *ḥn.* See note to Nf Gen 6:8, Num 11:25 above, Introd., III, 21; also *The Aramaic Bible* vol. 1A, p. 73.

[7]"Reqem de Ge'a"; HT: Kadesh-barnea. This is Nf's constant rendering of the Hebrew name (Num 32:8; 34:4; Deut 1:2, 19; 2:14; 9:23); also in Onq. (written with alef, *gy'h*), and Pesh. See McNamara, 1972, 200; G. I Davies, *VT* 22 (1972) 152–163.

cause they have *walked perfectly* after *the Memra of*[8] the Lord.' 13. And the anger of the Lord grew strong against Israel, and he made them wander about in the wilderness forty years, until all the generation that had done *what was hateful and abominable before*[r9] the Lord had ceased. 14. And behold, you have risen in your fathers' stead, an offspring of sinful men,[s] to increase further[t] the might of the Lord's anger against Israel. 15. And if you turn back from following *his Memra,*[u10] he will make *you wander about* again in the wilderness; and you will destroy all this people." 16. And they draw near to him and say: "We will build sheep folds[w] here for our flocks,[x] and cities[y] for our little ones. 17. And we will *pass over, armed,*[z11] before the children of Israel until such time as we have brought them in to their places; and our little ones shall dwell in *tall* cities against the inhabitants of the land. 18. <We will not return to our houses until each one of the children of Israel has taken possession of his inheritance>.[aa] 19. For we will not inherit[bb] with them on the other side of the Jordan and beyond, because *we have received* our inheritance[cc] for ourselves on this side of the Jordan to the east." 20. And Moses said to them: "If you will do this thing, if you arm[dd] yourselves before the Lord for the *army* of war,[ee] 21. and if every one who is armed of you will pass over the Jordan before the Lord, until such time as he *blots out* his enemies before him, 22. and the land is subdued[ff] before the Lord, after this you shall return and shall be free of responsibility *before* the Lord and before Israel; and thus the land shall be your possession before the Lord. 23. And if you do not do so, behold, you have sinned *before* the Lord; and know that your sins shall overtake[gg] you. 24. Build cities for your little ones, and sheepfolds[hh] for your flocks; and you shall perform what shall come forth from your mouths.[ii12] 25. And the sons of Gad and the sons

Apparatus, Chapter 32

[r] Nfmg: "(that had done) evil before (the Lord)."
[s] Nfmg: "(in your fathers' stead;) you shall increase the number of (evil) men, to increase the might of . . ."
[t] Nfmg: "yet"; = VN.
[u] Nfmg: "(from following) after him."
[w] Nfmg: "sheepfolds" (another form).
[x] Nfmg: "for our herds."
[y] Nfmg: "and cities" (another form).
[z] Nfmg: "we shall go up armed."
[aa] Missing in text and margin.
[bb] Nfmg: "we will not inherit" (another form).
[cc] Nfmg: "(because) our inheritance has come."
[dd] Nfi: "and if you arm yourselves."
[ee] Nfmg: "for battle array."
[ff] Nfmg: "and you subdue."
[gg] Nfmg: "it shall overtake (you)."
[hh] Nfmg: "sheepfolds" (another form); cf. v. 16.
[ii] Nfmg: "and do what has come forth from your mouths" (= what you have promised).

Notes, Chapter 32

[8]"the Memra of"; an addition in Nf.
[9]"hateful and abominable before"; HT: "evil in the eyes of."
[10]"from following his Memra . . .wander about"; HT: "from after him. . .abandon."
[11]"pass over armed"; HT: "equip ourselves for war hastily," *ḥšym;* or "in battle array," correcting to *ḥmšym.* A similar translation of *ḥlṣym* in 32:30 and of *ḥmšym* in Nf Exod 13:18.
[12]"what comes forth from your mouth," i.e., what you have promised.

of Reuben said[jj] to Moses, saying: "Your servants will do as my master[kk] has commanded. 26. Our little ones, our wives, our flock,[mm] and our entire herd, shall be there in the cities of Gileadah; 27. but your servants will pass over, every one who is armed for the *army of war,* before the Lord, to battle *array,* as my master[kk] has spoken." 28. And <Moses>[nn] gave command concerning them to Eleazar,[oo] and to Joshua bar Nun, and to the heads of the fathers' (houses) of the tribes of the children of Israel. 29. <And Moses said to them:>[nn] "If the sons of Gad and the sons of Reuben, every one who is armed for the *army* of *war,* will pass with you over the Jordan before you, you shall give them the land of Gileadah for a possession. 30. And if they do not pass over armed with you, they shall have possession[pp] among you in the land of Canaan." 31. And the sons of Gad and the sons of Reuben answered, saying: "What[qq] the Lord[rr] has spoken with your servants, this shall we do.[ss] 32. We shall pass over armed before the Lord into the land of Canaan, so that the inheritance of our possession[tt] (remain) with us beyond the Jordan." 33. And Moses gave to them, to the sons of Gad and to the sons of Reuben and to the half-tribe of Manasseh the son of Joseph, the kingdom of Sihon, the king[uu] of the Amorites, and the kingdom of Og, the king of *Motenim,*[ww][13] the land with its cities in its territory, the cities of the land round about. 34. And the sons of Gad built Dibon and Ataroth and *Lehayyath,*[14] 35. and Atroth-shophan and Jazer and Jogbahan,[xx] 36. and Beth-nimrah and Beth-*Ramatha,*[yy][15] *tall cities, and sheepfolds.*[zz] 37. And the sons of Reuben built[a] Heshbon and Elealeh and

Apparatus, Chapter 32

[jj] Lit.: "say"; Nfi: "and (the sons of Gad . . .) said"; cf. HT.

[kk] Nfmg: "our (master).

[mm] Nfmg: "our herds."

[nn] Missing in text; added in Nfi.

[oo] The word "priest" is missing.

[pp] Nfmg: "they shall have possession" (another form).

[qq] Nfmg: "all (that)."

[rr] Nfmg: "the Memra of the Lord."

[ss] Lit.: "thus (shall we do)"; Nfmg: "thus shall we do" (a different word for "thus").

[tt] Nfmg: "inheritance and possession."

[uu] Literally in text: "the kings of . . ." (*mlkyhwn*); Nfi: *mlkhwn,* "the king of . . ."

[ww] Or: Mutnim; MT: Bashan, also translated in Targum by "Butnin"; cf. 21:33.

[xx] Nfmg: "(and) Maklalta (= the crown) of Shophan and Mikwar and Jogbehah."

[yy] MT: Beth-Haran.

[zz] Nfmg: "and sheepfolds" (another form).

[a] Nfmg: "they build."

Notes, Chapter 32

[13]"Motenim" (*mwtnym*); HT: "Bashan," which is generally rendered as "Butnin" in Nf. See note to Nf 21:33.

[14]"Lahayyath"; MT: "Aroer." Nf has the same translation in the other occurrences of the word: Deut 2:36; 3:12; 4:48. According to Jastrow (II, 702f.), the word can mean "palisades," or in general "fortress" (as in Tg. (I) Est 9:27); or it may be a proper name (cf. Levy, p. 408). It is used in Onq. (and in Nf under the form *lḥwwt*) to translate Ar of Num 21:15 and Ar Moab of Num 21:28. See also the note to Nf Num 21:8.

[15]"Beth Ramatha"; rendering MT Beth-haran (not found elsewhere in the Pentateuch), as if it were Beth ha-ram as in Josh 13:27.

Kiriathaya,[b] 38. and Nebo and Baal-meon, *surrounded by high walls,*[c16] and Sibmah; and they called by their (new) names the names of the cities which they built. 39. And the sons of Mechir, the son of Manasseh, went to Gileadah and subdued it, and *blotted out* the Amorites who *were dwelling* within it.[d] 40. And Moses gave Gilead[e] to Machir, the son of Manasseh, and he settled in it. 41. And Jair, the son of Manasseh, went and subdued their villages and called them the villages of Jair. 42. And Nobah went and subdued Kenath and its *villages* and called it Nobah, after his own name.

CHAPTER 33

1. These are the journeys of the children of Israel, who came *redeemed*[1] out of the land of Egypt, according to their hosts, under the command[a] of Moses and Aaron. 2. And Moses wrote down their starting places, for their journeys, by command of *the decree of the Memra*[2] of the Lord. And these are their journeys according to their starting place.[3] 3. And they set out from *Pelusium*[b4] in the first month,[c] on the fifteenth day of the first month. After *the first festival day* of the

Apparatus, Chapter 32

[b] Cf. Ps.-J.'s rendering: "the city whose marketplaces are paved with marble (*be-marmera*), that is Berisha."
[c] Nfmg: "(and Baal-meon,) a city which is surrounded round about by their towers, on which are engraved the names of her princes and her heroes."
[d] Nfmg: "the Amorites who were there."
[e] Nfmg: "Gileadah."

Notes, Chapter 32

[16]"surrounded by high walls"; taking HT *mwsbwt šm* (RSV: "their names to be changed)" as "famed for being encircled"; cf. B. Barry Levy, 1987, 2, 169.

Apparatus, Chapter 33

[a] Lit.: "under the hands of . . ."
[b] A city in Lower Egypt; MT: Rameses.
[c] The month of Nisan.

Notes, Chapter 33

[1]"redeemed"; an addition in the manner of Nf; see above, Introd. III, 22.
[2]"decree of the Memra of. . ."; HT: "the mouth of."
[3]"(their) starting places," *mypqnyhwn;* HT: *mmwṣ'yhm* (RSV: "starting places"). Sokoloff (p. 324) renders as "extremity." Also in Frg. Tg. MS V, Num 34:5, 8, 9, 12.
[4]"Pelusium"; MT: "Rameses." The same translation is found in Nf in the other occurrences of the name: Gen 47:11; Exod 1:11, 12:37; Num 3:5.

Passover[5] the children of Israel came forth *redeemed, with head uncovered,*[6] in the sight[d] of all the Egyptians. 4. And the Egyptians were burying what the Lord[e] had *slain* among them, all the first-born; and upon their *idols*[f7] the Lord had executed *various* judgments. 5. And the children of Israel set out from <*Pelusium*>[g4] and encamped at Sukkoth. 6. And they set out from Sukkoth and encamped at Etham, which is on the borders of the desert. 7. <And they set out>[h] from Etham and *encamped*[8] at the *Taverns*[i] *of Hirata,*[9] which are near the *Idol* (of) Zephon;[j] and they encamped before[k] Migdol. 8. And they set out from before *the Taverns of Hirata*[9] and passed through the midst of the Sea into the wilderness; <and they went a journey of three days' *march* in the wilderness>[m] of Etham, and they encamped at Mara. 9. And they set out from Mara and encamped at Elim. And at Elim there were twelve springs[n10] of water *corresponding to the twelve tribes of Israel* and seventy *date*-palm trees *corresponding to the (seventy)*[o] *wise men of the children*[p] *of Israel;* and they encamped there.[q] 10. And they set out from Elim and encamped by the Sea of Suph. 11. And they set out from the Sea of Suph and encamped in the wilderness of Sin. 12. And they set out from the wilderness of Sin

Apparatus, Chapter 33

[d] Nfmg: "before."

[e] Nfmg: "the Memra of the Lord."

[f] Nfmg: "thus says the Lord" (corr.: "as the Lord has said").

[g] The text says wrongly: "of the philosophers" (*pilosopin* instead of *pilusin*).

[h] Missing in text and margins; VN: "and they set out from Etham and turned about to the Taverns of Hirata which is facing the idol."

[i] "Taverns": Greek loan word *pandokeion;* cf. Exod 14:2; Nfmg: "(Etham) and turned back to the Taverns . . ."

[j] Nfmg: "which is before the idol of Zephon."

[k] Nfmg: "opposite."

[m] Missing in text through homoeoteleuton; supplied in margin.

[n] "springs," Greek loan word *pêgê;* Nfmg 1°: "twelve fountains of water corresponding to"; cf. VN: "twelve fountains of water corresponding to the twelve tribes"; Nfmg 2°: "twelve sources of water corresponding to (the) twelve tribes."

[o] In the text "seven" (presumably by mistake); Nfi: "seventy."

[p] Nfmg: "ancients of the sons of."

[q] Nfmg adds: "by the sea," but the proper reading would be *'l my',* "by the waters"; cf. Ps.-J.

Notes, Chapter 33

[5]"the first festival day of the Passover"; HT: "after the morrow of (= day after) Passover." This is also Nf's translation throughout of the HT *mmḥrt hšbt,* Lev 23:11, 15, 16, and is the standard rabbinical interpretation on an issue of great calendrical importance in antiquity; see B. Barry Levy, 1987, 2, 38f, 169.

[6]"redeemed, with head uncovered"; additions, in keeping with Nf's usual manner of speaking of the Exodus from Egypt: "with head uncovered," *bryš gly,* is Nf's usual rendering of the HT *byd rmh,* "with a high hand" (RSV: "defiantly," etc.,) Exod 14:8; Num 15:30; 33:3. See note to Nf Num 15:30; also McNamara, 1966, 75–77.

[7]"idols"; HT: "gods."

[8]"encamped"; HT: "turned back to" (*wyšb*); rendering the HT *wyšb* (MT *wayyašob,* from the root *šwb*) as if it were from the root *yšb.* The LXX translates in like manner.

[9]"Taverns of Hirata"; HT: "Pi-hahiroth, *pwndqy ḥyrth* (*pwndqy* being a Greek loan word, *pandokion*). Nf renders in the same manner in the other occurrences: Exod 14:2, 9; Num 33:8. The word *ḥrth* ("Hirata") recalls the Hebrew *ḥerût,* "liberty," "licentiousness," and *Mek.* to Exod 14:2 interprets *ḥrwt* of Pi-ha-*ḥrwt* of the licentiousness of the Egyptians.

[10]The twelve springs and seventy palm trees are seen to correspond to the twelve tribes and the seventy sages of Israel. The seventy sages would be the members of the Sanhedrin, as noted in VN. See Apparatus.

and encamped at Dophkah. 13. And they set out from Dophkah and encamped at Alush. 14. And they set out from Alush and encamped at Rephidim, and there was no water there for the people[r] to drink. 15. And they set out from Rephidim and encamped in the wilderness of Sinai. 16. And they set out from the wilderness of Sinai and encamped at the Graves of *Those Who were Desirous.*[s 11] 17. And they set out from the Graves of Desire and encamped at Hazeroth. 18. And they set out from Hazeroth and encamped at Rithmah. 19. And they set out from Rithmah and encamped at Rimmon-perez. 20. And they set out from Rimmon-perez and encamped at Libnah. 21. And they set out from Libnah and encamped at Rissah. 22. And they set out from Rissah (and encamped)[t] at Kehalathah. 23. And they set out from Kehalathah and encamped at Har Shepher. 24. And they set out from Har Shepher and encamped at Haradah. 25. And they set out from Haradah and encamped at Makheloth. 26. And they set out from Makheloth and encamped at Tahath. 27. And they set out from Tahath and encamped at Terah. 28. And they set out from Terah and encamped at Mithkah. 29. And they set out from Mithkah and encamped at Hashmonah. 30. And they set out from Hashmonah and encamped at Moseroth. 31. And they set out from Moseroth and encamped at Bene-jaakan. 32. And they set out from Bene-jaakan and encamped at Hor-haggidgadah. 33. And they set out from Hor-haggidgadah and encamped at Jotbathah. 34. And they set out from Jotbathah and encamped at Abronah. 35. And they set out from Abronah and encamped at *Kerak Tarnogolah.*[u 12] 36. And they set out from *Kerak Tarnogolah*[12] and encamped in the wilderness of Zin, that is *Rekem.*[w 13] 37. And they set out from the wilderness of *Rekem* and encamped in Hor the Mountain[x] on the edges of the land of the Edomites. 38. And Aaron the priest went up Hor the Mountain according to *the command of the decree of the Memra of*[14] the Lord and died there, *at the end* of forty years,[15] at the time[16] the children of Israel came

Apparatus, Chapter 33

[r] Nfmg +: "of the congregation."

[s] Or: "of those who made requests"; Nfmg: "of those who asked for the flesh."

[t] Missing in text and margins.

[u] I.e., "Fort of the Cock"; MT: "Ezion-geber.

[w] MT: Kadesh.

[x] Nfmg 1°: "within Reqem"; Nfmg 2°: "in Taurus Amanus" or: "Yamanus" (*ymnws*); cf. Ps.-J.

Notes, Chapter 33

[11]"The graves of those who were desirous," (*qbry*) *š'ly š'lth;* HT: *Kibroth hatta'wah.* In the next verse Nf translates the same Hebrew words quite differently: *qbry twḥmdth,* "the graves of desire (or: 'Craving')." We are probably dealing with the translations of toponyms, not real place names. See note to 11:34 above.

[12]"Kerak Tarnogolah," *krk trnwglh,* lit.: "the Fort of the Rooster," translating HT *'ṣywn gbr* here, in v. 36 and Deut 2:8. The Aramaic form is probably the translation of the HT place name, as *gbr* in Mishnaic Hebrew also means "cock."

[13]"Reqem"; translating Kadesh of HT as elsewhere in Nf. See note to Nf Num 13:26; Gen 14:7; Smolar and Aberbach, 1983, 120, and McNamara, 1972, 199f.

[14]"the command of the decree of the Memra of"; HT: "(according to) the mouth of (the Lord)." See also note to 3:16.

[15]"at the end of forty years," *bswp 'rb'yn šnyn;* HT: *bšnt h'rb'ym lṣ't,* "in the forty (= fortieth) year (of the coming out of . . .)." Nf often adds *bswp* in such phrases (see Nf Gen 7:11, and note). Here the end of the year is not intended, since (as stated later in the verse) Aaron died in the fifth month. The phrase *bswp* can also mean "ultimately, finally."

[16]"at the time . . ." (etc.), lit.: "at the time of the coming out of. . ."; "redeemed" is added to HT, as often in Nf in such contexts; see above Introd. III, 22.

forth *redeemed* from the land of Egypt, in the fifth month, on the first[y] of the month. 39. And Aaron was a hundred and twenty-three years old at the time he died[z] on Hor the Mountain. 40. And the Canaanite, the king of Arad, heard *because* he was dwelling in the south in the land of Canaan, at the time the children of Israel came.[aa] 41. And they set out from Hor the Mountain and encamped at Zalmonah. 42. And they set out from Zalmonah and encamped at Punon. 43. And they set out from Punon and encamped at Oboth. 44. And they set out from Oboth and encamped at the *Passes*[bb] *of* Abarayya,[17] on the border of the Moabites. 45. And they set out from 'Iyyin and encamped at Dibon-gad. 46. And they set out from Dibon-gad and encamped at Almon-diblathaymah. 47. And they set out from Almon-diblathaymah and encamped at Mount Abarayya, before Nebo.[cc] 48. And they set out from the Mountains of Abarayya and encamped in the plains[dd] of Moab by the Jordan of Jericho. 49. And they encamped by the Jordan from *Beth*-Jeshimoth as far as Abel-shittim in the plains of Moab. 50. And the Lord[ee] spoke with Moses in the plains of Moab near the Jordan, saying: 51. "Speak with the children of Israel and say to them: 'When you pass over the Jordan to the land of Canaan, 52. you shall *blot out* all the inhabitants of the land from before you, and you shall make an end of all their *idols,* and you shall make an end of all their (images)[ff] of cast metal,[gg] and you shall destroy all their idolatrous altars.[hh] 53. And after you have blotted out *the inhabitants of the*[18] land[ii] you shall dwell in it; for I have given the land to you to inherit it. 54. And you shall give the possession of the land by lot to your[jj] families; for a *tribe of* many *people,* you shall enlarge its inheritance; and for *a tribe of* fewer *people,* you shall make smaller its inheritance; to each one where his lot falls, that shall be his. According to the tribes of your fathers shall you inherit. 55. But if you do not blot out the inheritances of the land from before you, all that you have left[kk] of them shall be as thorns in your eyes and as *spears* in your sides, and they shall afflict you in the land in which you dwell. 56. And I will do to you as I planned to do to them.'"

Apparatus, Chapter 33

[y] Nfmg: "(on the first) day."
[z] Nfmg: "(at the time) in which he was gathered."
[aa] Nfmg: "at the entrance of the sons of."
[bb] Cf. 21:11; Nfmg: "at the encampment."
[cc] Cf. 27:14; Nfmg: "(and encamped) at the encampment of the 'Abarayya, before Nebo."
[dd] Nfmg: "in the plain of."
[ee] Nfmg: "the Memra of the Lord."
[ff] Erased by the censor.
[gg] Nfmg: "and you shall smash (all the images) of cast metal(s)"; = VN.
[hh] Greek loan word *bomos,* reserved for idolatrous altars.
[ii] Nfmg: "you shall blot out the land"; instead of the verb "blot out" (*tywyṣwn*) we should probably read *ttbwn,* "the land, and you shall reside."
[jj] Nfi: "their (families)."
[kk] Nfi: "(all that) you leave"; Nfmg: "(all) that he left of them."

Notes, Chapter 33

[17]"Passes of Abarayya"; or: "passes (passing points)," *mgzh;* HT: *'yy h'brym;* RSV: Iye-abarim. Nf renders here as in Nf Num 21:11. In Num 13:29 Nf renders "beside the Jordan" as "by the passes (*mgyztyh*) of the Jordan." In Num 33:45 the HT uses only the form *'yym,* which Nf does not translate.

[18]"the inhabitants (of the land)"; added in keeping with Nf's general translation techniques (see above Introd. III, 23): the land cannot be annihilated. The HT has: *whwrštm ('t-h'rṣ)* (RSV: "you shall take possession of"), which Nf understands as meaning "to destroy" (a recognized, if rare, meaning); Nf renders in a similar manner also elsewhere, e.g., Num 14:12; Exod 15:9.

CHAPTER 34

1. And the Lord[a] spoke with Moses, saying: 2. "Command the children of Israel, and say to them: 'When you enter the land of Canaan—this is the land that shall fall to you as an inheritance,[b] the land of Canaan according to its boundaries—3. your boundary to the south[c] shall be from the wilderness of Zin to the *boundaries*[1] of *the* Edom*ites;* and your southern boundary shall be from the extremities of the Sea of Salt on the east. 4. And the boundary turns[d] for you to the south *from* the Ascent of Akrabbim, and shall pass by the *Mount of Iron;*[e2] and it shall come out[f] to the south of *Reqem de-Ge'a*[g3] and shall continue to *Tirat* Adarayya,[h4] and shall pass[i] by *the boundary of Shuq Masai*[j5] at *Qesem.* 5. And the boundary turns[k] from *Qesem* to the *Nile*[6] of *the* Egypt*ians,*[m] and shall come out[n]

Apparatus, Chapter 34

[a] Nfmg: "the Memra of the Lord."
[b] Nfmg: "(that) you shall take as possession."
[c] VN: "and your southern boundary shall be from the wilderness of Reqem opposite the boundary of the Edomites, and you shall have the southern boundary from the extremities of the Sea of Salt on the east."
[d] Nfmg: "shall turn"; VN: "and your southern boundary shall turn."
[e] MT: Sin (RSV: Zin); Ps.-J.: ". . . by the palm trees of the Mount of Iron" (*ṣyny ṭwr przl', ṣînê ṭûr parzela*).
[f] Lit.: "its comings forth"; "its exits."
[g] MT: Kadesh-barnea.
[h] VN: Dirat 'Adarayya; MT: Hazar-addar; Saadya translates by Raphiah; see v. 15.
[i] Nfmg: "(and shall pass) by Qesem"; MT: 'Asmon.
[j] Cf. v. 15.
[k] Nfmg: "and it shall turn"; = VN.
[m] MT: "to the Wadi (Torrent) of Egypt," i.e., the Wadi el-Arish (already Saadya); Nfmg: "of Egypt and its exit shall be to the west"; = VN.
[n] Lit.: "its exits."

Notes, Chapter 34

[1]"boundaries (of the Edomites)"; *tḥwmyhwn d-*; or: "boundary of. . . ," sing.; the *yod* representing a vocal shewa as elsewhere in Nf; HT: "along the side of (*'l/ydy*) Edom."

[2]"the Mount of Iron"; *ṭwr przl';* HT: Zin (*ṣn-h*). It is mentioned in Josephus, *War* 4, 8, 2, par. 454; cf. McNamara, 1972, 197, and above, Introd. IV, 42.

[3]"Reqem de-Ge'a"; *rqm dgy'h;* HT: Kadesh-barnea. See note to 32:8 and above, Introd. IV, 54.

[4]"Tirat Adarayya"; *ṭyrt 'dryyh,* "Enclosure of the Flocks," a translation of the HT *ḥṣr 'dr,* "Hazar-addar." Nf translates the HT *ḥṣr* (= *ḥaṣer,* "enclosure") as *ṭyrh* again in a toponym in Num 34:9, 10. For *ṭyr* the Frg. Tg. (VN), here and elsewhere, has *dyrt-*: "the courtyard of. . ." See also above, Introd. IV, 66.

[5]"Shuq Masai at Qesem," *šwq msyy* (Díez Macho emends to *mzyy*) *bqsm;* in an *Aruk* Pal. Tg. citation: *mzy.* HT: *'ṣmnh,* Azmon. The place name Azmon occurs only in Num 34:4-5 and Josh 15:4. The Frg. Tgs. (VN) translate simply as *qsm;* the other Targums retain the Hebrew form. The identifications of Shuq Mazai/Masai ("the street/district/market place/desire of Mazai") and of Qesem ("divination") are unknown; see also McNamara, 1972, 199, 201, and above, Introd. IV, 59, 60.

[6]"the Nile"; HT: "the Brook (of Egypt)." See above, Introd. IV, 46.

at the *west.*[7] 6. And the boundary *of the Great Sea*[o8]*—Ocean;* these are the *Waters of the Beginning,*[p] *its islands, its ports and the ships*[q] *with the Primordial Waters* that *are in it;*[r] this shall be for you the sea boundary.[s] 7. And this shall be for you the northern boundary: from the Great Sea you shall draw a line for yourselves to *Huminas*[t] *Taurus*[u9] in the *east;* 8. from *Taurus (U)manos*[w] you shall draw a line to the entrance[x] of *Antioch;*[10] and the boundary shall come out[y] *at the Aulon*[z] *of the*

Apparatus, Chapter 34

[o] I.e., the Mediterranean. The correct translation would have been: "and the western boundary" (*yam* is translated by "sea" instead of by "west"). PVN: "and the western boundary is Oceanus (or: 'Ocean'; generally the Mediterranean Sea; cf. Gen 1:7; Ps.-J.), the islands" (Greek loan word *nesoi*) and its harbors and the ships with the primeval waters of the Beginning (*br'šyt;* or: 'of Creation'). This shall be for you the western boundary."

[p] *br'šyt,* i.e., of Creation.

[q] Nfmg: "that is Oceanus, its islands and its harbors and the ships"; = PVN.

[r] *bgwwh;* or: "that are in the midst." Nfmg: "(the) primordial (waters) that are in it (*bgwwh;* or: 'in the midst'), that is the waters of the Beginning (*br'šyt;* or: 'of the Creation')."

[s] Nfmg: "the western boundary"; = PVN.

[t] = Amanos: the Tauros Amanos.

[u] Nfmg: "the Taurus in the east"; VN: "Tauros Menos" (*mnws*), cf. v. 8; MT: Hor ha-Har.

[w] *mnws;* as in PVN (*ṭwwrws mnws*).

[x] *m'lny;* in Nfi and Nfmg 1°; Nfmg 2°, there are three variant readings for "entrance": *m'ly, m'lh* and *m'lk;* PVN: "to the entrance to Antioch" (P, *m'ly,* VN, *m'l'*).

[y] Lit.: "and the exits of the boundary shall be."

[z] Lit.: "Awwlas" (= Ablas); VN: "*'wwl'*"; Nfi: "*d'l-.*"

Notes, Chapter 34

[7]"the west"; HT: "the Sea."

[8]The HT (RSV) has: "For the western boundary, you shall have the Great Sea and its coast; this shall be your western boundary." The Pal. Tg. paraphrase of v. 6 (Nf, PVN, Nfmg) is practically identical in all texts. This paraphrase seems to be a combination of geography and cosmological speculation; see A. J. Brawer, 1972, 415–420, at 417. The Great Sea, fundamentally the Mediterranean, is identified by a Greek or Latin loan word *ôkeanos.* In Greek tradition *ôkeanos* is the primeval water (or: the god of the primeval water) and the source of all smaller waters, conceived of as a great river which compasses the earth's disk, returning into itself; (see Liddell, Scott and Jones, *Greek-English Lexicon,* under *ôkeanos*). "These" (either the Great Sea and Okeanos, or their waters not explicitly mentioned) are further identified in Nf with "the Waters of Bereshit," presumably the primordial abyss of Hebrew tradition. After a mention of "its islands (in all texts the Greek loan word *nêsos*), harbors and ships," there is a further reference to "the primordial waters (*myy' qdmwyy*) that are in it," which also seem to refer to the waters of the primordial abyss. Hebrew thought would seem to have passed easily from mention of "the Great Sea" to reflection on the mythical waters of the abyss and their symbolism. See Ps.-J. Deut 11:24, where "the Latter Sea" of the HT is paraphrased; "the Sea of Okeanos; these are the waters of the beginning" (or: "of creation"). See above, Introd. IV, 48; also McNamara, 1966 (1978), 296, and A. M. Goldberg, 1970, 127–131 (for Pal. Tg. Deut 30:12 and Rom 10:6-7). On the loan word *ôkeanos,* see D. Sperber, 1986, 129.

[9]"Huminas Taurus," *hwmyns ṭwwrws;* Nfmg: *ṭwwrws;* VN: *ṭwwrs mnws.* Ps.-J. *ṭwwrys 'wmnys.* We should probably correct Nf to read: "Taurus Huminas," as in v. 8. HT: *hr hhr,* "Hor the mountain." This is a town on the northern border of Israel, distinct from the other Mount Hor, *hr hhr,* where Aaron died (Num 20:22-27, etc.), a name retained in the Targums. The original for Tg. Num 34:7 was probably "Tauros Amanus." A town of this name (*Tauromenium*), mentioned by Pliny, Cicero, etc., existed in the eastern part of Sicily (present-day Taormina). See further above, Introd. IV, 64.

[10]"Antioch" (on the Orontes); HT: Hamath. We have the same identification in the other occurrence of the name (Num 13:21; cf. also Gen 10:18). In Jerome's day (see *Hebr. quaest. in Gen.* 10:18), whereas most scholars identified biblical Hamath with Amath (Epiphania) in Syria (thus also Josephus, *Ant.,* 1, 6, 2, par. 138), some identified it with Antioch. See also above, Introd. IV, 1.

Cilicians.[aa][11] 9. And the boundary comes out[bb] at Zephirin and shall (go on and) come out at *Tirat Enwata,*[cc][12] which shall be for you the northern boundary[dd] 10. And you shall draw a line for the eastern boundary from *Tirat Enwata* to *Apamea.*[ee][13] 11. And the boundary goes down,[ff] from *Apamea* to *Daphne,*[gg][14] to the east of *Ayna;*[15] and the boundary goes down and touches on the extremities of

Apparatus, Chapter 34

[aa] Nfmg: "on the border of Al(as) of the Cilicians"; see Ps.-J.'s translation. MT: "From Hor ha-Har you shall draw a line as far as Lebo-Hamath and the boundary shall go and come out at Zedad."

[bb] Nfmg: "and it shall come out."

[cc] Correcting Nf text: *ṭirat 'Egebata* (*'gbth*). Nfmg: "Dirat 'Aynwata"; = VN; cf. v. 15.

[dd] Cf. Ps.-J.'s rendering. MT: "the boundary shall pass to Ziphron and end at Hasor-'Enan."

[ee] Nfmg: "as a western boundary between Derayyat 'Aynwata and Apamea (or: 'Paneas')." VN: "as a western boundary from Dirat 'Ayyanwata to Apimyas (*'pmyys*)"; Ps.J.: "Apamea." Probably Paneas is intended, at least in the case of Nf and Nfmg. In Nf the left bar of the *mem* is crossed out (though the stroke seems to be accidental), leaving it converted into the letter *nun;* likewise in Nfmg, as it seems, the *mem* has a small mark under the right bar leaving "Apamias" converted into "Apanias." MT: "from Hasar-'Enan to Shepham."

[ff] Nfmg: "it shall go down"; = VN.

[gg] VN: "and the boundary shall go down for you from Apimayas (*'pmyys*) to Daphne to the east of 'Aynwata and the boundary shall issue (lit.: 'reach') near the Sea of Genessar to the west" (error for "east" as in Nf., Ps.-J.?)"; MT: Riblah.

Notes, Chapter 34

[11]"the Aulon of Cilicia," *'wwlws dqylqy.* So also VN: *'wwl(s) dqylq'y;* Nfmg has: *'l-dqlq'y;* Ps.-J. *'bls dqylq'y* ("Abilas of the Cilicians"). HT: Zedad (*ṣddh*). The Frg. Tg. MS P simply has "Cilicia." (Cf. Nfmg). The exact original reading and identification of the place intended are uncertain; see further above, Introd. IV, 3. McNamara, 1972, 191f.

[12]"Tirat Enwata," *tyrt 'nbth;* "Enclosure of the Springs"; Nfmg, VN: *dyrt 'yynwwth;* HT: Hazar-enan. See also above, Introd. IV, 67.

[13]"Apamea"; *'pmyh;* Nfmg: *'pmyys.* In Nf and Nfmg the *m* has been corrected to *n,* (*'pnyh; 'pnyys*); VN: *'pmyys;* Ps.-J.: *'pm'ph.* It is uncertain whether the town originally intended was Apamea in Syria, or Paneas. See Alexander, 1974, 212; Le Deaut, 1979, 3 (*Nombres*), 323; McNamara, 1972, 191. The HT has: Shepham. In Jerome's day, however, the Jews identified biblical Shepham with Apamea; see Jerome, *Commen. on Ezek 47:18* with reference to Num 34:10-11 (*Sephama quam Hebraei Apamiam nominant,* CCL 75, 723; PL 25, 478). Le Déaut favors identification with Paneas (which would be written with a prosthetic *alef*), i.e., Caesarea Philippi. The next verse mentions Daphne, southwest of Paneas. See also above, Introd. IV, 2.

[14]"Daphne"; HT: Riblah, a name mentioned only here in the Pentateuch; elsewhere in the Bible it is also called Riblatah, Diblatah; "Riblah in the land of Hamath" (2 Kgs 23:33; 25:21; Jer 39:5; 52:9, 27). There were two places named Daphne at the northern borders of Israel: one a suburb of Antioch on the Orontes, known to Josephus (*Ant.,* 14, 15, 11, 451) and the rabbis, the other southwest of Dan (present-day Dafna); cf. Josephus, *War,* 4, 1, 1, 3. The rabbis identified Riblah with Daphnim (of Antioch; see the texts in Strack-Billerbeck, I, 33; II, 682; IV, 905, 998). (A variant reading in the Vulg. Num 34:11 translates as: *Rebla contra fontem Daphnim*—on the Orontes.) Perhaps the Targum has Daphne near Dan in mind. This is all the more probable if HT Shepham of vv. 10-11 is identified as Paneas (= Dan) rather than as Apamea. See further Alexander, 1974, 214–217; Le Déaut, 1979, 3 (*Nombres*), 323, and above, Introd. IV, 18.

[15]"Ayna"; a simple translation of HT "Ain."

the Sea of *Gennesar*[16] on the east.[hh] 12. And the boundary goes down to the Jordan and shall come out[ii] at the Sea of Salt. This shall be for you the land with its boundary round about.'"[jj] 13. And Moses commanded the children of Israel, saying: "This is the land which shall be possessed[kk] by lots, which the Lord[mm] commanded to give to the nine[nn] tribes and to the half-tribe; 14. for the tribe of the sons of Reuben[oo] according to their fathers' houses, and the tribe of the sons of Gad[pp] according to their fathers' houses had taken (their inheritance), and the half-tribe *of Manasseh* had received their inheritance. 15. The two tribes and the half-tribe of Manasseh were the first to receive their inheritance beyond[qq] the Jordan of

Apparatus, Chapter 34

[hh] Nfmg: "and the boundary shall go down and reach near the Sea of Gennesar (= Sea of Gennesaret) to the west"; see Ps.-J.; MT: "from Shepham the boundary shall go down to Riblah to the east of 'Ayn, and from there to touch on the eastern slopes of the Sea of Kinnereth."

[ii] Lit.: "and its exits shall be."

[jj] See rendering of Ps.-J.

[kk] Nfmg: "you shall possess."

[mm] Nfmg: "the Memra of the Lord."

[nn] Nfmg: "to the nine" (another form).

[oo] Nfmg: "of the Reubenites."

[pp] Nfmg: "of the Gadites."

[qq] Nfmg: "beyond the Jordan of Jericho, eastward (or: 'the first'), to the east. From the Plain of the Sea of Salt (= the Dead Sea) the boundary goes out for them to Kinnereth, fortress of the kingdom of the Amorites, and from Kinnereth, fortress of the kingdom of the Amorites, the boundary goes out for them to the Mount of Snow (= Mount Hermon) and to Humata of the Lebanon; and from the Mount of Snow and Humata (in Nfmg: 'Lehumata') of the Lebanon the boundary goes out for them to Hobah, which is to the north of 'Enewata (= the Springs) of Damascus, and from the north <of the Sources of Damascus (omitted?)> the boundary goes out for them to Dioqenes (*dywqnys*), to Turnegola (corr. from: Tur Talga, 'Mount of Snow') of Qesariyyon (= Caesarea Philippi), which is to the east, to the west of Dan; (from there) the boundary goes out for them to the Great River, the Euphrates, above (or: 'beside') which (have taken place) the battles . . ."; VN as Nfmg as far as: "the springs of Damascus." VN continue: "(north of the Springs of Damascus) the boundary goes out for them to Dioqtas (*l-dywqṭs,* in V; N: *l-dywqynws*) of the Cock (*twrngl'*) of Qesaryon (= Caesarea Philippi) which is to the east of the Cave (of Dan). And from Yoqtas of the Cock of Qesaryon, which is to the east of the Cave (of Dan), the boundary went out for them to the Great River, the River Euphrates (N alone adds: 'above' [or: 'besides'] which the war victories of the Lord are performed and from the Great River, the River Euphrates) the boundary went out for them to Qryn Zwwt' (Klein, 1980, 2: Sharp Corner) behind the city, all Trachon, Zimra, the place of the kingdom (or; 'the royal house') of Sihon, the king of the Amorites, and the place of the kingdom (or: 'the royal house') of Og, the king of Matnan (= Butnin = Bashan). It goes to Raphia and to Shuq Mazai until it reaches the border district of the Salt Sea. This is the portion of the two and half tribes."

Notes, Chapter 34

[16] "Sea of Gennesar," *ymh dgnysr;* Genessar in 1 Macc 11:67; HT: "the Sea of Chinnereth." Chinnereth is mentioned again in Deut 3:17, where Nf renders as "the Sea of Gennesar," and in Josh 11:2; 19:35; 1 Kgs 15:20, where the Targum renders as "Gennesar." The sea of Chinnereth is also mentioned in Josh 12:3; 13:27. See Alexander, 1974; L. Smolar and M. Aberbach, 1983, 114; Abel, 1933, 1, 495. See also above, Introd. IV, 23.

Jericho, eastward."[rr] [17] *The boundary went out for them to Kinnereth,* [18] *the fortress of the kings of the Amorites; the boundary went out for them to the fortress of Iyyon to the east of Beth Yerah;*[ss] [19] *and from the east of the Sea of Beth Yerah the boundary went out for them to Yadyoqita;*[20] *and from Yadyoqitos*[tt] *Tarnegol of Caesarea,*

Apparatus, Chapter 34

[rr] Or: "(as) the first ones (to take possession)."
[ss] Nfmg: "(to the east) of the Sea (add?: of Beth Yerah)."
[tt] The form of this word differs in Nfmg (*dywqynws*) and in VN (*ywqynws, dywqnws*).

Notes, Chapter 34

[17]Unlike the other tribes, chap. 34 gives no boundaries for the two tribes of Reuben and Gad, and the half-tribe of Manasseh, on the east side of the Jordan. The HT Num 34:15 simply says: "The two tribes and the half-tribe have received their inheritance beyond the Jordan at Jericho eastward toward sunrise." Their borders and territory are described in part in Num 32:33-42; Deut 3:1-17 (and for future, postexilic times) Ezek 47. The absence of frontiers in HT Num 34:15 has led to a developed midrash on these, which is inserted into the Pal. Tgs. The history of the development of this midrash is hard to unravel. Together with this we also have lists of the Holy Land frontiers in 1QapGen 21:8-20 and in the rabbinic texts *m. Hal.* 4:8 (R. Gamaliel II, c. 100 C.E.); *m. Sheb.* 6:1; *Sifre Deut.* 51 on 11:24 (Finkelstein, 117); *t. Sheb.* 4:11 (66); *j. Sheb.* 6, 36c (c. 200 C.E.); *m. Git.* 1:2. For a detailed study of these lists, see P. S. Alexander, 1974, esp. 218–252. See also G. Ogg, in Schürer, 1979, 2, 14–15, note 46; A. Neubauer, 1868; B. Barry Levy, 1987, 2, 175–180; H. Hildesheimer, 1886; S. Krauss, *Geographie;* Y. Sussman, 1976, 213–257; S. Klein, 1928, 197–259. I. Press, 2nd ed., 1951. The origin and purpose of this list of border names are uncertain; it may have been connected with Jewish halakah (what could be regarded as within Israel's borders for matters of halakah); see Brawer, 1972, cols. 415–416. G. Ogg, in E. Schürer, 1979, 2, 13, believes these lists are merely ideal and bear no relation to reality. With regard to Nf Num 34:15, the text of VN has basically the same list as Nf but in a somewhat different arrangement. This entire Pal. Tg. text seems to be very old and to have had a complex history of transmission. Note the emphasis here on the northeastern territory. B. Barry Levy, 1987, 2, 178f., notes that the greater part of the list focuses on the northern and eastern area, in and around Syria, from Lebanon to the Euphrates. He also notes (1986, 1, 121f.) Nf's interest in the Mesopotamian and Syrian place names in Gen 10:10, 11, 17, 18 and surmises that this may suggest a Syrian or Mesopotamian provenance for either the writing or editing of the text of Nf, or at least more familiarity with these places than the others in Gen 10.

[18]"to Kinnereth . . . to the fortress of Iyyon to the east of Beth Yerah." Deut 3:16-17 gives as the territory of the Reubenites and the Gadites "from Gilead as far as the valley of the Arnon, with the middle of the valley as the boundary, as far over as the river Jabbok, the boundary of the Ammonites; the Arabah also, with the Jordan as the boundary, from Chinnereth as far as the sea of the Arabah, the Salt Sea, under the slopes of Pisgah on the East." Nf renders "Chinnereth" of this text of Deuteronomy as "the Sea of Gennesar." In its paraphrase of Num 34:15, Nf leaves Chinnereth without identification. The name can indicate both a town and the sea, or the fruitful valley along the lake (Smolar-Aberbach, 1983, 114). Here most probably a town in Amorite territory is intended. (Nfmg and VN have "fortress"; Nf: "the fortress.") Heshbon was "*the* fortress" of Sihon, king of the Amorites. No *terminus a quo* is given for the border in Nf. Possibly, as is explicit in VN and Nfmg, the Dead Sea area is intended.

[19]"to the fortress of Iyyon to the east of Beth Yerah." Beth Yerah is at the southernmost point of the Lake of Tiberias (the Sea of Gennesar), near present-day Deganya. In *Gen. R.* 98, 17 (to Gen 49:21), R. Samuel b. Nachman identified Kinnereth of Gen 49:21 with Beth Yerah. See further McNamara, 1972, 192f. Nf gives Iyyon as east of Beth Yerah. The exact identification of this Iyyon is uncertain. Díez Macho, 1974, 4 (*Números*), 320, with reference to I. Press, 2nd ed., 1951, 696, col. 1a (*'Iyyon b*), thinks it appears to be 'Iyyôn, present-day 'Ayyun ("Wells"), two and a half kilometers to the north of Al-Hamma and four kilometers to the east of the Sea of Kinnereth. P. S. Alexander, 1974, 228, identifies the *'ywn* of *Sifre Num* 11, 25 (117) with the plain of *Merdj 'Ayun,* to the west of Hermon. The "fortress" would be to the north of the plain. In this case its present location in Nf, putting it near Tiberias (Kinnereth), would be due to a misunderstanding of the true situation by a glossator. See further above, Introd. IV, 29.

[20]"Yadyoqita" (*h-ydywqyṭ'*) later called in our text "Yadyoqitos Tarnegol Qesarian" (*ydywqiṭos trngwl qsrywn*). The form of the first name varies considerably in the recensions: Nf, *l-ydywqyṭ'; (m)-dywqyṭws;* VN, *l-dywqṭs/ywqts;* Nfmg, *l-kywqṭs;* Ps.-J. (Num 34:8) *dywwqynws.* The original form seems to have been *dywwqynws,* which is but a transformed or corrupt form of the Greek term *eikôn,* "image, idol." The full name would seem to have been *dywwqynos trngwl dqsrywn,* "The Image (or Idol) of the Rooster of Caesarea (Philippi)." This is, in the text of Nf, said to be on the east side of the west part (*m'rbh*) of Dan, *m'rbh* most probably being an error for *m'rh,* "cave." The cave is that of Paneas (see to v. 11), near Caesarea Philippi. See further above, Introd. IV, 71; also 15 and 30.

which is to the east of the (Cave) of Dan, the boundary went out for them to the Mount of Snow,[uu][21] *at the border of Lebanon, which is to the north of the Springs*[ww] *of Damascus;*[22] *and from the north of the Springs of Damascus the boundary went out for them to the Great River, the River Euphrates, beside*[xx] *which the arrays of the battle victories of the Lord were performed;*[yy] *and from the Great River, the River Euphrates, the boundary went out for them to Qeren Zawwe*[zz][23] *to Bathyra,*[zz bis] *and (to) the whole of Trachonitis*[25] *of Beth-Zimra,*[a][24] *the royal city*[b] *of Sihon, (king)*[c] *of the Amorites, and the royal city of Og, the king of Butnin,*[d][26] *whom Moses the Lord's prophet slew; it goes out to Raph(iah),*[e][27] *and to Shuq Mazai;*[28] *and to the Cave of*

Apparatus, Chapter 34

[uu] Cf. Ps.-J. Deut 3:9; 4:48; it is a name for Mount Hermon.

[ww] Or: "'Aynuta"; cf. vv. 9-11.

[xx] Or: "above (which)," or: "beside (which)"

[yy] Or: "(which there) have been done" (*mt'bdyn*).

[zz] VN: "Qiryan Zwwt'"; M. Klein: "Sharp Corner" (see note *qq* above); Etheridge: "the cities of Zawatha." Perhaps we should read: "the cities of Nave (capital of Batanea) and Betera" (= Bathyra) (also in Batanea).

[zz bis] Text has: (*lqrn zwwy*) *dbtryh,* ("to Qeren Zawwe) of Bathyra," or, as Díez Macho, 1974, 322, understands, "which is behind it."

[a] Beth-Zimra not identified. Perhaps we should read: "Nimra (Namara), a city of Batanea."

[b] Lit.: "house."

[c] In text: "the kingdom."

[d] In text: Botneyim = Bashan.

[e] In text we read Raphyon, which seems to be an error for Raphiah, and not Raphon (Raphana) of the Decapolis, badly written.

Notes, Chapter 34

[21]"The Mount of Snow," i.e., Mount Hermon, said to be "at the border of (*l-tḥwmh*) Lebanon—*tḥwmh* (like *ḥwmt'* of VN and Nfmg) being probably an error for *ḥmt',* "Hamath" (given as on the northern border in Ezek 47:16-17).

[22]The mention of the "springs of Damascus" is probably occasioned by Ezek 47:17: "Hazar-enon, which is on the northern border of Damascus." From the region of Damascus the border went to the Euphrates, "beside which the battle victories (lit.: 'the order of the battle victories') of the Lord had been performed." In Nf the Lord is said to have worked battle victories (*nṣḥny qrb-*) for Israel on various occasions: in Egypt (Exod 13:8; 14:14, 25), in the future (Deut 3:22, "the order of their battle victories"). What the battle victories performed by the Euphrates were we are not told.

[23]Qeren Zawwe, *qrn zwwy; qrn zwwt'* of VN and *qrn zkwt'* of Ps.-J. v. 9 should probably be corrected to *qryy zkwt',* "the villages of Zakutha" (present-day Zakiye, southeast of Damascus), which could be the *zkwt'* of *j. Ab. Zar.* 58b, mentioned in the frontier list of *Sifre Deut* 11:24 (118). See Alexander, 1974, 227; Le Déaut, 1979, 3 (*Nombres*), 332, n. 19. See also above, Introd. IV, 51.

[24]The Beth-Zimra is probably to be connected with the person named Zamaris, whom Herod is said to have put in charge of a group of Babylonian Jews (Josephus, *Life,* 54) in Batanea. This man "built fortresses and a town which he named Bathyra" (*Ant.,* 17, 2, 2; § 26); cf. Alexander, 1974, 426; Le Déaut, 1979, 3 (*Nombres*), 327, n. 45. See also Introd. IV, 7, 13.

[25]Trachon(a) in the Pal. Tg. generally renders Argob of the HT (Deut 3:4, 12f.): "Argob, the kingdom of Og of Bashan"; Nf: "Trachona, the kingdom of Og in Butnin." "Butnin" (text *bwtnyyn;* see note to Nf Num 21:33) is Batanea; HT: Bashan.

[26]"Butnin"; HT: Bashan. See note to 21:33; 32:33. See above, Introd. IV, 14.

[27]The border passed on to Raphion (*rpywn*) and Shuq Mazai. The Nf reading *rpyon* in the Transjordan is preferable to Raphiah (*rpyh*) of VN, south of Gaza. Raphion may be the *Raphôn* of 1 Macc 5:34 (= Josephus, *Ant.,* 12, 8, 4 § 342); the Raphana of Pliny (*Nat. Hist.,* 5, 18, 74). See further E. Schürer, 1979, 2, 137; Abel, *Géographie de la Palestine,* 2, 432. See also Introd. IV, 53.

[28]There is a Shuq Masai at Qesem also mentioned in Nf Num 34:4, as the terminus of one section of Israel's southern borders. In that text Shuq Mazai and Qesem seem to be towards Gaza. Here Shuq Mazai seems to be in the vicinity of En-Gedi and the Sea of Salt (i.e., the Dead Sea). Different towns may be intended. Díez Macho, 1974, 4 (*Números*), 322, believes the Shuq Mazai here = Sycamazon (Hirbet Suq Mazin), between Gaza and Raphiah, a short distance from the coast (with reference to Abel, *Géographie,* 2, 172, and Avi-Yonah, 1951, 118). See also Introd., IV, 59, 60.

Ain Gedi, until it reaches[f] *the border district of the Sea of Salt. This is the boundary of the two*[g] tribes and the half tribe." 16. And the Lord[h] spoke with Moses, saying: 17. "These are the names of the men who shall give you the land as a possession: Eleazar the priest[i] and Joshua bar Nun. 18. And you shall take one prince of every[j] tribe to give the land as a possession. 19. And these are the names of the men: of the tribe *of the sons* of Judah, Caleb bar Jephunneh. 20. And of the tribe of the sons of Simeon, Shemuel bar Ammihud. 21. And of the tribe *of the sons* of Benjamin, Elidad ben Chislon. 22. And of the tribe of the sons of Dan, the prince (Bukki)[k] ben Jogli. 23. Of the sons of Joseph, of the tribe of the sons of Manasseh,[m] the prince Hanniel ben Ephod. 24. And of the tribe of the sons of Ephraim, the prince Kemuel ben Shiphtan. 25. And of the tribe of the sons of (Zebulun),[n] the prince Elizaphan bar Parnach. 26. And of the tribe of the sons of Issachar, the prince Paltiel bar Azzan. 27. And of the tribe of the sons of Asher, the prince Ahihud bar Shelomi. 28. And of the tribe of the sons of Naphtali, the prince Pedahel bar Ammihud." 29. These (are the ones) whom the Lord[o] commanded *Moses* to give the landed possession to the children of Israel in the land of Canaan.[p]

CHAPTER 35

1. And the Lord[a] spoke with Moses in the plains of Moab near the Jordan of Jericho, saying: 2. "Command the children of Israel and let them give[b] to the Levites, from the inheritance of their possession,[c] cities to dwell in and (the) outskirts which are around about[d] (the) cities, you shall give them[e] to the Levites. 3. And the cities shall be theirs to dwell in; and their outskirts[f] shall be for their cattle and for their wealth and for all their property.[g] 4. And the outskirts[h] of the

Apparatus, Chapter 34

[f] Nfmg: "(king) of Batanea; it goes out from Raphiah to Shuq Mazai (text: 'to Raphiah and to Shuq Mazai') until it reaches . . ."
[g] Nfmg: "this was the portion of the two . . ."
[h] Nfmg: "the Memra of the Lord."
[i] Nfmg: "the high priest."
[j] Nfmg: "one prince for each tribe."
[k] Missing in text and margin.
[m] Nfmg: "of the tribe of the sons of Joseph, that is, of the tribe of the sons of Manasseh."
[n] "of Ephraim" in the text, but a dot above the word draws attention to the error.
[o] Nfmg: "the Memra of the Lord."
[p] Nfmg: "these are the tribes to which the Lord commanded to give possession of the land . . ."

Apparatus, Chapter 35

[a] Nfmg: "the Memra of the Lord."
[b] = "that they give."
[c] Nfmg: "of their possession" (with a verbal noun).
[d] Nfmg: "and the outskirts (*prwwly;* text, *prwyryn;* another pronunciation of the same word; that of VN) around the cities"; = VN.
[e] Nfmg: "(round about) them, (you shall give . . .)"; = VN.
[f] Nfmg: "and their outskirts"; = VN; cf. note *d* above. This variant is repeated in subsequent verses of Nf, with no PVN.
[g] Nfmg: "for their herds and all their riches."
[h] Nfmg: "and their outskirts"; cf. v. 4

cities which you shall give the Levites (shall reach) from the wall of the city[i] outwards for a thousand cubits round about. 5. And you shall measure outside the city, for the east side two thousand cubits, and for the *west*[j] side two thousand cubits, and for the north side two thousand cubits, and for the south side two thousand cubits, with the city in the center. These shall be for *you* the outskirts of the cities.[k] 6. And the cities which you shall give to the Levites shall be six cities of refuge, which you shall give so that the manslayers may flee there; and to these you *shall add* forty-two cities. 7. All the cities which you shall give to the Levites shall be forty-eight cities; these and their outskirts. 8. And as for the cities which you shall give from the possession of the children of Israel, from *the tribe* of many *people*[1] you shall take more, and from *the tribe*[m] of few *people* you shall take less; each one according to the possession which it had inherited, shall give of its cities to the Levites." 9. And the Lord[n] spoke with Moses, saying: 10. "Speak with the children of Israel and say to them: 'When you cross the Jordan to the land of Canaan, 11. you shall designate[o] cities for yourselves; they shall be cities of refuge for you, that the manslayer, *anyone who kills* a person inadvertently, may flee there. 12. And they shall be[p] for you cities for refuge from *the avenger of blood,*[q2] that the manslayer may not die until he stands before *the people* of the congregation[3] in judgment. 13. And the cities you shall give[r] shall be six cities of refuge[s] for you. 14. Three cities you shall give beyond the Jordan,[t] and three cities you shall give in the land of Canaan; cities (of refuge)[u] they shall be *for you.* 15. For the children of Israel and the sojourners, and for the residents who are among you, these six cities shall be for refuge, that the manslayer, anyone who *kills*[w] a person inadvertently, may flee there. 16. And if he struck him with an iron object and he dies,[x] he is a murderer; the murderer shall surely be put to death. 17. And if he strikes him with a stone (that) *fills* the hand, by which one may die, and he dies, he is a murderer;

Apparatus, Chapter 35

[i] Nfmg: "to the Levites, (shall he) from the wall of the city . . ." (a different word for "wall").

[j] Nfmg: "south."

[k] Nfmg: "these shall be for you the outskirts of the cities."

[m] Nfmg: "(from the tribe) of many (people) you shall give more numerous possession and from the tribe . . ."

[n] Nfmg: "the Memra of the Lord."

[o] Nfmg: "and (cities) shall be designated"; Nfmg, however, should probably be corrected.

[p] Nfmg: "and they shall (lit.: 'and it shall') be for you for refuge."

[q] Lit.: "of the blood"; Nfmg: "of blood."

[r] Nfmg: "which you shall set aside."

[s] Nfmg: "(shall be six cities;) and they shall be for you cities of refuge."

[t] Nfmg: "(three cities) of refuge you shall give in the land beyond the Jordan."

[u] Missing in the text; Nfmg: "they (lit.: 'it') shall be for you citi(es) of refuge."

[w] Nfmg: "he who kills."

[x] Nfmg: "and he kills him."

Notes, Chapter 35

[1]"tribe of many. . . of few people"; HT: "from the many . . .from the few."

[2]"avenger of blood"; HT: *go'el.*

[3]"people of the congregation"; HT: "the assembly."

the murderer shall surely be put to death. 18. And if he strikes him with a stick (that) *fills* the hand, by which one may die,[y] and he dies, he is a murderer; the murderer shall surely be put to death. 19. *The avenger*[z] of blood[2] shall himself put the murderer to death: when he meets him he shall put him to death. 20. And if he pushed[aa] him from hatred or threw (an object)[bb] at him in an ambush[cc] and he dies,[x] 21. or[dd] in enmity[ee] struck him with his hand and he dies,[x] the murderer shall surely be put to death; he is <a murderer>.[ff] *The avenger*[gg] of blood[2] shall put the murderer to death when he meets him. 22. But if suddenly[hh] and not from enmity[ee] he pushed him, or threw any object at him, but without lying in wait,[cc] 23. or any stone, by which one may die, without seeing him, and casts it upon him and he dies[x] although he did not hate him nor seek the harm *of his person,*[ii] 24. *the people of* the congregation[3] shall judge between the manslayer and the avenger of blood[jj] according to this legal procedure. 25. And the *people of the* congregation[3] shall deliver the manslayer from the hands of the avenger of blood; and *the people of* the congregation[3] shall return him to the city of refuge[kk] to where he had fled; and he shall dwell within[mm] until[nn] the high priest who was anointed with the oil *of the sanctuary* dies.[oo] 26. But if the manslayer shall come out beyond the boundary of his city[pp] of refuge to where he flees,[qq] 27. and the avenger of blood meets him outside the boundary of his city of refuge, and *the avenger* of blood slays the manslayer, he does not *have* the *guilt of shedding innocent* blood;[rr4] 28. for he must[ss] dwell in his city[pp] of refuge until the time the high priest dies; and after the high priest has died, the manslayer may return to the land of his possession. 29. And these (ordinances) shall be for you a statute of law[tt] for your generations in every place of your dwellings. 30. Anyone who *kills*[uu] a person, by the

Apparatus, Chapter 35

[y] Nfmg: "sufficient to die thereby."
[z] Nfi: "he who avenges."
[aa] Nfmg: "(and if) from hatred he pushes."
[bb] It is understood, as in the HT.
[cc] *bkmnh;* perhaps the text should be corrected to *bkwwnh,* "intentionally."
[dd] Nfi: "or," with HT.
[ee] Lit.: "as enemy."
[ff] Missing in text; added in Nfi.
[gg] Nfmg: "he who avenges."
[hh] Nfi: "suddenly" (written differently).
[ii] Nfmg: "(nor seek) his harm."
[jj] Nfi: "of his blood."
[kk] Nfmg: "to the city of his refuge."
[mm] Nfi: "there."
[nn] Nfmg: "in it until the time that"; cf. Ps.-J.
[oo] Nfmg: "with the oil of anointing"; cf. paraphrase of Ps.-J.
[pp] Nfi: "(of his) cities of . . ."
[qq] Nfmg: "(to where) he fled."
[rr] Nfi: "(does not have) blood." This variant which corresponds to HT seems to substitute for the following words of Nf: "the guilt (or: 'sin') of shedding innocent blood."
[ss] "the manslayer" is understood as subject.
[tt] Nfmg: "an ordinance for your generations."
[uu] Nfmg: "he who has killed."

Notes, Chapter 35

[4] "guilt of shedding innocent blood," paraphrases the HT: "blood"; as in Nf Exod 22:1.

declaration[ww] of witnesses[xx] shall the murderer be put to death; but one witness alone cannot testify[yy] against a person that he be condemned to death.[zz] 31. And you shall accept no *wealth* for the life of a murderer, since he is guilty of death; and he shall surely be put to death. 32. You shall not receive *wealth* for him who has fled to his city of refuge[a] to have him return to dwell in the land before the time the *high* priest dies. 33. And you shall not make the land in which you *dwell* guilty; for the blood shall make the land guilty[b] and no atonement[c] can be made to the land for the blood that has been shed in it except by the blood of him that shed it. 34. And *you* shall not defile[d] the land in which you dwell, since *the Glory of my Shekinah*[4] dwells in it; for I am the Lord who *has made the Glory of my Shekinah*[5] *dwell* in the midst of the children[e] of Israel."

CHAPTER 36

1. And the heads of the *tribes*[a] to[b] the family of the sons[c] of Gilead bar Machir, bar Manasseh[d] of the family of the sons of Joseph drew near, and spoke before Moses and before the princes of the fathers' (houses) of the children of Israel;[e] 2. and they said: "The Lord[f] commanded my master to give the land in possession by lots to the children of Israel; and my master[g] was commanded from *before* the

Apparatus, Chapter 35

[ww] Nfmg: "by a word of witnesses."
[xx] Nfmg: "(according to) witnesses."
[yy] Lit.: "respond; answer"; Nfmg: "he (cannot) bear witness."
[zz] See paraphrase of Ps.-J.
[a] Nfmg: "(and) you shall (not) take a bribe of money for a fugitive (or: 'to flee') to his city of refuge."
[b] Nfmg: "(is) that which makes guilty."
[c] Nfmg: "and the land is not atoned for . . ." (probably we should correct to: "and for the land atonement is not made"; cf. Ps.-J.).
[d] Nfmg: "(and) you shall (not) make guilty."
[e] Nfmg: "whose glorious Shekinah (lit.: 'that the glory of my Shekinah') dwells among the sons of . . ."

Notes, Chapter 35

[5]"glory of my Shekinah. . ."; HT: "I dwell. . .for I the Lord dwell in the midst. . ." On the phrase see *The Aramaic Bible,* vol. 1A, pp. 36f.

Apparatus, Chapter 36

[a] Thus both in Aramaic text and in Hebrew *incipit* of Nf; in HT, Nfmg, Onq., and Ps.-J.: "the heads of the families."
[b] Lit.: "according to"; cf. HT.
[c] Nfmg: "(the heads of) the families of the sons of . . ."
[d] After "Manasseh" the *sopher* wrote "ben Yoseph," which was then first of all canceled by two vertical strokes, one above each word, and later erased.
[e] Nfmg: "(of the fathers' houses) of Israel."
[f] Nfmg: "the Memra of the Lord."
[g] Nfmg: "our master."

Lord to give the possession[h] of Zelophehad[i] our brother to his daughters. 3. But if they become wives to one of the sons of the (other) tribes of the children of Israel, their inheritance will be held back[j] from the inheritance of their fathers and shall be added to the inheritance of the tribe to which they shall belong; and our inheritance will be taken away from the inheritance which falls to us by lot.[k] 4. And when the jubilee of the children of Israel comes, their inheritance[m] will be added to the inheritance of the tribe to which they belong; and their inheritance will be taken away from the inheritance of the tribe of our fathers." 5. And Moses commanded the children of Israel according *to the decree of the Memra of*[1] the Lord saying: "The tribe of the sons of Joseph *seeks*[n] what is right. 6. This is the word[o] which the Lord has commanded concerning the daughters of Zelophehad: 'They shall become wives to whomsoever is pleasing[p] in their sight; only they must marry within the family of the tribe of their fathers.[q] 7. And thus the inheritance of the children of Israel shall not pass from tribe to tribe;[r] for every one of the children of Israel shall cleave to the inheritance of his fathers. 8. And every daughter who inherits possession from a tribe[s] of the children of Israel shall become wife to a son of the family of the tribe of her fathers,[t] so that the children of Israel may each inherit the possession of his fathers. 9. Thus no inheritance shall pass from one tribe to another tribe; for each of the tribes of the children of Israel shall cleave to its own inheritance.'" 10. As the Lord[u] had commanded Moses, so did the daughters of Zelophehad do. 11. And Mahlah, Tirzah, Hoglah, Milcah, and Noh, the daughters of Zelophehad, (become wives)[w] to the sons[x] of *their father's brothers.*[2] 12. They married within the families of the sons of Manasseh, the son of Joseph, and their inheritance[y] remained in[z] the tribe of the *inheritance*[aa] of their father.[bb] 13. These are the precepts and the ordinances which the Lord commanded Moses concerning the children of Israel in the plains of Moab, near the Jordan[cc] of Jericho.

Apparatus, Chapter 36

[h] Nfmg: "the possession" (another form).
[i] Cf. 27:1-11.
[j] Nfmg: "our inheritance will be held back."
[k] Lit.: "from the lots of our inheritance."
[m] Nfmg: "our inheritance."
[n] Nfmg 1°: "that which (he seeks)"; Nfmg 2°: "they speak (what is right"; = Onq., Ps.-J.
[o] Nfmg: "the Memra of the Lord."
[p] Nfmg: "(according to) that which (pleases them)."
[q] Nfmg: "of their (fem.) father."
[r] Nfmg: "(from one tribe) to another."
[s] Nfmg: "(from) the tribes."
[t] Nfmg: "she shall become (wife) to one belonging to the families of the tribes of her father."
[u] Nfmg: "the Memra of the Lord."
[w] Missing in the text; in Nfmg: "they shall become wives."
[x] Nfmg: "to the sons of their (paternal) uncle(s)."
[y] Nfmg: "our inheritance."
[z] Correcting *kl* of text to *'l*, with HT, Ps.-J., Onq.
[aa] Thus in text contrary to HT.
[bb] Nfmg: "(in the tribe) of the families of their (masc.) father."
[cc] Nfmg: "the Memra of the Lord commanded through (lit.: 'by the hands of') Moses to the children of Israel in the Plain. . . ."

Notes, Chapter 36

[1]"decree of the Memra of"; HT: "the mouth of."
[2]"their father's brothers"; HT: "their uncles" (*ddyhn*).

INTRODUCTION TO TARGUM PSEUDO-JONATHAN: NUMBERS

I would refer readers to Michael Maher's introductions to Ps.-J. in volumes 1B–3 in this series (Genesis–Leviticus) for many specific details about the characteristics of the halakah, haggadah, and general editorial style of Ps.-J., and also to "The Brief Introduction to the Palestinian Targums of Numbers" by Martin McNamara at the beginning of this volume. The text of Ps.-J. is a literary work by a Targumic scholar who has demonstrated great literary skill in combining a literal translation with expansionary midrashic material. It may well be, as many scholars argue, that Ps.-J. is a literary work that was targeted for study by sages and highly educated Jews rather than for an ordinary synagogue congregation.

Shinan calls the text of Ps.-J. a "rewritten Bible."[1] Even if such terminology is acceptable because of the many expansions, Ps.-J. is a Targum nevertheless, since it follows the biblical order as regards the order of chapters and verses, unlike a text such as *The Genesis Apocryphon* (1QapGen). Whoever the author-editor was, he was dependent upon the Palestinian Targum tradition but modified it to suit his own predilections. Also, he was outside the mainstream of Judaism, as evidenced by the large variety of midrashic material he incorporated into his Targumic text, compared, for instance, with Tg. Onq.

With regard to the language of Ps.-J., E. M. Cook's dissertation demonstrates the complexity of the "dialect" used by the author.[2] The mixture of "dialect" may in some ways reflect the vagaries of rabbinic copiers whose familiarity with Aramaic is limited to that of Eastern Aramaic as known in the liturgical and Talmudic literature. As Kutscher has observed, "manuscripts copied in Europe cannot be considered as primary reliable sources from a linguistic point of view. . . . In Europe the Babylonian Talmud was primarily studied. Therefore, to the extent that the copyists knew Aramaic, they were familiar with Babylonian Aramaic, which is an Eastern and not a Western dialect."[3]

As far as a date for the compilation of Ps.-J. is concerned, having considered the discussion by Maher (vol. 1B, pp. 11–12) and noting that Greek words are frequently used

[1]M. Maher, *The Aramaic Bible,* vol. 1B, p. 8, n. 47, and A. Shinan, "The Chronicle of Moses," *Ha-Sifrut* 24 (1977) 100–101 (Hebrew).

[2]E. M. Cook, 1986.

[3]E. Kutscher, 1976, 2.

in Ps.-J., I would personally opt for an earlier rather than a later date, i.e., seventh/ eighth century.

McNamara has already discussed many of the translation techniques found also in Ps.-J. of Numbers (see section III, "Translation Techniques in Targum Neofiti Numbers," pp. 5–8 in this volume). I shall only add comments on items appearing in the text of Ps.-J. and not noted by him.

The HT *pqd,* "to take a census of the people," an idea central in all the Targums, occurs in chapters 1–4 and 26, with one instance in chapter 27 and two in chapter 31. Grossfeld[4] has examined all 356 biblical examples of the verb *pqd.* Considering earlier studies, he notes twenty-six different meanings but decides that all can be subsumed under four basic meanings dealing with (1) administrative/legal; (2) general; (3) theological; (4) military/census. He further notes that 114 cases of *pqd* occur under category (4) and, predominantly, in Num 1–4 and 26. In his examination of *pqd,* he limits his study to Tg. Onq. He is correct in saying that Tg. Onq. translates by the verb *mn'* and the noun *mny(y)n.* The only exception to this distribution in Tg. Onq. is in Num 1:2 and 31:49, where the idea of taking a census is expressed in the phrase *qbl hwšbn.*

I examined the eighty-six instances of HT *pqd* in Tg. Onq., Nf, and Ps.-J. noted by McNamara. In two instances where the HT *pqd* means "to appoint," all three Targums translated by *mn'* in 1:50, but in 31:14 all Targums diverge: Tg. Onq. *mn';* Nf *skm;* but Ps.-J. *'sṭrṭyq(ws),* "officer." The other instances are concerned with census-taking or counting. In these places Tg. Onq. always uses the root *mn'* with its derivatives, as Grossfeld concluded. However, when one examines Nf and Ps.-J., there are differences. Generally speaking, Nf translates the HT *pqd* by *skm* as a verb and *skwm* as a noun. We should note that in the three instances where the HT has the itpael of *pqd* (1:47; 2:33; 26:62), Nf has used the itpael of *skm.* When one turns to Ps.-J., the situation is conflating in the sense that Ps.-J. often combines derivatives of *mn'* and *skm.* In 1:44, 45; 3:39, 40, 43, Ps.-J. reads forms of *skwm mnyyn.* However, in the bulk of instances (thirty-five), Ps.-J. prefers *skm* (1:23-43; 2:4-30; 4:36-45 and every occurrence in chapter 26). In many ways the variation in words chosen in Ps.-J. to translate HT *pqd* makes for smoother translations.

There are eight instances of the phrase "decree/statute(s) of the Torah" in the HT of Numbers. Of these, in four instances (5:29; 6:13, 21; 19:14) the Targums approach the HT differently: Tg. Onq. *'wry(y)t';* Nf *gzyrt 'wry(y)t';* and Ps.-J. *'ḥwy(y)t 'wry(y)t'.* In 15:16 Tg. Onq. and Ps.-J. use only *'wry(y)t',* whereas Nf has *gzyrt 'wry(y)t'.* Tg. Onq. and Nf have *gzyrt 'wry(y)t'* in 31:21, and Ps.-J. precedes this phrase with *'hwy(y)t.* In two examples (27:11; 35:29) Tg. Onq. and Ps.-J. have *gzyrt dyn,* whereas Nf has *qyym d(d)yn.*

With regard to the HT *mšpt(ym),* "judgment(s)" (9:3, 14; 15:16, 24; 27:5, 21; 29:6, 33; 36:13), where Tg. Onq. has either *dyn* or *hwy,* Nf always has *sdr dyn,* "ordinances" (McNamara), "legal decision" (Sokoloff, 1990, 368), but Ps.-J. normally has only *dyn;* but in 29:6, 33; 36:13 Ps.-J., like Nf, has *sdr dyn.*

The HT *slḥ,* "to pardon," is normally translated by *šbq* in Tg. Onq. In Nf it is translated by *šry wšbq* (14:19, 20), but by *šbq* alone in 15:25, 26, 28; 30:6, 9, 13. In Ps.-J. the

[4]B. Grossfeld, 1984.

translation by *šbq* occurs only in 14:19, 20; 30:13. In all the other instances (15:25, 26, 28) Ps.-J. translates with the itpael of *šry*. However, in 30:6, 9 Ps.-J. has the double expression (*šry wšbq*).

In Ps.-J. the expression "consuming (*ṣlhb*) fire" (1:51; 3:4, 10, 38; 4:15, 19, 20; 11:1, 3) is added to explain God's anger, which in the HT is often expressed by the offender being "killed" or God's anger as "a fire kindled against the offender." The word *ṣlhb* appears only in Ps.-J. (Clarke, 1984, 496), except for one Nfmg (3:10). Sokoloff (1990, 464) translates *ṣlhb* as "reddish," but Jastrow (1282) sees the form as a palel of *ṣhb* with the meaning "to consume." Jastrow's meaning seems better here, since although the color of the fire may be "reddish," the idea expressed is the "consuming" power of the fire as expressing the anger of God.

In Ps.-J. the HT *twldwt* is translated by *yḥws gnyst'* (Clarke, 1984, 263), whereas in Nf the phrase is *yḥws zr'yyt'* (see McNamara, 10), but in 3:1 Ps.-J. translates the HT *twldwt* with only *yḥws*.

McNamara notes that Nf regularly adds "redeemed" to references to the Exodus from Egypt. Ps.-J. is less consistent, usually translating the HT literally except in 15:41 (twice); 24:8; and 24:7, where the idea of Messiah as redeemer is additional.

I have translated the HT *gr* (9:14; 15:15, 16, 26, 29, 30; 19:10; 35:15), which is *gywr* in the Aramaic, as "stranger" in the text of Ps.-J., unlike McNamara, who has translated *gywr* as "proselyte." Grossfeld in Tg. Onq. translates the word, in these passages, as "alien." Le Déaut (1979, vol. 3) likewise translates *gywr* as "immigrant" or "étranger." The context should be the determinate.

Many other variants in vocabulary between the three Targums have been noted in the various notes to specific words.

Targum Pseudo-Jonathan: Numbers

Translation

CHAPTER 1

1. And the Lord spoke[1] with Moses in the Sinai desert in the tent of meeting on the first *of the month Iyyar,*[2] that is the second month of the second year since their[3] departure from the land of Egypt, saying: 2. "Take a census[4] of all the congregation of the Israelites, according to their families, according to *their clans,*[5] by the number of their names, every male, one by one;[6] 3. from twenty years old and over, everyone in Israel entering the army[7] of Israel, you shall count according to their (place in the) army, you and Aaron. 4. And there shall be with you a man of each tribe, a man who is head of his clan. 5. These are the names of the men who shall stand with you: for Reuben, *Officer*[8] Elizur bar Shedeur; 6. for Simeon, *Officer* Shelumiel bar Zurishaddai; 7. for Judah, *Officer* Nahshon bar Amminadab; 8. for Issachar, *Officer* Nathaniel bar Zuar; 9. for Zebulon, *Officer* Eliab bar Helon; 10. for the sons of Joseph: for Ephraim, *Officer* Elishama bar Ammihud; for Manasseh, *Officer* Gamliel bar Pedahzur; 11. for Benjamin, *Officer* Abidan bar Gideon; 12. for Dan, *Officer* Ahiezer bar Ammishaddai; 13. for Asher, *Officer* Pagiel bar Ochran; 14. for Gad, *Officer* Eliasaph bar Deuel;[9] 15. for Naphtali, *Officer* Ahira bar Enan. 16. *These are the appointees of the people* of the congregation, chiefs of their clans, heads of Israel's thousands." 17. And Moses and Aaron took these men who had been specified by (their) name, 18. and they assembled all the congregation on the first *day of the month 'Iyyar,*[10] *that is* the second month. They were enrolled according to their descendants by their clans, by the enumeration of their names, twenty years old and over, one by one. 19. As the Lord commanded Moses, so he counted[11] them in the Sinai desert. 20. As for the sons of Reuben, Israel's firstborn son, their genealogies were (established), by their families, by their clans, by the enumeration of their names, one by one, every male twenty years and older, everyone entering the army: 21. the total[11] of the tribe of Reuben was forty-six

Notes, Chapter 1

[1]HT *dbr 'l* is translated in the Targums by *mll 'm,* suggesting reciprocation is involved.

[2]Ps.-J. tends to be specific when it comes to such references as month; see 1:18, etc.; see Clarke, 1984, 620, for Iyyar, and 674 for Nisan. In *Num. R.* 1,12 there is a detailed specification: "'in the wilderness of Sinai,' this indicates the region; 'in the tent of meeting,' this indicates the province; 'in the second year,' this indicates the precise year (after the Exodus); 'in the second month,' indicates the precise month; 'in the first day of the month,' indicates the precise day of the month; the era is indicated by 'after they were come out of Egypt.'" In *Num. R.* 1,15 Iyyar is mentioned specifically.

[3]Nf: "the children of Israel."

[4]*ḥwšbn:* Nf *ryš skwmyhwn,* "the sum total"; the same distribution of idiom in Ps.-J. and Nf is found in 1:49; 4:2, 22; 21:26, but in 26:2 Ps.-J. reads *skwm ḥwšbn.*

[5]Lit. "father's house."

[6]*lgwlgltwn:* lit. "by their poles"; most other translations: "head by head."

[7]HT: "to go forth to war" (*yṣ' ṣb'*) in Onq and here *npq ḥyl'* and Nf *npq ḥyl qrb'.* HT: *ṣb'* is understood liturgically in Num 4:3, 23, 30, etc.; 8:24, 25 but is understood usually in the military sense here and Num 31:7, 42.

[8]*'mrkl* added in Ps.-J.; see vv. 7–15.

[9]Num 2:14: Re'uel.

[10]See note 2 above.

[11]HT: *pqd* in the sense of "to number" is a verb; here *mny* and Nf *skm,* but usually in chs. 2–4 and 14:26, 29; 31:14, HT *pqd* as a noun is translated as *skwm,* "total," here and Nf.

thousand five hundred. 22. As for the sons of Simeon, their genealogies [12] were (established) by their families, by their clans, by the number of their names, one by one, every male twenty years and older, everyone entering the army: 23. the *total* of the tribe of Simeon was fifty-nine thousand three hundred. 24. With respect to the sons of Gad, their genealogies were (established) by their families, by their clans, by the number of their names, one by one, every male twenty years and older, everyone entering the army: [13] 25. the total of the tribe of Gad was forty-five thousand six hundred and fifty. [14] 26. With respect to the sons of Judah, their genealogies were (established) by their families, by their clans, by the number of their names, one by one, every male twenty years and older, everyone entering the army: 27. the total of the tribe of Judah was forty-seven thousand six hundred. 28. With respect to the sons of Issachar, their genealogies were (established) by their families, by their clans, by the number of their names, one by one, every male twenty years and older, everyone entering the army: 29. the total of the tribe of Issachar was forty-five thousand four hundred. [15] 30. With respect to the sons of Zebulon, their genealogies were (established) by their families, by their clans, by the number of their names, one by one, every male twenty years and older, everyone entering the army: 31. the total of the tribe of Zebulon was fifty-seven thousand four hundred. 32. With respect to the sons of Joseph: the sons of Ephraim, their genealogies were (established) by their families, by their clans, by the number of their names, one by one, every male twenty years and older, everyone entering the army: 33. the total of the tribe of Ephraim was forty thousand five hundred. 34. With respect to the sons of Manasseh, their genealogies were (established) by their families, by their clans, by the number of their names, one by one, every male twenty years and older, everyone entering the army: 35. the total of the tribe of Manasseh was thirty-two thousand two hundred. 36. With respect to the sons of Benjamin, their genealogies were (established) by their families, by their clans, by the number of their names, one by one, every male twenty years and older, everyone entering the army: 37. the total of the tribe of Benjamin was thirty-five thousand four hundred. 38. With respect to the sons of Dan, their genealogies were (established) by their families, by their clans, by the number of their names, one by one, every male twenty years and older, everyone entering the army: 39. the total of the tribe of Dan was sixty-two thousand seven hundred. 40. With respect to the sons of Asher, their genealogies were (established) by their families, by their clans, by the number of their names, one by one, every male twenty years and older, everyone entering the army: 41. the total of the tribe of Asher was forty-one thousand five hundred. 42. (With respect to) [16] the sons of Naphtali, their genealogies were (established) by their families, by

Notes, Chapter 1

[12] *yḥws* here and Nf.

[13] The phraseology follows the same pattern as in v. 22; see also vv. 24, 26, 28, 30, 32, 34, 36, 38, 40, 42.

[14] Nfmg: forty-five thousand six hundred.

[15] Nf and the *ed. pr.* of Ps.-J. read fifty-four thousand six hundred, but Nfmg reads forty-five thousand (four hundred).

[16] The preposition *lamedh* is omitted to conform with HT.

their clans, by the number of their names, one by one, every male twenty years and older, everyone entering the army: 43. the total of the tribe of Naphtali was fifty-three thousand four hundred. 44. These are the total numbers whom Moses and Aaron and the leaders of Israel had counted, twelve men, one for each clan. 45. And the sum totals of the Israelites of their clans from twenty years of age and older, everyone who entered the army in Israel (were counted). 46. And the sum totals were six hundred and three thousand five hundred and fifty.[17] 47. But the Levites, according to their ancestors, were not counted among them.[18] 48. And the Lord spoke with Moses saying: 49. "However, do not count the tribe of the Levites, and do not take their census among the Israelites. 50. But you shall appoint the Levites responsible for the tent of the testimony and for all the vessels and for all that belongs to it.[19] They shall carry the tent and all its vessels, and they shall minister to it; and they shall encamp around the tent. 51. And when the tent is to move, the Levites shall dismantle it; and when the tent is to rest, the Levites shall re-erect it. *A layman*[20] who approaches shall be killed *by consuming*[21] *fire from before the Lord.* 52. And the Israelites shall encamp each by his own camp and each by the standard according to their army. 53. But the Levites shall dwell around the tent of the testimony so that there be no (divine) anger against the congregation of the Israelites, and the Levites shall undertake the guarding of the tent of the testimony." 54. And the Israelites did according to all that the Lord had commanded Moses, thus they did.

CHAPTER 2

1. And the Lord spoke with Moses and with Aaron, *saying:* 2. "Everyone of the Israelites shall camp, each at his standard, by the emblems *which are marked out on the standards* of their clan."[1] 3. *The length of the camp of Israel was twelve miles,*

Notes, Chapter 1

[17]Exod 38:26; *Num. R.* 1,10.

[18]*Num. R.* 1,16-20; the tribe of Levi was not mentioned in the counting of all the Israelites.

[19]*Num. R.* 1,20. The Levites were appointed to minister to the tent of meeting and to erect and dismantle the tent when required because they are faithful to God. Other reasons for the preferential rôle of the Levites have to do with the Israelites making the golden calf.

[20]HT: *zr,* "stranger/foreigner": *ḥylwn,* i.e., a non-priest; *zr* is so translated in Ps.-J.; see Clarke, 1984, 275–276.

[21]*ṣlhb,* "reddish" (Sokoloff, 464); "flaming" (Dalman, 363); "to redden" or "to consume" from *ṣhb* (Jastrow, 1282). Although the matter of color seems to be basic, in the context of being killed or dying suggests "consuming" as the meaning.

Notes, Chapter 2

[1]This represents the MS reading; the *ed. pr.* adds: "they shall encamp, facing the tent of meeting, round about," as in HT.

and its width was twelve miles. And those who camp to the east towards the sunrise shall be under the standard of the camp of Judah;[2] according to their warriors *covering four miles(square). And their standard was of fine wool*[3] *tricolored, each (color) corresponding to the three jewels in the breastplate of the high priest: carnelian, topaz, and emerald.*[4] *On it was engraved and defined the name of the three tribes Judah, Issachar, and Zebulon. In its center is written: "Let the Lord arise and let your enemies be dispersed and your adversaries be put to flight before you."*[5] *On it was engraved the form of a young lion*[6] *because* the leader of the Judahites will be Nahshon bar Amminadab. 4. And the total *of its tribe*[7] and its warriors was seventy-four thousand six hundred. 5. Those who encamped close to him were the tribe of Issachar.[8] And the leader appointed over the warriors of the tribe of Issachar was Nathaniel bar Zuar. 6. And the total of its tribe[9] and its warriors was fifty-four thousand four hundred. 7. As for the tribe of Zebulon: the leader[10] *of the tribe* of Zebulon's warriors, who had been appointed, was Eliab bar Helon. 8. And the total of its tribe and its warriors was fifty-seven thousand four hundred. 9. The *total number of the* camp of Judah with respect to its warriors was one hundred and eighty thousand four hundred.[11] They set out first. 10. The standard of Reuben's camp, *encamped on the* south(side) by its warriors *covering four (square) miles,* was *of fine wool, tricolored, each corresponding to the three jewels in the breastplate: emerald, sapphire, and diamond.*[12] *On it were engraved and defined the names of the three tribes Reuben, Simeon, and Gad. In its center was written: "Hear, O Israel, the Lord our God*[13] *is one." On it was engraved the image of a young ram. There are those who wished to have on it the image of a young bull; however, the prophet Moses changed (altered) it so that they should not be reminded of their sin of the (golden) calf.* And the leader *who had been appointed over the warriors of* the tribe of Reuben was Elizur bar Shedeur. 11. And the total of its tribe and its warriors was 12.[14] 13. fifty-nine thousand three hundred. 14. And the tribe of Gad: its leader *who had been appointed over the warriors of* the tribe of the sons of Gad was Eliasaph bar Reuel.[15] 15. The total number *of the tribe's* warriors was forty-five thousand six

Notes, Chapter 2

[2]*Num. R.* 1,28-30 discusses much of the midrashic material found in vv. 3ff.

[3]Aramaic *mylt',* "fine wool" (Jastrow, 775), but Ps.-J. at Lev 16:4 *bwṣ mylt',* "fine linen."

[4]See Exod 28:17 (Ps.-J.); the order of precious stones listed here and in vv. 10, 18, 25 compared with those listed in Exod 28:17-20 differs among the various Targums.

[5]See Num 10:35 (Ps.-J.).

[6]See Gen 49:9; *Num. R.* 1,29 refers to Gen 49:9, where Judah is likened to a lion by Jacob in his final blessing.

[7]The MS reads "tribes," which is an error; read sing. as in *ed. pr.*

[8]MS reads incorrectly "Israel."

[9]MS omits "of the tribe."

[10]HT: *nsy,* "leader"; here and Nf: *rb' dhwh mmny* in ch. 2, but in other passages in Numbers HT *nsy* is translated only by *rb* (see 3:24, 30, 35; 7:3, 18; 13:2; 16:2; etc.).

[11]HT, Onq., and Nf: one hundred and eighty-six thousand four hundred; *ed. pr.:* one hundred and fifty-eight thousand four hundred.

[12]See Exod 28:18.

[13]Ps.-J. uses for "Elohim" the reverential form "Eloqim" (*'lqym*); see Maher, 1B, 1992, 16, n. 2.

[14]Vv. 11b–13a omit due to homoeoteleuton on *dšbṭyh.*

[15]See note on Num 1:14.

hundred. 16. The *complete* total of those *numbered* of Reuben's camp was one hundred and fifty-one thousand four hundred and fifty warriors. They were going forward second. 17. The camp of Levites (set) in the midst of the (other) camps shall carry the tent of meeting. *The extent of their camp shall cover four (square) miles. From its midst they set out.* As they encamp so shall they set out, every man in his set place according to their standard. 18. The standard of Ephraim's camp: according to their warriors *they camped in the west, and their camp covered four (square) miles. Its standard was of fine (wool), tricolored, each corresponding to the three jewels in the breastplate: zircon, agate, and amethyst.*[16] *On it were engraved and defined the names of the three tribes Ephraim, Manasseh, and Benjamin. In its center was written: "And the cloud of the Lord was over them by day in their going forward from the camp." On it was engraved the image of a young man.*[17] And the leader *who had been appointed over the tribe* of Ephraim's warriors was Elishama bar Ammihud. 19. And the total number *of its tribe* and its warriors was forty thousand five hundred.[18] 20. Those who were close to it were the tribe of Manasseh. And the leader *who had been appointed over the warriors of the tribe* of the sons of Manasseh was Gamliel bar Pedazur. 21.[19] 22. And the tribe of Benjamin: the leader *who had been appointed over the tribe* of the sons of Benjamin's *warriors* was Abidan bar Gideon. 23. And the total number *of its tribe* and its warriors was thirty-five thousand four hundred. 24. The *complete* total of those *numbered* of Ephraim's camp was one hundred and eight thousand one hundred according to the warriors. They set out third. 25. The standard of the warriors of Dan's camp, to the north, *the extent of its camp covering four (square) miles. Now its standard was of fine (wool), tricolored, each according to the three jewels in the breastplate: beryl, onyx, and jasper.*[20] *On it were engraved and defined the names of the three tribes Dan, Naphtali, and Asher. In its center was engraved and defined: "When (the ark)*[21] *halts he shall say, Return, O Lord. Dwell in your glory in the midst of the myriads of Israel."*[22] *On it was engraved the image of a venomous serpent.*[23] And the leader *who had been appointed over the tribe* of the Danite *warriors* was Ahiezer bar Ammishaddai. 26. And the total number of the tribe of Asher and its warriors (was) sixty-two thousand seven hundred. 27. Those who encamped beside him were (those of) the tribe of Asher. And the leader *who had been appointed over the* Asherite *warriors* (was) Pagiel bar Ochran. 28. And the total number *of the tribe* and its warriors (was) forty-one thousand five hundred. 29. And the tribe of Naphtali: the leader

Notes, Chapter 2

[16]See Exod 28:19.

[17]MS: *ryb',* as also Rieder; Ginsburger transcribes the MS *dyb'* and so emends to *dg',* "fish." Le Déaut follows Gen 49:27: "wolf"; *Num. R.* 1,30 considers "a bullock" (Deut 33:17).

[18]HT and Nf: forty-five thousand six hundred and fifty; Onq.: forty-six thousand six hundred and fifty; see Exod 28:20.

[19]MS omits.

[20]See Exod 28:20.

[21]See Num 10:33-36 (Onq.).

[22]See Num 10:36 (Onq.).

[23]See Gen 49:17: "a serpent in the way"; also *Num. R.* 1,29.

who had been appointed over the tribe of the Naphtalite *warriors* (was) Ahira bar Enan. 30. And the total number *of the tribe* and its warriors (was) fifty-three thousand four hundred. 31. The *complete* total of those *numbered* of the camp of Dan was one hundred and fifty-seven thousand six hundred. They set out last under their standards. 32. This is *the total numbers* of the Israelites according to their clans. All the numbers of the camps according to their warriors: six hundred and three thousand five hundred and fifty. 33. But the Levites were not numbered in the midst of the Israelites just as the Lord had commanded Moses. 34. The Israelites did according to everything that the Lord had commanded Moses. Thus they encamped by their standards and thus did they set out, every man according to his family, by his clan.

CHAPTER 3

1. These are the genealogies of Aaron and Moses *which were established on the day* when the Lord spoke with Moses on Mount Sinai. 2.[1] 3. And these are the names of the sons of Aaron, the priests, *disciples of Moses, lord of Israel,*[2] *who were called by his name on the day* they were installed in order *that they may present their offerings* in order to officiate. 4. But Nadab and Abihu died before the Lord *in a consuming*[3] *fire* at the time of their offering the alien fire *from the hearth.*[4] They had no sons. Eleazar and Ithamar *officiated* before Aaron, their father. 5. The Lord spoke with Moses, *saying:* 6. "Bring the tribe of Levi near and appoint it before Aaron, the priest, to serve him. 7. *They shall be divided into twenty-four sections.* They shall take charge of his service and the congregation's service before the tent of meeting by performing the service[5] of the tent (of meeting). 8. They shall take charge of all the vessels of the tent of meeting and the duties of the Israelites by performing the service of the tent. 9. You shall give the Levites to Aaron and his sons. They are given and *delivered as a gift* to him from among the Israelites. 10. You shall charge Aaron and his sons to observe their priestly duties. But *a layman*[6] who would approach shall be killed *by a consuming fire before the Lord.*"[7] 11. The Lord spoke with Moses, *saying:* 12. "As for me, behold I have brought[8] out the Levites from among the Israelites instead of every first-born who opened the womb

Notes, Chapter 3

[1]MS omits.
[2]Aramaic *rb dysr'l;* see Lev 24:12; Deut 9:19; 34:5 for the same expression in Ps.-J.
[3]Aramaic *ṣlhb;* see note on 1:51; see Clarke, 1984, 496.
[4]*Num. R.* 1,59-60: "ordinary secular fire"; see note on 1:51.
[5]Aramaic *pwlḥn.*
[6]See note on 1:51.
[7]HT, Onq. and Nf omit, but found, as here, also in Nfmg.
[8]HT: "take"; Onq. and here *qrb,* but Nf *prš;* see 31:48 and 8:6 for the same distribution; but 8:24 as Nf.

from among the Israelites. And the Levites *shall serve before me.*[9] 13. For all the first-born of the Israelites[10] are mine,[11] and on the day when I slew every first-born in the land of Egypt, I sanctified before me every first-born in Israel, both man and animal. They are mine. I am the Lord."[12] 14. The Lord spoke with Moses in the Sinai desert, *saying:* 15. "Count[13] the Levites according to their clans by their families. You shall count every male from a month old and over." 16. Moses counted them according to *the Memra of* the Lord[14] as he was commanded. 17. These are the Levites by their names: Gershon, Kohath, and Merari. 18. These are the names of the Gershonites by their families: Libni and Shimei. 19. The sons of Kohath by their families: Amram and Izhar, Hebron, and Uzziel. 20. The sons of Merari by their families: Mahli and Mushi. These are the families of the Levites by their clans. 21. To Gershon (belonged) the Libni family and the Shimei family. These are the Gershonite families. 22. Their numbers, counting every male from one month old and over; their total: seven thousand five hundred. 23. The *two* families *which descended* from Gershon shall camp behind the tent *to the west.* 24. The leader of the family *who was appointed over* Gershon's *two families* was Eliasaph bar Lael. 25. The charge (assigned to) the sons of Gershon in the tent of meeting shall be the tent, the curtain, its covering and the curtain which is at the door of the tent of meeting, 26. and the veil[15] of the courtyard, the curtain which is at the gate of the courtyard which is on the tent, and on the altar round about and its ropes (necessary) for all its service. 27. To Kohath (belong) the Amramite family, the Izharite family, the Hebronite family, and the family of Uzziel. These are the families of Kohath. 28. (In total), counting every male one month old and over; in total eight thousand six hundred charged with the duties of the sanctuary. 29. The *four* families *which descended from* Kohath shall camp on the south side of the tent. 30. The leader of the clan who was appointed over Kohath's family was Elizaphan bar Uzziel. 31. Their (assigned) charge was the ark, the table, the candelabra, the altars, and the vessels of the sanctuary with which they were serving, and the curtain and all (necessary for) its service. 32. The officer[16] *who had been appointed over* the leaders of the Levites was Eleazar bar Aaron, the priest. *It is he who inquired by the Urim and Thummim.*[17] *Under his supervision* the guards of the sanctuary's service *are appointed.* 33. To Merari (belong) the family of Mahli and the family of Mushi.

Notes, Chapter 3

[9]HT: "mine," as Onq. (*dyly*), but Nf "shall be for my name" (*lšmy*).

[10]MS reads "in the land of Egypt," which is an error at this place; Onq.: "for every first-born belongs to me."

[11]See note 9.

[12]HT, Onq., and here, but Nf "for my Name As the Lord said."

[13]HT: "number" (*pqd*); Onq. and here *mny,* but Nf *skm;* see note on 1:19, 21.

[14]HT: "according to the mouth of Yahweh"; here: *'l pm mymr;* Onq.: *'l mymr;* Nf: *'l pm gzrt mymr.* This distribution is found in 3:16, 39, 51; 4:37, 41, 45, 49; 9:18, 20, 23; 13:3. But in 27:21; 33:2; 36:5 Ps.-J. has only *'l mymr,* as in Onq. Here *'l pm* is considered a preposition, "according to" (Sokoloff, 407), even though it may appear as a literal translation of the HT.

[15]HT: "the hangings"; here *wwylwwt;* see McNamara's note on this verse concerning this word; see Num 4:26.

[16]Aramaic *'mrkwl* here and Onq., but Nf *rb;* but see Ps.-J., vv. 24, 30, 35 (*rb*).

[17]See Num 27:21.

These are the family of Merari. 34. Their total in numbers, every male from one month old and over: six thousand two hundred. 35. The leader of the clan *who had been appointed over* the family of Merari was Zuriel bar Abihail. They shall camp on the north side of the tent. 36. *And that which was assigned* to guarding by Merari's sons was the boards[18] of the tent, its bolts, its pillars, its sockets, and all (that concerns) its service, 37. the pillars of the courtyard round about and their sockets, and their pins and tent cords. 38. But those who encamp before the tent of meeting to the east were Moses and Aaron and his sons, taking charge of the duties of the sanctuary as a duty on behalf of the Israelites. *A layman*[19] who would approach shall be killed *by a consuming fire from before the Lord.* 39. *The total number* of Levites whom Moses and Aaron counted by the decree of *the Memra of* the Lord according to their families, every male from one month old and over: twenty-two thousand. 40. The Lord said to Moses: "Count all the first-born males among the Israelites from one month old and over and take the total number of their names. 41. Then you *shall bring*[20] the Levites *before me*[21]—I am the Lord—in place of all the first-born of the Israelites, and the cattle of the Levites in place of all the first-born cattle of the Israelites." 42. And Moses counted, just as the Lord commanded him, all the first-born of the Israelites. 43. All the first-born males, in *total number,* counting their names, from one month old and over, were according to their *total* number twenty-two thousand two hundred and seventy-three. 44. The Lord spoke with Moses, saying: 45. "Bring the Levites in place of the first-born of the Israelites, and the cattle of the Levites in place of their cattle. The Levites *shall serve before me.* I am the Lord.[22] 46. As for the redemption money for the two hundred and seventy-three first-born of the Israelites who are more than (the number of) Levites, 47. you shall take five selas[2I3] per head, by the sanctuary *sela,* taking twenty *ma'in*[24] to the sela. 48. You shall give the money to Aaron and his sons as the redemption money for those who were in excess." 49. Moses took (the money for) their redemption from those who remained in excess of those whom the Levites redeemed. 50. From the first-born of the Israelites he took the money: one thousand, three hundred and sixty-five *selas,* by the sanctuary sela. 51. Moses gave the redemption money to Aaron and his sons according to the command of *the Memra of* the Lord,[25] as the Lord had commanded Moses.

Notes, Chapter 3

[18]HT: "frames"; here and Nf: *lwḥ,* "tablets/boards" (Sokoloff, 279); Onq.: *dpy,* "planks."
[19]See note on 1:51.
[20]HT: "take"; here and Onq. *qrb,* but Nf *prš;* see also v. 45.
[21]Here and Onq. *qdmy,* but Nf *lšmy.*
[22]HT, here, and Onq.: "be mine. I am the Lord," but Nf: "be for my Name. I am the Lord."
[23]HT: "shekel." The biblical shekel is considered equal to a *sela* in targumic literature; also *b. Bek.* 50a: R. Hanina said whenever the word "silver" is mentioned in the Torah without specification, it means a *sela.*
[24]HT: "gerah."
[25]See note on v. 16.

CHAPTER 4

1. And the Lord spoke with Moses,[1] saying: 2. "Take a census[2] of the Kohathites from among the Levites, by their families and their clans, 3. from thirty years old and upwards to fifty years old, everyone who has come (of age) for service[3] to do the work in the tent of meeting. 4. This is the service of the Kohathites in the tent of meeting (concerning) the most holy of things: 5. whenever the camp is about to move, Aaron and his sons shall enter and remove the curtain which is spread out and (with it) cover the ark of testimony. 6. They shall put over it the covering of scarlet[4] skin and spread a simple cover of blue twisted thread[5] over it, and they shall set its poles in place. 7. And over the table of the display *bread* they shall spread a blue cover, and they shall put the dishes, censers, bowls, and libation goblets upon it; and the regular bread shall also be on it. 8. They shall spread over it a crimson-colored cover, and they shall cover it with a covering of scarlet skin, and they shall set its poles in place. 9. They shall take a blue cover and they shall cover the candelabra for lighting, and the lamps, and the snuffers, and the coal pans, and all the serving utensils with which they minister to it. 10. They shall put it and all its utensils into a covering of scarlet skin, and they shall put (it) on a yoke.[6] 11. And on the golden altar they shall spread a blue cover, and they shall cover it with a covering of scarlet skin,[7] 12. and they shall put them on a carrying pole. 13. They shall remove the ashes from the altar and spread upon it a cover. 14. Then they shall place upon it (the altar) all the vessels by which it is served—the coal pans, the forks, the shovels, the basins—all the vessels of the altar; and they shall spread a scarlet skin over it, and they shall set its poles in place. 15. When Aaron and his sons have finished covering the sanctuary and all the holy vessels, at the time of breaking camp, then the Kohathites shall enter to transport (it). But they must not come near to the sanctuary, lest they die *by a consuming fire.* Such is the assignment of the Kohathites in the tent of meeting. 16. And that which is handed over to Eleazar bar Aaron, the priest, (is) the oil for the light, the sweet incense, the perpetual cereal offering and the oil of anointment, the custody of the entire tent, and all in it, whether in the sanctuary or in its vessels." 17. Then the Lord spoke with Moses saying: 18. "*Do not be the cause* of the destruction of the tribe of the Kohath

Notes, Chapter 4

[1]Onq. and Nf add "and Aaron," as in HT.

[2]See note on 1:2.

[3]Aramaic *ḥyl:* also Onq. and Nf; See vv. 35, 43, 46. Here the military idiom found, e.g., in Num 1:3 is used to express liturgical service; see McNamara's note on 1:3.

[4]HT *tḥš* is difficult: "goatskin" (RSV); "porpoise hide" (NEB); all the Targums translate with an unfamiliar Aramaic word, *ssgwn'* (Sokoloff, 384, fails to translate). Jastrow (1009) says "it is the name of an animal skin used to cover the ark" but also suggests that it is the name of a color, i.e., "scarlet"; see also vv. 8–12, 14, 25 and McNamara's note on 4:6.

[5]As Nfmg.

[6]Here *'sl'* as in *ed. pr.,* but in MSmg *gwph,* "carrying frame," as in Nf; see Num 4:12: *gwp';* Num 13:23, where Nfmg reads *'sl'* for Nf *gwph.*

[7]MS omits part of vv. 11–12 due to homoeoteleuton on *ssgwn'.*

family[8] from the midst of the Levites. 19. But this *procedure* shall be followed for them so that they may live *the lives of the righteous ones* and not die *in the consuming fire:*[9] *they shall divert their eyes*[10] from the most holy of holies at the time of their approaching. Aaron and his sons shall enter and they shall appoint them man by man, each to his service and to his carrying. 20. And they[11] shall not enter *to look* when *the priests*[12 13] *enter* to cover[14] up the holy *vessels,* lest they die *in the consuming fire.*" 21. And the Lord spoke with Moses, *saying:* 22. "Take *a census*[15] of the Gershonites also those according to their clans by their families. 23. You shall count them from thirty years old and upwards to fifty years old, everyone who has come (of age) for service[16] to do the work in the tent of meeting. 24. This is the service of the Gershonite family: to serve and to carry. 25. They shall carry the curtains of the tent, and the tent of meeting, its curtains and the covering of scarlet which is on it above, and the curtain of[17] the door of the tent of meeting, 26. and the veil[18] of the courtyard, and the curtain of the entrance of the gate of the courtyard door that is by the tent,[19] round about, and their ropes, and all their service vessels, and everything that is delivered to them so that they may serve. 27. At the order[20] of Aaron and his sons shall be all the service of the sons of Gershon with respect to all their carrying and all their service, and you shall designate for them their assignment in the matter of carrying. 28. This is the service of the family of the Gershonites[21] in the tent of meeting, and their service shall be under the supervision of Ithamar bar Aaron, the priest. 29. You shall count the Merarites according to their family, by their clans. 30. You shall count those from thirty and upwards to fifty years old, everyone who has come (of age) for service to perform the service of the tent of meeting. 31. This is the burden of their carrying for all their service.[22] 32. You shall count by their name all the vessels in their charge to carry. 33. This is the service of the family of the Merarites for all their service in the tent

Notes, Chapter 4

[8]*Num. R.* 1,139ff.: "The Holy One . . . said to Moses and Aaron: Institute a measure for the protection of the children of Kohath, so that they may not be cut off from the world and so have no need to abandon the ark and flee."

[9]See vv. 15, 20; Sysling, 1991, 191–192, 261, which discusses life in the world to come and the place of the righteous; see also Num 31:50 (Ps.-J.).

[10]*Num. R.* 1,154: "for they would not die if they did not gaze upon the ark."

[11]Nfmg: "the Levites . . ."

[12]*Num. R.* 1,154: "the priests, sons of Aaron."

[13]Nfmg: "(when) the priests are covering the utensils of the sanctuary, lest they die." *Num. R.* 1,154 says that "the priests, sons of Aaron, should remove the ark and the curtain in front because they are priests and so the sons of Kohath will not see the ark and hence die."

[14]Not in HT; Onq. *ksy,* but here and Nf *šg',* "conceal" (Sokoloff, 565).

[15]*ḥwšbn;* see note on 1:2.

[16]See same expression in vv. 3, 30.

[17]Nf omits, but Nfmg reads as here and Onq.: *prš.*

[18]See note on 3:26.

[19]Nf adds "and the altar," as does HT.

[20]Here and Onq. *'l mymr',* but Nf *'l gzrt pmh;* see note on 3:16.

[21]*Num. R.* 1,168-169: "Moses and Aaron stationed the sons of Gershon . . . at their burdens and at their charges."

[22]MS omits the rest of v. 31 and part of v. 32 due to homoeoteleuton on *pwlḥnhwn;* see Onq. and Nf on Num 3:36-37.

of meeting under the supervision of Ithamar bar Aaron, the priest." 34. Moses and Aaron[23] numbered the Kohathites according to their families by their clans, 35. those from thirty and upwards to fifty years old, everyone who has come (of age) for service for work in the tent of meeting. 36. Their sum total according to their families: two thousand seven hundred and fifty. 37. These are *the total numbers*[24] of the Kohathite family: everyone who served in the tent of meeting whom Moses and Aaron counted according to *the Memra of* the Lord,[25] through Moses. 38. The *total number* of Gershonites according to their families and by their clans, 39. those from the age of thirty and upwards to fifty years old, everyone who has come (of age) for service, for work in the tent of meeting, 40. their sum[26] according to their family: two thousand six hundred and thirty. 41. These are *the total numbers* of the family[27] of the Gershonites, everyone who shall serve in the tent of meeting whom Moses and Aaron counted according to *the Memra of* the Lord.[28] 42. The *total numbers* of the family of Merarites by their families according to their clans, 43. from the age of thirty and upwards to fifty years old, everyone who has come (of age) for service, for work in the tent of meeting. 44. Their sum by their families: three thousand two hundred.[29] 45. These are *the total numbers* of the family of the Merarites whom Moses and Aaron counted according to *the Memra of* the Lord, through Moses. 46. The *total number* of Levites whom Moses and Aaron and the leaders of Israel counted, by their families and by their clans, 47. from thirty years and upwards to fifty years old, everyone who has come (of age) for service to perform the work of serving and the work of carrying in the tent of meeting. 48. Their sum: eight thousand five hundred and eighty. 49. According to *the Memra of* the Lord they were assigned through Moses, every man, his service and his carrying and the charges of each of them was as the Lord had commanded Moses.[30]

CHAPTER 5

1. And the Lord spoke with Moses, *saying:* 2. "Command the Israelites that they send away from the camp everyone who is leprous, and everyone who has a discharge, and everyone who is defiled *becoming unclean* through contact *with a dead*

Notes, Chapter 4

[23]*Num. R.* 1,168-169.

[24]Aramaic *mnyyn skwm* (vv. 38, 41–42, 45–46) but Onq. *mnyyn* and Nf *skwm* only; see Clarke, 1984, 409; see note on 1:19, 20.

[25]See Num 3:16 (Ps.-J.).

[26]*skwm;* see note 24.

[27]Here *gnyst;* omited in *ed. pr.*

[28]*Ed. pr.* adds "through Moses," as in vv. 45, 49. In *Num. R.* 1,172-177 the Midrash is concerned with lack of the phrase "by the hand of Moses" is not connected with the census of the Gershonites but only the Kohathites.

[29]Nf: three thousand five hundred.

[30]Nf: *'l ydwy dmšh,* "through Moses," as in v. 45, but contra Onq. and here.

person.[1] 3. Both male and female you shall put outside.[2] You shall put them outside the camp so that they not defile their camp wherein my *holy Shekinah* is dwelling amongst them."[3] 4. The Israelites did so and put those outside the camp. As the Lord spoke with Moses so the Israelites did. 5. Then the Lord spoke with Moses, *saying:* 6. "Say to the Israelites: A man or a woman who commits any of the sins of man by acting deceitfully[4] before the Lord,[5] that person shall be guilty. 7. They shall confess their sins which they have committed. *If he has extorted money from his neighbor* he shall repay his debt in its principal and add to it a fifth of its value. And he shall give *the principal and a fifth* to whomever he is indebted. 8. If the man has no close relative to whom to repay the debt, the debt being repaid before the Lord *shall be given* to the priest besides the ram of atonement by which atonement is made for him. 9. And all the offerings of separation[6] of all the holy things belonging to the Israelites, which they shall offer to the priest, shall be his. 10. And a man's *tithes* of his holy things shall be his *without his possessions being lessened.*[7] Whatever a man shall give to the priest, shall be his (the priest's)." 11. So the Lord spoke with Moses, *saying:* 12. "Say to the Israelites and command them: 'If any man's wife goes astray and acts deceitfully against him, 13. and *another* man has sexual relations with her, and it be hidden from her husband's eyes and she is undetected, she is defiled, since there is no certain witness *to witness* against her, and she is not caught, 14. and a fit of jealousy pass over him and he suspect his wife (of unfaithfulness) who is defiled;[8] or if a feeling of jealousy pass over him and he suspect his wife (of unfaithfulness) who had not become defiled: 15. and because *that* man *has not brought either a separation or a tithe, it is incumbent upon* him to bring his wife to the priest; *and because she has given the adulterer a taste of enjoyment,*[9] *it is incumbent upon her* to bring *her own appropriate*[10] offering—a tenth *of three seahs*[11] of barley flour *which is the food of animals;*[12] he shall not pour oil on it nor put frankincense on it, because it is a cereal offering of jealousy, a memorial cereal offering, recalling sin. 16. The priest shall bring her near and cause her to stand be-

Notes, Chapter 5

[1]HT and Onq. only *npš,* but here *npš mwt* and Nf *npš br nš.*

[2]Here *ptr,* but *ed. pr.* and Nf read *šlḥ,* as HT.

[3]Nfmg: "the glory of my Shekinah is dwelling among you."

[4]HT: *dlm' l m'l,* "by breaking faith" (RSV), is translated in Targums by *šqr,* "to deceive" (see also vv. 12, 27; Deut 32:51 Ps.-J.).

[5]Nf inserts "in the name of"; see McNamara's note on this verse.

[6]*'pršwt* for HT *trwmh,* "offering"; see Clarke, 1984, 488–490.

[7]*Num. R.* 1,229: an Israelite retains control over his various possessions.

[8]The MS inserts an unnecessary negative ("who is not defiled") which belongs with the alternative in the following section.

[9]*Num. R.* 1,281-282 here a discussion on "measure for measure." The guilty woman is brought to the Nicanor Gate to hear her judgment.

[10]*Sifre Num.* 8 (I,95) debates the need for a tithe of barley which is acceptable. Barley is specified because the normal sin offering is fine flour made from wheat.

[11]HT: "ephah": here and Onq. "seah," but Nf *mklth,* "a measure of capacity"; R. Hisda (*b. Men.* 77a) says the *ephah* and *bath* are the same and that therefore a *bath* is "three seahs."

[12]*Num. R.* 1,281: The woman received the "finest dainties" from the man "so her offering is the food of cattle." Likewise, she gave him "wine in exquisite flagons," so the priest shall give her "the water of bitterness to drink."

fore the Lord. 17. The priest shall take holy[13] water *from a laver*[14] *with a ladle*[15] *and put it* into a clay vessel *because she may have given the adulterer sweetened wine to drink in precious vessels.*[16] The priest shall take the dust that is on the floor of the tabernacle, *because the end of all flesh is dust,* and put it into the water. 18. And the priest shall make the woman stand before the Lord *and bind a rope on her loins and above her breast because she should have bound her loins with a girdle;*[17] and he shall uncover the woman's head *because she had plaited the hair of her head.*[18] And he shall put into her hand the cereal offering of remembrance, that is, the cereal offering of jealousy, while in the priest's hand shall be the bitter waters of investigation. 19. The priest shall cause her to swear *by an oath of the Great and Glorious Name, and the priest* shall say to the woman: If you have not acted unfaithfully, becoming defiled by having sexual relations without your husband's permission, you shall be cleared by these bitter waters *of investigation.*[19] 20. But if you have acted unfaithfully *without* your husband's *permission,* and if you are defiled *by having sexual relations,* and (another) man has used you sexually without your husband's *permission,* 21. then the priest shall make the woman swear by the oath of a covenant of chastisement, and the priest shall say to the woman: May the Lord make you a curse and an imprecation among *the children of* your people in that the Lord shall make your thighs to wither and your stomach to swell. 22. And may these waters *of investigation* enter your womb to cause your stomach to swell and your thighs to wither. And the woman *shall answer and say:* So be it![20] *If I have become defiled while betrothed; so be it! If I have become defiled since marriage.*[21] 23. The priest shall write these curses *on a scroll*[22] and wash it with the water *of investigation.*[23] 24. And he shall make the woman drink the bitter water *of investigation,* and the water *of investigation* shall enter her *for a curse.* 25. The priest shall take the cereal offering of jealousy from the woman's hand and raise the cereal offering before the Lord and offer it upon the altar. 26. And the priest shall take a handful[24] of the cereal offering, a memorial, and offer it at the altar, and afterwards he shall make the woman drink the water. 27. When he has made her drink the

Notes, Chapter 5

[13]HT and here "holy," but Nf *dky,* "pure"; Onq. *my kywr,* "water from a laver"; see Grossfeld, *The Aramaic Bible,* vol. 9, p. 85, n. 7.

[14]*Num. R.* 1,266: The laver was made from the mirrors of women (Exod 38:8).

[15]Here *nṭl';* see Exod 30:19, 21; 40:31 (Ps.-J.).

[16]*Num. R.* 1,269: "to drink out of exquisite cups so the priest gives her bitter water out of a piece of earthenware." *Sifre Num.* 10 (I,98–99) makes it clear that not all utensils are treated equal. In this instance a clay vessel is specified.

[17]Aramaic *ṣlṣwlyyn* (Jastrow, 1286).

[18]*Num. R.* 1,281: When a woman appears before the priest, she is all beautiful, but her hair must be unbound according to *Sifre Num.* 11 (I,101).

[19]HT: "bitterness" as Onq. and Nf, but here and Nfmg read *bdwq,* "investigation."

[20]Here *'mn,* "Amen."

[21]Nf and Frg.Tgs. (PV): "And the woman shall say: 'Amen, Amen that I have not been defiled, (and) Amen that I will not be defiled in the future.'"

[22]Nf: *spr',* "book."

[23]See note 19.

[24]MS reads *ṣryd;* see Lev 9:17 (Ps.-J.); J. Levy, II, 335, suggests "portion of offering not touched by oil."

water, it will happen that if she be defiled *by having sexual relations* and has acted deceitfully towards her husband, then the waters *of investigation* for a curse shall enter her and her stomach shall swell and her thighs shall wither and the woman shall become a curse among *the children of* her people. *Even the adulterer shall be detected by these waters of investigation, wherever he be.* 28. But if the woman has not been defiled *by having sexual relations* but is pure, she will emerge innocent[25] and *splendid from the river, and she shall find love before her husband and she shall* become pregnant with a *male* child.[26] 29. This is *the instruction of*[27] the law of jealousy when a woman has acted faithlessly *without* her husband's *permission* and has become defiled *by adultery,* 30. or a man, when the feeling of jealousy comes upon him and he is jealous of his wife and he makes his wife stand before the Lord, then the priest shall perform all this law. 31. But if the man be innocent *of sins,* then let that woman receive (the punishment for) her sin.'"

CHAPTER 6

1. And the Lord spoke with Moses, *saying:* 2. "Speak with the Israelites and say *to them:* 'If a man or a woman, *seeing a faithless woman in her moral corruption,* abstains *from wine or for any other known reason* shall take the vow of a *nazirite* by setting oneself apart for the Name of the Lord, 3. he shall abstain from new and old wine,[1] he shall not drink either vinegar (made from) new wine or vinegar (made from) old wine he shall not drink; any drink to which raisins are added he shall not drink, and he shall not eat either fresh or dried grapes. 4. All during his nazirite days he shall not eat anything that is made from the vine used for wine, neither the vine husks nor the pips[2] *within the grapes.* 5. During the time that he vowed to be a

Notes, Chapter 5

[25]HT: "she shall be free."

[26]HT: "conceive children" (RSV); Onq.: *t'dy 'dwy,* "be able to bear children"; *Sifre Num.* 19 (I,120–121) interprets these last phrases (free, male child) as "before giving birth" as pain but now "comfort" and "before producing females" now "males," etc. *Num. R.* 1,292 suggests that "the suffering of her false accusation is such that she should be given children as recompense."

[27]HT and Onq. omit, but Nf "the decree (*gzrt*) of the law"; see 6:13, 21 for the same distribution, but Num 19:2, 14 (Ps.-J.) adds *gzrt.*

Notes, Chapter 6

[1]HT: "wine and strong drink" (RSV) becomes in the Targums "new" and "old" wine; in *b. Ker* 13b "new" wine is any wine drawn from a vat, whereas "old" wine is "a fourth of a log of wine of forty days standing"; see Grossfeld, *The Aramaic Bible,* vol. 8, p. 87, n. 2.

[2]*zwg* raises questions: the HT *zwg* is "skin," as in Onq. *'yṣwr,* "shell of the grape" (Jastrow, 1074), but here it suggests the inner part of the grape; Nf translates *pgn,* "pip," and Nfmg uses *zwg* as here. Grossfeld, *The Aramaic Bible,* vol. 8, p. 87, n. 3, quotes *b. Naz.* 39a that *zwg* is the skin of the grape.

nazirite, a razor shall not pass over his head until the time when the period that he set himself apart to the Lord's Name has been fulfilled.[3] 6. During all the time of his being set apart to the Lord's Name, he shall not approach a man who is dead.[4] 7. He shall not defile himself either for his father or for his mother, or for his brother or for his sister at their death; for *the crown*[5] *of* his God is on his head. 8. All during his nazirite days he is consecrated before the Lord. 9. And if someone should die beside him suddenly[6] and defiles the head of the nazirite, then[7] his head, on the day of his purification, on the seventh day, shall he shave. 10. And on the eighth day shall he bring two turtledoves or two pigeons, *little doves,* to the priest at the door of the tent of meeting. 11. And the priest shall make one a sin offering and one a burnt offering and shall atone for him because he sinned *in defiling himself through the dead;* and he shall reconsecrate his head on that day. 12. He shall set himself apart again *before* the Lord the days his being a nazirite, and he shall bring a yearling lamb as guilt offering; but the preceding days shall be discounted because his nazirite (period)[8] has been defiled. 13. This is *the instruction*[9] *of* the Law concerning the nazirite. On the day when his time of being set apart is completed, let him bring *himself* to the door of the tent of meeting 14. and offer up his sacrifice *before* the Lord—a perfect yearling lamb as a burnt offering, and a perfect yearling ewe-lamb as a sin offering, and a perfect ram as a sacrifice *of holy things,*[10] 15. and a basket of unleavened cakes of finest flour mixed with *olive* oil, and unleavened wafers anointed with olive oil, and their cereal offerings, and their libations. 16. Then the priest shall approach before the Lord and shall offer up the sin offering and the burnt offering. 17. And he shall offer up the ram as a sacrifice *of holy things before* the Lord with the basket of unleavened cakes; and the priest shall offer up the cereal offering and the libation. 18. And the nazirite shall shave his consecrated head *outside, after slaughtering the sacrifice of holy things* at the door of the tent of meeting; he shall take the hair of his consecrated head and put it on the fire that is beneath *the cauldron*[11] of the sacrifice *of holy things.* 19. Then the priest shall take the *entire* cooked shoulder of the ram, and one unleavened cake from the basket, and one unleavened wafer, and shall put (them) in the hands of the nazirite after he has shaved (the head[12] of) his nazirate. 20. Then the priest *shall*

Notes, Chapter 6

[3]MS omits the last part of the verse; see Ginsburger, 1903, 236.

[4]Here *br nš,* but Onq. and Nf *npš;* see note on 5:2 for another distribution of the phrase in the Targums.

[5]HT and Onq. *nzr,* "separation," but here and Nf *klyl',* "crown"; by contrast, all the other occurrences in Ps.-J. translate *nzr* as "naziriteship"; see note on v. 19.

[6]HT: *bpt' pt'm;* in Targums *btkwp,* but in 35:22 Ps.-J. deviates from the other Targums with *šlw,* "unintentionally."

[7]*Ed. pr.* inserts *wyglh,* "let him shave (his head)."

[8]Nf, by adding *klyl',* "crown," suggests it is the "crown of the nazirite period" that is meant rather than simply "his naziriteship," as Onq. and Ps.-J.; the LXX reads "for the head of his vow was defiled."

[9]Nf: *gzrt,* "decree," but Nfmg "instruction"; see v. 21, where the same pattern is found; Onq. only "law"; see also note on 5:29.

[10]*nykst qwdšy'* is the usual translation for HT *zbḥ(y) šlmym* or *šlmym* alone; see Clarke, 1984, 385.

[11]According to *b. Naz.* 6:8, "take the hair . . . place it under the cauldron."

[12]Nf adds *klyl',* "crown"; see note 8.

raise them up as a leave offering. It is consecrated to the priest in addition to the breast of *the leave offering* and the thigh which is set apart. After this the nazir may drink wine. 21. This is *the instruction*[13] *of* the Law concerning the nazirite. He who has vowed his sacrifice *before* the Lord concerning his nazirate apart from that to which his hands adhere adequate to what he vowed with his vow, so shall he do according to the obligation of his naziriteship.'" 22. Then the Lord spoke with Moses, saying: 23. "Speak with Aaron and his sons, saying: 'Thus shall you bless the Israelites *while they (the priests) spread their hands upon the pulpit. In this language*[14] [15] *(Hebrew) they (the priests) shall speak to them:* 24. May the Lord bless you and guard you in all your endeavor *from (the demons of the) darkness and from frightening demons and midday demons and morning demons and destroyers and night demons.*[16] 25. May the Lord make the graciousness of his countenance shine upon you *in your study of the Law and reveal to you obscure things*[17] and protect you. 26. May the Lord show *the graciousness*[18] of his countenance to you *in your prayer*[19] and give you peace *in all your space.'*[20] 27. And they will place *the blessing of*[21] my *Name*[22] upon the Israelites and I, *by my Memra,* shall bless them."[23]

Notes, Chapter 6

[13]See notes on 5:29; 6:13.

[14]HT: "You shall say to them": *Sifre Num.* 39 (I,187–190) considers the phrase in Ps.-J. to refer to the priests and explains that the leader of prayers should give the instructions for Aaron and his sons as well as Moses and the priests to bless the whole congregation in the holy language (Hebrew). The priests should be standing (Deut 27:42), and the blessing is given face to face (i.e., priests facing the people and the people facing the priests); but it seems to refer to the fact that the blessing is spoken in Hebrew.

[15]According to *m. Meg.* IV.10 (*b. Meg.* 25b; *j. Meg.* 75c), the priestly blessing (Num 6:24-26) is not to be translated into Aramaic, which is so in Onq. and Nf. Here the *ed. pr.* cites the three verses before the addition in Aramaic, but the MS separates out the three verses, interspersed with the Aramaic translation; see Alexander, 1976, 177–191; Klein, 1988, 80–91.

[16]*Sifre Num.* 40 (I,191) understands "to keep you," i.e., from the demons.

[17]*Sifre Num.* 41 (I,193) understands this to mean the "light of the Torah."

[18]*Sifre Num.* 41 (I,194) discusses what "graciousness" means: "graciousness in the view of other people; in the mastery of Torah; in unmerited favor, etc."

[19]*Sifre Num.* 42 (I,199): "God hearing prayers of those who call upon him."

[20]*Sifre Num.* 42 (I,197–198) lists a whole series of instances when "great in peace" applies, but in many ways "the peace of the house of David" is the most inclusive, as Isa 9:6 says: "of the increase of his government, and of peace, there will be no end."

[21]This phrase is also found in Onq. to avoid direct reference to God.

[22]To avoid the direct contact of God's Name with mankind; in Nf "my Name, my Word" and in Nfmg and Frg.Tg. (P) "my sacred Name"; but *Sifre Num.* 43 (I,200–201) notes that the precise Name is mentioned only in the Temple, whereas in the provinces a euphemism is used.

[23]*Sifre Num.* 43 (I,200–201): for the people of Israel including women, proselytes and bondsmen are blessed by God.

CHAPTER 7

1. On the *first* day *of the month of Nisan,*[1] when Moses had finished erecting the tent, *not taking it apart again,*[2] he anointed it and consecrated it and all its vessels and the altar and all its vessels. He anointed them and consecrated them.[3] 2. Then the officers[4] of Israel brought an offering; the heads of their clans who were the chiefs of the tribes, *who had been appointed in Egypt*[5] *as officers* over the census. 3. And they brought their offerings to the Lord: six wagons *covered and equipped,*[6] and twelve oxen: a wagon between two officers, and an ox for each one. *But Moses did not find pleasure in taking them,*[7] so they brought them before the tent. 4. And the Lord said to Moses, saying: 5. "Accept them and *let the chips*[8] *be for the need of the service, oxen and wagons* shall be used in the service of the tent of meeting. You shall give them to the Levites, each man adequate for his service." 6. And Moses took the wagons and the oxen and gave (them) to the Levites: 7. two wagons and four oxen he gave to the Gershonites adequate for their service; 8. four wagons and eight oxen he[9] gave to the Merarites adequate for their service, under the direction of Ithamar bar Aaron, the priest. 9. But to the Kohathites he[10] gave *neither wagon nor oxen,* for on them was *imposed* the service of the sanctuary—carrying (it)[11] on the shoulder. 10. And the chiefs brought the offering for the dedication[12] *of the ointment* of the altar; on the day that they anointed it. The chiefs presented their offering before the altar. 11. And the Lord said to Moses: "Let an officer, each day, offer his offerings for dedication of *the ointment* of the altar." 12. And the one bringing his offerings, on the first day, was Nahshon bar Amminadab, *chief of the clan* of the tribe of Judah. 13. The offering *which he offered* (were): one silver bowl,[13] *heavily plated,* weighing one hundred and thirty *selas,*[14] *according the sanc-*

Notes, Chapter 7

[1]See note on 1:1.

[2]See Lev 9:1 (Ps.-J.); *Sifre Num.* 44 (I,205–207): "previously Moses had dismantled the tent daily, but on *that* day which is the first day of the month he did not do so."

[3]According to *m. Meg.* III.6, the synagogue liturgy of Hanukkah included the reading of Num 7:1-49.

[4]*'mrkly';* Onq. and Nf: *rbrb,* "chiefs."

[5]See Exod 5:14; *Sifre Num.* 45 (I,208) quotes Exod 5:14 that these officers of Israel were the same as were appointed over the people while still in Egypt.

[6]HT *ṣab* interpreted variously in the Targums: Onq.: *ḥpy,* "covered," as here; Nf: *zwg,* "yoked"; Nfmg comes closest to Ps.-J.: "loaded with tapestries when they are covered"; *Sifre Num.* 45 (I,208), i.e., canopied.

[7]According to *Sifre Num.* 45 (I,209), Moses did not accept anything until the Holy One said "Accept those . . ."

[8]*ṣyb',* "chips left from constructing the wagons" (Jastrow, 1274). This is a clarification not found in Onq. (nothing) and Nf ("them").

[9]As HT and Onq., but Nf: "Moses."

[10]See preceding note.

[11]Nf: "ark."

[12]Also Nfmg.

[13]Aramaic *pyyly.*

[14]See note on 3:47.

tuary sela,[15] one silver bowl *thinly* plated,[16] weighing seventy *selas,* according the sanctuary sela. *He brought these* two *vessels*[17] full of fine flour, *from that consecrated,* mixed[18] with *olive* oil for a cereal offering; 14. one censer[19] weighing ten *silver selas—it was of good gold; he brought* filled with *precious aromatic* incense, *from that consecrated;* 15. one young bullock *of three years,* one ram *of two years,* one yearling lamb: *these three, the chief of the tribe of Judah offered* as a burnt offering.[20] 16. One kid of the goats *he offered* as a sin offering; 17. and as a sacrifice *of holy things:*[21] two oxen, five rams, five goats, five yearling lambs. This was the *magnitude*[22] of the offering *which was brought from the goods*[23] of Nahshon bar Amminadab. 18. On the second day Nathaniel bar Zuar, *chief of the clan of the tribe of* Issachar, made offering. 19. He brought his offering *after Judah on the order of the Holy:*[24] one silver bowl, *heavily plated* weighing one hundred and thirty *selas, according the sanctuary sela;* one silver bowl, *thinly plated,* seventy *selas, according the sanctuary sela: these* two *vessels he brought* full of fine flour *from that consecrated,* mixed with *olive* oil for a cereal offering; 20. one censer[25] *weighing* ten *selas—it was of good gold; he offered* filled with *precious aromatic* incense *from that consecrated.* 21. *The chief of the tribe of* Issachar brought for a burnt offering one young bullock *of three years,* one ram *of two years,* one yearling lamb. 22. One kid of goats *he brought* for a sin offering 23. and, as a sacrifice *of holy things:* two oxen, five rams, five goats, five yearling lambs. This was the *magnitude* of the offering which Nathaniel bar Zuar *offered from his goods.* 24. On the third day Eliab bar Helon, *chief of the clan* of the sons of Zebulon, *made offering.* 25. The offering *that he brought* was one silver bowl *heavily plated,* one hundred and thirty *selas, according to the (sanctuary) sela,*[26] etc.;[27] 26. a silver bowl weighing, etc.; 27. one young bullock, etc.; 28. a kid of goats, etc.; 29. and for the sacrifice *of holy things,* etc. 30. On the fourth day *the chief of the clan* of the sons of Reuben, Elizur bar Shedeur, *made offering.* 31. The offering *which he brought* was a silver bowl, etc.; 32. one censer weighing, etc.; 33. one young bullock, etc.; 34. a kid of goats, etc.; 35. and, for the offering *of holy things,* etc. 36. On the fifth day the *chief of the clan* of the house of Simeon, Shelumiel bar Zurishaddai, *made offering.* 37. The offering *which*

Notes, Chapter 7

[15]Not in HT but here and Nf.

[16]*Sifre Num.* 49 (I,215): "the basin's plating is thick and the bowl's plating is thin," which makes the difference in the two types of vessels.

[17]Aramaic *m'ny'.*

[18]Aramaic *ptyk':* Nf "soaked," but Nfmg "mixed."

[19]Aramaic *bzyk';* see vv. 4–7, repeated for each of the twelve days; see Clarke, 1984, 95.

[20]*Sifre Num.* (I,217, 226) argues that all three animals are "suitable for a burnt offering."

[21]See note on 6:14.

[22]Aramaic *sdr.*

[23]*Sifre Num.* 48 (I,214): "he brought gifts from his own property and did not collect the cost from his tribe . . ."

[24]*Sifre Num.* 55 (I,220): It was on the explicit orders of the Holy One that the presentation of the offering was to be in the order in which the tribes are arranged for the journey.

[25]See note on 7:14.

[26]*Ed. pr.* adds "of the sanctuary."

[27]The MS abbreviated the text for vv. 25–82, where the formula is the same as earlier in the chapter.

he brought was a silver bowl, etc.; 38. one bowl weighing, etc.; 39. one young bullock, etc.; 40. a kid of goats, etc.; 41. and for the offering *of holy things,* etc. 42. On the sixth day *the chief of the clan* of the sons of Gad, Elisaph bar Deuel, *made offering.* 43. The offering *which he brought* was a silver bowl, etc.; 44. one censer weighing, etc.; 45. one young bullock, etc.; 46. a kid of goats, etc.; 47. and for the sacrifice *of holy things,* etc. 48. On the seventh day *the chief of the clan* the sons of Ephraim, Elishama bar Ammihud, *made offering.* 49. The offering *which he brought* was a silver bowl, etc.; 50. one censer weighing, etc.; 51. one young bullock, etc.; 52. a kid of goats, etc.; 53. and for the sacrifice *of holy things:* oxen, etc. 54. On the eighth day *the chief of the clan* of the sons of Manasseh, Gamliel bar Pedahzur, *made offering.* 55. The offering *which he brought* was a silver bowl, etc.; 56. one censer weighing, etc.; 57. one young bullock, etc.; 58. a kid of goats, etc.; 59. and for the sacrifice *of holy things:* two oxen, etc. 60. On the ninth day *the chief of the clan* of the sons of Benjamin, Abidan bar Gideon, *made offering.* 61. The offering *which he brought* was a silver bowl, etc.; 62. one censer weighing, etc.; 63. one young bullock, etc.; 64. a kid of goats, etc.; 65. and for the sacrifice *of holy things:* oxen,[28] etc. 66. On the tenth day *the chief of the clan* of the sons of Dan, Ahiezer bar Ammishaddai, *made offering.* 67. His offering *which he brought* was a silver bowl, etc.; 68. one censer weighing,[29] etc.; 69. a young bullock, etc.; 70. a kid of goats, etc.; 71. and for the sacrifice *of holy things:* oxen, etc. 72. On the eleventh (day) *the chief of the clan* of the sons of Asher, Pagiel bar Okran, *made offering.* 73. The offering *which he brought* was a silver bowl, etc.; 74. one censer weighing, etc.; 75. a young bullock, etc.; 76. a kid of goats, etc.; 77. and for the sacrifice *of holy things:* oxen, etc. 78. On the twelfth day *the chief of the clan* of the sons of Naphtali, Ahira bar Enan, *made offering.* 79. The offering *which he brought* was a silver bowl, etc.; 80. one censer weighing, etc.; 81. a young bullock, etc.; 82. a kid of goats, etc.; 83. and for the sacrifice *of holy things:* two oxen, five rams, five goats, five yearling lambs. This was *the magnitude* of the offering that Ahira bar Enan *offered from his goods.* 84. This was the dedication of the *ointment* of the altar on the day that they anointed it, from *the goods* of the chiefs of Israel: twelve silver bowls, *corresponding to the twelve tribes;* twelve silver sprinkling bowls, *corresponding to the twelve princes of the Israelites;* twelve gold censers *corresponding to the twelve signs of the zodiac.* 85. *The weight* of each silver bowl was one hundred and thirty *selas corresponding to the age that Yokebed was when she gave birth to Moses;* and seventy *selas* was *the weight* of each sprinkling bowl *corresponding to the seventy Elders of the great Sanhedrin;*[30] the total of the silver of (these) objects[31] was two thousand four hundred selas, according to the sanctuary sela. 86. Twelve gold censers *corresponding to the chiefs of Israel,* filled with *precious aromatic* incense; each censer had the weight of ten *selas, according to the sanctuary sela, corresponding to the ten*

Notes, Chapter 7

[28]*Ed. pr.* adds "two."
[29]*Ed. pr.* omits also in vv. 74, 80.
[30]See Sysling, 1991, 8, n. 73.
[31]Aramaic *mny'.*

commandments. And the gold censers were one hundred and twenty (selas) *corresponding to the years of life of Moses the prophet.* 87. The total of the bullocks for the burnt offering: twelve bullocks, one each *for (each) chief of the clan;* rams, twelve rams *because the twelve chiefs of Ishmael*[32] *will perish;* twelve yearling lambs, *because the twelve chiefs of Esau*[33] *will perish;* and their offerings, *because famine will be removed from the world;* and twelve kids of the goats *for the sin offering, because of the atonement for the sins of the twelve tribes.* 88. And all the oxen for the sacrifice of holy things: twenty-four oxen, *corresponding to the twenty-four orders*[34] *(of the priests);*[35] rams, sixty: *corresponding to the sixty years Isaac had lived when he begat Jacob;* goats, sixty: *corresponding to the sixty consonants in the priestly benediction;* the yearling lambs, sixty: *to atone for the sixty myriads of Israel.* This was (the offering) for dedication of *the ointment* of the altar *on the day that* they anointed it. 89. And when Moses entered the tent of meeting to speak with Him, he heard the voice *of the Spirit,*[36] which was conversing[37] with him, *descending from the highest heaven*[38] above the mercy seat which was upon the ark of the testimony between the two cherubim; *and from there the Dibbera*[39] *was conversing with him.*

CHAPTER 8

1. And the Lord spoke with Moses, saying: 2. "Speak with Aaron *and say to him:* 'At the time of *your lighting*[1] the lamps *opposite the candelabrum,* the seven lamps shall shine: *three towards the west and three towards the east, and the seventh in the middle.*'"[2] 3. And Aaron did this: opposite the front of the candelabrum *he lit* its

Notes, Chapter 7

[32]Contrary to Splansky (1981, 96–98), who thinks this may refer to the Twelve Shia Imams, assuming that Ps.-J. was composed at a time when the religion of Islam was supreme, Hayward (1989B) considers biblical verses (Gen 17:20; 25:13-15) for the imagery of Ishmael presented here.
[33]*Ed. pr.: prš,* "Persia"; see Gen 36.
[34]Aramaic *mṭrt'.*
[35]*Num. R.* (II,630): "twenty-four priestly and levitical divisions."
[36]HT: "voice"; Nf: "voice of the Dibbera."
[37]Aramaic *mtmll.*
[38]*Sifre Num.* 58 (I,228): a comparison between Moses and Balaam: To Moses God spoke directly "a voice would descend from Heaven to the area between the cherubim." *Sifre Num.* 58 (I,229) also discusses whether God speaks in "a great voice" (Deut 5:22) or in "a thin voice of silence" (1 Kgs 19:12).
[39]HT: "he"; Nf as here: *dbyr',* "God revealing his will." The *yodh* suggests the vocalization "Dibbera" rather than the later "Dibbûr." The word is less frequent in Ps.-J. (eight times: here only in Numbers and Deut 5:22-23; 10:4; 32:45) than in Nf and Frg. Tgs. (PV); see Muñoz León, 1974, 668–679. This concept is possibly less developed than "Memra."

Notes, Chapter 8

[1]HT: "set up"; here and Onq. *dlq,* but Nf *sdr;* see also v. 3.
[2]*Sifre Num.* 59 (II,3): The idea of seven lamps is based on Exod 25:37. These seven will illuminate from dusk to dawn (Lev 24:3); "three . . . to the east, three to the west, one in the middle so that all of them converge on the middle. R. Nathan says 'the one in the middle is the most honored of them all.'"

lamps just as the Lord ordered Moses. 4. Now this (is the way) the candelabrum was made: *a difficult*[3] *(to make) vessel* of gold, from its base until its lilies,[4] *the work of an artisan; it was wrought with a hammer:* so according to the vision which the Lord had shown Moses, thus Bezalel[5] [6] made the candelabrum. 5. And the Lord spoke with Moses, saying: 6. "*Advance*[7] the Levites from among the Israelites and purify them. 7. Thus shall you do to them to purify them: throw over them the water of purification and let the razor pass over all *the hair* of their body and let them wash their clothes and purify themselves *with forty containers of water.* 8. And they shall take a young bullock and its cereal offering of fine flour mixed[8] with olive oil; and a second young bullock shall you take for a sin offering. 9. And you shall bring the Levites before the tent of meeting, and you shall bring together the entire congregation of the Israelites. 10. When you will have brought the Levites before the Lord, the Israelites shall place their hands on the Levites. 11. Then Aaron shall raise up the Levites (as) a wave offering before the Lord, from the Israelites, and they shall be performing the service of the Lord. 12. And the Levites shall place their hands on the head[9] of the bullocks, and you shall make one a sin offering and one a burnt offering before the Lord, to atone for the Levites. 13. And you shall station the Levites before Aaron and his sons, and you shall present them (as) a wave offering *before* the Lord. 14. And you shall separate the Levites from among the Israelites, and the Levites *shall be ministering before me.*[10] 15. And afterwards the Levites shall enter to perform *the service of* the tent of meeting once you shall have purified them and presented them as a wave offering, 16. because they have been *expressly separated*[11] *before me* from among the Israelites; *I have brought them before me*[12] instead of everyone who opens the womb, that is, the first-born of everyone that is from the Israelites. 17. Because every first-born of the Israelites is mine, both man and animal. On the day that *I slew* all the first-born in the land of Egypt, I consecrated them *before me.*[13] 18. And *I have made* the Levites *approach* instead of every first-born among the Israelites. 19. And I have given and attributed the Levites from the midst of the Israelites to Aaron and his sons to perform

Notes, Chapter 8

[3]Aramaic *qšy',* "difficult to make rather than a reference to the hardness of the metal" (Jastrow, 1430), but *Sifre Num.* 61 (II,8–9): "hammered work is only what is made solid by a craftsman with a hammer" and not by the use of filings.

[4]HT: "flowers"; here and some Onq. MSS "lilies," but Onq. sing. "lily."

[5]HT: "he," i.e., Moses as in Onq., but here and Nf follow Exod 31:2-11, which assigns the task to Bezalel.

[6]*Num. R.* II,650: "Bezalel: you stood in the shadow of God" (*bzl 'l*) (Exod 31:2-11).

[7]Here and Onq., but Nf *prš,* "separate."

[8]See note on 7:13.

[9]Here sing. as Onq. and Nfmg, but Nf plural.

[10]HT: "be mine"; Nf: *lšmy,* "to my name."

[11]HT: "they were wholly given to me"; here and Onq. *prš,* but Nf: "they are given to me as a gift"; see 3:9 in all the Targums: "they are given (*ytn*) and delivered (*msr*)"; see Grossfeld, *The Aramaic Bible,* vol. 8, p. 93, n. 5, for another explanation that the Levites had separated themselves since the time of the golden calf (Exod 32:16, 18). But such an explanation really does not apply in this instance.

[12]See note 10.

[13]HT: "to me"; here and Onq. "before," but Nf "to my Name."

the service for the Israelites in the tent of meeting and to atone for the Israelites so that there not be death[14] among the Israelites, at the time the Israelites approach the sanctuary." 20. And Moses and Aaron and the entire congregation of the Israelites did with the Levites as the Lord commanded Moses; concerning the Levites thus the Israelites did to them. 21. And the Levites purified themselves and washed their clothes. Aaron *raised them as a wave offering* before the Lord; and Aaron made atonement for them in order to purify them. 22. And afterwards the Levites entered to perform the service in the tent of meeting before Aaron and his sons. As the Lord commanded Moses, concerning the Levites, thus they did to them. 23. And the Lord spoke with Moses, saying: 24. "This is *the instruction* for the Levites *lest they be disqualified by their (physical)*[15] *defect:* only from the age of twenty-five years old and upwards he (the Levite) shall participate in the work force[16] in the service of the tent of meeting. 25. And at fifty years of age he shall retire from the work force of the service and shall no longer serve. 26. But he may serve with his brothers in the tent of meeting to keep the watch; but the service he may not perform. Thus shall you do to the Levites with regard to their watch *until you enter the land.*"[17] [18]

CHAPTER 9

1. And the Lord spoke with Moses in the Sinai desert in the second year, at the time of their exodus from the land of Egypt in the first month saying: 2. "The Israelites shall celebrate[1] the Passover *feast in the evening* at its appointed time. 3. On the fourteenth day of that month in the evening you shall celebrate it at its appointed time according to all the statutes[2] and according to all the regulations shall

Notes, Chapter 8

[14]Nf *rgz,* "wrath."

[15]*Sifre Num.* 62 (II,13): There is debate whether the "presence of blemishes" makes one ineligible for priestly service or not. *Sifre* concludes that blemishes do not invalidate but age does.

[16]*lḥyyl' ḥyl',* lit. "to serve in the military," is intended here to refer to service in the sanctuary; see v. 25 and the note on 1:3. Nf has a different text: *l'yl yy'wl lḥyl qrbh,* but also intends sanctuary service rather than military.

[17]Omitted in *ed. pr.*

[18]*Sifre Num.* 63 (II,14): After fifty years of age the Levite "goes back to the work of locking the doors and carrying out the tasks of the Gershonites." *Sifre Num.* 63 (II,15) argues that unlike the Levites, priests are able to serve "until the end of their lives." However, the Levites, once they come unto the Lord, were invalidated only by losing their voice.

Notes, Chapter 9

[1]HT: *'śh,* "make/do," and in RSV "keep" is translated in the Targums with *'bd,* which Grossfeld (Onq.) translates as "offer" and McNamara (Nf) as "keep." I have translated as "celebrate."

[2]See Hayward, 1981, 68; here and Nf *qyymwy,* but Onq. *gzyrtyh.*

you do it." 4.[3] 5. And they celebrated the Passover on the fourteenth day of the month in the evening in the Sinai desert. As the Lord commanded Moses, so did the Israelites do. 6. However, there were men who had become defiled through *the defilement of* a human corpse[4] *who had died suddenly near them. Because the command (to honor the dead)*[5] *was imposed on them,*[6] they were unable to celebrate the Passover on that day, *for it was the seventh day*[7] *of their defilement,* and they drew near to Moses and Aaron on that day. 7. And these men said to him: "We are defiled by a person *who died near us.* Why, *now,* should we be prevented on that account *from sacrificing the Passover and sprinkling the blood* of the offering of the Lord *on the altar* at its appointed time *and to eat its flesh, purified,*[8] amidst the Israelites? 8. *This*[9] [10] *was one of the four legal cases that came up before Moses, the prophet, and he judged them by the Holy Memra. At the conclusion of some (cases) Moses was delaying, because they were cases concerning life (capital cases) and at the conclusion of others Moses was prompt, because they were cases concerning money (civil cases). And about these and about those, Moses said: 'I have not heard,' in order to teach the leaders of the Sanhedrin who were destined to arise after him that they should be delaying in capital cases but be prompt in civil cases; and that they should not be ashamed to question the case which was difficult for them because Moses, who was the lord*[11] *of Israel, needed to say: 'I have not heard.' Because of this,* Moses said to them: 'Wait until I hear what will be commanded from the Lord concerning you.' 9. And the Lord spoke with Moses, saying: 10. "Speak with the Israelites, saying: 'A man, *young* or old, when he becomes *defiled by the uncleanness of a person who has died, or a discharge, or leprosy, or who is unclean in a sexual matter by a nocturnal emission, or who is away from the threshold of his dwelling:*[12] If such things happen to you yourself or to your generations, *then you shall defer celebrating* the Passover *before* the Lord.' 11. In the second month, *that is the month of Iyyar,* on the fourteenth day in the evening shall they celebrate it; they shall eat it with unleavened bread and bitters. 12. They shall not leave any of it until the morning and they shall not break a bone of it.[13] They shall celebrate it according to

Notes, Chapter 9

[3]Omitted in MS.

[4]HT: *npš;* see McNamara's note on 9:6.

[5]See Num 6:9 (Ps.-J.).

[6]*Sifre Num.* 68 (II,26–27): The question here is the inability to perform the rite on a particular day because the rules about purification after contact with a corpse were still in effect; see Grossfeld, *The Aramaic Bible,* vol. 8, p. 89, n. 5.

[7]*Sifre Num.* 68 (II,26–27).

[8]*Sifre Num.* 68 (II,27–28) argues that the unclean gain the benefit of the sin offering insofar as the atonement of the blood rite was concerned and would refrain from eating the meat.

[9]The three passages where the same midrash is found are Lev 24:12; Num 15:34 and 27:5; see Le Déaut on Lev 24:12. In Nf, although the sense of the midrash is the same as here, the details are quite different; also the HT verse is translated at the end of the extended midrash; see Jaubert, 1964, 143–169; 1965, esp. 26–30.

[10]Ginzberg, *Legends,* III,242, VI,85: "This" refers to the unclean being allowed to participate in the eating of the Passover. Ginzberg notes other difficult cases.

[11]*rb;* see Lieberman, 1962, 82, for other titles of Moses.

[12]*Sifre Num.* 69 (II,31–32): a question of whether it is measured from Modiin or Jerusalem.

[13]See Exod 12:10.

every instruction of the Passover decree of Nisan. *But in the Passover of Nisan they may eat unleavened bread; however, the Passover sacrifice they shall not perform because of the defilement within them. Therefore, on the Passover of Iyyar they shall be purified and they shall offer it (then).*[14] 13. And the man who was (ritually) purified, *and in the ways of the world was not defiled,* and was not away from the threshold of his dwelling but neglected to celebrate the Passover *offering of Nisan,* that man[15] shall be cut off from his people because he did not offer up the Lord's sacrifice at its appointed time. That man shall bear his guilt. 14. However, if a stranger sojourns[16] amongst you and celebrates the Passover before the Lord, according to the instruction of the Passover decrees and according to its practice shall he celebrate it. One statute shall there be for you and for the immigrant and for the native born." 15. And on the day when the tent was erected, the cloud *of Glory* covered the tent; *and was covering* the tent of witness *by day,* and by night it was over the tent like the appearance of fire, until morning. 16. So it was continually: the cloud of Glory[17] 17. [18] above the tent. And afterwards the Israelites decamped.[19] 18. And according to *the Memra of* the Lord[20] they camped.[21] All the days that the cloud *of Glory* rested over the tent they also rested, encamped. 19. And when the cloud prolonged (its stay) over the tent many days, then the Israelites kept the watch of *the Memra of* the Lord and did not decamp. 20. And there is a time when the cloud *of Glory* will remain only a few days, *that is seven days of the week,* over the tent: according to *the Memra of* the Lord they remained encamped and according to *the Memra of* the Lord they decamped. 21. And there is a time when the cloud *of Glory* was (there) from evening to morning[22] and the cloud *of Glory* arose in the morning, so they decamped. Either by day or by night, when the cloud arose they were decamping. 22. Whether it be two days or a month *or a complete year,* whenever the cloud *of Glory* prolonged (its position) over the tent, by dwelling over it, the Israelites remained encamped and did not decamp. However, at the time it arose, they decamped. 23. According to *the Memra of* the Lord they remained encamped, and according to *the Memra of* the Lord they decamped. They kept watch of *the Memra of* the Lord according to *the Memra of* the Lord (transmitted) through Moses.

Notes, Chapter 9

[14]*Sifre Num.* 69 (II,33): All the instructions for the Passover mean keeping the rite itself.
[15]HT: "he," but here, Onq., and Nf "that man."
[16]HT: "if a stranger sojourns" (*ygwr gr*); here and Onq. *ytgyyr . . . gyywr',* but Nf *ytwtb . . . gywr* and Nfmg *ytgyyr;* see Num 15:14 (Ps.-J.).
[17]As in Nfmg.
[18]The end of v. 16 and the beginning of v. 17 are omitted in the MS due to homoeoteleuton on "cloud of Glory."
[19]MS omits the end of v. 17.
[20]HT: "by the command (mouth) of the Lord": here *'l pwm mymr'* and Onq. *'l mymar';* Nf *'l pm gzyrt mymryh;* see the same phrase in 20:23; see the note on 3:16.
[21]The verbs in the HT of vv. 16–23 are imperfect, which here and Onq. translate as perfect, but Nf retains the imperfect. The LXX renders the verbs as future.
[22]Lit. "from evening and just until (*w'd*) morning," as in Nf.

CHAPTER 10

1. And the Lord spoke with Moses, saying: 2. "Make for yourself, *from that which belongs to you,*[1] two silver trumpets, difficult (to make);[2] [3] the *work of an artisan* you shall make them. And they shall be yours to summon the congregation and to have the camp set out. 3. When they shall blow them, then shall the entire congregation meet before you at the door of the tent of meeting. 4. And if they blow on only one, then the leaders,[4] the heads of the thousands of Israel, shall meet before you. 5. When you blow an alarm,[5] then the camps stationed to the east will decamp. 6. When you blow an alarm a second time, then the camps stationed to the south will decamp; they shall blow an alarm for them to decamp. 7. And at the time of assembling the congregation you shall blow (the trumpet) but not sound an alarm. 8. And the sons of Aaron, the priests, *without blemish,*[6] [7] shall blow on the trumpets, and these (things) shall be for you a perpetual statute for your (future) generations. 9. And when, in your land, you enter *into the battle preparations* against the oppressors who oppress you, then you shall sound the alarm[8] with the trumpets; and your remembrance[9] *shall come* before the Lord your God *for good* and you shall be redeemed from your opponents. 10. And on the day of your rejoicing and of your festivals and at the beginning of your months, you shall blow on the trumpets, over your burnt offerings and over your sacrifices *of holy things.* And they shall become a *good* remembrance on your behalf before your God; *also Satan*[10] *shall be confounded at the sound of your alarm.* I am the Lord, your God." 11. And in the second year, in the second month, *that is the month of Iyyar,* on the twentieth of the month, the cloud *of Glory* arose from above the tent of testimony. 12. And the Israelites decamped on their journeys from the Sinai desert and the cloud *of Glory* came to rest in the desert of Paran. 13. And they decamped, at first, according to *the Memra of* the Lord[11] (transmitted) through Moses. 14. And the

Notes, Chapter 10

[1]*Sifre Num.* 72 (II,40): The biblical word "for yourself" implies that the trumpet should be made from "your own property." Others interpret the phrase "take for you" to say that the material belongs to the community. Still others make no distinction between the two phrases, but Ps.-J. clearly opts for the first.

[2]See note on Num 8:4.

[3]*Sifre Num.* 72 (II,40): "hammered work" suggests that the trumpets are "made from hard metal worked by a craftsman with a hammer."

[4]*rbrb.*

[5]*ybbt',* as in Onq., "trembling alarm" and Nf "alarm." The translation distinguishes between *ybb,* "to sound an alarm," and *tq',* "to blow a trumpet."

[6]*šlymy'.*

[7]*Sifre Num.* 75 (II,45): R. Tarfon says "unblemished or blemished," but R. Aqiba says only "the unblemished may blow the trumpet." Ps.-J. agrees with R. Aqiba.

[8]See note 5 above.

[9]See discussion in Sysling, 1991, p. 139, n. 11.

[10]See Num 29:1 (Ps.-J.).

[11]See note on Num 3:16.

standard of the camp of the sons of Judah decamped according to their armies. *And the chief who was appointed*[12] over the armies of the tribe of the sons of Judah was Nahshon bar Amminadab. 15. *And the chief who was appointed* over the armies of the tribe of the sons of Issachar was Nathaniel bar Zuar. 16. *And the chief who was appointed* over the armies of the tribe of the sons of Zebulun was Eliab bar Helon. 17. When the tent was dismantled, the sons of Gershon and the sons of Merari decamped, carrying the tent. 18. And the standard of the camp of Reuben decamped[13] by their armies. *And the chief who was appointed* over the armies of its tribe was Elizur bar Shedeur. 19. *And the chief who was appointed* over the armies of the tribe of the sons of Simeon was Shelumiel bar Zur Shaddai. 20. *And the chief who was appointed* over the armies of the tribe of the sons of Gad was Eliasaph bar Deuel. 21. And *the family of* Kohath, carriers of the sacred objects,[14] decamped and the tent would be erected[15] by the time of their arrival. 22. And the standard of the sons of Ephraim, according to their armies, decamped. *And the chief who was appointed* over the armies *of its tribe* was Elishama bar Ammihud. 23. *And the chief who was appointed* over the tribe of the sons of Manasseh was Gamliel bar Padah Zur. 24. *And the chief who was appointed* over the armies of the tribe of the sons of Benjamin was Abidan bar Gideon. 25. And the standard of the camp of the sons of Dan, rear guard of all the camps, according to their armies, decamped. *And the chief who was appointed* over the armies of its tribe was Ahiezer bar Ammishaddai.[16] 26. *And the chief who was appointed* over the armies of the tribe of the sons of Asher was Pagiel bar Okran. 27. *And the chief who was appointed* over the armies of the tribe of the sons of Naphtali was Ahira bar Enan. 28. These were the journeys of the Israelites according to their armies. *When the cloud of Glory arose from above the tent,*[17] they decamped. 29. And Moses said to Hobeb bar Reuel, the Midianite, Moses' father-in-law: "We are decamping from here to the place to which the Lord said: 'I will give it to you.' Come with us and we shall do good to you, for the Lord spoke about doing good to the strangers[18] [19] in Israel." 30. And he said to him: "I shall not go, but to my land and to my children I shall go." 31. And he (Moses) said: "Do not leave us thus.[20] For inasmuch as you know

Notes, Chapter 10

[12]This phrase in the following verses in Ps.-J. (15, 16, 20, 23, 26) is not found in HT or Onq. and only irregularly in Nf.

[13]Nfmg *ytlwn* (future) as in vv. 22, 25 but here in perfect; also Onq. and Nf.

[14]As Rashi explains, HT "carrying the holy things" (*ns' hmqdš*) does not mean "the sanctuary," which is the responsibility of the Gershonites and the Merarites; see v. 17.

[15]Lit. "they were erecting the tent."

[16]Nf: Ammi Nadab.

[17]See v. 34.

[18]HT "has promised good to Israel."

[19]*Sifre Num.* 78 (II,55–61): Although Moses would not enter the Promised Land, he promised that God would be good to his father-in-law, for Reuel was a friend of God (Prov 27:10).

[20]See Exod 18:1-11, which describes Jethro's knowledge of the miracles performed. Nf adds: "since you know the marvels that the Lord has worked."

when we were encamped in the wilderness *to judge and you taught us legal procedure:* and you are *as dear to us as the pupil*[21] *of our eye.* 32. And it shall be if you go with us, then that good which the Lord shall do to us we shall do to you *in the distribution of the land.*"[22] 33. And they decamped from the mountain, *upon which was revealed the Glory of the Shekinah*[23] *of* the Lord, journeying for three days and the ark of the covenant of the Lord traveling before them. *On that same day it went thirty-six miles,*[24] *and it was going before the camp of Israel,* journeying for three days *to prepare for* them a resting place.[25] 34. And the cloud *of Glory* of *the Shekinah of* the Lord was shadowing[26] them by day in their decamping from their encampment. 35. And it was whenever the ark *was desirous* of going forward, *the cloud was gathering itself up and standing still, and it was not decamping until Moses,*[27] *standing in his prayer, was praying and seeking mercy from before the Lord* and so he said: "*Let the Memra of* the Lord be revealed,[28] thus, *in the power of your anger;* and let the enemies of *your people* be scattered and let not their enemies be accustomed to stand[29] before you." 36. And when *the ark was desirous* of resting, *the cloud was gathering itself up and standing still and was not spreading while Moses was standing in his prayer and praying and asking for mercy from before* the Lord. And *so* he said: "May *the Memra of* the Lord return, thus, *in your good mercy and lead the people of Israel, and let the Glory of your Shekinah rest among them and show your mercy* to the myriads *of the house of* Jacob, *the multitudes of* the thousands of Israel."[30]

Notes, Chapter 10

[21]*Sifre Num.* 80 (II,63–64): Jethro's importance as a worthy proselyte for what he has seen because of his high position and because of the favor to be shown to proselytes. Onq. argues that Jethro should stay because he has seen the great deeds performed in the wilderness. Nf argues similarly, and Jethro is to be a witness to all this. Ps.-J. adds the idea of Jethro being as beloved as the orb of the eye (Deut 10:19). *Sifre Num.* would excuse those who did not see the miracles as Jethro did.

[22]*Sifre Num.* 81 (II,65): What applies to the Israelites in terms of blessings will apply also to Jethro.

[23]A very similar expansion in Nf; see Clarke, 1984, 269. Nf does not always expand the HT text in the same way, but see Exod 3:1; 18:5; 24:13 (Nf).

[24]*Sifre Num.* 82 (II,66): a distance of thirty-six miles.

[25]See McNamara's note on 10:33.

[26]HT: "was over them"; here *ṭll;* Onq. *mṭl,* "traveling," and Nf *mgn,* "shield."

[27]*Sifre Num.* 84 (II,71): The argument concerns an apparent conflict between Num 9:23, where God gives the command to camp and decamp, and here (v. 35), where it seems to be Moses who gives the command. The conclusion is that God gives the order, "but Moses so arranges matters as God wishes them."

[28]HT: "arise," which is too direct, so the Targums modify the imperative; Onq.: "reveal yourself" (*'tgly*); Nf: "arise, I pray" (*bb'w*).

[29]Aramaic *qwm qdm;* see Deut 33:11 (Ps.-J.).

[30]HT phrases "Return, O Lord" and "the ten thousand thousands of Israel" cause variations when the Targums try to rationalize the two ideas: Onq. adds to "return": "reside in your Glory among Israel's myriads of thousands"; Nf adds to "return": "from your powerful anger and come back to us in your good mercies and make the Glory of your Shekinah dwell midst the myriads . . . let the myriads be multiplied and bless the thousands of the children of Israel"; *Sifre Num.* (II,75) comments on this verse, quoting Deut 1:11: "May the Lord . . . add to your numbers . . . a thousand times over" and Ps 88:17: "With mighty chariotry, twice ten thousand, thousands upon thousands, the Lord came from Sinai. . . ." Both *Sifre Num.* and the Targums are obsessed with the magnitude of the Israelites in Sinai; see further McNamara's note on v. 36.

CHAPTER 11

1. But the wicked[1] among the people, like ones being troubled, *were devising and speaking*[2] evil *before*[3] the Lord; and it was heard[4] *before* the Lord, so his anger increased and a *consuming*[5] fire was kindled against them from before[6] the Lord *and destroyed some of the wicked ones who were*[7] on the outskirts of the camp, *those of the house* of Dan[8] *with whom there was an idol.* 2. And the people complained to Moses that *he should make inquiry for them.* Moses prayed before the Lord and the fire subsided there.[9] 3. So he[10] called the name of that place "Fire,"[11] because a *consuming* fire was kindled from *before* the Lord, against them. 4. Then *the strangers*[12] who *were gathered* among them *asked a question,*[13] and *even*[14] the Israelites cried again and said: "Who will feed us meat? 5. We remember the fish that we were eating freely in Egypt, *without legal*[15] *constraints:* cucumbers, melons, leeks, onions, and garlic. 6. And now our throat[16] is parched;[17] there is nothing except the manna *which we are looking on like a poor man who is looking out for the remains of a plate(ful)*[18] *from the hands (of his Master).*" 7. *Woe to the people whose food is bread from heaven! and who were grumbling!*[19] Because the manna was like

Notes, Chapter 11

[1]*Sifre Num.* 85 (II,80): HT "the people" is understood as "the wicked ones" as a number of biblical passages suggest (Exod 17:4; Num 14:11; etc.), but "my people," by contrast, refers not to people in general but only to "the suitable ones." Ps.-J. is the only Targum to adopt this distribution.

[2]*Sifre Num.* 85 (II,81): The intention of making the matter heard by the Omnipresent was the explanation for this phrase.

[3]Nf: "in the hearing of."

[4]HT: "the Lord heard"; note the use of the passive in the Targums for the HT active; see 12:2; Deut 1:34; 5:28; etc. (Ps.-J.) also Sysling, 1991, p. 141, n. 14.

[5]Aramaic *ṣlhb;* see note on 3:4 and Clarke, 1984, 496.

[6]HT: "fire of the Lord" is again expressed indirectly; see Sysling, 1991, p. 242, n. 64.

[7]This identification is different from *Sifre Num.* II,82, which says that on the outskirts of the camp are either proselytes or leading figures. Ps.-J. makes more sense.

[8]See Exod 17:8 (Ps.-J.); Num 22:41 and Deut 25:18 (Ps.-J.).

[9]*Sifre Num.* 86 (II,83): When the people complained and Moses appealed to God, God stopped the fire "on the spot."

[10]Here and Onq. as HT, but Nf "Moses."

[11]HT: "Taberah": here and Onq. *dlyqt'* and Nf *byt yqydh,* "the place of burning."

[12]*gywryy'* is understood as "proselytes" according to *Sifre Num.* II,84; Onq. *rbrbyn,* "mixed multitudes," and Nf *'rbwbh,* "motley crowd" (Jastrow, 1112), but Nfmg *'rbrwbh.*

[13]HT: "had a strong craving" (*t'w*), but here and Onq. *š'l,* and Nf *'tḥmd,* "craving." *Sifre Num.* (II,84–85) suggests that they were (1) complaining about meat which they did not have or (2) were "looking for a good excuse to abandon the way of the Omnipresent." It is clear that the point was that the people were prepared to ask questions, and even the Israelites.

[14]Aramaic *brm 'p.*

[15]Both Onq. and Nf consider the HT "for nothing" to mean without cost. Ps.-J., on the other hand, sees no legal constraints, i.e., no prohibition against those foods mentioned. *Sifre Num.* 86 (II,86), in discussing the meaning of "nothing," agrees with Ps.-J. and suggests that it has "nothing" to do with their religious duties.

[16]HT: *npš.*

[17]HT: "dried up" (RSV), also Ps.-J. and Nfmg, but Onq. "have a longing desire" (*d'yb'*) and Nf "empty" (*ryqwh*).

[18]*mgys'* "plate"; see Ps 123:2 (Tg.).

[19]*Sifre Num.* 88 (II,87): The people complained about the manna.

coriander seed, *white*[20] *when it descended from heaven,* and *when it was congealed,* its *appearance* was like the *appearance* of bdellium.[21] 8. *The wicked* of the people were grabbing and gathering and grinding in the mill; *but he who so wished* was pounding with the mortar and cooking it in the stewing pots and making cakes from it. For its taste was as the taste *of brisket*[22] *mixed*[23] *with oil.* 9. And when the dew descended on the camp at night, the manna also descended upon it. 10. And Moses heard the people lamenting, each man at the door of his own tent, *with their neighbors to whom (marriage) had been forbidden.* The anger of the Lord was increasing exceedingly. And in the eyes of Moses it was evil. 11. Then Moses said *before* the Lord: "Why do you treat your servant in an evil manner, and why have I not found mercy before[24] you in laying upon me the burden of this people? 12. Have I conceived *and cared* for this whole people *in my loins?* Are they *my children* that you said to me *in Egypt:* 'Carry *their burden* with *your strength*[25] as *a tutor*[26] carries the student[27] *until the time they arrive* at the land which you promised to their fathers'? 13. From where do I have meat to give to all this people, for they are crying to me, saying, 'Give us meat that we may eat'? 14. I am unable to carry all this people alone, for it is too heavy for me. 15. And if you do thus to me, *to leave all their burden upon me,* kill me now[28] *with the death in which the righteous rest;*[29] if I find mercy *before*[30] you, then I shall not see the misery which is on me."[31] 16. Then the Lord said to Moses: "Gather *in my Name* seventy *righteous* men from the elders[32] of Israel whom you knew *were* the elders of the people and their commanders[33] *in Egypt* and lead them to the tent of meeting, and they shall stand

Notes, Chapter 11

[20]MS reading; *ed. pr.: ḥzwr,* "apple-shaped ball" (Jastrow, 442).

[21]See Malina (1968) for a discussion of the manna tradition.

[22]HT: "rich cream" (*lšd*) is understood as *šd,* "breast," hence here "brisket"; Nf *ššyyn,* "pancakes"; Ps.-J. and Nf reflect two different interpretations. *Sifre Num.* (II,90–91) talks of "dough" (as in Nf "pancakes") and of "what is boiled" (as in Ps.-J.); see Grossfeld, *The Aramaic Bible,* vol. 8, p. 101, n. 9; Alexander, 1988, 227–228.

[23]*srbl,* "to interlace, mix," in contrast to *lwš,* "to knead," in Onq.

[24]Nf: "in your sight."

[25]HT: "your bosom": the Targum seeks to avoid suggesting a womanly function for Moses.

[26]HT: "nurse" (*'mn*): here *pydgg'* (Greek *paidagogos*), "instructor" (Sokoloff, 1990, 430); see McNamara's note on this verse for a different interpretation.

[27]*mynwq',* "boy/child," but here "student" because I translate *pydgg'* as "tutor."

[28]*Sifre Num.* 91 (II,97): Moses argues that God should kill him at once so that he would not see the punishment that is destined to come upon them as with Zedekiah (Jer 52:11), whose children were killed before his eyes were blinded.

[29]See Sysling, 1991, p. 216, n. 30 where there is a discussion of Num 4:19; 23:10 (Ps.-J.).

[30]See v. 11: "in your sight" (Nf).

[31]Nf: "the misery of your people"; see McNamara's note on v. 15.

[32]Nf: "wise men."

[33]*srk.*

ready with you there. 17. *And I shall be revealed in the Glory of my Shekinah,*[34] and I shall speak with you there, and I shall *increase* some[35] of the *prophetic* spirit[36] which is upon you and place (it) upon them. They shall carry with you the burden of the people, and you shall not carry (it) alone. 18. And to the people you shall say: '*Prepare* for tomorrow so that you may eat meat, for you cried *before*[37] the Lord, saying: Who can provide us with meat, because it was better for us in Egypt! Therefore the Lord shall give you meat and you shall eat. 19. Not one day shall you eat, nor two days, nor five days, nor ten days, nor twenty days; 20. but daily for a month, until *the stench*[38] goes out from your nostrils and it shall become an abomination[39] to you, because you have cut off[40] *the Memra of* the Lord, *whose Glorious Shekinah dwells* among you, and you cried before him saying: Why then have we gone out of Egypt?'" 21. And Moses said: "The people among whom *I dwell* are six hundred thousand *men* on foot and you said: 'I shall give them meat and they shall eat every day for a month.' 22. (If) the sheep *in Arabia* and the oxen *in Nabatea* be gathered for them, will it satisfy them? Or if all the fish of the *Great* Sea be gathered for them, will it satisfy them?" 23. And the Lord said to Moses: "*Can there possibly be a deficiency like this before the Lord?*[41] You shall see whether my words will come true for you or not." 24. Then Moses went out *from the tent, where the Shekinah resided,* and spoke with the people the words of the Lord. And he gathered seventy men from the elders *of Israel* and stationed them around the tent. 25. And the Lord *revealed himself* in the cloud of *Glory of the Shekinah*[42] and spoke with him. And he *increased*[43] some of the *prophetic* spirit which was upon him *but Moses, not lacking any,* and gave (it) to the seventy men, the elders. And it happened when the *prophetic* spirit rested on them, they prophesied *without*

Notes, Chapter 11

[34]HT: "I will descend"; Onq. "reveal myself" and Nf "be revealed in my Name."

[35]I.e., without reducing Moses' prophetic spirit; see v. 25; HT "set apart" (*'ṣl*), but Targums use *rby,* "increase" but Syr *bsr,* "diminish."

[36]HT: "spirit"; Nf and Frg.Tgs. (PV) "holy Spirit"; see also v. 25 and Sysling, 1991, p. 238 n. 33, but Onq. in vv. 25, 26, 29 as here.

[37]Nf: "in the hearing of."

[38]Expresses the intended meaning, which is only implied in HT: "it will come out . . ."

[39]HT: "something loathsome"; Onq. "obstacle" (*tql*), but here and Nf "an abomination" (*rḥq*), i.e., something from which we should remove ourselves.

[40]HT: "rejected"; Onq. "despised" and Nf "rebelled."

[41]HT: "is the Lord's hand shortened" (RSV) is here translated in the Targums to avoid an obvious anthropomorphism.

[42]See also 12:10; 17:7; Deut 1:31 (Ps.-J.) to avoid an anthropomorphism. Ps.-J. regularly defines the "cloud" in this manner.

[43]HT: "withdrew"; see note on v. 17.

ceasing.[44] 26.[45] But two men remained behind in the camp. The name of one was Eldad, and the name of the second was Medad *(the sons of Elisaphan bar Parnak. Yokebed, daughter of Levi, gave birth to them. for him at the time when Amram her husband divorced her and to whom she was married before she gave birth to Moses).*[46] *And the prophetic spirit rested upon them. Eldad*[47] *was prophesying and said: "Behold, Moses shall be gathered*[48] *from the world, and Joshua bar Nun*[49] *shall be standing in his place and leading the people of the house of Israel and bringing them to the land of the Canaanites and giving them possession of it." Medad*[50] *was prophesying and said: "Behold, quail*[51] *came up from the sea and were covering the entire camp of Israel and shall become a stumbling-block to the people." But the two prophesied as one and said: "Behold, a king shall arise from the land of Magog*[52] *at the end of days. (He shall gather kings crowned with crowns, and prefects attired in silken clothing, and all the nations shall obey him. They shall prepare for war in the*

Notes, Chapter 11

[44]HT: *yspw,* "but they did so no more" (RSV) understood the root to be *ysp,* whereas the Targums understood a root *swp,* "to stop, desist"; see Deut 5:22 (Ps.-J. and Nf) and Sysling, 1991, p. 237, n. 31.

[45]The expansion in this verse in the Pal. Tgs. reflects the literary remains of a book mentioned in the Athanasian Synopsis of the New Testament. The only extant phrase from that lost book is possibly preserved in *The Shepherd of Hermas* (*Visions* 2.3.4); (see K. Lake, *The Apostolic Fathers,* vol. 2, 22f.): "'the Lord (*kupios*) is near those who turn to him' as it is written in the Book of Eldad and Medad . . ." (note the Ps.-J. parallel: "the Lord (*kurios*) is near them at the hour of distress"). The reference in Num 11:26-27 is "a fertile field for aggadic interpretation" (Aberbach (1971) *EJ* vol. 6, 575–576). Ps.-J., Nf, and Frg.Tgs. (PV) contain the details of the prophecy of Eldad and Medad. There are variations in the form of the text, with Ps.-J. aligning its text with Frg.Tg. (V), while Nf's text alligns itself with Frg.Tg. (P).

Common to all the Targums is a prophecy about (a) the arrival of the quail, (b) the death of Moses and the succession of Joshua bar Nun, and (c) the coming of Gog and Magog or a king of Magog against the Israelites, who are delivered by a King Messiah (Nf, Frg.Tgs.) or the Lord (Ps.-J.). Ps.-J. adds the tradition about the genealogy of Eldad and Medad, who are born to Jochebed, mother of Miriam, Moses and Aaron (Exod 2:1ff. Ps.-J.), when she was married to Elisaphan from the tribe of Zebulon (Num 34:26) after she had divorced Amram, whom she later remarried (contra Deut 24:1-4). Pseudo-Philo, *Sifre Num.* 90 (II 94–95), *b. Sota* 12a, 13a contain parallels to the text of Ps.-J. and Frg. Tg. (V).

Ezek 37–39 seems to form the sources for the midrash in Ps.-J. The imagery of the Lord appearing in "the hour of need" and consuming the enemy with a blazing flame (Ezek 38:19) and birds of prey and wild beasts (Ezek 39:4) and burying the enemy in the land of Israel (Ezek 39:11). It is possible that the tradition both in the Pal.Tgs. and Rev 20:9 come from a common tradition based on Ezek 37–39; see McNamara, 1966, 233–237, for another interpretation of Num 11:26.

Part of the interpretation of the midrashic addition in Num 11:26 stems from the ambiguity of the last phrase in v. 25 stating that the seventy elders ceased to prophesy (HT) or did not cease (Tgs) while Eldad and Medad prophesied within the camp (v. 26). *Sifre Num.* 95 (II,107) interprets the end of v. 25 as the HT and contra the Targums and that the end of v. 26 meant that Eldad and Medad continued to prophesy "until the day of their death."

[46]Not found in Onq. or Nf.

[47]Nf: "Medad."

[48]Nf: *slq,* whereas here, Nfmg, and Frg.Tgs. (PV) *knš;* McNamara, 1986, 149, discusses the word play on *slq;* see Num 11:29 and Deut 34:5 (Ps.-J.).

[49]*Ed. pr.* adds "minister of the camp"; see Num 27:18-23, where Joshua bar Nun is Moses' successor; see *Sifre Num.* (II,107): the discussion is about the seventy elders who, according to v. 25, prophesied "but they did so no more," whereas in v. 26 Eldad and Medad prophesied that Joshua would succeed Moses in the camp and continued until the day of their death.

[50]Nf: "Eldad."

[51]See Num 11:31-33.

[52]See Ezek 37–39.

land of Israel against the sons of the exile. However, the Lord[53] *is near*[54] *them at the hour of distress, and all of them will be killed by a burning breath in a consuming fire that comes from beneath the throne of Glory;*[55] *and their corpses will fall on the mountains of the land of Israel. Then all the wild animals and birds of heaven shall come and consume their bodies. And after this all the dead of Israel shall live [again]*[56] *and shall delight themselves with the good which was hidden for them from the beginning.*[57] *Then they shall receive the reward of their labors.*[58] *And they belonged to the elders whose (names) were found inscribed on the registers.*[59] *They had not gone to the tent but they hid themselves in order to escape the honor*[60] *(which awaited them).I*[61] They were prophesying in the camp. 27. Then a young man ran and told Moses and said: "Eldad and Medad are prophesying now in the camp."[62] 28. So Joshua bar Nun, Moses' minister, replied and said: "My master Moses, *pray for mercy before the Lord that he may withhold the prophetic spirit from them.*" 29. And Moses said to him: "Is it *because they prophesy about me that I am to be gathered from the world and you are to serve in my place* that you are jealous for me? *I would desire* that all the Lord's people be prophets and that the Lord would place his *prophetic* spirit upon them." 30. Then Moses and *all* the elders of Israel reassembled at the camp. 31. And the wind *of a hurricane came out* and moved *angrily from* the Lord *and sought to submerge the world were it not for the merit of Moses and Aaron; and it blew over the Great Sea and caused the quail*[63] *to fly from the Great Sea and settle wherever there was little (occupants) in* the camp—about a day's journey *to the north* and about a day's journey *to the south—and they were flying about* two cubits above the surface of the ground *and were traveling among them at eye level in order that they (the people) should not be tired at the time of their gathering them.* 32. *And those lacking in faith among* the people arose all that day and all night and all the following day, and they gathered the quail. *He who was crippled and he who was limping* gathered ten *heaps.*[64] They spread them in layers

Notes, Chapter 11

[53]*qyrys* (Greek *Kurios*); Nf: "King Messiah"; see Le Déaut, vol. 3, p. 110, n. 30.
[54]*'ytymws* (Greek *etoimos*); see Clarke, 1984, 16.
[55]See Ezek 38:22; 39:4-6.
[56]See Ezek 37.
[57]See Ezek 39:17-20.
[58]Not in Nf.
[59]See *Sifre Num.* 95 (II,106) and *Num. R.* (663).
[60]According to Ps.-J. and contrary to *Sifre Num.* (II,107), Eldad and Medad avoided the promise of rewards. This apocalyptic idea expressed here and in Deut 32:39 (Ps.-J. and Nf) is discussed by Sysling, 1991, 264–265, where the idea of a reward for good works was fixed from the creation of the world (Gen 1:21 Ps.-J.). The apocalyptic idea that after the battle of Gog against Israel, the dead of Israel will arise again (here and Deut 32:39 Ps.-J.).
[61]*Sifre Num.* 95 (II,107) suggests that the two hid to escape the burden of prophecy.
[62]See McNamara's note on v. 27.
[63]*Sifre Num.* 97 (II, 110) explains that the wind blew the quail off course away from the camp (about a day's journey north and south) at about two cubits above the earth, so the people would not even have to bend to collect the birds; see also *Mekhilta on Exodus* 16:13 (II,109).
[64]*kwr,* "Kor," a measure of volume (Jastrow, 625).

all around the camp. 33. *The wicked ate some of the meat and did not offer thanks to him who had given (it) to them;* the meat, however, when it was between their teeth and was not *finished,* the Lord's anger intensified against *the wicked of* the people and the Lord slew them, among the people, with a very great *slaying.* 34. And he called the name of the place "The Graves *of Those Craving Meat,*"[65] for there they buried the people who asked for meat. 35. And from "The Graves *of Those Craving Meat*" the people decamped to Hazeroth and they remained in Hazeroth.

CHAPTER 12

1. And Miriam and Aaron *spoke words* against Moses *that were not worthy*[1] regarding the matter of the Cushite woman *whom the Cushites had married to Moses during his flight from Pharaoh, but he had separated from her* because as a wife *they had married him to the queen of Cush*[2] *and he had kept at a distance from her.*[3] 2. Then they said: "Does the Lord speak solely with Moses *because he has abstained from married life?*[4] [5] Does he not speak also with us?" And *it was heard before* the Lord. 3. And Moses was a man very humble *in his temperament,*[6] more than all mankind on the face of the earth, *but he did not consider their words.* 4. (Suddenly)[7] the Lord said to Moses, Aaron, and Miriam: "Go out, you three, to the tent of meeting." And the three of them went out. 5. And *the Glory of* the Lord *revealed* itself in the pillar of the cloud *of Glory* and stood at the door of the tent and called Aaron and Miriam. And the two of them went forward. 6. And he said: "Hear my words, I pray, *while* I speak.[8] Has there been any prophet *who has arisen from an-*

Notes, Chapter 11

[65]HT: "Kibroth-hattaavah"; here and v. 35 *qybry dmšyyly byšr',* "The Graves of Craving Meat" (in both verses Onq. is the same except for the omission of *byšr';* also Num 33:16-17 Ps.-J.); Nf *qbry š'lth,* "the Graves of the Craving," but in v. 35 Nf *qbry tḥmwdth,* "the Graves of the Desires" (also Deut 9:22 Ps.-J.). McNamara's note on v. 35 suggests that both ways of rendering the HT are acceptable.

Notes, Chapter 12

[1]See Deut 24:9 (Ps.-J.).

[2]Ps.-J. differs from Onq. (Moses' wife is beautiful—HT: *kšt*) and Nf and Frg.Tgs. (PV) (the Cushite woman was called Zipporah and was beautiful) but is aware of the more comprehensive interpretation in rabbinic tradition concerning Moses' marriage. A. Shinan, (1978) 66–78, suggests that sources for this tradition are Hellenistic Artapanas, Josephus, Ps.-J., and the medieval *Chronicle of Moses;* see also Grossfeld, *The Aramaic Bible,* vol. 8, p. 103, n. 1.

[3]Aramaic *rḥq* is a technical term for sexual abstention (Lev 15:19); see *Sifre Num.* 99 (II,116).

[4]See v. 8.

[5]*Sifre Num.* 99 (II,116-117).

[6]*Sifre Num.* 100–101 (II,119–120).

[7]MS omits but found in *ed. pr.* and Nf.

[8]*Sifre Num.* 102 (II,121–122).

cient times, to speak with them just as one has spoken with Moses? Because *the Memra of* the Lord is revealed *to them* in a vision, in a dream I[9] speak *with them.* 7. Such is not the *custom* with my servant Moses. Among the entire house of Israel, my people,[10] he is the (most) reliable. 8. *As one speaks to another,*[11] *I have spoken with him that he separate himself from married life;* directly,[12] and not *in secret, have I revealed myself to him at the bush.* He saw the likeness of *the back of my Shekinah.*[13] And why, therefore, have you not been afraid to speak such words against my servant, Moses?" 9. [14] and *the Glory of* the Lord's *Shekinah* went up from them and departed. 10. And the cloud *of the Glory of the Lord's Shekinah* went up from above the tent; and behold Miriam *was stricken* with leprosy. And Aaron looked at Miriam and, behold, she *was stricken* with leprosy.[15] 11. And Aaron said to Moses: "As a favor from you, my master, do not place upon us the guilt which we have foolishly and offensively committed. 12. As a favor from you *let not Miriam, our sister,* be declared (leprous),[16] *making (all) unclean in the tent* like[17] [18] the dead. For *she is like a child that has completed nine months in its mother's womb and who, as soon as it reaches term* to enter *into the world,* parts of its flesh is eaten. *When its mother is sitting on the birthstool, then the child dies, the midwife taking it out when it was thus in pieces. Likewise, when we were in the land of Egypt, our sister Miriam saw us in captivity, in our exile, in our dispersion, and in our oppression. And when the time of going out and possessing the land of Israel arrived, behold, thus she is held back from us! As a favor from you, my master, pray now for her that her merit*[19] *shall not be lost from the midst of the assembly.*" 13. Then Moses *prayed* and begged for *mercy from before* the Lord, saying: "I pray *by (your) mercy,* our merciful God! I pray, *O God, who has power over the breath of all flesh,* cure (her), *I pray.*" 14. And the Lord said to Moses: "If her father had severely *rebuked* her to her face, *would she not have been put to shame* and shut up for seven days? *And thus when I rebuke her, legally she should be put to shame for fourteen days. Only it is enough* that she be locked up for seven days outside the camp. *But I am delaying, for the sake of your merit,*[20] *the cloud of my Glory, the tent, the ark and*

Notes, Chapter 12

[9]MS "we."

[10]HT: "with all my house"; Onq.: "by all my people"; Nf: "in my whole world"; and Frg.Tgs. (PV): "in all my royal court."

[11]HT: "mouth to mouth" (*ph 'l ph*); in the Targums *mmll 'l mmll* (except in Nf *qbl* for *'l*); see Exod 33:11 (Ps.-J. and Nf); Deut 5:4 (Ps.-J. and Nf); 34:10 (Ps.-J. and Nf) for an almost identical expression.

[12]Lit. "and a vision."

[13]See Exod 33:23 (Ps.-J.).

[14]A translation of the HT "the anger of Yahweh blazed against them" is omitted in the MS.

[15]Onq. and Nfmg add "white as snow."

[16]MS omits.

[17]See Num 19:14 (Ps.-J.).

[18]*Sifre Num.* 105 (II,128).

[19]*bzkwt;* see v. 16 for the merits. The merit of Moses (the manna) and Aaron (the pillar of cloud) and Miriam (the well of water) are mentioned in rabbinic writings (Pseudo-Philo, *LAB* 20:7 (See Harrington's translation in Charlesworth, 1985, 2:329.

[20]*Ed. pr.:* "his."

all Israel, until she is cured. And afterwards she will be reinstated."[21] 15. So Miriam was shut up outside the camp for seven days, and the people did not decamp until the time when Miriam *was healed.*[22] 16. *But because*[23] *Miriam the prophetess became liable to be stricken with leprosy in this world, there is, in her case, a great law for the world to come that occurs to the righteous ones and to the keepers of the commandments of the Law. And although Miriam the prophetess watched a short time to know what would be Moses' fate,*[24] *it is for the sake of that merit that all Israel, being sixty myriads, totaling eighty legions, and the clouds of the Glory, the tent, and the well did not move, nor did they go forward until the time when Miriam the prophetess was healed.* After this the people went forward from Hazeroth and encamped in the desert of Paran.

CHAPTER 13

1. And the Lord spoke with Moses, saying: 2. "Send out *artful*[1] men that they might spy out the land of Canaan which I shall give to the Israelites. You shall send out one man for each of their[2] ancestral tribes of their fathers *from all the officers*[3] who are among them." 3. And Moses sent them out from the Paran desert according to the command of *the Memra of* the Lord;[4] all of them, *artful men, who were appointed* heads over the Israelites. 4. And these are the names *of the twelve men, reconnoitering:* For the tribe of Reuben, *messenger*[5] Shammua bar Zaccar. 5. For the tribe of Simeon, *messenger* Shaphat bar Hori. 6. For the tribe of Judah, *messenger* Caleb bar Jephunneh. 7. For the tribe of Issachar, *messenger* Yigal bar Joseph. 8. For the tribe of Ephraim, *messenger* Hoshea bar Nun. 9. For the tribe of Benjamin, *messenger* Palti bar Raphu. 10. For the tribe of Zebulun, *messenger* Gaddiel bar Sodi. 11. For the tribe of Joseph (i.e., for the tribe of Manasseh), *messenger* Gaddi bar Susi. 12. For the tribe of Dan, *messenger* Ammiel bar Gemalli.

Notes, Chapter 12

[21]Onq. as here, but Nf *'sy* "healed"; see v. 15.
[22]HT: "she may be brought in."
[23]*ed. pr.: 'p 'l gb* as Nf, but MS *lpwm;* see McNamara's note on this verse.
[24]See Exod 2:4 (Ps.-J.).

Notes, Chapter 13

[1]*Num. R.* 676-677 understands the biblical phrase "send me" to mean "send righteous men." These spies were only fools in that some of them returned an evil report. They were great men, but they made fools of themselves.
[2]MS reads "his," as does Onq., but Nf reads as here.
[3]Here *'mrkwl,* but Onq. *rb* and Nf *rbrb.*
[4]As Onq., but Nf *'l pm gzrt mymr.*
[5]*'zgd,* "messenger" (Sokoloff, 441); HT, Onq. and Nf omit; see following verse for a similar translation.

13. For the tribe of Asher, *messenger* Setur bar Michael. 14. For the tribe of Naphtali, *messenger* Nahbi bar Vophsi. 15. For the tribe of Gad, *messenger* Geuel bar Machi. 16. These are the names of the men whom Moses sent to spy out the land; and when Moses saw his humility,[6] he[7] summoned Hoshea bar Nun, Joshua. 17. And Moses sent them to spy out the land of Canaan, and he said to them: "Go up on this *side,* by the south, and you shall go up into the hill country. 18. And you shall see what the land is (like) and the people who live in it, whether they are strong or weak, few or many (in number); 19. and what the land is (like) in which they live, whether it is good or bad; and what (kind of) the cities are they, *in which they dwell,* whether they are *open cities* or with fortifications;[8] 20. what *the reputation* of the land is, whether *its produce* is rich or poor, whether there are *fruit-bearing* trees in it or not. *And you shall act possessively* and you take some of the fruit of the land." And the day *on which they left was on the twenty-ninth of the month of Sivan,*[9] the days on which there were the first fruits of the grapes. 21. And they went up and spied out the land from the Sin desert till *the highways*[10] *in the direction*[11] *of Antioch.*[12] 22. Then they went up from the south *side* and came[13] to Hebron, and there were Ahiman, Shesshai, and Talmai, *the sons of* Anak, *the giant.* And Hebron had been built seven years prior *to when Tanis* of Egypt *was built.* 23. And they came to the "River of the (Grape) Cluster,"[14] and there they cut a branch and a bunch of grapes, and carried it on a pole[15] *on the shoulder of* two of them, and also some pomegranates, and also some figs. 24. They[16] called that place the "River of the (Grape) Cluster" on account of the branch which the Israelites cut from there; *and wine was dripping*[17] *from it like a river.* 25. And they returned from spying out the land *on the eighth day of the month of 'Ab,* at the end of forty days. 26. And they came and went to Moses and to Aaron and to the entire congregation of the Israelites in the Paran desert, *at Reqem.*[18] They brought a report back to them and to the whole congregation and showed them the fruit of the land. 27. And

Notes, Chapter 13

[6]*'ynwwtnwtyh,* a quality used to describe Moses; in 12:3 (*'nwwtn*).
[7]HT and *ed. pr.:* "Moses," as also Onq. and Nf.
[8]HT: "camps or strongholds"; here *krk pṣyḥ* and *ḥqr,* but Onq. *pṣḥ* and *krk;* the text of Nf differs: *kpr* and *tlyl.*
[9]See v. 25; Onq. and Nf omit.
[10]HT, Onq., and Nf "Rehob," but here *plṭywwt* (Greek *plateia*).
[11]Lit. "as you enter."
[12]HT and Onq.: "Hamat"; here and Nf: "Antioch"; see Num 34:8 (Nf). Ps.-J. makes explicit the identification of Hamat in rabbinic terms. Antioch is outside the land of Israel according to the Rabbis; see Alexander, 1974, 183–184.
[13]*'tw,* "they came," here and Onq., but Nf identifies the subject as Caleb (*wmth klb*), which complies with Josh 14:13-14, which gives Hebron as Caleb's inheritance.
[14]HT: "valley of Eshcol"; Onq. and here *'tkl',* but Nf *nhl sgwlh;* the same distribution among the Targums is found in Deut 1:24.
[15]HT: "pole"; Onq. *'ryh',* "pole," here *'sl',* but Nf *gwph,* "basket," while Nfmg *'sl';* see Num 4:10 (Ps.-J.).
[16]HT, Onq. and Nf: "that place was called"; here and LXX plural.
[17]*nṭyp.*
[18]HT: "Kadesh," but in Onq., Nf, and here usually "Reqem"; see 20:14, 16; 27:14; 32:8; 33:26; 34:14. Josephus identifies it as Petra; see Davies, 1972, 152–163, and McNamara, 1972, 199–200.

they spoke about it and said: "We went to the land to which you sent us; indeed, *it produces* milk and honey, and this is its fruit. 28. But the people who live in the land are strong, and the cities *lived in* are very greatly fortified; and also we saw there some of *the sons of* Anak, *the giant.* 29. The Amalekites live in the south of the land; and the Hittites and the Jebusites and the Amorites live in the hill country; and the Canaanites dwell by the sea and *along the border*[19] *of* the Jordan." 30. And Caleb silenced the people and *made them listen* to Moses and he (Caleb)[20] said: "We shall indeed go up and take possession of it, for we shall indeed be able (to take) it." 31. But the men who went up with him said: "We shall be unable to go up against the people, for they are stronger than we are." 32. And they produced *an evil* report[21] for the Israelites about the land which they had spied out, saying: "The land that we passed through to spy out is a land which kills its inhabitants *with sickness;* and all its people in its midst are men, *masters of evil ways.*[22] 33. And there we saw *giants,*[23] the sons of Anak, *from the race of the giants;* and *we appeared* in *our* own estimation to be as locusts, and thus did we appear in their *own* estimation.

CHAPTER 14

1. And the entire congregation raised and gave forth their voice, and the people cried that night. *And it was appointed for them to cry on that night for their generations.*[1] 2. All the Israelites murmured[2] against Moses and against Aaron, and the entire congregation said to them: "Would that we had died in the land of Egypt, or in that wilderness would that we had died! 3. And why did the Lord bring us up to this land in order to cause us to fall by the sword *of the Canaanites,* and our wives and children to be plundered? Would it not be better for us to return to Egypt?" 4. And each man said to his brother: "Let us appoint *a king as* a head[3] *over*

Notes, Chapter 13

[19]HT: "along the Jordan"; here *tḥwm;* Onq. *kyp* and Nf *mgyzth,* "passes," but Nfmg *tḥwm.*

[20]See Onq.

[21]HT: "evil report"; here *ṭyb byš;* Onq. *šwm byš* and Nf only *ṭyb;* see also McNamara's note on this verse.

[22]HT: "men of great stature," as in Onq., but Nf "masters of evil eyes"; but Nfmg (*mykln byšn*) agrees with Ps.-J.

[23]HT: "Nephilim."

Notes, Chapter 14

[1]Refers to "future generations," as *Num. R.* 687 says: "For Israel had wept (at the report of the spies) on the night of the month of Ab and the Holy One, Blessed be He, had said to them, 'You have wept a causeless weeping before me. I shall therefore fix for you a permanent weeping for future generations.'"

[2]Itp *r'm.*

[3]Ps.-J. combines both the HT ("captain") and Nf ("king").

us, and let us return to Egypt." 5. And Moses and Aaron *bowed*[4] their faces before all the congregation[5] of the Israelites. 6. And Joshua bar Nun and Caleb bar Jephunneh of those who spied out the land tore their clothes. 7. And they said to the entire congregation, saying: "The land through which we passed to spy out is an exceedingly good land. 8. If the pleasure[6] of the Lord is with us, he will bring us up to this land and will give us it, a land *which is producing*[7] milk and honey. 9. Only do not treat with contempt the Lord's *commandments,*[8] and do not fear the people in the land, *for they shall be given into our hands; the power of their strength* has departed from them, and *the Memra of* the Lord *is assisting us;* do not fear them." 10. And the entire congregation gave command to stone them to death. And the Glory *of the Shekinah of* the Lord revealed itself[9] *in clouds of Glory* in the tent of meeting. 11. Then the Lord said to Moses: "How long is this people going to make me angry?[10] And for how long are they going to not believe *my Memra,* through all the signs that I have done among them? 12. I shall strike[11] them with *a deadly plague*[12] and destroy[13] them. Then I shall designate you as a nation, greater and stronger than they." 13. So Moses said: "When *the sons of* the Egyptians *who drowned in the sea* shall hear that you brought up this people with your power from amongst them, 14. they shall speak *with joy* to the dwellers of this land who heard that you are the Lord *whose Shekinah dwells*[14] among this people. For through *their* eyes they *saw,* O Lord, *the Shekinah of your Glory on Mount Sinai and received there your Law;* that your cloud was *a covering over them so that they should not be hurt by heat nor by rain;* and that in the pillar of cloud you led[15] them by day *in order to bring low the mountains and the hills and to raise up the valleys*[16] and by a pillar of fire to give light by night. 15. *And after all these miracles* you will kill this people as one man? And the nations that have heard the fame of *your strength* shall say, as follows:[17] 16. 'Since it was impossible for the Lord to bring this people into the land which he promised them, he killed them in the desert.' 17. And now let the power *grow strong,*[18] *before you,* O Lord, and let mercies be fulfilled upon them and

Notes, Chapter 14

[4]HT: "fell upon their faces"; Onq. and Nf *'šth,* "prostrate," but here and Nfmg *trk.*

[5]HT: *kl qhl 'dt;* Onq. *qhl knšt',* but Ps.-J. and Nf read only *knyšt'.*

[6]Here, Onq., and Nf *r'y,* to which Onq. adds "before the Lord"; Nfmg begins "if the Memra of the Lord . . ."

[7]*'bd.*

[8]HT: "rebel against the Lord"; Onq. "the Memra of the Lord," as does Nfmg, but Nf "the Glory of the Shekinah of the Lord."

[9]HT: "was seen."

[10]HT: "spurn" is moderated in the Targums by *rgz.*

[11]HT, Onq. as here, but Nf "kill."

[12]HT: "pestilence"; here *mḥt' dmwt'* and Onq. *mwt',* but Nf *dbr;* see 17:14, 25:9 (Ps.-J.).

[13]HT: "to disown/dispossess" (hiph *yrš:* here, Onq., and Nf shaphel of *yṣy,* "to destroy," in the sense of dispossessing from the world, in keeping with the tone of the first part of the verse. Sometimes Ps.-J. translated the HT with *trk,* "banish" (Num 32:21, 39; 33:52, 53, 55; Deut 7:17; 9:3).

[14]*šry:* an expression (as in Onq.) to smooth out HT "in the midst of."

[15]HT: "walk" is modified here, Onq., and Nfmg as "to lead," but Nf "walk."

[16]See Exod 12:37.

[17]*lmymr.*

[18]HT: "be great."

appoint me to a great nation just as you spoke, saying: 18. 'The Lord is long-suffering,[19] *and near in mercy, absolving* sinners, and *forgiving* offenses, justifying *those who return to the Law,* and not justifying *those who do not return,* visiting the sins of the wicked fathers on the *rebellious* sons to the third and fourth *generation.*[20] 19. So forgive the offenses of the people in the greatness of your beneficence, just *as you absolved* this people from *the time that they went out from Egypt* and until now." 20. And the Lord said: "I have forgiven *them*[21] according to your word. 21. However, *by a vow I promised* that the Glory[22] of the Lord shall fill the whole earth: 22. because the men who have seen my Glory, and the signs that I performed in Egypt and in the desert, have tested me already ten times[23] [24] but have not accepted *my Memra,* 23. *by a vow I say this,* none shall see the land which I promised to their fathers, and *none*[25] *of the generation* that angered me shall see it. 24. But my servant Caleb, because there was another spirit with him and he followed faithfully after *my Fear,*[26] I shall bring him into the land to which he was going and his *children* shall possess it.[27] 25. The Amalekites and the Canaanites live in the valley. Tomorrow, then, turn and travel into the desert, by way of the Reed Sea." 26. And the Lord spoke with Moses and with Aaron, saying: 27. "How long, (must I endure) the wicked congregation who have joined together against me? The murmurings of the Israelites that they are murmuring against me have been heard before me.[28] 28. Say to them: '*By oath, I exist.* According to how you speak before[29] me, so shall I treat you. 29. In this desert your bodies[30] shall be thrown down, the entire total of all those numbered from twenty years and over who murmured against me. 30. *By oath, I say,* that you shall not enter the land that *I promised to you by my Memra,* to settle you in it except Caleb bar Jephunneh and Joshua bar Nun. 31. But your children whom you said would become plundered, I shall cause them to enter (there), and they shall know the land which you have despised.[31] 32. And your corpses[32] shall be thrown into this desert; 33. and your

Notes, Chapter 14

[19]See McNamara's note on this verse.

[20]See Exod 20:5; 34:6-7 (Ps.-J. and Nf).

[21]Omitted in *ed. pr.*

[22]Nf: "Glory of the Shekinah."

[23]See Deut 6:16 (Ps.-J.).

[24]Ginzberg, *Legends,* III,350 and VI,121; *Aboth* 5:4 mentions the ten temptations. There are differences in which ten are meant. In III,350 notes the one in which the Israelites ask Moses what food he has for the starving children. The temptations result from the fact that God did not bring the Israelites directly to the Promised Land but let them wander for forty years in the wilderness.

[25]Reading with Le Déaut, vol. 3, p. 133, n. 17, *wkl,* as in Nf, instead of *wl'* to avoid a double negative.

[26]HT: "followed me"; here and Onq. *dḥlt',* but Nf "my Memra"; see 32:15. *dḥlt'* like Shekinah, *yqr* and Memra are substitutes to avoid direct contact with God.

[27]See Deut 1:36 (Ps.-J.).

[28]HT: "I have heard."

[29]Nf: "in my hearing."

[30]HT: "dead bodies"; here *gwšm,* but Onq. and Nf *pgr.*

[31]Here and Onq., but Nf *m's,* "reject."

[32]*pgr* as Onq. and Nf; see note on v. 29.

children shall go astray[33] in the desert for forty years, and they shall bear (the chastisement for) your sins until the time when your corpses are consumed in the desert. 34. During forty years you shall receive for your sins according to the number of days you were exploring the land, forty days, each day corresponding to a year, and you shall know *the consequence of* your murmuring *against* me. 35. I, the Lord, *have decreed by my Memra,* that I will do this[34] to all the[35] evil congregation who gathered themselves *to rebel* against me.' In this desert, they shall come to an end and there they shall die." 36. But the men whom Moses sent to spy out the land and who, when they returned, caused all the congregation to murmur against him by producing an evil report about the land, 37. (these) men who produced the *evil* report about the land shall die *on the seventh day of Elul: the worms coming out of their excrement*[36] *and going to their mouth and eating their tongue along with their palates. They were buried in death* before the Lord. 38. Only Joshua bar Nun and Caleb bar Jephunneh survived of those men who went to spy out the land. 39. And Moses spoke these words with all the Israelites, and the people mourned greatly. 40. And they arose early in the morning and went up to the top of the mountain, saying: "Behold, we are going up to the place of which the Lord spoke; for we have sinned." 41. And Moses said: "Why do you go against the decree of the Lord's *Memra?*[37] *Also* for it shall not succeed for you. 42. Do not go up, for the Lord's *Shekinah* shall not *rest* in your midst; and *the ark and the tent and the cloud of Glory shall not travel with you.* And be not crushed before your enemies. 43. Since the Amalekites and the Canaanites *are preparing* there for you, and you shall *be thrown down, slaughtered* by the sword. Because you turned away from *the worship of*[38] the Lord, *because of this, the Memra of* the Lord shall not be *your helper.*" 44. *And they armed themselves in the dark*[39] [40] *before dawn* to go up to the top of the mountain. But the ark, *where the Lord's covenant was,* no more than Moses, moved from the midst of the camp. 45. And the Amalekites and the Canaanites, who lived on that mountain, descended *and slew them and destroyed them and expelled them until their destruction.*[41]

Notes, Chapter 14

[33]HT: "roam"; Onq. *'ḥr,* "delayed," but Ps.-J. and Nf *ṭ'y,* "go astray"; Nfmg has quite a different interpretation: "shall nourish themselves for the merit of their fathers on the manna. . . ."; see 32:13.

[34]MS repeats *gzyrt bmymty,* but it is better to read with Onq. and Nf *d' ''byd.*

[35]*ed. pr.* and Nf: "this."

[36]*prt';* see Deut 21:8 (Ps.-J.).

[37]In all Targums for HT "mouth."

[38]Here *pwlḥn'* is used just as *dḥlt'* (v. 24) and Memra and Shekinah, etc., to avoid direct contact with God.

[39]HT *'pl,* "they presumed to go up" (RSV), is obscure: Onq. "they presumptuously (*'rš*) went up," but here *zrz bḥšwk',* "they armed themselves in the dark," and Nf *kmnw,* "they went up secretly."

[40]According to *Num. R.* (702), the HT "they presumed" (*y'plw*) implies that "they brought darkness (*'pl*) upon themselves and all of them remained in darkness" because the ark of the covenant did not depart the camp.

[41]HT and Onq.: "Hormah"; here and Nf *šṣy* replaces the place name; see 21:3 (Ps.-J.).

CHAPTER 15

1. And the Lord spoke to Moses saying: 2. "Speak with the Israelites and say to them: 'When you enter the land which I shall give you for your settlement, 3. and you shall prepare[1] *on the altar an offering before* the Lord, a burnt offering or a sacrifice *of holy things* for a vow explicitly expressed, or a freewill offering; or, *at the time of* your feasts you prepare *what is pleasurable for the Master of the world to be received in pleasure before* the Lord, from the herd or from the flock, 4. and *the man* who is offering a sacrifice *before* the Lord shall offer a cereal offering of a tenth of the finest flour[2] mixed with a fourth of a hin of *olive* oil. 5. And you shall offer with a burnt offering or a sacrifice *of holy things*[3] a fourth of a hin of wine *of grapes* for a libation, for each lamb. 6. Or for a ram, however, you shall prepare a cereal offering of two-tenths of the finest flour mixed with a third of a hin of *olive* oil; 7. and a third of a hin of wine *of grapes* shall you offer in bowls for the libation *so that it shall be accepted pleasurably before* the Lord. 8. Moreover, when you prepare a young bullock as a burnt offering, or the sacrifice for explicitly uttering a vow, or a sacrifice of *holy things*[4] *before*[5] the Lord, 9. let him offer in addition to the young bullock a cereal offering of three-tenths of finest flour, mixed with half a hin of *olive* oil, 10. and[6] half a hin of wine *of grapes for an offering*[7] *which is received with pleasure*[8] *before* the Lord. 11. In like manner shall it be done for each bullock or each ram or each young lamb or kids, 12. according to the number *of bullocks or lambs or kids* that you shall prepare *for the offering* so shall you prepare for each one, according to their total. 13. Every native-born *in Israel, but not among the gentiles,*[9] shall so prepare these libations *to offer a sacrifice which should be received with pleasure before* the Lord. 14. And if a stranger who sojourns[10] among you or *anyone* who is now among you since generations shall *offer a sacrifice which should be received with pleasure before* the Lord, just as you shall prepare, so shall he prepare. 15. For the *entire* assembly there is one statute:[11] for you and for the stranger who sojourns (among you). It is a perpetual statute for your genera-

Notes, Chapter 15

[1]HT: *'śh,* "do/make," is often translated here by *'bd* as Onq., but Nf *qrb.* In other places (e.g., v. 5) Ps.-J. and Onq. use *qrb.*

[2]*smyd':* Onq. and Nf *swlt'/slt.*

[3]HT: "the sacrifice"; in the Targums "holy things" is an addition. HT "peace offerings" (*šlmym*) is also regularly translated in the Targums by "a sacrifice of holy things."

[4]See note on v. 5.

[5]Nf: "to the name of the Lord"; see vv. 19, 22, 24.

[6]Ps.-J. omits the HT verb "to offer"; see Nf.

[7]*qwrbn;* see McNamara's note on v. 10.

[8]HT: "a pleasing odor" (RSV) (*ryḥ nyḥt*) as Nf, but Onq. and Ps.-J. only *(b)r'w'.*

[9]*Sifre Num.* 107 (II,147): Scripture says "all who are native . . . ," meaning: "these things an Israelite does. . . . but a gentile does not bring drink offerings."

[10]See discussion at Num 9:14.

[11]*Sifre Num.* 109 (II,150): "The purpose of Scripture is to treat as equivalent, for the purpose of all religious duties that are in the Torah, the Israelite and the proselyte."

tions: as it is for you, so shall it be for the stranger before the Lord. 16. The same regulation and the same Law shall there be for you and for the stranger who sojourns among you. 17. And the Lord spoke with Moses, saying: 18. "Speak with the Israelites and you shall say to them: 'On your entering the land to which I am bringing you, 19. it shall be when you eat of the bread *of the harvest* of the land, you shall set aside an offering *before* the Lord: *but not rice, nor millet, nor peas.*[12] [13] 20. You shall set aside one bread[14] from twenty-four from the first (batch) of your dough, as an offering *for the priest;* just as that which they are separating on the threshing place, so shall you separate it. 21. From the first (batch) of your dough shall you give as an offering *before* the Lord throughout your generations. 22. But if you should unintentionally fail to perform any one of these commandments that the Lord spoke with Moses, 23. all that the Lord commanded towards you through Moses from the day that the Lord commanded and onward throughout your (future) generations, 24. and if it be that an offense is done unintentionally without the knowledge of the congregation, then the entire congregation shall prepare a young bullock as a burnt offering *to be received with pleasure*[15] *before* the Lord, with its cereal offering and its libations *as are proper,* and a he-goat of pure strain[16] for a sin offering. 25. Then the priest shall make atonement for the entire congregation of the Israelites, and they shall be forgiven; for it was unintentional, and they have brought their offering, *a sacrifice before* the Lord, and they *offered before* the Lord a sacrifice for their transgression for their unintentional act. 26. The entire congregation of the Israelites will be forgiven *before* the Lord, as well as the strangers living among them, because it occurred to the people[17] unintentionally. 27. And if a *man* sins unintentionally, then he shall offer, for a sin offering, a goat of a year old *of pure strain.* 28. The priest shall make atonement *before* the Lord over *the man* who erred when he sinned unintentionally; by atoning for him, it will be forgiven him. 29. For the native-born among the Israelites and also for the stranger who lives among you, the same Law shall be for you and for whoever[18] shall act unintentionally. 30. But anyone who *performs a premeditated*[19] *sin,* whether he be a native-born or a stranger, and does not repent from his sins before the Lord, *he causes the anger of the Lord,* and that man shall be destroyed from among his people. 31. For he has despised the *initial* word that the Lord *commanded at Sinai*[20] and has negated the commandment *of circumcision;* that man will be destroyed in

Notes, Chapter 15

[12]*qyṭny:* a type of dry vegetable (Sokoloff, 490; Jastrow, 1326).

[13]*Sifre Num.* 110 (II,152): Excluded are rice, sorghum, poppy, sesame, and pulse, which cannot be used for unleavened bread, but wheat, barley, spelt, oats, or rye can be used.

[14]*ḥlh:* "a loaf, priest's portion of the dough" (Sokoloff, 201).

[15]See note on v. 10.

[16]See Lev 19:19 (Ps.-J.).

[17]HT: "the whole population" (RSV).

[18]MS: *wlmn.*

[19]HT: "with a high hand" (*byd rmh*); here *zdwn* (Jastrow, 380); Onq. *gly,* "defiantly"; Nf "with head uncovered," i.e., openly, publicly; see McNamara's note on this verse.

[20]See Exod 20:2-3 and *Sifre Num.* 112 (II,170): "to despise the word" is interpreted by some Rabbis as in Ps.-J.

this world (and destroyed) in the world to come, *because he shall give an account of his sins on the day of the great judgment.'"*[21] 32. When the Israelites were *encamped* in the desert, *the decree of the sabbath was made known to them, but the penalty of the sabbath was not made known to them. A man from the house of Joseph arose and said to himself: "I shall go and pluck wood on the sabbath day; and witnesses will see me and they will tell Moses. Then Moses will seek instruction from before the Lord that he might judge me, and, therefore, will make known*[22] *the penalty to all the house of Israel.*" And the witnesses[23] found the man when he was plucking and uprooting the wood on the sabbath day. 33. *After they had admonished*[24] *him, he had continued to pluck the wood; the witnesses brought him before Moses and before Aaron and before all the congregation.* 34. *This is one of the four legal cases*[25] *that came before Moses the prophet, and he judged them according to the Holy Memra. From these legal cases some of them were cases concerning money (civil cases), and some of them were cases concerning life (capital cases). With regard to the cases concerning money, Moses was quick. But with regard to the cases concerning life, Moses was deliberate. And with regard to each of these Moses said, "I have not heard," in order to teach the heads of the Sanhedrin,*[26] *who were to arise in the future, that they should be quick in the cases concerning money and deliberate in the cases concerning life, and not to be ashamed to inquire about the case that was difficult for them. For Moses, who was the master of Israel, himself had need to say, "I have not heard." Therefore* they restrained him in the place of confinement, for this case *had not as yet* been explained[27] what should *be done* with him. 35. Then the Lord said to Moses: "That man shall surely be killed. The entire congregation shall stone him to death outside the camp." 36. The entire congregation brought him outside the camp and stoned him, and he died according to what the Lord commanded Moses. 37. And the Lord spoke to Moses, saying: 38. "Speak with the Israelites and you shall say to them that they should make for themselves fringes[28] *not from cord nor from yarn nor from thread, but they should make them according to their category. And they shall cut the ends of their threads and shall hang them by five knots, in threes, on the four corners of their (prayer) cloaks in which they wrap themselves according to their generations; and they shall put on the (exterior) corner of their (prayer) cloak* a purple-blue twisted thread.[29] 39. And it shall be for you *the com-*

Notes, Chapter 15

[21]*Sifre Num.* 112 (II,171): The Scriptural statement that "his iniquity shall be upon him" is said to show that the sinner is "destined to give a full accounting of himself on the day of Judgment."

[22]*'štmwd'* is correctly a perfect but possibly confusion between *aleph* and *yodh.*

[23]*Sifre Num.* 113 (II,172–173): "they found . . ." indicates that Moses had appointed guards who found him "gathering wood."

[24]*Sifre Num.* 113 (II,173) suggests that they gave the man ample warning before bringing him before Moses and Aaron.

[25]See Lev 24:12; Num 9:8; 27:5; See Levy, 1987, 2:44-47 on Lev 24:12.

[26]MS: *sndry* but *ed. pr.: snhdry;* see Lev 24:12 (Ps.-J.).

[27]See McNamara's note on this verse.

[28]*ṣyṣyyt'* also in Nf, Frg.Tg. (V) and Pes, but Onq. *krwspd',* "edge" or "fringe."

[29]See McNamara's note on this verse.

mandment on fringes. And you shall see it *at the time that you are wrapping yourselves in them daily,* and you shall remember all my statutes[30] and you shall perform them, and you shall *not go astray by wandering after the impure fancies* of your mind[31] and after *the sights* of your eyes after which you are straying. 40. In order that you shall remember and observe all the commandments and shall be holy *just as the angels who minister before the Lord* your God. 41. I am the Lord, your God who *redeemed* and brought you *redeemed* from the land of Egypt in order to be your God. I *am* the Lord, your God."

CHAPTER 16

1. And Korah,[1] son of Izhar, son of Kohath, son of Levi, along with Dathan and Abiram, sons of Eliab,[2] as well as On, son of Peleth, sons of Reuben, each took[3] *his (prayer) cloak which was entirely purple,*[4] 2. and arose *with boldness and taught a (different) tradition regarding the matter of the purple, in Moses' presence. Moses had said: "I have heard from the mouth of the Holy One, may his name be blessed, that the fringes are to be white with one thread of purple in it. However, Korah and his friends made (prayer) cloaks whose fringes were entirely of purple, which the Lord had not commanded.* And two hundred and fifty men of the Israelites, officers[5] of the congregation *who were added at the time of the journeyings and campings, distinguished by their names, were aiding them.* 3. And they congregated against Moses and against Aaron and said to them: "Your authority is too great![6] Because all the congregation, all of them, is holy and among them *dwells the Shekinah of* the Lord; and why therefore are you lording it over the assembly of the Lord?" 4. When Moses heard this, *as if every one of them was jealous of his wife,*[7] *causing them to*

Notes, Chapter 15

[30]MS incorrectly *pyqwdyy;* Ginsburger and Rieder read *pyqwdy' dyy* as Onq., but Nf *mṣwwth dyy,* "precepts of the Lord."

[31]*lybkwn:* lit. "your heart."

Notes, Chapter 16

[1]Frg. Tg. (P) has an extensive midrash; see Klein (1980) on Num 16:1.

[2]See Num 26:5, 8, 9.

[3]Frg.Tg. (P) and Nfmg read both "took and separated" (*plg*). In *Num. R.* 18:16 several interpretations of the HT verb (*plg*) are given, including the idea that the HT verb "cannot but signify an expression of discord"; see Grossfeld, *The Aramaic Bible,* vol. 8, p. 113, n. 1, and McNamara's note on this verse.

[4]*Num. R.* (709): a cloak "entirely of blue . . . is subject to the obligations of the fringes."

[5]*'mrkwl,* but Onq. and Nf *rbrb.*

[6]*Num. R.* (711).

[7]*Num. R.* (732) and Ginzberg, III, 292, in Ps 106:16: "they were jealous (*qn'*) of Moses in the camp." The verb "jealous" is connected with adultery.

drink the trial water[8] *because of Moses* he fell on his face *because of the disgrace.* 5. Then he spoke with Korah and with the congregation *of his helpers,* saying: "Tomorrow the Lord shall make known who is worthy of him and who is holy and may draw near *to his service,* and he in whom he takes pleasure, he shall draw near *to minister*[9] to him. 6. This do; take for yourselves censers, Korah and the entire congregation *of his helpers.* 7. And put fire in them and tomorrow place there the *aromatic* incense before the Lord; and the man whom the Lord will choose shall be holy. You Levites have gone too far." 8. And Moses said to Korah *and his clan:* "Hear now, sons of Levi. 9. Is it too little for you that the God of Israel has separated you from the congregation[10] in order to draw you near to minister to him in performing the service of the tent of the Lord and to stand before all[11] the congregation to minister to them? 10. And he drew you near, you and all your brothers, sons of Levi, with you, and now you are demanding *even* the *high* priesthood.[12] 11. It is because of this that you and the entire congregation *of your helpers* are assembling against *the Memra of* the Lord. Also, Aaron, who is he that you are murmuring against him?" 12. And Moses sent *agents* to invite Dathan and Abiram, sons of Eliab, *to the house of great judgment.* But they said: "We shall not come up! 13. Is it too little a matter that you brought us out of the land *of Egypt,* which *produced* milk and honey, in order to kill us in the desert, that you are lording it over us? 14. Also, you have not brought us to a land producing milk and honey nor given us an inheritance of farms and vineyards. Have you blinded[13] the eyes of those men *who are in that land and overpowered them?* We shall not come up there." 15. Then Moses became exceedingly angry and said *before* the Lord: "*I pray* that you do not look at the gift[14] of their hands. For I did not requisition[15] a single one of your donkeys, nor have I done evil to even one of them." 16. And Moses said to Korah: "You and your entire congregation *of your helpers be ready tomorrow at the house of judgment before* the Lord, you and they, as well as Aaron. 17. Let each man take his censer and place in it (them) *aromatic* incense and draw near before the Lord, each man with his censer: two hundred and fifty censers. You and Aaron, each with his censer." 18. And each man took his censer and put fire in it,[16] and placed on it[17] *aromatic* incense, and they stood at the door of the tent of meeting *on one side,* and Moses and Aaron *on the other side.* 19. And Korah gathered against them the entire congregation at the door of the tent of meeting. *And he was overbearing because of*

Notes, Chapter 16

[8]See Num 5:18 (Ps.-J.).

[9]HT: "to him" as Nf, but Onq. and Ps.-J. make the idea specific with the verb *šmš* (*lšymwšyh*); see also v. 9.

[10]*Ed. pr.* adds "of Israel."

[11]*Ed. pr.* omits as HT, Onq., and Nf.

[12]Either the Levites were seeking this office or they were seeking a priesthood like the other priests who had fuller duties; see Grossfeld, *The Aramaic Bible,* vol. 8, p. 115, n. 7.

[13]Here *snwwr* (possibly a shaphel from *nwr;* Jastrow, 1005), but Nf *smy.*

[14]HT: *minḥah* is *qwrbn* in Onq. and Nf but *dwrwn* here.

[15]HT: "take" (*lqḥ*); here and Onq. *šḥr,* suggesting a forced levy, but Nf *ṭ'n,* "to load," and Nfmg *nsb.*

[16]"Them" in Onq., here, and Nf.

[17]See preceding note.

his wealth,[18] *for he found two treasures among the treasures of Joseph,*[19] *full of silver and gold; and he sought, with those riches, to banish Moses and Aaron from the world;*[20] *but* the Glory of the Lord was revealed to the entire congregation. 20. Then the Lord spoke with Moses and with Aaron, saying: 21. "Separate yourselves from among that congregation for I shall destroy them instantly." 22. Then *they fell prostrate in prayer* and said:[21] "O God, *who put* the spirit of life[22] *in the bodies of mankind* and *from whom is given* the spirit to all flesh, if one man sins, will (your) anger be against the entire congregation?" 23. And the Lord spoke with Moses saying: 24. "*I have accepted your prayers concerning*[23] the congregation. *Now speak to them,* saying: 'Withdraw from around the tents of Korah, Dathan and Abiram.'" 25. And Moses arose and went *to admonish*[24] Dathan and Abiram, and the elders of Israel followed him. 26. And he spoke to the congregation, saying: "Move, now, from the tents of these sinning men, *who have been sentenced to death from (the days of) their youth in Egypt. They have divulged my secrets when I killed the Egyptian; at the sea they angered the Lord, at Alush*[25] *they desecrated the sabbath day; now they have gathered against the Memra of the Lord. Therefore, see their banishment and the end of all their goods,* and do not draw near to anything which is theirs lest you are smitten because of all their sins!" 27. So they withdrew from around the tents of Korah, Dathan, and Abiram round about. Then Dathan and Abiram came out *with blaspheming words*[26] and stood, with their wives, their sons, and their little ones at the door of their tent, and made Moses angry. 28. And Moses said: "By this shall you know that the Lord sent me to perform all these works, that it is not of my own volition.[27] 29. If these (people) die *the death by which* all mankind dies, and (if) the final destiny of every man is applied to them, the Lord has not sent me. 30. But *if the death has not been created for them, from the days of the (beginning of) the world it is created for them now,*[28] *and if a mouth has not been created for the earth from its beginning, it is created for it now;* and the earth shall open the mouth and shall swallow them up and all that is theirs, and they shall go down *alive* into Sheol. Then you shall know that these men have angered the Lord." 31. And it happened when he had finished speaking all these words that the earth beneath them was

Notes, Chapter 16

[18]Josephus, *Ant.* IV,14.
[19]Ginzberg, *Legends,* III, 11, 286; *b. Sanh* 110a; *b. Pes* 119a.
[20]Aramaic *ṭrd mn ʿlm*.
[21]Incorrectly singular in MS.
[22]HT: *rwḥ* but here *nšmh;* see Num 27:16 (Ps.-J.).
[23]*Num. R.* (721-722): Moses seeks for God not to treat the wicked and the innocent in the same way and God agrees.
[24]Ginzberg, *Legends,* III, 292, 296.
[25]This name is found in the HT of Num 33:13-14; for allusions to why Dathan and Abiram angered the Lord, see Ps.-J. of Exod 2:13-14; 16:20; Ginzberg, *Legends,* III, 297.
[26]*Num. R.* (723): "insolence and contentiousness were in Dathan and Abiram and they came out blaspheming and reviling" and stood (*nsb*). *nsb* implies being blasphemous, according to *Num. R.*
[27]HT: "from my heart" (*mlby*); Onq. *rʿwty,* "ambition," and Nf *dʿty,* "designing." Ps.-J. seems to combined both HT and Onq. (*rʿwty lby*).
[28]Ginzberg, *Legends,* VI, 102.

split. 32. And the earth opened its mouth and swallowed them with *the men of* their houses and all of Korah's men and all (their) possessions.[29] 33. And they and all that was theirs descended alive into Sheol; and the earth covered over them and they perished from the midst of the assembly. 34. And all of Israel who were around them fled *from the terror* of their voice, *(those who were) shouting and saying: "The Lord is righteous, his judgments are true and these words of his servant Moses are true, and as for us, we are evil ones who rebelled against him."*[30] *And the Israelites fled when they heard, for they said:* "Lest the earth swallow us." 35. And a fire came out *in anger* from before the Lord and consumed the two hundred and fifty men who offered up the *aromatic* incense.

CHAPTER 17

1. And the Lord spoke with Moses, saying: 2. "Say to Eleazar bar Aaron, the priest, that he take away the censers from among the embers and scatter their fire far away, for they have been consecrated. 3. As for the censers of these wicked men *who were sentenced to death*[1] at the cost of their lives, they shall make them into hammered plates as coverings for the altar, for since they were brought before the Lord they were consecrated. And they shall be a (warning) sign for the Israelites." 4. Then Eleazar, the priest, took the bronze censers which those who died in the flames brought, and beat them into coverings *for the body of the altar, since from the beginning they were used at the altar.* 5. (This was to be) a reminder to the Israelites that no layman who is not from *the sons of* Aaron shall draw near to offer up the *aromatic* incense before the Lord; and that *no man shall be overzealous to the point of causing dissension regarding priestly matters,* as did Korah and the congregation *of his helpers. Their end is destruction; not a death as Korah's and his congregation in a conflagration of fire and being swallowed up by the earth but being smitten by leprosy.* As the Lord[2] spoke to Moses: "*Place your hand in your bosom*";[3] *and*

Notes, Chapter 16

[29]Aramaic *nyksy'* and Nfmg *mmwn;* Alexander, 1974, 198–199, suggests that the cleft in the rock at Petra called *es-sik* or "the Gates of Gehenna" (*bab es-sik*) is where Korah and his followers were swallowed up.

[30]*Num. R.* (733): Accordingly, it was desired that "the mouth of Gehenna be brought near to the rebels." Rab, son of Bar Hana, related that Arab merchants knew where the earth was cracked, and if one listened one could hear Korah and those swallowed up with him saying, "Moses and his Torah are true and they (Korah and associates) are liars."

Notes, Chapter 17

[1]HT: "at the cost of their lives" (*bnpštm*); Onq. and Nf *'tḥyybw,* "who have sinned"; Ps.-J. reflects the meaning of the HT.

[2]MS omits.

[3]See Exod 4:6.

his hand was covered with leprosy,[4] *so would it happen to him.* 6. The next day the entire congregation of Israelites murmured against Moses and against Aaron, saying: "*You caused the judgment of death*[5] *against* the people of the Lord." 7. And it was, when the congregation gathered against Moses and against Aaron *to kill them,*[6] they turned toward[7] the tent of meeting and, behold, the cloud *of the Glory of the Shekinah* covered it and *the Glory of* the Lord was revealed *there.* 8. Then Moses and Aaron went, *from before the assembly,* to the *door* of the tent of meeting. 9. And the Lord spoke with Moses, saying: 10. "Separate yourselves from the midst of this congregation, and I shall wipe them out instantly." Then *they fell*[8] *in prayer* on their faces. 11. So Moses said to Aaron: "Take the censer and put fire from upon the altar in it, and place *aromatic* incense *on the fire* and carry it quickly to the congregation and make atonement for their sake *for the Destroyer which had been restrained at Horeb whose name is "Ire"*[9] has come out *with a mandate* from *before* the Lord, to begin *to kill.* 12. And Aaron took (the censer) just as Moses had said and ran to the middle of the assembly and, behold, "Ire" *the "Destroyer"* had begun to destroy the people. He put on the *aromatic* incense and made atonement for the people. 13. *And Aaron*[10] stood *among them in prayer and made a partition with the censer* between the dead and the living; then the plague ceased. 14. And the number who died by the plague was fourteen thousand, seven hundred besides those who died because of Korah's secession.[11] 15. So Aaron returned to Moses at the door of the tent of meeting and the plague had ceased. 16. Then the Lord spoke with Moses, saying: 17. "Speak with the Israelites and take from them a staff, one staff per family, from all the officers[12] of their families—twelve staffs; you shall write each (man's) name on his staff. 18. But Aaron's name you shall write on Levi's staff, for there is but one staff for the chief of each family. 19. Then you shall deposit them in the tent of meeting before the Testimony where *my Memra* will meet *you.*[13] 20. However, it will happen that the staff of the one chosen *to minister before me* will blossom; and I alone shall quiet[14] the murmurings of the Israelites who are murmuring against you." 21. Then Moses spoke with the Israelites and every one of their officers gave him a staff, one staff per leader according to his family—twelve staffs; and Aaron's staff was in the midst of their staffs. 22. And Moses deposited

Notes, Chapter 17

[4]*Num. R.* (732): When Moses put his hand in his tunic and then withdrew it leprous, it implies the penalty of leprosy.

[5]HT: "kill," as also Nf, but Onq. and Ps.-J. soften the tone of accusation. The assumption is that Moses and Aaron themselves did not kill people.

[6]See Num 16:19 for the threat against Moses and Aaron. In Num 16:34 it is God who is the agent of the death of Korah, but in Num 17:6 it is Moses and Aaron who are responsible for Korah's death.

[7]Lit. "turned their face."

[8]HT: "fall," as Onq. (*npl*), but here itp of *rkm* and Nf itp of *šṭh.*

[9]See Deut 9:19 (Ps.-J.), where the five angels of destruction are listed.

[10]Nfmg: "Moses," following Deut 9:19.

[11]HT: "the affairs of"; here and Onq. "secession," but Nf "counsel."

[12]*'mrkwl.*

[13]HT: "you" (plural) as Onq. and Nf, but here singular, which Ginsburger corrects to plural.

[14]HT: "I will make to cease" (*whškty*); Onq. *nwḥ,* "put to rest," and Nf *bṭl,* "to cause to cease."

the staffs before the Lord in the tent of meeting. 23. And it came to pass on the next day when Moses entered the tent of testimony that, behold, Aaron's staff, for the house of Levi, bloomed and had produced buds, and blooms had sprouted from it *during the same night*[15] [16] and had produced almonds.[17] 24. And Moses brought out all the staffs from before the Lord to all the Israelites, who recognized (them) and each man took away his staff. 25. And the Lord said to Moses: "Return Aaron's staff before the Testimony as a sign to the rebellious people[18] that their murmurings should cease before me lest they die." 26. And Moses did just as the Lord commanded him, so did he. 27. Then the Israelites said to Moses, saying: "Behold, *some of us* were wiped out *by the burning fire, and some of us were swallowed up by the earth* and have perished. Behold, we are considered as though all of us have perished. 28. Anyone who approaches the tent of the Lord dies; truly, is our end to perish?"

CHAPTER 18

1. And the Lord said to Aaron: "You and your sons and your family along with you shall accept (the responsibility of) the guilt[1] (committed in connection with) the holy things *if you do not take care in offering them;* and you together with your sons shall accept the (responsibility of) the guilt (committed in connection with) your priesthood *if you do not take care in setting aside their priestly offering.*[2] 2. And even your brothers, the tribe of Levi, *who are called by the name of Amram,*[3] your father, shall you bring near to you that they may associate with you and minister to you while you together with your sons *shall stand* before the tent of testimony. 3. And they shall discharge the duty[4] to you and the duty of the whole tent; but they shall not approach the consecrated vessels or the altar lest they die, neither they nor you. 4. And they shall join you on the outside[5] and shall discharge the du-

Notes, Chapter 17

[15]As Nfmg.
[16]*Num. R.* (744): The budding and producing fruit is understood to have happened "on the same night."
[17]See McNamara's note on this verse.
[18]See Exod 16:32 (Ps.-J.).

Notes, Chapter 18

[1]HT: "incur the guilt" (*nś' 'wn*); here and Nf *qbl ḥwb,* but Onq. *šlh ḥwb,* "to affect forgiveness." The same HT idiom is translated in Onq. when there is no specific transgression except in v. 23. See Num 18:22, 23, 32, whereas Ps.-J. and Nf are always with *qbl;* see Grossfeld, *The Aramaic Bible,* vol. 8, p. 119, n. 1.
[2]*Sifre Num.* 116 (357) outlines the proper performance of the sacrifices.
[3]*Sifre Num.* 116 (359): "Amram erlangte es."
[4]HT: "duties"; *mṭrh,* "office, function, duty," in all the Targums.
[5]*Sifre Num.* 116 (364): "the priest inside and the Levites outside."

ties of the tent of meeting—all the service of the tent—but a layman[6] shall not approach you. 5. And you shall discharge the duties of the sanctuary and the duties of the altar so that there will not again be the anger which was against the Israelites. 6. As for me, I have advanced[7] near your brothers, the Levites, from the midst of the Israelites; they are a gift for you given *before* the Lord to perform the service of the tent of meeting. 7. While you together with your sons shall attend to your priesthood for every altar event and behind the curtain, and you shall serve according to custom:[8] as the service, so the food. I have given to you as a gift, the dignity of your priesthood, but laymen[9] who approach shall be killed." 8. And the Lord spoke with Aaron: "And I shall give to you with pleasure[10] the responsibility of my gift offerings:[11] *cakes and first fruits and* all the holy things of the Israelites. I give you them *as an anointing,*[12] and to your sons as an everlasting statute. 9. These shall be yours from the most sacred offerings; *what remains* from the burnt offering of *the sheep offered by fire,*[13] all their sacrifices which they bring *before* me of all their cereal offerings, of all their sin offerings, and of all guilt offerings. They are most sacred for you and for your sons. 10. You shall eat them in the most sacred (place),[14] every male among you[15] shall eat it in (a state of) purity;[16] it shall be sacred for you. 11. And this is what I have *granted* you: the separated portion of the gifts, all *the wave offerings* of the Israelites I have given to you, and to your sons and to your daughters together with you as an everlasting statute. Whoever is (ritually) pure in your family shall eat it. 12. All *the best olive* oil, and all *the best grape* wine, and the grain of their first fruits that they shall offer *before* the Lord have I given to you. 13. The firsts *of all the fruits of the trees* of their land that they shall bring *before* the Lord shall belong to you. Whoever is (ritually) pure in your family shall eat it. 14. All that is perfect[17] in Israel shall belong to you. 15. Whatever opens the womb of all flesh *among animals*[18] which they shall offer *before* the Lord, *according to the regulation*[19] applied to animals, *so shall be* the regulation applied to man with regard to belonging to you;[20] only you shall surely redeem the first-born of man *with*

Notes, Chapter 18

[6]HT: "stranger" (*zr*); see note on Num 1:51.
[7]HT: "take"; here and Onq. hap of *qrb,* but Nf *prš.*
[8]*Sifre Num.* 116 (367).
[9]See note on Num 1:51.
[10]*Sifre Num.* 116 (367); 117 (371).
[11]See note on Num 5:9.
[12]HT: "portion"; in Targums *rbw,* "anointing, consecration."
[13]The addition in Ps.-J. reflects *Sifre Num.* 117 (374), which discusses the sacrifices consumed by fire and suggests that the only sacrifices where something is still left over is the burnt offerings of cattle; see Grossfeld, *The Aramaic Bible,* vol. 8, p. 119, n. 3.
[14]*Sifre Num.* 117 (375): When the heathen are in the forecourt, then the faithful must eat within the temple precincts itself.
[15]MS.
[16]MS *dkwt'; ed. pr.: rbwt',* "sacred ointment.
[17]HT: "devoted thing" (*ḥrm*); also Onq., but here *gmr* and Nf *prš.*
[18]*Sifre Num.* 118 (383).
[19]*Sifre Num.* 118 (384).
[20]*Sifre Num.* 118 (384).

five selas and the first-born of unclean animals shall you redeem *with a lamb.* 16. And the redemption (price) of (a one-month old) *male* child shall you redeem according to *the sum of* your valuation by five selas of silver, according to the sanctuary sela, that is, twenty *main.* 17. But the first-born of cattle or the first-born of sheep or the first-born of goats you shall not redeem *because* they are sacred; their blood you shall sprinkle[21] on the altar, and their fat shall you offer up[22] as *a sacrifice that shall be received with pleasure*[23] *before* the Lord. 18. And their flesh shall be yours *for food;* just as the breast of the wave offering, so the right thigh shall belong to you. 19. Everything set aside of the holy things which the Israelites *shall consecrate before the Lord,* I give you and your sons and your daughters with you as an everlasting statute, *and it shall not be abolished; as* the salt *which seasons the flesh of the sacrifice,* because it is an everlasting statute before the Lord, so it shall belong to you and to your sons together (with you)." 20. Then the Lord said to Aaron: "In their land you shall not receive an inheritance *like the rest of the tribes,* nor shall there be a portion for you among them. I am your portion and your inheritance in the midst of the Israelites. 21. And I have given to the Levites, as an inheritance,[24] all the tithes in Israel in exchange for their services which they perform (in) the service of the tent of meeting. 22. And the Israelites shall not again approach the tent of meeting, incurring the sin leading to death. 23. As for *the Levites,* they shall perform the service of the tent of meeting, and they shall accept (the responsibility of) their sin *if they be not diligent during their service.* It shall be an everlasting statute for your (future) generations; but among the Israelites they shall have no inheritance. 24. Rather, I have given to the Levites, as an inheritance, the tithes of the Israelites which they set apart *before* the Lord as a gift,[25] because so have I said to them, that among the Israelites they shall not have an(other) inheritance." 25. And the Lord spoke with Moses, saying: 26. "And to the Levites (shall you speak) and say to them: 'Therefore shall you receive,[26] from the Israelites, the tithes that I give them as their[27] inheritance; and you shall separate from it a gift *before* the Lord, one tenth of the tithe. 27. And your gift shall be counted for you as the grain from the threshing floor or as the wine from the fullness of the wine press. 28. So shall you also set apart your gift *before* the Lord from all your tithes which you shall receive from the Israelites; and you shall give to Aaron, the priest, from

Notes, Chapter 18

[21]Read *tdrwq,* "sprinkle," as Onq. and Nf, but MS *tprwq,* "redeem."

[22]HT: "burn"; Onq. and here *slq,* but Nf *sdr,* "arrange."

[23]See Num 15:10.

[24]HT: "inheritance" as here, but Nf "my Memra is your inheritance"; see Grossfeld, *The Aramaic Bible,* vol. 8, p. 121, n. 10. Ps.-J. translates the HT, but in Onq. and Nf this phrase is explained as being priestly gifts. Nf further substitutes "Memra" for "I." *Sifre Num.* 119: "twenty-four priestly gifts did they give to the priests . . ."; see Deut 18:2 for a variant of the HT phrase in the Targums.

[25]HT: "offering"; in the Targums variants of the root *prš,* meaning "a portion set aside" or "a separated offering" (Sokoloff, 71).

[26]Lit. "take" (*nsb*).

[27]MS: "them" and "their" as HT "from them."

your gift *before* the Lord. 29. From all your donations (which you receive) shall you set apart a gift *before* the Lord; from all the finest of its best part[28] within it.' 30. And you shall say to them, *to the priests:* 'When you have set apart the finest of its best part, then it shall be counted for the Levites as *a gift*[29] *of grain* from the midst of the threshing floor or as *a gift of wine* from the midst of the wine press. 31. You shall eat it, *you the priests,* in every place, you and *the men* of your families; for it is your wages in exchange for your service in the tent of meeting. 32. And you shall not incur guilt because of it, at the time of your gift of the finest of its best part,[30] *by anyone eating of it who is unclean;* and you shall not desecrate the consecrated offerings of the Israelites, lest you die."

CHAPTER 19[1]

1. And the Lord spoke with Moses and with Aaron, saying: 2. "This is the decree of *the instruction*[2] of the Law which the Lord commanded saying: 'Speak with the Israelites that they bring you a red heifer, *two years old, from the separated offering (stored) in the chamber,*[3] *in which there is no blemish,*[4] *nor the mark of a hair of another (color), one which no male has come upon,*[5] *nor is there the discomfort of any severe labor, nor the bit, nor the yoke,*[6] *and has not been pricked by a goad or a wooden prick or a thorn or anything resembling* a yoke. 3. And you shall give it to Eleazar, *the chief*[7] *of the priests,* who shall take it *by itself* outside the camp *and shall arrange around it rows of wood of fig (trees);*[8] *and another*[9] *priest shall slaugh-*

Notes, Chapter 18

[28]HT: "all the best" (RSV); also Nf; Onq. "the best part," *śwpryh,* but here a superlative.
[29]*Sifre Num.* 122 (429).
[30]Same phrase in v. 29.

Notes, Chapter 19

[1]See the study by Hayward, 1992, 9–32, for a full discussion of this chapter. *Sifre Num.* (435-493) has many points related to this chapter.
[2]HT: "the statute of the law"; Onq. and Nf *gzyrt 'wryt';* Nfmg only *ḥwyyt',* whereas here *gzyrt ḥwyyt,* which seems to be a conflation of the two readings.
[3]*lškt':* the chamber where items for sacrifice are stored; see Num 28:2 (Ps.-J.).
[4]See McNamara's note on this verse.
[5]Ps.-J. elaborates the last phrase of the HT "on which no yoke has come up" by referring to another mishnaic ruling (*m. Parah* 2.1,4) that disqualifies a pregnant heifer.
[6]*qṭrb'* here, but at the end of the verse *nyr';* also in Onq. and Nf.
[7]*sgn,* "principal assistant to the chief priest" (Jastrow, 955). For *Sifre Num.* and later it is the chief priest himself who officiates, not the *sagan.*
[8]The specification of the wood of the fig tree is significant here because this wood is not mentioned in a dispute about the kind of wood to be used (*m. Parah* 3.8; 4.3).
[9]Nfmg: "another"; even LXX suggests another priest does the slaughtering.

ter it before him (by cutting) the two ducts,[10] *after the manner of the other animals, and shall examine her in accordance with the eighteen signs of Terefah.*[11] 4. And Eleazar, *in his white garments,*[12] shall take some of its blood with the finger of his right hand, *without collecting it in a vessel.* He shall sprinkle *toward the row of fig trees from the midst on the side opposite* in front of the tent of meeting *in one dipping (of the hand in the blood),* seven times. 5. *Then they shall go out from the midst of the rows (of fig trees), and another priest* shall burn the heifer while *Eleazar* looks on: the hide, and the flesh, and the blood, with its excrement shall he burn. 6. Then *another* priest shall take a piece of *cedar*[13] wood and *hyssop* and (wool) whose color turned into crimson and shall throw them into the midst of the burning of the heifer; *and he shall enlarge the flames to increase the ashes.* 7. And the priest *who slaughtered the heifer* shall rinse his clothes and shall wash his body *in forty seah* of water, and after this he shall enter the camp; but *that* priest shall be unclean, *before his immersion,* until the evening.[14] 8. *And the priest who was busy* with the burning shall rinse his clothes *in forty seah* of water and wash his body *in forty seah* of water; and he will be unclean, *before his immersion,* until the evening. 9. Then a ritually clean man, *a priest,*[15] shall gather the ashes of the heifer *into an earthenware receptacle covered with a clay seal.* Then shall he divide the ashes into three parts: *one shall be placed on the ramparts (of Temple), and another on the Mount of Olives, and the third portion shall be for all the Levitical keepers.* It shall be for the Israelite congregation as lustral water; for *it is for the forgiveness of the sin of the (golden) calf.* 10. *And the priest,* who gathered the ashes of the heifer, shall rinse his clothes and he shall be unclean, *before his immersion,* until the evening. And it shall be *for the cleansing* of the Israelites and the strangers that dwell among them as an everlasting statute. 11. Whoever touches *a dead body* of any man, *even a child of a few*[16] *months, either his body or his blood,* shall be unclean for seven days. 12. *He shall sprinkle*[17] *on himself the water (mixed with) these ashes* on the third day, and on the seventh day shall he be clean. But if he does not *sprinkle* on himself on the third day, *(the uncleanness) will tarry upon him,* and on the seventh day he will not be clean. 13. Anyone who touches *a dead body (of anyone), even a child of nine months, either its body or its blood,* and does not *sprinkle* himself, has defiled the tent of the Lord. That *man* shall be destroyed from Israel; for the waters of cleansing *were not sprinkled on him;* he is unclean; his uncleanness remains with him until he shall cleanse (himself) (on the third day) and repent; *and he may cleanse*

Notes, Chapter 19

[10]*symy',* "sign," i.e., the trachea and esophagus, where a ritual slaughter is effected.

[11]See Lev 11:1 (Ps.-J.).

[12]*bkyhwnyh* (*m. Parah* 4.1).

[13]*gwlmyš,* "a type of cedar" (Jastrow, 222); Onq. and Nf *'rz'.*

[14]See Lev 22:7 (Ps.-J.).

[15]Ps.-J., contrary to all other sources, e.g., Onq. and Nf, which suggest any clean man, stipulates he is to be a priest; see vv. 18, 19, 21.

[16]Ginsburger and Rieder read "nine"; see v. 13.

[17]*ndy* (see Clarke, 1984, 375) for HT *ḥt'* in ithp, "to purify oneself"; see Num 8:21; 19:12, 13, 20; 31:19, 20, 23. The Targums alternate between *ndy* and *dky.*

and immerse (himself) on the seventh evening. 14. This is *the instruction of* the Law:[18] If a man shall die *beneath a spreading cover of the tent,* anyone who enters into the tent *by way of the (principal) door but not (if he enters) from the sides when the (principal) door is open* and everything which is in the tent, *even its ground, its stones, its wood, and its vessels,* shall be unclean for seven days. 15. And every open *clay*[19] vessel, whose clay seal[20] was not attached to it, *completely around its mouth,*[21] *which would have separated it from the uncleanness, is defiled at the cover (of the tent) by the unclean air which touches its mouth to its interior, and not (by that which touches) its exterior.* 16. Whoever touches, in the open field—*and not even reckoning one (child) who died in his mother's womb*—one slain by the sword *or the sword that slew him or an entire dead body or even one of their bones, like a barley seed,* or a bone of a living man *which was separated from him,* or a grave, *or the covering stone, or the frame*[22] *(for the covering stone),* shall be unclean for seven days. 17. For whoever is unclean, they shall take, from the ashes of the burnt sin offering and put there *spring* water in a clay vessel. 18. Then a (ritually clean) man, *a priest,* will take *the three stalks* of hyssop *in one bundle* and dip them in *this* water; *at the moment of contacting the uncleanness,* he shall sprinkle the tent, all the utensils, and the men who were there, and him who touched the bone of a living man *which was severed from him and has fallen,* or the one slain *by the sword, or the one who died by plague,* or a grave, *or a covering stone, or a frame (for the covering stone).* 19. And the clean *priest* shall sprinkle over the unclean *man* on the third day and on the seventh day and shall declare him clean on the seventh day; and he shall rinse his clothes and shall wash himself with water and shall be clean in the evening. 20. But a man who has become unclean and does not sprinkle *himself,* that *man* will be destroyed from the midst of the assembly, for he has defiled the sanctuary of the Lord; the lustral waters shall not be sprinkled[23] on him; he is unclean. 21. And it shall be an everlasting statute *for you.*[24] *And especially the priest,* who sprinkles the cleansing[25] water, shall rinse his clothes, and whoever touches the lustral waters shall become unclean until the evening. 22. And anything whatever that the unclean person has touched, though he does not carry it, shall become unclean; and a clean man who touches it shall become unclean until the evening."

Notes, Chapter 19

[18]See note on 19:1.

[19]*pḥr,* whereas other Targums use *ḥsp. pḥr* is used twelve times in Ps.-J. (Clarke, 1984, 476) and *ḥsp* twice.

[20]HT: "cover" (*smyd*); see Grossfeld, *The Aramaic Bible,* vol. 8, p. 123, n. 2.

[21]The difficulty of the HT text is reflected in the different ways the Targums translate the phrase; see Grossfeld, *The Aramaic Bible,* vol. 8, p. 123, n. 2.

[22]*dwpq',* i.e., the uprights between which the rolling stones (of the door) move.

[23]Aramaic *zrq.*

[24]HT: "them" as Onq. and Nf, but some HT MSS read "you," as here.

[25]Aramaic *ndy.*

CHAPTER 20

1. And the Israelites, the entire congregation, came to the Zin desert *on the tenth day* of the month *of Nisan;*[1] and Miriam died there and was buried there. 2. *And because for Miriam's merit a well was given, when she died the well was hidden.*[2] [3] Then there was no water for the congregation, and they gathered against Moses and against Aaron. 3. So the people quarreled with Moses and they said, saying: "Would that we had died[4] when our brothers *died* before the Lord! 4. Why have you brought the assembly of the Lord to this desert to die here, we and our livestock? 5. Furthermore, why have you brought us up from Egypt to bring us to this evil place? It is *not* a place *suited* for a granary *or even for planting* figs, vines, or pomegranates; there is not (even) water to drink." 6. And Moses and Aaron went up from before *the murmuring of* the assembly to the door of the tent of meeting and *fell prostrate;*[5] then the Glory *of the Shekinah of* the Lord was revealed to them. 7. And the Lord spoke with Moses, saying: 8. "Take the staff *of miracles* and gather the congregation, you and your brother Aaron. Then *the two of you speak* to the rock *by the great and precise*[6] *Name* while they look on, and it shall give its water. *But if it refuses to bring forth, smite it, you alone, with the staff in your hand,* and water shall come forth for them from the rock, and you shall give the congregation and their livestock water to drink." 9. And Moses seized[7] the staff *of miracles* before the Lord, just as he had commanded him. 10. Then Moses and Aaron gathered the assembly before the rock and *Moses* said to them: "Hear now, rebels! *Is it possible for us* to bring forth water for you from this rock?" 11. And Moses raised his hand[8] and smote the rock with his staff twice: *the first time blood dripped, but the second time*[9] much water came forth, and he gave the congregation and their livestock (water) to drink. 12. And the Lord said to Moses and to Aaron: "*I surely swear,* because you didn't believe in *my Memra*[10] to sanctify me in the Israelites' eyes, therefore you shall not bring up this assembly into the land which I shall give them." 13. These are the "Waters of Contention" about which the Israelites contended *before* the Lord, *concerning the matter of the well which was hidden,* (where) he was sancti-

Notes, Chapter 20

[1]Onq. and Nf add "and the people stayed at Reqem"; Nfmg "Kadesh."

[2]See Num 33:46 (Ps.-J.) for another reason.

[3]*Mek. Exod.* 16:35 (128): When Miriam died the well was taken away but returned because of the merit of Aaron and Moses. But when Moses died all three—the well, the cloud of Glory and the manna—returned no more.

[4]HT: "expire" (*gw'*), but the Targums *mwt,* "died."

[5]Nfmg: "they fell down in prayer" (*bṣlw*).

[6]*mprš.*

[7]MS: *dbr,* but Onq., Nf, and *ed. pr. nsb.*

[8]HT: "hand," as here, Onq., and Nfi, but Nf *ḥwtrk.*

[9]Ginzberg, *Legends,* II, 322; III, 319: Before the water came from the rock, blood flowed at Meribah. In another passage the explanation for the blood is because Moses struck the rock with his rod rather than just speaking to the rock (Num 20:8 Ps.-J.) to bring forth the water.

[10]HT: "in me," here a standard translation; Nf "in the Name of my Memra," but by contrast Ps.-J. translates the end of the verse "sanctify me" literally.

fied by them, *by Moses and Aaron, when it had been given to them.* 14. Then Moses sent messengers *from Reqem*[11] to the king of Edom, *saying:* "Thus says your brother Israel, You know (well) all the troubles that found us. 15. Our ancestors went down to Egypt and have lived in Egypt many days. But the Egyptians dealt badly with us and with our ancestors. 16. Then we *prayed before*[12] the Lord and he heard *our prayer*[13] and sent *one of his ministering angels,* who brought us out of Egypt, and now we are in *Reqem,* a city *built* at the border of your territory. 17. Now let us pass through your land. *We shall not seduce your maidens, nor violate the betrothed, nor commit adultery with married women.*[14] We shall travel on the highway *of the King who is in the Heavens,* and we shall turn neither to the right nor to the left *to cause damage on the private roads* until we have passed through your territory." 18. But the Edomites said to them: "You shall not pass through *my territory,*[15] lest with a drawn sword shall I go forth against you." 19. Then the Israelites said to him: "Let us go by *the King's highway.*[16] If we drink your water, I and my livestock, then we shall give the price of *their value;* furthermore, let there be nothing *evil*[17] (to fear), *just*[18] let us pass through." 20. And he said: "You shall not pass through." And the Edomite(s) went out against them with a great army and with a powerful force. 21. And the Edomite(s) refused to allow Israel to pass through his territory. So Israel turned away from it, *because it was commanded from before the Memra of the Heavens*[19] *that they should not engage in battle with them. For*[20] *until now the time was not come for the punishment of Edom to be given into their hands.* 22. Then the Israelites, the entire congregation, decamped *from Reqem* and came to *Mount Amanus.*[21] 23. The Lord spoke with Moses[22] at *Mount Amanus* on the border of the land of Edom, saying: 24. "Aaron shall be gathered to his people, for he shall not enter the land which I have given to the Israelites because you rebelled against *my Memra*[23] at the 'Waters of Contention.' 25. Take

Notes, Chapter 20

[11]That is, Petra; see note on Num 13:26.
[12]HT: "we cried out to."
[13]HT: "our voice."
[14]See Num 21:22; the Targums base this interpretation on the three areas declared out of bounds: field, vineyard, and well in v. 17.
[15]*tḥwm,* lit. "borders," as in Onq. and Nf.
[16]Aramaic *'ysṭy'* = *strata.*
[17]HT: "nothing (more)."
[18]See Deut 2:27-28 (Ps.-J.).
[19]Le Déaut, 1979, vol. 3, p. 187, n. 21, discusses the use of "Heaven" as a surrogate for God in the Targums; see Maher, 1992, 1B, 8. The tradition found both here and in Nf and Frg.Tg. (V) says the Israelites did not fight Edom because of the divine command. Nf says it was "the Father in Heaven"; see Marmorstein, 1969, 105–107, and Urbach, 1975, 66–79.
[20]Ginsburger reads *mṭwl d,* but for the MS *d* is sufficient. The expression is found in all Targums. Israel avoided war with Edom because of God's command; see also Deut 2:5, 19.
[21]Onq. and Nf read "Mount Hor." Ps.-J. identified the place of Aaron's death and burial with that mentioned in Num 34:7.
[22]HT: "and to Aaron," as also Onq. and Nf, but reference to Aaron is not mentioned here because of the following verses.
[23]HT: "against my mouth"; Nf: "against the decree (*gzyrt*) of my Memra concerning" (*'l 'sp*).

Aaron and Eleazar, his son, and bring them up to *Mount Amanus.* 26. Then have Aaron remove his *glorious* garments *of the priesthood,* and you shall clothe Eleazar, his son (with them). Then Aaron will be gathered and will die there." 27. And Moses did just as the Lord commanded. And they ascended *Mount Amanus* while the entire congregation watched. 28. Then Moses stripped Aaron of his *glorious* garments *of the priesthood* and dressed Eleazar, his son. So Aaron died there on the top of the mountain. Then Moses and Eleazar descended from the mountain. 29. *And when Aaron's soul rested, the cloud*[24] *of Glory was lifted up on the first of the month of 'Ab.* Then the entire congregation saw *Moses descending from the mountain, his garments torn, and he was crying and said: "Woe to me, because of you, my brother Aaron, the pillar of Israel's prayers." Also, the men and the women of* Israel mourned for Aaron for thirty days.

CHAPTER 21

1. *And Amalek,*[1] who dwelt in the southern *land (he had changed* and had come to rule in Arad), heard *that Aaron's soul rested*[2] *(in death), and that the pillar of cloud which, through his merit,*[3] *advanced before the people, the Israelites*[4] had been removed; and that Israel came by the route of the spies[5] *to the place where they had rebelled against the Master of the World. For when the spies returned, the Israelites were camping at Reqem but turned back from Reqem to Moseroth*[6]*—six stages*[7] *in forty years. They decamped from Moseroth and returned to Reqem by the route of the spies. They came to Mount Amanus; then Aaron died there. Behold, therefore,*[8] he (Amalek) *came* and prepared for battle against Israel and took *some of* them captive. 2. Then Israel swore an oath *before* the Lord and said: "If you will hand over this people into (my)[9] hands, I shall destroy their cities." 3. And the Lord heard Israel's *prayer*[10] and delivered the Canaanites. He destroyed them and their

Notes, Chapter 20

[24]See Num 21:1 (Ps.-J. and Nf).

Notes, Chapter 21

[1]HT: "the Canaanite, the king of Arad"; Onq. and Nf as here.
[2]The midrash is only here, Nf, and Frg.Tg. (V); here *nwḥ;* Nf itp *slq,* "had been removed," and Frg.Tg. (V) *myt,* "died."
[3]*bzkwt:* see McNamara's note.
[4]The expanded text in Ps.-J. reflects somewhat Nf, but in Nf the midrash includes details on Miriam also.
[5]HT: "by way of Atharim" is interpreted in the Targums as well as the Vulg. as common noun ("spies").
[6]See Num 33:30, where Moseroth is mentioned.
[7]*Num. R.* (769-770) suggests seven stages backwards "based on Num 33:32-37, where the stages are listed but here counted in reverse."
[8]*h' bkyn.*
[9]HT: "my hand": here *yd',* but *ydy,* "my hand," in Onq. and *ydynn,* "our hands," in Nf.
[10]HT: "voice."

cities, and he called the name of the place Hormah. 4. So they journeyed from *Mount Amanus* by way of the Reed Sea, going around the land of Edom; but on the way the soul of the[11] people *became impatient.* 5. Then the people complained *in their hearts and talked against the Lord's Memra, and they quarreled*[12] with Moses: "Why did you bring us out of Egypt to die in the desert? For there is neither bread nor water, and we (our soul) have become impatient[13] with this *manna,* which is meager *food.*" 6.[14] *A divine voice*[15] *came from the heaven on high and so said: "Come, all mankind, see all the goodness that I have done to the*[16] *people. I brought them up, redeemed, from Egypt. I sustained them with manna from the heaven, and so they turned and grumbled against me. But behold, the serpent about whom I decreed from the day of the beginning of the world that dust shall be its food*[17] *does not grumble because of it, while my people grumbled against their food. Now, then, the serpents, which do not grumble against their food, shall come and bite the people who grumbled against their food." So the Lord's Memra* let loose against the people the *venomous*[18] serpents, and they bit the people and great numbers from Israel died. 7. Then the people came to Moses and said: "We have sinned, for we have *complained and talked against the Glory of the Lord's Shekinah and quarreled* with you.[19] *Pray before the Lord* that he remove the serpent's *plague* from us." So Moses prayed on behalf of the people. 8. Then the Lord said to Moses: "Make for yourself *a venomous bronze serpent*[20] and put it in *a place, aloft.*[21] Then it shall be (that) all whom *the serpent* bites, *when they look at it,* shall live, *if his heart pays attention to the Name of the Memra of the Lord.*"[22] 9. So Moses made the bronze serpent and placed it in *a place, aloft.* And it was whenever the serpent bit a man and he was looking at the bronze serpent *and his heart was paying attention to the Name of the Memra of the Lord,* then he lived. 10. So the Israelites decamped from *there* and camped in Oboth. 11. And they decamped from Oboth and camped in the plain of

Notes, Chapter 21

[11]"Soul of the"; thus text literally.

[12]HT: "speak against" (*dbr b*), but in the Targums there is a distinction between talking against God and quarreling with Moses; here there are two verbs (*hrhr* and itp of *nṣy*), whereas Onq. uses only itp of *r'm* and Nf *mll btr.* For "quarreling" here and Onq. *nṣy,* but Nf itp of *r'm.* The same distribution is found in v. 7.

[13]HT: "loathe"; here *qnt,* but Onq. and Nf *'wq,* "distressed."

[14]This verse contains a midrash common to all the Pal.Tgs. based on the phrase in Gen 3:14 concerning the serpent: "Dust you shall eat." The text in Ps.-J. is shorter and more compact, following more closely the HT and the text of Onq. than the one in Nf and Frg.Tgs. (PV), citing only the redemption from Egypt and the gift of the manna before introducing the role of the serpent, which in Nf "comes and rules over the people" in contrast to here; see also McNamara's note on this verse.

[15]*brt ql':* see McNamara's note on this phrase.

[16]*Ed. pr.:* "this."

[17]See Gen 3:14.

[18]*ḥwrmnyn* (Jastrow, 440).

[19]HT: "spoke against" (*dbr b*). Here a sharp distinction between the people's stance against God—criticizing—but outright quarreling (*nṣy*) with Moses; Onq. *lwn,* but Nf itp *r'm;* see note 12 and Num 20:3.

[20]HT: "fiery serpent" (RSV).

[21]*'l 'tr tly,* as in Nf, but Onq. *'t,* "standard," is closer to the HT *ns.*

[22]*Mek. Exod.* 17:11 (144): The Israelites "believed in Him who commanded Moses to do so; then God would send them healing."

Megaztha,[23] in the desert, *a place which overlooked* Moab, towards the sunrise. 12. From there they decamped and rested in the wadi *which produced*[24] *reeds, sedge, and violets.* 13. And[25] from there they decamped and camped beyond the Arnon *in a crossing* that is (found) in the desert that extends from below the Amorites. For the Arnon is the border of Moab, (situated) midway between Moab and the Amorites, and therein dwelt *a priesthood*[26] *of the worshipers of idols.* 14. Therefore it is said in the book *of the Law, where is written* the Wars of the Lord:[27] *Eth and Heb, who were (smitten) with the misfortunes of leprosy, were banished to the camp's extremities.*[28] *They announced to Israel that Edom and Moab were hidden among the mountains to ambush and destroy the people of the house of Israel. But the Master of the World hinted*[29] *to the mountains that they should draw near*[30] *one to the other: they died and their blood was flowing as torrents, close to the Arnon.* 15.[31] The torrents *of their blood* poured out,[32] *spreading to the dwellings of Lehayyath.*[33] *However, it was saved from this destruction because it had not been in their plan. And behold* it was (situated close)[34] to the border of Moab. 16. Then from there a well[35] *was given to them (the Israelites);* that is the well about which the Lord said to Moses: "Gather the people that I may give them water." 17.[36] *Therefore,* Israel *was giving praise* (in) that song *at the time when the well, which was given to them by the merit of Miriam, after it had been hidden, returned:* "Rise, O well! *Rise, O well!*" they were singing to it *and it rose.* 18. The well which the *patriarchs,*[37] *Abraham,*

Notes, Chapter 21

[23]HT: "Iye-Abarim"; Ps.-J. has difficulty with "Abarim," as is demonstrated here and in Num 27:12. But in Num 33:44 HT is translated in Ps.-J. as *mgzt 'ybr'y,* which is how Onq. and Nf translate Num 21:11; but see Deut 32:49 (Ps.-J.).

[24]HT: *zrd,* as in Onq. and Nf, is explained in Ps.-J. as producing plants.

[25]MS omits but is found in HT lemma of verse in MS.

[26]*kwmrny':* the word used to designate pagan priests.

[27]The following midrash, unlike Onq. and Nf, attempts to exegete the HT of v. 14. The problem in the text is connected with the HT "Waheb in Suphah." Onq. and Nf omit "Waheb" and exegete "Suphah" as from *swp,* "the Reed Sea," and the miracles that God performed there (see next note). Ps.-J. interprets *'et waheb* as two lepers: Eth and Heb; see *b. Ber.* 54a–b: "A Tanna taught 'Eth and Heb in the rear' (Num 21:14) were two lepers who followed in the rear of the camp of Israel"; see McNamara's note on 21:15 for other details.

[28]Here HT *swp* is understood as "extremity" (*swp*), but in Onq. and Nf it is interpreted as the "Reed Sea."

[29]Read *rmz* as in Nf v. 15.

[30]*Num. R.* (774): The Lord signaled to the mountains and the breasts of the mountains (i.e., the rocky projections), and they entered the caves where the enemy's armies had crushed them. The mountains moved because they belonged to the Lord of Israel.

[31]This verse introduces an extended midrash on the poetry found in the HT and the various proper names mentioned there. The expansions do not seem to belong to an organized midrash as in other sections of ch. 21; see the various following notes as well as McNamara's comments on these verses.

[32]HT: *'šd,* "slope," is interpreted in the Targums as the Aramaic *šdy* and translated *špk.*

[33]HT: "settlement of Ar" is translated in the Targums as here. J. Levy, 1966, 408, says it means "fortress"; see Grossfeld, *The Aramaic Bible,* vol. 8, p. 127, n. 9.

[34]Following Onq. *mstmyk* and Nf *smykh.*

[35]HT proper name "Beer"; vv. 16-20 contain a midrash on the idea of "Beer" as meaning "well"; see Pseudo-Philo, *LAB* 10:7; also McNamara's note.

[36]Ginzberg, *Legends,* III, 144; VI, 116; see note 28 above.

[37]HT: "princes," understood in the Targums as "the patriarchs" (lit. "fathers of the world").

Isaac, and Jacob, the leaders, dug from of old;[38] the chiefs of the people, *Moses and Aaron, the scribes*[39] *of Israel* (dug it; they)[40] measured it out with their staffs. And *from (the time of) the desert (sojourn) it was given to them as* a gift.[41] 19. *And because it (the well) was given to them as a gift, it turned to ascend the high mountains*[42] *with them, and from the high mountains it descended with them to the valleys,*[43] *going around the entire camp*[44] *of Israel and giving them drink, each and every one of them at the door of his tent.*[45] *20. And from the high mountains it descended with them to the deep valleys and disappeared*[46] *from them at the borders of* the Moabites, at the top *of the height*[47] *which* is oriented in the direction of *Beth-*Jeshimon,[48] *because they have neglected the words of the Law.* 21. Then Israel sent messengers to Sihon, king of the Amorites, saying: 22. "Let me pass through your country. *We shall not violate the betrothed one, nor seduce the virgins, nor commit adultery with the married women;* we shall travel on the highway of the King *who is in the Heavens,* until we have passed through your territory." 23. But Sihon did not permit Israel to pass through his territory. Sihon gathered all his people and went out before Israel to the desert, and he came to Jahaz[49] and prepared for war against Israel. 24. But Israel wiped him out *with the Lord's Name,*[50] *which kills* by the edge of the sword. It took possession of his land from the Arnon until the Jabbok up *to the border of* the Ammonites, for *Rabbath* at the border of the Ammonites was strong. *And until now it was their limit.* 25. And Israel took all these cities, and Israel lived in all the Amorite cities, in Heshbon and in all its villages. 26. For Heshbon was the city of Sihon, king of the Amorites. Now earlier he prepared for war against the king of Moab and had taken his entire land, from his control, up to the Arnon. 27. Therefore the poets say *allegorically:*[51] *"The righteous ones, who rule over their inclinations, are saying: 'Come and let us consider*[52] *the advantage of a*

Notes, Chapter 21

[38]According to Num 22:28 (Ps.-J.), the wells were created at the beginning of creation.

[39]HT: *mḥqq,* "scepter," is understood as from *ḥq,* "statute," and so the Targums interpreted as "scribe"; see Vermes, 1961, 45–55, esp. 52, where the distinction between the LXX ("ruler") and the Targums ("scribe") is discussed; see McNamara's note.

[40]The text of Ps.-J. seems repetitive. The text of Nf has a clearer syntax of the parts and avoids the repitition of "dug." Hence in Ps.-J., omit the second "dug."

[41]HT: "Mattanah" (a place name) is interpreted in the Targums as the gift of Torah, which was given in the wilderness period; see McNamara's note on this verse and also the next verse.

[42]HT: the place "Bamoth"; see McNamara's note.

[43]HT: the place "Nahaliel"; Ps.-J. inverts the order found in HT, Onq., and Nf.

[44]*Num R.* (776): encircled a large tract of land, "causing the sprouting of grass and trees. It was given in the wilderness so no one tribe could claim it exclusively."

[45]*Num. R.* (775): The princes stood by the well and drew water, "each one to his own tribe and to his own family."

[46]An explanation other than that suggested in Num 20:2 (Ps.-J.) about the disappearance of the well.

[47]HT: "Pisgah," interpreted as a height of land or a cliff rather than a place name; see Gray, 1903 292.

[48]HT: *hyšmn,* "desert, wasteland," is understood as a place name in the Targums; see 33:49.

[49]Spelled *yhṣ* in MS as in HT.

[50]The efficacy of the curse; also in Gen 42:37 (Ps.-J.); see Maher, *The Aramaic Bible,* 1992, 1B, 6.

[51]HT: *mšlym,* "ballad singers" (RSV); here *ḥwdt';* Onq. and Nf as Frg. Tg. (V) *mtl. Num. R.* XIX, 30 and XX, 7 contain the tradition that Balaam was the prophet employed by Sihon to curse the Moabites; Pseudo-Philo, *LAB* XVIII, 2.

[52]A play on Heshbon.

good work because of the compensation (it carries) and the compensation of an evil work because of the disadvantage (it carries); it will be perfectly instructive for him who is zealous to maintain the Law. 28. *For strong words*[53] *like fire are coming out of the mouths of the righteous, the masters of that calculation,*[54] *and strong merits*[55] *like the flames (leave) from those who read and maintain the Law; their fire has consumed*[56] *the enemy and the adversary, who were reckoned before them, like the worshipers of the altars of the idols*[57] *of the wadis of* the Arnon. 29. Woe to you, *O enemies of the righteous.* You have perished! O people who are withered[58] *who are eaters*[59] *of the words of the Law; they shall not have a remedy until their sons be constrained to exile themselves to a place where they were studying the Law;* and their daughters *are taken away as captives of the sword in the presence of those taking counsel in the counsel of the Law, interpreters*[60] *who are maintaining the Law.* 30.[61] *The wicked ones said: There is nothing high or exalted to the sight in all this. Your calculations shall perish which your souls shall end in weariness.*[62] *But the Master of the World shall hunt them until their souls expire and they become desolate, as he has desolated the cities of the Amorites and the palaces of the chiefs from the great gate of the royal palace to the street*[63] *of the smiths which is close to Medeba."* 31. And Israel, *after they had slain Sihon,* dwelt in the land of the Amorites. 32. Then Moses sent *Caleb and Phinehas* to spy out *Mikbar,*[64] and they captured *the villages* and *destroyed* the Amorites who were there. 33. Then they turned and went up the road to *Matnan.*[65] And Og, king of *Matnan,* went out to meet them, he and all his people *to engage in* war at Edrei. 34. *And it was, when Moses saw Og,*[66] [67] *he shook*

Notes, Chapter 21

[53]HT: "fire from" was interpreted variously in the Targums: Onq.: "an east wind as strong as fire"; Nf: "people of heroes burning like fire."

[54]HT: "Heshbon."

[55]HT: "a flame (from Sihon)" is interpreted also variously in the Targums: Onq. "waging war (as potent) as a flame"; Nf "warriors like the flame." These similes are related to Ezek 27:26, where "east wind" is rendered in the Targum as "the king who is strong as the east wind"; also Deut 32:22 interprets "fire" as "east wind."

[56]HT: "it devoured Ar of Moab, the Lord's height." "Ar" is identified in Onq. and Nf as "Lehayyath" (see also note on v. 15), but Onq. and Nf interpret the second phrase as here.

[57]HT: "heights" (*bmt*), i.e., where idolatrous worship was practiced.

[58]*kmyš':* a play on the god Cemosh.

[59]MS: *mdhnyt,* as in Deut 31:20 (Ps.-J.).

[60]*'mryn,* "Amoraim" (Jastrow, 76).

[61]The HT of this verse is difficult for the targumist: *wnyrm 'bd hšbn,* "their posterity perished from Heshbon", and *wnšym 'd npḥ,* "we laid waste until fire spread." These two HT phrases are variously exegeted in the Targums; Ps.-J. has the longest expansion and is not easily related to the text of Onq. and Nf. However, the idea of "perishing" and "desolation" and "laying waste" serves as the point for development in the Targums.

[62]*dbwn'* as an allusion to Dibon in the HT.

[63]*šwq'* as in Nfmg.

[64]HT: *y'zr;* see 32:1, 3 (Ps.-J.) and Onq. and Nf; *mkwwr* (Frg.Tgs. (PV) and Nfmg); here the spelling is with *beth* rather than double *waw.*

[65]HT: "Bashan," as also in Onq.; Nf "Butnim." Ps.-J. represents *b>m* and *š>t;* here the spelling is with *beth* instead of a double *waw;* see McNamara's note on this verse.

[66]MS reads "us" incorrectly.

[67]Ginzberg, *Legends,* III, 343–348, contains other traditions about the size and power of Og. The traditions found in Ps.-J. have some similarities but extensive differences with the traditions about Og found in other rabbinic literature.

and trembled before him. He said: "This is Og, the wicked one,[68] *who was scoffing at Abraham and Sarah, our ancestors, saying: 'You are like trees planted by the water channels but do not produce fruit.' That is why, the Holy One, blessed be he, kept him alive for generations that he might see great numbers of their children and that he might be delivered into their hands." So* the Lord said to Moses: "Do not fear him, for I have delivered him and all his people and his country[69] into your hand, and you shall do to him just as you did to Sihon, king of the Amorites, who dwelt in Heshbon." 35. *And it was,*[70] *when Og, the wicked one, saw the camp of Israel which was spreading for six miles, he said to himself: "I shall make war against this people, lest they do to me just as they did to Sihon." He went and dug up a mountain*[71] *extending for six miles and rested it on his head to hurl it against them. Immediately the Memra of the Lord prepared a worm, and it split the mountain; then it perforated it and his head was swallowed up in its center. He sought to draw it from his head but was unable to because the molars and the (other) teeth of his mouth were pulling hither and thither. Moses went and took an axe of ten cubits and leapt ten cubits and struck him on his ankle. So he fell and died far off from the camp of Israel. For thus it is written:* They struck him and his sons and all his people until not a single one of them remained to escape. Then they took possession of his land.

CHAPTER 22

1. Then the Israelites decamped and camped in the plains of Moab at the crossing of the Jordan (opposite) Jericho. 2. And Balak bar Zippor saw all that Israel had done to the Amorites. 3. And the Moabites feared greatly before the people for they were many,[1] and the Moabites were distressed *for their existence*[2] because of the Israelites. 4. Then the Moabites said to the elders of the Midianites, *a people and a kingdom*[3] *were they until this day:* "The assembly shall destroy[4] all our surround-

Notes, Chapter 21

[68]Also Nfmg.
[69]*Ed. pr.* reads "and all his country," but Nfi reads as here ("and his country").
[70]See Num 34:15 (Nf); Ginzberg, *Legends,* III, 345; VI, 120.
[71]*Deut R.* 2:31 (26).

Notes, Chapter 22

[1]HT: *rb* "many; here *sgy,* but Nf *tqp.*
[2]Here *bḥyyhwn;* see Exod 1:12 (Ps.-J.) for the same formula.
[3]That is, "a confederation"; Josephus (*JA* IV.vi.2 (sec. 102–104)) records that Moab and Midian were friends and allies, and the Midianites advised Moab to consult Balaam. Another view (*Sifre Num.* 157) suggests that Moab and Midian should unite because the common enemy, the Israelites, i.e., the leaders of the Israelites, "grew up in Midian."
[4]HT: *lḥk,* "to lick up," occurs twice in the verse. The first occurrence in all the Targums is the shaphel of *yṣy,* "to destroy." But for the second instance Ps.-J. has *b'y,* "to desire, require," but Onq. and Nf as HT *lḥk,* "to lick."

ings just as the ox consumes[4] the grass of the field." And Balak bar Zippor, *the Midianite, was king of* Moab at that time, *but not at another time, for so was the agreement between them, to have kings from here and there by turns.*[5] 5. He sent messengers to *Laban the Aramaean,*[6] *that is,* Balaam *(for he sought to swallow*[7] [8] *the people of the house of Israel),* the son of Beor, who *acted foolishly from the greatness of his wisdom. He did not spare Israel, the descendants of the sons of his daughters; and his dwelling house was in Paddan, that is Pethor, according to its name, "Interpreter of Dreams."*[9] *And it was built in Aram on the Euphrates,* a land in which the population *served and worshiped him*[10]—(and Balak sent) to call him, saying: "Behold, a people has come out from Egypt, and behold it obscures[11] the view of this land and is encamped before me. 6. And now come, I pray, curse for me this people, for they are stronger than I. Would that I could *reduce*[12] *them* and drive them from the land, for I know that whom you bless is blessed and whom you curse is cursed." 7. Then the elders[13] of Moab and the elders of Midian, with *the sealed objects*[14] *of divination*[15] in their hands, came to Balaam and told him Balak's words.[16] 8. And he said to them: "Lodge here tonight, and I shall reply to you an answer according to what the Lord shall speak with me." And the leaders[17] of Moab dined with Balaam. 9. *And a Memra*[18] *came from before the Lord* to Balaam and said: "Now, who are these men seeking[19] that they spend the night with you?" 10. And Balaam said *before the Lord:* "Balak, son of Zippor, king of the Moabites, sent *scouts* (to speak) to me. 11. Behold, a people came out of Egypt and obscures the view of the land, so now come, curse them for me. Would that I should be able to make war against him and drive him out." 12. Then the Lord said to Balaam: "Do not go with them! And do not curse the people, for they are blessed *by me*

Notes, Chapter 22

[5]That is, alternating between Moab and Midian.

[6]See Gen 31:24.

[7]See Num 31:8 (Ps.-J.) and Deut 26:5 (Ps.-J. and Nf).

[8]Ginzberg, *Legends,* III, 354; VI, 123: Balaam, by tradition, is identified as (a) Laban himself; (b) Laban's grandson; or (c) Laban's nephew. Balaam is called "devourer of Nations."

[9]*Num R.* (792); Onq. interprets "Pethor" as a place name, but Ps.-J. and *Num R.* take "Pethor" from the root *pšr,* "interpreter of dreams," combining both place name and the idea of interpretation; see McNamara's note.

[10]Balaam.

[11]HT: *ksh* "to cover, cover over" and Nf, but here and Onq. *ḥp'.*

[12]*Num R.* (793); HT: "defeat" is variously interpreted in the Targums: Onq. ap of *gyḥ,* "to fight"; Ps.-J. *z'r* and Nf shap of *yṣy,* "to destroy." *Num R.* agrees with Ps.-J.

[13]HT: "the elders"; here *rbrbny,* "leaders," as Nf, Nfmg, and Frg. Tg. (V).

[14]HT: "divination in their hands"; Nf reads *gryn,* and Díez Macho suggests emending the text to *'gryn,* "wages," but Aruk reads *gdyn* as MS of Ps.-J. (J. Levy: "sealed staffs of divination"). *gd* III, "luck" (Jastrow, 210) and *Num R.* considers them the objects or instruments of divination. Ps.-J. (*gdyn qysmyn*) seems to follow Onq. (*qsmy',* "divination materials") rather than the Nf text corrected by Díez Macho but closer to Aruk's reading; see McNamara's note.

[15]*Num. R.* 794: "instruments of divination" means that they carried "all manner of divining instruments by means of which divination would be performed."

[16]*pytgm* as Onq. and Nf, but Nfmg *mlwy.*

[17]*rbrby.*

[18]*mymr* in the MS has an indication for an abbreviation for *mymr'* (see v. 20), even though it is found in the middle of a line in this MS.

[19]*b'n* (from *b'y*) with Ginsburger, not *k'n* as MS.

from the days of their ancestors."[20] 13. So Balaam arose in the morning and said to the leaders *of Moab:* "Go to your land, *for it is not the Lord's pleasure*[21] to allow me to go with you."[22] 14. Then the leaders of Moab arose and came to Balak and said: "Balaam refused to come with us." 15. And Balak again sent more leaders,[23] more honored than those (who went before). 16. And they came to Balaam and said to him: "Thus said Balak, son of Zippor: 'You shall not refuse thusly to come to me; 17. for I shall surely honor you greatly, and everything which you say to me I shall do. So come now, curse for me[24] this people.'" 18. And Balaam replied again to the servants of Balak: "Even if Balak were to give me much of his *treasury*[25]—silver and gold—I would not have *permission* to transgress *the decree of the Memra of* the Lord, my God, to do a small or great *thing.*[26] 19. So now, I pray, *dine* here tonight so that I may know what *the Memra of* the Lord will speak with me again." 20. And *the Memra* came *from before the Lord* to Balaam and said to him: "If the men came to call you, arise, travel with them.[27] But only the word which I shall speak with you, shall you do." 21. So Balaam arose in the morning and saddled his *ass*[28] and went with the leaders of Moab. 22. But the anger of the Lord increased because he went to curse them. So an angel of the Lord was ready in the street to hinder him. And he was riding on his *ass* and his two lads, *Jannes and Jam(b)res,*[29] were with him. 23. When the *ass* saw the angel of the Lord standing in the street with his sword ready in his hand, the *ass* turned aside from the way and went into the field.[30] Then Balaam struck the *ass* to direct it towards the street. 24. But the angel of the Lord arose *in the narrow part which is in the middle among the vineyards, the place*[31] [32] *where Jacob and Laban erected a mound and a pillar* on this side here, *and a watchpost* on the other side, *and they contracted not to overstep this limit to (do) evil.* 25. When the *ass* saw the angel of the Lord, it pressed itself against *the hedge*[33] and pressed Balaam's foot against the hedge. So he struck it again, *the angel being hidden from him.*[34] 26. Then the angel of the Lord again passed and

Notes, Chapter 22

[20]Ginzberg, *Legends,* III, 359: " . . . from the time of Abraham and the patriarchs they have been 'the apple of my eye.'"

[21]*r'w' qdm yhwh;* see 23:27, where the expression is *r'w' mn qdm.*

[22]Various texts (*m. Aboth* V19) suggest the "haughty spirit and proud soul" of Balaam; see *Num R.* XX, 10.

[23]HT: "princes"; here and Onq. *rbrby,* but Nf *šlyḥyn,* "messengers."

[24]MS *lwty;* Nf *ly,* but Ginsburger suggests *bgyny* (see 23:7).

[25]MS reads *qwrṭwr,* "treasury, storehouse" contra *ed. pr.,* Onq., and Nf, which read *mly bytyh,* "house full of."

[26]*Num R.* 796: "unable to cancel the blessing: he has not given me permission to go and curse."

[27]*Num. R.* 798: "that a man is led in the way he desires to go . . . since you wish to go (and to perish from the world). Arise and go."

[28]Balaam is contrasted negatively with Abraham (Gen 22:3).

[29]The spelling is "Jambres" (Exod 1:15; 7:11 Ps.-J.). Jannes and Jambres were considered the sons of Balaam, who was one of the three counselors of Pharaoh (see Vermes, 1961, 137).

[30]*Num R.* 799 identified the HT "turned his ass into the road" as the ass turning aside to the field: Balaam was going to curse a whole nation "which had not sinned against him, yet he has to smite his ass to prevent it from going into the field."

[31]See Gen 31:45-52 (Ps.-J. and Nf); Balaam is identified as Laban the Aramaean already in Num 22:5.

[32]Ginzberg, *Legends,* III, 364; VI, 127: the tradition of Jacob and Laban erecting a wall is found only in Ps.-J.

[33]*syyg',* but Onq. and Nf *kwtl,* "wall."

[34]MS *mynh* must refer to Balaam, not his ass.

stood in a narrow place where there was no way to turn to the right or to the left. 27. And the *ass* saw the angel of the Lord, and it lay down beneath Balaam. And Balaam's anger increased and he struck the *ass* with a rod. 28. *Ten things*[35] *were created after the world was established, with the coming in of the sabbath between the suns: the manna, the well, Moses' staff, the diamond,*[36] *the rainbow, the clouds of Glory, the earth's mouth, the writing of the tablets of the covenant, the demons, and the mouth of the speaking ass.*[37] In that very hour *the Memra of* the Lord opened its (the *ass*'s) mouth *and prepared it to speak,*[38] [39] and it said to Balaam: "What did I do to you that you struck me these three times?" 29. And Balaam said to the *ass:* "Because you acted falsely[40] towards me. If there were a sword in my hand, I would indeed kill you now." 30. Then the *ass* said to Balaam:[41] *"Woe to you, Balaam, (you are) lacking knowledge, for I, an unclean animal, who will die in this world and who will not enter the world to come, you are unable to curse me; how much less*[42] *the children of Abraham, Isaac, and Jacob, by whose merits the world was created! But are you going to curse them? And so you have deceived*[43] *these people, when you said: 'This ass* does not belong to me. It is a loan to me, while my horses are resting in the meadow.'[44] Am I not your *ass* on which you have ridden from your *youth* until this very day? *Behold, have I profited from you sexually?*[45] [46] Have I ever had the habit of acting so with you?" And he (Balaam) said: "No." 31. Then the Lord uncovered Balaam's eyes and he saw the angel of the Lord standing in the street with his sword drawn in his hand, so he bowed and knelt (with) his face (to the ground). 32. Then the angel of the Lord said to him: "Why did you strike your *ass* these three times? Behold, I came out to oppose *you. But the ass feared, saw, and turned from the way. It was revealed*[47] *to me that you seek to go to curse the people, and the matter is not pleasing to me.* 33. And the *ass* saw me and turned before me these three times. If it were not for it turning from me, surely now I would have also killed you, but I would have spared it."[48] 34. Then Balaam said to the angel of the

Notes, Chapter 22

[35]See Gen 2:2 (Ps.-J.).

[36]Ginzberg, *Legends,* V, 53; VI, 299.

[37]A paraphrase found only in Ps.-J. (not in Onq. or Nf). *Num. R.* God opened the donkey's mouth to show that such activity is in God's power.

[38]*mmll.*

[39]*Mek. Exod.* 16:32 (II, 124).

[40]*šqr.*

[41]The following midrash is found substantially the same in Nf and the Frg. Tgs. (PV); see McNamara's notes on this midrash.

[42]*Num. R.* 779-780: the striking of the ass three times was recalling the patriarchs, who resisted the curses and persecution of their enemies.

[43]Ginzberg, *Legends,* III, 365.

[44]*Num. R.* 802: the princes of Moab were astonished at the ass which spoke, but Balaam said, "She is not mine" (and I have no experience of how to control it).

[45]Suggested by *rkb* as a term of bestiality.

[46]Ginzberg, *Legends,* VI, 128; *Num. R.* 802 discusses the idea that the ass had degraded Balaam, based on Lev 30:16, where a woman who lies with a beast is killed as well as the beast.

[47]HT: "because your way is peverse before me" (RSV) is translated as a passive in the Targums because the angel is speaking as God's agent here.

[48]*Num. R.* 803: God lets an angel cancel what God has said or done.

Lord: "I have sinned, for I did not know that you were standing[49] before me in the way. So if it is evil before you, I shall go back." 35. But the angel of the Lord said to Balaam: "Go with the men. But only the words that I shall speak with you, shall you speak." So Balaam went with Balak's leaders. 36. Balak heard that Balaam was coming, and he went out to meet him at a city of Moab that was on the border of the Arnon, which (was) at the limits of the territory. 37. And Balak said to Balaam: "Did I not surely send (men) to you to summon you? Why, then, did you not come to me? Indeed, truly, *did you say*[50] *that* I would be unable to honor you?"[51] 38. And Balaam said to Balak: "Behold, I have come to you now. Will I surely be able to speak anything? Only the word which *the Lord* will prepare in my mouth shall I speak." 39. So Balaam went with Balak and came to a city *surrounded by walls, to the plazas of the great city. It was the city of Sihon, that is (called) Berosha.*[52] 40. And Balak *slew*[53] oxen and sheep and sent (them) to Balaam and to the leaders who were with him. 41. And *at the time of* the morning,[54] Balak took Balaam and brought him up to *the high place of the idol,*[54] *Peor,*[55] from where he saw *the encampment of Dan,*[56] *which went at* the rear of the people[57] *who had been exposed from beneath the clouds of Glory.*

CHAPTER 23

1. Now *when* Balaam *looked at them, (he knew) that idol*[1] *worship*[2] was among them, and *he rejoiced in his heart* and said to Balak: "Build for me here seven (pagan) altars,[3] and make ready for me here seven oxen and seven rams." 2. And

Notes, Chapter 22

[49]Aramaic *'td;* see Clarke, 1984, 434 for the other occurrence of this word in Ps.-J., including Num 22:23; 23:6, 17, etc.
[50]*hwyt 'mr* here and in Onq., and the same idea (but different phrases) in Nfmg.
[51]*Num. R.* 804: Balaam finally departed in shame.
[52]HT: *qryt huṣoth,* "Kiriath-huzoth"; Ps.-J.: "Birasha," as Num 32:37 (Ps.-J.); Onq.: "in the city of its market places"; Nf: "the royal city, that is Maresha." The place name should possibly be read as in Ps.-J. if there is a change of *m*>*b;* Jastrow (166) suggests Baris; see McNamara's note on this word.
[53]HT: *zbh;* Ps.-J. *nḥr,* and Onq. and Nf *nks.*
[54]HT: *bbqr;* Onq. and Nf *bṣpr',* but here MS *'ydwny bṣpr'* is read as *b'ydwny ṣpr'* in Ginsburger or *l'ydwny ṣpr'* in Exod 14:27 (Ps.-J. and Nf).
[55]Here and Onq. *dḥlt',* "fear," but Nf *bmth,* "altars."
[56]See Num 25:3 (Nf).
[57]See Num 11:1 (Ps.-J.).

Notes, Chapter 23

[1]*nwkr'h.*
[2]See Num 22:41.
[3]HT: *mzbḥ;* Onq. and Nf (*mdbḥ*), but Ps.-J. uses *'gwryn* to designate a pagan altar.

Balak did as Balaam ordered, and Balaam and Balak[4] offered up an ox and a ram on (every pagan) altar. 3. Then Balaam said to Balak: "Stand by your burnt offering, and I will go. Perhaps *the Memra of* the Lord will meet me; and the thing that shall be shown to me I shall repeat to you." And he went, bent (double, crawling) like a serpent.[5] 4. *And the Memra from* before the Lord met Balaam, and he said *before* him: "I have arranged the seven (pagan) altars and offered up an ox and a ram on *every* (pagan) altar." 5. Then the Lord put a word in Balaam's mouth and said: "Return to Balak and thus shall you speak." 6. And he returned to him, and behold he was standing by his burnt offering, he and all the leaders[6] of Moab. 7.[7] And he took up the parable of his *prophecy*[8] and said: "From Aram *on the Euphrates,* Balak brought me, the king of the Moabites from the mountains of the east, 'Come, curse on my behalf *the house of Jacob,* come, *reduce*[9] Israel *for me.'* 8. How may I curse when *the Memra of the Lord is blessing them?* And who may I decrease[10] when *the Memra of the Lord multiplies them?* 9. *Balaam the wicked* said: *'I look upon this people who are being led by the merit of their righteous fathers who are like* the mountains, *and by the merit of their mothers who are like* the hills:[11] behold, (this) people, in their aloneness, *will in the future take possession of the world, because they are not being led by the laws*[12] *of the nations.'"* 10. *And it was when Balaam, the sinner, saw those of the house of Israel, their foreskin circumcised,*[13] *and hidden by the dust of the desert, he said: "Who will be* able to count *the merits of these strong ones?* Or number *the good works (found) in one of the four camps*[14] *of*

Notes, Chapter 23

[4]MS order, but HT, Onq., and Nf "Balak and Balaam." The Targums and Vulg. have both doing the sacrifice contra the LXX, Josephus, and Pseudo-Philo; see Vermes, 1961, 143.

[5]HT: *špy,* "a bare height" (RSV), causes problems; Onq.: "alone"; Nf: "solitary, tranquil heart"; Frg. Tg.: "tranquil heart." *Num. R.* 806: "until that moment he had been calm. . . . but then onwards he was confused"; LXX: "he went straight forward."

[6]*rbrby.*

[7]The messianic emphasis of 23:7-10 and 24:3-9, 15-24 is discussed by Fernández (1981). The vision of the Messiah revealed to Balaam had been hidden from all the prophets (see also McNamara, 1966, 242, and Vermes, 1961, 127–177). Much of the messianic or apocalyptic emphasis is based on the HT *štm* in Num 24:3 "whose eyes is opened"; see Chester, 1986, 199–202.

[8]LXX: "the spirit of God came upon him"; Philo (*VM* I, sec. 277) and Josephus (*Ant.* IV.vi.5) develop the idea of Balaam being possessed by the spirit of prophecy. *Num. R.* 807 proposes, contrarily, that Balaam is conscious of his trangression ("from Aram Balak brought me") and also Balaam is brought down from his glory.

[9]HT: *z'm* "curse Israel"; Onq. *trk,* "denounce"; here and Nf *z'r,* "diminish, curse," which is a synonym for the Aramaic *lwṭ,* "curse," in the first part of the verse; see Num 22:6 (Ps.-J.).

[10]See the note on the preceding verse as well as McNamara's note.

[11]*Num. R.* 810: "from the top of the rocks," that is, the patriarchs, and "from the hills," that is, the matriarchs. The Frg. Tgs. (PV) contain the same tradition as that in Ps.-J.; see McNamara's note.

[12]*nymws;* also Frg. Tgs. (PV); Onq.: "will be totally destroyed like the nations," the idea being that the nations will be punished/destroyed while Israel remains; see Vermes, 1961, 146–147.

[13]HT: *'pr* "dust," understood here as *'wrlt,* "foreskin," in Onq. as *d'dqy',* "the young ones," and Nf as *'wlm,* "young men." The Frg. Tgs. (PV): "who can count the youth . . . plentiful as the stars of heaven" (as Gen 15:5). Josephus has the same tradition as the Frg. Tgs.

[14]HT: *rb',* "the fourth part," is difficult; see McNamara's note and Grossfeld, *The Aramaic Bible,* vol. 8, p. 133, n. 5.

Israel?" Said Balaam the wicked: "If the house of Israel should kill me with a sword, already it has been announced to me that I have no share in the world to come; yet if I am going to die the death of the upright[15] ones, would that my end may be as *the smallest*[16] *among them."* 11. Then Balak said to Balaam: "What have you done to me? I brought you to curse my enemies, but behold with a blessing you have blessed them." 12. And he replied, and said: "Is it not whatever the Lord placed in my mouth that I will take care to speak?"[17] 13. Then Balak said to him: "Come now with me to another place from which you may see them; but you shall see only *the camp that travels* at the rear, and you will *be unable* to see all *their (other) camps.* Then from there you shall curse them[18] for me." 14. And he brought him to the "Field *of the Observatory*"[19] at the top of *the high place*[20] and built seven *(pagan) altars* and offered up an ox and a ram on every (pagan) altar. 15. And he (Balaam) said to Balak: "Stand here by your burnt offering, and I will withdraw[21] yonder." 16. And *the Memra from before* the Lord met with Balaam and put a word in his mouth and said: "Return to Balak and thus speak." 17. And he came towards him, and behold he was standing by his burnt offering and the leaders of Moab with him. And Balak said to him: "What did the Lord say?" 18. Then he (Balaam) took up the parable *of his prophecy* and said: "Arise, Balak, and listen! Listen to *my words,* son of Zippor. 19. Not like *the words of man is the Memra of the living and enduring God,* Master of all the ages, the Lord, for man speaks *then denies (it).*[22] *Neither can one compare his deeds to the deeds of the sons of flesh who ask advice and raise objections about what they decided. Yet, the Master of the entire world,*[23] *the Lord, says to increase this people as much as the stars of the heavens and to let them take possession of the land of the Canaanites, is it possible that* he speaks and does not do (it)? And *what* he has spoken, *is it possible that* he will not fulfill it?[24] 20. Behold, *I have received a blessing from the mouth of the holy Memra,* I shall not withhold *the series of their blessings from them."* 21. *Balaam the wicked said:* "I do not see *worshipers of idols*[25] among *those of the house of Jacob,* nor *are those who serve false idols established* among those of the house of Israel. *The Memra of* the Lord, their God, *is their support,* and the trumpets of the King Messiah *sound*

Notes, Chapter 23

[15]*qšyt;* see Deut 32:4 (Nf); see Frg. Tgs. (PV) for the same idea expressing Balaam's hope of being counted among the blest; see also McNamara's note.

[16]MS *kz'yry'.*

[17]See Vermes, 1961, 149 for a full discussion of the ancient writers on this verse.

[18]MS "it."

[19]HT: "field of Zophim"; here *skwt';* see Num 22:24 (Ps.-J.); Nf *skyyh,* "watchtowers."

[20]HT: "Pisgah," as in Num 21:20; Deut 3:27; 34:1. Targums: *rmt'.*

[21]HT: "meet," as Nf itp *zmn,* but here and Onq. itp of *'r'* and the Frg. Tg. (V), "will honor you."

[22]HT: "that he (God) should lie" is offensive to the targumist, and so he introduces "the Memra of God" as the actor.

[23]MS reads singular; *ed. pr.* reads *'lmy',* "ages."

[24]Frg. Tgs. (PV) "God speaks and acts, decrees and fulfills; and his decrees abide forever."

[25]HT: "he has not beheld misfortune (*'rm*) . . . nor divination": Nf: "I see no servants of falsehood . . . of foreign worship."

among them.[26] 22. To the God *who redeemed* and brought them out, *redeemed, from the land of* Egypt, *power, majesty, glory, and strength* are his.[27] 23. For those who use divination[28] are not *established* among *those of the house of Jacob,* nor are *the diviners of* enchantment *among the multitude of Israel.* At *this* time let it be said *to the house of Jacob* and *to the house of Israel:* "How praiseworthy *are these miracles and wonders which* God has done *for you!*[29] 24. Unique is *this* people; they *repose quietly* as a young lion *in strength,* and as a lioness, lift themselves up. They do not sleep[30] until they *have made a great slaughter of their adversaries and have taken possession of the spoils of the slain.*"[31] 25. Then Balak said to Balaam: "Neither (with) a curse shall you curse them, nor (with) a blessing shall you bless them." 26. Then Balaam said again to Balak: "Did I not speak with you from the beginning, saying: 'All that the Lord shall speak, I shall do'?" 27. So Balak said to Balaam: "Come, now, I shall bring you to another place. Perhaps it will be pleasing *before the Lord,* and there you shall curse him (Israel) for me." 28. Then Balak led Balaam *to the top of the high place*[32] *which* is oriented in the direction of *Beth Yeshimoth.*[33] 29. Then Balaam said to Balak: "Build for me here seven *(pagan) altars,* and set here for me seven oxen and seven rams." 30. And Balak did just as Balaam ordered, and he offered up an ox and a ram on *every* (pagan) altar.

CHAPTER 24

1. And Balaam realized[1] that it was good *before* the Lord to bless Israel. But he did not go, time after time,[2] to meet diviners. He set his face toward the desert, *to*

Notes, Chapter 23

[26]HT: *trw't mlk bw;* Onq.: *škynt mlkhwn bynyhwn,* "the Shekinah of their king is among them"; Nf and Frg. Tgs. (PV): *ybbqt zyw* (not in V) *'yqr mlkhwn mgn 'lhwn,* "the trumpets (of the splendor) of the glory of their king, is a shield above them."

[27]HT: *ktw'pt r'm lw,* "he has, like the horns (eminence) of a wild ox," is altered in the Targums to describe Yahweh's qualities (his eminence) to avoid likening God to an animal; see McNamara's note.

[28]*nḥšyn* possibly associated with *nḥš,* "serpent"; see McNamara's note.

[29]The Frg.Tgs. (PV) emphasize the joy of the future: "Happy are you, O righteous ones, that good reward is prepared for you with your Father in Heaven, for the world to come."

[30]HT: "lie down"; Onq., Nf, and Frg. Tgs. (PV) "rest," but Ps.-J. "sleep," as in Pesh. and LXX.

[31]HT: "drinks the blood of the slain" is avoided in all the Targums except Nf by speaking of taking possession of the possessions of the nations (Onq.)/the enemies (Frg. Tgs. [PV]) /slain, as here; see McNamara's note.

[32]HT: "to the top of Peor": *ryš rmth* here and Onq., but Nf *t'wwth,* "idols of Peor"; see McNamara's note.

[33]HT: *ha-jishimon,* "the desert," which all the Targums treat as a proper place name; see Num 21:20 ("Yeshimon"); 33:49 (as here).

Notes, Chapter 24

[1]*ḥm'.*

[2]HT: "as at other times," as Onq. (*kzmn bzmn*); Ps.-J. omits the comparative *kaph,* and Nf has different text: "as he used to go on every occasion"; also Frg. Tgs. (PV).

recall against them the matter of the (golden) calf that they had made there.[3] 2. So Balaam raised his eyes and saw Israel dwelling according to their tribes, *in their schools. Their doors (were) not aimed directly opposite the doors of their friends.* Then the spirit *of prophecy from before the Lord rested* upon him. 3.[4] And he took up the parable *of his prophecy* and said: "The word of Balaam, son of Beor; the word of the man *more honored than his father, because the hidden mysteries which were withheld from the prophets have been revealed*[5] to him, *and because he was not circumcised, he fell prostrate*[6,7] *while the angel stood before him;*[8] 4. The word of him who heard *the Memra from before the living*[9] *God;*[10] who has seen the vision *from before El*[11] *Shaddai. But when he sought that it be revealed to him, he prostrated himself,*[12] *and the hidden mysteries*[13] *which were hidden from the prophets,* were revealed *to him.* 5. How beautiful are *your schools*[14] *like the tents where* Jacob, *your father, ministered. And how beautiful is the tent of meeting*[15] *which is situated among you,* and your tents *which are around about it, O house of Israel.* 6. As streams *of water which grow stronger, so are they, of the house of Israel, dwelling as groups growing stronger by the teaching of the Law;*[16] and as gardens *planted* by the river *torrents,*[17] *so are their disciples as companions in their schools.*[18] *The expression of their faces shall shine as the appearance of the firmaments which the Lord created on the second day of the creation of the world* and extended for *the Glory of the Shekinah. They are exalted and raised up over all the nations* as the cedars *of Lebanon which are planted by the springs of water.* 7.[19] *Their king*[20] *shall arise from*

Notes, Chapter 24

[3]See Vermes, 1961, 155; Exod 32; see McNamara's note.

[4]The paraphrase of vv. 4–7 in the Pal. Tgs. should be compared with Tg. Gen. 49:1ff.

[5]HT: *štm,* "whose eyes are opened" (RSV), has several meanings. In Ps.-J. and Frg. Tgs. (PV) it is understood as a revelation to Balaam of what had been hidden to the prophets; see Grossfeld, *The Aramaic Bible,* vol. 8, p. 136, n. 3, for the other meanings of *štm.* Balaam fell prostrate before God because he was uncircumcised; see also Vermes, 1961, 156–157; Fernández, 1981, 250–252.

[6]See Gen 17:3 (Ps.-J.), explaining why Abraham could not stand upright before God.

[7]Ginzberg, *Legends,* III, 366; VI, 128: Balaam fell prostrate, for, being uncircumcised, he might not have listened to God if he had stood erect.

[8]This phrase not in v. 15.

[9]V. 16 omits.

[10]V. 16 inserts the phrase "who knew the hour when God most high was wroth with him."

[11]V. 16 omits.

[12]HT: *npl,* "to fall"; *Midrash R.* 634 contrasts Balaam's receiving a divine communication with Moses': "When He (God) spoke with Moses, the latter stood on his feet (Deut 5:28), but Balaam lay prone on the ground in the same situation (Num 24:4). Immediately after Balaam fell prostrate to the ground, his eyes were opened. This contrasts with Ps.-J. for the explanation of why Balaam prostrated himself (because he was uncircumcised)."

[13]See Gen 49:1 (Ps.-J. and Nf): Jacob reveals the hidden mysteries.

[14]HT: *'hlyk,* "your tents"; Onq. *'r'k,* "your land"; see Grossfeld, *The Aramaic Bible,* vol. 8, pp. 136–137, n. 7; Nf reads "tents" as HT, but Nfmg reads "your schools."

[15]HT: *mškntyk,* "your encampments"; Onq.: *byt mšrk,* "your dwellings; Nf: *mškmyh,* "his tents."

[16]The symbolism of water = the Law; see Vermes, 1961, 158.

[17]Onq.: "Euphrates."

[18]HT: *'hlym,* "aloes," understood as *'ohālim,* "tents," but then exegeted as in v. 5.

[19]All the versions differ widely from the HT. Basically the idea of water = righteousness = Messiah; see Vermes, 1961, 159–160.

[20]HT: "water."

them and their redeemer shall be from them and among them, and the descendants[21] *of the sons of Jacob shall rule over many nations.*[22] *The first who shall rule over them shall wage war against those of the house of Amalek* and shall be elevated over Agag,[23] their king. But *because he shall spare him,* his (Agag's) kingdom shall be taken[24] from him. 8. To God, who brought them out, *redeemed,* from Egypt *belong the power, the exaltation, the praise, and the strength. He*[25] *shall destroy* the nations, their enemies: *he shall break their might. He shall let loose the plague of his punishment against them and shall destroy them.* 9. *They* are resting and dwelling like a young lion and lioness, when sleeping, who will awaken? Those who bless them shall be blessed *like Moses the prophet, the scribe of Israel;* and those who curse *them*[26] shall be cursed *like Balaam, son of Beor."*[27] 10. And Balak's anger increased against Balaam and he clapped his hands; then Balak said to Balaam: "I brought you to curse my enemies and behold you have blessed them with a blessing these three times. 11. And now flee to your place; I had said that I would surely honor you, but behold the Lord has withheld honor from Balaam." 12. Then Balaam said to Balak: "Did I not speak with your messengers whom you sent to me, saying: 13. 'Even if Balak would give me the fullness of his *treasury,* silver and gold, I would not have the power to transgress *the decree of the Memra*[28] *of* the Lord to do good or evil of my own will; whatever the Lord will speak, I shall speak.' 14. And now, shall *I make an about-face* and go to my people? Come, I will advise you:[29] *Go, prepare inns,*[30] *and place there prostitutes,*[31] [32] *selling food and drink for less than their value; then bring this people*[33] *together so that they may eat and drink. When drunk, they will lie with them and denounce their God. In a short time they will be delivered into your hand, and many of them will fall. Yet after this they are destined to rule* over your people at the end of days. 15.[34] And he took up

Notes, Chapter 24

[21]HT: *zr',* "seed," is understood as both "descendants" and "power."

[22]HT: *mym,* "water," is understood as "many nations."

[23]See Vermes, 1961, 160–161; 1 Sam 15:9; the LXX including Aquila, Symmachus, and the Sam. Tg. substitute Gog as the eschatological enemy king.

[24]HT: *tnnś',* "be exalted"; Onq. and Ps.-J.: *ytnṭl,* "be taken away," to underline Saul's shame; Nf: *ytrwwm,* "be exalted," which agrees with the LXX that the messianic King will be exalted. Vermes, 1961, 161, notes that Frg. Tgs. (PV) and Nf preserve both meanings for the HT.

[25]Onq. and Nf: "the Israelites," but Ps.-J. and the Frg. Tgs. (PV) ascribe the whole action to God with no agent.

[26]HT: "you"; MS also reads "you."

[27]See Gen 12:3 (Ps.-J.) and Gen 27:29 (Ps.-J. and Nf).

[28]HT: "mouth (command) of the Lord."

[29]HT: "come let me advise you" but does not provide the advice: Onq., Nf, and Frg. Tgs. (PV) note only how to sin, but Ps.-J. is specific: fornication; see also *Sifre Num.* 137. This specific sinning provides a direct link between chs. 24 and 25. Although Balaam was prevented by God from cursing Israel, he obtained what he sought—the destruction of many Israelites; see Vermes, 1961, 162–164.

[30]*pwndqyn.*

[31]See Num 31:8.

[32]*Sifre Num.* 113 (509), Pseudo-Philo, *LAB* 18:14: "and afterwards the people were seduced after the daughters of Moab"; see also v. 25 and Num 31:16; Vermes, 1961, 169–172.

[33]The Israelites.

[34]4Q Test quotes vv. 15–17; see Fitzmyer, 1971, 79ff., 133.

the parable of his *prophecy* and said: "The word of Balaam, son of Beor; the word of a man *more honored than his father because the secret mysteries which were hidden from the prophet have been revealed to him.* 16. The word of him who heard *a Memra from before* God, who knew *the hour when* God most high *was wrath* with him, who saw the vision *before Shaddai. But when he was sought that it be revealed to him, he prostrated himself* and fell *on his face: and the hidden mysteries, which were hidden from the prophet, were revealed to him.* 17. I see him, but he is not here now; I observe him, but he is not near: *When the strong King*[35] *from those of the house of Jacob shall rule and the Messiah and the strong rod from Israel shall be anointed,*[36] *he will kill*[37] *the leaders*[38] of the Moabites *and make nothing* of all the children of Seth,[39] *the armies of Gog, who in the future will make war against Israel, and all their dead bodies shall fall before him.* 18. And they (the Edomites)[40] *shall be driven out, even the Gablaites*[41] will *be driven out from before Israel,* their enemy, and Israel *shall be strengthened with their wealth*[42] and shall take possession of them. 19. *Then a ruler* from among *those of the house of* Jacob *shall arise*[43] and lay waste *and destroy* the remnant[44] *(which remained from Constantinople,*[45] *the sinful city)*[46] *and lay waste (and destroyed the rebellious city) even Caesarea,*[47] *the strong*[48] city *of the Gentiles."* 20. And he saw *those of the house of* Amalek and took up the parable of his *prophecy* and said:[49] "The first of the nations *who made war against*

Notes, Chapter 24

[35]HT: "star"/"scepter"; Ps.-J. reflects a messianic interpretation of these words, as do Judaism and Christianity in general. The "star" which here destroys the Moabites, in Num 24:24 destroys all world powers; see also Rev 22:16, where Jesus is described as a "star."

[36]See Levey, 1974, 21, 23, for the interpretation of *rby* as "to anoint."

[37]HT: "crush" (RSV).

[38]HT: "forehead" (RSV).

[39]Onq.: "all mankind"; Frg. Tgs. (PV): "the people of the east" or, as here, the eschatological enemy, Gog.

[40]Omitted in the MS because the censor's perception of Edom is Rome.

[41]HT: "Seir."

[42]HT: "Israel does valiantly" is so interpreted in Frg. Tgs. (PV); here, Onq., and Nf *ḥyl* is understood as "to acquire wealth."

[43]HT of 24:19 has two themes which the targumist develops: (1) HT *wyrd,*" "one shall come down" (from a root *yrd*) or "one shall dominate" (from a root *rdh*); and (2) "a city shall perish." Onq. interprets *yrd,* "one will descend" (*nḥt*). Ps.-J., Nf, and Frg. Tgs. (PV) interpret the HT messianically. These three Targums interpret the first idea as "a king shall arise" (the second meaning of *wyrd*). The second idea is based on the indefinite identification of "a city." Onq. considers it to mean "a city of the nations." Nf has an erasure caused by the censor, but the Frg.Tgs. (PV) identify the city as Rome. So most likely "Rome" appeared in the space in Nf. Ps.-J. has the most expanded midrash on "a city," which is discussed in the following notes.

[44]MS *šyzbwt'* is abbreviated *šyz,* even though it is not at the end of a line in this MS.

[45]Frg. Tgs. (PV): "Rome," as does Rashi.

[46]HT: "a city"; Onq. "city of nations," but here and Nf "the sinful city," which Ps.-J. identified as Constantinople and Caesarea, "the rebellious city."

[47]Caesarea Maritima; Constantinople and Caesarea M. are two main representatives of the Roman Empire; see v. 24 (Ps.-J.).

[48]MS: *tqwp.*

[49]Nfi reads "the first of the kings and nations who waged war on the house of Israel were those of the house of Amalek. Joshua bar Nun of those of the house of Ephraim smashed them. The second who made war on them was Saul bar Kish, and he destroyed them; but their end will be destruction forever." According to *Esther Rabbah,* it is "Balaam the villain who commanded the Amalekites."

those of the house of Israel[50] was *those of the house of Amalek. Their end, in the days of the King Messiah,*[51] *is to make war along with the children of the east against those of the house of Israel.* But the end *of each of these* will be *everlasting* destruction." 21. Then he saw *Jethro,*[52] *who had converted,*[53] [54] and he took up the parable of his *prophecy* and said: "How strong are your camps, *whose dwelling* you set *in the clefts* of the rocks.[55] 22. Nevertheless, *it is decreed that the Shalmaites shall not be as spoil* until *Sennacherib, king of* Ashur, *comes* and takes you captive." 23. And he took up the parable of his *prophecy* and said: *"Woe to whoever is alive at the time when the Memra of the Lord is revealed, to give the good reward to the righteous ones, and to take revenge on the evil ones, and to cause nations and kings to form alliances,*[56] *and to incite one against another.* 24. *Now expeditions*[57] *shall be summoned with implements of war and shall come out with great numbers from Lombarnia*[58] *and from the land of Italy and be joined by legions who shall come out of Rome and Constantinople.*[59] They shall afflict the Assyrians and subjugate all *the children of* Eber.[60] *Yet the end of each of these shall be to fall by the hand of the King Messiah and to be forever destroyed."*[61] 25. Then Balaam arose and went and returned to his place. Alone, Balak went on his way and *he set up the daughters*[62] *of the Midianites in enclosures*[63] [64] *from Beth Yeshimoth to the Snow Mountain. And they were selling all types of desserts less than their value on the advice of Balaam the wicked at the dividing of the ways.*

Notes, Chapter 24

[50]See Exod 17:8.

[51]Frg. Tgs. (PV): "in the latter days"; Nf: "in the days of Gog and Magog." Here both eschatological idioms appear.

[52]The margin of the MS (also in v. 22) reads *šlmy',* "Shalmaite," as does the text of Onq. and Nf for Jethro; see Gen 15:19 and Grossfeld, *The Aramaic Bible,* vol. 6, p. 71, n. 17.

[53]See Exod 18:6 (Ps.-J.).

[54]Balaam's prophecy that the nations would be destroyed at the end of days exempted the descendants of Jethro, who will participate in Israel's joys and sorrows.

[55]Onq.: "in a fortified city."

[56]*ktt,* "to cause alliances" (Jastrow, 683), but *ktt* can also mean "to crush." Nf and Frg. Tg. (P) omit this phrase. In any case, the thrust of this verse is also eschatological.

[57]MS *ṣy'n* (çadeh) should be as in Onq. *sy'n.* The confusion may be because HT had *ṣym* with a çadeh.

[58]HT "Kittim" in Dan 11:20 and texts from Qumran are understood as "Rome." There is confusion in the various Targums: Onq. "Romans"; Nf has this phrase erased by the censor; Frg. Tg. (V) reads *blbrny',* "in naval craft from the provinces of Italy"; Frg. Tg. (P) reads *b'brbny',* "in confusion from the provinces of Italy which is Rome"; Ps.-J., as it appears, understands the reference to a place between Istria and Dalmatia; see also McNamara's note.

[59]See Le Déaut, 1979, 3, 241 n. 52, on dating the text. The "Kittim" is translated in the Targums as "Rome"; see Vermes, 1987, 28.

[60]HT: *'br,* "Eber," is understood in Onq. and Nf as "beyond the river, i.e., Euphrates."

[61]Again here the thrust is eschatological.

[62]Num 24:14; 25:15; 31:8 (Ps.-J.) suggest that Balak put his daughters into prostitution. This expression in v. 25 serves as an introduction to Israel's seduction in ch. 25.

[63]*qwlyn* (Jastrow, 1327).

[64]*Sifre Num.* 113 (509–510); Josephus, *Ant.* IV, 126–130; Pseudo-Philo *LAB* 18:13 speak of various activities of the Midianite woman as here described.

CHAPTER 25

1. And Israel dwelt *in a place which was called* Shittim *because of the folly*[1] [2] *and degradation which was among them.* And the people began *to desecrate*[3] *their holiness and to uncover*[4] [5] *themselves to the image*[6] *of Peor* and to debauch themselves with the daughters of the Moabites *who brought out the image*[7] *of Peor from under their girdles.*[8] [9] 2. Then they invited the people to sacrifice to their *idols,* and the people ate *at their banquets*[10] and bowed to their *idols.*[11] 3. *The people of the house of* Israel became associated with Baal-Peor[12] *like a nail in the wood which is not separated without splintering.*[13] The anger of the Lord increased against Israel. 4. Then the Lord said to Moses: "Take all the chiefs of the people *and appoint*[14] them *judges,*[15] *and let them give capital judgments for people who go astray after Peor. You shall crucify*[16] *them on wood before the Memra of the Lord against the sun in the early morning and with the sinking of the sun, you shall lower them and bury them.* Then the great anger of the Lord will turn away from Israel." 5. And Moses said to the judges of Israel: "Kill each man *of his tribe* who has joined[17] with *the idol* Peor." 6. And behold, an Israelite man[18] came *holding a plait of hair of a Midianite woman,* and brought her near towards his brothers in the sight of Moses and in the sight of all the congregation of the Israelites. *He answered and said to Moses: "What is it (that is wrong) to approach her? And if you say that it is forbid-*

Notes, Chapter 25

[1]Here *šṭwt'* is a pun on Dhittim.
[2]*Sifre Num.* 131 (502) says they began to act, drink, and bow down to the golden calf (Exod 32:6).
[3]HT: *wayyaḥel* can also be understood as *ḥll,* "to profane."
[4]*p'r* also suggests Peor.
[5]*Num. R.* (822): The sages suggest that the act of "uncovering oneself before Baal Peor" is tantamount to "worshiping it."
[6]*Sifre Num.* 131 (510): they reveled before the idol.
[7]*ṭwps'* = Greek *tupos.*
[8]*psyqyyhwn.*
[9]*Sifre Num.* 131 (511): they held the idol under their corseting and called it "Rabbi."
[10]*Sifre Num.* 131 (513).
[11]*ṭ'wwt.*
[12]As HT, but see v. 5.
[13]*Sifre Num.* 131 (513): such idol worship involves loss of life.
[14]HT: *ḥwq',* "hang them": a rare word in Hebrew; hip suggests a severe form of execution without specifying, but here, Nf, and Frg. Tgs. (PV) argue for a trial before condemnation. The leaders of the people are set up as judges in a Sanhedrin to judge and condemn everyone who is guilty to be crucified. The Pal. Tgs. were specific as citing the condemned as those who worship Peor. *Num. R.* (822) specifies the sin as "going to Peor." *Num. R.* adds: "if anyone has erred, the cloud will depart from him and the sun will not shine upon him . . . so that all will know who it is who has gone astray and will hang him"; see *Sifre Num.* 131 (518), *j. Sanh* X.2, and *Eccl. R.* III.16 for similar views; see also Grossfeld, *The Aramaic Bible,* vol. 8, p. 141, n. 2.
[15]*Sifre Num.* 131 (518). *Num. R.* (822) rejects the biblical notion of hanging the chiefs and instead says to make them "judges of those who have gone to Peor."
[16]*Sifre Num.* 131 (518); see also Gen 40:19; 41:13; Deut 21:22 (Nf).
[17]HT: *ṣmd,* "yoked themselves; here *dbq;* Onq. and Nf itp *ḥbr,* "who were associated with."
[18]*Num. R.* (823): Zimri is the name of the Israelite who seized the Midianite woman, daughter of Balak, by the plait of her hair.

den, did you not marry a Midianite woman, the daughter of Jethro?" And when Moses heard, he became excited and let himself go.[19] But they (the Israelites) wept[20] and recited the Shema, and stood at the door of the tent of meeting. 7. When Phinehas bar Eleazar bar Aaron, the priest, saw *this, he remembered the regulation*[21] *and answered:* "Whoever ought to kill, let him kill.[22] Where are the lions of the tribe of Judah?" When he saw that they were silent, he arose from among *his Sanhedrin* and took a spear in his hand.[23] 8. *Twelve miracles*[24] *were performed for Phinehas at the time when* he went after the Israelite man with the stranger:[25] *The first miracle (was) that he would have separated them but he could not. The second miracle (was) that their mouths were sealed and they could not shout, for if they would have shouted, they would have been saved. The third miracle (was) that he aimed with the spear and perforated together the Israelite man in his manhood and the Midianite woman in her womanhood.*[26] *The fourth miracle (was) that the spear remained fixed in the places of the perforation and was not dislodged. The fifth miracle (was) when he carried them aloft, the lintel was raised above him until he had gone out. The sixth miracle (was) that he carried them through the entire camp of Israel, which was six miles long, but was not weary. The seventh miracle (was) that he raised them with his right arm in the sight of all of their relatives;*[27] *but they were unable to do him harm. The eighth miracle (was) that the wood of the spear became strong and did not break from the load. The ninth miracle (was) when the iron (of the lance) extended into the two of them to its limit, it did not slip from them. The tenth miracle (was) that an angel came and turned the woman on her face and the man on his back, so that all the Israelites should see their shame.*[28] *The eleventh miracle (was) that they were kept alive while he walked them through the entire camp so that the priest should not be defiled by the dead.*[29] *The twelfth miracle (was) that their blood congealed and did not fall upon him; but when he carried them through the camp he shook (the lance), dropped them (to the ground), and they died. He answered and said before the Master of the World: "Can it be because of these*

Notes, Chapter 25

[19]Itp *šly; Num. R.* (823): When Moses heard Zimri's claim that Moses himself had married a Midianite, Moses "felt powerless and the Law slipped from his mind"; *b. Sanh* 82a says: "Moses forgot the halakah concerning marriage with a pagan woman."

[20]*Num. R.* (823) suggests that the people wept "because they became powerless at that moment."

[21]*Num. R.* (824): When Phinehas saw the act he remembered that Law, namely, that if a man cohabit with an Aramaean woman, i.e., any heathen, he is struck down by heathens.

[22]*Sifre Num.* 131 (519), i.e., "crucify."

[23]*Num. R.* (824-825): "he pierced them both as one lay on top of the other."

[24]Ginzberg, *Legends,* III, 386–388; *Sifre Num.* 131 (522–524); *Num. R.* (825) contains a list of twelve miracles, organized differently from Ps.-J.'s list. This is also true for the list in Ginzberg. In Ginzberg an angel plays a major role in Phinehas' activities, assisting him.

[25]MS: *ḥwṣ',* "the outsider"; *ed. pr.: mdyn'* (corrected to) *mdynyt'* (Rieder); Nfmg *hwṣ'* should be read *ḥwṣ'.*

[26]*bbyt htt twrph,* "genitalia" (Jastrow, 1658).

[27]That is, the tribe of Simeon; see v. 14.

[28]*Sifre Num.* 131 (524): the people establish the crime and administer death.

[29]Lit. "in the tent of a dead one"; see Num 19:14.

(two) that twenty-four thousand from Israel shall die?" Immediately the mercies of Heavens[30] *were unfolded, and* the plague was stopped from upon the Israelites. 9. And *the number* of those who died during the plague was twenty-four thousand. 10. And the Lord spoke with Moses, saying: 11. "The zealous[31] Phinehas bar Eleazar bar Aaron, the priest, has turned aside my anger from the Israelites because when zealous with my zeal *he killed the sinners* among them; and *because of him* I did not destroy the Israelites in my zealousness. 12. *In an oath* I say *to him in my name:* Behold, I have decreed to him my covenant of peace, and *I will make him an angel of the covenant, and he shall live eternally*[32] *to announce the redemption at the end of days.* 13. *And because they disgraced him, saying: Is he not the son of Puti*[33] [34] *the Midianite? behold, I will distinguish him by the high priesthood. Because he took the spear with his arm and struck the Midianite woman in her womanhood, and prayed with his mouth on behalf of the Israelite people, the priests shall be considered worthy*[35] of three gifts: the shoulder, the jaw, and the stomach.[36] And he and his sons after him shall possess an everlasting covenant of anointing because he was zealous for his God and he atoned for the Israelites." 14. And the name of the *slain* Israelite man who *had been killed* with the Midianite woman was Zimri bar Salu, a leader *of the clan of* the tribe of Simeon. 15. And the name of the *slain* Midianite woman was Cozbi, daughter of Zur, *who was called Sheloni, daughter of Balak,*[37] the chief of the people *of Moab,* whose *domicile* was in Midian. 16. And the Lord spoke with Moses, saying: 17. "Attack the Midianites *and kill them* 18. because they have attacked you with their deceitful advice when they deceived you regarding the idolatrous matter of Peor and that of Cozbi, daughter of the leader of Midian, their sister who *has been killed* on the day of the plague because of the (idolatrous) matter of Peor." 19.[38] And it was after the plague that the mercy of Heaven unfolded to redeem his people[39] with this punishment.

Notes, Chapter 25

[30]See note on Num 20:21.

[31]See Num 19:14.

[32]Phinehas is considered to be Elijah, who did not die, although he is not specifically so identified in the Targums; see Exod 4:13; 6:18; 40:10; Deut 30:4 (Ps.-J.); Hayward, 1978, 22–34.

[33]Puṭi, i.e., Puṭiel, Jethro's name in Exod 6:25 (Ps.-J.).

[34]*Sifre Num.* 132 (525); *Num R.* 25:12 (829).

[35]*zky.*

[36]See Deut 18:3; Le Déaut, 1970, 47.

[37]Ginzberg, *Legends,* III, 383: Balak had wanted his daughter to beautify herself to seduce Zimri, who had come with twenty-four thousand men. Zimri claimed to be greater than Moses because he was leader of the tribe of Simeon. But Moses denied Cozbi to Zimri.

[38]HT of v. 19 reads: "After the plague": Onq. translated the text of v. 19 as the first word of 26:1 (as does Le Déaut, 1979, 3, 251, without an explanation). Ps.-J. has an expansion of this phrase in v. 19, as does *ed. pr.;* Nf translated the HT literally as v. 19.

[39]See Num 31:3 (Onq.).

CHAPTER 26

1. Then the Lord said to Moses and to Eleazar bar Aaron, the priest, saying: 2. "Take *a total count*[1] of the entire congregation of the Israelites from twenty years old and up, everyone in Israel who is able to bear arms."[2] 3. So Moses and Eleazar, the priest, spoke[3] with *the officers*[4] *and gave orders to number* them on the plain of Moab, by the Jordan at Jericho, saying: 4. "You are to number them from twenty years old and up, as the Lord commanded Moses." Now (here are) the Israelites who came out of the land of Egypt: 5. Reuben, the first-born of Israel: Reuben's sons—(for)[5] Hanoch, the family[6] of Hanoch; for Pallu, the family of Pallu; 6. for Hezron, the family of Hezron; for Carmi, the family of Carmi. 7. These are Reuben's families and their count was forty-three thousand seven hundred and thirty. 8.[7] 9. And Eliab's sons: Nemuel, Dathan and Abiram—the same Dathan and Abiram who were summoning the congregation *who united* and made a schism[8] against Moses and against Aaron in the congregation[9] of Korah when *they united* and made a schism against the Lord. 10. Then the earth opened its mouth and swallowed them together with[10] Korah when the congregation of the wicked died when the fire consumed two hundred and fifty men; and they became an example.[11] 11. But Korah's sons *were not in the counsel of their father*[12] *but followed the teaching of Moses, the prophet. They did not die in the plague; neither were they smitten by the flames, nor were they engulfed in the swallowing of the earth.*[13] 12. Simeon's sons, according to their families: for Nemuel, the family of Nemuel; for Jamin, the family of Jamin; for Jachin, the family of Jachin; 13. for Zerah, the family of Zerah; for Saul, the family of Saul. 14. These are Simeon's families: twenty-two thousand two hundred. 15. Gad's sons according to their families: for Zephon, the family of Zephon; for Haggi, the family of Haggi; for Shuni, the family of Shuni; 16. for Ozni, the family of Ozni; for Eri, the family of Eri; 17. for Arod, the family of Arod; for Areli, the family of Areli. 18. These are the families of the Gadites according to their number: forty thousand five hundred. 19. Judah's sons: Er and Onan; but Er and Onan died *because of their sins*[14] in the land of Canaan.

Notes, Chapter 26

[1]*qbl skwm;* see note on Num 3:40.
[2]*npq lḥyl;* see note on Num 1:36.
[3]MS singular.
[4]Here *'mrkly'.*
[5]MS omits, but understood as in the following verses; see also vv. 23, 26, 30–32.
[6]Here *gnys',* but both Onq. and Nf *zr'.*
[7]MS omits.
[8]HT hip *nṣh,* "contend against"; Onq. translated as itp *knš;* Nf *plg,* but Ps.-J. has both words; see Grossfeld, *The Aramaic Bible,* vol. 8, p. 143, n. 2.
[9]HT: "company of Korah" (RSV); here and Onq. knyšt', "congregation," but Nf *'ṣth,* "counsel."
[10]Aramaic "and."
[11]Here and Nf *nysywn,* but Onq. *'t.*
[12]See Num 27:3 for the reason; also Frg. Tgs. (PV); see de Lange, 1976, 46.
[13]Nfmg has basically the same text as the expansion in Ps.-J.; see *Midrash R.* Psalms 45:1 (I, 449).
[14]See Gen 38:17-20; 46:12 (Ps.-J.).

20. And Judah's sons according to their families were: for Shelah, the family of Shelah; for Perez, the family of Perez; for Zerah, the family of Zerah. 21. Perez's sons were: for Hezron, the family of Hezron; for Hamul, the family of Hamul. 22. These are Judah's families according to their number: seventy-six thousand five hundred. 23. Issachar's sons according to their families: (for) Tola, the family of Tola; for Puvah, the family of Puvah; 24. for Jashub, the family of Jashub; for Shimron, the family of Shimron; 25. These are Issachar's families according to their number: sixty-four thousand three hundred. 26. Zebulon's sons (according to their families):[15] for Sered, the family of Sered; for Elon, the family of Elon; for Jahleel, the family of Jahleel. 27. These are Zebulon's families according to their number: sixty thousand five hundred. 28. Joseph's sons (according to their families): Manasseh and Ephraim. 29. Manasseh's sons: for Makir, the family of Makir; and Makir produced Gilead; for Gilead, the family of Gilead. 30. These are Gilead's sons: (for)[16] Iezer, the family of Iezer; for Helek, the family of Helek; 31. (for) Asriel, the family of Asriel; and (for) Shechem, the family of Shechem; 32. And (for) Shemidah, the family of Shemidah; and (for) Hepher, the family of Hepher; 33. however, Zelophehad, son of Hepher, had no sons, only daughters; and the names of Zelophehad's daughters: Makhlah, Noah, Hoglah, Milcah, and Tirzah. 34. These are Manasseh's families and their number: fifty-two thousand seven hundred. 35. These are Ephraim's sons according to their (families):[17] for Shuthelah, the family of Shuthelah; for Becker, the family of Becker; for Tahan, the family of Tahan. 36. And these are Shutelah's sons: for Eran, the family of Eran; 37. These are the families of Ephraim's sons according to their number: twenty-two thousand five hundred.[18] These are Joseph's sons according to their families; 38. Benjamin's sons according to their families: for Bela, the family of Bela; for Ashbel, the family of Ashbel; for Ahiram, the family of (A)hiram;[19] 39. for Shephupham, the family of Shephupham; for Hupham, the family of Hupham. 40. And Bela's sons were Ard and Naaman: *for Ard,*[20] the family of Ard; for Naaman, the family of Naaman. 41. These are Benjamin's sons according to their families and their number: forty-five thousand six hundred. 42. These are (Dan's)[21] sons according to their families: for Shuham, the family of Shuham; these are Dan's families according to their families. 43. The entire family of Shuham according to their *family:* sixty-four thousand four hundred.[22] 44. Asher's sons according to their families: for Jimna, the family of Jimna; for Jishvi, the family of Jishvi; for Beriah, the family of Beriah; 45. for the sons of Beriah: for Heber, the family of Heber; for

Notes, Chapter 26

[15]MS omits here and in v. 28.
[16]MS omits *lamedh;* see vv. 5, 23, 26, 31–32.
[17]MS and *ed. pr.* both read "number."
[18]Onq. and Nf read thirty-two thousand five hundred, as HT.
[19]MS reads *ḥyrm* for *'ḥyrm.*
[20]Onq., Nf, and *ed. pr.* of Ps.-J. omit, but found in MS.
[21]MS is in error reading "Gad"; see the end of the verse.
[22]HT: "number."

Malchiel, the family of Malchiel. 46. And the name of Asher's daughter was Serakh, *who was led by the sixty myriads of angels and was brought alive to the Garden of Eden because she told Jacob that Joseph was still alive.*[23] 47. These are the families of Asher's sons according to their number: fifty-three thousand four hundred. 48. Naphtali's sons according to their families: for Jahzeel, the family of Jahzeel; for Guni, the family of Guni; 49. for Jezer, the family of Jezer; for Shillem, the family of Shillem. 50. These are Naphtali's families according to their number: forty-five thousand seven hundred.[24] 51. These are the number of the Israelites: six hundred and one thousand seven hundred and thirty. 52. And the Lord spoke with Moses, saying: 53. "Among these *tribes* shall the land be divided as an inheritance according to the numbers of their names: 54. *to the tribe whose people* are many you shall increase their inheritance and to *the tribe whose people* are few you shall decrease their inheritance. Each according to their number shall be given its inheritance. 55. Yet the land shall be divided by lot; according to the number of the names of their ancestral tribe[25] shall they inherit. 56. According to lots shall their inheritance be divided, whether many or few. 57. And these are the numbers of the Levites according to their families: for Gershon, the family of Gershon; for Kohath, the family of Kohath; for Merari, the family of Merari. 58. These are the families of the Levites: the family of Libni, the family of Hebron, the family of Makhli, the family of Mushi, the family of Korah. And Kohath gave birth to Amram. 59. And the name of Amram's wife was Jochebed,[26] daughter of Levi, who was born to Levi[27] *on their entering into* Egypt, *within the walls.* She bore for Amram, Aaron, Moses, and their sister Miriam. 60. And to Aaron were born Nadab, Abihu, Eleazar, and Ithamar. 61. Then Nadab and Abihu died on their offering a strange fire from the hearth pots before the Lord.[28] 62. And their number was twenty-three thousand, (consisting of) every male from one month old and up. In fact, they were not counted among the Israelites because they were not given an inheritance among the Israelites. 63. These are the numbers (of the census)[29] when Moses and Eleazar, the priest, counted the Israelites on the plains of Moab by the Jordan at Jericho. 64. And among these there was not one (more) than the number when Moses and Aaron, the priest, counted the Israelites in the Sinai desert, 65. because the Lord had said to them that they would surely die in the desert; and not one of them remained except Caleb bar Jephunneh and Joshua bar Nun.

Notes, Chapter 26

[23]See Gen 46:17 (Ps.-J.), but according to Gen 49:21 (Ps.-J.), Nf, and Frg. Tgs. (PV), it was Naphtali who announced that Joseph was still alive.

[24]Onq.: forty-five thousand four hundred and forty, and Nf and HT forty-five thousand four hundred.

[25]MS reads singular.

[26]See Gen 46:27 (Ps.-J.), where some facts are expressed, including the fact that Jochebed was one of the seventy who entered Egypt with Jacob; see Maher, *The Aramaic Bible,* 1B, 1992, p. 151, n. 25. *Num. R.* (550-551) speaks of the marriage of Amram and Jochebed; see also Num 11:26 (Ps.-J.), where the divorce and remarriage of Amram are mentioned.

[27]MS: *ylydt* for *ytyldt.*

[28]See Lev 10:1 (Ps.-J.) and Num 3:4 (Ps.-J.).

[29]HT: *pqwdy;* variously translated as "numbers" (RSV); "detailed lists" (NEB); Nf translated both 26:63 and 31:14 by *skwm;* see Num 31:14, where Ps.-J. translated the HT as *'sṭrṭyy,* "military commander."

CHAPTER 27

1. Then the daughters of Zelophehad bar Hepher, bar Gilead, bar Machir, bar Manasseh of the family of Manasseh, bar Joseph approached *the court*[1] *when they heard that the land was being divided for the males (only) and they relied on the mercy of the Master of the World.*[2] And these are his daughters' names: Makhlah, Noah, Hoglah, Milcah, and Tirzah. 2. And they stood before Moses, *after* they had stood before Eleazar, the priest, and before the leaders and the entire congregation at the door of the tent of meeting (saying): 3. "Our father died in the desert. He was not among the congregation who murmured[3] and prepared to rebel against the Lord in the congregation[4] of Korah, but died for his own sins; *nor did he cause others to sin;*[5] and he did not have any *male* children. 4. Why should our father's name be omitted from the midst of his family because he had no male child? *If we are not considered as a (replacement for a) son, then our mother will be as observing the levirate.*[6] *Our mother shall take our father's portion and the portion of our father's brother.*[7] *But if we are considered as a son, give us an inheritance among our father's brothers.*" 5.[8] *This is one of the four legal cases that arose before Moses, the prophet, which he solved according to the Knowledge from on high.*[9] *Some of them were cases concerning money (civil cases), and some of them were cases concerning life (capital cases). With regard to the cases concerning money, Moses was quick; but with regard to cases concerning life, Moses was slow. And with regard to each of these, Moses said: "I have not heard," in order to teach the heads of the Sanhedrin of Israel who were to arise in the future that they should be quick in the cases concerning money but slow in the cases concerning life; and not to be ashamed to inquire about the case that was difficult for them. For Moses, who was the Master of Israel, himself had need to say: "I have not heard." Therefore* Moses brought their case before the Lord. 6. And the Lord spoke with Moses, saying: 7. "Zelophehad's daughters are correct[10] in what they are speaking: *This has been written before me:*[11] *but they are entitled for it had been said about them.*[12] You shall surely give them a hereditary possession among their father's brothers, and you shall transfer to them their father's in-

Notes, Chapter 27

[1]*Sifre Num.* 133 (537).
[2]*Sifre Num.* 133 (534-537): the daughters protested and appealed to God.
[3]*Sifre Num.* 133 (537): the people murmured as in Exod 16.
[4]Onq. as here (*knš*), but Nf "counsel"; see note on Num 26:9.
[5]*Sifre Num.* 133 (538): Zelophehad was without sin, and the daughters said that if he had had a male heir they would not be making their request.
[6]Ginzberg, *Legends*, III, 392; *Num. R.* (837): if no son, let our mother perform the levirate marriage. The daughters had used this argument with Moses if he would not recognize them as sons.
[7]*Sifre Num.* 134 (542): according to R. Eliezer.
[8]This section is found in Lev 24:12; Num 9:8; 15:24; *Sifre Num.* 68; Nf has a much longer midrash.
[9]See Num 15:34, where there is a similar phrase that refers to the Holy Word as the source.
[10]HT: "are right" (RSV); here and Onq. *y'wt*, but Nf *kdyn*, "rightly"; see McNamara's note.
[11]*Sifre Num.* 134 (540): refers to God.
[12]That is, the divine regulations expressed in the following verses (8–11).

heritance. 8. And with the Israelites shall you speak, saying: 'When a man dies and has no male child, then you shall transfer his inheritance to his daughter.[13] 9. And if he has[14] no daughters, then you shall give his inheritance to his *paternal*[15] brothers. 10. And if he has no *paternal* brothers, then you shall give his inheritance to his *paternal* uncles. 11. And if his father has no *paternal* uncles, then you shall give his inheritance to his nearest kinsman *from his father's family,*[16] and he shall inherit it. And it shall be as a legal decree of judgment, for the Israelites, just as the Lord commanded Moses.'" 12. Then the Lord said to Moses: "Ascend this mountain[17] and look over the land that I have given the Israelites. 13. And you shall see it, but you shall be gathered to your people, you alone, just as Aaron, your brother, was gathered; 14. *because* you rebelled against *my Memra* in the desert of Zin in the congregation *at* "The Waters of Contention"[18] (when it was proper) to sanctify me at the waters in their sight": these are the "Waters of Contention" at Reqem[19] in the Zin desert. 15. Then Moses spoke *before* the Lord saying: 16. "Let *the Memra of* the Lord, *which rules over the soul of man and from whom has been given* the breath *of life* to all flesh,[20] appoint a *trustworthy* man over the congregation, 17. who would go out before them to battle;[21] and who would come in before them *from the battle;* and who would take them out *from the hand of their enemies;* and who would bring them *into the land of Israel* so that the congregation of the Lord would not be *without wise men, so as not to go astray among the nations* as sheep that go *astray* when they have no shepherd." 18. Then the Lord said to Moses: "Take Joshua bar Nun, a man upon whom rests the prophetic[22] spirit *from before the Lord,* and place your hand upon him. 19. Then you shall make him stand before Eleazar, the priest, and before the entire congregation, and you shall give him command in their sight. 20. And you shall put upon him some of the splendor of your Glory[23] in order that the entire congregation of the Israelites will listen to him. 21. And he shall *minister* before Eleazar, the priest, and it shall be, *when a matter is hidden from him,* then he (Eleazar) shall inquire for him by these Urim before the Lord.[24] *According to the order of Eleazar, the priest,* shall they go out *to battle* and according *to his order* shall they go out *to render judgments,* he and all the Israelites with him, and the entire congregation." 22. So Moses did as the Lord commanded

Notes, Chapter 27

[13]*m. B Bat* 8:2.

[14]MS only *lyt,* not *lyt lyh* as Ginsburger.

[15]*Sifre Num.* 134 (544): the various hereditary possibilities are presented, and one of them, failing all others, is the brother of the father.

[16]*Sifre Num.* 134 (547): the important point is to preserve the inheritance in the father's family.

[17]HT: *har ha'brym,* "mountain of Abaraim," also in Onq. and Nf but not specified here.

[18]See Num 20:13.

[19]See Num 13:26; that is, Kadesh.

[20]See Num 16:22 (Ps.-J. and Nf).

[21]HT: *'yš,* "man," usually interpreted in the Targums as having special qualities.

[22]*Sifre Num.* 139 (570): one who has no fear just as one had no fear before Og; see Num 21:34.

[23]HT: "in whom is the spirit"; here and Onq. "prophetic spirit," but Nf "holy spirit."

[24]Onq.: *mzywk,* "some of your splendor," although Grossfeld translates it as "authority"; Nf misreads *mn* as from *m'n.* Better to read "some of your dignity"; see McNamara's note.

him and took Joshua and made him stand before Eleazar, the priest, and before the entire congregation. 23. Then he placed his hands upon him and gave him command as the Lord[25] *had commanded* Moses.

CHAPTER 28[1]

1. Then the Lord spoke with Moses, saying: 2. "Command the Israelites and say to them: 'The priests may eat my offering, bread of the arrangement[2] *of my table; but what you offer upon the altar no man has the right to eat. Is there not a fire which will consume it?*[3] *And it shall be received before me as a pleasant smell. My people, the Israelites, be careful to offer it from the levy of the chamber,*[4] [5] *an offering before me* in its time.' 3. And you shall say to them: 'This is *the order of the offerings* which you shall offer *before* the Lord: daily, two unblemished year-old lambs, as a regular burnt offering. 4. One lamb shall you prepare[6] in the morning *to atone for the sins of the night;* and the second lamb shall you prepare at twilight *to atone for the sins of the day.*[7] 5. And a tenth of three seah[8] of fine *wheat*[9] flour mixed with a quarter of a hin of pressed olive oil. 6. It is a regular burnt offering *as you offered* on Mount Sinai,[10] an offering *to be accepted with pleasure before the Lord.* 7. And its libation is a quarter of a hin for each lamb. From *the vessels of* the sanctuary shall the *old* wine be poured as a libation, *and if old wine cannot be found, bring forty day old wine as a libation before* the Lord. 8. And the second lamb shall you prepare (as a sacrifice) at twilight, according to the presentation[11] of the morning,

Notes, Chapter 27

[25]Nfi: "the Word of."

Notes, Chapter 28

[1]*m. Meg.* (e.g., 3:6) speaks of the regulations concerning the rules of this chapter. 28:11-15 is read at the beginning of the month (New Moon). The text of Ps.-J. v. 2 is more explicit than Onq. and Nf; see McNamara's note.

[2]HT: *lḥmy,* "my food" (RSV), raises a question, since God does not need or eat food: *lḥmy* is corrected to "bread of the arrangement" (*lḥym sydwr*); see Exod 25:30: "bread of the Presence," so called because of its arrangement in two rows; see Lev 24:6; *Num. R.* (843-847) clarifies that God requires neither eating nor drinking; see McNamara's note.

[3]That is, God will not consume it directly but the fire will; see McNamara's note.

[4]See Num 19:2 (Ps.-J.).

[5]*Sifre Num.* 142 (580): the offering should be made from sacrificial animals in the storehouse, not taken directly from the flock.

[6]*'bd* here and Onq., but Nf *qrb,* "offer."

[7]*Num. R.* (848): "transgressions of the night . . . transgressions committed during the day."

[8]HT: "ephah."

[9]*Sifre Num.* 142 (584): wheat flour rather than flour made from barley, spelt, or corn.

[10]*Sifre Num.* 143 (585).

[11]*dwrwn'* for *minḥah,* as in Onq. and Nf; see v. 26.

and according to its libation shall you prepare *the offering which will be accepted with pleasure before* the Lord. 9. And on the sabbath day (you shall offer) two perfect year-old lambs as a cereal offering and two-tenths of fine flour mixed with *olive* oil with the libation. 10. You *shall prepare* on the (same)[12] sabbath a sabbath burnt offering *in addition* to the regular burnt offering and its libation. 11. And at the beginning of *(the days)* of your *(menstrual)* month you shall offer a burnt offering *before* the Lord: two young bullocks without mixed genes, and one ram, seven perfect year-old lambs; 12. moreover, as a cereal offering three-tenths of fine flour mixed with *olive* oil for each ox, and two-tenths of fine flour for the cereal offering mixed with *olive* oil for each ram, 13. and for a cereal offering one-tenth of fine flour mixed with *olive* oil for each lamb of the burnt offering, *an offering to be accepted with pleasure before* the Lord. 14. And the libations *which are to be offered with them:* one-half of a hin of *grape* wine shall be for an ox, and one-third of a hin for a ram, and one quarter of a hin for a lamb. This burnt offering *shall be offered at the beginning* of every month *at the time of the renewal of* the beginning of *every (menstrual)* month of the year; 15. (in addition), one kid of the goats as a sin offering before the Lord *at the disappearance of the moonlight* in addition to the regular burnt offering shall be prepared (an offering) with its libations. 16. In the month of *Nisan,* on the fourteenth day of the month, (is) the sacrifice of Passover *before* the Lord. 17. And on the fifteenth day of this month there shall *be a festival.* For seven days unleavened bread shall be eaten. 18. On the first day of the festival (there shall be) a holy convocation.[13] No menial work shall you do. 19. You shall offer *an offering* (in the form) of a burnt offering *before* the Lord: two young oxen, one ram and seven year-old lambs. They shall be perfect to you. 20. And their cereal offerings of fine *wheat* flour mixed with *olive* oil, three-tenths for each ox and two-tenths for a ram shall you prepare. 21. One-tenth shall you prepare (as an offering), the *same* for the seven lambs. 22. (In addition) one kid for the sin offering to atone for you. 23. (In addition) to the morning burnt *offering* which is for a regular burnt offering, you shall prepare these offerings. 24. According to *these offerings of the first day* you shall prepare every day, for the seven days of the *festival, an offering*[14] *which shall be accepted with pleasure before* the Lord. In addition to the regular burnt offering shall it be prepared with its libations. 25. And on the seventh day you shall have a holy convocation; no menial work shall be done. 26. And on the day of first fruits when you offer a present[15] from the new *harvest before* the Lord at (the feast of) your Ingathering[16] *when seven weeks shall be completed,* you shall have a holy

Notes, Chapter 28

[12]*Sifre Num.* 144 (593): when one raises the question whether one can offer the sabbath offering on the following sabbath: on the specific sabbath and not on another sabbath.

[13]HT: *mqr' qdš,* "holy convocation," as here; but Onq. "a sacred occasion" (*m'r' qdyš*), while Nf has a double rendering: "a feast day" (*ywm ṭb*) and "a holy convocation"; see also v. 26; 29:1, 7, 12.

[14]Onq. and Nf add *lḥym,* "bread (offering)."

[15]*dwrwn':* see note on v. 8.

[16]HT: *šb't,* "weeks," is translated in Onq. and Ps.-J. as *'ṣrt,* "ingathering"; Nf: "Feast of Weeks," which Ps.-J. explains by the following phrase; Exod 23:15f.; 34:22; Lev 23:15-21.

convocation;[17] no menial work shall be done. 27. And you shall offer a burnt offering *to be accepted with pleasure before* the Lord: two young oxen and[18] one ram[19] and seven year-old lambs; 28. and their cereal offering (shall be) three-tenths of fine *wheat* flour mixed with *olive* oil for each ox, two-tenths for each ram, 29. one-tenth for each lamb and *the same* for the seven lambs. 30. In addition, one kid of the goats to atone for you 31. besides the regular burnt offering with its cereal offering shall you prepare. They shall be unblemished for you, with *the wine of* their libations.

CHAPTER 29

1. 'And in the seventh month, *that is the month of Tishri,* on the first of the month you shall have a holy convocation; no menial work shall be done; a day of trumpeting shall it be for you *to confound, by the sound of your trumpetings, Satan*[1] *who comes bringing charges against you.* 2. And you shall prepare a burnt offering *to be accepted with pleasure before*[2] the Lord: a young ox, a ram, seven perfect year-old lambs, 3. their cereal offerings of fine *wheat* flour mixed with *olive* oil: three-tenths for an ox and two-tenths for a ram, 4. and one-tenth for each lamb, *the same* for the seven lambs. 5. And one kid of the goats for a sin offering to atone for you. 6. Besides the burnt offering at the beginning of the month with its cereal offering, and the regular burnt offering with its cereal offering, and their libations according to the order of their appointment, an offering *to be accepted with pleasure before* the Lord. 7. And on the tenth day of the seventh month, *that is the month of Tishri,* you shall have a holy convocation, and you shall *deprive* yourselves *of food and drink, from the bath house and anointing yourself, from (wearing) sandals and using the (marriage) bed.*[3] No menial work shall be done. 8. Then you shall offer a burnt offering *before* the Lord *to be accepted with pleasure:* a young ox, a ram, seven perfect year-old lambs, belonging to you, 9. and their cereal offering of fine wheat flour mixed with *olive* oil: three-tenths for oxen, two-tenths for one ram, 10. one-tenth for each lamb, *the same* for the seven lambs; 11. (also) one kid of goats for a sin offering, besides *the sin offering* for atonement and the regular burnt offering

Notes, Chapter 28

[17]See note on v. 18.
[18]HT omits.
[19]HT plural but *Sifre Num.* 149 (604) explicitly states *one* (ram); Lev 23:18-20 prescribes *two* (rams).

Notes, Chapter 29

[1]See Num 10:10 (Ps.-J.).
[2]See vv. 6, 8, 13, 36; for a discussion of *qdm,* see Klein, 1979, 502–507; Ribera, 1983, 114–115.
[3]See Exod 19:15 (Ps.-J. and Nf); Lev 16:29 (Ps.-J.).

with their cereal offering and *the wine* of their libations. 12. And on the fifteenth day of the seventh month you shall have a holy *convocation.* You shall not do menial work, but you shall celebrate the festival *of Booths*[4] *before* the Lord for seven days. 13. Then you shall offer a burnt offering, an offering *which shall be accepted with pleasure before* the Lord: thirteen young oxen, *going each day and (hence) reducing their number; seventy (oxen) for the seventy nations,*[5] [6] *by thirteen orders (of priests) secure the offering:* two rams *that you will* offer *by two orders;* fourteen perfect year-old lambs that *eight orders* will offer: *six of them being offered two by two and two of them* one by one. They shall be perfect. 14. And their cereal offerings, three-tenths of fine *wheat* flour mixed with *olive* oil, for each of the thirteen oxen, two-tenths for each of the two rams, 15. and one-tenth for each of the fourteen lambs; 16. and one kid of the goats, a sin offering, *which will be offered by one order* besides the regular burnt offering and *the fine wheat flour* for the cereal offering and *the wine* for the libation. 17. And on the second day *of the festival of Booths you shall offer* twelve young oxen, *for twelve orders;* two rams *for two orders,* fourteen perfect year-old lambs *for nine orders: five of them shall offer two by two, and four of them one by one.* 18. And their cereal offering *of fine wheat flour* and *wine*[7] for their libations *which you shall offer* with the oxen and with the rams, and lambs by their numbers according to their prescribed ritual; 19. and one kid of the goats *for one order,* a sin offering, besides the regular burnt offering and *the fine wheat flour* for *their* cereal offerings and *the wine* for their libations. 20. And on the third day *of the festival of Booths you shall offer* eleven oxen *for eleven*[8] *orders;* two rams *for two orders;* and fourteen perfect year-old lambs *for ten orders: four of them shall be offered two by two, and six of them one by one;* 21. and their cereal offering *of fine wheat flour* and *wine* for their libations *which you shall offer with* the oxen and the rams and the lambs by their numbers according to the prescribed ritual, 22. And a kid for a sin offering *for one order* besides the regular burnt offering and *the fine wheat flour* for its cereal offering and *the wine* for its libation. 23. And on the fourth day *of the festival of Booths,* ten oxen *for ten orders;* two rams *for two orders;* fourteen perfect year-old lambs *for eleven orders; three of them shall be offered two by two, and eight of them offered one by one.* 24. Their cereal offering *of fine wheat flour* and *wine* for their libations *which you shall offer* with the oxen and the rams and the lambs by their numbers according to their prescribed ritual. 25. And one kid of the goats *for one order* as a sin offering, besides the regular burnt offering and *the fine wheat flour* for its cereal offering and *the wine* for its libation. 26. And on the fifth day *of the festival of Booths,* nine oxen *for nine orders;* two rams *for two orders;* fourteen perfect year-old lambs *for twelve orders: two of them shall be offered two by two, and twelve of them one by one;* 27. and their cereal offering *of fine wheat flour* for their cereal offering[9] and *wine* for their libations *which you shall offer* with

Notes, Chapter 29

[4]An addition in Ps.-J.; see vv. 20, 23, 26, 29; vv. 12–38 deal with the Feast of Booths.
[5]See Gen 11:8 (Ps.-J.); Deut 32:8 (Ps.-J.); Ginzberg, *Legends,* V, 194.
[6]*Num. R.* (851): "seventy as an atonement for the seventy nations."
[7]An addition also in Nf. Ps.-J. adds also in vv. 21, 24, 27, 30, 33, 37, but not in Nf.
[8]*Ed. pr.:* "twelve for twelve orders."
[9]Repeated in MS; but in *ed. pr.* omits because of HT lemma.

the oxen and the rams and the lambs by their numbers according to their prescribed ritual. 28. And one kid for a sin offering *for one order,* besides the regular burnt offering and *the fine wheat flour* for the cereal offering and *the wine* for its libation. 29. And on the sixth day *of the festival of Booths,* eight oxen *for eight orders;* two rams *for two orders;* fourteen perfect year-old lambs *for thirteen orders: one of them shall be offered (for) two (orders), and twelve of them one by one;* 30. and their cereal offering *of fine wheat flour* and *wine* for their libations *which you shall offer* with the oxen and the rams and the lambs by their numbers according to the prescribed ritual. 31. And one kid for a sin offering *for one order,* besides the regular burnt offering and *the fine wheat flour* for its cereal offering and *wine* for its libation. And a vase of water[10] shall be poured out on the[11] day *of the festival of Booths, a good remembrance for the showers of rain.* 32. And on the seventh day *of the festival of Booths* you shall offer seven oxen *for seven orders;* two rams *for two orders;* fourteen perfect year-old lambs *for fourteen orders. The number of all the lambs (are) ninety-eight in order to atone for the ninety-eight curses.*[12] 33. Their cereal offering *of fine wheat flour* and *wine* for their libations, *which you shall offer*[13] with the oxen and the rams and the lambs by their numbers according to the prescribed ritual. 34. And one kid for a sin offering *for one order,* besides the regular burnt offering and *the fine wheat flour* for its cereal offering and the *wine* for its libation. 35. And on the eighth day *you shall be gathering with joy from your booths*[14] *into your houses, a joyous gathering and a festival day, and you shall have a holy convocation;*[15] no menial work shall be done. 36. But you shall offer a burnt offering *which shall be accepted with pleasure before* the Lord; light[16] offerings—one ox (offered) *before the Lord,* one ram *for a unique people,* only seven perfect lambs *for the joy of seven days.* 37. Their cereal offering *of fine wheat flour* and the *wine* for their libations *which you shall offer* with oxen and rams and lambs by their numbers according to the prescribed ritual. 38. And one kid for a sin offering, besides the regular burnt offering and *the fine flour* for its cereal offering and *the wine* for its libation. 39. These shall *you offer before* the Lord *at the time of* your holidays besides your vow offerings *which you vowed during the festival which you brought on the festival*[17] and your freewill offerings (which you added) to your burnt offerings and to your cereal offering, and to your libations, *and for your holy offerings.'"*[18]

Notes, Chapter 29

[10]Also Nf; *m. Sukk.* 4:9 speaks of filling flasks at the Pool of Siloam and bringing them to the Temple on each of the seven days of the Feast of Booths, where water was mixed with wine. This practice is discussed in Gen 35:14 (Ps.-J.); see Forestell, 1979, 43 (#196) and 97; see further McNamara's note.

[11]MS leaves blank space for one word; Nf supplies *štytyh,* "sixth."

[12]Mentioned in Deut 28:16-68 (Ps.-J.).

[13]An addition also in Nf.

[14]See McNamara's note on v. 35.

[15]*Sifre Num.* 151 (607); Lev 23:35; Num 29:12; the phraseology found in Ps.-J. reflects both the phraseology of Ps.-J. ("holy convocation") and Nf ("a feast day"). *Sifre Num.* (Kuhn) considers (contrary to Horowitz, 151) that this extended phrase is a gloss in *Sifre Num.* The Targums (Ps.-J. and Nf) seem to have a double interpretation of the HT "a solemn assembly."

[16]*Num. R.* (852).

[17]*Sifre Num.* 152 (608): "gift" as a pilgrimage offering.

[18]HT: *šlmykm,* "your peace offerings"; see Exod 10:25. The general view is that "peace offering" is a "sacred offering"; see *m. Zeb.* 5:7.

CHAPTER 30

1. And Moses spoke with the Israelites all that the Lord had commanded Moses. 2. Then Moses spoke with the officers[1] of the tribes of the Israelites, saying: "This is the word that the Lord *spoke,*[2] *saying:* 3. 'If a man *of thirteen years*[3] made a vow *before* the Lord or swore an oath binding (himself) by an obligation to abstain from *anything which is permitted*[4] to himself, he shall not break[5] his word. *However, the court can release him (from his vow); but if they do not release him,* he shall act according to every (vow) that shall come from his mouth. 4. When a woman *who has not passed twelve years* shall have made a vow *before* the Lord or shall have bound herself by a vow, while in her father's house *until twelve years,*[6] 5. and her father shall hear her vow and the obligation that she herself made, being in agreement, her father shall be silent about it. All her vows shall stand, and every obligation which she herself made shall stand. 6. But if her father prohibit[7] her on the day that he heard, *or he did not agree to the oath and annulled it after he heard,* every vow and oath that she herself made shall not stand,[8] and (her father) shall be releasing and pardoning her before the Lord from the moment he (her father) released her from the power of the vow. 7. And if she is *given in marriage* to a man and her vow, on her or her lips, is binding, for she has bound herself *in her father's house and her father had not freed (her) while she was still unmarried, then when she is given in marriage to a man, they shall stand.*[9] 8. *But if after she was married she vowed* and her husband heard, if on the day that he heard he agreed to their fulfillment and he be silent to her, then her vow shall stand and her obligation which she herself made shall stand. 9. But if on the day that her husband heard, he prohibited her and released the vow which is incumbent on her and the utterance of her lips to which she bound herself, then she shall be freed before the Lord and she shall be forgiven. 10. But the vow of a widow or a divorced woman, everything that she herself makes binding shall stand against her. 11. Yet if (a woman), *while she was* in the house of her husband *or she was not of the age of majority,*[10] she herself made a vow or bound herself with an oath 12. and her husband heard of it and remained silent about it, and did not prohibit her *or he had died while she was not of the age of majority,* then all the vows shall stand and all the obligations that she herself made shall stand, *and her father shall not have the authority, at the same time, to annul*

Notes, Chapter 30

[1]Here *'mrkl,* but Onq. and Nf *r(')yš,* "chiefs."
[2]Here *mll,* but Onq. and Nf *pqd,* "command."
[3]*Sifre Num.* 153 (612): even a thirteen-year-old is considered a minor.
[4]*Sifre Num.* 153 (612): even though still a minor, he is responsible for his pledge.
[5]Here *pss;* see Clarke, 1984, 482, but Onq. and Nf *bṭl.*
[6]*Sifre Num.* 153 (617): a girl is considered a minor until twelve and a half years of age.
[7]*bṭl* here and Nf, but Onq. *'dy,* "cancel."
[8]plural; Nf *yqwm* (singular); see v. 12, where Nf and Ps.-J. both have plural.
[9]*Sifre Num.* 153 (625): a vow is binding whether in her father's or husband's house.
[10]That is, twelve and a half years of age.

them. 13. But if her husband surely release[11] them on the day that he heard, everything that came out of her lips to be a vow or to bind her own person shall not stand. And if her husband annuls them *and she did not know and acted,*[12] it shall be forgiven her *before* the Lord. 14. Every vow and every oath sworn to afflict the soul, her husband may fulfill or her husband may annul. 15. But if he (her husband) was surely silent and *agreed* to it from the day *that he heard* to *the next day,*[13] then every vow of hers or every obligation of hers shall stand. For *by his silence,* he confirmed them, because he was silent to her and he *agreed* and he did not release (her) *on the day that he heard.* 16. But if he surely shall release her[14] *one day* after he heard, *there is not much for her in the release, and if then the word be broken, her husband or her father* shall accept her sin.'"[15] 17. These are *the teachings of* the Laws that the Lord commanded Moses (concerning the relationships) between a man and his wife, between a father and his daughter *in the days* of her youth *while she is still* in her father's house, *but not in the days of her youth when she is in her husband's house.*[16]

CHAPTER 31

1. Then the Lord spoke with Moses, saying: 2. "Take revenge on the Midianites for the punishment (caused) the Israelites, and after that you will be gathered to your people." 3. So Moses spoke with the people, saying: "Equip men *among* you into an army that *will fight war* against Midian to mete out punishment[1] upon Midian on behalf of the Lord's people; 4. you shall send into the army a thousand men from every tribe of Israel." 5. *Righteous men, willing to surrender their lives, were chosen*[2] from the thousands of Israel, a thousand from each tribe, twelve thousand armed soldiers. 6. Then Moses sent them, a thousand from each tribe, to the

Notes, Chapter 30

[11]Here *šry,* but Onq. and Nf *bṭl.*
[12]*Sifre Num.* 154 (634).
[13]*Sifre Num.* 156 (641-642): i.e., in a twenty-four hour period.
[14]Here *šry lh.*
[15]*Sifre Num.* 153 (611).
[16]*Sifre Num.* 156 (643): so says R. Ishmael.

Notes, Chapter 31

[1]HT: "the Lord's vengeance" is modified in Ps.-J. to be unspecific, whereas Onq. has "punishment for justice on behalf"; Nf translated literally; parallels for Ps.-J. are found in 32:20, 22, 27, 29, 31; see Grossfeld, *The Aramaic Bible,* vol. 8, p. 151, n. 1, where he notes that rabbinic thinking says that the punishment is for the benefit of the people, even though the HT says "the Lord's vengeance."
[2]HT: "were provided" (nip *msr*); here and Onq. itp *bḥr,* but Nf itp *ḥyl,* "enlisted."

army, them and Phinehas bar Eleazar, the priest, to the army, along with the sacred *Urim*[3] *and Thummim by which to inquire;* and the trumpets *for sounding the alarm in his hands to gather (the people) together: to encamp or to move the camp of Israel forward.* 7. And they fought[4] against Midian *and surrounded her from three sides,*[5] just as the Lord commanded Moses, and they slew all the males. 8. Along with the slain of their camps they slew the kings of the Midianites: Evi, Reqem, Zur, *who is Balak,*[6] and Hur, and Reba, the five kings of Midian. And they slew Balaam bar Beor with the sword. *And it was when Balaam the sinner,*[7] *saw Phinehas, the priest, pursuing him, he made words of magic and flew in the air of the heaven.*[8] *Immediately Phinehas recalled the great and holy Name and flew after him and seized him by his head and brought him down, drew the sword, and sought to slay him; but he opened his mouth with words of prayers of supplication and said to Phinehas: "If you will spare my life, I promise you that all the days that I live I shall not curse your people." He answered and said to him: "Are you not Laban the Aramean*[9] *who sought to destroy Jacob our father, and went down to Egypt in order to destroy his descendants, and after they had come out of Egypt, you incited wicked Amalek against them, and now are you sent to curse them? But when you saw that your work did not take effect and the Memra of the Lord did not heed you, you persuaded the evil king Balak to put his daughters at the crossroads of the way to lead them astray,*[10] *and because of this twenty-four thousand of them fell. Therefore there is no possibility again of sparing your life." And immediately he drew his sword from its sheath and slew him.* 9. Then the Israelites took captive the Midianite women and their children, and they plundered all their cattle and all their flocks and all their belongings. 10. They burned with fire all their cities[11] and *houses of their princes and high places of their worship.*[12] 11. And they took captive all the plunder and all the booty of man and beast. 12. Then they brought to Moses and to Eleazar the priest and to all the congregation of the Israelites the captives, the booty, and the plunder at the camp in the plains of Moab near the Jordan at Jericho. 13. So Moses, Eleazar the priest, and all the officers[13] of the congregation went out to meet them outside of the

Notes, Chapter 31

[3]See Num 27:21; Ginzberg, *Legends,* III, 409: Moses gave Phinehas the Urim and Thummim "that he might, if necessary, consult God."

[4]HT: *wyyṣb'w* is translated by the itp *ḥyl,* although this is not the usual targumic translation of "to fight"; but the noun *ḥyl* translated the HT *ṣb',* "army." Onq., Ps.-J., and Nfmg translated with *ḥyl,* but Nf renders the HT *'zdyynw,* "they warred."

[5]Leaving the fourth side for escape; *Sifre Num.* 157(648).

[6]See Num 25:15 (Ps.-J.).

[7]Ginzberg, *Legends,* III, 409; VI, 143; *Sifre Num.* 157(648): "Balaam flies by means of sorceries."

[8]*Num. R.* (816): Balaam flies with five Midianite kings. Also when Balaam heard that twenty-four thousand Israelites had been slain, he returned to get his reward from the Midianite king.

[9]See Num 22:5 (Ps.-J.).

[10]See Num 24:14 (Ps.-J.).

[11]Onq. and Nf add "wherein they dwell," as in HT.

[12]*Sifre Num.* 157(649) HT "their strongholds" (*ṭyrtm*) in the Targums is as here based on *Sifre Num.* "and all their *ṭirotam*"—those places where they kept under guard their idol worshiping sanctuaries; as if the word is from *nṭr,* "to guard."

[13]Here *'mrkwl;* see note on Num 7:2.

camp. 14. And Moses was angry[14] with the military *commanders*[15] *who were appointed* over the army, the chiefs of the thousands and the chiefs of the hundreds who came from making war. 15. Then Moses said to them: "Have you spared every female?" 16. These are the ones who were *the stumbling block*[16] for the Israelites according to Balaam's *advice,* dealing falsely before the Lord about the matter of (the idol of) Peor so the pestilence[17] came upon the congregation of the Lord. 17. So, now, slay every male child and every woman who has known a man sexually; 18. but every female child, *place all before the glistening crown of holiness*[18] *and look upon her: whoever has been married to a man, her face shall become yellow, and* whoever does not know about sexual relation, *her face shall be red as fire;* and you shall spare them for you. 19. And as for you, remain outside the camp seven days; whoever slew a man or whoever approached a dead person, *you shall sprinkle*[19] on the third day and on the seventh both you and your captives. 20. *You shall sprinkle* every garment and whatever is of leather and every work of goat's hair, *horn or bone,* and every vessel of wood. 21. Then Eleazar the priest said to the men of war who returned from the war: "This is the instruction of the decree of the Law which the Lord commanded Moses: 22. *Yet,* (you shall pass through fire) these (articles) only *without their rust:* the gold, the silver, the bronze, the iron, the tin, and the lead, *the objects (which have been manufactured), but not the roughly shaped and simple ones;*[20] 23. everything *whose custom* is to be put into the fire: *cauldrons, pots, spits, and grills* you shall put in the fire and they shall be purified. *After this you shall sprinkle* them with water which is fit for purifying, the unclean. And all that cannot be put into the fire: *vessels, glasses, ladles, kettles* you shall pass through *forty seah of* water. 24. Then you shall cleanse your garments on the seventh day and purify (them), and after this you shall enter the camp." 25. Then the Lord said to Moses, saying: 26. "*Take the residue* of what you have taken as booty from the captives (men and animals) and you shall make the count, you and Eleazar the priest and the chiefs of the clans of the congregation. 27. Then you shall divide the plunder[21] among the reconnoitering troops *who captured the rich spoils in the war, who went out in the army,* and among the entire congregation. 28. And you shall set aside for the men, fighters of the war and who went out in the army, the

Notes, Chapter 31

[14]HT: "was angry" (*qṣp*), as Onq. and Nf (*rgz*), but here *kns.*

[15]HT: *pqwdy;* Nf *skwm,* as does Ps.-J. in Num 26:63; but here *'ysṭrṭygyn* (*strategos;* Jastrow, 92); see Clarke, 1984, 65, and McNamara's note; see also note on Num 1:21.

[16]See Num 24:25 (Ps.-J.); *twql';* see Clarke, 1984, 607.

[17]*mwtn'.*

[18]The high priest's diadem; see Exod 28:36; 39:30; Ginzberg, *Legends,* III, 413; VI, 145: Moses ordered men and women to be killed but "to spare the young girls." To determine their age, they were led in front of "the gold plate of the miter on the high priest's forehead." *Midrash Aggada* on Num 31:9 notes that it is the holy ark that replaces the high priest's diadem. In *Protoevangelium of James* 5:1 Joachim, the father of Mary, observed the high priest's miter to ascertain whether he (Joachim) was free from sin or not.

[19]HT: "you shall purify" (itp *ḥṭ'*): here and Onq. ap *ndy,* but Nf *dky;* also v. 20; see Clarke, 1984, 375.

[20]*Sifre Num.* 157(659).

[21]*dbrt'* from *dbr,* "to lead, to seize."

assessment[22] for the Name of the Lord: one woman out of five hundred, likewise (of the men),[23] the oxen, the asses, and the sheep. 29. You shall take from their half *which is the men's portion, warriors of the war,* and give (it) to Eleazar the priest as a separation offering in the Lord's Name. 30. And from the half (which is the portion) for the Israelites you shall take one of the captured out of fifty, *of the women,* of the oxen, of the asses, (of the sheep) and of all the animals, and give them to the Levites, keepers of the watch of the Lord's tent." 31. So Moses and Eleazar the priest did just as the Lord commanded Moses. 32. And *the sum of* the booty, the rest of the plunder which the people *who went out in the army* plundered, the number of the sheep were six hundred and seventy-five thousand; 33. and of the oxen, seventy-two thousand; 34. and of the asses, sixty-one thousand; 35. and of the human beings, of women who had not known a man sexually, the total number of persons, thirty-two thousand. 36. And the half, the portion *of the men* who went out in the army, makes the number of the sheep three hundred and thirty-seven thousand five hundred; 37. and the total of the assessment for the Lord's Name was from the sheep six hundred and seventy-five; 38. *and the total* of the oxen, thirty-six thousand; but the total of the assessment for the Lord's *name* was seventy-two, 39. and of the asses, thirty thousand five hundred; but the total of the assessment for the Lord's Name,[24] 40. thirty-two souls. 41. Then Moses gave to Eleazar the priest the total of the assessment of those set aside for the Lord, just as the Lord commanded Moses. 42. And the Israelite's half which Moses divided from (that of) the men who *went out* in the army; 43. and *the total of* the half of the congregation (consisted of) from the sheep, three hundred and thirty-seven thousand five hundred; 44. and *the total of* the oxen, thirty-six thousand; 45. and *the total of* the asses, thirty thousand five hundred; 46. and (the total of) *the women,* sixteen thousand. 47. Then Moses took from the half share of the Israelites, what was captured, one from fifty, both from the women and from the animals and gave them to the Levites, keepers of the duties of the Lord's tent, just as the Lord commanded Moses. 48. Then the military *commanders who were appointed* over the thousands of soldiers, the chiefs of the thousands and the chiefs of the hundreds, approached Moses 49. and they said to Moses: "Your servants have taken a census of the men, fighters of the war who had been *with* us, not one of us *went astray.*[25] 50. So we have brought our gift for the Lord's Name. *When the Lord delivered the Midianites into our hands and we conquered their land and their capital, and we entered into their chambers*[26] *and saw their daughters, fair, tender, and delicate, and every man*

Notes, Chapter 31

[22]HT: *mks,* "tribute"; Nf: "separated offering"; but see vv. 29, 41, 52 (Ps.-J.); see McNamara's note.
[23]Following the HT.
[24]MS omits due to homoeoteleuton on *lšm' dyhwh,* the end of v. 39 and most of v. 40.
[25]*šg':* in this sense Jastrow (1521) and also in Onq.; v. 50 suggests that the men did go astray in a moral sense; Ginzberg, *Legends,* III, 412; VI, 145: not one of the army neglected the slightest religious duty.
[26]Aramaic *ṭryqlyn* = Latin *triclinium.* The extended midrash here and in Nf seems to be based on the idea of self-discipline (Deut 21:10-14). The list of jewelry reflects the list in Gen 49:22 and Exod 35:22 (Nf).

who found on them jewels of gold loosened the diadems[27] *from their heads, the earrings from their ears, the necklaces from their necks, the bracelets from their arms, the rings from their fingers, the brooches*[28] *from their bosoms.*[29] *But with all of this far be it from us to raise our eyes! And we did not look at one of them in order not to sin with anyone of them and so that we not die by the death by which the wicked die in the world to come.*[30] *And may this be recalled in our favor at the day of the great judgment, to atone for our souls before the Lord."* 51. So Moses and Eleazar the priest took the gold from them, every article which was crafted. 52. And the *total* of all the gold set apart, which was separated for *the Name of* the Lord, was sixteen thousand seven hundred and fifty shekels, belonging to the chiefs of thousands and the chiefs of hundreds. 53. As for the warriors, they had taken spoil, every man for himself. 54. So Moses and Eleazar the priest took the gold belonging to the chiefs of the thousands and hundreds and brought it to the tent of meeting as a *good* remembrance for the Israelites before the Lord.

CHAPTER 32

1. And the Reubenites and the Gadites possessed much cattle in great abundance, and they saw the land of *Mikwar*[1] and the land of Gilead, and behold the place was one suitable for cattle sheds.[2] 2. So the Gadites and Reubenites came and said to Moses and to Eleazar the priest and to the leaders of the congregation, saying: 3. "Maklalta,[3] and Madbashta,[4] Mikwar, Beth Nimrin, Beth Heshbon, Maalath, Meda, Shiran, the Burial-Place-of-Moses and Beon,[5] 4. the land which the Lord conquered and *its inhabitants*[6] *destroyed* before the congregation of Israel is a

Notes, Chapter 31

[27]*qwryyh* here, Nf, and Frg. Tg. (V) raises the question of etymology: Sokoloff (506) "head ornament"; *m. Shab.* 6:1 "(go out) with a golden city," which Danby (1933, p. 104, n. 13) notes is a tiara shaped like the city of Jerusalem; see McNamara's note for additional information on this word.

[28]*mḥwkyy',* as in Onq., but Nf *m'zqyn.*

[29]Also Nf.

[30]Self-discipline is in evidence here as a reference to the future judgment: Gen 39:10 (Ps.-J. and Nf) and Deut 6:25 (Ps.-J.); 21:10-14 (Ps.-J.).

Notes, Chapter 32

[1]HT: "Jazer"; also Onq., but Nf "Mikbar"; at 21:32 (Ps.-J.) "Mikbar"; here we see a free interchange of double *waw* and *beth;* see also vv. 34–38; see Jastrow, 781. "Jazer" is a district in Piraea.

[2]See vv. 16, 24 (*dyryn d''n*), but vv. 1, 4 *byt b'yr.*

[3]Also some Onq. MSS.

[4]Ginzberg, *Legends,* III, 415; VI, 146; some Onq. MSS *mlbšt';* various place names suggest richness of the land.

[5]HT: "Ataroth, Dibon, Jazer, Nimrah, Heshbon, Elealeh, Sebam, Nebo, Beon," as also Onq., but Nf substitutes "Mikbar" for "Jazer," and "Simath" for "Sebam"; see vv. 34–38.

[6]HT: "congregation of Israel," as also Nf, but Onq. as here: "inhabitants."

land suitable for cattle sheds, and your servants have cattle." 5. Then they said: "If we find compassion before you, let that land be given to your servants, an inheritance. And let us not cross over the Jordan." 6. So Moses said to the Gadites and the Reubenites: "Shall your brothers go out to war while you live here? 7. And why should you *dismiss*[7] the ambition of the Israelites from crossing to the land which the Lord has given them? 8. So did your fathers do, when I sent them from Rekem Gea[8] to survey the land. 9. And they went up to the valley of Eshkol and saw the land; then they *dismissed* the ambitions of the Israelites, so that they would not enter the land which the Lord had given them. 10. And the Lord's anger was great on that day and he swore, saying: 11. 'The men who came out of Egypt from twenty years old and up shall not see the land which I promised to Abraham, Isaac, and Jacob, for they have not acted in perfect accord with my Fear; 12. none except Caleb bar Jephunneh the Kennizite and Joshua bar Nun, for they have walked with perfect reverence for the Lord's *Fear.*'[9] 13. And the Lord's anger was great against Israel, so he made them wander[10] in the desert forty years until the entire generation who did that evil *before* the Lord had come to an end. 14. And behold, you have arisen in your ancestors' place, disciples[11] of sinning men, to further increase the great anger of the Lord against Israel. 15. For if you turn back from following after *his Fear,* then he shall again delay[12] them in the desert and you shall destroy this entire people." 16. Then they approached him and said: "We shall build sheds for our cattle[13] here and cities for our children. 17. As for us, we shall go (fully) armed *among the* Israelites until we bring them into their (destined) place, and our children shall live in fortified[14] cities because of the inhabitants of the land. 18. We shall not return to our houses until the Israelites take possession, each man, of his inheritance. 19. For we shall not take possession with them across the Jordan and beyond, for our inheritance belonged to us across the Jordan to the east." 20. Then Moses said to them: "If you shall do this thing, if you shall go (fully) armed before the Lord*'s people*[15] to fight a war, 21. and if all those of yours who are armed shall cross over the Jordan before the Lord*'s people* to fight the war until he has driven out the enemies before him, 22. and the land be conquered before the Lord*'s people,* then after this you shall return and you shall be acquitted before the Lord and Israel; and that land shall be yours as an inheritance before the Lord. 23. But if you do not do this thing, behold you shall have sinned *before* the Lord, *your God,* and

Notes, Chapter 32

[7]Here *bṭl r'wt.*

[8]HT: "Kadesh"; see Gen 14:7 (Ps.-J.); Num 34:4; see Davies, 1972, 152–163, considers this place to be Petra; Alexander, 1974, 192–199.

[9]HT: "Lord"; here and Onq. *dḥlt',* "Fear," but Nf "Memra of"; see same expression and distribution in v. 15.

[10]HT: *n'm,* "to wander"; here and Nf *ṭlṭl,* but Onq. *'ḥr,* "to delay"; see v. 15.

[11]HT: *trbwt,* "offspring"; here and Onq. "disciples," but Nf literal (*trbw*); Nfmg and Frg. Tgs. (PV) *sgy,* "increase."

[12]HT: *'ḥr,* "to delay," as in Onq. and here, but Nf *ṭlṭl,* as in 32:13; see note 9 above.

[13]Nfmg: *nkysynn,* "our herds."

[14]Here *ḥqr'* = Akra, but Nf *tly,* "tall cities," and Onq. *kryk,* "fortified."

[15]HT: *lpny yhwh,* "before the Lord," as also Nf; here and Onq. "before the Lord's people"; see also vv. 21–22, 27, 29, 32.

know that your sin shall overtake you. 24. Build for yourselves cities for your children and sheds for your flocks, and what you have promised[16] you shall do." 25. And the Gadites and Reubenites said in agreement to Moses, saying: "Your servants shall do all that our lord[17] has commanded. 26. Our children, our wives, all our flocks, and our cattle shall remain[18] there in the cities of Gilead; 27. but your servants shall cross, all armed for war, before the Lord*'s people* to fight, just as our lord[19] has spoken." 28. Then Moses appointed over them Eleazar the priest[20] and the chiefs of the clans of the Israelite tribes. 29. Then Moses said to them: "If the Gadites and Reubenites, all armed for war, shall cross the Jordan with you, (before) the Lord*'s people,* and the land be conquered before you, then you shall give them the land of Gilead as an inheritance. 30. But if they shall not cross with you (fully) armed, then they shall have possessions among you in the land of Canaan." 31. So the Gadites and Reubenites answered *and said:* "All that the Lord spoke to your servant, so shall we do. 32. As for us, we shall cross (fully) armed before the Lord*'s people* to the land of Canaan, but with us our inheritance shall be retained on this side of the Jordan." 33. Then Moses gave to them, to the Gadites and the Reubenites, and to the half tribe of Manasseh, son of Joseph, the kingdom of Sihon, king of the Amorites, and the kingdom of Og, king of Matanan,[21] the land with its cities at the frontiers of the cities of the land round about. 34. The Gadites built *Madbashtha and Maklalta*[22] *and Lehayyat*[23] 35. *and Meklalat-Shophana and Mikwar*[24] *and Ramtha* 36. *and the great cities of Beth Nemrin* and Beth Haran, fortified cities with sheds for flocks. 37. The Reubenites built *Beth Heshbon and Maalath Mera, and the city of two streets paved with marble which was Berosha,*[25] 38. *and the Burial-Place-of-Moses and the city of Balak where they destroyed the idols of Peor in the dwelling of the house of the high places and the city which is surrounded by a wall, engraved* with the names *of its heroes,* and Shiran. *After they had rebuilt* (them), they called their (cities') names after the names of the men who built (them).[26] 39. Then the sons of Makir bar Manasseh went to Gilead and conquered it and drove out the Amorites who were in it. 40. So Moses gave Gilead to Makir bar Manasseh and he lived there. 41. And Jair bar Manasseh went and conquered their villages and called them the villages of Jair. 42. Then Nobah went and conquered Kenath and *its villages* and called it Nobah after his name.

Notes, Chapter 32

[16]Lit. "what has come out of your mouth."

[17]Lit. "our master."

[18]Lit. "be."

[19]See note 16.

[20]HT, Onq. and Nf: "and Joshua bar Nun."

[21]Also Nf, but "Butnim" in 21:33; Ps.-J. in 21:33 as here. A place east of the Sea of Galilee called "Battanaia" in Greek; see Josephus, *BJ* I 398.

[22]See v. 3.

[23]HT: "Aroer" as Onq., but Nf as here; Nfmg and Frg. Tg. (V) "fortress"; see 21:33 for a similar distribution. By contrast, Ps.-J. in Deut 2:36; 3:12; and 4:49 has "Aroer," as HT and Onq. but contrary to Nf.

[24]See note on 32:1.

[25]See 22:39; Onq. and Nf "Kiriathayim," as HT.

[26]Ginzberg, *Legends,* III, 416; VI, 146: the Israelites gave new names to places which suggested the idol Peor.

CHAPTER 33

1. These are the journeys of the Israelites who came out from the land of Egypt, according to their armies, *after miracles were performed for them*[1] under the leadership[2] of Moses and Aaron. 2. And Moses recorded their starting point for their (various) journeys according to *the Memra of*[3] the Lord, and these are their journeys according to their starting points. 3. And they moved from Pelusium[4] in the month *of Nisan. After having eaten the* Passover *feast,* the Israelites went out defiantly[5] in the sight of all the Egyptians. 4. And the Egyptians were burying all their first-born whom the Lord had slain, and *the Memra of* the Lord made judgment against their idols:[6] *the molten images were melted, the stone idols were shattered, the clay idols were broken into fragments, the wooden idols became ashes,*[7] *and the cattle (idols) were put to death.* 5. And the Israelites set out from Pelusium and camped in Sukkoth, *the place which seven clouds of Glory covered.*[8] 6. Then they set out from Sukkoth and camped in Etham, which was on the edge of the desert. 7. Then they set out from Etham and returned to *the entrance of* Hiratha,[9] a resting place before the idol Zephon, and they camped before Migdol. 8. And they set out from *the exodus of* Hiratha[10] and crossed in the midst of the sea. *Then they came out from the sea and went by the shore of the sea, gathering purple shells*[11] *and pearls.*[12] Then *after this* they went a three days' journey in the desert of Etham and camped at Marah. 9. Then they set out from Marah and came to Elim; and at Elim (were) twelve springs of water *(corresponding) to the twelve tribes* and seventy palm trees *corresponding to the seventy wise men,*[13] and they camped there *by the waters.*[14] 10. So they departed from Elim and camped *by the shore of* the Reed Sea.

Notes, Chapter 33

[1]*Num. R.* (864) considers Ps 77:21 "thou didst lead" to refer to the "wonders (*nifla'oth*) done for them," according to R. Joshua.

[2]Here *byd.*

[3]HT: "mouth of" and Nf "decree of the *Memra* of."

[4]HT: "Ramses"; see Clarke, 1984, 679.

[5]HT: *byd rm,* "triumphantly" (RSV); "boldly" (Jewish translation); see Exod 14:8: "defiantly" (RSV); Num 15:30; Nf "redeemed with head uncovered"; Onq. as here.

[6]HT: *'lhym,* "deities"; *t'wwt* in the Targums; see Grossfeld, *The Aramaic Bible,* vol. 6, p. 113, n. 20, on Gen 31:30.

[7]See Exod 12:12 (Ps.-J.) for a similar midrash; here the last phrase, "the cattle (idols) . . . ," is additional.

[8]See Exod 12:37; 13:20; Num 14:14; Deut 32:10 (Ps.-J.). *Mek.* to Exod 12:37 (I, 108) according to Aqiba interprets "Sukkoth" as "tents." Exod 12:37 (Ps.-J.) has a more extensive midrash.

[9]HT: Pi-haḥiroth"; Onq. as here, but Nf *pwndqy,* "taverns"; see Exod 14:2 (Ps.-J.), where *Mek.* to Exod 14:2 interprets *ḥrwt* as the "licentiousness of the Egyptians."

[10]HT: *mpny hḥyrt,* "from before Haḥiroth"; Onq. "from in front of Haḥiroth" and Nf "from before the taverns of Haḥiroth"; Ps.-J. *pyrwqy* is difficult and the root *prq* suggests "to separate, to release," hence "exodus," but there may also be confusion with the text of Nf *pwndqy* as in v. 7.

[11]Aramaic *'wnkyn:* Jastrow (29) corrects to *qwnkyn,* "purple shells"; see *mrglyyn w'bnyn ṭbyn,* "pearls and (precious) stones"; Exod 14:9 (Ps.-J.).

[12]Ginzberg, *Legends,* VI, 9; see Exod 14:9 (Ps.-J.).

[13]See Exod 15:27 (Ps.-J. and Nf) for the same expression; Frg. Tg. (V) notes the "seventy" as members of the Sanhedrin; Jaubert, 1971, 453–460 discusses the symbolism of the "twelve."

[14]HT: *'l ym swp,* but Ps.-J. is correct, since they are not yet at the Reed Sea.

11. And they set out from *the shore of* the Reed Sea and camped in the Sin desert. 12. And they set out from the Sin desert and camped in Dophka. 13. Then they set out from Dophka and camped at the fortified city.[15] 14. Then they set out from the fortified castle and camped at Rephidim; and *because their hands were neglectful*[16] *of the words of the Law,* there was no water there for the people to drink. 15. So they set out from Rephidim and camped in the Sinai desert. 16. And they set out from the Sinai desert and camped at the Graves *of Those Craving Meat.* 17. Then they set out from the Graves *of Those Craving Meat* and camped at Hazeroth, *the place where Miriam the prophetess was struck with leprosy.*[17] 18. Then they set out from Hazeroth and camped at Rithmah, *a place where there were many Broam trees.*[18] 19. So they set out from the place where there *were many Broam trees* and camped at Rimmon, *whose fruit is firm.*[19] 20. Then they set out from Rimmon, *whose fruit is firm,* and camped at Libna, *a place built of brick.* 21. And they set out from Libna and camped at Beth Rissa.[20] 22. Then they set out from Rissa and camped at Kehelathah, *a place where Korah and his company gathered against Moses and Aaron.*[21] 23. And they set out from Kehelathah and camped at the mountain whose fruits were beautiful.[22] 24. Then they set out from the mountain whose fruits were beautiful and camped at Haradah, *a place where they were anxious about the evilness of the plague.*[23] 25. So they set out from Haradah and camped at Makheloth, *a place of assembly.* 26. And they set out from Makheloth and camped in lower[24] Makheloth. 27. Then they set out from lower[24] Makheloth and camped at Terakh. 28. And they set out from Terakh and camped at Mithqa, *a place of Sweet Waters.*[25] 29. Then they set out from the place *of Sweet Waters* and camped at Hashmona. 30. And they set out from Hashmona and camped at the Place of Chastisement.[26] 31. Then they set out from the Place of Chastisement and camped at the Wells of Distress.[27] 32. And they set out from the *Wells of Distress* and camped at the Cliffs[28] and *the place was called* Gidgad. 33. Then they set out from *the Cliffs of* Gidgad and camped at Jotbath, *Good and Restful Place.* 34. Then they set out from the *Good and Restful Place* and camped at *the Ford.*[29] 35. And

Notes, Chapter 33

[15]HT: *'lwš,* "Alush," as Onq. and Nf, but here *krk tqyp.*
[16]*rpwn* here but omitted in Onq. and Nf; see Exod 17:1 (Ps.-J.), a play on "Rephidim."
[17]See Num 12:10.
[18]HT: "Rithmah"; here *'ylny rtmy* (Jastrow, 1503: "broom").
[19]HT: "Rimmon-perez"; "rimmon" is pomegranate in Hebrew; refers to the density of the fruit.
[20]See Gen 14:17 (Ps.-J.).
[21]See Num 16:3.
[22]HT: "Mount Shepher"; based on the root *špr,* "beautiful."
[23]HT: *ḥrd,* "to fear."
[24]HT: "Taḥath"; the Targums interpret as from *tḥt,* "under, below."
[25]*mtq,* "to be sweet."
[26]HT: *msrwt,* "Moseroth"; here *mrdwt',* "discipline."
[27]HT: *y'qn,* "Bene Jaakan."
[28]HT: *hr hgdgd,* "Hor Haggidgda."
[29]HT: "Abronah"; Aramaic *'br,* "to cross over."

they set out from *the Ford* and camped at *Kerak-Tarngolah.*[30] 36. Then they set out from *Kerak Tarngolah* and camped in the desert of Thorn-Palms, at the Iron Mountain[31] *which is Reqem.*[32] 37. Then they set out from Reqem and camped at Mount *Amanus,*[33] at the edge of the land of Edom. 38. Then Aaron the priest ascended Mount *Amanus* according to *the Memra of* the Lord and died there, in the fortieth year of Israel's exodus from Egypt in the fifth month on the first of the month. 39. And Aaron was one hundred and twenty-three years old when he died at Mount *Amanus.*[34] 40. And the sinner Amalek heard. He *joined with* the Canaanites and ruled at Arad; *his dwelling house* was in *the land to* the south.[35] When the Israelites came *he fought against them, but they destroyed them and their cities.* 41. Then they set out from Mount *Amanus* and camped at Zalmonah, *a place of briars and thorns*[36] *in the land of the Edomites. It was there that the soul of the people was distressed on the road.* 42. So they set out from Zalmonah and camped at Punon, *a place where the Lord let loose burning serpents*[37] *against them and where their complaints ascended into heaven.* 43. Then they set out from *the place where the Lord let loose against them the burning serpents* and camped at Oboth. 44. And they set out from Oboth and camped at *the Ford of* Abarayya on the Moabite border.[38] 45. So they set out from *the Ford* and camped at Dibon *the Chance.* 46. And they set out from Dibon *the Chance*[39] and camped at Almon Diblathayma; *even there the well was hidden from them because they had abandoned the words of the Law which are sweet as (dried) figs.*[40] 47. Then they set out from Almon Diblathayma and camped at Mount Abarayya before the Place of Moses' Grave.[41] 48. Then they set out from Mount Abarayya and camped on the plains of Moab by the Jordan (opposite) Jericho. 49. And they camped by the Jordan from Beth-Yeshimoth as far as the plain of Shittin in the plains of Moab. 50. Then the Lord spoke with Moses in the plains of Moab by the Jordan (opposite) Jericho, saying: 51. "Speak with the Israelites and say to them: 'When you have crossed the Jordan to the land of Canaan, 52. then you shall drive out before you all the inhabitants of the land and you shall bring to an end all their *places of worship,*[42] and all their molten images shall you bring to an end,[43] and lay waste all their *high places.*

Notes, Chapter 33

[30]HT: "Ezion-Geber"; see Deut 2:8 (Ps.-J. and Nf) *trngwlh,* "cock, watchtower"; here lit. "city of the Cock," said to be near Caeserea Philippi (Jastrow, 1700).

[31]See Alexander, 1974, 199ff.

[32]That is, "Kadesh"; see Gen 14:8 (Onq.); Num 13:26 (Nf); see McNamara, 1972, 199.

[33]HT: "Hor"; see Clarke, 1984, 620, for the fourteen occurrences of "Amanus" in Ps.-J. in Num and Deut.

[34]See Num 20:24.

[35]HT: "in the land of Canaan," as also Onq.; see Num 21:1 (Ps.-J.).

[36]See Tg. Isa 7:23; Stenning, 1949, 26–27.

[37]See Num 21:6ff.

[38]See Num 21:11ff.

[39]HT: "Dibon-Gad"; *gd* II "luck/fortune."

[40]*dblt'* (Jastrow, 277).

[41]HT: "before Nebo."

[42]HT: *mskyt,* "figured stones"; Targums *byt sygdt'* (*sgd*). The *mem* prefix in the HT suggests a place, hence *byt.*

[43]HT: "bring to an end" (*swp*), as Nf, but Onq. *'bd* "destroy."

53. And after you have driven out *the inhabitants* of the land, you shall dwell in it; for I have given you the land to inherit it. 54. So you shall take possession of the land by lots according to (the size of) your families; *to the tribe whose people are many you shall increase (the inheritance),*[44] *and to the tribe whose people are few you shall decrease (the inheritance).* According to where the lot falls, that shall be his (place); you shall take possession according to your ancestral tribes. 55. But if you do not drive out all the inhabitants of the land before you, then it shall be that those whom you spare *shall be looking with an evil eye* at you and *surrounding you as shields*[45] on your flanks and shall press in on you in the land in which you live. 56. And thus what I planned to do to them, I shall do to you.'"

CHAPTER 34

1. And the Lord spoke with Moses, saying: 2. "Command the Israelites and say to them: 'When you enter into the land of Canaan, this is the land *that shall be apportioned*[1] to you as the inherited portions, the land of Canaan within its borders.[2] 3.[3] And the southern border[4] for you shall be from the desert of the Thorn-Palms,[5] the Iron Mountain[6] on the borders of Edom; and the southern border for you shall be from the extremities of the Salt Sea on the east. 4. And your border shall go southward to the Ascent of Akrabbith[7] and shall cross to Thorn-

Notes, Chapter 33

[44]In HT, Onq., and Nf (*ḥsntyh*), "inheritance," is supplied.

[45]Aramaic *trysyn,* "shield" (Jastrow, 1698), but Onq. "take up arms" and Nf *rmmh,* "spears."

Notes, Chapter 34

[1]Here itp *plg.*

[2]The boundaries of the Promised Land are very important; see Alexander, 1974, 177ff., and Sussman, 1976, 213–257; see IQ Gen Apoc 21:14-19.

[3]Vv. 3–12 contain an extensive list of geographical names. Onq. identifies only two (vv. 4, 11); Nf and Frg. Tg. (V) are fuller, but Ps.-J. identifies all the more obscure place names. These lists of names are related also to two other lists found in Josh 15:2-4 and Ezek 47:15-20. As we shall see, Ps.-J. divides the list into places in the south (vv. 3–5), west (v. 6), north (vv. 7–9), east (vv. 10–12) relevant to the nine and a half tribes that crossed over to settle in the Promised Land. The territory of the three tribes Reuben, Gad and Manasseh, who dwelt east of the Jordan, are described in Num 32:33-42 and Deut 3:1-17. Alexander, 1974, 188–222, has a full discussion of these verses, which I am very dependent upon for the following notes.

[4]There are parallels to the distribution of the border areas. For "southern" see also Josh 15:2-4 and Ezek 47:19; 48:28.

[5]*ṣyny* for Zin (*ṣyn*).

[6]See Num 33:36; Josephus, *BJ* (IV, 454, region of Moab); *m. Sukk.* III.1 (valley of Hinnom); *1 Enoch* 67:4-13 (Callerrhoe); see McNamara, 1972, 197; Alexander, 1974, 189–190, who concludes: "it is east of the Jordan near Petra."

[7]Chief town in the toparchy of Acrabatene; modern Akraba, northeast of Nablus; Josephus, *BJ* III, 55; Alexander, 1974, 190–192.

Palms of the Iron Mountain, and its outer limits[8] shall be south of Reqem Gea,[9] and it shall culminate at the Tirath[10] Adarayya[11] and cross over *to Qesem.*[12] 5. Then the border shall turn from Qesem to the Nile of Egypt,[13] and its culmination shall be *to the west.*[14] 6.[15] Your *western*[16] border shall be the *Great* Sea, *the Ocean;*[17] and its limits: *these are the waters of creation with the primordial waters which were within its depths,*[18] *its upper spaces*[19] *and its outer areas,*[20] *its cities, and its provinces, its islands and its harbors, its ships*[21] *and its sailors.*[22] This shall be your *western* border. 7. And this shall be your northern border:[23] you shall draw a line from the Great Sea to Mount *Amanus.*[24] 8. From Mount *Amanus* you shall draw a line to the entrance of Tiberias;[25] and the limits of the border, *of its two sides,*[26] *drawing a line to the fortresses of Bar Zoemah*[27] *and to the fortresses Bar Sanigora,*[28] *of Divakinos,*[29] *and of Tarngola unto Caeserea,*[30] *from the entrance to*

Notes, Chapter 34

[8]Here "its going out."

[9]See note on Num 32:8 (Ps.-J.).

[10]Frg. Tg. (V): *dyrt,* "shed, storehouse" (Jastrow, 305), which Klein, 1980, translated "enclosure."

[11]HT: "Ḥasar-Addar"; here "enclosure of the flocks," from HT *ḥṣr;* see previous note; Nf *ṭyrt 'dryyh;* see also Num 34:3, 10.

[12]HT: *'smnh,* "Azmon"; here and Frg. Tg. (V) *qsm,* "divination"; see McNamara, 1972, 199, 201; Alexander, 1974, 199.

[13]HT: "Brook of Egypt," i.e., "the Nile," as in Nf; see Alexander, 1974, 182.

[14]HT: "the Sea."

[15]HT: "For the western boundary, you shall have the Great Sea and its coast; this shall be your western boundary." For v. 6 see McNamara's note.

[16]See Ezek 47:20.

[17]As in Nf and Frg. Tg. (PV). The reference to "ocean" extends the western limits to the Atlantic Ocean rather than stopping at the shores of the Mediterranean (Great Sea); see Deut 11:24 for a similar territorial limit. The term in Greek always refers to "the outer sea that girdles the island of the world," not to the Mediterranean; see Alexander, 1974, 47–48, 201, and also McNamara's note.

[18]See Alexander, 1974, 48, 201–202; *bgwwh,* "midst," but most likely a reference to the mythical waters and the primordial abyss, in a cosmological sense, which existed before the earth was created; hence *bgwyh.*

[19]*'byrwy* may be for Greek ἀήρ, although *'wyr* is usual transliteration; see Alexander, 1974, 202.

[20]*prbr,* "outerworks of the temple precincts" (Jastrow, 1213).

[21]Nf: "its islands, its ports and the ships"; Frg. Tg. (V): "its islands and its provinces and the boats (that are within it)."

[22]Here *'lgwwt* may be a corruption of "legion."

[23]See Ezek 47:15-17; 48:1, 28.

[24]Although Taurus Amanus may be a reduplication, Alexander (1974, 204–206) offers an extensive explanation of its association with the Taurus mountain range in Turkey, extending from the Mediterranean eastward. I have translated it as if from Aramaic *twr',* "mountain." The LXX and Vulg. recognize "Hor" as a possible Aramaic word, "mountain," the same as HT *hr.* Furthermore, the location of HT "Mount Hor" (Frg. Tg. [V]: "Taurus Minas"; Nf adds "in the east," as in vv. 3, 5) is in the north, west of Antioch, and not the mountain on which Aaron died (Num 20:22-27; 33:50), which is in the south. This Amanus, in the north, served as a fixed geographical point in Rabbinic toponomy; see Alexander, 1974, 203–206, for the many Rabbinic citations.

[25]HT: "Hammath," as Onq.; Nf and Frg. Tgs. (VP) "Antioch" (on the Orontes); an error in Ps.-J.; see Deut 3:17 (Ps.-J.) and Alexander, 1974, where there is a discussion of the strata of the text; see also Gen 10:18; 13:21.

[26]This is a secondary interpretation of HT "Zedad"; *sdd,* "side"; see McNamara's note.

[27]See Alexander, 1974, 225–226.

[28]*Op cit.,* 225.

[29]Meaning uncertain but possibly a transliteration of the Greek *eikon,* "likeness"; see Alexander, 1974, 220.

[30]*Op cit.,* 229, suggests emending phrase to "cock of Caesarea." The association with some place based on HT *gbr,* "cock," is uncertain. However, it may indeed refer to the image of a cock at Caesarea.

the Ablas[31] *of Cilicia.* 9. And the border shall go to *Keren Zekutha*[32] *and the Hill of Hatmana.*[33] And its limits shall be *to the wells of Beth Sekel and to the middle of the great courtyard*[34] *which is midway between Tirath*[35] *'Eynwwatha and Damascus.* This shall be your northern border. 10. And you shall draw a line with respect to the eastern border,[36] from the *Tirath 'Eynwwatha* to *Apamea.*[37] 11. Then the border shall go down from *Apamea* to *Daphne*[38] *to the east of 'Eynwwatha; and the border shall go down to the cave of Panias; and from the cave of Panias the border shall go down to the Mountain of Snow;*[39] *and from the Mountain of Snow the border shall go down to Enan;*[40] *and from Enan the border shall go down and surround the plain, the plain of the Arnon River. And it shall come to the Zin desert, the Mountain of Iron,*[41] *the Waters of Contention,*[42] *mourning*[43] *and resting*[44] *near Gennesaret,*[45] *the Castle of the Amorite*[46] *Kings, the possessions of the tribe of Reuben and Gad, and the half tribe of Manasseh.*[47] *And the border shall descend and surround the limits of the Sea of Gennesaret* to the east. 12. And the border shall descend to the Jordan, and its outlet will be at the Salt Sea; (the boundaries shall be) *Reqem Gea to the south, Mount Amanus to the north, the Great Sea to the west, the Salt Sea to the east.*[48] This shall be yours, the land of Israel, with the boundaries of its borders round about." 13. Then Moses commanded the Israelites, saying: "This is the land

Notes, Chapter 34

[31]HT: "Zedad"; Nf and Frg. Tg. (V) *'wwlws,* which is a variant of *'bls* of Ps.-J. Klein (1980, 2:167) derives the word from Greek *aulon,* "a narrow or hemmed-in place," associated with Cilicia. (The whole phrase is *'wwlws dqylq'y*). The reference must be to the Pass of Beilan; see Alexander, 1974, 207–208, for further discussion.

[32]HT and Onq. "Ziphron": Nf and Frg. Tg. (V) "Zephirin," whose identification is uncertain; "Keren" is derived from *qyryy',* "village"; see Alexander, 1974, 227.

[33]See also v. 15, where Nf and Frg. Tg. (V) have this material. The expression is based on Ezek 47:16-17; see Alexander, 1974, 209, 227.

[34]*Op cit.,* 209.

[35]HT: "Hazar-Enan"; here *dyrt* as in v. 4; Nf *tyrt 'gbth,* "enclosure of the Springs"; Alexander, 1974, 211, suggests a location in Trachonites. The plural "springs" suggest the springs of Daphne.

[36]See Ezek 47:18.

[37]HT: "Shepham"; here *'pmy'ph,* "Apamea," as Nf *'pmyh* and Nfmg *'pnyys.* We would understand Paneas, i.e., Caesarea Philippi. McNamara, 1972, 191, suggests the two possibilities: Paneas (Jastrow, 105) or Apamea in the valley of the Orontes; see Alexander, 1974, 211, 213. McNamara notes that in Jerome's day the Jews identified biblical Shepham with Apamea. Le Déaut, 1979, vol. 3, p. 323, favors Paneas.

[38]HT: "Riblah," southwest of Paneas; see McNamara's note and Alexander, 1974, 214–217; Le Déaut, 1979, vol. 3, p. 323.

[39]That is, "Hermon"; see Num 24:25; 34:15 (Nf); Deut 3:9; 4:48 (Ps.-J. and Nf).

[40]Possibly a variant from v. 10 or Hazar-Enan in Ezek 47:17.

[41]See Num 33:36 (Ps.-J.).

[42]Num 20:13, i.e., "the waters of Meribah."

[43]For the death of Aaron; Num 20:28-29; Ginzberg, *Legends,* III, 52, and Frg. Tg. (V) have a variant.

[44]The death of Aaron (Num 20:28-29).

[45]HT: "Sea of Chinnereth," as Deut 3:17 (Ps.-J. and Nf); Josh 11:2; 19:35; 1 Kgs 15:20; see Alexander, 1974, and Smolar and Aberbach, 1983, 114.

[46]According to v. 15 of Nf and Frg. Tg. (V), but the MS of Ps.-J. reads clearly "Edomites." This is apparently an error, given the geographical location.

[47]According to Alexander, 1974, 214, this belongs to a second stratum of the text; see also v. 15, where Nf and Frg. Tg. (V) record this material.

[48]This plus is found only here.

of which you will take possession by lots, which the Lord commanded to give to the nine tribes and the half tribe. 14. For the tribe of the Reubenites according to their clans, and the tribe of the Gadites according to their clans, and the half tribe of Manasseh have already received their inheritance. 15.[49] Two and a half tribes received their inheritances on the other side o the Jordan, to the east."[50] 16. So the Lord spoke with Moses, saying: 17. "These are the names of the men who shall take possession of the land: Eleazar the priest and Joshua bar Nun, 18. and you shall choose one officer from (each) tribe to take possession of the land. 19. And these are the names of the men: for the tribe of *the house of*[51] Judah, Caleb bar Jephunneh; 20. for the tribe of Simeon, Samuel bar Ammihud; 21. for the tribe of Benjamin, Elidad bar Kislon; 22. for the tribe of Dan, Officer[52] Bukki bar Jogli; 23. for *the tribe of* the sons of Joseph, for the tribe of the sons of Manasseh, Officer Hanniel bar Ephod; 24. for the tribe of *the house of* Ephraim, Officer Kemuel bar Shiphtan; 26.[53] for the tribe of Issachar, Officer Paltiel bar Azzan; 27. for the tribe of Asher, Officer Ahihud bar Shelomi; 25.[54] for the tribe of Zebulun, Officer Elizaphan bar Parnak; 28. for the tribe of Naphtali, Officer Pedahel bar Ammihud." 29. These are (they) whom the Lord commanded to give the Israelites possession in the land of Canaan.

CHAPTER 35

1. Then the Lord spoke with Moses in the plains of Moab by the Jordan at Jericho, saying: 2. "Command the Israelites that they give to the Levites, from the inheritance of their possession, cities for dwelling; and you shall give to the Levites

Notes, Chapter 34

[49]Nf and Frg. Tg. (V) have an extensive midrash in this verse, which Ps.-J. has partially distributed between vv. 8–11. Alexander, 1974, 218, considers that the additional material distributed in vv. 8–11 in Ps.-J. had originally stood in v. 15.

[50]Nf: "Jordan of Jericho, eastward"; Onq. "Jordan, across from Jericho, eastward in the direction of sunrise." Nf and Frg. Tg. (V) have an extensive midrash explaining the eastern border (omitted in HT) for the tribes of Reuben, Gad, and Manasseh. See Num 32:33-42 and Deut 3:5-20 for a description of the territory assigned to those three tribes; see Schürer, 1979, vol. 2, pp. 14–15, n. 46, for a discussion of the midrash; see Alexander, 1974, 218, who considers this midrash in Nf and Frg. Tg. (V) to be the source for the development in Ps.-J. in vv. 3–11; see McNamara's note.

[51]In the following verses in Ps.-J. there is a variation in idiom: "the tribe of the house of," "the tribe of," and "the tribe of the sons of"; Onq. is consistently "the tribe of" and Nf "the tribe of the sons of."

[52]Here *'mrkl,* but Onq. and Nf *rb'.*

[53]Beginning here the verses in Ps.-J. are out of order. The MS after v. 24 has the order: 26, 27, 25.

[54]V. 25 is misplaced in the MS, as noted in footnote 53; already Nf reads in the text "of Ephraim" incorrectly, but a dot is placed above the word, drawing attention to an error that must have already been found in an earlier vorlage, since in Ps.-J. the verse is misplaced.

suburbs[1] to the cities surrounding them. 3. And the cities shall be for them to dwell, and their suburbs shall be for their animals and possessions[2] and for all their *needs.* 4. And the suburbs of the cities which you shall give to the Levites (shall reach) from the wall of the city outwards for a thousand cubits round about. 5. And you shall measure two thousand cubits outside the city (on) the eastern side; and (on) the southern side two thousand cubits; and (on) *the western* side two thousand cubits; and (on) the northern side two thousand cubits, with the city in the middle. This shall be for you[3] the suburbs of the cities. 6. As for the cities that you shall give to the Levites, six cities of refuge, to which a murderer can flee; and in addition to them you shall give forty-eight[4] (other) cities 7. All the cities that you shall give to the Levites shall be forty-eight cities with their suburbs. 8. And the cities that you shall give from the inheritance of the Israelites. You shall take more *from the tribe whose people* are many. And you shall take less *from the tribe whose people* are few; each man shall give to the Levites from his cities according to his inheritance which he possesses." 9. Then the Lord spoke with Moses, saying: 10. "Speak to the Israelites and say to them: 'When you have crossed over the Jordan to the land of Canaan, 11. then you shall arrange for yourselves cities *with markets and stores providing foodstuffs.* You shall have cities of refuge to which a murderer who *slays a man* unintentionally may flee. 12. And you shall have cities for the refuge *of a murderer* from the avenger of *blood,*[5] so that the murderer will not die before he has stood trial[6] before the congregation. 13. And as for the cities that you gave, you shall have six cities of refuge *for the murderer:* 14. three cities shall you give on the other side of the Jordan, and three cities shall you give in the land of Canaan. They shall be cities of refuge. 15. For the Israelites and for the strangers and for the sojourners *among them,* these six cities shall be for refuge to which anyone who *slays a man* unintentionally may flee. 16. But if he smote him with *any* iron instrument and slew him, he is a murderer: the murderer shall surely be put to death. 17. Or if he smote him with stones (so great as to) *fill* his hand *which is sufficient* that it causes the death of someone and he *slew him,* he is a murderer: the murderer shall be put to death. 18. Or if he smote him with a piece of wood (so great as to) *fill* his hand *which is sufficient* that it causes the death of someone and he slew him, he is a murderer: he shall surely be put to death. 19. The avenger of blood may himself slay the murderer; when he meets him *outside of these cities, it is by the judgment*

Notes, Chapter 35

[1]*prwylyn* (Jastrow, 1218, *prwwr*) in v. 2 is spelled *prwdlyn* in the MS of vv. 3, 4, 7 and as *prwyryn* in Nf. The interchange between *resh* and *lamedh* point to a root *prwwr* as original (Sokoloff, 445).

[2]Aramaic *qnyn'* here translated as "possession" in the light of Nf *mmwn.*

[3]HT: "for them"; also Onq., but Nf "for you" as here.

[4]HT, Onq., and Nf read "forty-two." The confusion in Ps.-J. seems to be with the number in the following verse.

[5]HT: *g'l,* "avenger," in v. 12, but in vv. 19, 21, 24, 25 *g'l hdm,* "avenger of blood."

[6]Lit. "for judgment."

(of the court)[7] that he may slay him. 20. But if he (the murderer) assaulted him with hatred and *intentionally* knocked (him) down or cast beams[8] upon him with premeditation[9] and rolled upon him stones,[10] premeditatively, and slew him; 21. or *maintaining hatred against him* smote him with his hand and slew him, *he is a murderer:* the murderer shall surely be put to death. The avenger of blood may slay the murderer *when he has been found guilty.*[11] 22. But if unintentionally, *without maintaining hatred against him,* that he thrust him or cast upon him any instrument *but did not intend to slay him* 23. or with any stones that *were sufficient* that he die, *without intention,* and *cast upon him anything and slew him,* but he did not hate him and did not propose to do him harm, 24. then the congregation shall judge between the smiter and the avenger of blood according to *the rules of* these judgments. 25. And the congregation shall save the murderer from the hand of the avenger of blood and let him return to his city of refuge where he had fled. And he shall dwell there until the high priest dies, whom the chief[12] anointed with the oil *of anointing, because he did not pray on the Day of Atonement in the holy of holies concerning the three grave transgressions that the people of the house of Israel might not stumble by idolatry, nor by the incest, nor by the shedding of innocent blood,*[13] *it being in his power to annul them by his prayer; but he did not pray, therefore he was condemned to die that year.*[14] 26. But if, *while the high priest is yet alive,* the murderer indeed goes out from the limits of his city of refuge where he fled 27. and the avenger of blood finds him outside the limit of his city of refuge, and the avenger of blood slays the murderer, he (the avenger of blood) *shall not be subject to the sections (of the law dealing with) murderers,*[15] 28. for he (the murderer) should have dwelt in his city of refuge until the death of the high priest. And after the high priest is dead, the murderer may return to the land of his possessions. 29. And these (regulations) shall be the instructions for your regulating the procedure, for your generations, in all your dwellings. 30. Whoever *slays a man,* according to *the word of* witnesses who are fit *to testify against him, the avenger of blood or the law court*[16] shall slay the murderer; but one witness alone shall not *testify against a man* in order to be put to death. 31. And you shall not accept a ransom *to release a certain* murderer who is guilty of death, for he shall surely be put to death. 32. Nor

Notes, Chapter 35

[7]See v. 30.

[8]Aramaic *klwnsn,* "beam of a loom" (Jastrow, 640); see Le Déaut, 1979, vol. 3, p. 333, n. 13.

[9]*Sifre Num.* 160 (674): "particularly."

[10]*Sifre Num.* 160 (671): "a boulder or a column."

[11]HT: "when he meets him"; Onq. and Ps.-J. consider the HT to mean "after he has been convicted by the courts," which is the opinion of R. Eliezer in the Talmud; see Grossfeld, *The Aramaic Bible,* vol. 8, p. 161, n. 3.

[12]MS *sgn;* see Num 19:3.

[13]See Gen 13:13 and Deut 23:10 (Ps.-J.).

[14]Le Déaut, 1970, 46, quotes these words from *b. Melekoth* 11a; Le Déaut, 1974, 281–283, for comments on John 11:49.

[15]HT: "guilty of blood"; also Onq.; Ps.-J. *sydryn dqṭlwlyn* considers the legal regulation, but Nf *'dm zkyy,* "innocent blood," follows but expands the HT.

[16]*Sifre Num.* 161 (683): the law court and the witnesses must slay the offender.

shall you take a ransom for one who has fled to his city of refuge, so that he may return to dwell in the land before the priest dies. 33. Neither shall you defile the land[17] in which you are; for *innocent* blood *which is not revenged* shall defile the land. And as for the land, there is no atonement for the *innocent* blood which was shed in it except by *the shedding of* the blood of the one who shed it (in the first place). 34. *And you*[18] shall not defile[19] the land where you are; for *my Shekinah* dwells in its midst; for I am the Lord whose *Shekinah* dwells in the midst of the Israelites.'"

CHAPTER 36

1. Then the ancestral heads of the families[1] of the Gileadites, son of Makhir, son of Manasseh from the family of[2] Joseph, approached the court[3] and spoke before Moses and before the leaders of the ancestral heads of the Israelites. 2. Now they said: "The Lord commanded my lord[4] to assign the land for an inheritance to the Israelites by lot; and my lord was commanded from *before* the Lord to assign the inheritance of our brother Zelophehad to his daughters. 3. However, if they become wives to one of the sons of (another) tribe of the Israelites, their inheritance will be withheld from the ancestral inheritance and shall be added to the inheritance of the tribe to which they shall belong and our allotted inheritance will be diminished. 4. And when the Jubilee (year) occurs for the Israelites, their (the daughters') inheritance will be added to the inheritance of the tribe to which they belong, and their inheritance will be withheld from the inheritance of our ancestral tribe." 5. And Moses commanded the Israelites, according to *the Memra of* the Lord: "The tribe of the sons of Joseph appeals to the point. 6. This is the thing which the Lord has commanded: *not for the generation of the future, after the division of the land, but* for the daughters of Zelophehad by saying: 'They may become wives of whoever is pleasing in their sight, but they should become wives of the family of their father's

Notes, Chapter 35

[17]HT: hip *ḥnp,* "pollute (the land)"; Onq. and Nf *ḥwb,* "bring guilt upon," but Ps.-J. pa *ṭnp,* "soil, pollute" (Jastrow, 541).
[18]HT: singular but plural in Onq., Ps.-J., and Nf.
[19]HT: pi *ṭm'* "defile": Onq., Nf and Ps.-J. with *s'b* but Nfgl *ḥwb.*

Notes, Chapter 36

[1]Here *gnyst,* but Onq. and Nf *zr'yt,* "descendants."
[2]*Ed. pr.:* "family of the sons of."
[3]Aramaic *by dyn';* see Num 27:1 (Ps.-J.).
[4]Aramaic *rbwny,* as in Onq. and Nf.

tribe 7. *so that* the inheritance of the Israelites should not pass from one tribe[5] to another but the Israelite should remain attached to the inheritance of the ancestral tribe.'" 8. 9.[6] 10. Just as the Lord had commanded Moses, so did the daughters of Zelophehad. 11. Mahlah, Tirzah, Hoglah, Milkah, and Noah, daughters of Zelophehad, married the sons of their paternal uncles. 12. They married, then, into the family of the sons of Manasseh, son of Joseph, and their inheritance remained in the tribe of their ancestral family. 13. These are the commandments and regulations which the Lord commanded, through Moses, to the Israelites on the plains of Moab at the Jordan near Jericho.

Notes, Chapter 36

[5]HT: *sbb,* "be transferred from"; Onq. *sḥr,* "circulate"; here and Nf *nqp,* "to circle" (pass from one to another); see Num 36:9 (Nf).

[6]Vv. 8–9 omitted in the MS due to homoeoteleuton of *bny ysr'l* at the end of vv. 7, 9.

SELECT BIBLIOGRAPHY

Apart from the works mentioned here, for manuscripts of the Palestinian Targums, editions of Targum texts, and translations of Palestinian Targums of the Pentateuch, see either of the first two volumes of this series *(The Aramaic Bible,* vol. 1A, 231–233, or vol. 1B, 167–169).

1. Manuscript of Pseudo-Jonathan

London, BM Add. 27031

2. Editions of Targum Pseudo-Jonathan

Clarke, E. G., Aufrecht, W. E., Hurd, J. C., Spitzer, F.: 1984, *Targum Pseudo-Jonathan of the Pentateuch: Text and Concordance.* Hoboken, N.J.: Ktav.

Díez Macho, A.: 1977–89, *Biblia Polyglotta Matritensia.* Series IV. *Targum Palaestinense in Pentateuchum.* Additur Targum Pseudojonatan ejusque hispanica versio. Editio critica curante A. Díez Macho, adjuvantibus L. Díez Merino, E. Martínez Borobio, T. Martínez Saiz. Pseudojonatan hispanica versio: T. Martínez Saiz. Targum Pseudojonatan ex variis fontibus: R. Griño. Madrid: Consejo Superior de Investigaciones Cientificas. Vol. 4, *Numeri* (1977); vol. 5, *Deuteronomium* (1980).

Ginsburger, M.: 1903, *Pseudo-Jonathan (Thargum-Jonathan ben Usiël zum Pentateuch). Nach der Londoner Handschrift Brit. Mus. Add. 27031.* Berlin: Calvary.

Rieder, D.: 1974, 1984–85, *Pseudo-Jonathan: Targum Jonathan ben Uziel on the Pentateuch copied from the London MS (British Museum Add. 27031).* Jerusalem: Salomon's, 1974. Reprinted with Hebrew translation and notes. 2 vols. Jerusalem, 1984–85.

3. Translation of Pseudo-Jonathan

English: Etheridge, J. W.: *The Targums of Onkelos and Jonathan Ben Uzziel on the Pentateuch: With Fragments of the Jerusalem Targum: From the Chaldee.* Originally published London: Longman, Green, Longman, 1862, 1865. 2 vols. Reprinted in one vol. New York: Ktav, 1968.

French: Le Déaut, R., with J. Robert, *Targum du Pentateuque. Traduction des deux recensions Palestiniennes complètes.* 4 vols. Sources Chrétiennes 245, 256, 261,

271. Paris: Cerf. *Genèse,* 1978; *Exode et Lévitique,* 1979; *Nombres,* 1979; *Deutéronome,* 1980.

Spanish: Martínez Saiz, T., in Díez Macho's *Biblia Polyglotta Matritensia.* Series IV. *Targum Palaestinense in Pentateuchum.* Consejo Superior de Investigaciones Cientificas, 1980–88.

Hebrew: Rieder, D.: *Pseudo-Jonathan: Targum Jonathan ben Uziel on the Pentateuch copied from the London MS (British Museum Add. 27031).* Jerusalem: Salomon's, 1974. Reprinted with Hebrew translation and notes. 2 vols. Jerusalem, 1984–85.

4. Rabbinic Sources

Mekilta de Rabbi Ismael. Ed. J. Z. Lauterbach. 3 vols. Philadelphia: Jewish Publication Society, 1949 (reprint of 1933–35 edition).

Sifre on Numbers. Ed. K. G. Kuhn, *Sifre zu Numeri.* Stuttgart, 1959.

Sifre ad Deuteronomium. Ed. L. Finkelstein. Berlin, 1939; reprint New York, Jewish Publication Society, 1969.

Tosephta. Based on the Erfurt and Vienna Codices. Ed. M. S. Zuckermandel. Jerusalem: Wahrmann Books, 1963.

5. Translations of Rabbinic Works

Midrash Rabbah Numbers. Ed. H. Freedman and M. Simon; trans. J. J. Slotki. London, Soncino Press, 1939.

Midrás Sifre Números. Trans. M. Perez Fernández. Versión critica. Introducción y notas. Biblioteca Midrásica 9. Valencia: Institución San Jerónimo, 1989.

Sifre on Numbers. Ed. J. Neusner. Brown Judaic Series 118, 119. Atlanta: Scholars Press, 1986.

The Mishnah. Trans. H. Danby. Oxford: University Press, 1933.

Sifre. A Tannaitic Commentary on the Book of Deuteronomy. Ed. R. Hammer. New Haven, Conn.: Yale University Press, 1986.

6. General Works

Abel, F. M.: 1933–38, *Géographie de la Palestine.* 2 vols. 2nd ed. Paris.

Aberbach, M.: See Smolar, L., and M. Aberbach: 1983.

Alexander, P. S.: 1974, *The Toponomy of the Targumim with Special Reference to the Table of Nations and the Borders of the Holy Land.* Dissertation, Oxford University.

idem: 1976, "The Rabbinic List of Forbidden Targumim," *JJS* 27, 179–192.

idem: 1985, "The Targumim and the Rabbinic Rules for the Delivery of the Targum," *VTSuppl* 36, 14–28.

Allony, N.: 1975, "The Jerusalem Targum Pseudo-Jonathan. Rieder's Edition," *Beth Miqra* 61, 423–425 (Hebrew).

Attridge, H. W.: 1976, *The Interpretation of the Biblical History in the Antiquitates Judaicae of Flavius Josephus.* Missoula, Mont.: Scholars Press.

Avi-Yonah, M.: 1952; 3rd ed. 1962, *Ge'ografyah Historit shel Erez Yisrael le-min Shivat Ziyyon Reshit ha-Kibbush ha-Aravi* ("Historical Geography of Erez Israel from the Return to Zion until the Arab Conquest"). Jerusalem. English translations 1966, 1977.

idem: 1966A, *Atlas Carta le-Toledot Bayit Sheni ha-Mishnah ve-ha-Talmud* ("Carta Atlas of the Second Temple, Mishnaic and Talmudic Periods"). Jerusalem.

idem: 1966B, 1977, *The Holy Land from the Persian to the Arab Conquests (536 B.C. to A.D. 640): A Historical Geography.* Rev. ed. with a new extensive toponymic index, 1977. Grand Rapids, Mich.: Baker Book House.

Barnstein, H.: 1899, "A Noteworthy Targum MS in the British Museum," *JQR* 11, 167–171.

Beer, B.: 1857, "Eldat und Medad im Pseudojonathan," *MGWJ* 6, 346–350.

Bienaimé, G.: 1984, *Moïse et le Don de l'Eau dans la Tradition juive ancienne: Targum et Midrash.* Analecta Biblica 98. Rome: Biblical Institute Press.

Bloch, R.: 1978, "Note méthodologique pour l'étude de la littérature rabbinique," *RSR* 43 (1995) 194–227 (published in English as "Methodological Note for the Study of Rabbinic Literature," in *Approaches to Ancient Judaism: Theory and Practice,* ed. W. S. Green and W. J. Sullivan. Brown Judaic Studies 1. Missoula, Mont.: Scholars Press, 1978, 511–575).

Brawer, A. J.: 1972, "Geography." *EJ* 2 (1972) 415–420.

Brooke, G. L.: 1985, *Exegesis at Qumran. 4QFlorilegium in Its Jewish Context.* JSOT Supplements Series 29. Sheffield: JSOT Press.

Casson, L.: 1971, *Ships and Seamanship in the Ancient World.* Princeton, N.J.

Charlesworth, J. H., ed.: 1983, 1985, *The Old Testament Pseudepigrapha.* 2 vols. London: Darton, Longman and Todd.

idem: 1987, "From Jewish Messianology to Christian Christology: Some Caveats and Perspectives," in J. Neusner et al., *Judaism and Their Messiahs,* 225–264.

Chester, A.: 1986, *Divine Revelation and Divine Titles in the Pentateuchal Targumim.* Texte und Studien zum Antiken Judentum 14. Tübingen: J. C. Mohr (Paul Siebeck).

Cook, J.: 1983, "Anti-Heretical Traditions in Targum Pseudo-Jonathan," *JNSL* 11, 47–57.

Cooke, E. M.: 1986, *Rewriting the Bible: The Text and Language of the Pseudo-Jonathan Targum.* Dissertation, University of California, Los Angeles. Microfilm reprint.

Dalman, G. H.: 1897, "Die Handschrift zum Jonathantargum des Pentateuch, Add. 27031 des Britischen Museum," *MGWJ* 41, 454–456.

Dalman, G.: 1905, *Grammatik des Jüdisch-Palästinischen Aramäisch.* 2nd ed. Leipzig. Reprint with *Aramäische Dialektproben.* Darmstadt: Wissenschaftliche Buchgesellschaft, 1960.

idem: 1967, *Aramäisch-Neuhebräisches Handwörterbuch zu Targum, Talmud und Midrasch.* Göttingen, 1938; reprint Hildesheim: G. Olms, 1967.

Danby, H., trans.: 1933, *The Mishnah.* Oxford: University Press.

Davies, G. I.: 1972, "Hagar, El-Hegra and the Location of Mount Sinai with an Additional Note on Reqem," *VT* 22, 152–163.

Díez Macho, A.: *Neophyti 1.* Targum Palestinense. Ms de la Biblioteca Vaticana. Vols. 1–5. Madrid-Barcelona: Consejo Superior de Investigaciones Cientificas: 1 *Génesis,* 1968; 2 *Éxodo,* 1970; 3 *Levitico,* 1971; 4 *Numeros,* 1974; 5 *Deuteronomio,* 1978.

Esterlich, P.: 1967, "El Targum Pseudojonathan o Jerosolimatano," in *Studi sull'Oriente e la Bibbia offerti a P. Giovanni Rinaldi.* Genoa: Studio e Vita, 191–195.

Etheridge, E. W.: 1862, 1865, *The Targums of Onkelos and Jonathan ben Uzziel on the Pentateuch, with Fragments of the Jerusalem Targum: From the Chaldee.* 2 vols. London: Longman, Green, Longman. Reprinted in one volume, New York: Ktav, 1968.

Fernández, M. Pérez: 1989, *Midrás Sifre Números.* Versión critica, introducción y notas. Valencia: Institución San Jerónimo.

Finkelstein, L., ed.: 1939, *Sifre on Deuteronomy.* Berlin; reprint New York: Jewish Publication Society, 1969.

Fitzmyer, J. A.: 1971, *Essays on the Semitic Background of the New Testament.* London: Geoffrey Chapman.

Forestell, J. T.: 1979, *Targumic Traditions and the New Testament.* SBL Aramaic Studies 4. Chico, Calif.: Scholars Press.

Gignac, F. T.: 1955, *A Grammar of the Greek Papyri of the Roman and Byzantine Period 1, Phonology.* Testi e Documenti per lo studio dell'Antichità LV. Milan.

Ginzberg, L.: 1909–46, *The Legends of the Jews.* 7 vols. Philadelphia: Jewish Publication Society.

Ginsburger, M.: 1900, "Verbotene Thargumim." *MGWJ* 44, 1–7.

idem: 1903, *Pseudo-Jonathan (Thargum-Jonathan ben Usiël zum Pentateuch). Nach der Londoner Handschrift (Brit. Mus. Add. 27031).* Berlin: Calvary.

Goldberg, A. M.: 1970, "Torah aus der Unterwelt? Eine Bemerkung zu Röm 10,6-7." *BiblZeit* 14, 127–131.

Golomb, D. M.: 1985, *A Grammar of Targum Neofiti.* Harvard Semitic Monographs 34. Chico, Calif.: Scholars Press.

Gordon, R. P.: 1978, "The Targumist as Eschatologist." *VTSuppl* 29, 113–130.

Grabbe, L. L.: 1979, "The Jannes/Jambres Tradition in Targum Pseudo-Jonathan and Its Date." *JBL* 98, 393–401.

Greene, J. T.: 1992, *Balaam and His Interpreters: A Hermeneutical History of the Balaam Tradition.* Atlanta: Scholars Press.

Grelot, P.: 1963, "Jean VII, 38: Eau du rocher ou source du temple?" *RB* 70 (1963) 43–51.

Grossfeld, B.: "The Relationship Between the Biblical Hebrew BRḤ and NWS and Their Corresponding Aramaic Equivalents in the Targums—'RQ, 'PK, 'ZL: A Preliminary Study in Hebrew-Aramaic Lexicography." *ZAW* 91, 107–123.

idem: 1984, "The Translation of Biblical Hebrew PQD in the Targum, Peshitta, Vulgate and Septuagint." *ZAW* 96 (1984) 83–101.

idem: 1988A, *The Targum Onqelos to Leviticus and the Targum Onqelos to Numbers.* The Aramaic Bible 8. Wilmington, Del.: Michael Glazier.

idem: 1988B, *The Targum Onqelos to Deuteronomy.* The Aramaic Bible 9. Wilmington, Del.: Michael Glazier.

Hammer, R. (ed.): 1986, *Sifre. A Tannaitic Commentary on the Book of Deuteronomy.* New Haven, Conn.: Yale University Press.

Harrington, D.: 1985, "Pseudo-Philo," in J. H. Charlesworth, vol. 2, 297–377.

Hayward, C. T. R.: 1978A, "Phinehas—the same is Elijah: The Origin of a Rabbinic Tradition." *JJS* 29, 22–34.

idem: 1978B, "The Holy Name of the God of Moses and the Prologue of St. John's Gospel." *NTS* 25, 16–32.

idem: 1981, "Memra and Shekinah: A Short Note." *JJS* 31, 210–213.

idem: 1981, *Divine Name and Presence: The Memra.* Totowa, N.J.: Allanheld, Osmun.

idem: 1989A, "The Date of Targum Pseudo-Jonathan: Some Comments." *JJS* 40, 7–30.

idem: 1989B, "Targum Pseudo-Jonathan and Anti-Islamic Polemic." *JSS* 34, 77–93.

idem: 1991, "Pirqe de Rabbi Eliezer and Targum Pseudo-Jonathan." *JJS* 42, 215–246.

idem: 1992, "Red Heifer and Golden Calf: Dating Targum Pseudo-Jonathan." *Targum Studies* 1. Ed. P. V. M. Flesher. Southern Florida Studies in the History of Judaism 55. Atlanta: Scholars Press.

Hecht, R.: 1987, "Philo and Messiah," in J. Neusner et al., 1987, 139–168.

Heineman, J.: 1974, *Aggada and Its Development.* Jerusalem: Keter (Hebrew).

Hengel, M.: 1989, *The Zealots: Investigations into the Jewish Freedom Movements in the Period from Herod I until 70 A.D.* Edinburgh: T & T Clark.

Hildesheimer, H.: 1886, *Beiträge zur Geographie Palästinas.* Berlin.

Holler, R.: 1957, "The Meaning of PQD." Dissertation, McCormick Theological Seminary, Chicago.

Jastrow, M.: 1950 (etc.; reprints; preface 1903), *A Dictionary of the Targumim, the Talmud Babli and Yerushalmi and the Midrashic Literature.* 2 vols. New York: Pardes.

Jaubert, A.: 1963, "La Symbolique du puits de Jacob et Jean 4.12." *L'homme devant Dieu. Melanges offerts au Père Henri de Lubac.* Théologie: Études publiées sous la direction de Faculté de Théologie 56, vol. I, 63–73.

Jerome: *Hebraicae quaestiones in Genesim.* Ed. P. de Lagarde. CCL 72 (1959) 1–56. Turnhout: Brepols.

idem: *Commentarii in Hiezechielem.* Ed. Fr. Glorie. CCL 75 (1964). Turnhout: Brepols.

Jones, H. Stuart: See H. G. Liddell and R. Scott.

Josephus, Flavius: *Jewish Antiquities.*

idem: *Jewish War.*

Kasher, M.: 1983, *Torah Shelemah.* Vol. 35. *Aramaic Versions of the Bible. A Comprehensive Study of Onkelos, Jonathan, Jerusalem Targums and the Full Jerusalem Targum of the Vatican Manuscript Neofiti I,* vol. 2. Jerusalem: Beth Torah Shelemah.

Kish, G. (ed.): 1949, *Pseudo-Philo's Liber Antiquitatum Biblicarum.* Notre Dame, Ind.: University of Notre Dame Press.

Klein, M.: 1975, "A New Edition of Pseudo-Jonathan." *JBL* 94, 277–279.

idem: 1976, "Converse Translation: A Targumic Technique." *Biblica* 57, 515–537.

idem: 1979, "The Preposition *qdm* ('before'), a Pseudo-Anti-Anthropomorphism in the Targum." *JTS,* n.s. 30, 502–507.

idem: 1980, *The Fragment-Targums of the Pentateuch According to the Extant Sources.* 2 vols. Analecta Biblica 76. Rome: Biblical Institute Press.

idem: 1981, "The Translation of Anthropomorphisms and Anthropopathisms in the Targumim." *VTSuppl* 32, 162–177.

idem: 1982, *Anthropomorphisms and Anthropopathisms in the Targumim of the Pentateuch, with Parallel Citations from the Septuagint.* Jerusalem: Makor (Hebrew).

idem: 1982, "Associative and Complementary Translation in the Targumim." *Eretz Israel 16* (H. M. Orlinsky volume), 134*–140*.

idem: 1986, *Genizah Manuscripts of Palestinian Targum to the Pentateuch.* 2 vols. Cincinnati: Hebrew Union College.

idem: 1988, "Not to be Translated in Public—*l' mtrgm bsybwr'.*" *JJS* 39, 80–91.

idem: 1992, *Targumic Manuscripts in the Cambridge Genizah Collection.* Cambridge University Library Genizah Series 8. Cambridge: Cambridge University Press.

Klein, S.: 1928, "Das Tannäitische Grenzverzeichnis Palaestinas." *HUCA* 5, 197–259.

Krauss, S.: 1895, "Die biblische Völkertafel im Talmud, Midrasch und Targum." *MGWJ* 39 (1895) 1–11; 49–63.

Kuhn, K.G.: 1964, "Balaam." *TDNT* 1, 524f.

Kuiper, G. J.: 1972, *The Pseudo-Jonathan Targum and Its Relationship to Targum Onqelos.* Studia Ephemeridis "Augustinianum" 9. Rome: Institutum Patristicum "Augustinianum."

Kutscher, E. J.: 1976, *Studies in Galilean Aramaic.* Bar Ilan Studies in Near Eastern Languages and Culture. Trans. from Hebrew with annotation by M. Sokoloff. Jerusalem: Ahva.

Lagrange, M. J.: 1909, *Le messianisme chez les Juifs (150 av. J.C. à 200 ap. J.C.* Paris: Etudes Bibliques. Paris: Gabalda.

de Lange, N. A. M.: 1976, *Origen and the Jews: Studies in Jewish Christian Relations in the Third Century.* Cambridge: Cambridge University Press.

Le Déaut, R.: 1963, *La Nuit pascale. Essai sur la signification de la Paque juive à partir du Targum d'Exode XII, 42.* Rome: Pontifical Biblical Institute.

idem: 1970, "Aspects de l'intercession dans le Judaïsme ancien." *JSJ* 1, 35–57.

idem: 1974, "The Current State of Targumic Studies." *BibThB* 4, 3–32.

Le Déaut, R., with J. Robert: 1978, 1979, 1980, *Targum du Pentateuque. Traduction des deux recensions Palestiniennes complètes.* 4 vols. Trans. R. Le Déaut with J. Robert. Sources Chrétiennes 245, 256, 261, 271. Paris: Cerf. Vol. 1, *Genèse,* 1978; vol. 2, *Exode et Lévitique,* 1979; vol. 3, *Nombres,* 1979; vol. 4, *Deutéronome,* 1980.

Levey, S. H.: 1974, *The Messiah: An Aramaic Interpretation. The Messianic Exegesis of the Targum.* Monographs of the Hebrew Union College 2. Cincinnati–New York: Hebrew Union College–Jewish Institute of Religion.

Levine, E.: 1971, "Some Characteristics of Pseudo-Jonathan Targum to Genesis." *Augustinianum* 11, 85–103.

idem: 1971, "A Study of Targum Pseudo-Jonathan to Exodus." *Sefarad* 32, 27–48.

idem: 1972, "British Museum Additional MS 27031." *Manuscripta* 16, 3–13.

Levy, B. Barry: 1986, 1987, *Targum Neophyti 1. A Textual Study.* Vol. 1, Introduction, Genesis, Exodus; vol. 2, Leviticus, Numbers, Deuteronomy. Lanham, N.Y.–London: University Press of America.

Levy, J.: 1881, *Chaldäisches Wörterbuch über die Targumim und einen grossen Theil des rabbinischen Schriftthums.* Leipzig; reprints Köln: Melzer, 1959, 1966.

Liddell, H. G., Scott, R.: 1940, *A Greek-English Lexicon.* Rev. ed. H. S. Jones. Oxford: Clarendon.

Lieberman, J.: 1955, *Tosefta ki-fshuta (The Tosefta).* New York.

Lieberman, S.: 1962, *Hellenism in Jewish Palestine.* New York: Jewish Theological Seminary.

Lund, S., and J. Foster: 1977, *Variant Versions of Targumic Traditions Within Codex Neofiti 1.* SBL Aramaic Studies 2. Missoula, Mont.: Scholars Press.

Luzarraga, J.: 1973, *Las tradiciones de la nube en la Biblia y en el judaismo primitivo.* Analecta Biblica 54. Rome: Biblical Institute Press.

McCarthy, C.: 1981, *The Tiqqune Sopherim and Other Theological Corrections in the Masoretic Text of the Old Testament.* Orbis Biblicus et Orientalis 36. Freiburg (Schweiz): Universitätsverlag and Göttingen: Vandenhoeck & Ruprecht.

McNamara, M.: 1966A (reprint with supplement 1978), *The New Testament and the Palestinian Targum to the Pentateuch.* Analecta Biblica 27. Rome: Biblical Institute Press.

idem: 1966B, "Some Early Rabbinic Citations and the Palestinian Targum to the Pentateuch." *Rivista degli Studi Orientali* 41, 1–15.

idem: 1972, *Targum and Testament. Aramaic Paraphrases of the Hebrew Bible: A Light on the New Testament.* Shannon: Irish University Press.

idem: 1991, "Early Exegesis in the Palestinian Targum (Neofiti) Numbers Chapter 21." *Studien zum Neuen Testament und seiner Umwelt* 16:127–149.

idem: 1992, *Targum Neofiti 1: Genesis.* The Aramaic Bible 1A. Collegeville, Minn.: The Liturgical Press.

idem: 1993, "Early Exegesis in the Palestinian Targum (Neofiti 1) Numbers Chapter 24." *PIBA* 16, 57–79.

McNamara, M., M. Maher, R. Hayward: 1994, *Targum Neofiti 1: Exodus.* Translated, with Introduction and Apparatus by M. McNamara and Notes by R. Hayward. *Targum Pseudo-Jonathan: Exodus.* Translated with Notes by M. Maher. The Aramaic Bible 2. Collegeville, Minn.: The Liturgical Press.

Maher, M.: 1971, "Some Aspects of Torah in Judaism." *ITQ* 38, 310–325.

idem: 1990, "The Meturgemanim and Prayer." *JJS* 40, 226–246.

idem: 1992, *Targum Pseudo-Jonathan: Genesis.* Translated with Introduction and Notes. The Aramaic Bible 1B. Collegeville, Minn.: The Liturgical Press.

idem: 1993, "The Meturgemanim and Prayer (2)." *JJS* 44, 220–234.

idem: 1994, *Targum Pseudo-Jonathan: Exodus.* See above under McNamara, M., M. Maher, R. Hayward.

Malina, B. J.: 1968, *The Palestinian Manna Tradition: The Manna Tradition in the Palestinian Targums and Its Relationship to the New Testament.* Leiden: Brill.

Maneschg, H.: 1981, *Die Erzählung von der ehernen Schlange (Num 21, 4-9) in der Auslegung der frühen jüdischen Literatur. Eine traditionsgeschichtliche Sudie.* Frankfurt am Main–Bern: Peter D. Lang.

Maori, Y.: 1983, "The Relationship of Targum Pseudo-Jonathan to Halakhic Sources." *Te'uda* 3, 235–250 (Hebrew).

Marmorstein, A.: 1905, *Studien zum Pseudo-Jonathan Targum*. Pozsony: Alkalay.

Martin, D. J.: 1973, "New Directions in Biblical Scholarship. Targum Yerushalmi to the Pentateuch Tradition." *Journal of Orthodox Thought* 13/14, 201–208.

Martin, E. G.: 1985, "Eldad and Modad," in J. H. Charlesworth, 1985, 2, 463–465.

Muñoz (Léon), D.: 1971, *Apéndice sobre el Memra de Yahweh en el MS Neophyti I,"* in *Neophyti 1*, vol. 3: *Levitico,* 70*–80*.

idem: 1974, "Dibbura y Memra, 2," in *Dios Palabra. Memrá en los Targumim del Pentateuco.* Granada: Santa Rita-Monachil, 668–679.

idem: 1977, *La Gloria de la Shekina en los Targumim del Pentateuco.* Madrid: Consejo Superior de Investigaciones Cientificas. Instituto "Francisco Suarez."

idem (ed.): 1986, *Salvación en la Palabra. Targum. Derash. Berit. En memoria del profesor Alejandro Díez Macho.* Madrid: Ediciones Cristiandad.

Neubauer, A.: 1868, *La géographie du Talmud.* Paris: Frères.

Neusner, J., et al.: 1987, *Judaisms and Their Messiahs at the Turn of the Christian Era.* Cambridge–New York: Cambridge University Press.

Noth, M.: 1968, *Numbers: A Commentary.* Old Testament Library. London: SCM.

Ogg, G.: 1979, revision of E. Schürer, paragraph 22: "The Cultural Setting," *The History of the Jewish People.* Vol. 2, 1–80.

Ohana, M.: 1975, "La polémique judéo-islamique et l'image de Ismaël dans Targum Pseudo-Jonathan et dans Pirke de Rabbi Eliezer." *Augustinianum* 15, 367–387.

Panciera, S.: 1956, "Liburna. Rassegna delle fonti, caratteristiche della nave, accezioni del termine." *Epigraphica* 18 (1956) 130–156.

idem: 1958, "Liburna," in *Dizionario epigrafico di antichità romane.*

Patai, R.: 1979, *The Messiah Texts.* Detroit: Wayne State University Press.

Pérez Fernández, M.: 1981, *Tradiciones Mesiánicas en el Targum Palestinense.* Estudios exegéticos Institución San Jerónimo-Casa de Santiago.

Philo: 1956/623, *Philo with an English Translation.* Ed. F. H. Colson and G. H. Whitaker. Cambridge, Mass.: Harvard University Press (reprint of 1929–41 edition).

Philo: *On the Life of Moses (De Vita Mosis).*

Press, I.: 1951, *Historical-Topographical Encyclopedia of Palestine* (Hebrew). 2nd ed. 4 vols. Jerusalem.

Pseudo-Philo: 1949, *Pseudo-Philo's Liber Antiquitatum Biblicarum.* Ed. G. Kish. Notre Dame, Ind.: University of Notre Dame Press.

Rappaport, S.: 1930, *Aggada und Exegese bei Flavius Josephus.* Vienna: Alexander Kohut Memorial Foundation.

Revel, D.: 1924-25, "Targum Jonathan to the Torah." *Ner Mar'aravi* 2, 17–122 (Hebrew).

Ribera, J.: 1983, “La expresión *mn qdm* y su traducción.” *Aula Orientalis* 1, 114–115.

Rieder, D.: 1988, “On the Ginsburger Edition of the ‘Pseudo-Jonathan’ Targum of the Torah.” *Leshonenu* 32, 298–303 (Hebrew).

Schabert, J.: “Das Verbum PQD in der Theologie des Alten Testaments.” *BibZeit* 4 (1960) 209–226.

Schürer, E.: 1973, 1979, 1980, *The History of the Jewish People in the Age of Jesus Christ (175 B.C. 4–A.D. 135).* A New English version revised and edited by G. Vermes, F. Millar, M. Black. 3 vols. Edinburgh: T & T Clark.

Shinan, A.: 1975, “‘Their Prayer and Petitions.’ The Prayers of the Ancients in the Light of the Pentateuchal Targums.” *Sinay* 78, 89–92 (Hebrew).

idem: 1975–76, *“lyšn byt qwdš’* in the Aramaic Targums of the Torah.” *Beth Miqra* 21, 472–474 (Hebrew).

idem: 1979, *The Aggadah in the Aramaic Targums to the Pentateuch.* 2 vols. Jerusalem: Makor (Hebrew).

idem: 1982–83, “On the Theoretical Principles of the Meturgemanim.” *Jerusalem Studies in Jewish Thought*, vol. 2, 7–32 (Hebrew).

idem: 1983A, “Folk Elements in the Aramaic Targum Pseudo-Jonathan.” *Studies in Aggadah and Jewish Folklore Presented to Dov Noy on His 60th Birthday.* Ed. I. Ben-Ami and J. Dan. Jerusalem: Magnes, 139–155 (Hebrew).

idem: 1983B, “Miracles, Wonders and Magic in the Aramaic Targums of the Pentateuch.” *Essays on the Bible and the Ancient Near East. Festschrift I. L. Seeligman.* Ed. A. Rolfé and Y. Zakovitch. Vol. 2, 419–426. Jerusalem: Rubinstein (Hebrew).

idem: 1983C, “The Angelology of the ‘Palestinian’ Targums on the Pentateuch.” *Sefarad* 43, 181–196.

idem: 1985, “The ‘Palestinian’ Targums—Repetitions, Internal Unity, Contradictions.” *JJS* 36, 72–87.

idem: 1986, “On the Characteristics of Targum Pseudo-Jonathan to the Torah, 2.” *Proceedings of the Ninth World Congress of Jewish Studies.* Jerusalem: World Union of Jewish Studies, A, 109–116.

idem: 1990, “Dating Targum Pseudo-Jonathan: Some Comments.” *JJS* 41, 57–61.

Singer, I., et al.: 1901–7, *The Jewish Encyclopedia.* New York: Funk and Wagnalls.

Smolar, L., and M. Aberbach: 1983, *Studies in Targum Jonathan to the Prophets.* New York.

Sokoloff, M.: 1990, *A Dictionary of Jewish Palestinian Aramaic of the Byzantine Period.* Ramat-Gan: Bar-Ilan University Press.

Speiser, E. A.: 1958, “Census and Ritual Expiation in Mari and Israel.” *BASOR* 149, 17–25.

Sperber, D.: 1982, *Essays on Greek and Latin in the Mishna, Talmud and Midrashic Literature*. Jerusalem: Makor.

idem: 1984, *A Dictionary of Greek and Latin Legal Terms in Rabbinic Literature*. Ramat-Gan: Bar-Ilan University Press.

idem: 1986, *Nautica Talmudica*. Ramat-Gan: Bar-Ilan University Press; Leiden: Brill.

Splansky, D. M.: 1981, *Targum Pseudo-Jonathan: Its Relationship to Other Targumim, Use of Midrashim and Date*. Dissertation, Hebrew Union College, Cincinnati.

Stemberger, G.: 1991. See under Strack, H. L., and G. Stemberger.

Stenning, J. F.: 1949, *The Targum of Isaiah*. Oxford: The Clarendon Press.

Story, C. K. J.: 1947, 1948, "What Kind of Messiah Did the Jews Expect?" *Bibliotheca Sacra* 104 (1947) 483–494; 105 (1948) 102–114, 233–247.

Strack, H. L., and G. Stemberger: 1982, *Einleitung in Talmud und Midrasch*. 7th ed. Beck'sche Elementarbücher. Munich: Beck. Eng. trans. by M. Bockmuehl, *Introduction to the Talmud and Midrash*. Edinburgh: T & T Clark, 1991.

Sussman, Y.: 1976, "The Boundaries of Erets-Israel." *Tarbiz* 45, 213–257.

Syrén, R.: 1986, *The Blessings in the Targums. A Study on the Targumic Interpretations of Genesis 49 and Deuteronomy 33*. Acta Academiae Aonensis, Series A, vol. 64, nr. 1, Åbo, Åbo Akademi.

Sysling, H.: 1991, *Techiyyat Ha-Metim. De opstanding van de Dodem in de Palestijnse Targumim op de Pentateuch en overeenkomstige Tradities in de Klassieke Rabbijnse Bronnen*. Zutphen: Terra.

Urbach, E. E.: 1975, *The Sages: Their Concepts and Beliefs*. Jerusalem: Magnes Press.

Van Hooser, J. B.: 1962, "The Meaning of the Root PQD in the Old Testament." Dissertation, Harvard Divinity School.

Van Unnik, W. C.: 1974, "Josephus' Account of the Story of Israel's Sin with Alien Women." *Travels in the World of the Old Testament*, 241–261. Assen: Van Gorcum.

Vermes, G.: 1955, "Deux traditions sur Balaam—Nombres xxii.2-21 et ses interprétations midrashiques." *Cahiers Sioniens* 9, 289–302.

idem: 1961A (1973), *Scripture and Tradition in Judaism*. Studia Post-Biblica 4. 2nd rev. ed. 1973. Leiden: Brill.

idem: 1961B, "The Story of Balaam." *Scripture and Tradition in Judaism*, 127–177.

idem: 1963, 1975, "Haggadah in the Onkelos Targum." *JJS* 8, 159–169. Reprint in G. Vermes, *Post-Biblical Jewish Studies*. Studies in Judaism in Late Antiquity. Leiden: Brill, 1975, 127–138.

idem: 1987, *The Dead Sea Scrolls in English*. Sheffield: JSOT Press. New York: Penguin; 3rd revision.

York, A. D.: 1974, "The Dating of Targumic Literature." *JSJ* 5, 49–62.

idem: 1979, "The Targum in the Synagogue and the School." *JSJ* 10, 74–86.

INDEXES TO TARGUM NEOFITI 1: NUMBERS

HEBREW BIBLE

Deuteronomy

APOCRYPHAL/DEUTEROCANONICAL BOOKS

OLD TESTAMENT PSEUDEPIGRAPHA

NEW TESTAMENT

TARGUMIM

Targum Neofiti

Numbers

Deuteronomy

Neofiti Margin

Targum Onqelos

Targum Pseudo-Jonathan

Palestinian Targum General

Fragment Targum P

Fragment Targum V

Fragment Targum N

Fragment Targum L

Cairo Genizah Palestinian Targum Fragments

Other Targums

Samaritan Targum

Targum Citations

ANCIENT VERSIONS

Septuagint

Peshitta

Vulgate

QUMRAN TEXTS

JEWISH WRITERS

RABBINIC LITERATURE

I. Tosefta, Mishnah, Talmud

II. Midrash

EARLY CHRISTIAN WRITERS

PAGAN WRITERS

MODERN AUTHORS

INDEXES TO TARGUM PSEUDO-JONATHAN: NUMBERS

HEBREW BIBLE

APOCRYPHAL/DEUTEROCANONICAL BOOKS

QUMRAN TEXTS

NEW TESTAMENT

TARGUMIM

Targum Pseudo-Jonathan

Targum Neofiti and Neofiti Glosses

Targum Onqelos

Fragment Targums (PV)

ANCIENT VERSIONS

Septuagint

RABBINICS

I. Mishnah and Talmud

II. Midrash

ARAMAIC WORDS

INDEX OF SUBJECTS

INDEX OF AUTHORS